John Brown, Abolitionist

John Brown, Abolitionist

The Man Who Killed Slavery,
Sparked the Civil War,
and Seeded Civil Rights

David S. Reynolds

Alfred A. Knopf
New York
2005

THIS IS A BORZOI BOOK
PUBLISHED BY ALFRED A. KNOPF

Knopf, Borzoi Books, and the colophon are registered
trademarks of Random House, Inc.

Library of Congress Cataloging-in-Publication Data
Reynolds, David S., [date]
John Brown, abolitionist : the man who killed
slavery, sparked the Civil War, and seeded civil
rights / David S. Reynolds.
p. cm.
Includes bibliographical references and index.
ISBN 0-375-41188-7
1. Brown, John, 1800–1859.   2. Abolitionists—United
States—Biography.   3. Antislavery movements—United States—
History—19th century.   I. Title.

E451.R49   2005
973.7'116'092—dc22
[B]   2004048864

Manufactured in the United States of America

First Edition

To Suzanne and Haig,

for their encouragement and support

Contents

Preface   ix

1. The Party   3

2. The Puritan   14

3. The Pioneer   29

4. The Patriarch   40

5. The Pauper   66

6. The Plan   95

7. Pottawatomie   138

8. Pariah and Legend   179

9. The Promoter   206

10. Plotting Multiculturally   239

11. Practice   268

12. Preparation   288

13. Problems   309

14. Pilloried, Prosecuted, and Praised   334

15. The Passion   370

16. Positions and Politics   402

17. The Prophet   438

18. Posterity   480

Notes   507

Acknowledgments   553

Index   555

Preface

A word about my subtitle. The Abolitionist John Brown (1800–1859) did not *end* American slavery. The Thirteenth Amendment, ratified by the states six years after his death, did that. But he can be said to have *killed* slavery in the way described by his contemporary Wendell Phillips, who said that after Brown's raid on Harpers Ferry, Virginia, slavery was like a fallen pine, still green but dying. In a speech at Brown's funeral Phillips declared, "John Brown has loosened the roots of the slave system; it only breathes,—it does not live,—hereafter." "Kill" is an apt word for Brown, who went to murderous extremes, unlike other Abolitionists, most of whom were pacifists who disavowed violence.

By the same token, Brown did not *cause* the Civil War, which resulted from a host of social, political, and cultural forces. But he *sparked* the war to a degree that no other American did. "Begin" is the word Frederick Douglass chose: "If John Brown did not end the war that ended slavery, he did, at least, begin the war that ended slavery."

Nor did Brown *bring about* civil rights. *Brown v. Board of Education*, the Supreme Court decision of 1954 that banned school segregation, got moving that project, which was carried on by the activists of the 1950s and '60s and is still ongoing. But Brown *planted seeds* for the civil rights movement by making a pioneering demand for complete social and political equality for America's ethnic minorities. His demand was heard by African American leaders from Frederick Douglass to W. E. B. Du Bois and many others who admired Brown more strongly than they did any other white man in American history.

This book argues for Brown's achievements in these areas and more. It also shows that none of these achievements would have been possible had Brown's unique vision not intersected with the particular cultural and social conditions of nineteenth-century America. In a different time and place Brown could have fallen from view, discarded as a forgettable crank or a heinous criminal. As it happened, he had an impact on the course of national events matched by few in American history. This cultural biography attempts to explain how and why he did.

John Brown, Abolitionist

The Party

One of the most symbolic events of the Civil War occurred in a mansion. The event was the reception held on January 1, 1863, at the Medford, Massachusetts, estate of the businessman George L. Stearns to celebrate the Emancipation Proclamation, which had been issued that afternoon by President Lincoln.

Stearns called the affair "the John Brown Party." The highlight of the evening was the unveiling of a marble bust of John Brown, the antislavery martyr who had died on a scaffold three years earlier after his doomed, heroic effort to free the slaves by leading a twenty-two-man raid on Harpers Ferry, Virginia.

Brown's presence was felt elsewhere in America that day. The Union general Robert H. Milroy, stationed near Harpers Ferry, read Lincoln's proclamation aloud to his regiment, which spontaneously thundered forth the war song "John Brown's Body," with its heady chorus about Brown "mouldering in the grave" while "his soul keeps marching on." The Emancipation Proclamation made General Milroy feel as though John Brown's spirit had merged with his. "That hand-bill order," he said, "gave Freedom to the slaves through and around the region where Old John Brown was hung. I felt then that I was on duty, in the most righteous cause that man ever drew sword in."

In Boston, a tense wait had ended in midafternoon when the news came over the wires that the proclamation had been put into effect. At a Jubilee Concert in the Music Hall, Ralph Waldo Emerson read his Abolitionist poem "Boston Hymn" and was followed by performances of Handel's Hallelujah Chorus, Beethoven's Fifth Symphony, and Mendelssohn's "Hymn of Praise." That evening at Tremont Temple a huge crowd cheered as the proclamation was read aloud and exploded into song when Frederick

Douglass led in singing "Blow Ye the Trumpet, Blow!," the joyous hymn that had been Brown's favorite and had been sung at his funeral.

A number of people missed the Boston celebration because they had gone to George Stearns's twenty-six-acre estate in nearby Medford for the John Brown Party. The party was, in its own way, as meaningful as Lincoln's proclamation. It celebrated the man who had sparked the war that led to this historic day. Lincoln's proclamation, freeing millions of enslaved blacks, sped the process that led eventually to civil rights. John Brown's personal war against slavery had set this process in motion.

Gathered in Stearns's elegant home was a motley group. Stearns himself, long-bearded and earnest, had made a fortune manufacturing lead pipes. His guests included the bald, spectacled William Lloyd Garrison and the volatile Wendell Phillips, pioneers of Abolitionism; the stately, reserved philosopher Ralph Waldo Emerson, magus of Transcendentalism; his idealistic cohort Amos Bronson Alcott, who was there with his daughter, Louisa May, soon to captivate young readers with *Little Women;* Franklin Sanborn, the Concord schoolteacher whose students included children of Emerson, John Brown, and Henry James, Sr.; and the red-haired, vivacious Julia Ward Howe, writer of "The Battle Hymn of the Republic." They represented cultural threads that had once been aimed in various directions but were now unified in their devotion to the memory of John Brown.

Garrison and Phillips had since the 1830s called for immediate emancipation of the slaves or, barring that, separation of the North and the South. Garrison, long committed to pacifism, had advocated moral argument as the sole means of fighting slavery until John Brown's self-sacrificing terrorism inspired him to espouse a more militant stance. Phillips, long driven by his disgust with slavery to curse the Constitution and the American Union, had come to espouse Brown's vision of a unified nation based on rights for people of all ethnicities.

Emerson had begun his career alienated from the antislavery cause but had taken it up with growing zeal that culminated in his famous statement that John Brown would "make the gallows as glorious as the cross." Along with Thoreau, who had died the previous year, he had been chiefly responsible for rescuing Brown from infamy and oblivion. Alcott, too, had played a part in the resuscitation of Brown, whom he called "the type and synonym of the Just." If, as Alfred Kazin suggests, without John Brown there would have been no Civil War, we would add that without the Concord Transcendentalists, John Brown would have had little cultural impact.

And without Julia Ward Howe, John Brown may not have become fused with American myth. The wife of Samuel Gridley Howe, one of those who had financed Brown, she wrote "The Battle Hymn of the Republic" to the tune of "John Brown's Body," retaining its "Glory, glory hallelujah" and changing "His soul goes marching on" to "His truth is marching on." With her memorable images of a just God "trampling out the vintage where the grapes of wrath are stored," and loosening "the fateful lightnings of His terrible swift sword" against the slaveholding South, she caught the essence of John Brown, a devout Calvinist who considered himself predestined to stamp out slavery. She had coupled his God-inspired antislavery passion with the North's mission and had thus helped define America.

Another of Stearns's guests, Frank Sanborn, helped define John Brown. In 1857 he had introduced Brown to several reformers who, along with him, would make up the group of Brown's backers known as the Secret Six. A zealous Brown booster, he would perpetuate the legend of the heroic Brown in his writings of the post–Civil War period.

As for George Stearns, besides having been the chief contributor of funds and arms to Brown, he was largely responsible for pushing Brown's ideal of racial justice toward civil rights. He once declared, "I consider it the proudest act of my life that I gave good old John Brown every pike and rifle he carried to Harper's Ferry." Just as Brown had assigned prominent positions to blacks in his antislavery activities, so Stearns led the recruitment of blacks for the Union army. After the war, Stearns would fight for passage of the Fifteenth Amendment, which gave suffrage to blacks.

That these and assorted other reformers, writers, and society people would gather on Emancipation Day to honor John Brown was more than fitting. From their perspective, it was inevitable. Everyone present believed that without John Brown this day would not have come, at least not as soon as it did.

Several at the party had doubts about President Lincoln. Despite his deep hatred of slavery, Lincoln had acted with politic moderation early in his presidency. Hoping to preserve the Union by conciliating the South, he had supported the Fugitive Slave Act of 1850 (anathema even to some of the most conservative Northerners), had endorsed a constitutional amendment preserving slavery where it already existed, had revoked an emancipation proclamation in Missouri, and had advocated colonization for blacks, who, he said, could never live on equal terms with whites in America due to racial differences. In response, Wendell Phillips had written a bitter article, "Abraham Lincoln, Slave-hound of Illinois." Garrison was so angry that he wrote of Lincoln, "He has evidently not a drop of anti-slavery blood in his veins; and he seems incapable of uttering a humane or generous sentiment respecting the enslaved millions in our land."

As strange as such statements appear today, they were not so to those who had known John Brown and had absorbed his progressive racial views. There was good reason Stearns had organized a John Brown Party instead of an Abraham Lincoln Party.

Although Stearns and his guests were overjoyed by the president's proclamation, they saw Lincoln as a latecomer to emancipation, a goal for which John Brown had given his life. In 1861, two years before Lincoln's proclamation, Stearns, Sanborn, Phillips, and other followers of Brown had formed an Emancipation League, whose aim was to win over Lincoln to the idea that freeing the slaves must be the primary mission of the Union war effort. The league issued a public document demanding emancipation "as a measure of justice, and as a military necessity." As a first step, Stearns wrote in a letter to Lincoln, black troops were needed to ensure a Union victory. Lincoln accepted the strategy after Stearns had devoted most of 1862 traveling thousands of miles throughout the North and organizing ten black regiments, including the famous 54th Massachusetts, led by Colonel Robert Gould Shaw.

The use of black soldiers was just one of Brown's forward-looking measures that impelled George Stearns to single out John Brown for tribute that evening.

Although the white marble bust of Brown, which Stearns and his wife had commissioned Edwin A. Brackett to sculpt in 1859 while the imprisoned Brown awaited execution, had long been a fixture in the Stearns mansion, unveiling it anew on Emancipation Day gave it fresh significance. The bust, which many compared to Michelangelo's *Moses*, was an idealized rendering. It invested the stern, hatchet-faced Brown with a calm Jovian dignity. It gleamed against the black walnut wainscoting on the landing of the Stearnses' curved staircase as the hushed crowd below heard Emerson read his "Boston Hymn" and Julia Ward Howe give a powerful recitation her "Battle Hymn of the Republic."

The journalist James Redpath would later see the bust in the Boston Athenaeum amid Roman statuary and would comment that it might well be Moses but certainly was not John Brown. True: But, then, who *was* John Brown?

Perhaps the most significant meaning of the John Brown Party was that everyone present was joined by an idealistic vision of a man who, in other circles, was branded as a murderer, a thief, and an insane fanatic. The pristine purity of Brackett's bust was as distant from John Brown's real looks as the starry-eyed hero worship of Stearns's guests was from a true appraisal of his achievements.

Marble bust of John Brown by Edwin A. Brackett, 1859.
BOYD STUTLER COLLECTION OF JOHN BROWN,
WEST VIRGINIA ARCHIVES.

The fact is that during his life and after it Brown gave rise to significant misreadings that shaped the course of American history. Brown himself had misread the slaves and sympathetic whites among the locals, whom he expected to rally in masses to his side as soon as his raid on Harpers Ferry began. The blacks he liberated misread him, since, by most reports, few of them voluntarily joined him in the battle against the Virginia troops—a fact that may have contributed to the fatal delay on the part of Brown, who had expected "the bees to hive" as soon as his liberation plan became known among the slaves.

Most important, Brown himself became the subject of crucial misreadings. Although after the raid he was at first denounced by most Northerners, a few influential individuals, especially the Transcendentalists, salvaged his reputation by placing him on the level of Christ—a notable misreading of a man who, despite his remarkable virtues, had violent excesses, as evidenced by the nighttime slaughter of five proslavery residents he had directed in Pottawatomie, Kansas. The Transcendentalist image of Brown spread throughout the North and was fanned by books, melodramas, poems, and music—culminating in "John Brown's Body," the inspiring song chanted by tens of thousands of Union troops as they marched south.

At the same time that this misreading swept the North, an opposite one was pervading the South. The South's initial grudging admiration for Brown's courage was quickly overwhelmed by a paranoid fear that he was a malicious aggressor who represented the entire North—a tremendous and tragic misreading, since virtually everyone in the Northern-led Republican Party, from Lincoln to Seward, actually disapproved of his violent tactics. The South's misreading was fanned by Democratic Party propaganda that unjustifiably smeared the Republicans with responsibility for Harpers Ferry. In this view, "Black Republicanism" meant not only "nigger-worship" but also deep alliance with John Brown, whom the Democrats characterized as a villain of the blackest dye.

These dual misreadings, positive and negative, were perpetuated in biographies of Brown. The early biographers were mainly people who had known Brown personally and who idolized him—they therefore twisted facts to make him seem heroic, at times godlike. In reaction, there arose a school of biographers intent upon exploding this saintly image. They swung to the other extreme of portraying him as little more than a cold-blooded murderer, horse thief, inflexible egotist, fanatical visionary, and shady businessman.

These extremes of hagiography and vilification were in time answered by scholarly objectivity. Several biographers—most notably Oswald Garrison Villard and Stephen B. Oates—present information about Brown's life factually, unfiltered by partisan bias. Villard and Oates pitilessly expose Brown's savagery at Pottawatomie and question the wisdom of his provisional constitution and his attack on Harpers Ferry, even as they praise his humanitarian aims.

Still, there is a danger to an overstrict insistence on impartiality. One reviewer's comment on Villard—i.e., that he "holds a position of impartiality, and almost of aloofness"—speaks for the best modern biographies. For example, biographers have waffled on the issue of Brown's sanity, leaving it as an unsolved problem. One can be objective without remaining impartial about the crucial moral, political, and human issues that Brown's life poses.

My stand on some key issues is: (a) Brown was not insane; instead, he was a deeply religious, flawed, yet ultimately noble reformer; (b) the Pottawatomie affair was indeed a crime, but it was a war crime committed against proslavery settlers by a man who saw slavery itself as an unprovoked war of one race against another; and (c) neither Brown's provisional constitution nor the Harpers Ferry raid were wild-eyed, erratic schemes doomed to failure: instead, they reflect Brown's overconfidence in whites' ability to rise above racism and in blacks' willingness to rise up in armed insurrection against their masters.

The current book develops these and other arguments by placing Brown fully in historical context. This is emphatically a *cultural* biography, a term that demands explanation. Cultural biography is based on the idea that human beings have a dynamic, dialogic relationship to many aspects of their historical surroundings, such as politics, society, literature, and religion.

The special province of the cultural biographer is to explore this relationship, focusing on three questions: How does my subject *reflect* his or her era? How does my subject *transcend* the era—that is, what makes him or her unique? What *impact* did my subject have on the era?

Cultural biography takes an Emersonian approach to the human subject. As Emerson writes, "the ideas of the time are in the air, and infect all who breathe it. . . . We learn of our contemporaries what they know without effort, and almost through the pores of our skin." The cultural biographer explores the historical "air" surrounding the subject and describes the process by which the air seeped through the pores of his or her skin. "Great geniuses are parts of the times," Melville wrote; "they themselves are the times, and possess a correspondent coloring." Once the biographer accepts the cultural environment as a viable area of study, new vistas of information and insight open up. John Brown emerges in cultural biography not as an isolated, insane antislavery terrorist but as an amalgam of social currents—religious, reformist, racial, and political—that found explosive realization in him.

Most standard biographies, of course, contain some information about a subject's historical milieu. Cultural biography, however, analyzes this milieu not as window dressing—not as something "out there," on the fringes of personal life—but rather as a dynamic entity constantly seeping into the subject's psyche and shaping his or her behavior. Character traits usually explained psychologically have social dimensions. Cultural signifiers color the most private thoughts. If John Brown's effort to wipe out slavery by raiding Virginia with a tiny band of men seems absurd when viewed as an isolated military act, it makes sense when seen in light of the slave revolts, guerilla warfare, and revolutionary Christianity that were major sources of inspiration for him.

Cultural biography illuminates not only the subject's life but also national history. John Jay Chapman noted in 1910, "John Brown and his raid are an epitome, a popular summary of the history of the United States between the Missouri Compromise and the Gettysburg celebration. . . . He is as big as myth, and the story of him is an immortal legend—perhaps the only one in our history." Similarly, the novelist Albion Tourgée wrote, "John Brown! . . . Cause and Consequence! . . . The climax of one age and the harbinger of another!"

Despite such statements made long ago, little has been done to fit John Brown into American history. Although the Harpers Ferry raid is widely acknowledged as a major event leading to the Civil War, the historical forces that contributed to and resulted from the raid have yet to be described with care. A main obstacle to a historical understanding of Brown has been the long-standing view of him as a crazed terrorist with few links to mainstream American history. A large part of this book is devoted to tracing such links. As shall be seen, placing John Brown fully in his times freshly illuminates, among other things, the legacy of Puritanism, the significance of slave revolts, the varieties of antislavery activism, racial attitudes, the social impact of Transcendentalism, and, more generally, the causes of the Civil War. Literary history, too, is illuminated, since many imaginative writers—Melville, Whitman, Whittier, Victor Hugo, to name a few—wrote eloquently about Brown. Finally, new dimensions of popular culture come to light, since Brown was a cultural icon variously championed and denigrated in popular literature, music, and art.

A potential danger of using a subject's life to explore history is that the subject can get lost in the process. If a person is described as an amalgam of social and cultural currents, what happens to the notion of individuality? Since society and culture influence everybody, why is it that we isolate one person from the rest? What makes him or her special?

Cultural biography, rightly executed, reveals not only how a subject *reflects* the social environment but also how he or she *transcends* it. Once again Emerson's philosophy sheds light on the subject. In Emerson's view the "representative" human being mirrors the social environment while at the same time remaining unique. Emerson's most memorable concept, self-reliance, asserts the utterly original, self-contained nature of the fully developed individual. Cultural biography can lapse into flaccid history without repeated reminders of the ways in which the subject, while influenced by cultural surroundings, contributed something new, often startlingly so, as a result of his or her unique angle of vision.

A comparison of John Brown with his contemporary Walt Whitman is useful here, since they were people of different temperaments and convictions responding to the same set of social conditions. Their most memorable contributions—the early editions of Whitman's *Leaves of Grass* and

Brown's antislavery activities in Kansas and Virginia—occurred almost simultaneously, between 1855 and 1860. The two men shared a deep concern for the fate of their nation, which they saw torn over slavery. The distinction between the two lies in their radically different, wholly original responses to the national crisis. Whitman, fearing the impending separation of the North and the South, created all-embracing poetry meant to become a model of togetherness and cohesion for the divided nation. Brown, concerned solely with ending slavery, resorted to terrorist tactics to disrupt the South's peculiar institution. Whitman sought to provide America with healing and reconciliation through poetic language; Brown sought to purge America of its greatest injustice through military action.

Although both envisaged a transformed American society in which people of all races enjoyed equal rights, the method each chose to bring about this society was unique. Whitman's sweeping, inclusive free verse and all-absorbing poetic persona were unlike anything else in antebellum literature. Likewise, Brown's brand of antislavery terrorism was sui generis. An important task of my cultural biography is to identify *how* John Brown was unique in his espousal of violence and *why* he became so.

As Emerson saw perhaps more clearly than anyone else did, a person's uniqueness need not isolate him or her from the surrounding culture. To the contrary, the more confidently individualistic someone is, the greater the influence that person is likely to have. The self-reliant individual has social repercussions. "A man Caesar is born," Emerson wrote, "and for ages after we have a Roman Empire. . . . An institution is the lengthened shadow of one man; as, the Reformation, of Luther; Quakerism, of Fox; Methodism, of Wesley; Abolition, of Clarkson. . . . [A]ll history resolves itself very easily into the biography of a few stout and earnest persons."

Whereas standard biographies typically end with the subject's death, cultural biography recognizes that in many cases death is just the start of a person's real significance. One of the Transcendentalists' paradoxical points about John Brown was that he didn't truly live until he had died. "He is more alive than he ever was," Thoreau said after Brown was hanged. "He has earned immortality. . . . He is no longer working in secret. He works in public, and in the clearest light that shines on this land."

To gauge Brown's impact properly, the cultural biographer must analyze his powerful influence on the Civil War. At the end of the war, Emerson wrote in his journal, "It has been impossible to keep the name & fame of John Brown out of the war from the first to the last." He was right. The disgruntled proslavery journalist Charles Chauncey Burr, confronted with the South's impending defeat, in 1863 castigated Lincoln for having waged "a stupendous John Brown raid" on the South. Tracing Lincoln's war aims to John Brown, Burr lamented, "No man can support such a war without being a disciple and follower of the old thief and assassin of Osawatomie [i.e., Brown]. . . . You are either for Lincolnism or against it."

There was some truth in Burr's assessment of the Civil War as a "John Brown raid" on a large scale. The war increasingly reflected John Brown's strategies and goals. In 1861, at the beginning of the war, Lincoln's main aim was not to stamp out slavery but to save the Union; as seen, his pronouncements about the war seemed so conservative with regard to slavery that Abolitionists like Garrison and Phillips excoriated him. By 1863, following the lead of John Brown's supporters, Lincoln had become a warrior for emancipation. The Gettysburg Address, following on the heels of the Emancipation Proclamation, mirrored John Brown's social vision, since it broadened American egalitarianism, as described in the Declaration of Independence, to include blacks. Moreover, Lincoln's embrace of the tactics of "total war," as waged by his generals Sherman and Grant, echoed John Brown's approach to ending slavery through all-out violence. Like John Brown before them, they were willing to take extreme measures, including attacks on civilians, to defeat their proslavery enemies. Given Lincoln's increasingly Brown-like vision, it is understandable that his Second Inaugural Address, in which he declared that a sternly judgmental God might make the war last "until every drop of blood drawn with the lash, shall be paid by another drawn with the sword," coupled antislavery passion with Calvinistic images in a manner strikingly reminiscent of many of Brown's pronouncements.

Brown's long-term impact has been manifested in many ways, perhaps most significantly among African Americans. Viewed as a whole, Brown's career anticipated a panoply of civil rights goals, some of which America is still struggling to achieve. The right to vote; the right to participate in government; the right to be paid equally for equal work; and the right to live in an integrated society free of prejudice—John Brown had envisaged all these rights for blacks and other minority groups. No other white person, not even Lincoln, has been so widely admired among American blacks as has John Brown. W. E. B. Du Bois, Langston Hughes, Malcolm X, and many other prominent figures have extolled him. Although the fully integrated society Brown envisaged, in which people of all races and both sexes participate equally in America's democratic system, is still far from being realized, social conscience on racial issues has improved markedly as a result of increasing acceptance of the ideals he lived and died for.

Which takes us back to the John Brown Party at George Stearns's home on Emancipation Day. Stearns, the champion of civil rights policies he had learned from Brown, chose the African American J. B. Smith to cater his function. Even though Smith, who had distinguished himself by earning a living catering functions at Harvard, was usually punctilious about collecting money for his work, he refused to bill the Stearnses for the evening. He wanted to contribute his services in honor of the man who had given his life to free 4 million members of his race.

The Puritan

A Southern political cartoon of 1863 spoke volumes about the paranoia John Brown had aroused in the Confederacy. The cartoon, titled "Worship of the North," pictures an altar with the word PURITANISM blazoned across its base and FREE-LOVE, SPIRIT RAPPING, ATHEISM, and NEGRO WORSHIP on the bricks above it. On the altar sits an ugly Lincoln, beside whom lies the dying American Union. Flanking the altar are antislavery leaders of the Republican Party, including Charles Sumner and William Henry Seward. An African in tribal dress looms at the side of the group holding an odd-looking spear. Hovering over all are Satan and a statue of John Brown, both also holding spears.

The cartoon illustrates the often-neglected fact that the Civil War was far more than a struggle between the North and the South over social issues such as slavery, economics, and states rights. These social issues were intensified by profound cultural differences, real and perceived. John Brown was at the epicenter of this conflict.

The South's view of him as a demonic Northerner is made clear in the cartoon, where his statue stands like an idol above the altar on the same level as Satan. From the South's perspective, the "Worship of the North" was devil worship, and John Brown was Satan's main accomplice.

The spears held by the statue, Satan, and the African represent the pikes John Brown had distributed at Harpers Ferry among the blacks he temporarily freed from slavery. He had designed the pikes, made of bowie knives attached to poles, to be used as weapons by the blacks against white pursuers. For Southerners, the John Brown pike epitomized the twin horrors of Northern aggression and slave revolts.

The other images in the cartoon were also linked with the satanic Brown. Lincoln and his antislavery cronies, from this Southern perspective,

"Worship of the North" (proslavery political cartoon; unattributed).

were Brown's worshipers. The moribund American Union was his victim. The armed African was the product of his raid, as was the North's sympathy for blacks, parodied in the racist phrase NEGRO WORSHIP.

The remaining words on the altar indicated the depth of the South's hostility. SPIRIT RAPPING and FREE-LOVE were two of the countless "isms" the South associated with Northern society. Movements such as spiritualism, free love, Fourierism, Transcendentalism, and women's rights had, in fact, sprouted prolifically in the antebellum North, a society caught in the throes of reform and creative ferment. These Northern movements prompted both disgust and smugness in the South. For Southerners, Northern society was wild and anarchic, given to ever-shifting fads that were essentially godless (hence the ATHEISM on the cartoon altar). Abolitionism was an especially wicked example of Northern fanaticism. The South, which considered itself a stable society supported by the "civilizing" institution of slavery, regarded the North as a chaos of homegrown theories rooted in that Ur-source of subversiveness: New England Puritanism.

The PURITANISM at the base of the cartoon was as telling as was the Brown statue at the top. From the South's perspective, seventeenth-century

Puritanism had contributed to the Northern cultural evils that found their culmination in Brown.

Normally, Puritanism does not factor in histories of the Civil War. A widely held view is that Puritanism, far from stirring up warlike emotions, had by the nineteenth century softened into a benign faith in America's millennial promise. Supposedly, it buttressed mainstream cultural values, fostering consensus and conformity.

For many in the Civil War era, however, Puritanism meant radical individualism and subversive social agitation. In 1863, the Democratic congressman Samuel Cox typically blamed the Civil War on disruptive New England reform movements that he said were rooted in Puritanism. He insisted that fanatical Abolitionism caused the war, and, in his words, "Abolition is the offspring of Puritanism. . . . Puritanism is a reptile which has been boring into the mound, which is the Constitution, and this civil war comes in like a devouring sea!" Charles Chauncey Burr, another defender of the South, bewailed "this terrible Puritan war." Burr painted the history of the North as a dark drama of aggressive Puritanism:

> The nature of Puritanism is to tolerate nothing that it dislikes, and to fight every thing that dislikes it. . . . Nothing escapes it. About a third of a century ago it drove at slavery—swore that it would either break up slavery, or break up the Union. . . . It organized, sent forth agents and lecturers, printed tracts and newspapers, to fill the Northern mind full of its own fanaticism, and to teach the slaves how to poison or murder their masters. . . . On, on, this implacable Puritanism drove, destroying social unity, and sowing the seeds of anarchy, despotism and war, until its harvest of death was ready to be gathered.

This demonization of Puritanism made its way into Southern war songs, such as "The Southern Cross," which painted the South as peaceful and free until ruined by the "Puritan" North:

> *How peaceful and blest was America's soil,*
> *'Till betrayed by the guile of the Puritan demon,*
> *Which lurks under virtue, and springs from its coil,*
> *To fasten its fangs in the life blood of freemen.*

What linked Puritanism with Northern reform was its powerful heritage of antinomianism—the breaking of human law in the name of God. Antinomian rebels from Anne Hutchinson onward put divine grace above social codes. In the nineteenth century this spirit fostered a law-flouting individualism that appeared variously in militant Abolitionism, Transcendentalist self-reliance, and the "individual sovereignty" championed by anarchists and free-love activists—a pervasive individualism parodied in "Worship of the North" by the word EGO that beams from two suns in the top corners of the cartoon.

Northerners, like Southerners, associated these movements with radical Puritanism, but often from a positive perspective. In his 1844 lecture "New England Reformers," Emerson declared that the "fertile forms of antinomianism among the elder puritans seemed to have their match in the plenty of the new harvest of reform." Emerson admired the self-reliant spirit behind the reforms. "In each of these movements," he said, "emerged a good result, an assertion of the sufficiency of the private man." A Northern journalist went so far as to say: "Puritanism and nothing else can save this nation. . . . The Puritan element, which demands religious freedom, as the birth-right of Heaven, in matters spiritual, is the nourisher of that civil liberty which releases the body from secular despotism in matters temporal."

Northern soldiers were proud to accept the sobriquet "Puritan." A Union marching song, "My Northern Boy to the War Has Gone!" pictured a Union soldier at Antietam carrying his grandfather's sword, which linked him to the Puritan past:

> *His Puritan Grandsire's sword gleamed bright*
> *Where hosts were in strife engaging;*
> *And many a Rebel eye clos'd in night,*
> *While the contest fierce was raging!*

Southerners made a contrast between the supposedly refined Norman "cavaliers" who they said occupied the South and the lowly Saxon "Puritans" of the North. Blaming the Civil War on "the irreconcilable antithesis and utter incompatibility of the two sections," one writer typically declared that the real conflict was between the "cavalier element predominating in Southern civilization" and the "Puritan element which underlies the fabric of Northern civilization." Stressing this "antithesis of the Puritan and Cavalier," the writer insisted that the North's uncontrolled democracy would foster endless social revolutions there, whereas the slave system kept the South orderly and structured. Another journalist claimed that the Northern Puritan is "at once a religious fanatic and a political agitator and reformer," while the Southern Cavalier was "the builder, the social architect, the institutionialist, the conservator." Yet another contrasted "the

principles of [Northern] Calvinistic *insubordinatism* and [Southern] Episco-
pal *subordinatism*. The first is iconoclastic in all things. The second teaches
respect and reverence in all things. The first aids all effort to destroy the
Constitution. The second assists all effort to maintain the Constitution."

How accurate were these generalizations about the Southern cavalier?
Not very. While it's true that many aristocratic families had fled to the
American South when Oliver Cromwell drove them out of England in
1651, by the mid nineteenth century the Southern white population did not
wholly—or even predominantly—derive from blue-blooded cavalier stock.

As history often reminds us, though, cultural myths can be just as powerful as facts. When Mark Twain said that the historical novelist Walter
Scott caused the Civil War by fanning the South's pride in its "chivalric"
heritage, he tapped into the self-deception inherent in the myth of the
noble cavalier. To cover up the horrors of slavery, the South paraded socio-
logical half-truths and ersatz history. How convenient to present slavery as
a "civilizing" institution that allowed cultured whites to care for ignorant
blacks! One article on the Southern cavalier said, "The institution of
domestic slavery alone has sufficed to make the South conservative and religious, and its absence to render the North anarchical and infidel." Another
described slavery as "a benevolent system of tutelage by a superior race over
an inferior race," emphasizing the crucial importance of sustaining the
institution: "Let us strengthen slavery by every possible appliance, regarding that institution as the very base, the corner-stone of our system, which
once rudely framed, the whole superstructure will totter in the imminent
peril of hopeless ruin."

What about the notion of the North as Puritan? That, too, was only
partly accurate. Although the North had been Puritan during the seventeenth century, by 1850 it had become so polyglot that the term described it
inadequately. One nineteenth-century Northerner, however, *was* a bona
fide Puritan: John Brown.

For the South, Brown was the natural result of anarchical, criminal
Puritanism. Samuel Cox, to illustrate his point that "the history of Puritanism is a catalogue of murders, maimings, extortions, and outrages,"
noted the appropriateness of the North's favorite war song, "John Brown's
Body," which he called "a hymn of apotheosis to a horse-thief and a murderer." Another proslavery commentator generalized: "Everybody who
ever saw a Puritan, or who ever heard or read of a Puritan, knows that from
the days of Calvin and Knox, down to those of Cotton Mather, and still
later to . . . John Brown—everybody knows that they have been the same

arrogant, self-righteous, conceited race—each man thinking and acting on the belief of his own infallibility and of other people's fallibility."

If the South saw Brown as an arrogant lawbreaker, the North, once it overcame its initial doubts about him, heralded him as a freedom-fighter in the Puritan tradition. His uniqueness among nineteenth-century Americans is captured in many contemporary accounts of him as a throwback to an earlier era. Franklin Sanborn remarked, "He was, in truth, a calvinistic Puritan, born a century or two after the fashion had changed; but as ready as those of Bradford's or Cromwell's time had been to engage in any work of the Lord to which he felt himself called." Another associate called him "a Puritan of the Puritans," and another commented: "In religion and character Brown was the last of the Puritans." The Abolitionist Richard J. Hinton, similarly, described him as "a puritan brought back from the days of Cromwell or a vision of the old Revolutionary times, to show the world that all the fearless energy and strong integrity that characterized these epochs, has not yet faded out."

Both enemies and friends of John Brown, then, considered him a deep-dyed Puritan. They were right. He was a Calvinist who admired the works of Jonathan Edwards. He was proud of his family roots in New England Puritanism. He patterned himself after the Puritan warrior Cromwell, to whom he was often compared. He had an astounding sincerity of faith, so that his letters and speeches were more often than not lay sermons. He was willing to die for his utter belief in the word of the Bible, which he interpreted without mediator, like a true Puritan.

Like the arch-Puritan Cromwell before him, he came to have a notably divided reputation, with many seeing him as a bloodthirsty terrorist and others viewing him as a saintly liberator. The truth is that, like Cromwell, he was both of these things. He was a terrorist *because of* his own interpretation of Puritan beliefs. Far from enforcing tame conformity, Puritanism unleashed militant individualism and warfare against institutions.

How could Puritanism fuse with antislavery passion with such intensity in John Brown that he believed he could single-handedly free America's 4 million slaves? His family background and his early life in Connecticut and Ohio yield some clues.

John Brown's paternal ancestry reached to early Puritan times, though the details are unclear. Some genealogists say that he was descended from the carpenter Peter Brown, who arrived in America on the *Mayflower* in 1620, resided in Plymouth and then Duxbury, was married twice and had four children, and died in 1634. Others claim that the family began in

America with another Peter Brown, who settled in Connecticut around 1650.

I find the *Mayflower* story plausible. Brown and his contemporaries were certain of it. In his 1857 autobiographical letter to the young Henry Stearns, Brown, using the third person, identified himself as "a decendant on the side of his Father of one of the company of the Mayflower who landed at Plymouth 1620."*

In any case, what matters is that Brown's earliest male ancestor was a New England Puritan. By the mid seventeenth century, the Browns were in Windsor, Connecticut, where Peter Brown (1632–92) and his wife, Mary, raised four sons, the oldest of whom, John, became the first of four John Browns of successive generations, including a Revolutionary War captain and his grandson, the martyr of Harpers Ferry.

On his mother's side, Brown descended from Peter Wouter van der Meulen of Amsterdam, who fled Holland soon after the siege of Leyden, settling, like the Browns, in Windsor. His son, known as "Peter the Miller," anglicized the family name to Mills. Peter's son Gideon entered the ministry after graduating from Yale and died before the American Revolution. His son, also Gideon Mills (the grandfather of John Brown), served as a lieutenant in the war and in 1800 moved to Ohio.

Religious devotion was intense on both sides of the family. John Brown was related on his father's side to the Reverend Nathan Brown, a missionary to India and Japan, and on his mother's to the well-known Reverend Luther Humphrey and the Reverend Dr. Heman Humphrey, one of the first presidents of Amherst College.

Calvinistic piety filled the life of John Brown's father. Born in West Simsbury, Connecticut, in 1771, Owen Brown was five when his father, who had joined the Connecticut 18th Regiment as a captain, died of dysentery in a Continental Army camp north of New York City. Owen and his ten siblings were left in the care of his resolute but long-suffering mother, who struggled to keep the family fed. Owen recalled her as "one of the best of mothers, active and sensible," but the crops failed for lack of help, and the brutal winter of 1778–79 killed off most of the livestock. To economize, she sent Owen to live with his married sister, Asubah, who trained him in reading and religion. After a year he moved back home and helped raise corn and wheat. He then lived briefly with another relative, Elijah Hill, who worked him hard and paid him little. By 1782 he was home again. That

---

*Because of the large number of errors in spelling, grammar, and usage in Brown's writings and other primary texts, I do not use "[*sic*]" for each error. The quotations are in their original form.

summer a religious revival swept the area, causing the conversion of his mother, his older sisters, and a brother.

The revival was a major turning point for Owen Brown, who devoted much of the rest of his life to a search for signs of salvation in himself and his loved ones. Calvinists believed that a sovereign God freely gave grace to totally depraved humans, certain of whom He "elected" to be saved. Predestined to go either to heaven or to hell, humans received conversion not as a reward for good works but as a gift arbitrarily bestowed by the Divine Judge. Angry because of Adam's disobedience, God mercifully sent Christ to rescue some souls from eternal damnation. Conversion, which was an opening up to this freely given grace, brought delight but not complacency. For example, the famous preacher and theologian Jonathan Edwards testified that after his conversion he tasted the sweetness of God's grace but at the same time became far more conscious of his own sinfulness and helplessness than he had been before it.

Owen knew that although he had already won "the name of a good boy," he could not be sure he was one of God's elect. He turned wholly to religion, hoping to receive assurance of grace. With his family he studied the Bible constantly and joined a church choir, entering "into an association with the better class of people." Around 1784 the Reverend Jeremiah Hallock of the West Simsbury Congregational Church began taking him into his home for periodic religious instruction. A thin, sober teenager with an embarrassing stutter, Owen spent his summers farming and the rest of the time learning the craft of shoemaking. At sixteen he became a traveling cobbler, going from town to town in nearby Massachusetts, returning home the next year to resume his farming and shoemaking there. All the while his mind was on God. He was delighted when the Reverend Hallock hired him for six months, giving him more religious lessons. At that time Owen "was under some conviction of sin" (a good sign) but still wasn't sure about salvation. He later recalled, in self-flagellating Calvinist fashion, "Whether I was pardoned or not, God only knows—this I know I have not lived like a Christian."

When he was twenty, he met the prim, chaste Ruth Mills. A descendant of Congregationalists and Presbyterians, with ministers in her family background, she was ideal for him. He courted her for two years, and on February 13, 1793, they were married in West Simsbury. The Reverend Hallock worried like a parent over the newlyweds' spiritual state, but he could have spared his concern, for they were strongly focused on religion. As devout a Calvinist as her husband, Ruth helped keep his thoughts trained on God. He declared, "I never had any person such an assendence over my conduct

Owen Brown, father of John Brown.
LIBRARY OF CONGRESS.

as my wife, . . . and if I have been respected in the World I must ascribe it more to her than to any other Person."

The couple moved to Norfolk, Connecticut, enjoying a modest prosperity as result of Ruth's frugality and Owen's hard work as a farmer, tanner, and shoemaker. But adversity soon arrived. In 1794, Ruth bore a son, Salmon, who died when he was two, and a year later a second child died shortly after birth. Both husband and wife took ill, and the tanning business suffered. But the last two years of the century brought new blessings. A daughter, Anna, was born in July 1798; and a series of religious revivals that began that year led both Owen and Ruth to feel assured of their salvation. As Owen would recall, "My wife and self made a profession of religion, which I had so poorly manifested in my life."

Like other orthodox Calvinists, Owen could believe himself saved and yet never be free of self-doubt or fear for the souls of his loved ones. To the end of his days, he would express worry over the spiritual condition of those close to him. If a child died, his first concern was whether he or she "died in Christ." Even after a lifetime of praying and Bible-reading, he would begin his scribbled autobiography with this self-critical statement: "My life has been of little worth. Mostly filled up with vanity."

Uncertain of his spiritual state, he nonetheless was definite about a key social issue, American slavery, which he saw as sinful. The Revolutionary War had liberated America from England but had not freed enslaved blacks. The war left slavery intact in twelve of the thirteen states, including all but one in the North (Vermont). Owen was familiar with slavery from his childhood in Connecticut, where slaves were used on farms. At one point his widowed mother, needing help with the crops, had borrowed a neighbor's slave, Sam, a native of Guinea on the African coast. Owen loved playing with the kindly Sam, who carried him on his back, and he was devastated when Sam suddenly died.

If Owen accepted slavery as a child, he came to detest it in early manhood. After slavery had been abolished in Connecticut by gradual-emancipation acts in 1784 and 1787, he overhead the Reverend Hallock discourse on the immorality of slavery to a minister from Rhode Island, where slavery still existed. Also, Hallock showed Owen an antislavery sermon by Jonathan Edwards, Jr.

What further ignited Owen's hatred of slavery was an episode of the 1790s that prefigured the Dred Scott case. A Southern clergyman had traveled north during the Revolution and had left a family of slaves in Norfolk, Connecticut, for reasons of safety. In 1797 or '98, he returned to Norfolk to reclaim the slaves, who resisted him, saying they were now Northerners. The male slave managed to escape, but his wife and children were left in the hands of their ex-master. At a local hearing the minister argued that as a resident of a Southern state he was justified in claiming his property. He was roundly criticized by a panel of local residents, and evidently he returned south without the slaves. Owen later said of the incident: "Ever since, I have been an Abolitionist; I am so near the end of my life I think I shall die an Abolitionist." Indeed, he became a reliable agent for the Underground Railroad, and he once withdrew his support from Western Reserve College in Ohio because it refused to admit blacks.

Into this unusual family atmosphere of fervent Calvinism and equally fervent Abolitionism, John Brown was born on May 9, 1800, in Torrington, Connecticut. Had he appeared at a different historical moment, it is quite possible that Harpers Ferry would not have happened—if so, the Civil War might have been delayed, and slavery might not have been abolished in America as soon as it was. Given the importance of that moment, it is worthwhile to reflect on the antislavery sentiment of that time.

There was no organized Abolitionist movement yet. That would come in 1832 with William Lloyd Garrison's New England Anti-Slavery Society. The founding fathers had given a mixed message about slavery. Jefferson had written human equality into the Declaration of Independence and had prophesied that slavery would eventually lead to a cataclysmic war between the races. But he believed that if the slaves were ever freed they would have to be colonized abroad, and he himself owned over a hundred slaves. George Washington was also a slave-owner. Although the Constitution didn't condone slavery—or even mention it—it tacitly recognized it in its provision for returning "fugitives from labor," its instructions to Congress for quelling insurrections, and the three-fifths clause, which counted three-fifths of each state's slave population when apportioning congressional representation.

Abolitionism, such as it was, came in bits and spurts. The earliest anti-slavery writings voiced sentiments that John Brown would later act upon. The Calvinist judge Samuel Sewall in his 1700 pamphlet *The Selling of Joseph* argued that slavery violated the Golden Rule. "Whatsoever ye would that men should do unto you, do ye even so them," he wrote, applied to blacks, since "These *Ethiopians*, as black as they are; seeing they are the Sons and Daughters of the First *Adam*, the Brethren and sisters of the last ADAM, and the offspring of GOD; They ought to be treated with a Respect agreeable." An obvious Christian point, it would seem. Yet in the two centuries after Sewall made it, shockingly few white Christians admitted that blacks were included in the Golden Rule. An exception was the British revivalist George Whitefield, who during a tour of America in 1739 denounced slavery in a public letter to Southern slaveholders, telling them that it was sinful to use slaves "worse than if they were brutes" and warning, "*The blood of them, spilt for these many years, in your respective provinces, will ascend up to heaven against you!*" Another exception was the New Jersey Quaker John Woolman, who in 1746 reminded slave-owners of the Bible's statements that God "was no respecter of persons" (that is, God's rule was above all human rules) and that holding slaves was "not . . . doing as we would be done by." John Brown would use both the "no respecter of persons" phrase and the Golden Rule as moral weapons against the slave power.

His other main weapon was the Declaration of Independence. He once explained his antislavery stance to George Stearns: "I believe in the Golden Rule, sir, and the Declaration of Independence. I think that both mean the same thing; and it is better that a whole generation should pass off the face of the earth—men, women, and children—by a violent death than that one jot of either should fail in this country. I mean exactly so, sir."

This conflation of the Golden Rule, the Declaration, and visions of apocalyptic violence was extremely unusual for its day. It was made by someone who was descended on both sides from Revolutionary War soldiers and who was born into a Calvinistic family in a state that was among the first to emancipate slaves.

Intense Calvinism and a republican belief in human rights would combine uniquely in John Brown. He never surrendered the Calvinistic doctrines—predestination, total depravity, God's sovereignty, and so forth—he had learned from his parents. Their religion was not the modified Calvinism of nineteenth-century preachers like Charles Grandison Finney or Lyman Beecher, who made room for human agency. Instead, it harked back to the orthodox Calvinism of Puritan times. Owen Brown, describing his conversion, said of the religious revivals of 1798–99: "Perhaps there has never been so general a revival since the days of Edwards and Whitfield." He was linking his conversion to the Great Awakening of the 1740s, when the Massachusetts minister Jonathan Edwards and the traveling British revivalist George Whitefield had prompted mass conversions through their Calvinistic preaching. The most famous sermon in American history, Edwards's "Sinners in the Hands of an Angry God," was delivered in 1741 in Enfield (then in Massachusetts), a few miles from where the Brown family lived.

The fact that Owen Brown prized the tradition of Jonathan Edwards, whose works John Brown would read along with the Bible, reveals the strength of the family's connection to the Puritan past. The Calvinism of Jonathan Edwards was total. For him, God was *absolutely* sovereign, and humans were *absolutely* helpless in the face of God's power. There was no middle ground. Nor would there be for John Brown, who believed that God determined everything. He would tell Frederick Douglass that God had made the Allegheny Mountains as a haven for escaped slaves. When his Harpers Ferry raid misfired, he considered it predestined. As he wrote a friend from his Virginia prison, "The disgrace of hanging does not trouble me in the least. In fact, I know that the very errors by which my scheme was marred were decreed before the world was made."

There was, however, a key distinction between the religion of Edwards and that of Brown. The latter's was permeated with a republican insistence on social rights for all. The American Revolution had made a difference. Its impact was visible in Jonathan Edwards's clergyman son, who shaped Brown's Abolitionism. The religion of Jonathan Edwards, Jr., was perhaps even more severe than his father's, since he described the delights of salvation with less passion than had the elder Edwards, while he still emphasized sin and damnation. But the younger Edwards devoted himself to combatting not only his father's main opponent—liberal religion—but also the institution of slavery. Like Jefferson, Edwards Jr. had a belief in social equality that fostered a hatred of slavery. But he had neither Southern loyalties nor slaves that qualified this hatred.

Why, though, did the younger Edwards, and John Brown after him, adopt Abolitionism when most other Calvinists of their day did not? The fusion of Abolitionism and Puritanism can be seen as a rare product of Protestant ferment at a moment when republican feelings were fresh and the disestablishment of religion had recently occurred. John Brown may have thought he was predestined from all eternity to free the slaves, but in fact it was by mere chance that he was born at a moment when American Protestantism had just hit the fan of disestablishment, sending it in all kinds of directions. In the seventy years just after the Revolution, an amazing variety of Protestantisms would arise. To give some notorious examples, the Shakers would recommend celibacy, the perfectionists under John Humphrey Noyes would introduce complex marriage (many sexual partners for each woman), the Millerites would predict the imminent end of the world, and the Mormons would practice polygamy—all under the aegis of Protestant Christianity.

By the mid twentieth century more than 250 Protestant sects and denominations would exist in America. Each would announce itself as the final word about God and the Bible, when in fact each was a mutation of ever-evolving American Protestantism. The Abolitionist Calvinism of Jonathan Edwards, Jr., and Owen Brown's family was no exception to the rule. It was a chance mutation. Unlike many other Protestant mutations, which gave rise to large churches, it won few converts because of the near-universal racism of American whites at that time.

In the early going, most Protestant offshoots arose in the North. The South remained the domain of more conservative Protestant strains such as Episcopalianism and Methodism. Small wonder that Southerners called Abolitionism another bizarre Northern Protestant craze. Northern Calvinism, with its emphasis on individual interpretations of the Bible, seemed especially culpable to the South. As George Fitzhugh, the South's leading critic of Abolitionism, argued, "History will show that Geneva [John Calvin's home] was the birthplace of modern *isms*, modern infidelity, anarchy, and military despotism. . . . In America, the Revolution placed all churches on the political Calvinistic platform, for it freed them all equally from a political head. . . . The result has been that all Northern churches have exhibited anarchical and schismatic tendencies, while all Southern churches have become eminently conservative, kind, and respectful to each other."

Although this claim misrepresented many Northern movements, which were often Protestant without being specifically Calvinistic, it accurately described the Christian Abolitionism promoted by Jonathan Edwards, Jr., and by the Brown family. The Revolution indeed had freed American churches "equally from a political head," so that Protestants were more able than ever to offer individual versions of Christianity. The version offered by the younger Edwards branded slavery as a violation of both the Bible and American principles. In a typical sermon of 1791, Edwards said, "To hold any man in slavery, is to be every day guilty of robbing him of his liberty, or of *man-stealing*. Fifty years from this time it will be as shameful for a man to hold a slave as to be guilty of common theft or robbery." The fact that Owen Brown's Abolitionism was influenced by a sermon by the younger Edwards shown to him by Hallock establishes that John Brown's Abolitionism was truly in the Puritan Calvinist tradition.

To say John Brown was rooted in New England Puritanism begs the question: Wasn't that also true of many other reformers? What made him different?

While many reformers—including Emerson, Theodore Parker, George Stearns, and Samuel G. Howe, to name some who were close to Brown—had deep Puritan roots, what distinguished Brown was that he *remained* an old-style Puritan. All these reformers had either rejected Calvinism in favor of liberal religion or, in the case of Emerson and Parker, had jettisoned Christianity altogether. Thomas Wentworth Higginson, a Secret Six member also descended from early New England, noted: "John Brown is almost the only radical abolitionist I have ever known who was not more or less radical in religious matters also. His theology was Puritan, like his practice; and accustomed as we are now to see Puritan doctrines and Puritan virtues separately exhibited, it seems quite strange to behold them combined in one person again."

When he called Brown "almost the only" Puritan Abolitionist he knew, he may have been thinking as well of Wendell Phillips, the dynamic anti-slavery orator who, like Brown, was a devout Calvinist. Notably, Phillips came the closest to Brown, among the antebellum reformers, in the urgency of his demands for full social rights for American blacks. If Brown was the *least* racist white person among the pre–Civil War public figures I've investigated, Phillips was a close second—proof again of the social radicalism generated by Puritanism.

To mention Phillips, however, is to highlight another aspect of Brown's uniqueness: his lowly background and his humble lifestyle. Phillips, weaned in the Boston Brahmin society, was a Harvard graduate distanced from the blacks he defended. Although he was a reformer in the militant Puritan mold, he was also one of the wealthiest men in Boston, and he occasionally betrayed a patrician attitude.

Brown, in contrast, emerged from generations of plain folk, and for most of his life he straddled the poverty line. Unlike the Boston moguls and Concord philosophers who backed him, he approached social reform not from "above" but from ground level—one is tempted to say dirt level. If he later based his Abolitionism on the Bible's injunction to "suffer with those in bonds as bound with them," it is partly because his democratic sympathies grew from a hardscrabble existence.

It is impossible to review Brown's childhood without feeling that the rigors of his family's Calvinistic faith were matched by the rigors of his daily life. Long before he battled American slavery, he was both toughened and humanized by a grueling pioneer life in ethnically diverse environments.

The Pioneer

In 1805 the Browns moved from Connecticut to Hudson, Ohio. The thirty-four-year-old Owen Brown, having struggled as a tanner and farmer in New England, had visited Hudson the year before. He had found the small community there "very harmonious and middling prosperous, and most united in religious sentiments." He bought land in the center of Hudson, deciding it would be a good place to try surveying and perhaps set up his own tannery.

He was following in the tracks of other Connecticut Calvinists who had relocated to Ohio's Western Reserve. Hudson, founded in 1799 by Deacon David Hudson, was by 1805 a frontier township in which twenty-five to thirty families occupied an area of some twenty-five square miles. Whites were a small minority in the region, which consisted mainly of Indian tribes, including the Senecas, the Oneidas, the Chippewas, the Ottawas, the Onondagas, and the Mingoes. Four years before the Brown family came, the Indians had seen the arrival of the Reverend Joseph Badger, a clergyman who traveled some 1,700 miles by horseback to spread Calvinistic Christianity. Other Connecticut settlers followed, and soon the Western Reserve was also known as New Connecticut.

In migrating to Ohio, Owen Brown was repeating the "errand into the wilderness" his Puritan forefathers had attempted when they had first settled New England. Having recently experienced his religious conversion, Owen believed that in New Connecticut he would join a community of saints engaged in winning the American West for the Lord, just as, in his mind, Peter Brown had come on the *Mayflower* to New England to Christianize the New World.

What Owen could not realize was that his own errand into the wilderness, guided by his unusual brand of Christianity featuring respect for people of all ethnicities, would prepare the way for the pioneering antislavery activities of his oldest son.

The trip west was beset with dangers. In a small ox-drawn wagon train, Owen set out on June 9, 1805, with his thirty-three-year-old wife Ruth and their four children: Ruth, who was seven; John, five; Salmon, three; and the one-year-old Oliver. Along with them were the eleven-year-old Levi Blakeslee, whom they had adopted, and the Connecticut schoolmaster Benjamin Whedon and his kindly wife. Their route took them through southern New York and Pennsylvania to Pittsburgh, where they crossed the Allegheny River and followed the Beaver River to the Mahoning Indian Trail, which led them through Ohio's Western Reserve to Hudson, about twenty-five miles south of Cleveland.

One of John Brown's earliest memories was the grueling forty-eight-day journey, which for him was an endless source of adventure. He later recalled his thrill at trekking through "a wilderness filled with wild beasts, & Indians" and encountering packs of "Rattle Snakes which were very large; & which some of the company generally managed to kill." His father let him help drive the oxen and ride the horses, giving him a sense of accomplishment.

In Hudson the Browns lived in a log house that Owen built. There was only one room, about fourteen-by-sixteen feet, with a small loft—a necessity, since seven people occupied the house. The door hung on wooden hinges and was barred by a rough plank. The iron pots in the fireplace produced little besides cornmeal mush, johnnycakes, and bread. The Browns planted corn the first spring after their arrival, but blackbirds and squirrels ate most of the seeds, and the crop was damaged by an unexpected summer frost. Owen survived by surveying land parcels in the Western Reserve. Soon he had earned enough to buy a better house and start a tannery.

The community of saints he had envisaged took the form of the Ecclesiastical Convention of New Connecticut, a religious group devoted to spreading Calvinism and building Congregational and Presbyterian churches throughout the Western Reserve. From 1805 to 1808, Owen Brown was a delegate to the convention, along with three other leading Hudson citizens, Captain Heman Oviatt, Deacon Stephen Thompson, and Hudson's founder, Deacon David Hudson.

If the Browns were pioneers in their errand into a wilderness, they were also pioneers in forging friendly relations with people of different races. Owen's childhood friendship with the likable African native Sam, along with his Christian Abolitionism, had rid him of racial prejudice. He forbade his family to discriminate against people of color.

Unlike earlier Christian settlers from Columbus through Cortés to William Bradford, the Browns did not let feelings of so-called ethnic or religious superiority poison their view of the natives. For them, Indians were not savage "others" to be conquered but rather fellow humans to be respected.

The Browns were unusual not only among previous explorers but even among their fellow whites in Hudson. Owen would later explain that his kindly attitude toward the natives was not generally shared: "When we came to Ohio the Indians were more numerous than the white People but were very friendly and I beleave were a benifet rather than injery there [were] some Persons that seamed disposed to quarel with the Indians, but I never had."

Owen Brown was a rare instance of a white American completely committed to Christianity but at the same time intent on not forcing his religion or customs on the Indians. Though he had come to Hudson, as he explained, "with a determination to help . . . in the seport of religion and civil Order," he had not come to proselytize or dominate the natives.

To the contrary, he had a mutually beneficial relationship with them. He exchanged meal and bread for the turkey, venison, and fish they brought him. Sometimes they were late in filling their side of the bargain, but they always proved "faithfull to pay their debts." When in 1806 the Cayahoga Indians were threatened by another tribe, they appealed to Owen, who organized the building of a protective cabin for them. If he wanted to win over the natives to Christianity, his tactic was one of comradeship and example, not violence. When the disruptive War of 1812 resulted in the departure of many of the area's natives, Owen Brown was not happy, as were many of his neighbors. "The Indians," he wrote, "left these parts mostly, and rather against my wishes."

The result of his racial openness was a truly multicultural upbringing for his son John, who mixed freely with the natives in the Hudson area. The rifle-toting natives at first frightened John, but, in his words, he "used to hang about them quite as much as was consistent with good manners; & learned a trifle of their talk." They taught his father how to skin deer, and soon John was wearing buckskin, like the Indians. At six, he would later recall, he "was installed a young Buck Skin"—a reference, perhaps, to a play initiation ceremony into a tribe concocted by his young Indian friends. One poor Indian boy gave him a yellow marble that he treasured. He lost the marble—the cause of great sorrow to him, as was the loss of a bobtail squirrel he had found in the woods and tamed.

Although his parents doubtless approved of John's friendship with the natives, they must have sometimes worried about his spiritual condition. The boy resisted their Christian teachings and chafed under their harsh discipline. Never would John forget the punishment he received from his mother when he lied about stealing three brass pins from a girl who lived with them. His mother drew a confession from him, and then had him brood over his guilt for a day before giving him "a thorough whipping." His father was quick with the rod, evidently for good reason, since John had a wild streak. He was sent to a schoolhouse in Hudson, but he recalled enjoying it only for "the opportunity it afforded to wrestle, & Snow ball & run & jump & knock off old seedy Wool hats." Such scampish activity was for him "almost the only compensation for the confinement, & restraints of school."

His schooling was intermittent, for his father needed his help at the tannery, where John learned how to make leather from the skins of many kinds of animals, including squirrels, cats, and raccoons. John preferred working hard at home to going to school, though he went often enough to know that he disliked arithmetic. He enjoyed reading after a friend introduced him to some volumes of history. He never bothered to perfect his grammar: When Thoreau said that John Brown would leave a Greek accent falling the wrong way but would right a fallen man, he was being kind. Brown had enough trouble with English punctuation and spelling to worry about Greek. Still, he developed a sinewy writing style forceful enough to elicit high praise from Emerson and Lowell—and especially from Thoreau, who said that Brown's prose, with all its technical errors, defined standard English.

John Brown's courage was visible early on. Although not given to picking fights, he "was *excessively* fond of the *hardest & roughest* kind of plays; & could *never get enough* [of] them." The boys in Hudson formed rival gangs, the "Federalists" and the "Republicans," according to their parents' political views. John's father was a Federalist who opposed Republicans such as Jefferson and Madison because they were slaveholders. Once a play fight turned cruel when the Republican boys pelted John's group, the Federalists, with heavy, wet snowballs that threatened injury. Infuriated, John ran headlong into the Republican gang, scattering it single-handedly.

He needed courage to face the loss of his mother, who died in childbirth on December 9, 1808. Both eight-year-old John and his father were devastated by the loss. Owen, left with six children to care for, including the adopted Levi Blakeslee, didn't let much time pass before he looked for another wife. Within a year, he was married to the twenty-year-old Sallie Root. John, who felt he would never recover from his mother's death, had trouble accepting his stepmother. He called her "a sensible, inteligent, & on many accounts a very estimable woman" but admitted he "*never adopted her in feeling.*" He pined after his mother for years.

By the time John was twelve, the population of Hudson had grown to 202. Sawmills and gristmills had sprung up, and the farms were stocked with swine, sheep, and cows. Doctor's offices, lawyer's offices, saloons, and a few shops bordered the town's dirt streets, which were muddy in the winter and dusty in the summer. Rude log cabins still dominated the area, but Deacon Hudson, the town's founder, had built a white New England–style frame house that signaled the future.

The War of 1812 once again tested the pioneering spirit of the Brown family. Owen Brown became a chief provider of beef and horses for General William Hull's army on the Detroit front. He had to make regular hundred-mile cattle drives northwest around the shore of Lake Erie and up into Michigan to Hull's camp. He often took John along and at least once sent the boy to drive a herd alone on the wilderness trail.

It was during one of these long cattle drives that John Brown had two revelations that would inform the rest of his life. One related to the army. The profanity, disobedience, and mutinous talk of Hull's soldiers appalled him, and he vowed never to serve in the military. As he later recalled, "The effect of what he saw during the war was to so far disgust him with Military affairs that he would neither train, *or drill*; but paid fines; & got along like a Quaker untill his age finally has cleared him of Military duty."

His second revelation was that slavery was evil. His parents had prepared him for this discovery by teaching him that the Golden Rule applied to people of all races—a rare notion for American whites of that era. On one trip he befriended a slave boy his own age owned by the family he was lodging with. The boy was intelligent and benevolent. John rankled at the preferential treatment that he, as a white, received from the family. The slave's master praised the twelve-year-old John for his good sense and his ability to travel far from his family, but he maltreated the black boy, beating him with household tools and making him sleep in the cold in rags. John instantly recognized "the wretched, hopeless condition, of *Fatherless & Motherless* slave *children:* for such children have neither Fathers nor Mothers to protect & provide for them." He would call this incident a main factor in the process that "in the end made him a most *determined Abolitionist,*" leading him "to declare, *or Swear: Eternal war* with Slavery."

These childhood revelations distinguished him from most of his contemporaries. Other white reformers of his day would adopt ardent antislavery positions much later in life than he. For many, it took significant public events to spark active involvement in the antislavery movement. For Wendell Phillips, the motivating events for such involvement were the 1835 mobbing of William Lloyd Garrison and the 1837 murder of the antislavery editor Elijah Lovejoy. Nathaniel P. Rogers's conversion to Abolitionism was caused by the 1835 lecture tour of the British antislavery reformer George Thompson. For Emerson the touchstone moments were the 1832 emancipation of slaves in the West Indies and the proslavery Compromise of 1850; for Lincoln, the Mexican War and the failure of an emancipation bill in Kentucky; for Thoreau, the Mexican War and the rendition of the fugitive slave Anthony Burns; and so on.

John Brown, too, would be deeply affected by such events. What set him apart was that antislavery passion was rooted in his family background and in his childhood friendship with the pitiable slave boy. From a young age, hatred of slavery flamed in the core of his being.

This early disgust with slavery helps explain the extreme measures he would later take against the institution. The other Abolitionists were, by and large, pacifists, and they would maintain their pacifism, embracing violence against the South only as a last resort. John Brown began as a pacifist in his rejection of the military but would take the unique step of dismissing pacifism when he realized the depth of the South's devotion to slavery. His antislavery convictions overwhelmed his pacifism, because they were not acquired over time: they simmered within him from childhood onward.

Little would have come of these convictions, however, had they not fused with religious fervor. In his early teenage years John Brown wrestled with sin in typically Calvinistic fashion. Helpful around the tannery and gifted with practical intelligence, he impressed his elders, whose flattery led him to think highly of himself. As he would recall, he became "quite full of self-conceit," and, despite a tendency to bashfulness, he admitted to being dictatorial with his peers. He knew that he was ignoring the Bible's warnings against vanity. He also felt guilty because he had grown "quite skeptical" of religion. He was ripe for a conversion.

It came when he was sixteen. Following his parents' example, but at a much earlier age, John Brown made a public profession of faith. Guided by the Reverend Mr. Hanford, in 1816 he announced his repentance and his acceptance of Christ in the small schoolhouse that served as the Hudson Congregational Church. He turned to religious studies. He avidly read the Bible, accepting its "divine authenticity" and aiming to commit its "entire contents" to memory. He also memorized most of the pieces in Isaac Watts's famous hymnal. Intending to pursue his religious studies, at seventeen he set out for the East with his fourteen-year-old brother Salmon and a family friend, Orson M. Oviatt. They rode horses that they sold when they reached New England.

Their first stop was at the home of his family's mentor, the Reverend Jeremiah Hallock, who advised them to attend a school in Plainfield, Massachusetts, run by a relative, Moses Hallock. By the fall of 1816 the three boys were enrolled in the school. Moses Hallock would recall Brown as a tall, sedate boy devoted to his studies, which included rhetoric, grammar, math, Latin, and Greek. John had brought with him some large pieces of leather he had tanned at home. One was for resoling his shoes, and another was for other students to pull on. On a dare, Hallock's father boasted he would snap the piece by pulling it with his hands. He struggled mightily but failed; his son long recalled "the very marked yet kind immovableness of [John Brown's] face, on seeing father's defeat."

John remained in this school only a few months, transferring that winter to the Morris Academy in Litchfield, Connecticut. The other two boys followed. The school's director, the Reverend William R. Weeks, and his young assistant, Herman L. Vaill, found John to be a serious young man ready to assume a fatherly role with his rambunctious brother Salmon. Once when Salmon committed an infraction, John asked Vaill if he planned to punish the boy, saying that their father would if they were at home and announcing his intention to do so if Vaill refused. When Vaill demurred, John flogged Salmon.

Wishing to devote his life to religion, John aimed to train for the ministry. Decades later Vaill would remind him of the Morris Academy years "and how we had religious meetings for religious conferences and prayers, in which your own voice was so often heard." John hoped to receive his divinity training at Amherst College. Funds were running short, however, and an eye inflammation interfered with his studies. By the summer of 1817, he had returned to Ohio, having reluctantly abandoned his ministerial plans.

He resumed his work at his father's tannery but before long decided to go into business for himself. With his adopted brother Levi Blakeslee he started a tannery about a mile northwest of the center of Hudson, on the road toward Cleveland. They built a barn where they soaked, dried, and cured leather. Nearby they erected a cabin where they kept what they called a "Bachelor's Hall," with John doing the cooking and baking.

John Brown at eighteen was a lean man of five feet ten inches, with dark hair brushed straight back and a chiseled face whose determined look was accented by hollow cheeks, a sharp jaw, and glittering gray-blue eyes. Plain in dress, he was fastidiously neat. By reading the lives of what he called "great, wise & good men," he had grown to dislike "vain & frivolous" conversation and people. Purposeful and tenacious, he liked establishing plans and sticking to them, confident of success.

Success, however, would rarely come, at least in the financial sense. Although he had good instincts as a tanner and later as a surveyor, farmer, and wool dealer, he lacked the tact and flexibility it took to succeed in business. Also, like many other aspiring businessmen, he would be buffeted by the financial panics that periodically struck the American economy before the Civil War.

He might have avoided financial distress had he heeded the experience of his father. Owen Brown had put himself in a precarious position by buying large land parcels on speculation. Between 1819 and 1823 the first great economic depression of the nineteenth century came and nearly wiped him out. "Money became scarce," he recalled, "property fell, and that which I thought well bought would not bring its cost." His bad timing in business would rub off on his son, but so would his stoical acceptance of failure. Owen conceded that the economic panic had left him "a heavy loser" but turned to religion for solace: "I can say the loss or gain of property in a short time appears but of little consequence, they are momentary things, and will look very small in eternity. Job left us a good example."

If the father and son were not destined to be pioneers of capitalism, they did become unwitting pioneers of American race relations. Without an awareness of doing anything extraordinary, believing they were simply practicing Christianity—even though most American Christians would have considered their tolerant racial attitudes heretical—they risked their reputations and even their lives to defend oppressed slaves.

Their first known test came in 1817, a significant year because it also saw the founding of the first large antislavery organization, the American Colonization Society. Colonizationists argued that slaves should be emancipated and deported to Africa or elsewhere, since equal rights were impossible for blacks to achieve in the United States. Although little came of the movement other than sending a number of boatloads of blacks to Liberia, colonization had a surprisingly wide impact on American culture. Jefferson was an ardent colonizationist, as were Henry Clay, Harriet Beecher Stowe, and Abraham Lincoln, to name a few. Colonization also engendered William Lloyd Garrison's American Anti-Slavery Society, which arose in protest against the colonization scheme, considering it racist and impractical.

Owen and John Brown were worlds apart from the colonizationists in their view of slavery. For them, blacks were not inferior beings to be excluded from America; instead, they were equals to be integrated into white society. As will be seen, John Brown would often welcome blacks into his home. His first step in this direction came shortly after his return from the East, when a fugitive slave approached him and Levi Blakeslee, begging for help in evading a band of white pursuers. While Blakeslee went to town for supplies, Brown took the fugitive into his cabin. When the sound of approaching horses was heard, he told the black man to flee through a window and hide in the brush. The sounds turned out to be neighbors returning to town. Brown went to retrieve the fugitive, whom he found cowering behind a log. Like the incident of the maltreated slave boy, this one led Brown to vow "eternal enmity to slavery."

For the next two decades, this kind of direct aid to individual blacks would be John Brown's chosen method of combating slavery. Hudson was a popular station on the Underground Railroad, that network of secret links facilitating the flight of black fugitive slaves from the South to the far North or Canada. Owen and John Brown were active workers for the Underground Railroad, ready at all times to hide fugitives and help them on their way north.

As important as antislavery activity was to John Brown, at this point it was not a deliberate program but something he did unself-consciously and instinctively, like breathing. It was part of his other daily activities. In his late teens, he was mainly concerned with running his tannery. He also eyed work as a land surveyor. Using Abel Flint's *System of Geometry and Trigonometry Together with a Treatise on Surveying*, he struggled to decipher the tangents, logarithms, and scientific tables needed to master surveyor's instruments.

By early 1820 his duties at the tannery necessitated his use of a housekeeper for chores around the cabin. He took in a widow from the neighborhood, Mrs. Amos Lusk, who, like him, was descended from the New England Puritans. Helping her with the housekeeping duties was her nineteen-year-old daughter Dianthe, a short, plain woman of deep piety who loved singing hymns and praying alone in the woods. Although humorless, she was pleasant and disarmingly candid. John Brown, encouraged by his father and attracted by Dianthe's quiet virtue, engaged in a brief courtship that resulted in their marriage on June 21, 1820, probably in Hudson's new Congregational meetinghouse, which had been dedicated that March.

Until her death after childbirth on August 10, 1832, Dianthe would be a guiding presence in John Brown's life. He later recalled her as a "neat industrious & economical girl; of excellent character; earnest piety; & good practical common sense" who through mild admonitions "maintained a most powerful; & good influence" over him. She bore seven children, five of whom—John Jr., Jason, Owen, Ruth, and Frederick—would survive to adulthood.

Despite Brown's fond recollections of Dianthe, their marriage was not problem-free. Her family had a history of mental illness; two of her sisters supposedly showed symptoms of it. Although Dianthe was stable through much of her marriage, she reportedly exhibited some derangement, especially toward the end. Her two oldest sons, John and Frederick, would also have bouts of "insanity." These mental problems, along with apparent aberrations among others of John Brown's extended family, including some of his blood relatives, would be brought up at Brown's 1859 trial as a last-minute gesture toward an insanity defense. Brown rejected the tactic vigorously, insisting he was not insane.

In light of everything I've read by and about him, I believe him. His wife's condition remains unclear. John Jr.'s problems were intermittent. Frederick, as Brown himself admitted, was the most consistently disturbed of the immediate family—though even he enjoyed long periods of normalcy. But I cannot categorize John Brown as insane, as some have done.

Insanity, a fuzzy term anyway, was particularly so in an era when phrenology with its bump-reading and brain "organs" was accepted as high science, and when "monomania" was a catchall word for any dogged behavior out of the ordinary. At the very least, it is impossible, given the evidence, to brand Brown as insane simply on the basis of the fact that some of his relatives had symptoms of what was then called insanity.

More relevant to Brown's later development than his wife's mental state was a difficulty that arose in his relationship with her brother, Milton Lusk. Milton was very close to Dianthe, calling her "my guiding star, my guardian angel," and saying she sang to him beautifully and sometimes took him to pray with her in the woods. When she became John Brown's housekeeper, he tried to visit her Sundays, his day off. John Brown, a firm believer in the holiness of the Sabbath, refused the Sunday visits. Milton became enraged and declared, "John, I won't come Sunday or any other day." An open quarrel ensued, and Milton declined to attend his sister's wedding.

What makes this squabble significant is Brown's utter insistence on the sanctity of the Sabbath. He was willing to risk upsetting his beloved Dianthe in order to adhere to his belief in the Sabbath. Although strict sabbatarianism was not rare among nineteenth-century Americans, Brown would twice prove himself unique—on May 25, 1856, at Pottawatomie and on October 16, 1859, at Harpers Ferry—when he chose Sundays to carry out his terrorist campaigns against slavery.

In other words, he could refuse Sunday visits, but he could commit murder on Sunday. The apparent paradox resulted from the fact that his passionate sabbatarianism eventually fused with his antislavery zeal. He chose Sunday in order to put an exclamation point on his holy war against slavery. On the Sunday he began the Harpers Ferry raid, he woke his men early and called them to worship to pray for success in their effort to topple slavery.

Back in June 1820, however, the newly wed John Brown was thinking not of antislavery battles but of starting a family and succeeding in business. He could not foresee how large his family would grow or how often death would visit his household.

Least of all could he anticipate how his antislavery battles would consume his life and would spark the bloodiest war in American history.

4

The Patriarch

John Brown fathered twenty children by two wives. Even in a time when families were large (the average American household had around nine children), this number was extraordinary. More typical was the percentage of his children who did not make it to adulthood. Only eight—four by each wife—would outlive him. Among the remainder, two died shortly after being born, six were victims of childhood illnesses, and one was scalded to death in a kitchen accident.

Such early deaths were, tragically, all too common in the era before modern medicine. Although these deaths were not unusual, those of three others—Frederick, Oliver, and Watson—were. These sons died while accompanying their father in his war against slavery. Three more sons, John Jr., Owen, and Jason, also risked their lives in this private war, escaping death only by ingenuity and luck. As for the four surviving daughters, they accepted their brothers' deaths with stoic approval.

How did John Brown breed these antislavery martyrs? The same unique mix of Calvinistic religion, racial tolerance, and antislavery passion from his childhood carried over into his offspring, intensifying exponentially as the slavery crisis deepened. The clan raised by John Brown was the only white family in pre–Civil War America willing both to live with black people and to die for them.

Not long before his death, John Brown advised his sons to pattern their lives after the biblical patriarchs. He himself had done so. His interpretation of Calvinism drew equally from the Old and the New testaments, both of which he knew as well as any preacher. From the Old he derived a belief in a stern, judgmental God who commanded humans to fight for justice and to "increase and multiply." From the New he absorbed the idea of a loving, self-sacrificing Christ and a sympathy for "those in bonds." Joined with an absolute belief in predestination, which was inherited from Jonathan Edwards, this religious outlook made Brown and his children come to believe that they were chosen by God to free millions of enslaved blacks.

In the early going John Brown was more interested in increasing and multiplying than in rescuing slaves, even though their plight was never far from his mind. Just as biblical patriarchs like Abraham and Jacob felt they were God-directed in founding a religious race, John Brown was driven to disseminate piety by creating a religious family. He did so with a strictness that rivaled that of the God he believed in, yet with moments of genuine tenderness.

"Family" for John Brown meant more than his wife and children. It meant everyone around him, especially his employees at the tannery. James Foreman, who began at the tannery in 1820, recalled that Brown, who never sat down to a meal without praying, ruled "that his apprentices and journeymen must under all circumstances attend church every Sabbath and family worship every morning."

This religious stricture did not set well with all of the workers. One of them, rebelling against Brown's severity, stole a piece of fine calfskin from the tannery and gave it to his brother. Brown discovered the theft and gave the man a verbal thrashing that made him weep. The worker threatened to leave and never return, but Brown said if he did so he would prosecute him "to the end of the law." Brown then ordered that none of the other workers could talk with the thief for two months. Foreman commented, "I think a worse punishment could not have been set upon a poor human being than that was to him, but it reformed him and he afterwards became a useful man."

John Brown even disciplined complete strangers as though they were family. Once, when his wife Dianthe was ill after giving birth, he galloped off in search of a doctor. On the way he passed an apple orchard where he spotted two men taking fruit that was obviously not theirs and putting it into large bags, which they tied to their horses. Forgetting his wife's condition, Brown halted his horse and chased the men down. Commanding them to empty the bags, he said he wouldn't report their crime if they owned up to it then and there. They obeyed, and he lectured them on the wickedness of stealing.

Long before Pottawatomie and Harpers Ferry, then, John Brown was engaged in vigilante justice. In his mind God was the only true judge, and he, God's servant, was the enforcer of divine law.

The way he ran his business did not jibe with the practices of the emerging capitalist economy. Although the era of a smile and a shoe shine was still a long way off, the antebellum period had its own kinds of commercial hype, such as the countless ads for homespun medicines—only $1 a bottle!—promising to cure everything from rheumatism to cancer, or the dime shows exhibiting two-headed chickens, bearded ladies, and similar freaks.

John Brown was the opposite end of the spectrum from such ploys. He was too honest to succeed as a capitalist. Only later, when he was raising money and guns for his antislavery terrorism, would he become an effective salesman, though even then it was sincerity rather than slickness that won contributors.

At his Hudson tannery he was ready to lose customers in the name of probity. He refused to sell his leather unless it was in perfect condition. If any moisture remained in a piece after it had been soaked and dried, he wouldn't allow a customer to take it even if he or she had traveled ten miles for it. Nor did he manage his hiring and firing normally. Hearing that a family in the neighborhood was destitute, he charitably hired the father even though he had no immediate opening, giving him clothing and food as advance payment.

If he wasn't maximizing his profits, he was earning a good name for himself. He taught Sunday school in the Congregational meetinghouse. He joined a local Masonic lodge, though he later quit the Masons after they became embroiled in the scandal surrounding the disappearance of William Morgan, an upstate New York man who was allegedly murdered by members of the group. The tannery prospered sufficiently so that by 1824 he could buy several nearby land parcels and replace his cabin with a white frame house.

Meanwhile, children came, initially in a trickle. The first was a boy, born on July 25, 1821, whom John Brown named after himself. Nineteen months later came Jason, followed by Owen in November 1824. These children arrived when their father was in the first flush of his magisterial sternness. John, Jason, and Owen received the brunt of his Old Testament–style discipline. They were not allowed to play or have visitors on the Sabbath. His later children would benefit from his growing tenderness.

John Jr. would never forget his father's means of controlling his sometimes-recalcitrant boys. "Father had a rule not to threaten one of his children. He commanded, and there was obedience." Usually, but not always. When obedience did not come, the rod or the switch was always ready.

John Brown believed that his own sinfulness was reflected in his children's disobedience. This explains the masochistic extremes to which he could take his punishment of them. He kept a sharp eye on his oldest son, taking note of even minor wrongdoing. He put John to work in the tannery, having him drive a blind horse in a circle to grind bark. The task was tedious, and the boy habitually daydreamed, looking out the window at neighborhood children at play. This was one of the offenses that appeared in a list his father kept in a ledger:

John, Jr.,

For disobeying mother.........................8 lashes

For unfaithfulness at work ....3 lashes

For telling a lie ....8 lashes

John Brown often showed his son the book, ordering him to reform. Finally, he decided that the boy's "debits" outnumbered his "credits," leaving him "bankrupt." He took him into the barn for an "accounting." He seized a beech switch and gave the boy a third of his apportioned number of lashes. He stopped unexpectedly, took off his shirt, and bent down. He commanded his son to whip him. The terrified boy administered the whip softly. His father cried, "Harder; harder, harder!" until he had "received the balance of the account." Blood bubbled on the father's back. The boy could not understand why the innocent should suffer at the hands of the guilty. "But at that time," he later wrote, "I had not read the ponderous volumes of Jonathan Edwards's sermons which father owned."

The Edwards reference was apt. Although there is no record of Jonathan Edwards ever having been whipped, either by one of his children or by himself, his autobiographical *Personal Narrative* reveals that he subjected himself to spiritual self-flagellation that was as painful as any physical beating. Even after his conversion, as he reported, he "often had . . . very affecting views of my own sinfulness and vileness; very frequently so as to hold me in a kind of loud weeping, sometimes for a considerable time together." This tradition of the self-flagellating American Calvinist was familiar enough to Nathaniel Hawthorne that in *The Scarlet Letter* he featured the tormented Puritan preacher Arthur Dimmesdale, who is consumed by guilt and applies a lash to his own back. John Brown, by having his son whip him, was not just making a parental point. He was expressing a Calvinistic conviction of sin.

His attention to such spiritual matters was always interwoven with his practical affairs. Although he had developed a solid tanning business, Hudson had grown quickly and had lost its rural feel. All his life he would love wild spaces and living off the land. He remained as devoted to the subsistence lifestyle that had predated the capitalist economy as he was to the Puritan values of the past. He would later congratulate three of his sons who chose to be farmers or shepherds for following "the pursuit of the patriarchs." His own role as a biblical patriarch could be better filled in the wilderness than in an expanding town.

In the spring of 1825 he heard of large, inexpensive land tracts for sale in northwestern Pennsylvania in Randolph Township, Crawford County, some ninety miles east of Hudson. He visited the area and loved its openness. He bought a two-hundred-acre parcel and moved there with his wife and three children in May 1826. To many, Randolph (soon renamed New Richmond) would have seemed forbidding, since it was a wilderness filled with bears, wolves, deer, and wild turkeys. But for a man bent on resurrecting the primitive ways of the Bible, it was ideal.

If the Old Testament patriarchs founded races, John Brown founded an American community. In his nine years in the township he became the area's first businessman and first postmaster, and he founded its first school and its first church. His "family" now extended beyond his home and work—it included many of those living in that section of Pennsylvania.

It took him just four months to clear twenty-five acres of timbered land and build a log house, a barn, and a tannery. The house stood on a rise of land a hundred feet from the state road that ran to the nearest town, Meadville, twelve miles away. It was divided into two large rooms: a family room that served as a kitchen and a dining area; and another room used as a library and schoolroom. Fireplaces flanked both rooms. Sleeping quarters consisted of tiny compartments above and in the tannery. The tannery itself was an impressive frame structure, measuring twenty-six by fifty feet, that held eighteen vats. Within a year of his arrival, Brown had hired ten to fifteen workers.

He had been drawn to the area by its abundance of the kinds of bark used in the leather-tanning process. However, because sheep and cattle herds were sparse in the region, hides were more difficult to come by than they had been in Hudson. Also, the area's scattered population precluded easy sale of his leather.

He tried to overcome these difficulties through a business arrangement that made sense but proved precarious. He had a distant relative, Seth B. Thompson, who raised cows and sheep in Trumbull County, near the Ohio-Pennsylvania line. The two struck a deal whereby Thompson provided cattle that Brown sold to supply beef to his area. In turn, Brown, the only tanner in New Richmond, used the cattle hides to make leather he sent to Thompson, who sold it in his more populated region. Also, Thompson often sent Brown his own cowhides to be tanned in exchange for barrels of salt pork.

For a time, the partnership worked and the tannery thrived. By June 1831, Brown was able to give his apprentice James Foreman a 116-acre farm parcel as a reward "for faithful service." The next month he bought 200 additional acres for $600.

Problems arose over the exchange of money with Thompson. A bumbling capitalist, Brown began a pattern of operating on credit that would in later years lead to bankruptcy and legal tangles. Those who bought beef from him were often slow in paying him, and he was forced to take bank loans with promissory notes signed by Thompson. Brown kept afloat by selling off land parcels, first a ninety-one-acre one and then a hundred-acre one, but by the spring of 1832 he was so stretched he could not afford even the down payment on an ox team. Although Thompson took the situation well, the relationship became strained.

Brown never had a head for the financial side of the tanning business— or of any business, for that matter. His main interest in tanning was the opportunity it gave him to live around animals and have the sense of being a shepherd like the prophets of old.

His growing family also answered to his patriarchal proclivities. John Jr. was turning into a large, quiet boy with curly hair. Jason was bright and sensitive. He once insisted a dream he had was real and got a terrible thrashing from his father, who warned him against such fantasies. The copper-haired Owen suffered an obscure childhood injury that crippled his left arm for life.

Not long after their move to Pennsylvania, the boys gained a new sibling, Frederick, who proved to be a sickly (possibly mentally handicapped) child who had terrible headaches and who died when he was four. On February 18, 1829, a daughter, Ruth, arrived; she would grow into a black-haired, moody girl. The next year a second Frederick was born. Simple-minded and unstable, Frederick would prove ill-starred, ending as a victim of the Kansas slavery wars.

Not an easy brood to control, it would seem, yet John Brown did so with combined firmness and tenderness, along with large doses of religion. In his own childhood, as he remembered to his shame, he had told many lies. With his children he nipped this failing in the bud, demanding complete honesty. Ruth would recall receiving many whippings for telling lies, all but one of which she considered fair—and in that case she was too scared to tell the whole truth. Once when she found a piece of calico belonging to a girl in the neighborhood, he told her to return it to learn how valuable even a "trifling thing" was to its owner. Another time, when she was tempted to get a brother to write a school essay for her, her father scolded her and advised, "Never appear what you are not,—honesty is the best policy."

He came to be less overbearing with time and to regret his early severity. His wife's growing problems brought out his softer side. He must have also pitied the first Frederick, doomed to an early death, and the weak-minded second Frederick as well. By the early 1830s he showed himself capable of great compassion. Ruth would say, "He sometimes seemed very stern and strict with me; yet his tenderness made me forget that he was stern." Because Dianthe was often incapacitated, he tended the children when they became ill. To care for a sick child he would stay up all night, for several days if necessary. Scarlet fever once struck the home, and he administered to several cases at once, earning a local reputation as a good doctor.

His compassion extended to the elderly and to animals. He made his children always give up their seats for older people, quoting the Bible verse, "Thou shalt rise up before the hoary head, and honor the face of the old man." He was a careful shepherd. When his adult sheep contracted a disease called grub-in-the-head, he ensured the survival of their newborns by spending hours holding the lambs to their supine mothers for feeding. Often he would revive an apparently dead lamb by bringing it into the house, bathing it and wrapping it in blankets, and spoon-feeding it warm milk.

He launched into community building. He surveyed for roads and served as the postmaster of New Richmond from January 7, 1828, until May 27, 1835. Since there was no school, he and a neighbor, George B. Delamater, improvised one. Brown taught his own children and Delamater's, along with others from the area, in his own house for part of the school year. For the remaining months Delamater did the same at his house, four miles away. In time Brown replaced himself in the classroom with a woman he hired, and he built a small schoolhouse on his property. A strong advocate of physical exercise, he organized wrestling matches in his house in which he frequently participated.

Few aspects of local life escaped his influence. A man in the neighborhood was jailed for stealing a cow but then released when it was discovered he was extremely poor and had to be home to support his family as best he could. John Brown was indignant, holding that justice must be served no matter what. He badgered a constable into rearresting the man and returning him to jail. But Brown displayed compassion by supplying the man's family with abundant provisions until the jail term ended.

Brown also served as a librarian for the region. He distributed among the neighbors "good moral books and papers" in order "to establish a reading community." Doubtless among the books he lent were favorites from his own library: *Aesop's Fables*, John Bunyan's *Pilgrim's Progress*, Jonathan Edwards's works, Franklin's *Autobiography* and *Poor Richard's Almanac*, and Richard Baxter's *Saints Everlasting Rest; or, A Treatise of the Blessed State of the Saints in the Enjoyment of God in Glory* (a seventeenth-century account of heaven and hell that Brown thought no one could read without becoming a Christian). Brown never lost a chance to quote Franklin's sayings, such as "Diligence is the mother of good luck"; "God gives all things to industry"; "One today is worth two rich tomorrows"; "If you would have your business done, go; if not, send"; "God helps those who help themselves"; and "If you would have a faithful servant and one that you like, serve yourself."

In short, Brown was a model citizen. His neighbor Delamater said that "it almost became a proverb" when "speaking of an enterprising man" to say, "He was as enterprising and as honest as John Brown and as useful to the country." In his personal habits he was neat and simple. James Foreman recalled, "He would never wear expensive clothing of the reason that it was [a] useless waste of money which might be better given to the poor."

This is not to say that John Brown was a tiresome goody-goody. He had a sense of humor. Foreman noted, "In his habits he was jocose and mirthful when the conversation did not turn on anything profane or vulgar." He could get into laughing fits in which his body shook uncontrollably while no sound came from his mouth.

Firm in his convictions, he admired self-reliance in others. As Foreman said, "He despised any man who would on all points coincide with him in opinion, he must have ideas of his own or Brown could not bear him."

He loved to choose some political, social, or religious topic and debate it with his students and family members. Like Benjamin Franklin, he drew out opponents with adept questions until his own position was proven superior.

He used this technique memorably on a Methodist clergyman he met at a neighbor's home and again at the tannery. The flippant, fluent clergyman, considering Brown a bumpkin, argued against predestination, a basic doctrine of Calvinism that the Methodist faith denied. His snide attitude drew remarks from Brown, who demanded a public debate on the issue. The preacher agreed to the debate but was offended by Brown's surliness, asking if he had actually said he was "no gentleman, let alone a clergyman." Brown retorted, "I did say you were no gentleman. I said more than that, sir . . . I said, sir, that it would take as many men like you to make a gentleman as it would wrens to make a cock turkey."

The debate came off, conducted in questions and answers. The

Methodist wasn't prepared for an opponent weaned on Jonathan Edwards, the subtlest Calvinist theologian in American history. Brown ran circles around the minister, asking him difficult questions about free will, human sinfulness, and Satan. The baffled preacher cut off the debate after a few questions, conceding defeat.

On the most popular reform of the day, temperance, Brown had mixed feelings. The Bible seemed to condone wine drinking. Brown believed that "a free use of pure wines in the country would do away with a great deal of intemperance, and that it was a good temperance work to make pure wine and use it." The key word was "pure." The average American in 1830 consumed the equivalent of four gallons of absolute alcohol a year—an astonishing amount, especially since much of it was laced with brain-ravaging additives such as lead, logwood, and tartaric acid. "Pure" wine may have been permissible in Brown's view (two of his sons would run vineyards until their scruples made them quit), but the firewater consumed by most Americans was not. In 1830, Brown declared himself a teetotaler, a full decade before total abstinence became the watchword of the temperance movement. Evidently, he did not drink for the rest of his life. Nor did he approve of hunting or fishing, which he regarded as a waste of time, though he developed into a good marksman by the time of Bleeding Kansas.

He was also a lay minister. His failure to earn his divinity degree did not prevent him from holding religious services in his barn, tannery, or the schoolhouse he built later. Some Sundays he called in a preacher. On others he did the preaching, giving extemporaneous sermons or reading those of others. With typical Calvinist severity, he declared in one sermon, "Our stupidity ingratitude & disobedience we have great reason to mourn & repent of," and in another, "Is not the reflection that full & complete justice will last be done enough to make a very Heavens & Earth to tremble?" He read Jonathan Edwards's admonitory sermons, such as "Sinners in the Hands of an Angry God," "The Eternity of Hell's Torments," and "The End of the Wicked Contemplated by the Righteous." Since New Richmond did not have a church, he founded one in 1832, composing the articles of faith himself.

His faith was severely tested in the early 1830s, which brought not only financial setbacks but also three painful deaths. Frederick, the sickly four-year-old, died on March 31, 1831. Seventeen months later Brown's wife Dianthe, after a problematic pregnancy, gave birth to a son who died soon after birth. Dianthe contracted what was called "childbed fever," accompanied by severe heart palpitations. Anticipating her death, she spoke blissfully of heaven and gave parting advice to her family. She died on August

10, 1832. The next day Brown wrote his father, "We are again smarting under the rod of our Heavenly Father. Last night about eleven o'clock my affectionate, dutiful and faithful Dianthe (to use her own words) bade 'farewell to Earth.' " In a letter to Seth Thompson he put on a brave face, saying, "I have felt my loss verry little" because Dianthe had died "composed and happy in mind."

But the grief ran deep. He confessed to Thompson, "I have been pretty much confined to my house for a number of weeks. . . . I find I am getting more & more unfit for every thing . . . I have been growing numb for a good while." He was in what Emily Dickinson would call "the Hour of Lead," a time when sorrow stiffens the spirit.

Dianthe's passing left him in the difficult position of having to tend to five children while running the tannery and carrying on his civic activities. His employee James Foreman, newly married, took the Browns into his home to help care for the bereaved family. Brown paid board. Even in his gloom Brown was able to think of those less fortunate than he. While at the Foremans, in the dead of winter, he heard of a destitute family living four miles away. Brown donated food and clothing to the family, refusing remuneration despite his own straitened circumstances.

The Foremans soon saw they couldn't handle having six extra people in their household. Brown moved back into his own home and took on a housekeeper whose sixteen-year-old sister, Mary Day, came occasionally to spin cloth. Mary caught his eye as she sat at her spinning wheel. Tall and deep bosomed, she had striking black hair and a sturdy frame. The daughter of Charles Day, a blacksmith and farmer in nearby Troy Township, she had had little formal education but impressed Brown as a practical, hardworking woman.

It wasn't long before Brown, too bashful to propose verbally, presented her with a written offer of marriage. The girl nervously put his note under her pillow and slept on it a night before opening it. After reading it, she grabbed a bucket and rushed off to a spring to fetch water. Brown followed her. By the time the two returned to the house, he had received the answer he wanted. They were married on June 14, 1833. Ten months later a baby girl, Sarah, arrived.

Unlike the erratic Dianthe, Mary would prove to be a rock of stability for John Brown. Staunch and stoical, she set a tone of quiet courage that would influence the whole family. At the time of her marriage she was only half Brown's age and four years older than his oldest son, but her stepchildren would always call her "Mother." She would endure the deaths of nine of the thirteen children she had with John Brown, including four in one terrible week in 1842. Only four of her children outlived her. She stood behind her husband in times of poverty, long separation, and mortal danger. During his trial friends suggested that she try to save him by testifying that he was insane. She replied flatly, "It would be untrue, and therefore impossible."

She went along with Brown's settled rituals, including the home religious services he led each morning. In the winter months the family breakfasted before the sun rose, and then he distributed Bibles. He required each family member to read Bible passages. He stood to pray, resting his hands on the back of a chair and leaning slightly forward as he gave religious exhortations and recited biblical sayings, often from memory. Among his favorites were these:

> "Remember them that are in bonds as bound with them."
>
> "Whoso stoppeth his ear at the cry of the poor, he also shall cry himself, but shall not be heard."
>
> "He that hath a bountiful eye shall be blessed; for he giveth his bread to the poor."
>
> "A good name is rather to be chosen than great riches, and loving favor rather than silver and gold."
>
> "Whoso mocketh the poor reproaches his Maker, and he that is glad at calamities shall not be unpunished."
>
> "He that hath pity upon the poor lendeth unto the Lord, and that which he hath given will he pay him again."

As these passages indicate, in his daily prayers Brown was passing on the socially conscious religion of his youth. Sympathy for the poor and oppressed, especially for enslaved blacks, pervaded the atmosphere of his household. Antislavery commitment was not learned by his children, but absorbed at all times.

Brown kept an eye on antislavery activity in the public sphere. In the 1820s he had been a Whig and had supported John Quincy Adams, an opponent of slavery. But the rising prominence of Henry Clay, the Kentucky slaveholder who advocated colonization, made him disgusted with the Whig Party. He also detested another famous slaveholder, the Democrat Andrew Jackson. It is likely that after the early 1830s he never voted in a presidential election. Several years before William Lloyd Garrison rejected the American politicians as corrupt tools of the slave system, Brown launched his own private rebellion by withdrawing from political participation.

To mention Garrison is to contrast Brown's Abolitionism and that of the era's leading Abolitionist journalist. Brown reportedly saw issues of Garrison's landmark antislavery newspaper the *Liberator* in either 1831 (its first year of publication) or 1832 during a visit to his father in Ohio. If so, Garrison's vitriolic rhetoric—"I will be as harsh as truth, and as uncompromising as justice— ... I will not retreat a single inch—AND I WILL BE HEARD"—must have resonated within Brown and stirred his militancy. There were, however, significant differences in the antislavery views of the two men.

Like almost all other antebellum reformers besides Brown, Garrison espoused antislavery relatively late in life. The son of an alcoholic seaman, he became a writer of sensationalistic journalism and then took up the temperance cause. It was only when he met the Quaker Benjamin Lundy in 1828 that the twenty-three-year-old Garrison became interested in antislavery. Soon he was the nation's leading spokesman for immediate emancipation.

But his antislavery energy went in different directions than did Brown's. Garrison championed nonresistance, believing that by persuasion alone slaveholders could be taught the error of their ways. Rejecting Calvinism, he became a Christian perfectionist who believed that through exemplary sinlessness reformers could be models for Southerners to follow. If these models were not heeded, Garrison advocated the separation of the North and the South.

Although Garrison wrote eloquently against racism, he did not exhibit racial openness sufficiently to prevent some blacks from complaining that they been overlooked for positions in his American Anti-Slavery Society. Later, Garrison stunned many of his colleagues by trying to disband the Society after the Thirteenth Amendment had abolished slavery, not recognizing how much work had to be done to prevent blacks from being virtually reenslaved in the South. As the war was ending he initially opposed the enfranchisement of blacks, whom he thought must be educated before being granted full social rights.

It is not surprising that when Garrison and Brown met in Boston in 1857 they quarreled about the goals and tactics or antislavery reform. Nor is it surprising that Garrison's first response to the Harpers Ferry raid was negative. He called it "misguided, wild, and apparently insane," "utterly lacking in common sense."

Rebellion by slaves against their masters was the issue that crystallized the difference between Garrison and Brown. Slave revolts repelled Garrison and contributed to his pacifism. In contrast, they inspired Brown and contributed to his violence—so much so that many contemporaries (both opponents and supporters) assumed that he modeled his antislavery terrorism after the violence of rebellious slaves.

Among the scores of slave revolts and conspiracies before the Nat Turner rebellion of 1831, four stand out: the uprising in New York City in 1712; the plot by a slave named Gabriel to seize Richmond, Virginia, in 1800; the large slave uprising near New Orleans in 1811; and Denmark Vesey's plan to take over Charleston, South Carolina, in 1820. Although two of these rebellions, those of Gabriel and Vesey, were discovered before they could be carried out, all were designed to terrorize whites through vindictive violence. As the historian Eugene Genovese has noted, "No slave revolt that hesitated to invoke terror had a chance." Because slaves had little knowledge of or access to firearms, cruder instruments—knives, axes, or, in Gabriel's case, handmade pikes—were the weapons of choice. The only avenue to success, the blacks knew, led through a sea of blood.

Violent in aim, the revolts elicited reprisals by whites that were even more violent. During the 1712 New York rebellion nine blacks were killed outright, and later eighteen were executed, some horribly: three were burned at the stake, one was broken on a wheel, and one was manacled and starved to death. Six more committed suicide. The Gabriel plot, which caused no actual damage because it was prevented, nonetheless resulted in mass executions; twenty-six blacks were hanged, and one hanged himself. The Vesey conspiracy, also aborted, prompted the execution of thirty-five blacks and the sale of thirty-seven others to slaveholders outside of South Carolina. Most grisly of all was the aftermath of the New Orleans incident of 1811, in which some two hundred blacks had begun a rampage in southern Louisiana. The rebellion was quickly stifled, with the slaves having killed only two or three whites. Still, sixty-six blacks were slaughtered on the spot and sixteen more were executed later. As a warning to other would-be slave rebels, the heads of the blacks were cut off and placed on poles along the road between New Orleans and the plantation where the revolt had begun.

Nat Turner's rebellion in August 1831 outdid all the others in carnage on both sides. The short, stocky Turner had been raised on a plantation in southeastern Virginia, where, unlike most slaves, he received a rudimentary education. Intensely religious, he developed a messianic image of himself as a liberator of his race. He had visions of black and white angels fighting in the heavens, and he saw blood on corn—portents, he believed, of his forthcoming victory over his white oppressors. In the summer of 1831 he spread a plan among nearby slaves for a violent takeover of Southampton County, followed, if necessary, by a retreat to the Virginia mountains or the Great Dismal Swamp, twenty-five miles away.

On the night of Sunday, August 31, the revolt began. Turner and six cohorts, armed with swords and axes, went from plantation to plantation, killing men, women, and children as they slept. Not until they had killed fifty-five were the whites in the area able to organize a pursuit. An untold number of blacks—reportedly hundreds—were slaughtered in the chase. Turner managed to evade capture for nearly two months, hiding in a cave within five miles of his plantation until a dog, sniffing his provisions, led farmers to him. When he was caught on October 31, he was cool and composed, and he remained firm through his trial and on his way to his hanging a month later. Sixteen other blacks were hanged as well, and twelve more were sold out of state.

The incident sent a shock wave of fear and outrage throughout the South. Thousands of slaveholders trembled for their lives, as the suspicion spread, in the words of a Virginia congressman, that "a Nat Turner might be in every family, that the same bloody deed might be acted over at any time and in any place."

Garrison and Brown reacted in different ways to the Turner rebellion. Garrison had criticized David Walker's 1829 incendiary *Appeal*, which encouraged slave revolts. While Garrison admired Nat Turner's motives, he was appalled by the bloody violence of his insurrection. Garrison and his cohorts were terrified by such incidents and wanted to prevent more of them. Thus, they stressed a nonviolent solution to the slave problem, one based on the use of moral suasion to induce the South to free its slaves or, barring that, the dissolution of the Union, so that the North would remain secure against the taint of slavery and the possibility of bloody vengeance by blacks.

Even before the Turner rebellion, Garrison had said that if no remedy to the slavery problem were reached soon, the "gigantic cannibal" of the vindictive black man would rise up in the South. "A cry of horror, a cry of revenge," he wrote, "will go up to heaven in the darkness of midnight. . . . Blood will flow like water." Denouncing slave revolts, he wrote in the *Liberator*, "We do not preach rebellion; no, but submission and peace." When Nat Turner rebelled, Garrison said his worst fears were now realized; this was "the first step of the earthquake" that would shake down the whole nation. "We are horror-struck," he wrote of Turner. "What we have so long predicted,—at the peril of being stigmatized as an alarmist and declaimer, has commenced its fulfillment." The ultimate result of such violence would be "a war of extermination" between the races. He embraced nonresistance partly in response to his fear of such a race war.

In his newspaper he printed pieces that emphasized the brutal savagery of blacks. One poem gave a white person's view of the Turner revolt, with a shriek, a startled eye that saw "The gleaming axe, and the ear just caught / the sable fiend's hurra!" and then "Out on the polished floor / Ran the ensanguined flood; / The babe slept on its mother's breast," while the "unripened virgin" lay on the cold stone floor, "Crushed in her budding loveliness." A story titled "Another Dream" envisaged a race war that engulfed American whites, who were "subjected to all that the vengeance of infuriated slaves could inflict." As the narrator recalls: "Three savage negroes rushed into my house and killed my wife and child before my face. Oh! the unutterable agony of that moment!"

Despite his fulminations against racism, then, Garrison came close to accepting Southern whites' stereotypical view of blacks as potentially vicious beasts. To be sure, his emphasis was different from that of Southerners. The latter thought blacks must be *kept down* in order to avoid a race war. Garrison thought they should be *liberated* to avoid one. The Southerners believed that ungrateful *blacks* caused insurrections like Turner's. Garrison insisted that oppressive *whites* did. Still, both slave-owners and Garrison were driven by a deep-seated terror of the cataclysmic possibilities of a war caused by slave revolts.

John Brown, in contrast, admired slave rebels and learned from them. In fact, as I discuss later, he perhaps viewed them at times too idealistically, basing his antislavery ventures on his observations of individual cases.

One of his daughters would recall that among his black heroes "Nat Turner and Cinques stood first in his esteem." Cinque was the leader of an 1837 rebellion by some fifty enslaved blacks who were being transported from Cuba to Spain on the Spanish schooner *Amistad*. After breaking free of their chains belowdecks, the blacks swarmed the ship and killed the captain and three crew members. Cinque ordered the ship's owners to conduct the vessel to Africa. Through nighttime trickery the blacks were instead taken to America, brought ashore on Long Island, and submitted to a trial. To the delight of Abolitionists, they were eventually exonerated on the basis of America's prohibition of the international slave trade. Thirty-five of the blacks were returned to their homeland; the remainder died either in prison or at sea.

The fact that Brown admired both Turner and Cinque shows the breadth of his appreciation. Cinque, he knew, was a rebel many Northerners could appreciate. Even Garrison, despite his objections to Cinque's violence, condoned the *Amistad* revolt. As historian Henry Mayer has pointed out, this rebellion was easier for Abolitionists to swallow than previous ones because it was launched against Spanish authorities on the open seas, not against whites on American soil.

Unlike Garrison, Brown particularly liked Cinque because he succeeded *without* much violence. Brown's preference was for peaceful emancipation of slaves, as happened in the West Indies in 1832. Where he departed from the likes of Garrison and Emerson was his belief (and time proved him right) that voluntary liberation was unlikely to happen in America, since Southerners' devotion to their peculiar institution was steadily strengthening.

Given the unlikeliness of a peaceful solution, Brown got clues from slave rebellions. If a rebellion succeeded without excessive violence, as with Cinque, all the better. His daughter declared, "How often have I heard him speak in admiration of Cinques' character and management in carrying his points with so little bloodshed!" If Garrison looked to pacific whites to set an example of nonresistance, Brown looked to rebellious blacks to set an example of courage. To inspire members of his all-black League of Gileadites in 1850, he would refer to the *Amistad* revolt: "Nothing so charms the American people as personal bravery. Witness the case of Cinques, of everlasting memory, on board the 'Amistad.' "

But it was Nat Turner, not Cinque, whom Brown would eventually emulate. As the intransigence of slaveholders became clearer during the 1850s, he resorted to the kind of terrorist tactics Turner had used. There were a number of similarities between Brown and Turner. Both knew much of the Bible by heart, and both saw themselves as chosen by God to liberate America's slaves. Turner in Southampton County and Brown at Pottawatomie chose the terrorist tactic of killing defenseless people at night, using similarly crude weapons, although Turner was indiscriminate in his slaughter. Brown at Harpers Ferry adopted Turner's plan of a retreat to the wilderness, a strategy that had been used with success by the maroons of Jamaica. When captured, both candidly confessed their motives—emancipation of the slaves—and both endured their incarceration and execution with unflinching firmness.

Brown's contemporaries were quick to connect him with Turner. For example, just after Brown's hanging, the *Anglo-African Magazine*, edited and written by blacks, ran a long article comparing the two. In the comparison Brown came off the better. The essayist noted that Turner's "terrible logic" could only conceive of the liberation of one race along with "the extirpation of the other," while Brown fought for an integrated society in which blacks and whites were equal. So close was the association between the two figures that a nineteenth-century historian of American blacks described Turner as a "Black John Brown."

Why did Brown embrace the same insurrectionary violence that drove other Abolitionists to pacifism? He did so because he was thoroughly open to all aspects of the black experience, including the violence of slave rebels. He would trigger the Civil War through his antislavery terrorism—and this terrorism itself was largely black-inspired. To see John Brown as the main link between African American culture and the Civil War is to recognize that blacks were prime movers in American history.

In the early 1830s, when his chief concerns were running his tannery and supervising his young family, John Brown had no plan to imitate antislavery terrorism. However, the emotional background to his later activities was being formed. Sensitivity to the experience of blacks was ever-present and instinctive with him. He built a special room in his barn that served as a hiding place for fugitive slaves. A neighbor noted, "He considered it as much his duty to help a negro to make his escape as it was to help catch a Horse thief."

He not only taught his children to be kind to blacks; he urged them to be close friends with them and to be open to living with them. His daughter Ruth recounted a particularly moving appeal he made to her one evening after he sang her his favorite hymn, "Blow Ye the Trumpet, Blow!":

> He asked me how I would like to have some poor little black children that were slaves (explaining to me the meaning of slaves) come and live with us; and asked me if I would be willing to divide my food and clothes with them. He made such an impression on my sympathies, that the first colored person I ever saw (it was a man I met on the street in Meadville, Penn.), I felt such pity for him that I wanted to ask him if he did not want to come and live at our house.

The notion of living with blacks was more than just family talk. John Brown did his best to act upon the idea. In an 1834 letter to his brother Frederick he described two plans he had to help African Americans. One was to adopt "at least one negro boy or youth" and "bring him up as we do our own—viz., give him a good English education, learn him what we can about the history of the world, about business, about general subjects, and above all, try to teach him the fear of God." The other was to start a school for blacks. Before Prudence Crandall scandalized Connecticut residents by opening a school for black girls, John Brown declared that he had harbored his scheme "for years."

Behind his plan was his conviction that education was the pathway to freedom for blacks. He hoped that others would adopt his ideas. He explained that if Americans generally set about "to work in earnest to teaching the blacks, the people of the slaveholding States would find themselves constitutionally driven to set about the work of emancipation immediately."

He was on the right track. As anyone familiar with Frederick Douglass's *Narrative* knows, for slaveholders the educated slave was the dangerous one. Illiteracy rates among Southern blacks ran well above 80 percent, and for good reason. Whites wanted to keep blacks ignorant. Many Southern states passed laws against educating slaves, since, in the words of the North Carolina law, "teaching slaves to read and write tends to excite dissatisfaction in their minds and to produce insurrection and rebellion."

Brown's design of educating blacks, then, was innovative and potentially useful. His faltering financial status, however, prevented the plan from reaching fruition. He hoped in vain that some "Christian slaveholder" would free a slave voluntarily and turn him or her over to Brown for adoption. To his brother he said he even wanted to tap into his already scanty resources and "submit to considerable privation in order to buy one."

His dreams were for naught, at least for now. By early 1835, money was tight in Randolph County. It was ever more difficult for Brown to collect payments for old debts or for his livestock and hides.

In Hudson, Ohio, which Brown had left nine years earlier, a wealthy businessman, Zenas B. Kent, invited him to run a tannery with him. Since Brown didn't have enough money to relocate, Kent loaned him $25. On May 18, 1835, Brown gave up his postmastership of Randolph County. He and Mary packed their meager belongings and, with the six children, moved to Hudson.

Within six months of the move, on October 7, 1835, a son, Watson, was born, adding yet another mouth to feed. The struggling family was crammed into a small rented house in Hudson. Brown and the fourteen-year-old John Jr. worked at building a new tannery for Kent in the town of Franklin, some six miles away. It was agreed that they would run the tannery as soon as it was finished. Kent, however, had a change of heart and decided to rent the building to his son.

Stymied in the tannery business, Brown took temporary work on a crew digging a new canal, four feet deep and thirty feet wide, which was projected to run through Franklin. While engaged in this tedious labor, he came up with a fresh plan for financial security: land speculation. The canal, to go east-west across Ohio into Pennsylvania, promised to bring rapid development to Franklin. Zenas Kent's Franklin Land Company had bought some five hundred acres near the Cayahoga River with the design of profiting from what appeared to be an imminent real estate boom in the area. Kent had apportioned sites for a factory, a water supply plant, and a mill.

What was good for a shrewd businessman like Kent was good enough for John Brown. Adjacent to the Franklin Land Company's property, in the village of Franklin Mills, was a 92.5-acre farm owned by Frederick Haymaker. John Brown was confident that someday this site would be prosperous and heavily populated. As in Pennsylvania, he had the urge to build a community. Now there was the added incentive of climbing out of poverty for good. He would segment the land into lots and later sell them at a profit.

With money borrowed from his brother Frederick, he put a small down payment on the property and moved with his family into the large Haymaker farmhouse that came with the purchase. He used his surveyor's compass and chain to map out a town. On a grid he sketched a plan for 150 industrial lots and broad streets extending on both sides of the canal, which was projected to run through the center of the community. He assigned names to the streets, including Cayahoga, Hale, Prospect, and Franklin. On the corner of what he called Magadore and Summit streets he oversaw the construction of a block building to be used as a factory warehouse and as a hotel for the businesspeople he knew would be flocking to the area.

Ironically, digging on the canal was suspended as a change of its course was contemplated, while digging on a new financial hole for John Brown continued apace. Brown persuaded Seth Thompson to go in on the Haymaker project, assuring him that lots in the area were going for as high as $900 an acre. They called the land "Brown & Thompson's Addition to Franklin Village." In January 1836, Thompson (who should have known better after the hides-for-cattle debacle) put down $1,134 on half of the property, promising an additional $1,866 shortly and four payments of $1,000 each to be made until January 1840. Brown contributed his portion by borrowing around $7,000 from Frederick Wadsworth and the farmer and merchant Heman Oviatt.

He had visions of money pouring in from settlers buying parcels in his carefully plotted development. He was not far wrong, at least with the regard to the settlers. By the time of the Civil War, the Haymaker property would be covered with homes and shops. But his luck and timing, as was usual with his business pursuits, were poor. He bought the property at exactly the wrong moment, when land prices peaked. Until the canal project resumed, the lots Brown had so carefully laid out were unsalable.

By the summer of 1836 Brown was so hard up he had to borrow $250 from Thompson to buy an ox team. With his land scheme in abeyance, in July he left Franklin Mills and took his family back to Hudson, where he purchased a tract of land with $350 his father lent him. Though still hopeful that Haymaker would eventually pay off, he started a tannery on the Hudson property, located in northeast Hudson near Ravenna Road, about three miles from the center of town. Money was so scarce that he sometimes had to trade pieces of leather for food for his family, which kept growing: on October 2, 1836, a son, Salmon, arrived, followed by Charles on November 3, 1837.

Despite his rising debts, Brown continued to relish his patriarchal role. On the Hudson land was a tremendous rock, covering nearly half an acre and bubbling with spring water. In the warm months the children loved chasing each other over the rock. The house on the property was smaller than the Haymaker one, but also cozier. On winter evenings the family often sat in the living room by the huge fireplace, ten feet wide with oversized andirons and a crane with hooks that held kettles. John Brown would gather two or three children on his lap and sing hymns or discuss national affairs, an increasing source of concern for him. He continued his community service, winning local attention for his abilities as the teacher of a men's Bible class in Hudson.

If his return to Ohio began a long downward economic spiral for him, it also opened new vistas of antislavery activity. During his nine years in New Richmond, Brown had served as a lone antislavery policeman in the Pennsylvania wilderness, helping an occasional stray fugitive slave and, as a friend reported, interviewing each new settler to determine whether he or she was "an observer of the Sabbath, opposed to Slavery, and a Supporter of the Gospel and common schools." By returning to central Ohio, he left such piecemeal reform work behind. He was now in a region where the contest over slavery raged as heatedly as it did anywhere else in the nation.

The appearance of Garrison's *Liberator* in 1831 had set the region on fire. Western Reserve College, founded in Hudson in 1826, was the setting of a bitter quarrel between faculty members and students who favored the colonization of blacks and those who took up Garrison's banner of immediate emancipation. Among the Garrisonians were Elizur Wright, Jr., whom Brown knew from his school days in Hudson and who was now a professor of mathematics and natural philosophy; the Reverend Beriah Green, professor of religion and sacred literature; and the Reverend Charles Backus Storrs, professor of morals and sacred theology and president of the college. After battling with the colonizationists, Storrs died in 1833 of a pulmonary hemorrhage. The other two resigned from the college and went elsewhere, Wright to New York, where he became secretary of the American Anti-Slavery Society, Green to assume the presidency of a college in Whitesboro, New York.

John Brown's father was involved in this fight, which gained national attention. Owen Brown had been a proponent of Western Reserve College but in protest of its advocacy of colonization joined the board of trustees of nearby Oberlin Collegiate Institute, which had been founded in Hudson in 1833 and reorganized in 1834–35 as an antislavery institution. He remained on the Oberlin board from November 1835 until August 1844. He also started a dissident church, variously called the Free Church or the Oberlin Church, where the college's professors could sermonize against slavery.

The most progressive college in the country, Oberlin opened its doors to women and blacks. Its administration and faculty were cut in the Garrisonian mold. Asa Mahan, its president from 1835 to 1850, was a vigorous proponent of immediate emancipation, as were most of its faculty members, including the Reverend Charles Grandison Finney, the famous evangelist from New York. Finney was appointed as a professor of theology at Oberlin in 1836 under the aegis of Arthur and Lewis Tappan, wealthy Manhattan philanthropists who were officers in the American Anti-Slavery Society. The Tappans, who had built a brick tabernacle for Finney in New York, sent to Oberlin a huge tent to be used for antislavery rallies. A hundred feet in diameter, with ten tall peaks, the "Oberlin tent" became a key symbol of the Abolitionist zeal that took over the region.

This zeal was also manifested in antislavery societies that sprang up in several Ohio towns. In Hudson, Owen Brown helped found the Western Reserve Anti-Slavery Society in 1833, serving as its treasurer. By 1837 there were more than 200 antislavery societies and some 17,000 citizens opposed to slavery in the Western Reserve.

Hudson was an important stop on the Underground Railroad—so much so that there was a sign outside town that read DIS DE ROAD TO HUDSON. Because the Fugitive Slave Act of 1793 and Ohio's black laws (first passed in 1804) were in effect, slave-hunters roamed in search of escaped slaves. But Abolitionists there had great success in aiding fugitives. Oberlin Collegiate Institute would gain the distinction of never losing a fugitive slave to federal authorities.

Even though the fines for helping fugitives were steep—$1,000 for each one assisted—John Brown accepted the risk and became a busy stationmaster in the Ohio branch of the Underground Railroad. Upon his arrival in Hudson, he established the town's tenth station, constructing a hiding place for fugitives beneath a haymow in his barn. Regularly, he made nighttime rides to transport blacks to stations farther north, such as Barlow, Deavertown, or Cleveland.

Despite mounting antislavery activity in the Western Reserve, severe discrimination against the region's 10,000 free blacks persisted, enforced by the state's black laws. According to the laws, blacks were treated unequally with whites in residency requirements, legal rights, jobs, and education. On January 18, 1837, John Brown addressed a crowd of Abolitionists and free blacks in Cleveland in support of a petition to the state legislature to repeal the black laws. The laws, however, remained on the books for a dozen more years.

Brown took action not only against legal discrimination but also against discrimination on a more personal level. In the summer of 1836, just after the Brown family had moved into the Haymaker farm, the Western Reserve got what was perhaps its first exposure to a totally nonracist white person (even the Abolitionists in the Reserve were known to accept the prevailing racial stereotypes of the era). John Brown had hired two blacks, a man and wife, to help on the farm as he surveyed the property. One day during a religious revival he went with them to the Franklin Congregational Church and was stunned to see them and other blacks sit at the rear of the church, out of sight of the minister and choir. Furious, Brown made a point the next time he visited the church of escorting several blacks down the aisle to his own preferred pew. He reminded the congregation of the Bible's instruction that God "was no respecter of persons," and then returned to the back of the chapel, where he and his family took the seats vacated by the blacks.

His action struck the congregation "like a bomb-shell." The next day the church deacons called Brown in for a going-over, but, as John Jr. laconically put it, "they returned with new views of Christian duty." On each of the remaining days of the revival, the Browns continued to exchange their seats for those of the blacks.

A year later, after the Browns had moved to Hudson, they received a letter from the Franklin church informing them that they had been expelled because they had been absent for a year without reporting themselves. The statement didn't fool the Browns, who knew that their unconventional fairness to blacks, not their absence from church, was behind the expulsion. From that date, John Jr. claimed, he never set foot in a church again; nor did his brothers. Their father, too, was so disgusted that he reportedly went to church thereafter at most intermittently, perhaps not at all, even though his religious faith was unwavering. Like the Garrisonian "come-outers" who would later flee churches in droves, the Browns in 1837 came out of an institution which they realized paid the merest lip service to concepts like charity and brotherly love.

John Brown was not content with confining his antislavery work to the Underground Railroad or helping local blacks. Events occurred on the national stage in the mid-1830s that brought out in him a potent militancy that must have at first surprised even him.

Specifically, proslavery forces in America turned aggressive. The Nat Turner rebellion had unleashed a paranoid reaction among Southerners, who suddenly demonized Northern Abolitionists. William Lloyd Garrison, despite his firm denunciations of Turner's violence, was charged with causing the insurrection, and he received assassination threats. When Garrison tried to deliver an antislavery address in Boston in May 1835, he was seized by a proslavery mob, bound, and pulled by a rope through the city's streets to a chorus of cries such as "Lynch him!" and "Turn him a right nigger color with tar!"

Similar crowd actions flared up with such frequency that the mid-1830s have been identified as a generative time for much of the proslavery violence that raged through the rest of the antebellum period. In 1838, Lincoln declared in alarm, "Accounts of outrages committed by mobs, form the every-day news of the times. They have pervaded the country, from New England to Louisiana."

Especially significant in its impact was the November 1837 murder of the Illinois antislavery editor Elijah P. Lovejoy. Lincoln called the murder of Lovejoy "the most important single event that ever happened in the new world." John Quincy Adams said it sent "a shock as of an earthquake through this country."

A Presbyterian minister who had been trained at Waterville (later Colby) College in Maine and Princeton Theological Seminary, the muscular, snub-nosed Lovejoy had been a colonizationist but had espoused a tougher antislavery stance when he moved to the rough-and-tumble city of St. Louis, Missouri. When a proslavery mob destroyed the press in his newspaper office after he had editorialized against the lynching of a black, he moved his operation across the Mississippi River to Alton, Illinois. There he braved several assaults on his antislavery newspaper, the *Alton Observer*, staving off his attackers with a rifle, though his press was thrown into the river three times. Faced with the suspension of his newspaper at a town meeting, he boldly defended his right to free speech and invited antislavery martyrdom. Referring to a black Missourian named McIntosh who had recently been burned to death by a mob, he declared, "You may burn me at the stake as they did McIntosh at St. Louis; or you may tar and feather me, or throw me into the Mississippi as you have often threatened to do; but you cannot disgrace me." He added that Jesus Christ "died for me; and I were most unworthy to bear his name, should I refuse, to die for him." On the evening of November 7 a furious mob of proslavery citizens over-powered twenty guards that had been assigned to protect Lovejoy's printing press. In the melee Lovejoy was fatally wounded by a shotgun blast.

The repercussions of the Lovejoy incident and other mob actions of the 1830s were immense. Like slave revolts, mobs embodied violence, but of a different—in some ways more terrifying—sort: violence on the part of white Americans, usually proslavery ones. Slave revolts, as frightening as they were, could at least be suppressed. Mobs, in contrast, threatened to get out of control. This was especially true in the pre–Civil War era, when police forces were disorganized and ineffective. It is not surprising, then, that mobs had profound and widely varying effects.

Mobs were a key factor in Lincoln's rejection of revolutionary impulses and his faith in the law, the Constitution, and the political process. In his speech to the Young Men's Lyceum in Springfield, Illinois, given two months after the Lovejoy incident, he identified the "mobocratic spirit" as the main threat to the American system. "Whenever the vicious portion of the population," he said, "shall be permitted to gather in bands of hundreds and thousands, and burn churches, ravage and rob provision stores, throw printing presses into rivers, shoot editors, and hang and burn obnoxious persons at pleasure, and with impunity; depend on it, this Government can-not last."

During the two decades after the Lovejoy affair, Lincoln shied away from any actions or movements that posed a threat to social order or peace. Unlike most antislavery figures, he derived little inspiration from the European revolutions of 1848. He also dismissed the wild "isms" of the 1850s. In his debates on slavery with Stephen Douglas, he used logical persuasion and homely metaphor rather than violent emotion. He rebuked extreme antislav-ery measures, including John Brown's raid on Harpers Ferry. He remained so loyal to the Constitution that he accepted its fugitive slave clause. Even when forced by the bombing of Fort Sumter to resort to war, he initially sent Northern troops to restore the Union as it was, not to eradicate slavery.

If mob action fostered moderation in Lincoln, it pushed other antislav-ery figures toward nonresistance and a rejection of church and state. Garri-son responded to his own mobbing and the Lovejoy murder by calling violence a proslavery tool he would not use. He said that though Lovejoy was "certainly a martyr—strictly speaking—he was not . . . a Christian mar-tyr," since he had taken up arms in self-defense. Not only did Garrison recoil to pacifism, but he also renounced the political process, the military, the church, and the Constitution—all of which he believed were corrupted by the slave system and its accompanying violence.

The schism that developed in the American Anti-Slavery Society in 1840 between Garrison's followers and those of James Gillespie Birney (an Abolitionist editor whose press was several times destroyed by mobs) resulted partly from differing attitudes toward the disruptions created by mobs. Both the Garrisonians and the Birneyites shrank from such disruptions, but differently. The former turned to what they saw as the "higher law" of God, which they viewed as overriding politics and human institutions. The latter repudiated this belief in the higher law, saying it was potentially just as anarchic as mob action. Birney's followers instead embraced politics, arguing that mob-related wildness could be best countered by the calm exercise of voting and due process. Birney founded the Liberty Party, which ran on an antislavery platform in 1840 and which set the stage for the Free Soil and Republican parties.

The Lovejoy case also resonated among the Transcendentalists. Signals of their later apotheosis of John Brown emerged in Emerson's response to Lovejoy. "The brave Lovejoy," he wrote, "has given his breast to the bullet . . . and has died when it was better not to live. There are always men enough ready to die for the silliest punctilio; to die like dogs . . . but I sternly rejoice that one was bound to die for humanity and the rights of free speech and opinion." For Emerson, Lovejoy was the self-reliant individual who stood in brave opposition to the thoughtless mob. Later on, both Emerson and Thoreau would greatly expand on this idea of idealistic self-reliance in their defense of John Brown.

The self-sacrificing individualist they idealized was himself shaped by the Lovejoy killing. John Brown heard of the incident at a prayer meeting led in Hudson by Laurens P. Hickock, an antislavery professor of theology at Western Reserve College. Hickock had already conducted a memorial meeting for Lovejoy at his college; it was the second meeting, held in the town's Congregational church, that John Brown and his father attended. Hickock described the murder and then excoriated proslavery mobs. "The crisis has now come," he declared. "The question now before American citizens is no longer alone, 'Can the slaves be made free?' but, 'Are we free or are we slaves under Southern mob law?'" He proposed the founding of another antislavery newspaper with another editor to keep alive Lovejoy's spirit. "If a like fate attends them," he said, "send another, till the whole country is aroused; and if you can find no fitter man for the first victim, send me." Similar speeches followed.

John Brown and his father sat silently through the harangues. As the meeting drew to a close, John Brown suddenly rose, lifted his right hand, and said, "Here, before God, in the presence of these witnesses, from this time, I consecrate my life to the destruction of slavery!" His aged father then stood up and with his characteristic stammer added, "When John the Baptist was beheaded, the disciples took up his body and laid it in a tomb and went and told Jesus. Let us now go to Jesus and tell him." Tears flowed down his wrinkled face as he led the meeting in prayer.

No longer was John Brown working in secret. A murder committed by a proslavery mob had drawn from him a vow to fight slavery. The circumstances of his oath were telling. He was responding to a man who was an inchoate version of what he would later become. Elijah Lovejoy had risked his life by defending blacks publicly, as would Brown. Also like Brown, he persevered in his battle despite setbacks, and when faced with defeat he consciously chose the role of the Christ-like martyr.

Perhaps most significantly, he was the victim of proslavery violence. Hickock's question "Are we free or are we slaves under Southern mob law?" set a fire of retaliatory vengeance within Brown. The Lovejoy episode turned other Abolitionists away from violence. It sped Brown on the path toward it.

If family legend is to be believed, he openly announced his commitment to antislavery violence around this time, repudiating Garrisonian pacifism. His sons John and Jason never forgot the day when John Brown persuaded family members to pledge themselves to armed warfare against slavery. The two were sitting by the fire with Owen and Mother when their father addressed them soberly. As John Jr. recalled, he told the four of "his determination to make war on slavery—not such war as . . . 'was equally the purpose of the nonresistant abolitionists,' but war by force and arms. He said that he had long entertained such a purpose." He asked the four if they were "willing to make common cause with him in doing all in our power to 'break the jaws of the wicked and pluck the spoil out of his teeth.' " After they assented, he kneeled in prayer and asked each to take an oath of "secrecy and devotion to the purpose of fighting slavery by force of arms to the extent of our ability."

By the late 1830s, John Brown had become a patriarch on a large scale. His "family" had by now expanded well beyond his immediate relatives or his own town and state. It included the nation's ever-growing population of enslaved blacks. In his mind he was already the patriarch of patriarchs, the Moses who would lead a race out of bondage.

5

The Pauper

Few successful people in history have failed so miserably in so many different pursuits as John Brown. He failed as a tanner, a shepherd, a cattle trader, a horse breeder, a lumber dealer, a real estate speculator, and a wool distributor. From a jaundiced view, he can even be said to have failed as an antislavery warrior: in Kansas he committed murder and lost a son; in Harpers Ferry he lost a battle, two more sons, and, after a trial and conviction, his life.

In pre–Civil War, America, however, success and failure, like patriotism and treason, were often reversible. A number of extraordinary individuals took pride in "failing," as American society defined that term. "It is now my settled purpose to write novels that are said to 'fail,' " declared Melville on the eve of writing *Moby-Dick*. He knew that his novel, with its philosophical depth and stylistic adventurousness, would hold little appeal for conventional critics or a public that feasted on sentimental fiction and pulp romances. Such shallow literary tastes prompted the lines "Poverty—be justifying / For so foul a thing" as "Publication" from Emily Dickinson, who went virtually unpublished in her lifetime and who qualifies as the greatest poet who ever "failed." Another proud "failure" was Walt Whitman, whose magnificent 1855 edition of *Leaves of Grass* met with widespread vilification from critics, including one who labeled it "a mass of bombast, egotism, vulgarity, and nonsense."

Even more pertinent to John Brown is Emerson, who would become one of Brown's most eloquent defenders. In "Self-Reliance" (1841) Emerson insisted that society's views of failure and success were skewed. "If our young men miscarry in their first enterprises," wrote Emerson, "they lose all heart. If the young merchant fails, men say he is *ruined*." College graduates are considered a failure if they are "not installed in an office within one year afterwards in the cities or suburbs of Boston or New York." But, Emerson argued, the supple person who "in turn tries all the professions, who *teams it, farms it, peddles,* keeps a school, preaches, edits a newspaper, goes to Congress, buys a township, and so forth, in successive years, and always like a cat, falls on his feet, is worth a hundred of these city dolls."

Although this was written sixteen years before Emerson met John Brown, it described Brown even more accurately than it did Thoreau, whom Emerson had in mind when he wrote it. Brown, in fact, did all the things Emerson mentioned except edit a newspaper and go to Congress (and he would do even these things, metaphorically, in the months after his death, when the universal interest in him made one observer comment that "John Brown the friend of the slave, has edited every paper, [and] presided over . . . every Legislature, Judicial and Executive department of government").

Somehow, unbelievably, Brown always ended up on his feet, like Emerson's cat. He endured poverty and countless lawsuits, while caring for a family that was ever growing and ever dying off, yet still remained confident of success. Later he killed five people and not only escaped prosecution but was subsequently revered by sages and business leaders as a second Christ. At the end he suffered the disgrace of being convicted for murder and treason yet remained cheerful in prison and looked forward to the gallows with joy. He did so because his idea of success had little to do with conventional definitions and because he lived in an era when institutions appeared to him (and to some others) as secondary to the "higher law" of justice and morality.

Observing the higher law for him frequently meant ignoring human codes and customary practices. Among the customary practices he neglected were business ones. Although Brown loved to quote Benjamin Franklin, he didn't heed his warnings about debt, such as "he that goes a-borrowing goes a-sorrowing" or "creditors have better memories than debtors." Between 1836 and 1842, Brown lived on debt and nearly lost everything he owned. And the picture remained almost as bleak for him in the decade after that.

If in his mind he was Franklinian, in his heart he was Emersonian, evidently without having read Emerson. Despite his many business endeavors, he had little interest in what Franklin called "the way to wealth." In his letters there is much about his effort to provide for his family but nothing about the pursuit of money for its own sake. In fact, he felt guilty at those moments when it looked like he might succeed financially. He worried that money might interfere with higher pursuits.

Also, he chafed in any role in an organization, whether it was a business, a church, or a reform society. Unconsciously, he accorded with Emerson's criticism of society's rage for specialization, by which, as Emerson wrote, "functions are parcelled out to individuals, each of whom aims to do his stint of the joint work, whilst each other performs his." For Emerson, society reduces man to "a thing, into many things"; the food-gathering "Man on the farm" becomes the mere farmer, the businessman a moneymaker, the attorney a statute-book, the mechanic a machine, Man Thinking the bookworm, and so forth.

John Brown enjoyed his work but did not want to lose his soul in the process. He was more inclined to be what Emerson would call the "Man on the farm" rather than the farmer—or, to make other coinages, the tender of animals and producer of fine leather, not the seller of hides; the expert in wool instead of the wool dealer; or the designer of communities rather than the real estate salesperson. In his fight against slavery, he saw himself as a God-inspired person who acted upon sympathy for oppressed blacks, not as an antislavery reformer. In his slave-battling role he managed to make a mark on history, since slavery was an issue on most Americans' minds, and he forced the issue in an unprecedented way. In his other roles he failed signally, because he was out of step with the times.

There was a problem with trying to live according to the philosophy of work that Emerson (and Thoreau more famously) expressed, the one John Brown unwittingly lived by. America was hurtling toward industrialization. The first two decades of the nineteenth century have been identified as the key transitional moment between the subsistence economy of the past and the capitalist economy of the future. In the bygone subsistence economy, Americans lived off the land, producing most of the goods they consumed. Under capitalism, they generally worked outside the home and purchased goods that were manufactured by others. Along with industrial capitalism came competition and specialization. There was less and less room in this economic landscape for the self-sufficient "Man on the farm," and increasingly more for factories, machines, corporations, commercial farms, and the other capitalist appurtenances that ushered in the depersonalized jobs the Transcendentalists loathed. Moreover, the overweening power of the market created sharp fluctuations, which were particularly threatening in the era before effective government controls.

Just as John Brown's religion was a throwback to Puritanism, so his economic attitudes harked back to precapitalist America. In his mind, he lived in a subsistence economy. He had enjoyed a subsistence lifestyle as a child in the Ohio wilderness, and he would regain one when he moved in 1849 to the remote North Elba in upstate New York, where he chose to spend his final years and where he would request to be buried.

In the intervening years, however, he suffered endless tribulations trying to survive in the new world of capitalism. It would be tedious to detail his labyrinthine financial woes. Still, an overview of them is useful, because they provide an instructive case history of an earnest, stubborn man victimized by the risky new American economy.

Moreover, his economic travails contributed to his antislavery views. Labor reformers of his day claimed that the class divisions created by capitalism made workers "wage slaves." Brown's sympathy for "those in bonds" intensified as a result of his own experience as an oppressed "slave" of the capitalist system.

Brown's financial problems resulted from his overreliance on borrowed money and the economic downturn of 1837–42. During these years he juggled four business projects: the Haymaker real estate scheme, another land project involving a farm named Westlands, a cattle business, and a wool business.

The two land parcels would have paid off had Brown been able to hold on to them for decades and had he lived beyond fifty-nine: between 1860 and 1880, when they contained a railroad crossing, factories, and other businesses, their combined worth rose into the hundreds of thousands of dollars. The cattle and wool businesses might have succeeded had Brown not dug himself such a deep hole of debt in his real estate ventures that he had to resort to desperate maneuvers to obtain money.

It did not help matters that he attempted this balancing act at precisely the wrong moment, during the most severe depression before the Civil War. In 1836 the American economy, exacerbated by uncertainty in the world markets, went into an inflationary spiral. In the fall of 1837 a panic over specie (hard money) led to a sudden collapse of prices abroad and at home. A massive run on banks caused business failures and soaring unemployment nationwide. By the middle of 1838, half a million Americans were out of work. Hard times lingered for four years.

Not a propitious moment for a reluctant tyro to launch into business. But launch Brown did, and with abandon. Years later he would look back on the purchase of the Haymaker farm on credit as the start of "my extreme calamity." He told his son John all his misfortunes "grew out of one root,—doing business on credit." He should have thought of that to begin with, when he reached deep into other people's pockets to finance both the Haymaker property and the Westlands farm, which he purchased around the same time.

Located in Twinsburg, outside of Hudson, Westlands was, in Brown's view, the perfect farm. Since he lacked the money to buy it, in the fall of 1838 he got a loan from the Western Reserve Bank of Warren and, as security, signed a promissory note for $6,000 over to six people, principally Heman Oviatt, a farmer in nearby Richfield. Brown considered Westlands a farm he could live on and develop in the future, with the help of money he would earn from the Haymaker speculation.

Despite his mounting debts, his optimism survived the economic panic of 1837. In July 1838 he moved from Hudson back to the Haymaker house in Franklin Mills to keep a close eye on possible land sales there. He had heard that the state planned to apportion $420,000 for the Pennsylvania and Ohio Canal, the completion of which would make his land valuable. Ominously, however, it soon became clear that not only would the canal be rerouted away from the Haymaker area but also water was to be drained from the Cayahoga River, lessening the water supply (and hence the value) of the property. Still, Brown remained hopeful.

Hope could not solve the problem of his creditors. A number of suits were filed against him. One was initiated by the Western Reserve Bank, which called up his loan on Westlands. Lacking funds, Brown referred the bank to the promissory note for $5,260 he had signed to Heman Oviatt, against whom judgment was brought. To placate Oviatt, Brown signed over to him the penal bond of conveyance that had come with the property in lieu of a deed, which Brown did not have because he had not come close to meeting the asking price for the land. The understanding was that the farm belonged to Oviatt if Brown failed to come up with $5,260.

Oviatt was not the only person Brown had tapped in his real estate gambit. Smaller loans from others (Milo Hudson, William Astromo, Alpheus Hoskins, and William Folger) subjected him to several other lawsuits filed by banks in the Portage County Court of Common Pleas.

Brown had a brainstorm—not a good thing for an entrepreneur with his spotty track record to have during a major economic depression. He would herd cattle from his area to Connecticut, to be sold there by a firm he knew, Wadsworth & Wells, which would give him part of the proceeds of the sale. While he was in the East he would visit New York and Boston in search of yet another loan, which would allow him to pay off his creditors in Ohio.

He was about to jump from mud into quicksand.

He rounded up cattle owned by his father, Seth Thompson, and Heman Oviatt (all of whom should have known better than to go into the business), promising to reimburse them as soon as the money came in from Wadsworth & Wells. In November 1838 he made the arduous trip east, driving his cattle, probably via the Erie Canal and the Hudson River, to West Hartford, Connecticut. Unaware of his questionable business capacities, Tertius Wadsworth and Joseph Wells were thrilled at the prospect of having him as the Ohio partner in their firm. He would drive some two hundred cattle each year to Connecticut, and they would sell the animals in the East.

Leaving his cattle with them, Brown proceeded to Manhattan, arriving there on December 1. He dropped off a surveyor's compass to be fixed, and he visited Wall Street and William Street, evidently in search of a loan. In his letters home he kept up a brave face. On December 5 he wrote to his family, "I have not yet succeded in my business, but think the prospect such that I do not by any means despair of final success. As to that, may Gods holy will be done."

"Final success" would indeed come to him, but not in business. Success would spring from what was instinctive in him: compassion for blacks. He was always ready to communicate this compassion, even in the midst of his business troubles. Leaving New York, he headed for Boston and on the way stopped in his native town, Torrington, Connecticut. While there, he was taken to a grade school, where he gave an impromptu lesson in racial justice. On a classroom map he pointed to Africa and lectured on the evils of slavery and the slave trade. He asked the students how many of them would fight "against this great curse, when you grow up." Many boys raised their hands, and then he declared, "Now I want those who are *quite sure* that they will not forget it, who will promise to use their time and influence toward resisting this evil, to rise." Two boys stood up. John Brown put his hands on their heads and blessed the boys in the name of God, "who is your Father, and the father of the African," the Son, "who is your Saviour and the Saviour and master of the African," and the holy Spirit, "which gives you strength and which gives strength and comfort to the African."

This spontaneous prayer demonstrated just how free of racism Brown was. To instill a commitment to human brotherhood in schoolchildren, he spoke of a Holy Trinity that was equally attentive to the Caucasian and the African.

His quick plunge into his deepest social passions seems to have made him more careless than ever about more practical pursuits. His handling of finances in the months following the school episode was irrational.

The day after Christmas he arrived in Boston not as the dispenser of holiday cheer but as a beggar. He looked up three rich Bostonians, associates of Zenas Kent, whom he had met in Ohio: Henry Hubbard, George D. Munroe, and Edmund Munroe. He petitioned them for a loan. He was confident enough of getting the money that when he returned west through Connecticut he paid $130 for a flock of fine Saxony sheep that he drove back to Ohio.

The return to Franklin Mills only brought more anxiety. While suits piled up against him, he kept waiting for the loan from Boston to come through. By March 1839 he was convinced that only a second trip east would rescue him. He now needed a loan of perhaps as much as $20,000. Apparently he had managed to repay his father, Seth Thompson, and Heman Oviatt for the cattle he had taken on the first trip, for these three provided him with another herd for this trip.

Once more he drove a large cattle herd to West Hartford to be sold by Wadsworth & Wells. He stayed on there for two months to help with the sale. Over a hundred cattle were sold, but his mind was on the expected loan from Boston. On May 28, 1839, he wrote Seth Thompson, "I can only say that I still expect to obtain money at Boston, & that I expect to start for that place this week, or within a day or two."

Early June saw him in Boston checking on the loan. He must have received promising news, because soon he was back in West Hartford expecting the money any day. However, his hopes had dimmed by June 12, when he wrote his wife: "I am now somewhat in fear that I shall fail of getting the money I expected on the loan. Should that be the will of Providence, I know of no other way but we must consider ourselves very poor; for our debts must be paid, if paid at a sacrifice. Should that happen (though it may not) I hope God, who is rich in mercy, will grant us grace to conform to our circumstances with cheerfulness and true resignation."

This Calvinistic reliance on the "will of Providence" and God's "grace" may have bolstered him, but it did not pay bills. His financial frustration drove him to do something that was at best unethical. He borrowed (to put it kindly) $5,500 from Wadsworth & Wells without telling them. It is unclear whether he simply held on to the proceeds of the cattle sale or pilfered the money from the cash box in the West Hartford office. At any rate, he immediately sent the money back to Ohio to pay part of the loan on the Westlands farm. He made sure that a deed for the property was made out in his name. He did not report what he had done to Heman Oviatt, to whom he had signed over his initial bond of conveyance for the farm.

Tertius Wadsworth and Joseph Wells were not happy when they discovered that $5,500 was missing from their account. Brown would later say in court that he felt justified in borrowing the money since he was a partner in the firm and had been active in the cattle sale. Still, he should have told his partners about taking the funds. Wadsworth and Wells threatened to have him arrested. To keep them at bay, he told them he would turn over to them the Boston money, which he said would arrive at any moment.

A boon came from an unexpected source. While he was pondering his situation, he met George Kellogg, an agent of the New England Wool Company of Rockville, Connecticut. Kellogg was delighted to learn that Brown raised sheep and was an expert in fine wool. On June 15 he gave Brown $2,800 as an advance on wool that Brown promised to send him later from Ohio.

Sinking ever more deeply into his borrow-from-Peter-to-pay-Paul bog, Brown in desperation gave Kellogg's money to Wadsworth and Wells. He left Connecticut around June 18, arriving in Ohio in July. By early August, Kellogg had learned what had happened with his money and wrote Brown demanding an explanation.

Brown did not reply until August 27, when he wrote Kellogg, "I have found it hard to take up my pen to record, & to publish, my own shame, & abuse of the confidence of those whom I esteem, & who have treated me as a friend, & as a brother." With disarming candor, he described what had happened. He explained that on the day he was about to leave Connecticut, he faced the choice of going to jail or giving the $2,800 to his partners. He had done the latter in the expectation that within a month $5,000 would arrive from Boston. He had come home to a mountain of debt, leaving him virtually penniless. Besides, he noted, wool prices were now extremely high, so that he would not have risked buying wool even if he had kept Kellogg's money. But he promised to repay Kellogg soon. He signed himself "Unworthily yours."

Two weeks passed with no news of the Boston loan. On September 12, Kellogg wrote a note in which he attributed Brown's difficulties to the post-1837 depression. He wondered, though, about Brown's behavior. Brown answered immediately saying, "I utterly deny . . . a fraudulent or trickish design." He added that on August 29, as protection against his creditors, his property had been turned over to a trustee, George B. De Peyster. He still held out hope that he would pay Kellogg back, but several months later he confessed that he was unable to do so. By then he had left Franklin Mills and moved back to the Hudson property. He explained that he had "no less than a family of 10 to provide for," several of them ill.

He would have found himself less straitened had he taken a cue from the Shakers, who practiced celibacy in their communities. Lack of money was not going to swerve John Brown from the image of himself as a patriarch with a divine injunction to increase and multiply. Oliver Brown was born at

Franklin Mills on March 9, 1839, followed by Peter Brown, born at Hudson on December 7, 1840.

Fortunately for Brown, George Kellogg did not press charges for his lost money. The exchange of letters had convinced him of Brown's sincerity and good intentions.

Time would prove Kellogg right. Nothing in Brown's letters betrayed intentional deception. In fact, Brown was so sincere that in October 1842, after he had been legally cleared of debt by declaring bankruptcy, he sent Kellogg's wool company a formal agreement to repay the loan "and the interest thereon, from time to time, as divine Providence shall enable me to do so." Brown admitted that he had "imprudently pledged the [money] for my own benefit, and could not redeem it." Although Brown did not have to make this commitment, he did so, as he said in the agreement, "in consideration of the great kindness and tenderness of said Company toward me in my calamity and more particularly of the moral obligation I am under to render all their due." For the rest of his life he would periodically send Kellogg small sums, and in his will he left $50 toward the loan, which, however, he never came close to repaying in full.

Too late Brown came to the realization that credit had ruined him. He later explained to a friend, "I started out in life with the idea that nothing could be done without capital, and that a poor man must use his credit and borrow, and this pernicious notion has been the rock on which I, as well as so many others, have split. . . . Running into debt includes so much of evil that I hope all my children will shun it as they would a pestilence."

More than his dependence on credit, however, did him in. His awkwardness as a businessman stemmed also from lack of judgment and bullheadedness. He manifested these characteristics in two more botched efforts that came in 1840: a real estate deal with the Oberlin Collegiate Institute and a fight to retain the Westlands farm.

In April 1840 his father tried to arrange for his besieged son to move to western Virginia, where land was cheap and he could get a new start. Although Virginia was a slave state, its extreme western section was inhabited by poor whites, few of whom owned slaves. As a trustee of Oberlin, Owen Brown was aware that Gerrit Smith, a wealthy New York philanthropist, had given the college a large tract of land there. This fertile region, south of the Ohio River and eighty miles west of the Allegheny Mountains, needed to be surveyed because of boundary and title issues. At his father's urging, John Brown offered his services to Oberlin. He proposed going to Virginia and surveying the land, adding that if he were given acreage he could move there and farm it at a profit for the college. Oberlin's board of trustees, appointing him as an agent of the college, agreed to pay him a dollar for every day he worked, plus expenses, and to give him a thousand acres of land very cheaply when he was done.

With his compass and chain, he set off for Virginia and worked at his surveying during the rest of April and part of May. In July he submitted his survey for examination by the Oberlin Prudential Committee. On August 14 the committee got authorization from the trustees for a deed to a thousand acres of Virginia land to be issued to "Bro. John Brown of Hudson."

But Brother John had other plans. He was mulling over a possible partnership with Heman Oviatt in sheep and cattle farming in Richfield, Ohio. By late fall he thought the Oviatt plan might not work, and he looked back regretfully at the Oberlin offer. On January 21, 1841, he wrote the college's secretary, saying he was now ready to accept the land. The college was experiencing financial problems, however, and withdrew its offer. Brown sent Oberlin an angry letter and, after haggling, received a $29 settlement from the college.

So much for a thousand acres of good real estate, virtually free.

One wonders what he could have done with the land even had he taken it when he could. Just as he was allowing the Oberlin offer to slip away, he was preoccupied with an auction of his possessions and a fight for Westlands. The auction was held in the summer of 1840. Although he did not declare bankruptcy (that would come later), many of his household items and farm instruments were sold publicly so that he could raise money to pay his debts. He felt little attachment to worldly goods, yet he hated to lose the Saxony sheep he had brought from Connecticut.

The auction left him with his Hudson property, where he now lived. He also had nominal ownership of Westlands, though that was in jeopardy. The Ohio State Supreme Court ruled that Westlands must be sold in order to repay $1,202.28 to Daniel C. Gaylord, one of those who had given Brown a loan on the property. At a public auction on October 12, 1840, Amos Chamberlain of Hudson, an acquaintance of Brown, purchased the farm for $1,681, the low price reflecting the depressed real estate market.

Brown's reaction to the sale was an early signal of his violent reaction to anything that stirred him viscerally. So far, he had remained surprisingly calm and even cheerful in the face of his difficulties, constantly assuring his family that brighter days were ahead and impressing even his most frustrated creditors with his integrity. His equanimity owed much to Calvinistic fatalism but just as much to his emotional disengagement from the monetary schemes he was pursuing. As far as capitalist ventures went, he was, like Whitman's persona in "Song of Myself," "Both in and out of the game, and watching and wondering at it."

Westlands was a different story. His feelings for it related not only to his imperiled finances but also to his dreams. It was his perfect farm, a beautiful property where, if only his luck would change, he could settle down with his growing family and become the "Man on the farm." Maybe he could recapture the subsistence life he had known as a child.

He was ready to fight to keep the dream alive. When Amos Chamberlain tried to take possession of the land, Brown issued a trespass warrant against him through a friend who was a justice of the peace. Then he prepared for battle, even while appealing to Chamberlain's sympathy. He wrote Chamberlain begging him to allow him to keep the farm as defense against his creditors. He gave muskets to his three oldest sons—John, Jason, and Owen (nineteen, seventeen, and fifteen)—and put them in an old log hut near the border of the farm. Warning them that Chamberlain or someone else might be coming, he instructed them, "Shoot him if he puts his head inside." Chamberlain went to a local constable, who sent a posse that retreated at the sight of the guns. A few days later the county sheriff arrived at the farm and arrested John Brown and two of his sons (the third, Jason, was hiding in the woods). The Browns were taken to Akron jail but released almost immediately, since the sheriff decided he couldn't hold sincere men who were defending their own property. During their incarceration, Amos Chamberlain angrily went to Westlands and tore down the log hut.

Chamberlain occupied the farm, but a prickly issue remained: the bond of conveyance on the property that Brown had given one of his other creditors, Heman Oviatt, two years earlier. Who now owned Westlands— Chamberlain or Oviatt?

Actually, the situation was even more complicated. John Brown, in temporary efforts to patch up various debts, had mortgaged or taken liens against his different properties, involving a number of people—not only Oviatt but also Gaylord, Wadsworth, and Wells. Oviatt, feeling he was the rightful owner of Westlands, filed a claim against Brown and these three men. He appealed the case to the Ohio Supreme Court, which decided against him. Amos Chamberlain was granted ownership of the farm.

It is a testament to John Brown's ability to project decency that Oviatt, the biggest loser in the credit competition, showed no bitterness against him. Like Kellogg, Oviatt believed in Brown's integrity. Also like Kellogg, he would receive from Brown an unsolicited written promise to repay the money Brown owed him (now totaling over $5,600 plus court costs) in small payments as "Divine Providence" would allow.

Even as he was pursuing Westlands in court, Oviatt accepted an offer by Brown to establish their long-contemplated tannery partnership. In January 1842 an agreement was made for Brown to tend Oviatt's sheep and make leather out of the hides Oviatt would provide. In return, Oviatt would sell the leather and put half of the wholesale price toward Brown's long-standing debt to him on the Haymaker acreage. Under the arrangement, Brown and his family temporarily moved into a house on Oviatt's Richfield property.

Although Brown was settling matters with Oviatt, he had lost the Haymaker farm, which was being fought over by two creditors. Also, Tertius Wadsworth and Joseph Wells filed a suit against him for land mortgages he had signed over to them.

This suit was the last straw. By the summer of 1842 Brown was so poor he had trouble buying postage. He filed for bankruptcy, which was granted on September 28. In return for protection against creditors, he was stripped of his possessions except for modest necessities.

The court's inventory of the possessions he was allowed to keep reveals a pathetically humble lifestyle. His household items, with their assessed values, included "1 Pot Cracked 0.50," "4 Wooden pails old 1.12½," "6 Bedsteads old 5.25," "3 Bags old 1.00," "6 Feather beds old & poor 6.00," "2 Spinning Wheels 2.00," "4 Milk Pans 1.00," "1 Glass Bottle 0.10," "1 tin Cannister 0.09," and "2 Earthen Pots broke," of no value. The list suggests that the children, who now numbered twelve, ranging from the twenty-year-old John to an infant, Austin, born on September 14, were crammed into five beds.

The food listed was equally sparse, including dried apples, corn, potatoes, beans, lard, pork, and sugar. For farm animals the family was allowed two horses, two hogs, two cows, seven sheep, three lambs, and nineteen hens. Farm tools included "1 Pitch fork 0.25," "4 old Axes 1.75," "1 crow bar 1.37," and "1 shovel 0.25." Some rough clothes and a handful of other items were also permitted. The only abundant items in the household—"11 Bibles & testaments 6.50"—reflected John Brown's priority: religion.

He would need religion more strongly than ever in 1843, a tragic time for his family. The year began on a modestly hopeful note when Brown found a house to rent in Richfield, not far from his place of work, Oviatt's farm. The house was a whitewashed log cabin, in which the fourteen

Browns crowded around a table eating porridge and johnnycakes. On the property was a millpond and a creek dam where the boys hunted for mud turtles, which they took home to be cooked for dinner.

Whatever happiness the Browns had regained was shaken by the sudden deaths of four children. On September 4, 1843, Charles came down with dysentery, caused, perhaps, by the primitive, unsanitary conditions in which the family lived. Charles, a strapping six-year-old with long legs that made him a good runner, was a sandy-haired, quietly brave boy. After a week of diarrhea, fever, and vomiting, he died. Within a few days three others—the infant Austin, and Peter and Sarah (ages three and nine)—showed symptoms of the illness. They died on three successive days late in the month. The four children were buried in Fairview Cemetery in Richfield. Their names and their parents' names appear on the gravestone above a religious verse.

Salmon, who was turning seven at the time, would later say that these deaths were "a calamity from which father never fully recovered." John Brown recalled having "a steady, strong, desire; to die" around this time, perhaps referring to a wish to rejoin his lost children in the afterlife.

But he faced the tragedy with Calvinistic resignation. He wrote John Jr., who had gone off the previous year to attend the Grand River Institute, a manual labor school in Ashtabula County, "This has been to us all a bitter cup indeed, and we have drunk deeply, but still the Lord reigneth and blessed be his great and holy name forever." Four other family members, he added, had caught the illness but were recovering. With poignant understatement, he said of the departed ones, "They were all children towards whom perhaps we might have felt a little partial but they all now lie in a little row together." Comfort could be taken, he noted, that Sarah died happily in expectation of seeing her Maker. Jason, twenty, added a pious postscript: "These days are days of rebuke and severe trial with us. . . . Let us not murmur, The Judge of all the Earth, has done, and will do right."

In a few months the Judge of the Earth did right. In January 1844, John Brown visited Akron and looked up Colonel Simon Perkins, a well-to-do sheep farmer he had once met. Perkins proved to be his rescuer, at least for the time being.

Simon Perkins (the "Colonel" was an honorary title) was the son of a War of 1812 general who had helped found Akron. A diminutive and affable man with a goatee, Perkins admired John Brown's abilities as a judge of wool. He also pitied Brown in his misfortunes. He offered to go into a partnership by which Brown would move to Akron to merge his small sheep herd with Perkins's large one, tend the sheep and supervise shearing, and send wool to distributors in the Northeast. Brown would share profits and losses with Perkins, who would provide feed and shelter for the animals as well as a house in Akron that Brown could rent for just $30 a year.

At last, Brown found a viable way out of his financial mire. That spring he would actually send money to John Jr. and Ruth, both of whom were enrolled in the Grand River Institute. In a letter to John he wrote, "Divine Providence seems to smile on our works at this time. . . . I think this is the most comfortable and the most favourable arrangement of my worldly concerns that I ever had, and calculated to afford us more leisure for improvement, by day, & by Night, than any other. I do hope that God has enabled us to make it in mercy to us, & not that he should send leanness into our soul."

These words, cheerful as they were, had an ominous tinge. Although Brown believed that his "worldly concerns" would now be comfortably arranged, how about his spiritual ones? By worrying that "leanness of soul" might accompany success, Brown was expressing his old animus against business pursuits for their own sake.

He was right to worry, even at this happy moment. The new partnership with Perkins would eventually founder on his old "Man on the farm" syndrome. He cared about sheep and wool but not about the realities of the market economy. The kindly Perkins would keep the business going for eight years. At times it would work, but generally it barely broke even, and in the end it collapsed, largely because of Brown's reluctance as a capitalist. Once again, Brown would end up in court facing creditors.

Such a calamitous ending was far from his mind when he took his family to Akron in April 1844. The Browns occupied a modest farmhouse across the road from Perkins's elegant brick mansion. With his oldest sons and his dogs, Brown worked hard on Perkins's large farm herding some 1,500 sheep and gathering wool. Brown had such an intimate knowledge of the sheep that he could tell them all apart.

For all his enjoyment of such work, he was not the ideal shepherd. He used dogs, Perkins said, "because it was then the fashion to use them, as much for company as anything else; but they did more harm than good." He could distinguish between the sheep but was not deft in keeping them in line. Perkins's conclusion was that Brown "was a rough herdsman, but a nice judge of wool." Brown elicited respect from local farmers for his knowledge of the various breeds of sheep and reportedly wrote articles on the subject for local papers. He even came up with a remedy for bots, a disease caused by larvae in farm animals' stomachs.

Although Brown was good to have around the farm, Perkins also used him as an agent for the company. Frequently, Brown took trips throughout the surrounding region and to the East, where he bought sheep or arranged to sell wool. Jason stayed on the farm and tended the flocks, while Frederick, an unbalanced but tenderhearted fifteen-year-old, helped out with the younger children.

Through all the bad times he had not forgotten the slaves. While in Akron he kept up his involvement in the Underground Railroad. Some 2,000 slaves a year were now escaping through Ohio, coming up from Kentucky and Virginia and passing on to Canada. John Brown regularly hid fugitives in Akron and conducted them, sometimes five or six at a time, to stations north.

Besides slaves, he had growing concern for another group of oppressed people: working-class whites. The rise of the American labor movement in the 1830s and '40s resulted from the sharp class divisions created by capitalism. The same social tensions that abroad engendered Karl Marx's *Communist Manifesto* (1848) manifested themselves in the United States by an increasing disparity between the wealthy "upper ten" and the impoverished "lower million." Labor unrest resulted in various reform movements: George Henry Evans's land reform, associated with the agrarianism that would lead to the Homestead Act of 1862; workers' unions, early versions of the big labor unions of the late nineteenth century; and utopian experiments of many types, ranging from the Associationist Brook Farm in Massachusetts to the free-love community Modern Times on Long Island.

Without joining a movement, John Brown shared the spirit of the labor reformers. In his travels for Perkins he became increasingly angry at what he saw as a conspiracy on the part of companies who he believed cheated farmers by colluding on wool prices, depriving the hardworking farmers of a fair profit.

His resentful view of business leaders resembled the conspiratorial vision of labor reformers of the period. The most popular novel of the 1840s, *The Quaker City; or, The Monks of Monk Hall,* by the vituperative labor unionist George Lippard, dramatized a plot on the part of America's social rulers—bankers, lawyers, moguls, clergymen, and so on—to defraud and corrupt everyday Americans. In an age before government controls on business and safety nets for the poor, radicals like Lippard imagined that the so-called idle rich were conspiring against common workers.

John Brown had a similar idea that eastern capitalists were unfairly holding down wool prices. His idea of an organized conspiracy was neither more foolish nor more accurate than was Lippard's—both were in some ways right, in other ways off the mark. Although Brown was correct in thinking that wool growers did not get enough for their best fleeces, there is no evidence of complicity on the part of buyers.

In March 1846 he approached Perkins with a plan for combating the supposedly nefarious buyers. While Perkins remained in Akron overseeing the flock, John Brown and two of his sons would move to Springfield, Massachusetts, and run a wool distribution center. Brown would warehouse wool from growers in Ohio, Pennsylvania, New York, Vermont, and Virginia, sort the wool and price it according to quality, and then arrange for sales to eastern companies.

For growers the plan would ensure that their wool would be priced fairly according to grade. For buyers it would guarantee that the wool they bought would be accurately sorted by Brown's trained eye. Although Brown would receive a commission of 2 cents per pound of wool sorted and sold, his main goal was to correct a perceived wrong, not to make money.

Although Perkins was skeptical of the plan, he was impressed by Brown's earnestness and supplied the capital necessary for starting the business. By June, Brown was in Springfield, a town of 11,000 on the Connecticut River, stocking an old warehouse on Water and Railroad streets with bales of wool that were already arriving from growers. As the business grew, he moved it into a building on North Main Street with stores below and apartments above. Jason had come along to help, and John Jr., having finished at the Grand River Institute, joined them in July. They lived successively in various rented apartments.

Just as Brown was establishing himself in Springfield, another tragedy struck his Ohio home. In early November came the devastating news that Brown's youngest daughter, Amelia, who had been born in Akron in June 1845, was scalded to death in a household accident caused by Ruth. In a letter of November 8, addressing his family as "MY DEAR AFFLICTED WIFE & CHILDREN," he gave what consolation he could. "This is a bitter cup indeed," he wrote, "but blessed be God: a brighter day shall dawn; & let us not sorrow as those that have no hope." Ever the Calvinist, he added, "I humbly hope this dreadful afflictive Providence will lead us all more properly to appreciate the amazeing, unforeseen, untold, consequences; that hang upon the right or wrong doing of things seemingly of trifling account." Three weeks later he advised Mary to "try to maintain a cheerful self command while we are tossing up & down, & let our motto still be Action, Action; as we have but one life to live."

He lived by this motto in Springfield, where he and his sons worked indefatigably. In 1846 and '47 they sorted and graded as many as three hundred tons of wool. Brown put in long hours at the warehouse, dividing his time between handling wool and keeping neat account books.

With his resolution and vigor, why didn't he succeed?

E. C. Leonard, a businessman who worked down the block from him, gave a reason for his failure. Referring to Brown familiarly as "Uncle John," Leonard described his business strategies: "Uncle John was no trader: he waited until his wools were graded, and then fixed a price; if this suited the manufacturers they took the fleeces; if not, they bought elsewhere, and Uncle John had to submit finally to a much less price than he could have got. Yet he was a scrupulously honest and upright man,—hard and inflexible, but everybody had just what belonged to him. Brown was in a position to make a fortune, and a regular-bred merchant would have done so. . . . But, as I said, it was a failure."

Brown's partner, Simon Perkins, made similar comment: "Brown managed according to his own impulses: he would not listen to anybody, but did what he took into his own head. He was solicitous to go into the business of selling wool, and I allowed him to do it; but he had little judgment, always followed his own will, and lost much money."

A stubborn, dictatorial spirit, then, proved to be Brown's undoing once again. But the Springfield venture differed notably from his previous ones. This time, Brown was driven by a deep bitterness against what he regarded as exploitative corporations. Having long been a shepherd and farmer, he saw such rural workers as innocent pawns of scheming capitalists. Never a capitalist himself, he now launched his own war against those who he believed were taking advantage of farmers.

In his own way he was a labor reformer. Thomas B. Musgrave, an experienced wool dealer, said that "warehousing of wool at Springfield and elsewhere was a new feature introduced by Brown, in order to enhance prices in the interest of the farmers."

John Brown, Jr., who late in life became a socialist, declared that in the 1840s "Father's favorite theme was that of the *Community plan of cooperative industry*, in which all should labor for the common good; 'having all things in common' as did the disciples of Jesus in his day. This has been, and still is, my Communistic or Socialist faith."

This assessment was only half right. By no stretch of the imagination could John Brown, who verged on anarchism in his hatred of government and other institutions, be called a communist. But his son was accurate in emphasizing his belief in "cooperative industry." Brown's economic vision had nothing to do with the Marxist materialism that underlay communism.

Instead, it can be related to the utopian socialism of the pre–Civil War period. More than twenty-five utopian communities were founded during this time, many of them based loosely on the ideas of the French visionary Charles Fourier. Despite great differences between the communities, most attempted to provide alternative models of work in order to counteract the perceived evils of capitalism. They tried to make work attractive and cooperative instead of selfish and competitive.

John Brown had his own model, one allied with what today would be called the producers' cooperative, in which producers organize for mutual support and financial equity. In a widely distributed circular titled "To Wool Growers," Brown stated that as the middleman between farmers and capitalists he could gain fair treatment for producers of wool.

Given the improvisational, homespun nature of his cooperative, his hopes for it were just as chimerical as the Fourierist fantasies of the reformers at Brook Farm, memorably satirized in Hawthorne's *The Blithedale Romance*. But Brown's plan was bold. Whereas the utopian reformers retreated to isolated rural locations to experiment with their models, Brown put his to the test in a bustling commercial town, becoming directly engaged with capitalists all over the Northeast. Had he been flexible in his pricing of the various grades of fleeces, he might have succeeded.

There was the rub. He was *not* flexible. He ignored the first law of the market economy: supply and demand. He established prices he thought were fair and stuck to them. If, as was often the case, his warehouse was bulging with unsold wool, he would not initiate a planned price reduction. Instead, he would retain his prices, which were often out of line anyway.

Although he was an excellent judge of wool, he had little expertise in deciding its market value. Setting the price of his finest wools too high and his poorest ones too low was his habitual error (a reflection, no doubt, of his emotional response to excellent versus low-quality fleece). As a result, buyers gobbled up his inexpensive grades and waited on the fine ones until he was forced to sell them at highly reduced prices.

His price-fixing idea was wrongheaded not only because it ignored the changeable American market but also because it met challenges from abroad. A tariff law passed by the U.S. Congress in 1846 reduced duties on imported wool, the supply of which ballooned while prices fell. Brown was more inclined to fulminate against those who passed the tariff than he was to adjust his prices accordingly. He blamed "doughfaces" (Northerners with Southern sympathies) for passing the tariff and pursuing war with Mexico, which, like most Abolitionists, he saw as a plot to extend slavery. He expressed dismay to Perkins about "the panic that now exists in the wool market on account of the Tarriff. The prospect of good & brisk sales is very different from what it was before the Dough faces passed the bill through the house."

Brown might not have succeeded, however, even if the market or the tariff were not considerations. Capitalism runs on self-interest and financial incentives. Brown was careless of both of these elements of capitalism. His carelessness came out in small ways and in a more general sense as well. His account books were neatly written but far from meticulous: though he entered credits and debits, he balanced his books erratically and was often clueless about available funds.

His disregard for the bottom line was linked to his overall distaste for business. He wanted to help wool farmers, but he did not want to enter into a cutthroat competition for money. If the Emersonian "Man on the farm" syndrome had precluded his success as a commercial farmer, a Thoreau-like "I hate trade" one prevented his advance in business. Thoreau says in *Walden* (1854) that he once "tried trade" (in his father's pencil business) but "found that it would take ten years to get under way in that, and that then I should probably be on my way to the devil." Convinced that "the ways by which you may get money almost without exception lead downward," Thoreau abandoned business and pursued a higher "economy."

Brown could sound like Thoreau in his rejection of materialism and his dedication to things of the spirit. His concern that worldly business might bring "leanness of the soul" resurfaced in his letters from Springfield. After ten months of work there had brought no significant improvement of his family's financial picture, he still distinguished sharply between monetary and spiritual success. Replying to a letter from his father, he wrote: "I am quite sensible of the truth of your remark that my family are quite as well off as though we possessed millions. I hope we may not be left to a feeling of ungratitude or greediness of gain, & I feel unconscious of a desire to become rich. I hope my motive for exerting myself is higher. . . . My only motive [in moving his family to Springfield] would be to have them with me, if I continue in my present business; *which I am by no means atached too.*"

Ready to move his large family to Springfield but "by no means attached" to his work there? By early 1847 his dream of helping wool growers was rubbing up against the realities of the market. If he could not reform the workplace to protect farmers, what attached him to Springfield? Why not move back to Ohio?

Most importantly, as discussed in the next chapter, new opportunities for antislavery work opened up while Brown was in Springfield.

Also, he hadn't given up on the wool operation. In January 1847 he sent

House in Springfield, Massachusetts, where
John Brown lived in the 1840s.
BOYD STUTLER COLLECTION OF JOHN BROWN, WEST VIRGINIA ARCHIVES.

a circular to Ohio farmers announcing that he would speak at a convention for sheep farmers the next month in Steubenville. He wrote, "We want to see every wool grower in Washington Co[unty] there then as we have something to tell them about the wool market that every one should hear." In February he traveled to Steubenville and addressed the meeting, giving such an impressive account of his method of grading and sorting that the group named him the eastern representative for Ohio's growers.

For his hard-pressed family, moreover, Springfield offered a fresh start. Ohio had proven a dead end, and Springfield opened new vistas. At least he had a sure job there for the foreseeable future. His business strategies may have puzzled Simon Perkins, but his assiduity and integrity were undeniable. Perkins would remain supportive of him to the end, even after the business failed.

Before the whole family moved from Ohio in July 1847, John, Jason, and John Jr. had been living in a boardinghouse. The arrival of Mary and the younger children necessitated a move to larger quarters. They tried several rental houses before settling into a two-and-a-half-story frame dwelling on Hastings Street (later 51 Franklin Street).

Situated in a nondescript working-class neighborhood around the corner from the wool warehouse, the house was simple but handsome, with a front piazza supported by fluted columns and a wing in the back connecting to a small barn. The inside was spartan. The Browns bought only basic furniture, voting as a family to send money instead to the aid of fugitive slaves in upstate New York. Frederick Douglass, who visited the home in November 1847, noted that it had "no sofas, no cushions, no curtains, no carpets, no easy rocking chairs inviting to enervation or repose." Meals—"none of your tea and toast sort, but potatoes and cabbage, and beef soup"—were served at a table "innocent of paint, veneering, varnish or tablecloth, [which] announced itself unmistakably and honestly pine and of the plainest workmanship." Altogether, said Douglass, the home had "an air of plainness about it which almost suggested destitution." (He couldn't know that it was the finest one the Browns ever inhabited.)

In the spring of 1847, John Jr. was again at the Grand River Institute, where he met a woman named Wealthy Hotchkiss. A brief courtship led to their marriage in July. They settled in Springfield so that he could continue working with his father. Jason, meantime, wanted a life of his own. That year he was married to Ellen Sherbondy. They moved back to Ohio. Brown's oldest daughter, Ruth, had remained in Ohio when the rest of the family moved east.

John Brown at forty-seven seemed taller than his five feet ten inches. Wiry and erect, he had not yet developed the stoop that would later lead to the popular image of "Old Brown." His dark hair, flecked with gray, stood out in short bristles around his head, giving him a feral look accented by his prominent ears. His hawklike nose curved toward his firmly set mouth, which stretched in a grim line across his face. His blue-gray eyes flashed when he was excited or mirthful and settled into a snakelike gaze in calm moments. He dressed in simple snuff-colored cloth outfits and wore cowskin boots. Often he walked with his hands clasped behind his back and with his eyes fixed on the ground as though he were preoccupied.

A "reading" of his physiognomy made in February 1847 by Orson S. Fowler, the era's leading phrenologist, was revealing. Brown was doing nothing unusual in consulting a phrenologist. Others who did so included Walt Whitman, Edgar Allan Poe, Margaret Fuller, and Mark Twain. Phrenology, an early version of pop psychology, held that a person's attributes were told by the contours of the skull. The idea was that that the brain consisted of more than thirty "organs"—"ideality" (expressing religious devotion), "amativeness" (heterosexual desire), "adhesiveness" (comradeship), and others—that created bumps and valleys on the skull. Reading the bumps was considered therapeutic, for the patient was told whether a certain bump was unusually large or small and therefore was urged to use willpower to quell or enhance a certain attribute (e.g., "Your bump of amativeness is too big; watch out for promiscuity").

John Brown in 1846. The earliest known daguerreotype of
Brown, probably taken in Springfield by a black photographer whose
name is unknown. The banner Brown grasps with his left hand may be
inscribed with the initials S. P. W., signifying Subterranean Pass
Way, Brown's name for the Underground Railroad.

BOYD STUTLER COLLECTION OF JOHN BROWN, WEST VIRGINIA ARCHIVES.

Fowler's reading of Brown was, we know today, largely conjecture based on facial expression, but it was at least partly accurate. Fowler was off the mark in a couple of areas, as when he said, "You have not enough devotional feeling, nor of what we term 'spirituality of mind,'" but he was generally accurate about Brown's traits, as confirmed by other evidence. His statement that "you are positive in your likes and dislikes, 'go the whole figure or nothing,' and want others to do the same" spoke to Brown's bull-headedness, which he manifested even in small ways, such as insisting that people around him drink tea instead of coffee. Fowler's comment that Brown was "practical rather than theoretical" was right, as were his pronouncements about Brown's powerful ego, as attested by the rocklike firmness confirmed by other contemporary descriptions of him as well as by photographs. "You would rather lead than be led," Fowler said, "—have great sense of honor, and would scorn to do anything mean or disgraceful. You might be persuaded, but to drive you would be impossible. You like to have your own way, and to think and act for yourself—are quite independent and dignified, yet candid, open, and plain; say just what you think, and most heartily despise hypocrisy and artificiality, yet you value the good opinion of others though you would not stoop to gain applause."

Conjecture, yes, but a fair enough appraisal. Brown himself was sufficiently moved by the consultation that two weeks later he wrote Mary a contrite letter admitting to some of the faults Fowler had noticed. Fowler had called him "too blunt and free-spoken," saying he was prone to "give offence when you do not intend to" and to criticize others in a "plain, pointed, manner" instead of in a "bland and affable" one. In his letter Brown apologized to Mary for "my harsh rough ways," adding, "I often regret that my manner is no more kind & affectionate to those I really love, & esteem; . . . I want your face to shine even if my own should be dark, & cloudy."

He would have every excuse for his face to be dark and cloudy many times over the next two years. In January 1848 his son Oliver nearly died from swallowing a hemlock root he mistook for a carrot. He vomited, passed out, and was saved only by powerful emetics.

The economy, which had been strong since 1844, dipped in early 1848, putting more pressure than ever on the wool business. Wool sales fell, and Brown's warehouse filled up with tons of unsold bales. Alarming debts piled up; for instance, Perkins & Brown owed $57,000 to the Cabot Bank.

The winter of 1848–49 brought no respite from suffering. Several members of Brown's family came down with severe colds. The eighteen-year-old Frederick, the most unstable of the children, endured excruciating headaches perhaps associated with dementia. Owen, now twenty-four, had pain and stiffness in his crippled arm, relieved somewhat by applications of a galvanic battery. Death visited the family again. The youngest child, Ellen, died three weeks before her first birthday. A cold had developed into pneumonia, and she passed away in her father's arms on April 30, 1849.

Brown hoped that the gold rush of 1849 would indirectly benefit the wool business, but it did not. Debt and unsold inventory had risen too high for Perkins & Brown to recover. Brown became increasingly angry at American manufacturers who toyed with his pricing system, refusing to buy until he got desperate and reduced his prices to ruinously low levels.

Worse, the very people he had been trying to serve, wool growers, were complaining loudly. Many had shipped him wool for which they never received payment. In July 1849 he tried to make amends by traveling through Pennsylvania and Ohio to distribute payments, but he became ill, perhaps with cholera, and had to leave money with agents while he rushed on to Akron to recuperate.

Even in the midst of his afflictions, he had his eye on the current cultural scene. Although an aficionado of phrenology, he had serious doubts about another popular craze, mesmerism. America at the time was flooded with traveling hypnotists, who amazed audiences with displays of their seemingly miraculous powers. One of them, the genial Le Roy Sunderland, on one of his periodic appearances in Springfield's Hampden Hall, was putting on his usual show one evening when a stern-faced man in the audience stood up and pronounced the affair a humbug. It was John Brown, who said he was especially dubious of Sunderland's claims to make his subjects insensible to pain. Brown proposed a test. He would allow himself to be subjected to the same test as one of Sunderland's subjects to prove that willpower, not hypnotism, blocked pain.

The next day Brown appeared with cowhage (or "cow-itch"), a nettle that stabs like pins when applied to the skin. Sunderland first rubbed the cowhage across the neck and upper chest of a woman he had put under a spell. She showed no signs of pain until the spell was momentarily lifted, when she screamed in agony. Next the prickly substance was applied to Brown. A combination of his tough skin, leathery from long-term exposure to the elements, and sheer stoicism kept him from crying out. However, when Sunderland passed ammonia under his nose, he automatically threw back his head in shock. The same test had provoked no reaction from the hypnotized woman. Brown managed to restrain his response to the cowhage until he got outside the auditorium, where he clawed his neck in frenzy and rubbed himself against poles to relieve the pain. He was up all night. The next morning he saw a doctor for his pain, and he wrote a letter to a local paper saying that perhaps there was something to mesmerism.

Brown never forgot American blacks, to whom his life was increasingly dedicated. He had known for some time about a large area of land in upstate New York that the wealthy antislavery reformer Gerrit Smith had opened to settlement by free blacks and fugitive slaves. As his wool business faded, he developed a strong desire to move to the area so that he could help the blacks establish a community by surveying their properties and guiding them in farming. He bought from Smith 244 acres at a dollar an acre in the isolated village of North Elba, far in the Adirondacks near Lake Placid. About a third of the acreage was arable. Since he had to remain in Springfield to attend to his business, in May 1849 he sent the rest of the family to North Elba to live in a rented house until he was able to go there and build one.

His frustrations with the American wool market prompted a new idea: selling his wool abroad. A Scottish wool agent had told him that the finest

American fleeces were enjoying a healthy sale at good prices in England. John Brown believed he could save his company if he tapped into the European market. Having arranged for ten tons of high-quality wool to be shipped, he set sail on August 15 for Liverpool, where he landed on the twenty-sixth, proceeding to London the next day.

His impressions of England were mixed. He called it "a fine country, so far as I have seen; but nothing so very wonderful has appeared to me." Unlike most American travelers, he was not there for culture. He reserved his comments for matters closer to his heart. In a letter to John Jr. he said he found the farming and stonemasonry "very good," the cattle "middling good," but the horses "will bear no comparison with those of our Northern States, as they average." "Their hogs," he continued, "are generally good, and mutton-sheep are almost everywhere as fat as pork."

At this moment, though, the last thing John Jr. cared about was the quality of English livestock. With his father abroad, he was left alone fending off anxious wool growers, who assaulted him with what he called "many importunate letters and some saucy ones" asking about their unsold wool. He held out a vague promise that they might receive positive news when "our Mr. Brown" got back from Europe.

But Mr. Brown's news from Europe would not be positive. Learning from the Pickersgill firm that his wool would be auctioned in mid-September, he crossed the channel to Calais and took a train to Paris, where he met with representatives of the manufacturing firm Thirion Maillard & Co. who said they would go to England to inspect his wool when it went there. He continued on to Brussels and went to investigate the nearby Waterloo battlefield, making a personal assessment of mistakes Napoleon had made. Then he traveled to Hamburg, staying in the Hôtel de l'Europe. His travels during the eleven or twelve days after he left Hamburg are unknown. He would later report that as part of his preparation for an invasion of the South he learned about military strategy by watching military reviews in various European countries, but if he did so, there is no documentary evidence. It is surmised that after Germany he went on to Switzerland and Italy. At any rate, by September 17 he was back in England, with high hopes of selling his wool.

His hopes were again dashed, this time with devastating results. His wool attracted low prices at auction, partly because buyers were suspicious of it. A number of the bales that he had not inspected were opened up and found to have in them mud, wood, and other refuse wool growers had included to falsify weight. Desperate to sell the suspect wool, he traveled to Wortley, Branley, and elsewhere but found he could get no better prices anywhere. When he returned to London, he confronted a maddeningly ironic situation. Some of his wool was to be sold to American buyers for lower prices than had been his original asking price in America. The Pickergills actually lent money to a New York firm for this purpose. The Massachusetts wool merchant Thomas B. Musgrave paid 52 cents a pound for fleece for which he had previously offered Brown 60 cents a pound.

And so Brown lost triply on his wool: in America, then in England, and then in America again. True, his trip abroad had been satisfying in some ways. He won a medal at the world's fair in London for some fine Saxony sheep he had brought with him. Also, he gave the British a comeuppance when a jocose buyer, testing his knowledge of wool fibers, handed him poodle hair instead, asking him to grade it. "Gentlemen," Brown declared after feeling the hair, "if you have any machinery that will work up dog's hair, I would advise you to put this into it."

But the outcome of the trip for Perkins & Brown was disastrous. All told, the firm lost at least $40,000 in the fiasco. Brown returned home only to find growers more furious than ever about their wool, which either remained unsold or had been virtually given away.

The time had come to close the agency, but many accounts had to be settled first. In April 1850, Brown consulted with Perkins in Burgettstown, Pennsylvania. Perkins was as gracious as he could be, given the European debacle, which had stunned him. He knew that the end of their business was in sight. He accepted the situation, as Brown related, "without a frown on his countenance, or one syllable of reflection; but, on the contrary, with words of comfort and encouragement," setting "an example worthy of a philosopher, or of a Christian."

The incorrigible Brown felt "nerved to face any difficulty while God continues me such a partner"—not good news for Perkins, who doubtless squirmed at the prospect of further dealings with Brown. Perkins was magnetized, though, by Brown's indisputable integrity, finding him "thoroughly honest and honorable in all his relations."

For the remainder of 1850, Brown made a number of trips through Pennsylvania, western Virginia, and Ohio to deal with growers, settling accounts with some and trying to placate those he could not pay. He had time in September to return to North Elba, where he showed his prize Devonshire cattle in a county fair and witnessed Ruth's marriage to Henry Thompson, a North Elba neighbor who was a staunch Abolitionist. Invigorated, he went to Springfield in October to close the agency.

Having finished with the wool business, Brown did what he always did—he planned yet another business. In November he wrote Jason, who had a vineyard in Ohio, to find two "Junk Bottles," clean them, and fill them "with the Cherry Wine being verry careful not to rile it up before fill-ing the Bottles providing good Corks & filling them perfectly full." The bottles were to be sent to him in Springfield to be used as samples toward sale. His new dream was a beverage business that could help the temper-ance cause. "We can effect something to purpose by producing unadulter-ated Domestic Wines," he wrote confidently. "They will command great prices."

Nothing came of the wine idea. Not only did Brown lack capital, but he was preoccupied with creditors left over from the wool operation.

He spent much of 1851 and '52 in court. Rushing from trial to trial, he zigzagged between Pittsburgh, Troy, Utica, Vernon, Boston, New York, and other cities. The history of his court appearances will never be known in detail. Brown found himself at a loss for words when he tried to recount them. In a typically frenetic moment he wrote, "To give you a full history of all that has worked to delay this tedious business, will require more time than I have now to write," explaining that "I must have some days to pre-pare for the Burlington case, & also for the Pittsburgh business." His perennial optimism flickered dimly under the weight of his frustration. "I feel sorely disappointed," he lamented, "in not being able to get through with this business, now, as I do not know how we are to get along about money, but hope there will be some way."

Some sample cases give a taste of what he was going through during these years. Henry Warren of Pittstown, New York, charged him with ship-ping his wool to Burlington Mills Manufacturing Company of Vermont without paying him an adequate price for it. He claimed he had shipped the fleece to Brown in 1847 but was reimbursed in lower 1848 prices. Brown countered that Warren's wool had not arrived until 1848 and that there was no telling where much of it went, since it was mixed with other wool. The court judged in Brown's favor, but an appeals court reversed the decision, leaving Brown furious. Meanwhile, Burlington Mills filed a suit against Brown for not sending promised shipments. The case dragged on until 1853, when Brown's lawyer persuaded him to settle out of court, a decision Brown later regretted when he won a similar case in New York. Cabot Bank won a judgment against Perkins & Brown for its sizable loan. Although Perkins funded the trials, Brown lost much time and energy in the dizzying succession of cases.

In addition to his legal snarls, Brown continually dealt with severe per-sonal misfortune. An infant son born on April 26, 1852, in Akron, Ohio, died twenty-one days later. This was the seventh of the thirteen children of his second marriage to die. In December 1851 the unstable Frederick had a particularly bad spell. As Brown reported to John Jr., "One serious difficulty has been with Frederick, who has been very wild again."

But John Jr. himself was problematic. Along with his brother Jason, he had rejected his father's religion and had become an agnostic. Worse yet, a number of the younger Brown children had grown skeptical. In January 1852, Brown penned a sober letter to his children. "When I look forward as regards of the religious prospects of my numerous family (the most of them)," he wrote, "I am forced to say, & to feel too; that I have little, very little to cheer." Ever the Calvinist, he took the blame on himself: "That this should be so, is I perfectly well understand the legitimate fruit of my own planting; and that only increases my punishment." Noting apostasy among both his older and younger children, he gave a general benediction: "God grant you *thorough* conversion from sin, & full purpose of heart to continue steadfast in his ways through the *very short* season of trial you will have to pass."

He became even more upset when John Jr. sent him a letter in which he defended his skepticism. The father's reply was a six-page sermon. He noted with poignant sarcasm that his younger sons "appear to be a *little in advance* of my older ones" by discovering the Bible to be "all a fiction" at an earlier age. As for John Jr.'s letter, it gave him "little else than pain & sorrow." To rebut his son's argument, he used exhortation, not logic. Assuming that everything in the Bible was self-evidently true, he strung together quotations from the Old Testament about evil backsliding, false prophets, human wickedness, God's judgment, and so on.

Evidently, John Jr. was not won over by the recitation of dreary passages he had heard from infancy. Along with most of his siblings, and with most Americans of his generation, he had abandoned the Puritan-based Calvinism of his father.

Still, John Brown never gave up looking hopefully for signs of religious conversion in his children. He exulted over a pious letter from Ruth and her husband Henry Thompson in June 1853. Two months later, though, he harped again on backsliding in his family. Expressing hope that his doubting children would "through the infinite grace and mercy of God . . . be brought to see the error of your ways," he added sternly, "I do not feel 'estranged from my children,' but I cannot flatter them; nor 'cry peace when there is *no* peace.' "

His letters were also full of Calvinistic self-flagellation. In a letter to Ruth and Henry he discussed practical matters and then got to his own sinfulness. "Yesterday I began my 54th year," he wrote, "& I am surprised that one guilty of such an incredible amount of sin & folly should be spared so long; & I certainly have reason to be surprised. I still Keep hopeing to do better hereafter."

In 1853 he went to Ohio, as usual financially pressed. He had a vague plan of renewing his farming partnership with Perkins. He spent most of the year on the sheep farm, trying to make the business work. But by January 1854 it was clear that his time as a business associate of the good-hearted Simon Perkins was at its end. They dissolved their partnership on friendly terms. Brown wanted to go on to North Elba immediately, but he had to earn money to do so. He rented a couple of farms and worked them for many months, but a drought destroyed most of his crops. He was cheered by the arrival on September 25 of his twentieth and last child, named Ellen in memory of the infant who had died five years earlier. But another child was another mouth to feed. In the winter he moved back to North Elba, as poor as ever.

Poor financially, but not spiritually. During the same years when he was headed "downward," as Thoreau described his own experience in business, his thoughts about slavery and race were broadening notably. The period from 1838 to 1854 was a time of worldly failure but inward growth for Brown.

The way he became a man who changed the course of American history is a story of its own.

6

The Plan

It was during John Brown's Springfield years that he first revealed his plan to invade the South to free the slaves.

When had the plan first come to his mind? What made him turn to violence to combat slavery? What were his precedents? How did his proposed solution to the slavery problem compare with that of others of his time?

Surprisingly, these questions have never been addressed with care. Although historians agree that John Brown was a catalyst of the Civil War, no one has traced in detail the backgrounds of his antislavery vision. Important sources of the Civil War have therefore been given short shrift.

Though John Brown did not live to see the war, he embodied its spirit in advance. What Abraham Lincoln became by the end of the conflict—an antislavery warrior who resorted to extreme violence and who humbled himself before what he called (in the Second Inaugural) "the providence of God" and "the judgments of the Lord"—is a heightened version of what John Brown, the God-directed fighter against slavery, had been when he died on the scaffold six years earlier.

No single person came closer than Brown to anticipating the war. True, others had *predicted* war. As early as 1787, Jefferson had prophesied that the injustices of slavery could lead to cataclysmic racial conflict. "Indeed I tremble for my country," he wrote, "when I reflect that God is just." Three decades later John Quincy Adams wrote in his diary: "A dissolution [of the Union] for the cause of slavery would be followed by a servile war in the slaveholding States, combined with a war between the two severed portions of the Union"—a "calamitous and desolating" prospect, he believed, but one that would rid America of its "great and foul stain," slavery. The Republican senator Charles Sumner in his famous speech "The Crime Against Kansas" (1856) said he saw signs of an approaching "civil war," a "fratricidal, parricidal war" that would have "an accumulated wickedness beyond that of any war in human annals." Similarly, a correspondent to the *Boston Traveller* asserted, "This nation is going steadily toward a war which, should it come, will be the darkest, deadliest, and most awful which ever cursed this planet."

But John Brown not only *predicted* war; he *made* war. At Pottawatomie he led a slaughter of five proslavery citizens. In Missouri he liberated eleven slaves from their owners, killing a white man in the process, and led the blacks on a precarious thousand-mile flight to freedom. His armed seizure of the federal arsenal at Harpers Ferry, Virginia, resulted in a battle in which seventeen died.

Because we now view the antebellum period retrospectively through the lens of the bloodiest conflict in our history (in which more Americans died than in all the nation's other wars *combined*), it is perhaps difficult to see just how unusual John Brown's antislavery violence was for its time.

Most white Abolitionists strongly opposed violence. Satanic cruelty and discord, they maintained, governed the slaveholding South and could be counteracted through Christ-like nonresistance. The era's most prominent antislavery reformer, William Lloyd Garrison, founded the New England Non-Resistance Society in 1838, largely in response to the ferocity of proslavery mobs.

During the 1840s the Society attracted many leading Abolitionists who joined Garrison in rejecting the American Constitution because it implicitly supported the violent institution of slavery. Disunion became the watchword of the Garrisonians, who were convinced that the Constitution bound the North to the South in an unholy alliance of violence. Because of the Constitution's clause about suppressing insurrections, Garrison insisted, Northerners were "liable to be drafted at a moment's warning" in order "to put down a black rebellion in the south" and thus to aid in "subduing or exterminating the blacks." Since the South's "security lies in northern bayonets," Garrison argued, the North must separate itself peacefully from the Union with the expectation that slavery would soon die out as a result of the economic and social instability of an isolated South.

Although a number of Abolitionists became more militant after 1850, nonviolence left an impact on the antislavery movement. Garrison admired Harriet Beecher Stowe's meek Uncle Tom because of his willingness "to be 'led as a lamb to the slaughter,' returning blessing for cursing, and anxious only for the salvation of his enemies," showing the glorious "nature, tendency, and results of CHRISTIAN NON-RESISTANCE." Even in 1855, after the infamous Kansas-Nebraska Act had aroused violence in several previously mild reformers, such as Thoreau and Henry C. Wright, Garrison could affirm, "Non-resistance makes men self-governed. The kingdom of God is within them."

The later 1850s saw an increasing number of converts to a more confrontational stance. Garrison came to endorse slave insurrections (though not invasions of the South by whites), and during the war he was a flag-waving supporter of the Union war effort. Nonresistance survived, however. In an 1863 antislavery convention, for example, Stephen S. Foster, supported by his wife, Abby Kelley Foster, denounced the war with the assertion: "If you are battling with slavery upon the field of blood, you are not on my platform. That is an aggressive weapon, that we repudiated at the outset; and we pledged ourselves never to use it. . . . For one, I will continue as I ever have done."

When we look for examples of the opposite strain in the antislavery movement—those who endorsed armed violence early on—we find only scattered voices. Around the time of the Revolution, in the fresh fervor of republicanism, a handful of Americans speculated about the use of violence to free the slaves. John Adams wondered if the slave problem could be settled "only by force," an idea seconded by his wife, Abigail, who found it "a most iniquitous scheme . . . to fight our selves for what we are daily robbing and plundering from those [i.e., slaves] who have as good a right to freedom as we have." The Reverend Isaac Skillman asked in 1772 whether an enslaved black should "be deemed a rebel that supports his own rights?" In the 1790s some reformers expressed sympathy for the slave revolt on Haiti. In 1822 four whites were convicted of encouraging blacks to join Denmark Vesey in his plan to seize Charleston, South Carolina.

The rising sectional tensions of the 1830s and '40s brought more explicit calls for antislavery violence, but still not many. What might be called the White-Abolitionists-for-Violence Club was small indeed.

One member was Jabez D. Hammond, a prominent judge, congressman, and author from upstate New York who made several statements about the need for force to free the slaves. In 1839, Hammond told his fellow Abolitionist Gerrit Smith that he believed blacks could win freedom only through a mass revolt aided by whites. Wealthy himself, he asked Smith to add funds toward military schools for blacks in Canada and Mexico. Smith demurred but by 1842 insisted to the American Anti-Slavery Society that slaves had the right to fight their way to freedom. The erratic Smith swung between moderation and militancy, at first recommending colonization, then becoming John Brown's main supporter, and, after the failure of the Harpers Ferry raid, lapsing into a period of insanity followed by long years of denial of Brown and his cause.

Jabez Hammond, meanwhile, kept up his interest in the violent overthrow of slavery. In *Life and Opinions of Julius Melbourn* (1847), an unduly neglected novel, he took on the persona of an emancipated slave who travels around America discussing slavery with important people, from Thomas Jefferson to John Quincy Adams. Julius Melbourn discounts moral persuasion as a means for liberating America's slaves. Sounding much like John Brown, he declares: "The relation between master and slave is necessarily a state of war. The slave is a prisoner to his master, not by natural or moral right, but by physical force alone." The only answer to the slavery dilemma, he indicates, is disunion followed by war. "If the slave states were severed from the free," he says, "and if a well-organized army of 10,000 men were to land in a slaveholding state, protected by a competent naval force, with provisions, and arms, and munitions of war sufficient for an army of 60,000 men, the slaveholding states would be subdued in less than six months." This idea stuck with Hammond, who in 1852 wrote Gerrit Smith of his dream that an army of "10,000 men with an able commander, and arms munitions of war and provisions for 50,000 men, would march through the Southern states and liberate every slave there in six months." This was a bold but quixotic statement upon which Hammond had no means of acting.

There were others who did act and who inspired John Brown. When Brown in 1850 wanted to stir up rebelliousness among his all-black League of Gileadites, he declared, "Think of the number who have been mobbed and imprisoned on your account! Have any of you seen the Branded Hand? Do you remember the names of Lovejoy and Torrey?"

The three men Brown mentions here were notable victims of proslavery violence. As seen earlier, the editor Elijah Lovejoy's murder at the hands of an Illinois mob in 1837 prompted Brown to pledge himself publicly to the destruction of slavery. The two other figures mentioned, Charles T. Torrey and Jonathan Walker (famous for his branded hand), were especially aggressive operators on the Underground Railroad.

The Reverend Charles T. Torrey made successful efforts to wrest blacks from slavery and became known for his courageous martyrdom. Torrey was a Yale-educated Congregational clergyman who held pastorates in New Jersey and Massachusetts before giving up the ministry and moving to Maryland with the aim of challenging slavery. He had regular secret meetings with slaves in the Baltimore area and conducted many of them northward. Finally, he was arrested for slave-stealing and was sentenced in 1844 to six years in a Baltimore prison. Receiving indications that he could be released from jail if he admitted to committing a crime, he refused, asserting, "I cannot afford to concede any truth or principle to get out of prison." He died of tuberculosis in jail on May 9, 1846, at age thirty-three. His body was taken to Massachusetts for interment, and a memorial service in his honor at Boston's Tremont Temple attracted a huge crowd.

Torrey embodied the paradox that John Brown later represented more famously: in a time of immoral laws, patriotism looks like treason—a paradox verbalized by Secret Six member Thomas Wentworth Higginson when he told Brown that he was "always ready to invest money in treason." By liberating slaves, Torrey was breaking a state law but obeying the natural law of human equality announced in the Declaration of Independence. He was a traitor to human law but a patriot to higher law. James Russell Lowell captured the paradox in the opening verse of his poetic eulogy to Torrey:

> *Woe worth the hour when it is crime*
> *To plead the poor dumb bondsman's cause,*
> *When all that makes the heart sublime,*
> *The glorious throbs that conquer time,*
> *Are traitors to our cruel laws!*

Another lawbreaker Brown admired, Jonathan Walker, earned the sensational sobriquet "the Branded Hand" after an unusually painful punishment inflicted by proslavery authorities. Born in Cape Cod in 1799, Walker had a young manhood much like Melville's. He went to sea at seventeen, was stranded on an island in the Indian Ocean for a time, and then led a desultory sailor's life before returning to America. He settled in Pensacola, Florida, where he was active in the Underground Railroad. In 1844 he was approached by blacks who expressed their desire for freedom in militant terms: "Do you know that if we had the privilege of fighting for it as the revolutionary fathers had, how gladly we would avail ourselves of the blessed opportunity?" Walker chose a course almost as risky as fighting: escape by sea in a small boat. Along with seven blacks, he set sail by night for the Bahamas, but within a few days he collapsed of exhaustion. The boat drifted and was overtaken by two sloops, which towed it to Key West. The blacks were returned to slavery, and Walker was imprisoned, remaining in solitary confinement in heavy irons for a year. His later trial and conviction was followed by a severe sentence: seven years in jail, a fine of nearly

$5,000, a public pelting with rotten eggs, and the letters "S.S." branded on his palm.

The brand was a weapon ready-made for Abolitionists to hurl at proslavery laws. Walker himself sarcastically called it "the seal, the coat-of-arms, of the United States." The Abolitionist poet John Greenleaf Whittier memorably reversed the mark's meaning in his 1846 poem "The Branded Hand." Calling Walker's punishers "loathsome moral lepers" who "Give to shame what God hath given unto honor and renown," he said the "S.S." actually signified "Salvation to the Slave," since it would become the standard of the "Puritan" North when it took stern revenge on the South.

There were other slave rescuers Brown never mentioned but surely knew of. In July 1841 three Illinois Abolitionists—Alanson Work, James E. Burr, and George Thompson—crossed the Mississippi River to Missouri and tried to entice a group of enslaved blacks to freedom. When one of the blacks reported the three to his master, they were arrested and sentenced to a long jail term for slave-stealing. Three years later in Kentucky, Calvin Fairbank and Delia A. Webster were arrested after they had carried the future black leader Lewis Hayden and his family across the Ohio River to be taken north. In 1848 the New York Abolitionist William L. Chaplin hired two adventurers, Daniel Drayton and Edward Sayres, to spirit nearly eighty slaves out of the Washington, D.C., area in the hold of a schooner. Soon captured, Drayton and Sayres received a heavy fine, while Chaplin, not implicated in the incident, went on to attempt another rescue in August 1850, when he made a botched effort to carry two slaves north in a carriage.

As bold as these antislavery figures were, none had the militancy of another Abolitionist well known to Brown, Lysander Spooner. A lawyer and an anarchist who argued for the right of resistance to government, Spooner rose to prominence in the 1840s by arguing that the Constitution did not endorse slavery, directly opposing the Garrisonians, who branded the Constitution "a covenant with death and an agreement with hell" because they thought it did. Spooner argued that since slavery was by definition illegal and immoral, enslaved blacks had the right to bear arms against their oppressors and to seek aid from sympathizers in other states.

In 1858, Spooner printed a circular giving instructions for the violent overthrow of slavery. Preparations should be made, Spooner declared, for groups of whites to descend upon the South and wage a war of liberation. Wherever possible, these groups should free enslaved blacks. At the same time, free blacks and escaped slaves in the South should "form themselves into bands, build forts in the forests, and there collect arms, stores, horses, everything that will enable them to sustain themselves, and carry on their warfare upon the Slaveholders." "The state of slavery," Spooner continued, "is a state of war, in this case a *just* war, on the part of the Negroes—a war for liberty." Blacks deserved financial reparation for years of unrequited toil, and they had the right to capture and flog their former masters. With revolutionary ardor Spooner wrote, "The tea must be thrown overboard, the Bastille must be torn down, the first gun must be fired, by private persons."

Reactions to the circular among Abolitionists reveal the uniqueness of John Brown. The evangelical Arthur Tappan took the typical nonresistance line, insisting that he was "a peace-maker, and abjure all resort to deadly weapons to secure our rights." Hinton Helper, author of the controversial antislavery volume *The Impending Crisis of the South*, called Spooner's proposal "Immature-Impractical-Impolitic." Even the radical Wendell Phillips was ambivalent, saying Spooner's plan "would be a good one if it were only *practicable*" and was of little use since it was not. More positive, but still guarded, responses came from a few others, including Thomas Wentworth Higginson and Theodore Parker.

Unlike all of them, Brown considered Spooner not too radical but too tame, because Spooner failed to act on his words. By the time the circular appeared, Brown, who had been contemplating an invasion of the South for two decades, was finalizing plans for Harpers Ferry. He did what he could to suppress the distribution of Spooner's document, since he thought it might jeopardize his own plan by association.

Even though no white person came closer to expressing his own plan for slave liberation than Spooner, Brown sensed basic differences between himself and the anarchist thinker. These differences became clear in Spooner's response to Brown's preparations for a Southern invasion. When Spooner met Brown and learned of his plan, he wrote Gerrit Smith in disapproval of it. Neither blacks nor whites in the South, he said, were yet ready for the kind of rebellion Brown envisaged. Both groups must be emotionally primed and educated in strategy before a revolt could be initiated. Brown's plan was foolhardy because it expected too much from ignorant slaves and unprepared whites.

After Brown's attack on Virginia, Spooner was sympathetic and even devised a plan to rescue Brown from prison, aborted due to lack of funds. Still, differences between the two men remained. Spooner was a theorist of violence, whereas Brown was an activist. For all of his militant notions, Spooner, a cerebral deist, was a stickler for reason and ideas—so much so that he disapproved of the Civil War simply because he thought the North was devoted too strongly to restoring the Union instead of to ending slavery. Brown, in contrast, was a passionate Calvinist who believed in action rather than talk.

An even deeper difference, on the issue of race, divided Brown from Spooner and the other Abolitionists. Brown's plan for liberating the slaves was free of the racism that more or less tainted the views of the others. In this regard, Spooner and Higginson were the least culpable of the group, since they both believed blacks capable of independent military action. Like Phillips, however, they sometimes assumed a patronizing attitude toward blacks, whom they felt needed instruction and guidance before they would be ready to rebel. As Higginson wrote to Spooner, "The great obstacle to anti-slavery action has always been the apparent feebleness & timidity of the slaves themselves." Higginson's ambiguous attitude toward blacks would carry into the Civil War, when he commanded blacks troops whom he treated as docile and childlike, and would harden into conservatism toward the end of Reconstruction, when, ignoring the rise of Jim Crow, he insisted that blacks had made sufficient gains and needed no further help from white reformers.

As for the other Abolitionists mentioned above, two who stand out for their close association with Brown, Hinton Rowan Helper and Theodore Parker, had racial views that were downright reactionary. Helper's link to Brown was hardly intentional. Helper vilified not only Spooner's circular but also the Harpers Ferry raid, about which he said defensively, "I had nothing to do, and never expect to have anything to do, with any such ill-advised proceeding. It is impossible to achieve victory on the Brown basis." His denials notwithstanding, in the anti-Abolitionist frenzy that swept the South after Harpers Ferry, he and Brown were held up as demonic coconspirators behind a plot by the "Black Republican" party to assault Southern institutions. The Virginian Edmund Ruffin went so far as to label the Republicans "the Brown-Helper party."

Ruffin and other Southerners did not recognize that a hatred of slavery was just about the only thing Helper and Brown had in common. Helper opposed slavery not on moral grounds but because he thought it was hurting the South economically. An unabashed racist from North Carolina, he wanted slavery to be abolished so that blacks, whom he believed had little to contribute to America, could be expelled from the nation and intelligent, efficient whites could save his section's economy.

Theodore Parker was a different story. An enthusiastic member of the Secret Six, he agreed thoroughly with Brown about the need for blacks to be freed from wicked oppression through revolutionary violence. But the similarity stopped there. A liberal clergyman and learned scholar (he knew twenty languages), the Harvard-educated Parker occupied a different religious and social realm from Brown. More to the point, his racial stance was surprisingly hidebound. "No doubt the African race is greatly inferior to the Caucasian in general intellectual power," he once wrote, "and also in an instinct for liberty which is so strong in the Teutonic family."

John Brown never manifested such racism. A chief source of inspiration for him was black culture in its varied dimensions. Harpers Ferry would not have happened had he not had a profound knowledge of this culture.

Significantly, Brown felt most comfortable about discussing his military plans with blacks. He mixed with free blacks in Springfield; there were some 270 living in the town and 130 elsewhere in Hampden County. Among the first people outside the family with whom he discussed his invasion plan was Thomas Thomas, a black porter who worked for Perkins & Brown.

Although Thomas showed little interest in the plan, several other blacks did. On a business trip to New York State, Brown met the black Abolitionists Rev. J. W. Loguen of Syracuse and Rev. Henry Highland Garnet of Troy. Brown found them receptive, especially Garnet. Having escaped with his family from slavery in 1825, Garnet was a Presbyterian preacher famous for his inflammatory speech delivered in Buffalo in 1843, *Address to the Slaves of the United States of America*. "Brethren, arise, arise!" Garnet had declared. "Strike for you lives. Now is the day and the hour. . . . Let your motto be resistance! *resistance!* RESISTANCE!" This revolutionary language struck home with Brown, who reportedly tried to get Garnet's *Address* published in a pamphlet along with David Walker's *Appeal*.

Loguen and Garnet passed word of Brown to their friend Frederick Douglass, who had escaped slavery in 1838 to become the era's leading black Abolitionist. Tantalized by his friends' whispered descriptions of John Brown and his plan, Douglass interrupted a lecture tour in November 1847 to visit the Brown home. Brown opened up to Douglass, whose famous *Narrative*, published two years earlier and still selling well, had dramatized heroic resistance to the slave system through self-education and physical force. One evening after dinner Brown sat Douglass down at his large family table and laid out his planned invasion. Their animated discussion began at 8 p.m. and continued until three the next morning.

Spreading out a large map on the table, Brown, his eyes aflame, traced in a curved line the Appalachian mountain range that extended some 2,200 miles from Maine to Georgia. "These mountains," Brown proclaimed, "were placed here to aid the emancipation of your race; they are full of natural forts, where one man for defense would be equal to a hundred for attack; they are also full of good hiding places, where a large number of men could be concealed and baffle and elude pursuit for a long time. I know these mountains well and could take a body of men into them and keep them there in spite of all the efforts of Virginia to dislodge me, and drive me out."

The plan was to invade a Southern state with "at first twenty-five picked men" who would be stationed in separate groups of five in a southward line along the mountain range. Periodically, these groups would raid nearby plantations, liberate enslaved blacks, arm them, and retreat with them to the mountain hideaways. The more timid blacks would be sent north to freedom on what Brown called the Subterranean Pass Way. The rest would remain with the liberators, whose number would grow so that eventually a colony of free blacks would be living in the mountains.

The goal was to weaken the institution of slavery by terrorizing slaveholders, whose power over their human chattels would become insecure, and by stimulating intensified antislavery activity in the North. Although Brown did not plan a general slave insurrection, he said he was "not averse to the shedding of blood" if his groups were threatened by pursuers. Arming the blacks would give them a sense of strength and independence. "No people could have self-respect or be respected," he said, "who would not fight for their freedom." Besides, he averred, "Slavery was a state of war to which the slaves were unwilling parties and consequently they have a right to anything necessary to their peace and freedom."

Douglass was fascinated but dubious. Why the recourse to violence? Might not the South be persuaded to abandon slavery through peaceful means? No, Brown insisted; "he knew [the Southerners'] proud hearts and that they would never be induced to give up their slaves, until they felt a big stick about their heads." Wouldn't the slave-owners pursue Brown's men with dogs and guns? Yes, Brown answered, but through crafty use of caves and precipices "we would whip them."

He told Douglass he had been developing the plan for a number of years and was waiting for the opportunity and funds to execute it. Although Douglass was skeptical of the scheme, and would remain so up to the Harpers Ferry affair and beyond, he was astonished by Brown's empathy for blacks, unmatched by any other white person he knew. In his newspaper the *North Star* he said that Brown, "though a white gentleman, is in sympathy a black man, and as deeply interested in our cause, as though his own soul had been pierced with the iron of slavery."

Frederick Douglass.
LIBRARY OF CONGRESS.

Actually, Brown was even more deeply sympathetic to black culture than Douglass appreciated. Although Douglass always had the highest regard for Brown and came to think that he more than anyone else was responsible for ending slavery, he always had doubts about the practicability of the invasion plan.

But the plan had a greater chance for success than Douglass acknowledged. It grew mainly out of the tradition of slave insurrections in America—not just the United States but also the West Indies.

Of the slave rebellions in the American South, Nat Turner's was by far the most important to Brown. It had a sensible design: a quick strike by a small group to be followed by retreat to the wilderness. It also had powerful results: in the short term, Turner evaded pursuers by hiding out for over a month; in the long term, his revolt lingered in the communal unconscious of the South like a recurring nightmare. Brown once explained the plan for his invasion by comparing it to Turner's use of wilderness hideouts: "Nat Turner, with fifty men, held Virginia for five weeks; the same number, well organized and armed, can shake the system out of the State.... Twenty men in the Alleghenies could break slavery to pieces in two years."

Brown's plan was overly optimistic but not insane, as it has been called.

Recent times have provided vivid examples of small, poorly armed groups using wilderness topography to outwit or elude vastly superior forces. The mountains of Afghanistan, in particular, provided protection for guerillas resisting the Russian army and later for Osama bin Laden and his followers in their evasion of the United States military. There was sense in Brown's statement that "a ravine is better than a plain. Woods and mountain-sides can be held by resolute men against ten times their force."

There were a number of precedents for Brown's plan for guerilla action in a wilderness setting. He was intimately aware of guerilla warfare in European history. One of his favorite books, Joachim Hayward Stocqueler's *Life of Field Marshal the Duke of Wellington*, contained what he called "valuable hints" about the ability of a small force to defeat a huge one by making use of mountain defenses. Especially intriguing to him was Stocqueler's account of effective resistance to Napoleon's army in the Pyrenees Mountains by Portuguese guerillas who, "acquainted as they were with the different passes in the mountains, and the by-roads through the country . . . could assemble at any given point, or disperse, without the possibility of defeat." Brown was stirred by the description of mountain areas with "huge fallen masses of rock and earth, yawning fissures, deep and narrow defiles, where 300 men would suffice to check an army."

But Brown had more than warfare in mind. His plan also included the establishment of a growing community of blacks and sympathetic whites that would eventually form an independent mountain colony. It was for the governance of such a colony that he wrote his "Provisional Constitution and Ordinances for the People of the United States" in 1858.

Here, Brown's admiration for African and Native American culture had its greatest impact on his strategy. Brown knew that the rebellious slaves of the West Indies and the Seminole tribe of Florida had not only resisted capture but also had established communities in the wilderness. A contemporary article pointed out this aspect of his plan: "[Brown] would use natural strongholds; find secret mountain passes to connect with one another; retreat from and evade attacks he could not overcome. He would maintain and indefinitely prolong a guerilla war, of which the Seminole Indians in Florida and the Negroes in Haiti afforded examples."

John Brown was a man of action and passion but in certain areas a student as well. His reading was not broad, but it was deep. Among the fields he knew well was the history of maroons. Maroons—the word derives either from the French *marronage*, meaning "flight," or from the Spanish *cimarrones*, meaning "unruly," "wild"—were rebellious slaves who fled into the wilderness and founded communities there, protecting themselves with guerilla tactics.

In his dream of creating a maroon community, Brown tapped into one of the oldest American traditions. Maroons in America predated the landing of the Pilgrims by nearly a century. When the Spanish explorer Lucas Vásquez de Ayllón established a colony in South Carolina in 1526, probably at the mouth of the Pedee River, he brought nearly a hundred black slaves, some of whom fled into the wilderness and lived among the natives. Soon the Spaniards relocated to Haiti. The fugitive blacks they left behind became, in the words of historian Herbert Aptheker, "the first permanent inhabitants, other than the Indians, in what was to be the United States."

From the mid seventeenth century through 1864 more than fifty maroon communities arose, scattered across the country. Aptheker notes that "the mountainous, forested, or swampy regions of South Carolina, North Carolina, Virginia, Louisiana, Florida, Georgia, Mississippi, and Alabama (in order of importance) appear to have been the favorite haunts for these black Robin Hoods." A popular area for maroon settlement was the Great Dismal Swamp in North Carolina and Virginia, the setting of Harriet Beecher Stowe's novel about slave rebellion, *Dred*. Some of the maroon settlements lasted a long time, preserved by guerilla resistance to white invaders and by foraging of nearby farms. Florida, a favorite haven for fugitive slaves before its annexation by the United States in 1819, was the site of an important society of maroons and Seminole Indians. During the Second Seminole War of 1835 to 1843, a small but potent force of blacks and Indians launched guerilla battles in which some 1,600 whites were killed. The federal government had to spend a staggering $30 million to $40 million to win the war. The blacks, though outnumbered by their Indian allies five to one, reportedly were "the most formidable force, more blood-thirsty, active, and revengeful than the Indians."

If Brown was inspired by the history of his country's maroons, he was even more inspired by those of the West Indies, as was attested by close associates. Richard Realf, one of his followers in Kansas, reported that Brown had studied all the books on insurrectionary warfare he could find, paying special attention to the maroons of Jamaica and Toussaint L'Ouverture's liberation of Haiti. Another friend, Richard Hinton, affirmed that Brown knew the story of Jamaica and Haiti "by heart." According to Thomas Wentworth Higginson, part of Brown's plan was "to get together bands and families of fugitive slaves" and "establish them permanently in those [mountain] fastnesses, like the Maroons of Jamaica and Surinam."

The places mentioned here—Surinam, Jamaica, and Haiti—illustrated the possibility of creating a black community in the wilderness forged and maintained by unconventional military action.

The largest maroon population in the western hemisphere was in Surinam, where enslaved blacks escaped into that country's bush country and fended off European pursuers in a war that lasted half a century. The blacks, known as the Bush Negroes, destroyed so many plantations and killed so many whites that they finally won an agreement allowing them to exist as a virtual state within a state.

Jamaica's history exemplified the way in which maroons could use terror tactics to win freedom for blacks. The island had been left undeveloped during 150 years of Spanish occupation but entered a new phase when the British took it over in 1655. The black population, which grew from around 40,000 in 1700 to over 300,000 by 1830, proved extraordinarily successful in breaking the yoke of slavery. Between 1655 and 1738, enslaved blacks who fled into the towering Blue Mountains provoked panic among sugar farmers by destroying plantations, stealing additional slaves, and resisting capture through ambushes and mountain skirmishes. In March 1739 the whites were forced to sign a treaty that gave freedom and land to the Leeward Maroons in return for a cessation of hostilities. The maroons created a number of villages, including Trelawny Town, Charles Town, Nanny, and Accompong. Even though slavery remained on the island, the maroon presence, and a massive slave uprising in December 1831, sealed its demise.

The society of blacks that was by far the greatest inspiration for John Brown was the one created in Haiti by Toussaint L'Ouverture. Haiti, known as the Land of Mountains because of the tall ridge running through it, had been first settled by the Spanish, who founded the town of St. Domingo, the name by which the island was then commonly known. Conflicts developed when British and French settlers occupied other sections of the island. François Dominique Toussaint, the grandson of an African prince and the slave of a French settler, emerged at a young age as a brilliant, magnetic leader. In 1791 he led a slave rebellion that resulted three years later in the liberation of his people by France's new revolutionary government. After gaining his freedom, he helped the French drive their Spanish and British rivals off of the island, and he was appointed as the French commissioner of the island.

Napoleon, however, grew jealous of Toussaint and, at the urging of advisers and relatives, decided to reestablish slavery on Haiti. In 1802 he sent 60,000 troops to the island with the mission of conquering and enslaving the blacks living there. Toussaint (whose appellation "L'Ouverture" sig-nified "opening the way everywhere") led an effective guerilla resistance that, when combined with a deadly epidemic, kept the French army at bay. The French used a trick to capture Toussaint and deport him to Europe, where he was imprisoned in a dungeon. Kept in chains in a dank cell, he soon died and became recognized as a martyr to the cause of black freedom. Inspired by his heroism, his followers in Haiti strengthened their guerilla war and in 1803 succeeded in driving the French from the island.

The war for Haiti had been a notably bloody one, with atrocities com-mitted by both sides, but especially by the French, who burned and tor-tured blacks. By the end, some 20,000 French soldiers and 60,000 white civilians were killed in the struggle. The blacks gained complete control of the island.

The names Haiti and Toussaint L'Ouverture resonated in pre–Civil War America, exacerbating tensions over slavery. The American slave rebels Gabriel Prosser and Denmark Vesey found in the Haitian insurgents exam-ples they tried to follow. For militant antislavery figures the Haitian revolt stood out as a realization of the full potential of blacks. "Surely no more convincing argument in proof of the capacity of blacks could be required, than their achievement of such a revolution," wrote a magazine essayist in 1821. The black Abolitionist J. Theodore Holly considered Haiti the cap-stone of the history of blacks, whose rebelliousness and autonomy it exhib-ited. "In the case of Hayti," declared Holly, "the question of negro capacity stands out a naked fact, as vindication of itself, not only without any aid whatever from the white man, but in spite of his combined opposition to keep down in brutal degradation these self emancipated freemen." Tous-saint, Holly added, was the most inspirational of history's black heroes—an opinion seconded by a black journalist who called him "one of the greatest men the world ever saw." Wendell Phillips repeatedly delivered a speech on Toussaint that contained the rousing line: "The only race in history that ever took the sword into their hands, and cut their chains, is the black race of St. Domingo."

From the proslavery perspective, Haiti epitomized the horrors of slave insurrection. Ignoring the fact that the atrocities committed by the white invaders far exceeded those committed by the blacks, defenders of the South gave hyperbolic accounts of the alleged savagery of the Haitians.

Both the positive and negative views of Haiti would influence reactions to John Brown's raid on Harpers Ferry. In the view of Wendell Phillips, John Brown carried on Toussaint's spirit, and his five black soldiers at

Harpers Ferry were like Toussaint's warriors. "Some doubt the courage of the Negro," Phillips declared. "Go to Haiti. . . . And if that does not satisfy you, come home, and if it had been October 1859, you might come by way of quaking Virginia, and asked her what she thought of Negro courage." If George Washington, he continued, was "the bright, consummate flower of our earlier civilization," then John Brown is "the ripe fruit of our noonday" along with "the soldier, the statesman, the martyr, Toussaint L'Ouverture."

The Haitian overtones of Brown's raid appalled his critics. In a Union meeting in Boston shortly after the attack, the statesman Edward Everett described Brown's plan in lurid terms: "It was an attempt to do on a vast scale what was done in St. Domingo in 1791, where the colored population was about equal to that of Virginia." Had Brown succeeded, he asserted, he would have unleashed horrors similar to those of the Haitian blacks, such as "the midnight burnings, the wholesale massacres, the merciless tortures, the abominations not to be named by Christian lips in the hearing of Christian ears,—some of which, too unutterably atrocious for the English language, are of necessity veiled in the obscurity of the Latin tongue."

This "unutterably atrocious" behavior unnamable except in Latin was the nineteenth-century tag for sodomical rape. This false charge against the rebellious slaves, and by association against Brown, reveals the extraordinary fear that both the Haitians and Brown aroused. Recent historians have shown that insurgent blacks rarely raped their white victims, even though as slaves they were often subject to the predatory sexuality of whites. Few slave rebels in the western hemisphere committed rape, and in all the slave revolts on U.S. soil, no evidence of even a single rape has yet been found. As for the "merciless tortures" for which Everett held slave rebels responsible, that, too, was a bogus charge, one that was more descriptive of whites than of blacks. Whites whipped and mutilated blacks when they owned them and regularly tortured them when they caught them rebelling. In Haiti, blacks were burned at the stake, eaten alive by hungry dogs or birds of prey, or nailed to trees or ships' masts.

Actually, if Brown erred at Harpers Ferry, it was in the direction not of violence but of clemency. As he admitted after his capture, his concern for the welfare of his hostages and their families contributed to the fatal delay in his flight to the mountains. It would seem that he had taken too sanguine a view of the experience of maroons and of slave insurrections generally.

To understand the influence of slave revolts on his planned invasion of the South, it is useful to follow his ideas for such an invasion as they evolved over the years.

Thomas Wentworth Higginson stated in 1859 that Brown's notion of attacking the South originated "twenty years ago this summer." That would suggest 1839 as the year that Brown came up with a nascent version of the plan. This date makes sense, coming as it did at the end of a decade of the Nat Turner revolt, the slave uprising in Jamaica, the mobbing of Garrison, and the murder of Lovejoy—all of which, as we've seen, had a strong impact on John Brown.

It is unlikely that at that early date Brown had Harpers Ferry or any other specific target in mind. The western Virginia idea may have come from the land-surveying he did in that state in the spring of 1840 for the Oberlin Collegiate Institute. Although the tracts he surveyed lay some eighty miles west of the Allegheny Mountains, it is possible that he took time from his surveying to explore the mountains or that he visited them at some other time. At any rate, his familiarity with the mountains was confirmed by a number of people who knew him well.

Brown's detailed description of the plan to Frederick Douglass in 1847 did not mention Harpers Ferry. The first recorded mention of that site was during the period between 1849 and 1851, after Brown had moved to live among the blacks at North Elba. His daughter Sarah recalled that at this time he laid out his design on Harpers Ferry, drawing sketches of felled trees and log forts of the type he intended to use as protection in the mountains near Harpers Ferry. He described the plan with such intensity that at school her heart raced and she shivered in dread whenever the town was mentioned in her lessons. She said he discussed the plan with a black neighbor, Lyman Epps, whom he tried vainly to recruit for the effort, corroborating Higginson's declaration that Brown had moved to North Elba with the intention of raising a force of black soldiers for his attack on the South.

If the information up to this point is accurate, it tells us a lot about John Brown. It says that his idea of using violence to battle slavery came to him very early and that the plan became increasingly radical over time. Not only did he lay out his plan mainly to blacks, but also his vision of organizing an army of blacks and liberating slaves who would fight to preserve their freedom in the mountains stemmed directly from the maroon cultures he knew well.

It would also make sense that he named Harpers Ferry as his objective around 1850, a momentous year in the conflict over slavery. Harpers Ferry, a town of around 5,000 at the confluence of the Potomac and Shenandoah rivers in what is now West Virginia, was the home of a federal arsenal that produced a large percentage of the weapons and munitions used by the

United States military forces. The town was crucial to the government, both practically and symbolically, so much so that during the war Union and Confederate forces battled fiercely for the town, which traded hands thirteen times. Eighteen fifty was the year in which the congressional compromise over slavery, ushering in a strict new fugitive slave law, instilled in many Northerners a deep hostility to the federal government, which now seemed clearly allied to the proslavery cause. In choosing Harpers Ferry as the site of his planned assault, John Brown was not only targeting slavery but also challenging the national government.

His eagerness to attack the site grew with additional instances of government malfeasance. In 1854, the year the Kansas-Nebraska Act opened up the western territories to slavery, Brown's rage against the government reached a new level. A few days after the infamous bill was introduced to Congress, Brown wrote a public letter, published by Frederick Douglass in his newspaper, denouncing governmental "fiends in human shape" who pass "abominably wicked and unjust" laws, doing "what in their power lies to destroy confidence in legislative bodies, and to bring magistrates, justices, and other officers of the law into disrespect amongst men." His anger would deepen that summer when proslavery forces vowed to win Kansas for the South, backing up their words in November with the first of several rigged elections in which Missouri "border ruffians" seized polls in Kansas and illegally voted for proslavery candidates.

Also appalling was the news in May that a Boston black man, Anthony Burns, had been seized by federal authorities and detained to await the probate court's decision on a request by a Virginia farmer to reclaim him as a fugitive slave. At the time, Brown was in Vernon, New York, where he was contesting a lawsuit. A friend of his recalled that when Brown heard the news about Burns, he rose excitedly from his chair and announced he was going to Boston. Pacing about nervously, he declared, "Anthony Burns must be released, or I will die in the attempt." His friend talked him out of the plan. No doubt Brown was thrilled by the effort of Thomas Wentworth Higginson and others to free Burns but disappointed by the failure of the attempt. He must have seethed when federal troops led the chained Burns through the streets of Boston, taking him to a ship that would return him to slavery.

His discussions of Harpers Ferry now became more frequent and more radical than before. His daughter Anne, eleven at the time, heard him speak often about his scheme. Later she wrote, "I think I may say, without any intention of boasting, that I knew more about his plans than anyone else, at least anyone else who 'survived to tell the tale.' " He didn't have to warn her or other family members not to reveal the plot. Everyone knew it was a secret. To Anne, he said simply, "I know I can trust you."

In late 1854 or early 1855, Brown visited Colonel Daniel Woodruff, a veteran of the War of 1812, in Ohio to solicit his help in the Virginia invasion. According to another friend who was present, "Brown spoke of the evil days in Kansas, then existing, and he wished to relieve Kansas and to retaliate by striking another point. He wanted to attack the arsenal of Harpers Ferry: First, to frighten Virginia and detach it from the slave interest; second, to capture the rifles to arm the slaves; third, to destroy the arsenal machinery, so they could not be used to turn out more arms for the perhaps long guerilla war that might follow; and to destroy whatever guns were already stored there that he could not carry away."

Although in 1855 he followed three of his sons to Kansas to challenge proslavery elements there, Harpers Ferry was never far from his mind. By 1857 he had presented his plan in detail to Hugh Forbes, a British soldier of fortune who had fought in the Italian revolution under Garibaldi and whom Brown hired to train men for the Virginia invasion. Brown's revelations to Forbes indicate just how optimistically he read the history of slave rebellions in the United States and the West Indies.

Brown's idea was to attack the Harpers Ferry area with twenty-five to fifty blacks and whites, moving first against a large plantation to free as many slaves as possible. Forbes protested that such a raid would elicit little response from the ignorant slaves, who were wholly unprepared for such an event. Brown brushed aside the objection, saying he was sure that on the first night he would be able to get between two hundred and five hundred blacks to join him. Half of this number he would use to attack the federal arsenal to seize as many arms as possible, destroying the rest to hinder pursuit. The remaining blacks would be split into five or six groups, each directed by a few of the original raiders, that would liberate slaves on several different plantations. If federal troops chased him, he averred, "he could easily maintain himself in the Alleghenies," while "his New England partisans would in the meantime call a Northern Convention, restore tranquility and overthrow the pro-slavery administration."

Brown predicted confidently that "the planters would pursue the chattels and be defeated. The militia would then be called out, and would be defeated." The movement "would strike terror into the heart of the slave States by the amount of organization it would exhibit, and the strength it gathered. . . . The design was to make the fight in the mountains of Virginia, extending it to North Carolina and Tennessee, and also the swamps of South Carolina, if possible. The purpose was not the expatriation of one or a thousand slaves, but their liberation in the States wherein they were born, and were held in bondage."

Forbes disputed Brown on many points, arguing that a slave insurrection fomented by men lacking in education and experience would either have little effect or would rapidly "leap beyond his control, or any control, when it would become a scene of mere anarchy and would assuredly be suppressed."

The plan Forbes offered in response had only superficial connections to Brown's scheme. It aimed, like Brown's, to weaken slavery through armed invasion, but there the similarity stopped. Forbes would position the invaders in the northern frontier of slave states, especially Maryland and Virginia, making intermittent raids on plantations to liberate slaves and direct them immediately north to freedom. Such raids would occur at first twice a month and then, if successful, once or twice a week. The emancipated blacks would be sent north so quickly that pursuit of them would be fruitless. The raiders' position would slowly push southward in the expectation that the South's defenders in their "excitement and irritation" would "commit some stupid blunders."

The differences between Brown's and Forbes's plans boil down to the former's unquestioning faith in blacks. Brown, inspired by the militancy of slave rebels like Nat Turner (whom he mentioned to Forbes), was convinced that slaves would rise up speedily once they saw a window to freedom and would join his battle for liberation. Forbes, in contrast, took a conservative approach: slaves would first have to be roused up and prepared before they would take the probably self-destructive step of rebelling. Besides, Forbes suggested, the blacks wouldn't know how to handle their sudden freedom and would either be recaptured or would act wildly. Brown, with his admiration of maroons, felt confident he could establish and defend a community of blacks in the mountains. This community, run according to Brown's provisional constitution, would not remain separate forever from mainstream society. As Forbes noted, Brown's ultimate goal was not "expatriation" but "liberation in the States in which they were born"—that is, integration into white society as soon as slavery was abolished.

Brown's plan, free of racism to begin with, was by 1857 informed by a truly progressive vision of racial justice. Brown envisaged blacks fighting their way out of slavery, freeing others of their race, establishing a community with a constitution that favored them, and eventually being integrated as equals into American society. As will be seen, the plan would become even more racially broad-minded as time passed, culminating in the actual raid on Harpers Ferry. Before we trace the plan's further developments, however, it would be useful to explore Brown's racial views in greater detail and to compare them with those of other Americans of his day.

American slavery was justified by the ever-strengthening racism of the South. Southerners around the time of the Civil War looked back with mixed feelings on the founding fathers. On the one hand, they patriotically used the founders' ideas about liberty and independence to defend states rights and the agrarian way of life. They also took pride in the fact that several of the founders held slaves and that the Constitution permitted slavery. On the other hand, they believed the founders had not been strong enough in defending slavery. The antebellum South saw itself, ironically enough, as more sophisticated, humane, and Christian than the Revolutionary generation, because it accepted the principle that chattel slavery was, in John C. Calhoun's phrase, "a positive good." The so-called Puritan North was for the South the anarchic arena of devilish Abolitionists who preached the irreligious doctrine of the equality of the white and black races. Alexander H. Stephens, vice president of the Confederacy, declared in 1861 that the North was filled with "insane" and "fanatical" people who believed the races are equal, whereas the South adhered to the "great truth" that while all whites, of whatever class, are equal, it is "not so with the Negro. Subordination is his place."

Such racist rhetoric filled proslavery journals and newspapers. Charles Chauncey Burr's *Old Guard* was typical. "To attempt to elevate the Negro to the white man's level, is an insult to manhood, a crime against society, and a sin against God," wrote Burr. Enslaved blacks, he declared, were fortunate, because they were removed from the barbarism of Africa: "The Negro, when a 'slave' to a Caucasian, is vastly higher in the scale of humanity, than when in his native state." Although improved by the society of whites, he continued, the black person can only be improved to some degree, "because our heavenly Father made him an inferior being, a perpetual child." The "repulsive antagonism" whites feel toward blacks "is not prejudice, but a holy principle implanted by our Creator in the hearts of all His superior children." Drawing on the pseudoscientific notion of polygenesis, Burr claimed that black people were of a different species from whites, with a small brain, baboonlike cranium, monkey features, and distinct internal organs. As for the North, its belief in the equality of whites and blacks made it Satan's den. Burr explained, "The irreligion of Puritanism, which crops out and runs to seed in all manner of infidelisms, as we see in

Massachusetts, is attempting to undo the works of the Almighty, by proclaiming the equality of beings eternally unequal."

Blacks would have had at least some hope in America had such assessments of the North's racial attitudes been accurate. Sadly, they were not.
Racism was hardly just a Southern phenomenon. The black journalist
William J. Watkins insisted that "prejudice at the North is much more vir-
ulent than at the South." "*Such* Free Soilism," he wrote sourly, "is infinitely
worse than rampant pro-slaveryism." Similarly, William Lloyd Garrison
asserted, "The prejudices of the north are stronger than those of the
south." When he went to England in 1832, Garrison was astounded to find
that the signs of racial discrimination he was accustomed to in the North—
separate seating in restaurants; arguments over seats in coaches; indignities
in church—were absent from British life. The black author William Wells
Brown made a similar assessment. In an 1856 speech, after citing several
personal encounters with American racism, he declared: "You see nothing
of this hatred abroad. A black man is treated in Europe according as he
behaves, and not according to his colour. This feeling is one of the great
hindrances to the abolition movement."

Racial prejudice was virtually inescapable in America. The word "nigger" had alarmingly wide currency. In 1837 the black minister Rev. H. Easton of Boston noted the ubiquity of the word. He declared: "Nigger lips,
nigger shins, and nigger heels, are phrases universally common among the
juvenile class of society." Whites are told "if they do thus and so, they will
be poor or ignorant as a nigger; or that they will be black as a nigger; that
they will have hair, lips, feet, or something of the kind, like a nigger. . . . See
nigger's thick lips—see his flat nose—nigger eye shine—that slick looking
nigger—nigger, where you get so much coat?—that's a nigger priest—are
sounds emanating from little urchins of Christian villagers, which continually infest the feelings of colored travellers, like the pestiferous breath of
young devils; and full grown persons, and sometimes professors of religion,
are not unfrequently heard to join in the concert." In school rooms there
are "nigger seats" where bad students are sent, and "the same or similar use
is made of nigger pews or seats in meeting-houses. Professing Christians,
where these seats exist, make them a test by which to ascertain the amount
of their humility." ·

The demeaning epithet was so widely accepted that even enlightened
people—Whitman and Lincoln, for example—could use it. The word
appeared often in minstrel shows, melodramas, pulp novels, and other
forms of popular entertainment. Mark Twain's use of "nigger" more than

two hundred times in *Huckleberry Finn* has aroused bitter controversy in our time but was a realistic register of nineteenth-century American culture.

Racism gained a dangerous veneer of authenticity from the primitive pseudosciences of the day. Phrenology gave rise to the notion that people of different races had different head structures that denoted varying characteristics and capabilities. The press was full of pictorial charts that purported to show "typical" heads of different races. Inevitably, a good-looking Caucasian head was placed at the top of such charts and was associated with qualities such as reason, cultivation, and efficiency, while a brutish-looking African head always came at the bottom, described in terms of passion, sensuality, and laziness. During the Civil War so-called ethnographic science would supposedly confirm such racial differences and would help engender eugenics by "proving" the inherent superiority of the Caucasian line.

So pervasive was racism in America that Lincoln could say, with little exaggeration, that he had never met "a man, woman or child who was in favor of producing a perfect equality, social and political, between Negroes and white men." Lincoln himself, though deeply opposed to slavery, stated in August 1858, "I have no purpose to introduce political and social equality between the white and black races. There is a physical difference between the two, which in my judgment will probably forever forbid their living together upon the footing of perfect equality." The next year he expressed himself more concisely: "Negro equality! Fudge!!"

Such comments by Lincoln point up the surprising fact that even many people who detested slavery nonetheless accepted the prevalent racial views of the day. The Kentucky Republican Cassius Clay, a vigorous antislavery orator, stated: "I have studied the Negro character. They lack self-reliance—we can make nothing out of them. God has made them for the sun and the banana!" White members of the American Anti-Slavery Society loudly denounced racism yet failed to free themselves of it. Even Garrison, its leader, had his lapses, as when his squabble with Frederick Douglass led him to say that the "sufferers" of slavery could not understand its evils as much as white Abolitionists—a comment that leads the biographer Henry Mayer to speculate that "it is possible that there is a substratum of racism in every white American." Mayer also notes that blacks were "not destined to play a central role" in the Anti-Slavery Society. This hypocrisy angered blacks such as William Watkins, who insisted that Abolitionists are well intentioned, but *"they lack a practical exemplification of the doctrine they inculcate."* "What are the facts in the case?" he asked. "Do the Abolitionists themselves act towards us as though they were devoid of prejudice against color, or condition? They do not."

It is ironic, then, that "Black Republicanism," intended to point up Abolitionists' alleged fondness for blacks, became the catchall name that the South assigned to Northern political sentiment. Racism infected not only the mores but also the laws of the North. The black leader James McCune Smith complained in 1854 that the oppression of blacks in the North, ranging from Jim Crow laws to denial of voting rights to antimiscegenation codes, formed a huge mass of antiblack sentiment. Smith noted, "There may be counted two thousand distinct forms of oppression scattered among the hundred and seventy-six thousand free colored people in the free States."

One of the South's favorite charges against the North—that it endorsed miscegenation—was mistaken. Some of the most vehemently Abolitionist states had the strictest laws against intermarriage of whites and blacks. Massachusetts had passed such a law in 1705 that was replaced by much harsher laws in 1786 and 1836 that established the penalty for blacks marrying whites as six months of hard labor in the common jail along with nullification of the marriage. Rhode Island passed similar laws in 1833 and 1844.

In this cultural sea of racism, John Brown stands out for his utter lack of prejudice. This is not to say that he was the only nonracist white in North America. Racism came in all degrees, from the self-righteous bigotry of Southern fire-eaters to the occasional hypocrisy of Garrison. Moreover, there were antislavery leaders, particularly Wendell Phillips and Alexander Milton Ross (a Canadian associate of Brown's on the Underground Railroad), who showed no signs of prejudice.

But Brown was the only one to model both his own lifestyle and his plans for abolishing slavery on black culture. He did not denounce racism in the lecture hall and then retreat to a mansion, as did the well-heeled Phillips, nor did he alternate between antislavery activity and dabbling in horticulture and poetry, as did the cerebral Dr. Ross. He immersed himself in black culture, learning much from it and giving much back to it.

His immersion reached new depths when he was living in the 1840s in Springfield. The town offered many opportunities for Abolitionist activity, such as a local antislavery group and a station of the Underground Railroad. But even the latter, once a main preoccupation, did not win his involvement. He remained committed to the education of blacks, expressing an interest in creating an "African high school" in either the United States or Canada.

Although the school did not materialize, for lack of time and money, he did what he could for the public education of blacks in 1847 by writing "Sambo's Mistakes," a column for the black-run newspaper *The Ram's Horn*. This essay has not been appreciated as the radical document it is. The oversight is understandable, for the piece has a didactic purpose that makes it seem old-fashioned. In it, Brown assumes the persona of a free black, Sambo, who admits to many errors in his daily behavior that he promises to correct. Sambo tells us that he is given to reading novels and newspapers instead of history books, to chewing and smoking tobacco, to showing off, to wasting his money on expensive clothing and jewelry, to quarreling with friends over religious doctrines, and so forth. Sambo says that in committing many of these errors he is aping some of the worst habits of whites. He assures the "editor" that he can easily fix each flaw and will do so immediately.

When viewed in the context of the era's racism, this seemingly innocuous tale delivers a powerful message: blacks are not moronic brutes but rather are intelligent beings fully capable of improving themselves. They are not hopelessly mired in ignorance and immorality but are as perfectible as whites. Even if in the past Sambo has spent too much time "devouring silly novels & other miserable trash," he is now intent on reading serious books that will lead to his advance in American society. Such books, he says, will store "[his] mind with an endless variety of rational and practical ideas," so that he can profit from "the experience of millions of others of all ages" and fit him "for the most important stations in life" by fortifying his mind "with the best & wisest resolutions, & noblest sentiments, & motives."

The piece does not pretend that such self-improvement guarantees social justice for blacks. To the contrary, it identifies racism as a force against which blacks must fight. As his name implies, Sambo has always been too submissive in the face of the bigotry he sees everywhere, and he knows he must become bolder in challenging racism. As he says, "I have always expected to secure the favour of the whites by tamely submitting to every species of indignity contempt & wrong instead of nobly resisting their brutal aggressions from principle & taking my place as a man, a citizen, a husband, a father, a brother, a neighbour, a friend as God requires of every one (if his neighbour will allow him to do it)."

There is pathos in the parenthetical clause—*if* whites permit, blacks will exercise their dignity and manhood, taking their places as citizens in American society. The real problem, Brown knew, was that American whites were doubly resistant to the idea of racial equality: they were corrupted not only by racism but all too frequently by acquiescence to proslavery political forces. Brown, as Sambo, compares the inability of blacks to realize their full manhood with the failure of Northern whites to stand up boldly for racial justice. As Sambo says, "I find that I get for all my submission about the same reward that the Southern Slaveocrats render to the Dough faced Statesmen of the North for being bribed & browbeat, fooled & cheated, as the Whigs & Democrats love to be, & think themselves highly honored if they may be allowed to lick up the spittle of a southerner." In other words, Northern doughfaces kowtow to the South just as blacks are forced to submit to whites. A shocking moral flabbiness characterizes all aspects of the racial issue.

Confronted with his society's racism, which he saw as omnipresent, Brown entered sympathetically into black culture to a degree unmatched by any other white person of his day. "Sambo's Mistakes" was one of his sympathetic gestures. If Walt Whitman merits praise for empathetically assuming an African American persona at moments in his poetry (for instance, "I am the hounded slave," or "I am oppressed. . . . I hate him that oppresses me, / I will either destroy him, or he shall release me"), Brown deserves recognition for doing so in his essay.

Although Brown lacks Whitman's lyricism, he can be said to be ahead of the poet in theme. The message of "Sambo's Mistakes"—that blacks are fully capable of improving themselves and assuming their role as equal citizens of American society—was in line with what progressive blacks of his day were saying. The Reverend Nathaniel Paul enjoined his fellow free blacks to rid themselves of "the odious stigma which some have long cast upon us, that we were incapacitated by the God of nature, for the enjoyment of the rights of freemen" by proving themselves educable and upright, with "judgment capable of discerning, and prudence sufficient to manage our affairs with discretion." The educator Mary Ann Shadd Cary wrote to Frederick Douglass in 1849, "The great fault of our people, is in imitating [the white man's] follies; individual enterprise and self-reliance are not sufficiently insisted upon." The Abolitionist Martin R. Delany wrote in 1852, "The elevation of the colored man can only be completed by the elevation of the pure descendants of Africa," in order "to establish the equality of the African with the European race." The journalist J. Holland Townsend argued that blacks must demonstrate their "individual manhood" and win the respect of whites through education: "Educate men and you melt the chains from their limbs; liberty becomes a fire in their bones, that all the penal enactments in the world can never effectually put out."

It was this kind of knowledge, energy, and self-confidence that Brown recommended for American blacks in "Sambo's Mistakes." But he did far more than write sympathetically about blacks. Here he differed significantly from Whitman, who in his poetry was open to black experience but in private life could be racist. John Brown put action behind his words. In Springfield he founded a black cadre, the League of Gileadites. In North Elba he lived in a colony of blacks whom he helped and worked with.

He formed the League of Gileadites in January 1851 in response to the recently passed Fugitive Slave Act. The notorious law, which gave federal marshals the right to pursue and reclaim fugitive slaves, drew many acidic words from Northerners. It enraged Emerson, pulling him from his pedestal of philosophic aloofness. "I do not often speak to public questions," he admitted, but this "immoral law" impelled him to voice "the secret of the new times, that Slavery was no longer mendicant, but was become aggressive and dangerous." "This law," declared Thoreau, "rises not to the level of the head or the reason; its natural habitat is in the dirt. It was born and bred, and has its life, only in the dust and mire," fit only to be tread upon like a "venomous reptile" by lovers of freedom.

From some quarters came calls for violent resistance to the law. Wendell Phillips said that any black threatened by a federal marshal "should feel justified by using the law of God and man in shooting that officer," though he advised nonresistance for whites. The reformer William P. Newman wrote Frederick Douglass: "I am frank to declare that it is my fixed and changeless purpose to kill any so-called man who attempts to enslave me or mine." A committee of Philadelphia blacks passed a resolution saying that the Fugitive Slave Act was "so wicked, so atrocious" that they vowed "to resist to the death any attempt to enforce it upon our persons."

As combative as such positions were, none was as groundbreaking as John Brown's. Brown was convinced that God sent the new law to warn whites to shed their racism and blacks to prepare for armed battle against whites. He wrote Mary, "It now seems that the fugitive slave law was to be the means of making more abolitionists than all the lectures we have had for years. It looks as if God had his hand in this wickedness also." Responding to the law, in the fall of 1850 he converted his wool warehouse into a station for the Underground Railroad.

The capture of a fugitive slave in New York that winter drove him to more aggressive action. In January 1851, still in Springfield closing down the wool business, he organized a group of local blacks. The name he gave the group referred to Mount Gilead of the Old Testament, where Gideon (meaning "hewer" or "warrior") was directed by God to save Israel from an invading tribe by determining who was the bravest among his troops.

John Brown had long loved the hymn "Blow Ye the Trumpet, Blow!" and now he got a chance to put its martial spirit and images into action. In the Bible story, Gideon is inspired to take up the sword when the angel of the Lord blows his trumpet. Gideon raises an army of 22,000 that the angel commands him to winnow down. The angel declares, "Now therefore come, proclaim in the hearing of the people, saying, 'Whoever is afraid and trembling, let him return and depart from Mount Gilead.' " Ten thousand remain on the mountain, but God instructs Gideon to reduce the force even further. Through a test, 300 men are selected. Gideon breaks up his force into three groups of 100 each, telling them to face the enemy, blow trumpets in unison, and cry, "The sword of the Lord, and of Gideon." They do so, producing a deafening sound. The enemy soldiers are thrown into such confusion that they attack each other and run away in fear. Gideon is left the leader of Israel.

Like earlier American Puritans, John Brown accepted the typological idea that the saintly settlers of the New World reenacted biblical stories. In his mind the Fugitive Slave Act was God's trumpet waking him to military action. He was the American Gideon, called upon to raise a small but potent army against a formidable enemy, the Southern slave power and its doughfaced sympathizers in the North. He knew his troops would be few, consisting as they did of willing blacks he could find in Springfield, but they would be highly motivated.

He managed to get forty-four blacks, many of them fugitives passing through town on the Underground Railroad, to convene as the League of Gileadites on January 15, 1851. He addressed them in words whose combative message must have shocked even the angriest of them.

Members of the group, he declared, must arm themselves, learn about their weapons, and be ready to use them at all times. Should they see a marshal or a Southern overseer approach a fellow Gileadite, they must attack the slave-catcher as a group. Many hearts in his all-black audience must have raced when he instructed with emphasis: *"Do not delay one moment after you are ready; you will lose all your resolution if you do. Let the first blow be the signal for all to engage; and when engaged do not do your work by halves, but make clean work with your enemies,—and be sure you meddle not with any others."* He told them to swiftly kill whoever posed a threat, then retreat. That way, the enemy's allies would be thrown into confusion and could not respond effectively. Should Gileadites be chased after the incident, they should flee into the homes of whites in the area known to be sympathetic to the antislavery cause. The whites would either defend them, take the blame for harboring them, or dishonor themselves by turning them over to the authorities. In the case of the capture and trial of a group member, other Gileadites should appear in the courtroom with concealed gunpowder, cause an explosion to create disarray, and then spirit the prisoner away.

This speech was a first in American history: a white person's detailed strategy for preemptive armed warfare to be waged by blacks against proslavery forces. Brown's plan was revolutionary at every step, from the initial arming of the blacks to the quick murder of a slave-catcher to the flight to the homes of whites (who therefore might be charged as accessories to the murder) to the detonation of gunpowder in the courtroom.

The address was innovative in other ways as well. Membership in the group was not restricted to able-bodied men. Brown stated: "We invite every colored person whose heart is engaged for the performance of our business, whether male or female, old or young. The duty of the aged, infirm, and young members of the League shall be to give instant notice to all members in case of an attack upon any of our people." Brown welcomed the participation of *all* blacks: women, children, old, or handicapped. The latter three groups would serve as scouts. Healthy women would join in the male Gileadites in attacking slave-catchers.

His inclusion of women as part of the attack force brings up an unappreciated fact about Brown: he was forward-looking on the issue of gender. He sympathized with the women's rights movement, which began with the famous convention in Seneca Falls, New York, in 1848. He made a point of attending feminist lectures whenever possible. As his daughter Anne Brown Adams recalled, "John Brown was strong for women's rights and women's suffrage. He always went to hear Abby Kelley Foster and Lucretia Mott, even though it cost him considerable effort to reach the place where they spoke." Around the home, John Brown was a patriarch but not "patriarchal" in the modern male-chauvinist sense. Without fanfare, he made sure that males and females shared tasks equally, with no regard to gender stereotypes. The girls did some of the outdoor work, and the boys shared in the housekeeping duties. Even Frederick Douglass, who was active in the feminist movement, was surprised by the switching of gender roles in the Brown household. "The mother, daughters and sons did the serving, and did it well," Douglass noted. "Supper over, the boys helped to clear the table and wash the dishes. This style of housekeeping struck me as a little odd. I mention it because household management is worthy of thought."

His observation was corroborated by one of Brown's sons, who wrote, "There were no drones in the Brown hive . . . there was no pampering; little petting. The boys could turn a steak or brown a loaf as well as their mother." Another son noted that Brown himself had much of "the woman in him," as evidenced by his willingness to perform work normally reserved for women.

Another way in which the League of Gileadites reflected Brown's values was that it was jingoistic at the same time that it was revolutionary. The full name of the group—"a branch of the United States League of GILEAD-ITES"—was intended as a patriotic gesture, showing that the league was not set *against* the United States but wanted to work *within* it, to help its core values be fully realized on the racial level. Brown had the league members sign a pledge that contained the words "As citizens of the United States of America, trusting in a just and merciful God, whose spirit and all-powerful aid we humbly implore, *we will ever be true to the flag of our beloved country, always acting under it.*" This language was falsely optimistic, since many of those present were not counted as "citizens of the United States of America"—and soon the Dred Scott decision would strip *all* American blacks of citizenship.

Brown's optimism, however, was not blind. He of course knew that many in his league were not citizens and that even the free blacks had enjoyed few social rights. He also realized his league could only be ephemeral, since many of its members were on their way to Canada. But he appears to have formed the group as an immediate shot of confidence for Springfield's blacks, not as a long-term project; after all, he knew he had North Elba and many lawsuits ahead of him. Two days after the Gileadite meeting, he reported to Mary that he had been busy "with the colored people here, in advising them how to act, and in giving them all the encouragement in my power. They very much need encouragement and advice; and some of them are so alarmed that they tell me they cannot sleep on account of either themselves or their wives and children. I can only say I think I have been enabled to do something to revive their broken spirits. I want all my family to imagine themselves in the same dreadful condition."

His effort "to revive their broken spirits" had led him to prevaricate in his speech, not only about citizenship issues but also about racial attitudes. Though he knew the deep racism of American whites, he reminded his black listeners of martyrs like Elijah Lovejoy and Charles Torrey, insisting there were a good number of other whites ready to help blacks challenge slave-catchers. "Colored people," he proclaimed, "have ten times the number of fast friends among whites than they suppose, and would have ten times the number they now have were they but half as much in earnest to secure the dearest rights as they are to ape the follies and extravagances of their white neighbors." Such reassurance undoubtedly lifted spirits even if it misrepresented reality.

His optimism also energized his approach to his experiment in multicultural living at North Elba. He had many reasons to view the project with trepidation. Located near Lake Placid in an isolated region in the Adirondacks, North Elba was beautiful but forbidding. Neither the natural setting nor the social environment was welcoming. Brown's main goal was to help free blacks and fugitive slaves establish a farming community—no easy task in a rocky, mountainous region where winter stretched from late October to May. Day-to-day life was an exercise in survival. Once Brown nearly died when he was walking at night in a blizzard on a mountain road; a passerby neglected his calls for help, and he barely managed to make it through the blinding storm to the next farmhouse.

Gerrit Smith, who lived some 230 miles away in Peterboro, New York, had bought the North Elba land because he realized that a settlement of blacks would not be welcome close to mainstream communities. However, there were whites scattered throughout in the region who resented the sudden incursion of blacks in the late 1840s and who overcharged them for provisions, draining their resources. A near famine resulted.

In 1848, even as his wool business was floundering, Brown shipped five barrels of pork and five of flour to be distributed among the blacks in North Elba. By January 1849 his mission was to move there. He wrote his father from Springfield, "I was on some of the Gerrit Smith lands lying opposite Burlington Vermont last fall that he has given away to the blacks & found no objection to them [the lands] but the high Northern Lattitude in which they lie. They are indeed rather inviting on many accounts. There are a number of good colored families on the ground: most of whom I visited. I can think of no place where I think I would sooner go; all things considered than to live with those poor despised Africans to try, & encourage; & show them a little so far as I am capable how to manage."

An immediate reason for his rush to move there in the spring of 1849 was to defend the blacks against corrupt whites, including a swindling surveyor whom he replaced. In June of that year he reached into his nearly empty pockets and sent Gerrit Smith $225 to pay for a land parcel for a black settler who was being swindled.

Relocating to North Elba was like going back in time for the Browns,

The farm in North Elba, New York, where John Brown
lived and was buried. In the foreground is his gravestone.
BOYD STUTLER COLLECTION OF JOHN BROWN, WEST VIRGINIA ARCHIVES.

who exchanged the lively commercial world of a Massachusetts town for the primitive conditions of mountainous upstate New York. About a quarter of the Browns' 244-acre tract had been cleared for farming. The family struggled to raise crops and livestock amid boulders and burned-out tree stumps. During the times John Brown was forced to be away from North Elba on business matters, the rugged, red-haired Owen and the sturdy Ruth, both in their twenties, worked along with the dour-faced, persevering Mary to oversee their property.

In the North Elba census of 1850 the Brown farm, worth $500, was listed as having five cows, four oxen, some swine, sheep, and chickens, twenty bushels of oats, thirty bushels of potatoes, and one hundred pounds of butter. The family had a subsistence lifestyle. A visitor commented, "They never raise anything to sell off that farm, except sometimes a few fleeces. It was well, they said, if they raised their own provisions, and could spin their own wool for clothing."

For John Brown, who had failed in the competitive world of American capitalism, a subsistence life among blacks he could help was exactly what he wanted, though trips often kept him away. His community, like his other projects, was destined to fail economically, but it was a daring effort at interracial cooperation. If the twenty-odd utopian communities in antebellum America tested all kinds of strange theories—about free love, "attractive" labor, complex marriage, the water cure, and so on—North Elba tested a theory that, for its day, was as bizarre as any of them: the theory that blacks and whites could live and work together on equal terms.

Most of the blacks who owned property at North Elba were from New York State or Connecticut. Among those there in 1850 were the thirty-six-year-old Lyman Epps and his thirty-one-year-old wife, Ann, who lived in a log house worth $100 along with their four children and Lyman's widowed mother, age seventy-seven; Josiah and Susan Hasbrook, both thirty-four, crammed with their six children into a $25 log hut; Thomas and Jane Jefferson, with their three sons in a rude frame house; and William and Eliza Carasaw, in their twenties, who were about to start a family.

John Brown treated these and the many other black families in the area on terms of complete equality. He worked with them, surveyed their lands, and socialized with them, often visiting their homes and taking them into his. Lyman Epps, Jr., would never forget the kindness Brown showed toward his family. Epps recalled Brown as "a true friend of my father's," adding, "He'd walk up to our house on the Table Lands and come in and play with us children and talk to father. Many's the time I've sat on John Brown's knee. He was a kind and friendly man with children." Since North Elba was a station on the Underground Railroad, fugitive slaves arrived continuously. Once when Brown did not have room in his home for a fugitive who had just arrived from the South, he dropped him off at the Eppses' for the night before taking him the next day to Canada, some 250 miles to the north.

A memorable portrait of Brown at North Elba came from Richard Henry Dana. The New York author, famous for his adventure novel *Two Years Before the Mast*, was hiking in the Adirondacks in late June 1849 with two friends when his party got lost. The three groped through the densely forested hills until they came upon a clearing that turned out to be the Brown property. Brown's single-story frame house stood starkly amid charred tree trunks on a rolling field framed by a lush pine forest and mountains, with a glimpse of the azure Lake Placid in the distance. Towering over the lake was the 4,867-foot Whiteface, with a bald slope that had been created by a landslide. To the south was the taller Mount Marcy, whose Indian name, Tahawus, meant "Cloudsplitter," made famous in Russell Banks's fine novel about John Brown.

Dana and his companions were welcomed into the Brown home. Mary was not around, but Dana reported, "There were a great many sons and daughters,—I never knew how many: from [Ruth], a cheerful, nice, healthy woman of twenty or so, and a full-sized red-haired son [Owen], who seemed to be foreman of the farm, through every grade of boy and girl, to a couple that could barely speak plain." Ruth tended to the visitors' insect bites and prevented them from filling themselves with water and milk so that she would have time to cook heartier fare for them. John Brown was off surveying land. Dana and his friends learned that he was an Abolitionist who had come to Gerrit Smith's tract to help struggling blacks, for whom he was "a kind of king."

Late in the afternoon Brown arrived, carrying his surveyor's instruments and walking with his son Frederick next to a wooden wagon on which sat two black men. The gaunt, dark-complexioned Brown struck Dana as "a grave, serious man . . . , with a marked countenance and a natural dignity of manner." Brown greeted and talked with Dana, who found him "well informed on most subjects, especially in the natural sciences." He had books in his home, and clearly he had read them.

Brown invited the visitors to dinner. Dana was taken aback when the two blacks he had met and another one sat at the table along with the rest. He was even more shocked by the way Brown treated the blacks. He addressed each politely, just as he did the whites. His introductions went, "Mr. Dana, Mr. Jefferson," "Mr. Metcalf, Mrs. Wait," and so forth. The blacks, who had never encountered such respect from a white person, appeared befuddled. Still, Brown continued with the decorum throughout the dinner, making sure that everyone at the table was integrated into the conversation.

On leaving, Dana offered to pay Ruth for the meal, but she refused his money. He continued pressing her, offering her a five-dollar bill and several one-dollar bills. She took one of the latter, ran upstairs, and returned with change. "It was too piteous," Dana recalled. "We could not help smiling, and told her we should feel guilty of highway robbery if we took her silver. She consented to keep the one dollar, for the three of us—one meal apiece and some extra cooking in the morning."

Dana and his friends spent the next day exploring the Lake Placid area, and then on the way home revisited the Browns to say goodbye. "We found them at breakfast, in the patriarchal style," Dana wrote, with the huge family and the hired men and women, including three blacks, seated around the large table. "Their meal was neat, substantial, and wholesome."

Although the scene charmed Dana, he saw nothing remarkable in it. He could not imagine, as he wrote later, that ten years after it this plain farmer would be "the central figure of a great tragic scene, gazed upon with wonder, pity, admiration, or execration by half a continent! That this man should be thought to have imperiled the slave empire in America, and added a new danger to the stability of the Union! That his almost undistinguishable name of John Brown should be whispered among four millions of slaves, and sung wherever the English tongue is spoken, and incorporated into an anthem to whose solemn cadences men should march to battle by the tens of thousands! That he should have done something toward changing the face of civilization itself!"

If Brown's forthcoming impact on America was unimaginable to Dana, it was because he did not appreciate the magnitude of John Brown's radicalism during the North Elba visit. He should have realized that for an American white to live equally among blacks—sitting at dinner with them, making friendly visits to their homes, staying with them on trips, helping the imperiled flee north and the impoverished develop farms, treating all of them with dignity and respect—was, for its time, as earth-shaking in its implications as Harpers Ferry was in fact.

Six years after Dana's visit, Walt Whitman wrote in a poem:

> *This is the meal pleasantly set . . .*
> *. . . I make appointments with all,*
> *I will not have a single person slighted or left away,*
> *The keptwoman and sponger and thief are hereby invited . . .*
> *the heavy lipp'd slave is invited. . . . the venerealee is invited,*
> *There shall be no difference between them and the rest.*

Exhilarating in their affirmation of human equality, these lines were, unfortunately, utopian rather than descriptive of nineteenth-century reality. Even Whitman, who manifested signs of the prevailing racism, had difficulty living up to his own radically democratic words.

John Brown came as close to doing so as any antebellum figure I am aware of. His triumphant ability to overcome his culture's racism explains the fact that he has been singled out appreciatively by American blacks of contrasting viewpoints, from W. E. B. Du Bois and his circle, who founded the Niagara Movement on nonresistant principles, to aggressive militants such as Malcolm X and H. Rap Brown. Describing Brown as "the man who of all Americans has perhaps come nearest to touching the real souls of black folk," Du Bois wrote, "John Brown worked not simply for Black Men—he worked with them; and he was a companion of their daily life, knew their faults and virtues, and felt, as few white Americans have felt, the bitter tragedy of their lot."

The approval these later black leaders expressed for Brown was already present among the blacks of his own day. In a memorial service for him held in Cleveland shortly after his death, the black reformer Charles H. Langston declared, "I never thought that I should ever join in doing honor to or mourning for any American *white* man." In John Brown, however, he found "a lover of mankind—not of any particular class or color, but of all men. He knew no complexional distinctions between God's rational creatures. . . . He fully, really and *actively* believed in the equality and brotherhood of man. . . . He is the only American citizen who has lived fully up to the Declaration of Independence. . . . He admired Nat. Turner as well as George Washington."

The connection made here between Brown's racial openness and his regard for Nat Turner brings us back to the plan he had for battling slavery. Only a white who could esteem Turner as much as he did Washington could have come up with a plan like the one Brown was fashioning during his years at Springfield and North Elba. The Harpers Ferry area he eventually selected as the site of his raid had many associations with George Washington, who had surveyed the area as a young man, thinking it had commercial potential, and had suggested to his brother Charles that he move there. Charles did so, and he became the founder of Charles Town (where John Brown would be tried and hanged). Also in the region was a house George Washington designed and built for another brother, Samuel, as well as the plantation of a great-grandnephew, Colonel Lewis W. Washington.

It was the latter Washington who had special significance for John Brown's plan. Brown knew that among Colonel Washington's possessions were two emblematic heirlooms: a sword that Washington's great-granduncle, the first president, had reportedly received as a gift from Frederick the Great, as well as a pistol that had been given to the president by the Marquis de Lafayette, the French general who had aided America during the Revolution.

On the night of his raid on Harpers Ferry, Brown directed a small party of whites and blacks to go to Lewis Washington's plantation, set free the slaves there, and take hostage the colonel, who was forced to hand over the sword and pistol to Osborne Anderson, one of five blacks among Brown's invaders. When Washington was carted to the engine house at the Ferry where Brown was headquartered, Brown handed pikes to several of the just-liberated blacks and had them guard Washington and other hostages, ordering them, "Keep these white men inside." By giving blacks such power over whites, Brown was creating a richly symbolic racial role reversal. In effect, he was putting Nat Turner in control of George Washington—an astonishing feat, even though it proved only temporary.

It is unknown at what moment in his planning for the Virginia invasion the role-reversal idea came to him. My guess is the summer or fall of 1854, when his growing anger over the American government's proslavery gestures made him focus on the federal arsenal at Harpers Ferry as his specific target. Probably, his line of thinking was: As the system first presided over by George Washington is now increasingly devoting itself to the oppression of enslaved blacks, I will answer with the resonant act of putting blacks in control of a descendant of George Washington.

Even if his plan was not quite this precisely formulated in 1854, the instinct for such a role reversal was firmly in place. At least since the Springfield meeting with Frederick Douglass in 1847, a reversal of racial roles was the essence of the plan, which showed deep traces of Nat Turner and the maroons of the West Indies. Brown's engagement with black culture gained a deeply personal dimension at North Elba, where he may have failed to find recruits for his planned raid but where he gained new familiarity with and respect for individual African Americans.

The other utopian communities of the period either died out or were transformed into commercial ghosts of themselves: Oneida, for instance, moved from "complex marriage" to silverware production, and Amana would become a manufacturer of household furniture. The North Elba community did not, literally speaking, become anything: figuratively, it can be said to have become an idealized version of America. It raised a prospect that in that day seemed sheer nonsense: that is, blacks and sympathetic whites can live together in harmony in a community in which people of both races have an equal say in day-to-day affairs.

This aspect of North Elba came through even in negative portrayals of the community. Jibing "Gerrit Smith's abortive attempts at Negro colonization," an essayist of 1859 called the experiment "an utter failure," noting that only two or three of the settlers remained there. The colony has barely survived, the essayist continued, "although at one time [it was] so numerous that it seemed probable the anomalous political aspect would be exhibited in a town in New York controlled by negro suffrage, and represented in the County Board by colored supervisors."

The essayist was in one sense right. An American town politically controlled by blacks—that *would* have been an anomaly. But the essayist was also dead wrong: North Elba was *not* an utter failure. It would become Exhibit A in the defense of John Brown among blacks from Frederick Douglass through W. E. B. Du Bois to the civil rights leaders of the late twentieth century. It established a model for racial togetherness that even today is rarely achieved in America.

Because of this, it became John Brown's favorite place. For him, North Elba was home. Shortly before he died, even though the colony could be said to have "failed," he told Mary he hoped she would continue living there after his death. She did so for a while, and she honored his wish to be buried there.

In death as in life, then, Brown was a North Elban. The blacks of North Elba affected the course of American history by helping him decide upon the direction of his antislavery activities. What would have happened had the Harpers Ferry raid come off four years earlier than it did? No one can say, but there is evidence that it could have occurred as early as 1855, possibly even 1854. Largely because of a decision made by the black colonists at North Elba, Brown deferred his plan.

The summer of 1854 was a turning point in the conflict over slavery because of escalating tensions in Kansas. For Southerners, the Territory was important to win for slavery because of an implied domino effect: if Kansas went to slavery, so would Nebraska and many other states farther west that would be formed in the future. Proslavery forces gathered in Kansas in July and issued a resolution pledging to drive from the state any people who stood opposed to slavery extension. Antislavery forces, especially the New England Emigrant Aid Society under Eli Thayer of Worcester, established the opposite goal of winning Kansas for freedom by flooding the state with Northern settlers opposed to slavery.

The rising conflict stirred the Browns to action. Three of the sons—Owen, Frederick, and Salmon, all then residing in Ohio—departed in October 1854 for Kansas, where they wanted to be counted among the antislavery settlers. They left Ohio with ten cattle, three horses, and some personal possessions, going through Chicago to Meridosia, Illinois, where they spent the winter. By late April 1855 they were in Kansas, establishing a camp eight miles west of the town of Osawatomie.

Springtime swelled rivers, allowing two other brothers, John and Jason, to travel with their families from Ohio to Kansas by boat. They took the Ohio and Mississippi rivers to St. Louis, where they bought tents and farm tools. They boarded a steamer, the *New Lucy*, headed for Kansas by way of the Missouri River. The boat, they found, was crowded with Southerners. John Jr. wrote that "their drinking, profanity, and display of revolvers and bowie-knives—openly worn as an essential part of their make-up—clearly showed the class to which they belonged, and that their mission was to aid in establishing slavery in Kansas."

An unforeseen tragedy occurred when the four-year-old Austin Brown, the oldest of Jason's two children, became the victim of a cholera outbreak among the passengers. When the *New Lucy* stopped at Waverly, Missouri, the Browns disembarked and buried Austin's small body during a violent thunderstorm. The steamer's captain, a Southerner, played a cruel joke on them by pulling away before they could reboard, even though they had paid their fare to go on to Kansas City. Stranded in a slave state, they had to continue by stage. En route they tried to buy food from farmers who rejected their requests when they sensed from the Browns' accents that they were Northerners. On May 7 they at last reached their brothers' camp, which they called Brown's Station, near Osawatomie.

John Brown felt a strong urge to join his sons but had other matters on his mind. Even as he gave his sons the go-ahead, he backed off from joining them. On August 21, 1854, he wrote to John Jr., "If you or any of my family are disposed to go to Kansas or Nebraska, with a view to help defeat *Satan and his legions in that direction, I have not a word to say; but I feel committed to operate in another part of the field*. If I were not so committed, I would be on my way this fall." The other "part of the field" was Harpers Ferry, which he evidently hoped to invade soon with a force he was recruiting in Ohio, where he spent much of the year farming.

In the fall of 1854, with his Ohio ventures failing, he had three viable options open to him: to return to North Elba with Mary and the remaining children, including the newborn, Ellen; to begin the journey west to join his sons in Kansas; or to round up a small invasion force and begin the Harpers Ferry "operation" right away. His rage over the Kansas-Nebraska Act may have driven him to choose the latter option had his black friends not advised otherwise.

Having dedicated his life to blacks, he now requested them, along with his family, to decide his immediate fate. On September 30, five days after the birth of Ellen, he wrote to a number of his children who were in North Elba: "After being hard pressed to go with my family to Kansas as more likely to benefit the colored people *on the whole* than to return with them to North Elba; I have consented to ask for your *advice & feeling* in the matter; & also to ask you to learn from Mr. Epps & all the colored people (so far as

Mary Day Brown with eight-year-old Anne (left)
and five-year-old Sarah (right) in the early 1850s.
BOYD STUTLER COLLECTION OF JOHN BROWN, WEST VIRGINIA ARCHIVES.

you can) how they would wish, & advise me to act in the case, all things considered. As I volunteered in their service; (or the service of the colored people); they have a right to vote, as to the course I take."

These words show that his *only* concern now other than his family was for American blacks, how to help them and how to follow their wishes. His phrasing was significant. What course of action, he asked, was the most "likely to benefit the colored people *on the whole*"? How did "all the colored people" advise him to act in the case? Since he had given his life to "the service of the colored people," they had the "right to vote" on his course of action.

This was far more than a call for black suffrage, which would have been rare for that era. It was a request by a white person for blacks to vote on his private actions—rare for any era.

The North Elba colonists were not the only blacks he consulted. He wrote letters to a number of black leaders, including Frederick Douglass and the physician James McCune Smith, asking their advice.

He decided to move for the time being to North Elba, with the obligation of returning to Ohio periodically to finish his affairs there.

Leaving Mary and the younger children behind in Akron until they could join him, he went east, arriving at the North Elba homestead on November 14, 1854. The next day Ruth described his arrival in a note to her mother, reporting that he had a cold but had brought joy to the community. Ruth wrote, "We are rejoiced to hear that he has given up the idea of going to Kansas, but will move here this winter, if he can get feed for his cattle." His return meant Mary's as well—more good news for Ruth, who noted to her mother, "We need you here as much or more than you will be needed in Kansas." Ruth said she knew John Jr. was in Cincinnati preparing to go join his brothers in Kansas, adding that she hoped John's wife, Wealthy, would visit North Elba before heading west with him.

John Brown divided his time that winter and the next spring between North Elba and Akron, as he still owned livestock and farm materials in Ohio he had to sell. It was not until the summer of 1855 that he could bring the Akron contingent en masse back to North Elba. The family settled into a primitive, unplastered four-room home that his son-in-law Henry Thompson had built. This would be the main home for the Browns as long as they stayed in the region, through Harpers Ferry and beyond.

By that time, however, John Brown's mind was trained mainly on Kansas, where the steady buildup of proslavery forces were provoking alarmed letters from his sons. Salmon wrote, "There are slaves owned within three miles of us." John Jr. asked his father to raise money for guns, which were to be shipped west as quickly as possible. "The storm every day thickens," he wrote, "its near approach is hourly more clearly seen by all." He predicted that "the great drama will open here, when will be presented the great struggle in arms, of Freedom and Despotism in America. Give us the arms, and we are ready for the contest."

Heeding the call, John Brown raised money for arms at a convention of reformers, the Radical Political Abolitionists, in Syracuse on June 28. Members of the group included Gerrit Smith, Lewis Tappan, Samuel J. May, and Frederick Douglass. These and others present had split with Garrison over American politics, which they embraced, and over women reformers, whom they frowned upon. John Brown made a passionate plea for contributions of funds for weapons and received $60. This was a paltry amount, considering the fact that the convention pledged nearly $5,000 to other Abolitionist causes, but it gratified Brown. He wrote Mary, "The convention has been one of the most interesting meetings I ever attended in my life; and I made a great addition to the number of warm-hearted and honest friends."

Brown went on to Springfield, where he shipped some guns and flasks to Cleveland, and then to North Elba, where he prepared for his trip to

Kansas. It was decided that the twenty-one-year-old Watson would stay in North Elba to run the farm. Henry Thompson, Ruth's husband, would accompany Brown to Kansas, as would the sixteen-year-old Oliver, whom they would meet in Illinois, where he was working.

Brown and Thompson left North Elba on August 13 and reached Chicago fifteen days later. Along the way they stopped in Ohio, where Brown gave some antislavery speeches and collected weapons, including revolvers, rifles, ammunition, and several short, heavy broadswords. He and Thompson went through Cleveland to Rockford, Illinois, where they picked up Oliver. The three proceeded to Chicago, where they bought a young horse for $160. With their wagon loaded with provisions, surveying equipment, and concealed weapons, they continued to Missouri. Their pace slackened to some sixty-eight miles a day when their horse got sick. They lived on crackers, herring, eggs, tea, and prairie chickens they shot on the wing. Thompson had a rough bout of ague (malarial fever), and all three developed bowel complaints for lack of wholesome water. At Waverly, Missouri, they stopped and exhumed Austin's body, so that it could receive a proper burial in Kansas.

They met Missourians who boasted about their exploits against "d——d Abolitionists" across the line in Kansas. "No man of them," Brown reported, "would blush when telling of their cruel treading down & terrifying of defenceless Free State men." He was revolted by "the coarse, vulgar, profane, jests, & the bloodthirsty brutal feelings to which they were giving vent continually."

When the three travelers arrived at Brown's Station on October 7, they had only 60 cents between them. The scene they encountered was worse than they had anticipated. Earlier that year John Brown had received letters from his sons extolling the fertility of the Kansas soil and describing the abundance of their crops. But torrential rains in August followed by cold, cutting winds in the fall had spoiled some of their crops and had brought on illness. Brown's Station was no more than a few flimsy tents by a campfire. Everyone but John Jr.'s wife, Wealthy, and their three-year-old son, Tonny, was suffering from ague. Crops lay unreaped and rotting in the fields, and provisions were sparse.

As Henry Thompson and Oliver unpacked the wagon, John Brown tended to the sick ones, who were shivering in the wind near the fire. Jason and Ellen thanked him for bringing them Austin's corpse, which they ceremoniously reburied.

A week after his arrival, John Brown wrote his father, "I felt very much disappointed at finding all my children here in such very uncomfortable circumstances." Circumstances grew even more uncomfortable in late October, when sleet and icy blasts swept the region. Frederick came down with a terrible fever, and several of the others suffered relapses.

For a time John Brown was virtually the only healthy person at Brown's Station. He had a surprising energy that belied his appearance. Now fifty-five, he was gray, wrinkled, and stooped. But he was still lithe, and so vigorous that he could get by on just three or four hours of sleep a night.

He set about fortifying the community for the coming winter. He gathered what crops he could, stacked hay, husked corn, and tended to the animals. For Jason, Ellen, and their child he built a log hut with a tent roof and a crude chimney. For John Jr. and his family, he and Salmon constructed a cabin in a brushy hollow near a creek.

By November 15 he could report to Mary that "matters in general are once more in a progressive state; & a tolerable degree of cheerfulness seems to prevail." Even the political situation in Kansas seemed propitious. The Browns had recently gone to an election site well armed to fight border ruffians, but none had showed up. The Free State Party was scheduled to "get a Constitution adopted making *Kansas Free*; & as we understand them to be a decided Majority; we believe the great victory will follow before long."

But this was only the calm before the storm. John Brown would soon be making use of his weapons—most memorably those menacing two-bladed broadswords he had brought from Ohio.

7

Pottawatomie

To some John Brown was a crazed fanatic who became a criminal when he supervised the murder of five men on Pottawatomie Creek, Kansas, in May 1856. To others he was a heroic antislavery warrior whose courage was epitomized in his battle three months later against proslavery forces at nearby Osawatomie.

The debate concerns more than John Brown. It involves competing interpretations of the causes of the Civil War. The generation of Civil War historians known as the revisionists accepted the negative view of Brown and of other Abolitionists. They regarded both the Abolitionists and the proslavery fire-eaters as fringe fanatics who stirred up trouble and brought on the war with their frenzied denunciations of the opposing side. In this reading John Brown was the most fanatical of the fanatics, the craziest of the crazy. Allan Nevins typically called Brown a neurotic afflicted by "paranoia" who should have been confined "in an asylum for the criminally insane." According to this view, the Civil War might have been avoided had not extremists like Brown agitated as belligerently as they did.

The civil rights movement of the 1960s brought a more positive reading of the Abolitionists, who were seen as ethical crusaders who helped start a war of liberation. Still, the idea of John Brown as a fringe fanatic persisted. Although Brown is now regarded as a key figure, it has proven difficult to place him in overviews of the pre–Civil War period. He is commonly seen as an anomaly, a lone gun, not as an integral part of the larger forces that led to the war.

Undeniably, John Brown *was* an anomaly—he was an Abolitionist who believed in violence and who actually made war. Moreover, he was not representative of a mainstream movement, nor even of a perimeter one such as Garrisonian Abolitionism. And he did direct a horrible crime.

It is hard to admire a cold-blooded killer. It is also challenging to position the anomalous Brown in the pattern of events that led to the Civil War. His historical importance becomes clear only if we change the terms of the discussion. The Pottawatomie killings were not admirable or legally defensible. But they were explainable, given John Brown's makeup as it intersected with special conditions of time and place, and given the long-term social tensions that led to these conditions.

As for Brown's place in the larger picture, that is revealed when we explore not only Brown himself but also how he was perceived, and how events swept him to fame. In 1856, after all, he was no more of a fringe figure than was a gangly Illinois lawyer named Abraham Lincoln who had once been a Whig congressman but who had since fallen into obscurity. Just as Lincoln would rise to power when the Republican Party needed an antislavery spokesperson who was firm but moderate, so John Brown would fill a need for Northerners who were looking for a hero to admire in a time of immoral laws and spineless politicians. To some of these Northerners, as shall be seen, Brown's violence was justifiable and his integrity was unimpeachable. They accepted Brown's bloody tactics and his treasonous designs because of their ardent faith in the man they called Osawatomie Brown. This faith proved contagious, becoming a major source of inspiration to the Union army during the Civil War.

For most of the time John Brown was in Kansas, it was in a state of war and near anarchy. After the passage of the Kansas-Nebraska Act, violence was endemic to the Territory. As Lincoln wrote a friend, "I look upon the [Kansas-]Nebraska law not as a *law*, but a *violence* from the beginning. It was conceived in violence, is maintained in violence, and is being executed in violence."

Lincoln, who instinctively opposed violence, chose to combat slavery in Kansas through persuasive eloquence. In his debates with Senator Stephen Douglas he argued logically about the dangers of slavery extension in the territories. For John Brown and his sons, who had long plotted violence against the South's peculiar institution, Kansas provided an opportunity to fight proslavery forces.

John Brown came armed to Kansas in the fall of 1855 for good reason. From his sons' letters and from a flood of press reports, he was keenly aware of the South's intention to seize Kansas for slavery, with force if necessary.

For many Southerners, Kansas was an all-or-nothing proposition. If it went for slavery, the rest of the territories would do so as well. If it went for Abolition, slavery extension was stymied, perhaps doomed. Warren Wilkes, a South Carolinian who led an armed force of Southern settlers in Kansas, wrote:

> Kansas is . . . the turning-point in the destinies of slavery and aboli-
> tionism. If the South triumphs, abolitionism will be defeated and
> shorn of its power for all time. If she is defeated, abolitionism will
> grow more insolent and aggressive, until the utter ruin of the South is
> consummated. If the South secures Kansas, she will extend slavery
> into all territory south of the fortieth parallel of north latitude, to the
> Rio Grande; and this, of course, will secure for her pent-up institu-
> tion of slavery an ample outlet, and restore her power in Congress. If
> the North secures Kansas, the power of the South in Congress will be
> gradually diminished, and the slave population will become valueless.
> All depends upon the action of the present moment.

Many other supporters of slavery voiced this view as well. Particularly insistent on winning Kansas for slavery were landowners in the neighboring state of Missouri. In 1855 there were some 90,000 slaves in Missouri. Although only one in eight Missouri families owned slaves (as opposed to one in two in the Deep South), among these families were the prominent ones that inhabited the state's western counties, bordering Kansas.

The slave-owner David Rice Atchison got his fellow Missourians moving across the border on a proslavery crusade. A blustery, physically imposing man—he stood six feet two and weighed over two hundred pounds—Atchison was nicknamed "Old Bourbon" for his love of hard liquor. A senator from Missouri, he laid claim to having served briefly as both the president and the vice president of the United States: in the one-day interim between the presidencies of James K. Polk and Zachary Taylor, he was, as the head of the Senate, allegedly the nation's ex officio president; and after the death of Franklin Pierce's vice president, William R. King, he was acting vice president from April 18, 1853, until December 4, 1854.

Forcing slavery upon Kansas was Atchison's cause célèbre. Atchison had persuaded Stephen Douglas to make the repeal of the Missouri Compromise a part of the Kansas-Nebraska Act, which, as acting vice president, he signed into law along with President Pierce. Atchison encouraged Missourians to go to nearby Kansas and vote for proslavery candidates to counteract antislavery emissaries from the East. He declared: "If a set of fanatics and demagogues a thousand miles off [in New England] can afford to advance their money and exert every nerve to abolitionize Kansas and exclude the slaveholder, what is your duty, when you reside within one day's journey of the Territory, and when your peace, quiet, and property depend on your action?"

It mattered little to Senator Atchison and his ilk that interstate voting was illegal. As one of his Missouri confederates, General B. F. Stringfellow, said in a speech, "To those who have qualms of conscience as to violating laws, state or national, I say the time has come when such impositions must be disregarded, since your rights and property are in danger. And I advise you, one and all, to enter every election district in Kansas . . . and vote at the point of the bowie-knife and revolver."

Such calls for violent lawbreaking fell on willing ears. Thousands of Missourians were ready at election time to go into Kansas, take over the polling booths there, and cast their ballots for proslavery candidates. Armed with bowie knives, shotguns, and pistols, they crossed over on horses or in wagons stocked with whiskey jugs and festooned with hempen rope brought along to hang any "d——d Abolitionist" who got in the way.

By most accounts, they were a scurvy bunch, well deserving of their moniker: border ruffians. One Free State man described them as the most "rough, coarse, sneering, swaggering, dare-devil looking rascals as ever swung upon the gallows," another as "groups of drunken, bellowing, blood-thirsty demons." The *New-York Tribune* portrayed the typical border ruffian as tall, slim, hairy-faced, with a yellow complexion, whiskey-red eyes, and walnut-colored teeth, wearing a dirty flannel shirt and dark pants held up by a leather belt from which protruded a bowie knife.

These Missourians did their assigned work. In the election for a Kansas delegate to Congress on November 29, 1854, they elected a proslavery candidate by casting 1,729 fraudulent votes. The election on March 30, 1855, saw even worse fraud, as the invaders cast more than 80 percent of the 6,307 recorded votes, ensuring that thirty-nine of Kansas's forty representatives supported slavery. The border ruffians terrorized the few polling officials who dared to try to stop the outrage.

The proslavery leaders "elected" by the ruffians organized a bogus legislature that passed stringent laws protecting slavery in Kansas. These so-called black laws mandated absurdly severe punishments for antislavery activity: two to five years of hard labor for anyone possessing an Abolitionist publication; five years of hard labor for writers or publishers of antislavery writings; and the death penalty for those who induced slaves to revolt. To speak against slavery was a felony. B. F. Stringfellow boasted in September 1855, "We now have laws more efficient to protect slave-property than any State in the Union"; he insisted that the laws "have already silenced Abolitionists; for in spite of their heretofore boasting, these know they will be enforced to the very letter and with the utmost rigor."

His assertion proved hollow, for the black laws (among the worst violations of civil liberties in American history) were so extreme as to be virtually unenforceable. Still, the laws created an atmosphere of violence and reprisal. In August 1855 opponents of slavery in Kansas organized a Free State convention in Lawrence to challenge the bogus legislature, which was meeting at Shawnee Mission. The next month, Free State Kansans convened at Big Springs to select antislavery candidates, oppose the black laws, and form a committee (on which John Brown, Jr., served) for counting votes during elections. The convention passed a resolution stating: "We owe no allegiance or obedience to the tyrannical enactments of this spurious Legislature . . . and will resist them to a bloody issue so soon as we ascertain that peaceable remedies shall fail, and forcible resistance shall furnish any reasonable prospect of success."

Bloody issue was not long in coming. That fall a Boston woman visiting Kansas wrote home about border ruffians who had recently shot down a Free State man with no provocation. "The border Missourians," she explained, "are a horseback people; always off somewhere; drink a great deal of whiskey, and are quite reckless of human life. . . . To shoot a man is not much more than to shoot a buck."

As iniquitous as was the proslavery element in Kansas, the Free State side was not much better. The antislavery settlers sent from the East by emigrant aid societies were often low- or lower-middle-class people ripe for ridicule as "scum" hired to control the vote in Kansas. Missourians variously dubbed them "the lowest class of rowdies," "the most unmitigated looking set of blackguards," "hellish emigrants and paupers whose bellies are filled with beggars food," men of "black and poisonous hearts." Worst of all, in the eyes of the Missourians, was that these Yankee settlers were "nigger-lovers" dedicated "alone to the one idea, sickly sycophantic love for the nigger," obsessed with running off slaves and "taking to their own bed and their own arms, a stinking Negro wench."

On this score, however, the criticism was misdirected. Most of the Free State settlers had as little affection for blacks as did the Missourians themselves. "Free State" meant free of *any* blacks, whether slaves or not. The Free State convention at Big Springs specified that "the best interests of Kansas require a population of free white men," demanding "stringent laws excluding all negroes, bond and free, from the Territory." It also denounced interfering with slavery where it existed, declaring "that the stale and ridiculous charge of Abolitionism so industriously imputed to the Free-State party . . . is without a shadow of truth to support it."

Like many antislavery whites elsewhere in America, then, the Free State Kansans were, in the main, shameless racists. One Free State leader reported, "There is a prevailing sentiment against admitting negroes into the Territory at all, slave or free." Another took pride in helping organize what he called "the 'free white State party,' " whose motto was " 'slavery before Negroes.' "

This distaste for blacks was codified in the constitution of a Free State government presented at a convention in Topeka on October 23, 1855. Most of the thirty-four people present, directed by the Free State leader James H. Lane, favored exclusion of blacks from Kansas but decided to let the people decide the issue. When the constitution was offered for ratification, its "Negro Exclusion Clause" passed overwhelmingly, as three-quarters of the Territory's Free State settlers voted for it.

Economics buttressed this racist sentiment for "negro exclusion." Most of the Free State settlers migrated to Kansas not in the cause of Abolition but in hopes of starting new lives under the auspices of the eastern emigrant aid societies, which ran as businesses. The leaders of the societies, such as Eli Thayer of Worcester and Amos Lawrence of Boston, were businessmen trying to turn a profit in Kansas. They were white supremacists who hated the name "Abolitionist" sometimes given them by Southerners. They opposed slavery not on moral grounds but because they wanted to foster laissez-faire capitalism in the Territory.

The emigrants they funded were lured by the cheap land prices in Kansas, where a 160-acre parcel sold for $1.25 an acre. On August 1, 1854, less than three months after the Kansas-Nebraska Act was passed, twenty-nine emigrants sponsored by Thayer's society formed a community on the south bank of the Kaw River in what later became Lawrence, a New England–like town with brick buildings, frame houses, and a Free State hotel that also served as a fort. More than 650 additional settlers came in the fall, with new arrivals steadily increasing over the next year. Soon many Free State towns—Topeka, Humboldt, Osawatomie, Claflin, Manhattan, and others—had sprung up. They immediately found themselves in competition with proslavery towns such as Leavenworth, Easton, and Atchison that tried to dominate commerce in northeastern Kansas along the Missouri River. These proslavery settlements consisted mainly of solid Missouri farmers, though there were also land speculators, businesspeople, and some ne'er-do-wells of the border ruffian variety.

Although John Brown's sons had moved to Kansas partly for economic reasons, they distinguished themselves by their staunch Abolitionism. Early in their stay there they were delighted by the fertile soil and the beautiful rolling prairie, covered in the warm months with tall grass and flowers. In April 1855, John Jr. wrote home, "Arrived in Kansas, her lovely prairies and wooded streams seemed to us indeed like a haven of rest. Here in prospect we saw our cattle increased to hundreds and possibly to thousands, fields of corn, orchards, and vineyards."

He and his four brothers made land claims some eight miles from Osawatomie, a town that had been founded as a capital investment by three businessmen. The Brown brothers' rural claims were near the homestead of their father's half-sister Florilla and her husband, the Reverend Samuel Lyle Adair.

It was not long before the brothers staked another kind of claim: to their identity as antislavery warriors. Soon after their arrival, they were approached by a group of heavily armed border ruffians who inquired about the Browns' political views. The ruffians must have been stunned by the bold answer one of them, probably John Jr., gave: "We are Free State, and more than that, we are Abolitionists."

The Missourians were put on guard. These men were not typical Free State settlers; they actually opposed slavery on moral grounds. Jason recalled: "They rode away at once, and from that moment we were marked for destruction. Before we were in the Territory a month, we found we had to go armed, and to be prepared to defend our lives." Less than a year after the encounter, one of the Missourians in the group, the Reverend Martin White, would murder Frederick Brown in cold blood.

Such violent death was not completely unexpected. The Browns knew their antislavery brashness did not sit well with the border ruffians. John Jr., who was elected vice president of a Free State society in June 1855, was especially outspoken. After the proslavery convention at Shawnee Mission passed its infamous black laws, John risked a felony charge by telling a slaveholder that no one had the right to hold a slave in Kansas. The next day he wrote his stepmother, "If any officer should attempt to arrest me for a violation of this law and should put his villainous hands on me, I would surely kill him so help me God." His wife, Wealthy, announced blithely, "Perhaps we shall all get shot for disobeying their beautiful laws, but you might as well die here in a good cause as freeze to death there [in North Elba]."

The Browns were justified in sensing a mounting threat from the proslavery side. A number of Free State figures had already met death or humiliation at the hands of the border ruffians. In the spring of 1854 the Kansas courts denied the self-defense case of the Free State settler Cole McCrae in the shooting of a border ruffian simply because his lawyer, James H. Lane, refused to swear allegiance to the proslavery legislature. Around the same time a proslavery committee commanded the prominent Free State lawyer William Phillips of Leavenworth to leave Kansas. When Phillips refused to obey, he was seized and taken to Rialto, Missouri, where his head was shaved and he was disrobed, tarred and feathered, and ridden on a rail before being sold for a dollar by a black man forced to conduct the mock auction. Phillips remained uncowed and returned to Kansas but later was killed by Missourians.

In August 1855, as John Brown began his journey from the East to Kansas, the Reverend Pardee Butler, a Free State clergyman of Atchison, was tied aboard a raft that was set adrift on the Missouri River by ruffians who pelted him with stones as he floated away. The ruffians had festooned the raft with flags inscribed with derisive messages such "The way they are served in Kansas," "Eastern Emigrant Aid Express," "For Boston," and "Let future emissaries from the north beware. Our hemp crop is sufficient to reward all such scoundrels."

The violence escalated in the fall. On October 25, two weeks after Brown arrived at his sons' camp, Patrick Laughlin, a proslavery settler, killed Samuel Collins, a Free-Stater who had a shoot-out with him over membership in a secret Free Soil club. Laughlin was wounded but recovered and settled in Atchison. He was never punished for the killing.

Kansas was such a tinderbox that crimes unrelated to slavery could inflame war. In late November, Charles Dow, a Free State Ohioan who lived south of Lawrence, was shot in the back by Franklin N. Coleman, a proslavery settler from Alabama. Although the dispute originated over Coleman's cutting timber on Dow's land, word spread that the murder resulted from a quarrel over slavery. A proslavery sheriff, Samuel J. Jones, wanted to prevent Dow's housemate, Jacob Branson, the only witness to the killing, from testifying against Coleman. Jones raised a posse and arrested Branson on false charges, setting an impossibly high bail that would prevent him from appearing in court. A party of fifteen well-armed Free State men approached Jones's posse, rescued Branson, and took him to safety in Lawrence.

Even though the rescue of the wrongly arrested Branson was justifiable, Jones used it as an excuse to plan an attack on Lawrence, the antislavery stronghold. He went to Kansas's governor, Wilson Shannon, requesting at least 3,000 troops so that he could storm Lawrence and enforce the proslavery laws of the Shawnee legislature. Shannon began mustering militia forces.

Thus began the so-called Wakarusa War, the first conflict in which John Brown participated. A force of some 1,200 proslavery men gathered on the Wakarusa River, a tributary of the Kaw, south of Lawrence. Shannon claimed the troops were from the Kansas militia, but in fact they consisted mainly of Missouri border ruffians eager to launch an all-out assault on the Free State town. Their martial frenzy was fanned by overheated appeals in proslavery newspapers, such as this one in the *Leavenworth Herald*, reprinted as a widely distributed handbill:

> **TO ARMS! TO ARMS!**
>
> It is expected that every lover of Law and Order will rally at Leavenworth, on Saturday December 1st, 1855, prepared to march at once to the scene of the rebellion, to put down the outlaws of Douglas county. . . . Come one, come all! The laws must be executed. The outlaws, it is said, are armed to the teeth and number one thousand men. Every man should bring his rifle, ammunition, and it would be well to bring two or three days' provisions. . . . Every man to his post, and to his duty.

The undisciplined, drunken mob of Missourians that gathered on the banks of the Wakarusa could hardly have organized a march on Lawrence. Still, the threat of violence alarmed Free State settlers, who came to Lawrence individually and in groups from surrounding towns.

Aroused by the prospect of battle, John Brown sent out John Jr., who returned in a gallop to Brown's Station with the report that a large proslavery force was threatening to burn Lawrence. On December 6, John Brown and several of his sons broke camp and set out for Lawrence. Jason, Owen, and Henry Thompson were ill and had to stay behind.

An arduous overnight expedition brought the Browns to Lawrence, where they found Free State troops drilling and building earthworks. The Browns, armed with revolvers and broadswords, were a formidable sight when they rumbled into town on a wagon bordered with poles with bayonets attached to them.

They went at once to the Free State Hotel, where appalling news greeted them. The evening before, Thomas Barber, a Free State Kansan from Ohio, had been killed. He and his brothers, who lived ten miles outside of Lawrence, had been coming to the town for a week to help build fortifications. As they were going home after work on December 6, even though they were few and unarmed, they were fired upon by a band of ten to fifteen Missourians. Barber was shot in the hip area and soon bled to death. His body was taken to the Free State Hotel, where it remained for several days.

John Brown's reaction to the Barber murder and the ruffian army outside Lawrence said much about his instincts. He had not come to Kansas with a definite idea of making war. In fact, he had reported in a recent letter that "matters in general" were "in a progressive state" there and that the Free State side would soon win "a great victory" when it passed its constitution. When directly confronted with proslavery outrages, however, he went on the offensive.

While the Free State leaders Charles Robinson and James Lane occupied themselves with negotiating with Governor Shannon in the hotel, Brown improvised a plan for attacking the army of border ruffians, which he estimated to be 1,500 strong. He spoke of the plan to Robinson, who appointed him on the spot as a captain in the "First Brigade of Kansas Volunteers," in command of a company called the Liberty Guards, consisting of Brown's sons and fifteen others. His plan was to surprise the Missourians by attacking them at night while they were sleeping.

Fired with the idea, Brown stormed out of the hotel and went to the earthworks on the outskirts of town in search of volunteers for the nighttime assault. He gave instructions on how to fire rifles (aim low, he said), and exhorted his followers to stand firm against a possible attack by the ruffians.

But his day for war had not yet arrived. Back in the hotel Robinson and Lane worked out a deal with Governor Shannon to end hostilities. Shannon, who had initially ordered up the Kansas militia, was not well disposed to the rowdy pack of Missourians that had answered his call to arms. Relaxed by the brandy Robinson and Lane served him, he agreed to order the proslavery forces to retreat and to give up a Free State officer they had seized. Thereafter, Shannon did not try to enforce the infamous black laws of the bogus legislature.

The Wakarusa War left John Brown more certain than ever that slavery would be abolished in Kansas. Amused by proslavery claims of having won the war, he wrote, "We learn by their papers they boast of a great victory over the *Abolitionists*," when in fact they had retreated "after incurring heavy expences; suffering great exposure, hardships, & privations, not having fought any Battles, Burned or destroyed any infant towns or Abolition

Presses; leaving the Free-State men *organized & armed,* & in *full possession* of the Territory." He added confidently, "Free-State men have only hereafter to retain the footing they have gained; and *Kansas is free.*"

This confidence buoyed him during the early part of the winter, which was so severe that it temporarily quieted quarrels over slavery. Temperatures often ranged from ten to twenty-eight degrees below zero. The snow, driven by harsh winds over the Kansas prairies, halted mail for a time and enveloped the Browns' makeshift cabins on North Middle Creek. Food ran out, and John Brown trudged east through the snow to Westport, Missouri, staying there a week to buy pork, flour, and corn. Henry and Jason shivered with ague, Owen and Oliver had frozen toes, and Frederick suffered a relapse of his mental trouble, accompanied by agonizing headaches. Pressed for money, John Brown was forced to sell his horse and wagon. On February 1, 1856, he bravely wrote Mary, "Our present wants are tolerably well met; so that if health is continued to us we shall not probably suffer much."

Poignant letters came from his eighty-five-year-old father, who sent $50 along with prayers for the salvation of his extended family. Aged and ill, Owen Brown knew death was approaching; it would come on May 8. A Calvinist to the end, he worried over his own spiritual condition and that of his loved ones. He wrote: "My sins are ever before me which ma God parden through the merits of Christ. I have great anxiety for my children even to the fourth generation. . . . Now I can do but little more than to commit them to the care of a mursafull God."

John Brown, though as devoutly Calvinistic as his father, was far more concerned about the sins of his nation than about his own or those of his family. The new year started propitiously enough, as on January 5 Brown served as chairman of an Osawatomie Free State convention that selected candidates for state office, including John Brown, Jr., for membership in the legislature.

But the election, held ten days later, reignited the clash over slavery. Although the heavily armed Browns met no illegal voters at their local voting place, at Leavenworth skirmishes broke out. Border ruffians hacked to death the Free State leader Reese P. Brown (no relation to John Brown), using hatchets and knives. They left Brown mortally wounded at the door of his cabin as his wife screamed in horror.

When he heard of this brutal murder and other attacks against Free-Soilers, John Brown prepared for war. He wrote home, "We have just learned of some *new;* & shocking outrages at Leavenworth: and that the Free-State people there have fled to Lawrence: which place is again threatened with an attack. *Should* that take place, we may soon again be called upon to 'buckle on our armor;' which by the help of God we will do."

Developments on both the local and national scene between January and May 1856 had a profound impact on Brown. These months marked an important turning point for him. The most controversial act of his life, the Pottawatomie slaughter, occurred on May 26. The incident has led some to dismiss John Brown as a psychopath who had come to Kansas only to stir up trouble and who gave vent to his murderous impulses at Pottawatomie. Brown's defenders have explained the act as retaliation against proslavery aggressions in Kansas.

Larger forces, however, contributed to the massacre. John Brown was no designing troublemaker; if anything, he had ended 1855 with an overly optimistic view of the Kansas situation, which he thought had moved clearly to the Free State side. Nor was his deed simply a payback to his enemies in Kansas. It can best be explained as an act of terrorism improvised at a moment when outside forces—some local and recent, others national and long-developing—converged in his psyche and set off within him an explosion of vindictive rage.

The first two months of 1856 brought a whole new dimension to the slavery conflict when President Franklin Pierce officially supported the proslavery legisature in Kansas. The handsome, affable Pierce had been elected in 1854 largely because he was expected to forge compromises on the slavery issue. But for him compromise meant weak-kneed concession to the South. Not only did he support the proslavery measures of the Compromise of 1850, but he signed into law the Kansas-Nebraska Act and endorsed slavery for Kansas.

When the first territorial governor he appointed, Andrew H. Reeder, turned against slavery in the summer of 1855, Pierce dismissed him and replaced him with the pliable Wilson Shannon. In spite of the atrocities committed by the border ruffians, Pierce stated that nothing illegal or immoral had taken place in Kansas. Worst of all, on January 24, 1856, he proclaimed the proslavery legislature at Shawnee Mission legitimate and its opponents treasonable. On February 11 he added that the United States government supported the proslavery Lecompton constitution and stood opposed to the Free State government in Topeka.

Supporters of slavery in the Territory were exultant. As Horace Greeley noted in his antislavery paper the *New-York Tribune*, "The Border Ruffians have been raised entirely off their feet by Pierce's extraordinary Messages, which they regard as a complete endorsement of all their past outrages and an incitement to persevere in their diabolical work."

It appeared, then, that Kansas had been officially given to slavery. John Brown, who had been sanguine about Free Soil's prospects in Kansas, was rudely awakened by Pierce's proclamations. On February 20 he wrote to Mary: "We hear that Franklin Pierce means to crush the men of Kansas. I do not know how well he may succeed; but I think he may find his hands full before it is over." On the same day he wrote Joshua R. Giddings, the antislavery senator from Ohio, that the federal government had sent troops to Kansas supposedly to expel Missourians from Indian land but actually "in readiness to act in the enforcement of those *Hellish enactments* of the (so called) Kansas Legislature; absolutely abominated by a great majority of the inhabitants of the Territory; and spurned by them up to this time." Brown asked Giddings what Congress could do to help the situation.

He could only have been frustrated by Giddings's equivocal reply that national troops would never attack Free State Kansans since such an attack would "light up the fires of civil war throughout the North." Nor could he have predicted that the Republican Party, formed in Pittsburgh on February 22, would turn into a large organization that during the next four years would galvanize the North against slavery.

Even his ostensible allies in Kansas, the Free State leaders, proved tepid in their resistance to the slave power. On March 4, the Free State legislature met in Topeka and chose governmental representatives, including James Lane and Andrew Reeder as U.S. senators, but proposed a compromise resolution pledging that the Free State Party would not attempt to enforce its laws unless Kansas became a state. John Brown, Jr., who served on two state committees, proved to be the most radical member of the group, since he was the only one present who voted against the resolution. He did, however, sign a petition to Congress requesting the admission of Kansas to the Union as a free state. He returned to Brown's Station on March 22 convinced that violence alone would settle the conflict over slavery in Kansas.

The other members of the family agreed. Their expectation in December had been that Kansas would quickly become free, but the Territory now seemed to be rushing toward slavery. The president of the United States had recognized the Lecompton constitution, and the Free State legislature in Kansas had proven weak in its counterproposals.

The Browns now assumed personal vengeance against the slave power. They suddenly felt they were in a state of war. Their letters to North Elba blazed with defiance. John Jr.'s wife, Wealthy, wrote on March 23 that "those miserable Missourians, barbarous scamps," were "getting together arms, men, and means, to make another desperate attempt to drive out the

Free State men here, but let them come, the people here are quite well supplied with arms, and have for the last six months had military Companies formed and are ready and determined to go forward and defend their rights even if it must be by bloodshed."

A week later John Jr. wrote a friend back east to spread the news that emigrants headed to Kansas should "by all means come thoroughly armed with the most efficient weapons they can obtain, and bring plenty of ammunition." With uncanny prescience, he predicted a war over slavery that would start in Kansas and later engulf the whole South:

> The question here is, shall we here be freemen or Slaves? The South is arming and sending in her men, the North is doing the same thing, it is now decreed and certain that the "Slave power" must desist from its aggressive acts upon the settlers of Kansas or if they do not, the war-cry heard upon our plains will reverberate not only through the hemp and tobacco fields of Missouri, but through the "Rice swamps", the cotton and sugar plantations of the Sunny South.

His notion that national war was "decreed and certain" unless slavery ceased its aggressions appears in retrospect so accurate a prophecy of the Civil War that it may seem that armed violence was then on the minds of many Kansans. It was not. The Free State leaders at Topeka had resolved not to enforce antislavery laws until Kansas was officially admitted as a Free State. Perhaps the ease with which they had won the Wakarusa War in December had fooled them into thinking that the slavery problem could be resolved through negotiation—eased, if necessary, with liquor. At any rate, by selecting two U.S. senators, they had chosen the route of politics, not violence.

Most Kansans, then, did not think that war was inevitable. But the Browns had come to think so. John Jr. said war was "decreed and certain" if the slave power remained belligerent. His father took a step beyond this vindictive attitude. He actually hoped proslavery forces would increase hostilities so that he could retaliate in kind. Having heard that federal courts in Kansas were planning arbitrary arrests of Free State settlers, he wrote home on April 7, "For One I have no desire (all things considered) to have the Slave power cease from its acts of aggression. 'Their foot shall slide in due time.'"

He gave this famous sentence from Deuteronomy fresh meaning. His favorite theologian, Jonathan Edwards, had made it the text of his sermon "Sinners in the Hands of an Angry God." For Edwards the statement signified the precarious state of sinful humans, doomed to slide at any moment into hell. For Brown it predicted the perils in store for supporters of slavery, not only in the afterlife but also in this life. Since Brown did not see anyone else in Kansas ready to answer proslavery violence with antislavery violence, he was prepared to buckle on God's armor and go it alone, joined only by his sons and a handful of others he had captained in the Wakarusa War. He felt he was commissioned by God to make the feet of the proslavery enemy "slide in due time."

He displayed his attitude at a public meeting held by Free-Soilers at Osawatomie on April 16. Initially, the tenor of the meeting, like that of the Topeka one the month before, was conciliatory. The topic was how Free State settlers should respond to President Pierce's proclamations. The Reverend Martin White, who straddled the fence between the antislavery and proslavery side, argued that since the weight of the federal government was now unequivocally behind the Shawnee laws, it would be treasonous for any Kansan to break these laws or to refuse payment of taxes in protest.

John Brown rose angrily and denounced this position, declaring, as White later recalled, that he was "an Abolitionist of the old stock—was dyed in the wool and that negroes were his brothers and equals—that he would rather see this Union dissolved and the country drenched with blood than to pay taxes to the amount of one-hundredth part of a mill."

This is the first recorded instance of Brown's mentioning a national bloodbath in connection with his antislavery convictions. That he came up with this image of "the country drenched with blood" at this time, in April 1856, suggests that national events had pushed him beyond any residual qualms about war into a military frame of mind.

He framed the image in radical racial terms. He said he was a "dyed in the wool" Abolitionist who saw blacks as "his brothers and equals." This declaration was revolutionary. He knew that most Free-Soilers in Kansas detested Abolitionism almost as strongly as did their proslavery opponents, especially when it was coupled with a belief in the equality of the races.

Although his outburst led some allies at the meeting to support a resolution denouncing Lecompton, it impelled Martin White and several others to walk out in disgust. White, realizing that his views on race accorded with those of the Missourians, soon switched to the proslavery side. Four and a half months later, on August 30, Martin White, leading an attack on the Free State community at Osawatomie, would kill John Brown's son Frederick.

The intervening period was the most controversial in John Brown's life. Convinced he was now at war, Brown, along with his sons and followers,

John Brown in Kansas, 1856.

committed violent deeds unprecedented in the history of American anti-slavery activism.

He now welcomed confrontations with the partisans of slavery. According to his son Salmon and others, he disguised himself as a federal surveyor and ran his chain through a camp of 400 proslavery troops led by Colonel Jefferson Buford. He overheard Buford's men boast that soon they would annihilate every one of "those damned Browns" and would stand by the Lecompton laws "until every damned abolitionist was in hell." Salmon recalled tersely, "They did not know at that time that they were talking to old Puritan stock," adding that John Brown returned home "well served up for future action."

Although this anecdote could be apocryphal, there is no doubt that proslavery elements in the region hated and feared the Browns. At the end of April, a proslavery judge, Sterling G. Cato, issued warrants for the arrest of John Brown and his sons, either because they had attended the April 16 Free State meeting or simply because their overt Abolitionism was against the law. Cato held a court session in a tavern near Osawatomie owned by Henry Sherman, a proslavery settler.

To test Cato, John Brown sent his son Salmon and his son-in-law Henry Thompson on a ten-mile trek to the session to see if the judge would dare to arrest them. If he did, Brown planned to rescue them the next day. Salmon, uncomfortable at being used as Abolitionist bait, recalled, "I thought father was wild to send us, but he wanted to *hurry up the fight.*"

The scene at Cato's court bristled with animosity. When the appearance of Salmon and Henry failed to provoke an arrest, John Brown, Jr., entered the courtroom as the judge was declaring on behalf of the Shawnee laws. Seeing what Cato was about, John left and reentered, demanding whether or not the judge planned to enforce the iniquitous laws. When Cato insisted that the court was not to be disturbed, John went outside and shouted, "The Pottawatomie Rifle Company will meet at the parade ground." Some thirty armed men obeyed the command. The show of force had an effect, since Cato, who had indicted three Free State men for petty crimes, did not serve the indictments. He broke up the session and left for Lecompton, the proslavery center. Never again would he try to hold court in the Osawatomie region.

Several of the proslavery men present that day at the court would become John Brown's victims on Pottawatomie Creek a month later. The owner of the tavern where Cato held court, Henry Sherman, would escape Brown's violence through the lucky accident of being away the night Brown invaded his cabin, but his brother William was killed.

The three Sherman brothers, bachelors known as Dutch Henry, Dutch Bill, and Dutch Pete, had moved to Kansas from Oldenburg, Germany, in 1844. They typified foreign emigrants from Germany and Ireland, most of whom supported slavery when they settled in the American territories. Dutch Henry, a towering hulk of a man, ran his store and tavern at a section of Mosquito Creek that came to be known as Dutch Henry's Crossing. His main customers were the cross-country emigrants passing east or west, from whom he was wont to pilfer horses or cows.

There is no way of confirming neighbors' rumors that the Shermans were drunkards who sexually harassed Free State women and pimped for Native American women they captured and forced into prostitution. But by all accounts they were a brutal trio cut in the mold of border ruffians. Dutch Henry once threatened to hang a local merchant, the elderly Squire Morse, for selling Frederick Brown lead to be used for Free State bullets.

Also present at Cato's court were James P. Doyle, who sat on the grand jury, and his oldest son, the twenty-two-year-old William, who served as bailiff. Both would be murdered, along with William's twenty-year-old brother Drury, by Brown's band at Pottawatomie.

James Doyle and his illiterate wife, Mahala, were indigent whites who had left Tennessee in November 1855, when they felt financially squeezed as nonslaveholders in a slave state. Relocating to Kansas with their daughter and three sons, they at first objected to slavery on economic grounds but became avid members of the proslavery Law and Order Party because they hated Abolitionists far more than they did slavery.

The Doyles considered blacks to be brutes. Henry Thompson got a taste of their racism when he met them at a Kansas polling booth late in 1855. Referring to a supposed lack of intelligence and feeling among slaves, James Doyle declared, "Sell husband, wife or children; they do not care anything about it." Thompson retorted, "Look here, old man! I've seen colored men as much smarter than you are as you are smarter than that little dog running along yonder." Doyle replied, "That is incendiary language, and you will have to pay for it yet."

Another who would be killed by Brown's men, Allen Wilkinson, appeared as district attorney at Cato's court that day. A man of some education, Wilkinson had migrated from Tennessee to Kansas, where he built a cabin that doubled as a post office a mile north of Dutch Henry's Crossing on Mosquito Creek. Wilkinson was briefly a Free-Soiler before turning strongly proslavery. Elected by voter fraud, he was a member of the Shawnee legislature that in 1855 passed the notorious laws against Abolitionism. George Grant, a Free State settler, later said of Wilkinson: "He was a dangerous man. Everybody feared him. He was the most evil-looking man I ever saw. He abused his wife shamefully. She was a very nice woman, and well-liked by the neighbors." Grant's comments may have been exaggerated; Wilkinson's wife denied them, insisting that her husband was a loyal Law and Order man who did not abuse her.

Still, there was no question about Wilkinson's fierce hatred of Abolitionists, which he shared with the Shermans and the Doyles. All were known to desire the extermination of Abolitionists. According to one report, the night before he was killed, Wilkinson had told his wife of a plan to kill all the Free State people living in the region.

Such threats from individual proslavery settlers, however, formed only a small part of the background for the killings John Brown carried out at Pottawatomie. Several events between late April and mid-May—the shooting of the proslavery sheriff Samuel J. Jones; continued assaults on Free State people; the sack of Lawrence by border ruffians; and news of the vicious caning of Charles Sumner by Preston Brooks in the U.S. Senate—added fuel to John Brown's desire for retaliatory vengeance.

Sheriff Jones wanted to get back at the Free State men who had in

December taken from him his prisoner Jacob Branson, whom he had arrested on false charges in the shooting of Charles Dow. Jones now issued equally bizarre arrest warrants against six people on the charge of contempt of court. On April 23 he got into a quarrel with an antislavery man who punched him in the face. He organized a posse of ten to take the charged men into custody. That evening, while he was sitting in his tent, he was shot by Charles N. Riler, a Free-Soiler from New York.

Although Jones was not seriously wounded, the proslavery press, to provoke vengeance against the Free State faction, spread the news of his "murder." The *Squatter Sovereign* on April 29 wrote, "We are now in favor of levelling Lawrence and chastising the Traitors there congregated, should it result in total destruction of the Union." A week later the same paper wrote, "In a fight, let our motto be, 'War to the knife, and knife to the hilt.' Jones' Murder Must Be Revenged!!"

Proslavery violence increased. The Reverend Pardee Butler, who had bravely returned to Kansas after being tied to a raft and stoned the year before, was tarred, cottoned, and left stranded on the open prairie; he was told that if he returned to Atchison he would be hanged. On May 5, John Stewart died after ruffians shot him in the back simply because he had said he was an Abolitionist. When three Free State men rode out to investigate the crime, one of them, Charles Lenhart, asked the guilty ruffians where they were going. The answer was a shot that killed Lenhart.

Free State settlers found themselves endangered when Judge S. D. Lecompte, responding to President Pierce's support of Kansas's proslavery laws, ordered a grand jury to indict members of the Topeka legislature for treason. Indictments for the arrest of several Free State leaders, including Robinson and Lane, were issued.

The supporters of slavery now saw ample justification for attacking Lawrence, the Free State capital. By definition most of the people living there, including Robinson and Lane, were traitors. On May 11 the federal marshal, J. B. Donaldson, made the spurious claim that rebellious people in Lawrence had interfered with the execution of the proslavery indictments. He issued a call for "law-abiding citizens of the territory" to gather for an attack on the town.

Some 750 Missouri border ruffians and recently arrived Southerners led by Jefferson Buford answered the call. The tipsy ruffians, dressed in their customary red flannel shirts, mingled with the Southerners, many of whom had come from Alabama to save Kansas for slavery. The South Carolina flag, with its crimson star and the state motto, Southern Rights, waved above the throng, as did a transformed American flag, with a tiger in place of the stars. Also flapping in the breeze were banners with inscriptions such as THE SUPREMACY OF THE WHITE RACE, ALABAMA FOR KANSAS — NORTH OF 36 DEGREES 30, and YOU YANKEES TREMBLE, / AND ABOLITIONISTS FALL, / OUR MOTTO IS, / SOUTHERN RIGHTS TO ALL.

A group of terrified Lawrence settlers issued a statement promising obedience to the Shawnee laws, but to no avail. A leader of the ruffians told his men to be brave and orderly, but "if any man or woman stand in your way, blow them to hell with a chunk of cold lead!" His troops, who were in their usual state of raucous intoxication, gleefully ignored the command to be orderly and looked forward to following the one about blowing Free-Staters to hell.

They were disappointed, because on May 21 they swarmed into Lawrence virtually unchallenged. Free State leaders, including Lane and Robinson, had fled the town, believing that defense was hopeless. The ruffians ransacked the offices of two antislavery newspapers, the *Herald of Freedom* and the *Kansas Free State*, destroying equipment and hurling type into the Kansas River. They burned Robinson's house and looted other homes. They destroyed the Free State Hotel with gunpowder and thirty-two shots from a cannon. In all, they inflicted more than $200,000 in damages.

The sight of the smoldering ruins of the hotel delighted Sheriff Jones, who declared: "This is the happiest moment of my life. I determined to make the fanatics bow before me in the dust, and kiss the territorial laws; and I have done it—by G—d, I have done it." The next morning's *Lecompton Union* said of the demolished hotel, "*Thus fell the abolition fortress;* and we hope this will teach the [New England Emigrant] Aid Society a *good lesson for the future.*"

The Browns heard about the attack too late to do anything about it. On May 21 a messenger came to Brown's Station reporting that Lawrence was about to be attacked. John Jr., who had been planting corn, called together the Pottawatomie Rifles, now thirty-four strong, and led them in a gallop up Ottawa Road toward Lawrence, twenty-five miles away. By evening his father and brothers joined up with them on California Road near Middle Creek.

The group camped for the night at Mount Vernon and at daybreak resumed the ride. When a second messenger reported that Lawrence was being razed without resistance, the men proceeded to Middle Ottawa Creek, where their Indian ally Ottawa Jones gave them a quick breakfast of milk and cornmeal. While they were eating, another messenger brought the terrible news that the ruffians had completed their damage and had retreated. John Brown urged the volunteers to move forward to engage the enemy, which had regathered at Lecompton and controlled the crossing of the Marais des Cygnes River. A vote was taken, however, to stay for the night on Middle Ottawa Creek and wait for reinforcements.

John Brown now had one thing on his mind: violent retribution. Infuriated by the failure of the Free-Staters in Lawrence to defend themselves, he became, as a friend said, "wild and frenzied, and the whole party watched with excited eagerness every word or motion of the old man." Sometime during the night of May 22, in the camp on Middle Ottawa Creek, he came up with a "radical retaliatory measure" that would punish "designated men prominent in enforcing Border Ruffian laws." The plan would involve "some killing."

The next morning over the breakfast campfire he consulted with several of the men in the group, including his close allies James Townsley and Theodore Weiner. Townsley, a painter who lived near Pottawatomie Creek, said glumly, "We expect to be butchered, every free state settler in the region." Weiner, a Jewish storekeeper described by Salmon Brown as "a big, savage, bloodthirsty Austrian" who "could not be kept out of any accessible fight," added that Dutch Bill Sherman and other proslavery Germans along the Pottawatomie had threatened to kill the Free State settlers who failed to leave the area.

John Brown's steel-blue eyes glared. "Something *is going to be done now,*" he declared. "We must show by actual work that there are two sides to this thing and that they cannot go on with impunity."

After breakfast he gathered the rifle company and called for volunteers. Weiner volunteered and went with him to Townsley, who offered his lumber wagon for carrying men and weapons to the Pottawatomie area. John Jr. pleaded, "Father, be careful and commit no rash act." His plea would prove as ineffective as Atchison's request for orderliness among his mob of ruffians. Brown had his men sharpen the two-bladed broadswords he had brought with him from Akron.

The final spark for his murderous violence was the news of Preston Brooks's beating of Senator Charles Sumner. The incident had occurred the day before, May 22, and probably news of it reached Lawrence late that afternoon. Sumner, the eloquent antislavery senator from Massachusetts, had offended Brooks by criticizing his kinsman Senator Andrew P. Butler of South Carolina in his speech "The Crime Against Kansas." In denouncing the western spread of the South's peculiar institution, Sumner had mockingly compared Butler to the "chivalrous knight" Don Quixote, in love with the ugly "harlot Slavery."

Brooks, a self-styled Southern gentleman with a tall frame and a stylish goatee, was infuriated by the speech. At the end of the Senate's session on May 22, he approached Sumner, who was sitting alone at his desk reading papers. After uttering a one-line rebuke for the insult to his state and his relative, Brooks hammered Sumner with the gold head of his gutta-percha cane. The stunned Sumner at first lurched toward his assailant, but his long legs were trapped under his fixed desk, and he quickly became a supine target for Brooks's blows, which came so fast that the floor was slippery with blood. After beating Sumner senseless, Brooks calmly walked out of the Senate chamber.

Jason Brown never forgot the reaction of his father and his followers when they heard about the assault on Sumner from a messenger who rushed into the camp. Jason recalled, "At that blow the men went crazy—*crazy*. It seemed to be the finishing, decisive touch." When someone advised Brown to use caution, he snapped, "Caution, caution, sir. I am eternally tired of hearing that word caution. It is nothing but the word of cowardice."

He was taken over by an instinct for violent revenge. Although the immediate reasons for this revenge—the events of the past three months, culminating in the sack of Lawrence and the caning of Sumner—were compelling, they do not sufficiently explain the murders he was about to commit. To account for them, we must look at their social and cultural contexts.

The slaughter at Pottawatomie was far more than a payback for individual misdeeds by the border ruffians or by Preston Brooks. It was an impetuous expression of long-delayed retaliation for years of Southern violence against Abolitionists and against blacks.

At Pottawatomie, John Brown gave the South some of its own medicine. Up to that time, social violence had manifested itself far more frequently in the South than in the North. John Brown showed that the North, too, could use the tactics of murderous force.

As historians have shown, the antebellum South was a culture of violence and vigilante justice, characterized by eye-gouging, bowie-knife stabbing and scalping, hanging, burning over slow fires, whipping, tarring and feathering—all reflected in the extraordinary violence of Old Southwest humor.

To be sure, the North also experienced social violence. But, as historian David Grimsted notes, there were significant differences between the violence of the two sections. "In the South," Grimsted writes, "social violence of most kinds was only rarely repressed or punished, so it became a tolerated, even sanctioned mode of social control. . . . Northern criminals and mobs tended to endanger property rather than injure people, while proto-typical Southern rioters, like their counterparts in crime, attacked persons more than property." When Northern mobs *did* target people, they focused on minority groups or Abolitionists, much like the Southerners—a phe-nomenon epitomized during the Civil War by the New York City draft riots, an explosion of Negrophobic violence.

Judge Lynch ruled in the South to an extent that it never did in the North. And the judge ruled mainly on race- and slavery-related issues. Abolitionists (or, rather, anyone even faintly suspected of pro-Northern feeling) were common victims of Southern violence. "Acts of Southern public violence which drew little or no official response provide a stomach-churning catalog of butchery," writes Grimsted, who adds that "in well over 90 percent of these Southern criminal mobs, there was no legal protection of victims nor legal action against perpetrators." Southern "murderers were commonly expected to leave the area or submit to arrest, but they were sel-dom pursued by the law."

Southerners committed murders for the paltriest of reasons. A code was established whereby "killing was all right if any prior threat had occurred." It was common practice in the South to assault people when they were defenseless: "sneak attack, attack from ambush, attack on the unarmed or even the sleeping, attack on one by several did little to detract from the honor of these public maulings or murders."

The South's penchant for violence was well known among both the opponents and the supporters of slavery. "Pistols, dirks, bowie knives, or other instruments of death, are generally carried throughout the slave states," wrote the Abolitionist Theodore Dwight Weld in 1839, "and . . . deadly affrays with them, in the streets of their cities and villages, are mat-ters of daily occurrence." Southerners took pride in such violence, associat-ing it with chivalric manliness. Henry A. Wise, a Virginia politician who was the state's governor when John Brown was captured there, bragged that with the bowie knife alone the South could defeat the North with all its armaments. "The best way to meet the abolitionist," Wise declared, "is with cold steel and Dupont's best [gunpowder]!"

The duel was an accepted way of settling disputes among Southerners, as typified in the famous duels of Henry Clay against John Randolph, William J. Graves against Jonathan Cilley, and Thomas L. Clingham against William L. Yancey. No one thought the less of President Andrew Jackson because he had once killed an opponent in a duel and had assaulted another with a gun and a knife.

The deadly interfamily feud was also commonplace, accounting for no less than a fifth of the killings and maimings in the antebellum South. Mark Twain's portrait in *The Adventures of Huckleberry Finn* of the feuding Shepherdsons and Grangerfords reflected a gruesome reality. Buck Grangerford tells Huck: "A feud is this way. A man has a quarrel with another man, and kills him; then that other man's brother kills him; then the other brothers, on both sides, goes for one another; then the *cousins* chip in—and by and by everybody's killed off, and there ain't no more feud."

The act that was the immediate trigger of John Brown's murderous rage—Preston Brooks's assault on Charles Sumner—epitomized Southern violence. It involved not just family honor but *distant* family honor; the man Brooks avenged was a cousin of his father. The provocation for the attack, Sumner's mild political insult, was negligible. The mode of confrontation, the pummeling of a defenseless opponent, was typically cruel. The outcome, too, was predictable: the North was outraged, while the South viewed Brooks as a hero.

Far from trying to cloak his crime, Brooks brandished it. Reporting that he had landed "about thirty first-rate stripes" with his cane, he boasted: "Every lick went where I intended. For about the first four or five licks he offered to make a fight, but I plied him so rapidly that he did not touch me. Towards the last he bellowed like a calf. I wore my cane out completely but saved the head, which is gold. The fragments of the cane are begged for as sacred relics. Every Southern man is delighted and the abolitionists are like a hive of disturbed bees. They are making all sorts of threats. It would not take much to have the throats of every Abolitionist cut."

He was right about Southerners being delighted. Editors, mass meetings, and student groups hailed him throughout the South. Huge cheering crowds greeted him wherever he appeared, and he was showered with gifts, including canes with the inscriptions such as HIT HIM AGAIN and USE KNOCK-DOWN ARGUMENTS. The *Richmond Enquirer,* the South's leading paper, called antislavery senators "a pack of curs" who "have become saucy, and dare to be impudent to gentlemen" and thus "must be lashed into submission. . . . Let them once understand, that for every vile word spoken against the South, they will suffer so many stripes, and they will soon learn to behave themselves like *decent dogs*—they never can be gentlemen."

John Brown, in his camp in Kansas, did not witness the South's reaction to "Bully" Brooks, but he could have predicted it, since the Territory's proslavery press was full of such vitriol.

Newspapers in Kansas and Missouri seethed with savage threats against Abolitionists. B. F. Stringfellow in the *Squatter Sovereign* did everything he could to prompt violence against Free State Kansans. It was useless to expect peace in the Territory, he announced, "as long as one enemy of the South lives upon her soil, or one single specimen of an abolitionist treads in the sunlight of Kansas territory." Elsewhere he fulminated, "We cannot feel safe while the air of Kansas is polluted with the breath of a single Free-soiler. . . . Self-preservation requires the total extermination of this set." Goading border ruffians to bloody action, he wrote: "We are determined to repel this Northern invasion, and make Kansas a Slave State; though our rivers should be covered with the blood of their victims, and the carcasses of the Abolitionists should be so numerous in the territory as to breed disease and sickness, we will not be deterred from our purpose."

Along with such rant went a smug contempt for what was seen as the spinelessness of Abolitionists. Grimsted notes that of all the charges leveled by Southerners against the Abolitionists "none was pushed harder than that they were cowards." Advocates of slavery taunted their opponents, saying that bowie knives, hemp, and tar and cotton were waiting for Northerners who ventured south. The Richmond preacher William L. Plummer spoke for many Southerners when he said, "Abolitionists are like infidels, wholly unaddicted to martyrdom for opinion's sake. Let them understand that *they will be caught* [lynched] if they come among us, and they will take good heed to keep out of our way. There is not one man among them who has any more idea of shedding his blood in this cause than he has of making war on the grand Turk."

In the Wakarusa War, when the Free State side put up resistance to the ruffians, a contemporary witness noted, "This was entirely unexpected on the part of the invaders. They never imagined the possibility of the abolitionists showing fight." The ease with which Lawrence fell was attributed to the cowardice of the Free State settlers. The ruffian leader David Atchison raised cheers among his men by boasting, "Boys, to-day I'm a Kickapoo Ranger, by God! This day we have entered Lawrence, and the abolitionists have not dared to fire a gun!"

The South's violence prompted both self-criticism and self-justification among Abolitionists. William Lloyd Garrison was frustrated by the North's weakness in the face of proslavery threats. He asserted, "It is only for some few seditious hot-spurs at the South to brandish their cowskins or bowie knives, and shout, 'We'll dissolve the Union!' and straightway we turn pale, our knees smite together, our tongues cleave to the roofs of our mouths!" At the same time, Garrison's distaste for slaveholders' violence nurtured his pacifism, which stood in opposition to what he called "the supremacy of the bowie knife, the revolver, the slavedriver's lash, and lynch law" in the South.

Many Northerners conceded that their own weakness put them at a disadvantage in the slavery conflict. A New England journalist said it was widely assumed that "Kansas would of course become a slaveholding State" because "the peaceable and industrious people of the free-labor States were not familiar with the use of the bowie-knife and revolver, and therefore not likely to place themselves in any dangerous proximity to the armed champions of Slavery."

The lack of tough antislavery warriors in Kansas was of great concern to the Free State editor G. W. Brown, who lamented in a letter to Eli Thayer: "We do not love to blush for New England, and yet we are often compelled to do so for her degenerate sons. It is a common subject of remark among Missourians that the New Englanders are mere Sunday School *Children*, and that they are not adapted to border life. In any other place than Kansas it would be a high compliment to them; but here we want sterner material." He said above all he wanted "to prevent *cowards* from coming here, as we prefer no emigration at all to the miserable platroons who fly at the first approach of danger."

True, some Free State Kansans *talked* about violent reprisal against their proslavery foes. Charles B. Stearns, a former Garrisonian nonresistant, assumed a violent stance when he moved to Kansas from the East. Calling the border ruffians "drunken ourang-outangs" and "wild beasts," he claimed it was his "duty to aid in killing them off." He explained, "When I deal with men made in God's image, I will never shoot them; but these proslavery Missourians are demons from the bottomless pit and may be shot with impunity."

Such talk, however, was rarely accompanied by action. The historical record indicates that the proslavery side committed most acts of violence. Of the fifty-two who died in the Kansas slavery battles of 1855 to 1858, almost 75 percent were Free State settlers. Of the thirty-six Free State casualties, twenty-eight were murders; the remaining eight occurred during battle. In contrast, only eight on the proslavery side were murdered. Among the rest, five died in battle, two were killed accidentally by their own violence, and one was shot when he disturbed a Free State meeting.

The eight proslavery people murdered included the five John Brown killed at Pottawatomie. It was John Brown who, more than anyone else, "brought Southern tactics to the Northern side," as a contemporary journalist put it. There was appropriateness in Brown's using terror to avenge the sack of Lawrence and the caning of Sumner, typically Southern acts of violence met by characteristic Northern timidity. Sumner's helpless passivity before Brooks's sadistic attack was not unlike the inability of the citizens of Lawrence to resist the invading border ruffians. The Missourian David

Atchison told his troops outside Lawrence that the gutless Free-Staters, who had not fired a shot, "tonight . . . will learn a Southern lesson they will remember." The federal officer Nathaniel Lyon sneered at "the wanton cowardice" and "the craven fear of Northern men in abandoning their helpless families to the merciless outrages of the inexorable savages."

John Brown agreed with these sentiments. He called the Free State residents of Lawrence "cowards, or worse" for not resisting the border ruffian invasion. At Pottawatomie he would prove that a Northern group could slaughter the enemy just as Southern mobs had for decades: on a negligible pretext, using a sneak attack when the enemy was defenseless, and with disregard for possible punishment—punishment that for Brown, as for 90 percent of the antebellum Southerners involved in mob action, never came.

A crucial question remains: How could John Brown square murder with his religious faith? He was, after all, a Christian, and most Abolitionists of his day used Christianity to endorse pacifism, not violence. Even if we say that Kansas was in a state of war, how could he, as a Christian, commit what amounted to a war crime?

By mid-May 1856 the events in Kansas and on the national scene made the Old Testament God of Battles seem more relevant to him than the New Testament's Prince of Peace. In this sense he followed the example of his greatest hero among white Christians, Oliver Cromwell.

The leader of the English civil wars of the mid seventeenth century, Cromwell was the historical figure with whom John Brown was most often associated. Brown loved to peruse Joel Tyler Headley's sympathetic biography *The Life of Oliver Cromwell* (1848).

Brown patterned himself after this Puritan warrior to such a degree that he was known in his day as a second Cromwell. For Wendell Phillips, it was Brown the "Cromwellian" who made social violence, once a Southern phenomenon, a Northern one as well. Phillips pointed out that in former decades the "men of violence, men who trusted in their own right hands, men who believed in bowie knives" were mainly Southerners attacking Abolitionists. The violence "was all on that side," Phillips declared; but now "the tables have been turned . . . and men who believe in violence, the five points of whose faith are the fist, the bowie knife, fire, poison, and the pistol, are ranged on the side of Liberty." John Brown had changed everything. Phillips explained, "You cannot expect to put a real Puritan Presbyterian, as John Brown is—a regular Cromwellian, dug up from two centuries—in the midst of our New England civilization, that dares not say its soul is its own. . . . Put a Christian in the presence of a sin, and he will spring at its throat if he is a true Christian."

It was not only the Calvinistic Phillips who linked Brown with Cromwell. Many others did so as well, including William Lloyd Garrison, who declared, "He was of the old Puritan stock, a Cromwellian, who believed in God and at the same time in 'keeping his powder dry.' "

Brown matches Cromwell more closely than he does any other historical figure. Both were devout Calvinists who ascribed their deeds to God. Both had lowly beginnings: Cromwell started as a farmer, as did Brown. Both lost sons by their side in battle. Both saw themselves as warriors against oppression. Both demanded discipline, morality, and sobriety among their followers; both were harsh, unrelenting men with a tender domestic side. And both were murderers. They are hard to admire wholeheartedly, because they took innocent human life.

Cromwell, having led English Puritans to victory over the royalists, directed the beheading of the king (standard procedure in revolutions) and then committed war atrocities (*not* standard). Many of Charles I's followers had fled to Ireland, which was full of Catholics, anathema to Cromwell. As the new commander in chief and lord lieutenant of Ireland, Cromwell presided over massacres in several Irish towns where his army met resistance. After taking over Drogheda, he ordered his troops to kill by the sword every armed citizen and every tenth Irish soldier. Over 2,000 were killed in this way. The streets were strewn with corpses, and the gutters ran with blood. Not only did Cromwell praise God for assisting him in this work, but he conducted similar slaughters at Wexford and Tredah. Understandably enough, to this day Cromwell's name is reviled in many parts of Ireland.

Despite Cromwell's obvious shortcomings, many nineteenth-century Americans, especially New Englanders like those who funded John Brown's raid on Virginia, idolized him. The North's reverence for Cromwell, an unacknowledged source of the Civil War, is discussed in the next chapter. Brown, who often quoted Cromwell's phrase about trusting in God and keeping one's gunpowder dry, was familiar with the Puritan leader's use of violence to enforce what he considered Christian principles.

The most positive way to view Cromwell's and Brown's crimes is to regard them as what Doris Lessing calls "good terrorism"—that is, terrorism justified by obvious social injustice. Terrorism is violence that avoids combat, is used against the defenseless (often civilians), and is intended to shock and horrify, with the aim of bringing about social change. Cromwell's massacres in Ireland and Brown's Pottawatomie murders may qualify as terrorism on these counts.

It might be argued that excessive force in each case challenged real social injustice: centuries of oppressive British royalty in Cromwell's case and the twin horrors of chattel slavery and Southern violence in Brown's. Just as the populists of late czarist Russia, to whom John Brown was compared in the nineteenth century, are sometimes called "good" terrorists because they envisioned a free, nonviolent society, so Brown is open to a sympathetic interpretation because he used violence in order to create a society devoid of slavery and racism.

Choice of victims is a consideration in gauging whether terrorism is "good." Wholesale slaughter of numerous innocents, as in the September 11, 2001, attack on the World Trade Center, resists this affirmative reading.

Was Brown justified in his choice of victims at Pottawatomie Creek? The most extreme statement he was known to have made on the topic was his declaration to the Free State settler James Hanway that he "proposed to sweep the creek . . . of all the proslavery men on it." If this statement accurately describes Brown's intentions, it avoids the stigma of indiscriminate killing, but just barely. It specifies its victims by politics ("proslavery") and by gender ("men"); but the phrase "sweep the creek" sounds arbitrary, as though he were out to kill any political enemy he could find in the area. If, however, Pottawatomie was a response to long- and short-term proslavery outrages waged against carefully selected targets, it becomes less random and thus more defensible.

Brown's sons Jason and John Jr. insisted that their father did not go on an unsystematic murder spree but instead chose his victims, who were active in proslavery politics and had challenged the Browns personally. As mentioned, three of the victims—James P. Doyle, his son William Doyle, and Allen Wilkinson—had served at the proslavery hearing of Judge Cato, who had issued warrants for the arrest of the Browns. Another victim, William Sherman, was part of the family whose tavern at Dutch Henry's Crossing was the local center for proslavery activities, including Cato's trial. William's brutish brother Henry Sherman had threatened to lynch a merchant who sold lead to Jason Brown.

That John Brown at Pottawatomie was responding to the combined forces of proslavery violence and personal threats was the view of James Hanway, a Free State judge who was a reliable witness because he knew all the parties involved and wrote careful notes in his memorandum book about the incident when it occurred.

An Englishman who had settled in the area in 1856, Hanway reported that the men who would be Brown's victims had constantly threatened opponents of slavery. James Doyle and his oldest son had warned an antislavery store owner they would kill him unless he left the Territory. Dutch

Henry Sherman had often terrorized Free State residents, saying he would "shoot & exterminate" them. When he heard about the sack of Lawrence, he raised a red flag over his cabin to celebrate the beginning of all-out war. Allen Wilkinson, said Hanway, was so abusive of Free State people that his wife upbraided him for opening himself up to deadly retribution.

These Pottawatomie settlers, Hanway argued, reflected the mentality of proslavery violence that Brown answered in kind. Hanway reported that "a base conspiracy was on foot to drive out, burn, and kill;—in a word the Pottawatomie creek from its mouth to its fountainhead was to be cleared of every man, woman, or child who was for Kansas being a free state." A typical proslavery newspaper praised the destruction of Lawrence and urged ruffians to exterminate every "black hearted abolitionist and drive them from the Territory." After John Brown's killings on the Pottawatomie, Hanway claimed that the proslavery forces had gotten their due:

> They advocate assassination and now that 5 persons have been murdered on their side perhaps they will learn that such hellish sentiments when carried into effect, will work equally to the destruction of the pro-slavery men of the territory. Such [proslavery] men are the immediate instigators of all such bloody tragedies we have witnessed—they should be held responsible at the bar of public opinion.

There was also a racial element in the murders. Most of the other killings in Kansas occurred in the familiar arena of gun battles, road skirmishes, and vigilante-type executions. They were "typical" of violence on the part of white frontiersmen.

John Brown's sword murders, in contrast, were primitive. They shared the spirit of the retaliatory savagery of two minority groups John Brown knew well, rebellious slaves and oppressed Native Americans. The murders were related to such atrocities as Nat Turner's bloody nocturnal rampage or the scalping raids of Indians. John Brown not only wanted to kill proslavery people, he wanted to do it in a way that insurrectionary slaves or embittered Indians would have done it.

His act of violence surged from the heart of racial oppression. Like his later revolutionary schemes—including his stealing of eleven Missouri slaves, his convention of blacks in Chatham, Canada, and his plan for a massive slave rebellion in the South to be sparked by the Harpers Ferry raid—it stemmed from his racially motivated vindictiveness.

Pottawatomie's connection to the Nat Turner affair (both of them nighttime murders of proslavery people by knife-wielding antislavery bands) seems obvious but actually is less relevant than its link to the Native American issue.

In Kansas there was a close link between the incursions of slavery and the maltreatment of Native Americans. As late as 1854, Kansas was still so sparsely settled that no settlement there could be identified as a white town or village. Native Americans, many of whom had been forced out of the East, were the main inhabitants of the Territory. Although white towns formed as proslavery and antislavery forces competed for supremacy after the passage of the Kansas-Nebraska Act, Indians were by far the largest ethnic group during the time John Brown was there.

In warring against proslavery forces, John Brown was defending the rights of not only African Americans but also of Native Americans. Indian tribes occupied the finest lands in Kansas. From 1854 onward, proslavery settlers took control of most of these lands through unfair bargains, outright confiscation, or deadly force. A contemporary journalist noted, "Nearly all of the Indian agents [i.e., white officials who dealt with the natives] were slavery propagandists, and many of them owned slaves." The first to introduce slavery into Kansas was the Reverend Tom Johnson, an illiterate, coarse, slaveholding minister who appropriated some of the Shawnee tribe's finest land and converted it into Shawnee Mission, a proslavery center.

Thereafter, proslavery settlers attempted to spread the so-called blessings of the South's culture, including its incongruous mixture of Christianity and slavery. Nearly 100,000 Cherokees, Creeks, and Choctaws established Christian communites in the territory south of Kansas, in what is now Oklahoma. These Indian communities had newspapers, churches, and, shockingly, slavery. Many Cherokee farmers owned black slaves.

Most of the natives who remained in Kansas, however, adopted few white customs other than excessive consumption of firewater. For the most part, the natives in Kansas were cheated or displaced by the invading whites.

Both proslavery and antislavery whites were prejudiced against the natives. The Free State settlers loathed the prospect of Indians remaining in Kansas as strongly as they desired the exclusion of blacks.

John Brown and his family were as unusual on the Native American issue as they were in their opinion of blacks. John Brown's respect for Native American culture dated from his Ohio childhood and ran through his adulthood. A story dating from his period in western Pennsylvania during the 1820s, when he was starting his family near Meadville, showed his deep sympathy for Indians. Every winter, natives from western New York would flock to the Meadville area to hunt. Many times the Browns welcomed groups of natives, supplying them with food and provisions. Some local white families, incensed over the annual arrival of the Indians, went with guns to John Brown's house, asking him to join them in driving off the natives. John Brown replied firmly, "I will have nothing to do with so mean an act. I would sooner take my gun and help drive you out of the country."

His notion of fighting racist whites while aiding Indians was fully realized in Kansas, where he befriended the natives as he battled the proslavery types who were trying to displace them. From the start, the Browns established friendly relationships with local tribes such as the Sacs, the Foxes, and the Ottawas. Bands of thirty to forty natives would frequently pass back and forth near Brown's Station. Often four or five would break off from the pack and ride over to talk with the Browns. "While we were in Kansas," recalled Jason Brown, "I did not know, or hear of a single act of unkindness by any of these Indians to the white settlers."

In the summer of 1855, John Jr. visited a nearby Indian chief, who was so pleased with their meeting that later he sent members of his tribe to the Browns bearing gifts of melon and corn. The chief made it clear to John that he would have nothing to do with the efforts of whites to "civilize" Native Americans. Civilization, the chief indicated, was corrupting. "We want no houses and barns," he said. "We want no schools and churches. We want no preachers and teachers." He added with a laugh, "We bad enough now." His tribe met in council and chose the Browns as the surveyors of its land, sensing it would thereby be protected against proslavery settlement.

On the eve of the Pottawatomie killings the Browns found that racism tainted even their close followers. John Jr., after seeing his father off with an anxious warning not to do anything "rash," liberated two enslaved blacks (a teenaged boy and girl) from a farm a dozen miles outside of Lawrence. His subordinates in the Pottawatomie Rifles denounced this bold action, calling it "a great mistake and a terrible outrage upon humanity."

His brother Jason reported later that the freeing of the slaves "raised a good deal of commotion and division among us" on the issue of race. He explained: "It was objected to by the 'Free White State' men, as they called themselves, who wanted Kansas only for whites, when it should be admitted into the Union as a State, leaving out the broken and disheartened remnants of eleven or twelve tribes of 'red man' around us, for another removal and the black man to be sent into a still more hopeless bondage." The volunteers, who "did not want to mix up with 'niggers' or abolitionists," voted to return the blacks to their owner. They also voted to relieve John Jr. of his command of the company.

The incident showed that the problems of blacks and Indians were intermingled. In the eyes of the Browns, the "hopeless bondage" of the slaves and the removals of "broken and disheartened" native tribes were equally despicable. For " 'Free White State' men," in contrast, both blacks and Indians were loathsome creatures to be banished from the presence of whites. Most Free State whites in Kansas were just as racist as their proslavery opponents, whom they were more inclined to compromise with than to murder.

John Brown's actions around the time of his Pottawatomie raid show how distanced he was from such racism. Not only did he respect Native Americans, but his closest ally, other than family members, was the half-breed John Tecumseh "Ottawa" Jones. He finalized his plan on the reserve where Jones lived, and after the killings he spent much of his time there. He later credited his Indian friend with saving him and his family from starvation in the desperate months just after the raid.

Ottawa Jones was a prosperous and well-educated farmer who lived on the ten-mile-square Ottawa reserve along with more than three hundred other Indians. He had attended Hamilton College and in 1845 was married to a Maine woman who had come to Kansas as a missionary to the Indians. He owned over a hundred cattle and fourteen horses, and his three-hundred-acre farm produced 4,000 bushels of grain annually.

Jones was familiar with the cruelty and treachery of whites. He had established a large hotel that was burned to the ground by forty proslavery men, who also stole money from his wife. His total loss was between $6,000 and $10,000. He had also witnessed the apostasy of Dutch Henry Sherman. For years Sherman had worked on Jones's farm, until he earned enough to venture out on his own. While working for Jones, Sherman had been equivocal on slavery, but when he left to run the store on Mosquito Creek he became a rabid proslavery activist.

On the Joneses' reserve, near Middle Ottawa Creek, was a way station where Brown and his party camped the night of May 22. Brown's group used a large grindstone there to sharpen the two-edged broadswords that had been brought from Ohio. The swords, inscribed with eagles, were reportedly left over from a failed filibustering scheme to take over Canada. Now they were going to be put to the service of a new kind of filibuster: one against slavery and racism, one that coupled the gratuitous violence of Southern lynchings with the bloodiness of revolts by enslaved blacks and massacres by Native Americans.

While he was at Middle Ottawa Creek, John Brown consulted with the Free State resident Henry H. Williams, telling him he and his group were "going back there to break up Cato's court and get away with some of his vile emissaries before they got away with us." Although Williams gave Brown the names and locations of several members of the court who lived along Pottawatomie Creek, he recoiled from the prospect of the murders.

He was not alone in his doubts. James Townsley would claim that upon hearing the details of Brown's murderous scheme, he tried to back out of it, relenting only when Brown insisted that he was vital to it. John Jr. warned his father against rash action, and Frederick and Oliver were unwilling participants in the raid.

But the plan aroused enthusiasm among those who, like John Brown, thirsted for reprisal. In the early afternoon of Friday, May 23, Brown and six others—his sons Frederick, Salmon, Oliver, and Owen, his son-in-law Henry Thompson, and James Townsley—rolled out of the Ottawa Creek camp in Townsley's lumber wagon. They were armed with rifles, revolvers, and the broadswords. Beside them, on a pony, rode Weiner, the volatile Austrian. As they left, cheers erupted from those left behind.

Brown conducted the group to a grassy ravine in the woods a mile north of Dutch Henry's Crossing. The eight men spent the night and the following day there, making preparations for the attack. When Salmon expressed doubts about the planned slaughter, Brown declared that it was time to "fight fire with fire," to "strike terror in the hearts of the proslavery people." He insisted that "it was better that a score of bad men should die than that one man who came here to make Kansas a Free State should be driven out."

Around ten o'clock at night on Saturday, May 24, the men seized their weapons and walked a mile north on California Road to Mosquito Creek, wading across it to the area near the Pottawatomie where the proslavery settlers lived. They went first to the cabin of one of the settlers (most likely J. H. Mentzig, who had been a juror on Cato's court) to draw him out. The muzzle of a rifle poked at them through a chink, and they backed off. They went on to the nearby home of James Doyle and his family.

Near the Doyle property, two savage bulldogs attacked them, barking furiously. Townsley killed one of them with his sword; the other fled howling into the woods.

In the cabin James Doyle, his wife, Mahala, and their six children lay asleep. A sharp rap on the door drew Doyle out of bed. He asked the identity of the caller and was answered by a man asking directions to Allen Wilkinson's house. As soon as Doyle opened the door to explain, five armed men barged into the house. The leader, John Brown, who wore a straw hat and a black cravat, announced that they were from the Northern Army and were taking Doyle prisoner. Mahala Doyle, bursting into tears, cried to her husband, "Haven't I told you what you were going to get for the course you have been taking?" He grumbled, "Hush, mother, hush."

She watched in horror as the invaders led him and her two oldest sons, William and Drury, out into the night. She begged them to spare her sixteen-year-old son, John, and they did, knowing that he was not a member of the proslavery Law and Order Party, as the others were. As terrified as she and the young children were, they could not have imagined the atrocity that was about to happen.

Brown's band led the three captives two hundred yards up the road that led into the woods. Owen and Salmon fell on them, hacking away with the heavy swords. In the melee, horrible wounds were inflicted. Drury Doyle's fingers and arms, raised to fend off blows, were severed, and his head and chest were gashed. His brother was stabbed through the head, jaw, and side, and the father was wounded in the breast. Although John Brown did not participate in the attack, he fired a single shot into the head of the senseless James Doyle to make sure of death.

The group proceeded half a mile to the cabin of Allen Wilkinson, who had been the acting district attorney at Cato's trial in April. His wife roused him when she heard the dog barking outside, but he mumbled that it was only passersby and dozed off again. In a few minutes loud knocking brought him to the door. He asked the callers who they were. The reply was a shouted request for directions to Dutch Henry's cabin. He began to answer but was told to come out and show the way.

When he opened the door, he found himself surrounded by four men. He was asked curtly to explain his position on slavery. When he indicated that he opposed the Free State party, one of them declared, "You are our prisoner. Do you surrender?" Having no choice, he responded, "Gentlemen, I do."

He requested to be allowed to go off in search of help for his wife, who had the measles, promising to return by morning and give himself up. When John Brown asked the sick woman if there weren't any neighbors who could stay with her, she replied that they were away and she was too ill to look for them. Brown muttered, "It matters not." He told Wilkinson to dress and led him outdoors before he could put on his shoes. As he was taken away, one of Brown's group returned to the cabin and took two saddles, informing Mrs. Wilkinson that her husband was being taken "a prisoner to the camp."

A hundred and fifty yards from the cabin Wilkinson met the same fate as the Doyles. Henry Thompson and Weiner, possibly with the help of one of the younger Browns, slashed him to death, stabbing him in the head and side. They heaved his body into dead brush.

The final victim, William Sherman, was staying at the home of a proslavery friend, James Harris, on the other side of the Pottawatomie. Brown's party waded across the creek toward Harris's cabin. By this time, midnight had passed. The pious John Brown, once so careful about observing the Sabbath that he accepted no visitors on Sunday, was now prepared to kill on that day.

Intent on finding another proslavery person, he and the others—except for Frederick, Weiner, and Townsley, who stood guard outside—broke into Harris's cabin at sword point. They found Harris along with three house-guests, William Sherman, John S. Wightman, and Jerome Glanville. Sherman's views on slavery were well known to them, but those of the others were not. Wightman, a traveler who had stopped at Harris's for the night, must have persuaded them he was not an active supporter of the proslavery side, for they left him alone.

They were less sure about Glanville and Harris, who were taken outside successively for interrogation. Had they ever threatened Free State settlers? Had they hosted border ruffians? Had they participated in the sack of Lawrence? They answered the questions satisfactorily and remained unharmed.

When Brown and his party learned that Dutch Henry, their main target, was out on the prairie searching for lost cattle, they decided upon his brother Dutch Bill instead. They led Sherman to the edge of the creek, where Brown's two youngest sons, along with Weiner and Thompson, felled him. The next morning James Harris found the partly submerged body. There was a deep hole in the chest, and one of the hands was sliced off, connected to the arm only by a piece of skin. Brains oozed into the creek through a gash in the skull.

The bloody work was done. Having confiscated horses and other property from his victims, Brown and his followers washed their swords in the creek and then rode back to the camp on Middle Ottawa Creek. A messenger had preceded them there with the news that five proslavery men had been "horribly cut and mangled" on the Pottawatomie and that "they said old John Brown did it." John Jr. was at first exultant but soon became confused and then deranged. Most in his rifle company were appalled, calling the act "barbarous & inhuman."

Adrenaline had carried the murderers through the night, but now emotions were frayed. Owen, usually stoical, wept convulsively. As dawn broke he said to Townsley, "There shall be no more such work as that." At Ottawa

Jones's place, Jason Brown asked his father if he had killed those men. Brown replied that he had not committed the murders but had directed them. Jason denounced the slaughter as "an uncalled for, wicked act." His father responded, "God is my judge. It was absolutely necessary as a measure of self-defence, and for the defence of others."

As it turned out, God was the only judge John Brown would have to face for the Pottawatomie murders. Vigilante justice ruled in the Territory, and many previous killings over the slavery issue had gone unpunished. Although a proslavery court issued an indictment for the arrest of Brown on charges of murder, the case was not taken up immediately due to the chaotic state of the Kansas legal system. In the meantime, Brown and his followers hid out in the wilderness, resurfacing occasionally to battle proslavery forces. By the end of September, he had left Kansas for the East to raise funds for his war against slavery.

James Townsley, a reluctant member of the band, remained in Kansas and, ironically, took the burden of blame. The case, initially named *Territory v. John Brown, Senior et al.*, was changed in the court records to *Territory v. James Townsley, for murder*. Four murder indictments were served on Townsley, who was arrested on November 24. However, the confusion of the territorial justice system, along with an absence of witnesses, caused long delays, and ultimately the case was dropped.

In the weeks just after Pottawatomie, the proslavery press, predictably, bellowed about the "Abolitionist" murders. The *Border Times*, in an article reprinted in two other proslavery papers, swelled the number of Brown's victims. The headline declared,

**WAR! WAR! EIGHT PRO-SLAVERY MEN MURDERED
BY THE ABOLITIONISTS IN FRANKLIN COUNTY,
K. T. LET SLIP THE DOGS OF WAR!**

By this time, such shrieking headlines about war and extermination were so common in the local papers that the real horror of the Pottawatomie incident did not stand out in the general mayhem. It wasn't long before the real facts about the murders became known. On June 5 the *St. Louis Morning Herald* reported: "The blood-curdling story of the murder by night of *five men* who were at the time quietly sleeping, thoughtless of danger, in their own homes, is fully confirmed. . . . The accursed wretches *mangled and mutilated the bodies they had slain!*"

Brown's responsibility for slayings became common knowledge. A proslavery manifesto against Abolitionist "robbers and assassins" who kill "law-abiding citizens" denounced "Brown and his banditti with the blood of the murdered Wilkinson, and Sherman, of Doyle and his sons, not yet cold upon his hands." Similarly, a Leavenworth paper excoriated "Brown, the notorious assassin," and the *Squatter Sovereign* blasted "Brown the notorious assassin and robber." A St. Louis paper portrayed Brown as the leader of a large band of killers: "John Brown, Sen., known as the Osawattomie Murderer, is still at large, at the head of about 300 thieves and murderers, who, like himself, are not only outlaws here, but were so in the states from which they came."

Garbled versions of the story reached the eastern papers, and John Brown was associated with the killings. Again, however, the unique quality of the slayings was underemphasized because of what was seen as the generally explosive state of affairs in Kansas. Newspapers were still abuzz over the sack of Lawrence and the assault on Sumner, which had preceded Pottawatomie and which helped muffle its immediate impact.

The incident proved to be one event in a crescendoing string of violence that sent Kansas into a state of anarchic war. William A. Phillips, the most reliable contemporary historian of Kansas, noted that within a month of Pottawatomie, "outrages were so common that it would be impossible to enumerate them. Murders were frequent, many of them passing secretly and unrecorded." Likewise, editor O. C. Brown reported a "reign of terror" in the region, as "almost daily murders are committed . . . and nothing done." Another witness noted proslavery atrocities "of brutal ferocity from which the wildest savages might have shrunk with horror," including thirteen slaughtered men "who had been seized and brained, some of them being shot in the forehead, and others down through the top of the skull, whilst some were cut with hatchets and their bodies shockingly and disgustingly mutilated."

Did Pottawatomie end slavery's prospects in Kansas? Not the way John Brown had intended. His supporters overstated the matter when they claimed that his violent act frightened proslavery settlers so much that many of them left Kansas, leaving it to the Free State side.

True, the Pottawatomie area was no longer a comfortable place for proslavery people. Brown's brother-in-law, the Reverend Samuel L. Adair, who lived near the scene of the killings, reported, "Some pro-slavery men took the alarm & fled." Likewise, James Townsley claimed that "the proslavery men were dreadfully terrified, and large numbers of them soon left the territory. It was afterward said that one free-state man could scare a whole company of them."

But it is wrong to think that Brown's crime cleared all or even a significant part of Kansas of slavery's supporters. Battles between the opposing sides would rage through the remainder of 1856 and through the first half of 1857, with no single event standing out as a deciding one. Kansas, despite its violent birth throes, would be admitted to the Union in 1858 as a Free State mainly because of the steady buildup of Northern settlers who would finally succeed in prohibiting slavery by the ballot.

If Pottawatomie had only a minimal impact on slavery in Kansas, it was destined to have a huge, if oblique, impact on the nation. It initiated the South's misreading of the North as aggressively Abolitionist. Although Pottawatomie was unprecedented in Abolitionist annals, Southerners called it characteristic of the Northern antislavery party.

The germ of the misreading appears to have been a widely reprinted letter that first appeared in the proslavery *Kansas Weekly Herald of Leavenworth* shortly after the murders. The letter was written on May 30 by Henry C. Pate, an irascible captain in the Missouri state militia and a correspondent of the paper who had gone to Osawatomie to help federal troops hunt down John Brown and his sons. Pate called Brown's group "an organized band of Abolitionists, armed and equipped to thieve, murder, and resist all law. Such is the Free-State party here."

This erroneous pairing of John Brown's murderous band and "the Free-State party" launched a series of misreadings that snowballed as time passed. In early June the *Squatter Sovereign* announced, "Midnight murders, assassinations, burglaries, and arson seem now to be the watchwords of the so-called Free State party." Shortly thereafter Mahala Doyle, who had fled to Missouri, testified against John Brown before a Jackson County justice of the peace. Her devastating testimony, printed in the *Kansas Weekly Herald*, presented Brown as the satanic leader of the Kansas Free State sector: "With an eye like a snake, he looks like a demon. Apparently a miserable outlaw, he prefers war to peace, that pillage and plunder may the more safely be carried on. And this is a leader of the Free State party in Kansas."

John Brown was *not* "a leader of the Free State party in Kansas." Nor, for that matter, was he ever linked to *any* antislavery political organization or reform group. But this wild inaccuracy became the most common charge against him—not just in Kansas and Missouri but throughout the South.

The misreading gained a national audience later that summer when an essayist for *DeBow's Review*, the South's most widely read journal, pointed to Pottawatomie as proof that the Abolitionists "have secret military organizations for resisting the laws" and killing proslavery people. "By such banditti the murders near Ossawatomie, on Pottawattamie creek, were committed," the writer averred. After giving many gory details of the slayings—and embellishing them with the report that Allen Wilkinson was "flayed alive, his nose and ears were cut off, his scalp torn from his head"—the essayist generalized:

> Incredible as these things may seem, they unquestionably happened in Kansas Territory in the latter part of last month; yet what is more incredible, but not less true, is the undeniable fact that these outrages are not, as some pretend, the mere extravagances of a few irresponsible individuals, but on the contrary are justly chargeable to the abolition party, as the legitimate fruit of their party measures and party discipline, and as naturally resulting from the public teachings, advice, and counsel of their chief men and most distinguished leaders.

The statement was absurd. Far from being "justly chargeable to the abolition party," Pottawatomie was an utterly anomalous event, even by Kansas standards. The midnight slashings were at the farthest remove from the antislavery movement's "public teachings," whether those teachings took the form of Garrison's pacifism, Harriet Beecher Stowe's Christian reformism, Lincoln's temperate nonextensionism, or Horace Greeley's antislavery columns in the *New-York Tribune*.

Pottawatomie was so anomalous that it even caused dissension and confusion among those closest to John Brown. Owen agonized over his part in the incident. John Jr. soon lapsed into temporary insanity. When Jason, who excoriated his father for the deed, asked Fred if he had killed any of the men with his own hands, Fred broke into tears and said, "No; when I came to see what manner of work it was, I could not do it."

Even John Brown sent mixed signals. A couple of weeks after the event he wrote Mary deceptively that he was fleeing authorities because he was "accused of murdering five men at Pottawatomie." Over time he would change his tune about the killings. His usual story—that he directed the killings but did not participate in them—was, by the best evidence, true. But his retellings ranged from self-indictment (he once reflected that perhaps he was guilty of murder) to self-righteousness (another time he said God had ordained his five victims to be murdered).

As for Free State people outside Brown's family, they too were sharply divided about the murders. Judge Hanway, Rev. Adair, O. C. Brown, and others saw them as justified retaliatory strikes that intimidated slavery's defenders. In contrast, Amos Hall, Edward Bridgman, and John T. Grant condemned them as barbaric and unmerited.

When neither the murderer's family nor the murderer himself nor the

Free State Kansans could agree on the meaning of his crime, how could the *DeBow's* essayist claim that this crime reflected the "party measures" and "public teachings" of Northern antislavery leaders? The essayist was the first to make what would become a common misreading of John Brown—i.e., that he epitomized Northern antislavery sentiment—which fed directly into the Civil War.

Brown had changed the terms of the slavery struggle. Before Pottawatomie, the Abolitionists were considered laughable cowards who either shirked war, as at Lawrence, or could be whipped into submission, as in the caning of Sumner. After it, they seemed like ferocious criminals intent on attacking Southern institutions.

John Brown had aroused a new emotion in slavery's defenders: fear of Northerners. As a contemporary observer noted, "There is no one for whom the ruffians entertain a more wholesome dread than Captain Brown. They hate him as they would a snake, but their hatred is composed nine tenths of fear."

If Pottawatomie fanned Southern hostility, it also set the stage for his eventual deification among Northerners. It made John Brown a marked man in Kansas, and border ruffians and federal forces pursued him. It was his stubborn resistance to capture in the aftermath of Pottawatomie that nurtured the legend of his seemingly superhuman heroism, a legend that eventually gained wide currency in the North.

Like most legends, this one was part truth and part myth. The year just after Pottawatomie saw John Brown displaying real courage in the antislavery battle and then winning strong support by peddling himself as a mythic American warrior.

8

Pariah and Legend

The John Brown legend was built upon the dramatic events of the summer of 1856. Some of the events involved extraordinary pain, others extraordinary courage. The painful ones would elicit pity from Brown's supporters, the courageous ones admiration.

Pity was aroused by the image of Brown as a persecuted pariah cruelly treated by proslavery forces in Kansas. Brown would exploit the image in his fund-raising tours in the East, emphasizing the extreme suffering he endured fighting slavery in Kansas.

Left out of his self-presentation was the fact that he was, in one sense, a lucky man, not a victim. He had literally gotten away with murder. Although he spewed violent words against slavery, he knew the Pottawatomie killings would be a hard sell, even to those aware of his involvement in them. Instead of trying to capitalize on them, therefore, he emphasized his afflictions during that chaotic summer.

None of the afflictions was more pitiable than the experiences of his immediate family. John Jr. temporarily lost his sanity and endured months of incarceration and maltreatment at the hands of proslavery forces. Jason was also imprisoned and tormented by his captors. Then, at the end of the summer, Frederick was murdered.

The story later arose that these sorrows drove John Brown into a mad fury and prompted his antislavery violence—an obvious inaccuracy, since his most extreme violence had come *before* that summer. The summer of 1856 did not drive John Brown crazy, but it did make him more committed than ever to the forceful overthrow of slavery.

The Pottawatomie incident threw his Kansas family into confusion. John Jr. and Jason left Middle Ottawa Creek for Osawatomie, where their wives had fled. When they reached the cabin of their Uncle Samuel and Aunt Florilla Adair, they were delighted to find their wives there. The Adairs at first did not invite them in, fearing that proslavery troops would burn their cabin at any moment. They relented only when Jason assured them that neither he nor John had participated in the Pottawatomie slaughter.

They did, however, turn away Owen, who showed up at 2 a.m. on a horse he had stolen from the enemy. The Adairs sent him off, declaring, "You endanger our lives. . . . You are a vile murderer, a marked man!" Owen replied defiantly, "I intend to be a marked man!" and rode in search of his father, who was hiding in the wilderness with Theodore Weiner and several others.

Jason stayed with the Adairs two nights before leaving to seek federal troops who, he thought, might give him protection when he told them he was innocent of wrongdoing. John, increasingly deranged, passed a sleepless night in the cabin and then fled into the bush, believing pursuers surrounded him. He was captured in a ravine by a band of roaming Missourians led by Captain Henry C. Pate.

A former newspaper editor from Westport, Missouri, Pate had been born in Virginia and was the archetypal Southern gentleman: handsome, suave, and ardently proslavery. He had participated in the sack of Lawrence. After Pottawatomie he scoured the Osawatomie region with his Shannon's Sharp Shooters in search of the Browns. One of his lieutenants explained to a local paper, "We were heading down to the southern part of the territory, expecting to see rattlesnakes and abolitionists, and took our guns along."

Given this trigger-happy attitude, it is surprising the Sharp Shooters did not murder either of the Brown brothers when they captured them. It would seem that Pate, although full of proslavery bluster, feared possible reprisal from John Brown should his sons be killed.

Jason Brown met Pate's troop on a road near Ottawa Jones's. Thinking that only bravado would save him, Jason tore open his shirt and offered his chest as a target, declaring, "I have never knowingly injured a human being. Now if you want my blood for that, there is a mark for you." The tactic worked, for Pate held his men off, turning Jason over to a federal cavalry officer, Captain Wood, who drove him on a forced march to Paola to be held pending further investigation. He was kept inside a house under armed guard.

On his third night there, he was joined by his brother John, whom Pate had also handed to Wood. John was in chains. His mind had collapsed under the combined pressures of Pottawatomie, his rifle company's apostasy, and recent beatings at the hands of Wood's soldiers, who mistook him for one of his father's murderous band. He was so out of touch with reality that later on, when Missourians entered the house, he pointed to the chest of his sleeping brother and told one of them where to strike with his bowie knife. Instead of following the mad command, the ruffians roused Jason, bound him, and took him away, out of reach of the crazy John.

The brothers remained apart for two weeks and then were taken from Paola to Osawatomie, nine miles distant. Jason rode in a wagon, but John was forced to trot on foot. His wrists and upper arms were bound tightly behind him, and a forty-foot rope was tied around him so that he could be tugged. By the time the company reached the new camp, he was, as Jason reported, "a maniac and in a terrible condition." His arms were bleeding and so swollen that the rope around them was no longer visible. His feet had been severely lacerated by flints from creek bottoms that had punctured his boots.

At the camp he was attached to a tent pole by ox chains. In his wild state he believed he was the commander of the camp. He shrieked orders and heaved about in his chains. Jason was told to quiet him but replied, "I can't keep an insane man still." He attempted to calm John, who did not respond. When three guards tried pummeling John into silence, Jason yelled, "Don't kill a crazy man!" John sank into unconsciousness.

The brothers, along with five other Free State men, were next taken to Lecompton, where a proslavery court was to examine them. The sixty-five-mile journey was torturous. The Free-Staters were chained together by the ankles and forced to walk more than twenty miles a day. At one point they passed the Adair cabin. From the doorway Aunt Florilla cried, "What does this mean in this Land of the Free? What does this mean that you drive these men like cattle and slaves!" The *New York Times* reported that the forced march had "no parallel in republican government."

After a court investigation Jason was released, but John was charged with high treason because of his record as a Free State politician. Jason returned to Brown's Station only to find that Missourians had destroyed the family's two cabins. He then found his way to his father's wilderness camp. John would remain a prisoner until September 9, when he was released on bail.

Jason and John showed what could happen to Free State people if they took a weak position toward the proslavery side. Their father did the opposite: he went on the offensive. In doing so, he not only won a surprising victory, at Black Jack, but also succeeded morally even when he was defeated, at Osawatomie. The courage he displayed in the summer of 1856 did not save Kansas from slavery, but it lay the basis for the John Brown legend, which would prove to be a vital force behind the Civil War.

While the Pottawatomie killings provoked guilt or frenzy among most members of John Brown's Kansas family, they had little immediate effect on him other than making him more determined than ever to avoid cowardice. As always, he displayed more venom against the weakness of the Free State side than against the proslavery ruffians. In the June letter to Mary he denounced the Free State leaders who had "decided, in a very cowardly manner, not to resist any process having any Government official to serve it, notwithstanding the process might be wholly a bogus affair." He blamed the sack of Lawrence on this cowardice.

One of his followers reported that one night around the campfire Brown said to his band, "If the cowardice and indifference of the free-state people compel us to leave Kansas, what do you say, men, if we start South, for instance to Louisiana, and get up a negro insurrection, and thereby compel them to let go their grip on Kansas?"

Above all, he wanted to maintain a brave front. On May 26 he rode to Brown's Station with eight others: his sons Owen, Frederick, Salmon, and Oliver, his son-in-law Henry Thompson, Theodore Weiner, James Townsley, and August Bondi, a Hungarian Jew of Free State sympathies. Brown found his family's homes ruined and the area desolate. In the afternoon there arrived a Free State resident, O. A. Carpenter, who requested Brown's help in defending Prairie City, a village near Palmyra Township strategically located on the road between Lawrence and Osawatomie. Carpenter reported that Pate's band was preparing to seize the village, thereby threatening to cut off the Free State route between central and southern Kansas.

Agreeing to defend the village, Brown gave the order at dusk to make the twenty-mile northeasterly ride. The group, now ten with the addition of Carpenter, was armed with revolvers, muskets, and the broadswords used at Pottawatomie. Due to the shortage of saddles, the three youngest— Frederick, Oliver, and Bondi—rode bareback. On Brown's command, Frederick rode first, followed by Owen and Oliver, and then Brown himself, with the others in pairs behind him. As they approached the Marais des Cygnes River, they spotted a camp of what Carpenter recognized as federal dragoons commissioned to enforce the Territory's laws.

With typical brazenness Brown faced the soldiers head-on. He ordered Frederick and Carpenter to ride steadily forward. An armed sentinel saw them approach and cried out, "Who goes there?" "Free-State!" Frederick yelled. As the sentry hurried off to fetch an officer, Brown brought the rest of his party forward. The officer arrived and questioned the group. All except Carpenter remained silent.

Carpenter said he and his fellows were farmers who had heard Osawatomie was going to be attacked and had gone there to defend it against Missourians. They had seen none and were now going home. Carpenter repeated the story to a lieutenant who arrived late. The lieutenant bought the farmer story. When one of his men suggested holding the visitors for further investigation, he said sternly, "I have no orders to stop peaceable travellers, such as these people are; they are going home to their farms." Turning to Brown's group, he said, "Pass on! pass on!"

Slowly, Brown and his men rode through the federal camp and forded the stream beyond it. Once out of sight of the camp, they sped until four the next morning, when they stopped to recoup for a few days in a forest clearing half a mile from Ottawa Creek.

Brown was looking for an excuse to pick a fight with the proslavery side, and he got one on May 29 when two Free State men of the Prairie City area, Captain Samuel T. Shore and Dr. Westfall, arrived at his camp and told him that Missourians were stealing horses and threatening an attack on Willow Springs, twelve miles away. Brown asked Shore how many men he could muster and was disappointed to learn that the local residents were intimidated by the Missourians and disinclined to fight. Incensed, Brown asked Carpenter why he had brought him all this way if no reinforcements were forthcoming. Shore begged Brown to stay, insisting that his presence was all that prevented the Missourians from overrunning the area. Shore offered to try to gather volunteers. Brown gave him two days to do so.

In the interim, an unexpected visitor, James Redpath, arrived on the scene. The Kansas correspondent for the *New-York Tribune*, Redpath would later become Brown's first major biographer and an avid promoter of the John Brown legend. He chanced upon Brown's camp when he got lost near Ottawa Creek while looking for a preacher who had promised to take one of his newspaper pieces to Kansas City for mailing to New York. In the dense forest he encountered the physically imposing, wild-looking Frederick Brown, who recognized him as a Free State reporter and led him to the camp.

Along the way Frederick talked distractedly about Pottawatomie, insisting his family had nothing to do with the incident. If Redpath suspected Frederick of protesting too much, he never indicated it, since he later denied John Brown's involvement in the killings.

Redpath would never forget the wilderness camp. In the primeval setting of a clearing surrounded by huge logs were nine men, some lounging on blankets, others working or standing guard. Saddled horses were tethered near a creek, and rifles and swords were stacked against trees. John Brown, bent over a fire with his sleeves rolled up as he poked a roasting pig with a fork, was a picture of shabby dignity. A week's growth of white beard bristled on his cragged face, his clothes were soiled, and toes protruded from his worn boots.

He presented a noble image to Redpath, whom he recognized and welcomed. Unlike Frederick, he betrayed no anxiety. He deflected Redpath's questions about Pottawatomie and forbade his men to discuss the incident. He sensed that his words might reach a large audience, since the paper Redpath wrote for, the *New-York Tribune*, was the North's most influential antislavery paper. The pariah, detested by his enemies and doubted even by members of his own family, became in the presence of the New York journalist a persuasive promoter, explaining the cause with which he believed God had entrusted him.

If the Pottawatomie murders were on his mind, he showed no guilt, having evidently accepted them as divinely ordained. Although he had committed what many later called a heartless crime, he seemed the embodiment of virtue. He was moral to the point of prissiness. Redpath noted that no swearing or drinking was permitted in the camp.

At the same time, he left no doubt that antislavery violence was his main aim in life. For him violence was not only justified but also necessary, as long as it was carried out in the name of principle. He told his visitor, "I would rather have the small-pox, yellow fever, and cholera all together in my camp, than a man without principles. It's a mistake, sir, that our people make, when they think that bullies are the best fighters, or that they are the men fit to oppose these Southerners. Give me men of good principles; God-fearing men; men who respect themselves—and with a dozen of them, I will oppose any hundred such men as these Buford ruffians."

He soon got a chance to put this philosophy into action. The next day, Shore reappeared and reported that a force of Missourians and federals under the command of Captain Pate had gathered on the Santa Fe Road. Three of them had raided a building in Palmyra and had demanded some weapons, which the Free State people there handed over without resistance.

This cowardly capitulation by the Free-Staters inflamed Brown. Pate had taken two of his sons, had destroyed Brown's Station, and had chased him through the wilderness. It was time to turn the tables. When Shore announced that the next morning (Sunday, June 1) he would gather local residents for an attack on the Missourians, Brown declared, "We will be there!" Brown roused his men early and gave the order to march to Prairie City to join Shore's company. He was again preparing for violence on a holy day.

The nine men he commanded made a ragtag group. After eight days of bushwhacking, the men wore only "memories of what had once been boots and hats," as one of them said. As they left their forest hideaway on their stolen horses, they snickered over their own appearance. Only their captain, riding in the lead position, remained deadly serious.

At Prairie City, Brown found that Shore had gathered twenty volunteers, bringing the total to twenty-nine. Brown was told that the previous evening Pate had taken prisoner three Free State men: a doctor, a Baptist minister, and an Englishman named Lymer.

Before the day was over, the Free-Staters got a chance to retaliate. That evening, while Brown and the rest were at a religious service in Prairie City, a contingent of Pate's group attacked the village, assuming it would fall easily. In the middle of the service, someone yelled, "The Missourians!—They are coming!" The worshipers, including Brown, seized their guns and ran outside, firing on the six invaders and capturing three of them.

Brown learned that Pate's force was positioned in Black Jack, a boggy area (named for its blackjack oaks) four miles outside of Prairie City. In the dark of night he and Shore led their troops toward Black Jack, reaching the area at four the next morning. Two hours later a sentry for the proslavery group, having spotted Brown and his men, ran frantically to Pate, shouting, "The abolitionists are coming!" When Pate asked for details, the scout cried that "a hundred" abolitionists were advancing toward them across the prairie. Pate rapidly arranged his troops, some fifty-five strong, in a defensive position behind three wagons placed as a barricade between a sloping prairie and a ravine.

Since Brown could have no idea that the enemy had greatly overestimated his number, he approached the battle carefully. He left the horses with Frederick in a camp to the north of Pate, then had his men file forward in pairs, using declivities in the prairie as protection. Upon approaching the slope that stretched downward to Pate's barricade, he wisely broke to the right with a small group of fighters, descending into the ten-foot-deep ravine that passed around the enemy troops.

His fellow commander, Shore, bravely but foolishly headed over the open prairie toward Pate's barricade, receiving heavy fire. Realizing his precarious position, Shore soon joined Brown in the ravine. Rifle fire filled the morning air. In the heat of battle both sides experienced desertions. When

Brown saw a number of his men go to the safety of a distant hill, he went over and ordered them to take aim at the enemy's horses. They did so, and soon Pate's horses and mules were decimated.

Despite his small force, Brown was winning the battle when a bizarre event sealed the victory. Suddenly, Frederick, of all people, appeared on Owen's horse, Red Ned Scarlet, galloping across the battlefield, waving a sword and screaming, "Hurrah! Come on, boys! We've got 'em surrounded; we've cut off all communication." The Missourians shot at Frederick without hitting him. Frederick's words, which in his excited state he evidently meant, frightened Pate, who ordered his men to surrender. Pate sent out one of his Southern soldiers and a Free State prisoner carrying muskets with white flags tied to them.

The firing stopped, and the two men walked up the slope to Brown, who asked the Southerner if he was the captain of his group. When the Southerner replied negatively, Brown told him to stay with him, sending the other back to fetch the captain. Pate came forward and introduced himself as a representative of the Territory's federal marshal, saying he didn't suppose Brown would want to be waging war against the U.S. government. Brown cut him off with a brusque retort: "Captain, I understand exactly what you are, and do not wish to hear more about it. Have you a proposition to make me?" When Pate hesitated, Brown interjected, "Very well, captain; *I have one to make to you*—that is, your unconditional surrender."

Pate was not used to seeing such nerve in an Abolitionist. Brown and eight of his men went down to the wagon barricade, where Brown told Pate's lieutenant to command the proslavery troops, who now numbered twenty-three, to surrender their arms. The lieutenant balked and looked at Pate, who also hesitated. Brown quickly cocked a pistol and pointed it at Pate's head, hissing, "Give the order!" Within seconds, the proslavery force handed over their weapons, which Brown's party loaded into wagons to be hauled away. And so, with only nine on his side, Brown took twenty-three prisoners, as well as camp provisions and the few remaining horses.

In some ways, the Battle of Black Jack was as silly as its name. The threadbare Free State troops who laughed at themselves; the imaginary horde of Abolitionists who alarmed Pate into an overly defensive posture; the deserters who helped Brown win the battle by taking potshots at the enemy's horses; the crazy Frederick terrifying the Missourians into surrender—all lent an air of absurdity to the affair.

But if Black Jack was like a Monty Python movie, it had John Wayne playing the lead. For the first time, an Abolitionist made proslavery ruffians cower. If, as some say, "Bleeding Kansas" was the opening episode of the

Civil War, then Black Jack was its first real battle. Four of Pate's men were killed and many others were wounded. Eight Free-Staters received wounds, Henry Thompson and O. A. Carpenter serious ones. (After the battle Salmon Brown was crippled by an accident that was not combat-related.) Black Jack revealed that violent Abolitionism, when it took up arms, could puncture Southern intimidation and bluster.

It suggested, too, that John Brown brought more than violence to the antislavery side; he brought military skill. His ally, Shore, committed a mistake that during the Civil War would lead to numerous defeats and thousands of needless deaths on both sides—that is, opting for the heroic but self-defeating open-field charge against superior numbers. Had he continued down the slope to Pate's barricade, he would have been, in miniature, like Ambrose Burnside at Fredricksburg or George Pickett at Gettysburg.

In contrast, Brown employed a technique that he would use more famously at Osawatomie and that was the backbone of his Virginia plan— counteracting numerical superiority with guerilla attacks that took advantage of natural defenses. It was his side-angle shooting from a ravine and his men's long-range slaughter of the enemy's animals from a distant hill that explains Pate's growing terror, leading to his paranoid overreaction to Frederick's triumphant cry.

In one of the many coincidences that associated Brown's career with the Civil War, two Southerners connected with Black Jack, Henry C. Pate and J. E. B. Stuart, would become distinguished Confederate officers. After Harpers Ferry, Pate would visit Brown in his jail cell, and in the war he would rise to colonel of the Fifth Virginia Cavalry, dying on May 11, 1864, at Yellow Tavern, Virginia, on the same day and within a hundred yards of where the celebrated Stuart was killed. Stuart, for his part, was among the federal troops that arrived at Brown's camp a few days after Black Jack; three years later, under the command of another future Confederate leader, Robert E. Lee, Stuart would capture Brown at Harpers Ferry and would participate in the hanging of Brown.

Victorious on the battlefield at Black Jack, Brown was also clement as a captor. He took Pate and his men back to his camp, where he supplied them with whatever food he could muster. He drew up a treaty whereby he would let go of Pate and a lieutenant in exchange for the release of his sons Jason and John.

Unluckily for Brown, a copy of the treaty made its way to the U.S. garrison at Paola, alerting the federal officers there of the capture of Pate's force. On June 5, three days after the battle, Colonel Edwin Sumner, with a fifty-man cavalry force, arrived at Brown's camp, announcing that he was under orders from the president and the governor to disband armed groups throughout the Territory. When Brown told him of the treaty with Pate, Sumner gave lip-service assent to its terms, liberated Pate and his men, and retrieved the booty Brown had seized. Brown was furious to learn that he had upheld his side of the treaty, while the release of his sons would be delayed. Still, he must have been relieved that Sumner, perhaps because of his Free State leanings, did not arrest him despite the murder warrant against him.

Brown knew he had won a symbolic victory at Black Jack, one that he could parlay into eastern support for his cause. Early the next month he contributed a vivid account of the battle to the *New-York Tribune*. Without crowing, he communicated the major message of the battle: proslavery forces could be effectively challenged through courage and military skill.

It was Brown's courage, above all, that would impress his eastern backers, most of whom would be directly or indirectly linked to the Concord Transcendentalists. The group's philosophical leader, Emerson, would feature Brown in his lecture "Courage," and Thoreau would emphasize valor in his speech "A Plea for Captain John Brown." By the 1850s, in response to spinelessness in high places, the Transcendentalists had given their earlier notions a political edge, praising not just self-reliance but brash temerity, not just nonconformity but outright rebellion in the name of principle. Because they saw these qualities in Brown, they and their circle embraced the Kansas warrior when he arrived in Boston in early 1857.

What they did not know was that he had voiced ideas akin to theirs, evidently without having read them. August Bondi, one of Brown's Kansas group, recalled him saying that individuals must never "acknowledge laws and institutions to exist as of right if [their] conscience and reason condemned them." Brown "admonished us not to care whether a majority, no matter how large, opposed our principles and opinions. The largest majorities were sometimes only organized mobs, whose howlings never changed black into white, or night into day. A minority conscious of its rights, based on moral principles, would, under a republican government, sooner or later become the majority."

Brown's notion that individual conscience surpassed laws and majorities echoed Transcendentalist writings from Emerson's "Self-Reliance" through Thoreau's "Civil Disobedience" and *Walden*. It might seem odd that Brown, a Calvinist, arrived at ideas similar to those of the Transcendentalists, who rejected not only Calvinism but Christianity. Actually, though, Calvinistic Puritanism carried the seeds of Transcendentalism.

Puritans who held that God's indwelling grace superseded human law anticipated Emerson's concept of intuition as the highest law.

In one important respect, however, Brown was different from both the bygone Puritans and the Transcendentalists: that is, in his ability to avoid prejudice against people of different races, creeds, and classes. It is significant, for example, that Bondi, to whom he made the above remarks, was a Jew from Austria. Not only did Brown confer with Bondi on serious topics, but he also impressed him with his thoughtfulness. "He exhibited at all times the most affectionate care for each of us," Bondi wrote. "We were united as a band of brothers by the love and affection toward the man who with tender words and wise counsel, in the depths of the wilderness of Ottawa creek, prepared a handful of young men for the work of laying the foundation of a free commonwealth."

For an ultra-Protestant like Brown to be so close to a Jew was remarkable in the 1850s, when raging nativist sentiment impelled many American Protestants to anathematize Jews and Catholics, newly arrived from Europe. Nativists of the decade formed the American Party, the name referring to a bias in favor of WASPs born in the United States. Actually, John Brown was more American than the American Party, not because he was a New England–born WASP but because he embodied a basic democratic principle the party ignored: toleration.

His toleration extended to everything but slavery. He had what was then called monomania on that issue. Some thought this made him unbalanced, especially in the summer after Pottawatomie. Samuel Walker, a Kansas compatriot who joined Brown's group for a while, wrote to Free State judge James Hanway, "He was a great man but you and I know he was Insane in the summer of 56." Once, when Walker roused the sleeping Brown, he snapped awake, grabbed his rifle, and fired at Walker, who barely averted the bullet by pushing away the muzzle. A photograph of Brown from that summer shows a strange look about the eyes and mouth that is absent in other pictures of him.

The pressures of the moment—Pottawatomie, the imprisonment of Jason and John Jr., Black Jack, the burning of family homes, his weeks as a fugitive in the wilderness—made him more excited and intense than ever.

Still, to say that he went insane is going too far. Luke F. Parsons, who joined Brown at Black Jack and was close to him for over a year, wrote: "He always impressed me as a sane man. No one of his followers questioned this. It was evident to all that he was a man of intense convictions, a 'crank' on the subject of slavery and of absolutely fixed beliefs on it, but he was in

John Brown in 1857 (the so-called mad photograph).

every sense of the word sane." He recalled that Brown prayed often, asked God's blessing before meals, and "never tolerated profanity or foul talk among his men." "There was something strangely mysterious in his manner that commanded universal respect," Parsons added. "Where he was everyone acknowledged his leadership. No one ever questioned his authority because he spoke and acted as one who was to be obeyed."

Obedience to Brown meant breaking the law, at least the proslavery law of the Kansas Territory. He acted upon the Old Testament sanction for enjoying the spoils of the enemy. On June 3 and 4 he led a raid on a store in the California Road near the Franklin-Douglas county line, where he stole horses, cows, and some $3,000 to $4,000 in supplies. Here and in the future, all such gains, ill gotten or not, were directed toward the destruction of slavery.

In the chaotic state of Kansas, such plundering was commonplace on both sides of the political divide. Colonel Edwin Sumner, for example, injured and robbed several Free State citizens shortly after retrieving Brown's Black Jack booty and prisoners—"in good keeping," Brown wrote wryly, "with the cruel and unjust course of the Administration and its tools throughout this whole Kansas difficulty."

Brown and his small group spent June living, in his words, "like David of old, . . . with the serpents of the rocks and wild beasts of the wilderness; obliged to hide away from our enemies." Although he reported to Mary he was "not disheartened," since he believed God approved his actions, he was still irate over the Free State cowardice that had led to the destruction of Lawrence and the dwellings around Oswatomie. "It is said," he wrote disgustedly, "that both the Lawrence and Osawatomie men, when the ruffians came down on them, either hid or gave up their arms, and that their leading men counselled them to take such a course."

Determined to set an example of boldness, he came out of hiding on July 1. He left his company, which now numbered twenty-two, camped by the Wakarusa River, and rode into Lawrence, where he sent his letter about Black Jack to the *New-York Tribune* and made plans for what appeared to be a forthcoming battle stemming from a meeting of the Free State legislature to be held on the Fourth in Topeka.

While in Lawrence, he called on the antislavery journalist William A. Phillips, who was staying at the Eastern House. Phillips was born in 1824 in Scotland, had emigrated to America in his teens, and in 1855 became a Kansas correspondent for the *New-York Tribune*. He would soon publish the well-received history volume *The Conquest of Kansas by Missouri and Her Allies*; later he served as a Union general in the war and then as a three-term congressman from Kansas.

Brown intrigued Phillips. "He was always an enigma," he recalled, "a strange compound of enthusiasm and cold, methodic stolidity,—a volcano beneath a mountain of snow." That hot July 3 in the Eastern House the two discussed military strategy. Brown reported having visited several European forts, which he found to be out of date, explaining that principled soldiers were stronger than any fort. He showed Phillips two military manuals by the British revolutionary Hugh Forbes, whom he would later hire as a drill instructor, and he displayed an innovative repeating rifle with a range of eight hundred yards, though he stressed the superiority of fighting at close quarters.

Phillips decided to go with Brown on his trip to Topeka. Late that afternoon the two rode out of Lawrence to the summit of Mount Oread, where Brown's company was to join them. While they waited, Phillips admired the sunset view of prairies, rivers, and hills. "What a magnificent scene, captain!" he exclaimed. "Yes," replied Brown drily; "a great country for a free State."

They met up with the rest of the group on California Road. Brown was reticent—to keep discipline, he said—as he led his party toward Topeka. He became extra vigilant when the road passed near Lecompton, the proslavery capital. Near midnight he ordered a rest stop on a hillside southwest of Big Springs. The horses were picketed, and the company napped while he and Phillips, their heads on their saddles, stretched out on the dew-drenched grass and continued talking.

Brown revealed unexpected depths of knowledge and thought. Surveying the night sky, he pointed out the constellations, telling the time by them. His rapture over their beauty suggested to Phillips that "a poetic and impulsive nature lay behind that cold exterior." "The whispering of the wind on the prairie was full of voices to him," Phillips wrote, "and the stars as they shone in the firmament of God seemed to inspire him." All of nature, Brown said, "moves in sublime harmony in the government of God." Ever the Calvinist, he added, "Not so with us poor creatures." Human nature was flawed, erratic; nothing showed this more graphically than America's social ills.

These ills were not confined to slavery, Brown declared. America was plagued by "an infinite number of wrongs." Sounding like Thoreau, he insisted that capitalism diverted Americans from higher goals. Sounding like George Henry Evans and other land-reformers, he condemned "the sale of land as chattel," arguing that land speculators traded land for money without thinking of the poor.

None of these problems, however, approached the seriousness of slavery, the "sum of all villainies." Slavery must be abolished before other problems could be addressed. If it was not, "human freedom and republican liberty would soon be empty names in these United States."

Abolition required action, not talk. Kansas was an egregious example of the debilitating effects of slavery. The proslavery ruffians he dismissed as "brutal and coarse." He was equally disapproving of the Free State side, which he said consisted of timid compromisers who "would rather pass resolutions than act" and who "criticized all who did the real work."

Eager to set an example of action, he roused his company at 2 a.m. (neither he nor Phillips had slept) and resumed the trip. To avoid Tecumseh, a proslavery town, he left the road and headed across the open country toward Topeka, using the stars as his guide. The way was difficult, and the morning found his men floundering in a creek bottom. Before noon they arrived at the outskirts of Topeka. Brown parted ways with Phillips, who went into the town to attend the Free State meeting.

For all his talk of action, Brown chose not to fight the proslavery troops that had come to Topeka to break up the Free State legislature. Perhaps he found few natural defenses in the area that would help him defeat the large force led by Edwin Sumner. Probably, too, he was concerned for the safety of John Jr., who was being held nearby as a prisoner and thus risked being killed in reprisal for resistance to Sumner. Besides, four of his other sons— Owen, Salmon, Frederick, and Oliver—were sick, so that his force was not at top strength.

At any rate, Brown remained on a farm outside of Topeka while Sumner took over the Free State convention hall and quashed the forthcoming meeting. In a letter home Brown noted bitterly that Sumner's action was done "in the name of Franklin Pierce." Showing a brave face, he wrote, "A dreadful state of things exists here but I have not doubt but that in the end *Right* will triumph."

His appearance belied his optimism. He was fifty-six, but his gaunt, grizzled face made him look older. With four of his sons ill, another in prison, his son-in-law nursing his battle wounds, and the Kansas Free State party in disarray, he needed to recoup. He decided to go to Nebraska City in the neighboring Nebraska Territory, where two Free State leaders, James H. Lane and Charles Robinson, were to confer over tactics for Kansas.

Meanwhile, Kansas had risen to national prominence in ways unimaginable three months before. The sack of Lawrence and its stormy aftermath had made the Territory a cause célèbre for the new Republican Party, which at its convention on June 17 made the admission of Kansas into the Union as a Free State a chief plank of its platform. The National Kansas Committee, aimed at providing funds and weapons to Free State settlers, was founded in Buffalo, New York, and spread rapidly to all the other Northern states except Massachusetts, which already had several emigrant aid societies.

Before long, Brown would be milking these eastern organizations for support. For now, though, he prepared for fresh battles in the Territory. Such preparation was especially difficult now that the crippled Salmon and the injured Henry had lost their will to fight and Owen was reduced to a skeleton by ague. Brown put the three, along with Frederick and Oliver, who were also ill, into an ox wagon and, with other members of his company, rumbled toward Nebraska City.

Along the way there occurred an incident that contrasted with the generally solemn events of that summer. Oliver wanted to present a revolver he had captured at Black Jack to Lucius Mills, one of the company. John Brown objected, insisting that Mills, who had served as a nurse rather than as a soldier in the battle, would never use the gun. Brown got so worked up that he struggled with Oliver for the gun. Oliver, a tough man who had once thrown thirty lumberjacks in a day, easily restrained his father, Salmon later reported. "Father was like a child in his hands." Pinned against the ox cart, Brown shouted, "Let me go!" Oliver retorted, "Not until you agree to behave yourself." Overpowered by his muscular son, Brown at last relented and let Mills have the revolver.

Despite the momentary humiliation, Brown learned on the trip how famous his Kansas exploits had made him. On August 3 a group of Free-Staters led by Captain Samuel Walker, who was also going to Nebraska City to see James Lane, overtook Brown's party on the road. As the Free-Staters passed Brown, one of them pointed at him and cried, "There he is!" Deafening cheers filled the air. If the applause stirred Brown, he didn't show it. Driving his oxen slowly forward, he remained indifferent, glancing now and then at the passing soldiers. Fixed on the road ahead, in his worn hat and soiled clothes, he looked like a hard-pressed farmer on his way to work.

At Nebraska City he had strategy sessions with Lane and Walker. On August 7 he met Aaron Dwight Stevens, one of Lane's commanders, who would soon become an important member of Brown's cadre. The tall, dark-haired Stevens, who went under the alias of Charles Whipple, was a twenty-five-year-old Connecticut native who had fought in the Mexican War and in campaigns against the Indians of the western plains. Jailed in New Mexico after rebelling against a harsh officer, he escaped from prison in January 1856 and made his way to Kansas, where he lived among the Indians and became an effective Free State warrior. He joined Brown's force in Nebraska City and remained faithful to the end, cheerfully following his leader by dying on a Virginia scaffold for participating in the raid on Harpers Ferry.

As with August Bondi, John Brown's closeness to Stevens showed his complete tolerance of people of sundry faiths. In religious views, Stevens was as distant from the Calvinistic Brown as was the Jewish Bondi. An agnostic and a deist, Stevens liked to read aloud from Thomas Paine's *The Age of Reason*, which attacked Christianity as superstitious and false. "The Christian religion never looked consistent to me," Stevens once wrote, "and therefore I have had to look elsewhere for religion, and found it in the great Bible of Nature." Like many others of his era who rejected Christianity, he became a devout spiritualist, discovering in séances and table-rappings evidence of an afterlife. Although John Brown hated both deism and spiritualism, he prized Stevens because of his antislavery militancy. Once again, hatred of slavery became a higher religion that bonded Brown to a person of utterly different beliefs.

Brown needed followers like Stevens, since the family nucleus of his Kansas campaigns had broken up. After Nebraska City, illness and disenchantment with antislavery violence induced several of the Browns to leave the Territory. Owen, Salmon, Oliver, and Henry Thompson went to Iowa City, Iowa, where Owen would remain, while the others left variously for North Elba and Ohio.

John Brown remained so dedicated to the salvation of the Territory from slavery that he reentered the Kansas fray. With him was Jason, who remained healthy, and the simple Frederick, incognizant of danger and ever loyal to his father. The decision cost Frederick his life but led to his father's heroic performance at the Battle of Osawatomie, an effort that would give rise to the legend of "Osawatomie Brown."

Ironically, the South contributed to the legend, distorting the facts about Brown in order to demonize him but in the process setting him up for sanctification by the North. Atchison and Stringfellow, the leading proslavery editors, blamed Brown for antislavery actions he had nothing to do with. They insisted that he was behind August raids on proslavery strongholds at Fort Saunders, New Georgia, Fort Titus, and Treadwell, pumping up the raids with overblown headlines such as "War! War!! War!!! The Bloody Issue Begun!!" In fact, Brown knew of these raids but did not join them.

The proslavery smear tactics, repeated before a national audience when the August issue of *DeBow's Review* fantastically linked the Pottawatomie killings with Republican policy, contributed to Brown's mythic stature. A correspondent for the *New York Times* noted that Brown was not just another Free State warrior but was now known as the "terror of all Missouri" and the "old terrifier." As John Jr. wrote to his family from prison on August 16, "Father . . . is an omnipresent dread to the ruffians. I see by the Missouri papers that they regard him as the most terrible foe they have to encounter." The mere report that "John Brown is coming!" broke up many a proslavery meeting.

It was the *idea* of John Brown that terrorized the South. He was a new phenomenon: an Abolitionist who was committed to armed warfare against slavery and who showed no signs of relenting. As a Free State associate, R. G. Elliott, wrote, "Brown was a presence in Kansas and an active presence all through '56. Yet it was his presence more than his activities, that made his power,—the idea of his being. He was a ghostly influence. No man in Kansas was more respected. Yet after Pottawatomie he moved much in secret."

Nothing shows more clearly how "the idea of his being," rather than his activities, counted than the events of August 1856. For those who accepted the John Brown legend, it was during this month that Brown proved himself a brilliant military strategist and fearless antislavery warrior. For those who doubted the legend, it was then that Brown revealed himself as a malicious horse thief, a blundering captain, and a military loser.

Actually, both views were partly true. Brown's deeds that month were at best only moderately successful, at worst unethical, even illegal. The Battle of Osawatomie, destined to become the chief ingredient of the John Brown legend, was, unlike Black Jack, a military failure.

Nonetheless, Brown's courage and antislavery commitment were indisputable, and his strategy at Osawatomie was, in general, intelligent. Time would prove that it was the *idea*, not the reality, of the Battle of Osawatomie that gave rise to the myth of Osawatomie Brown.

The events leading up to the battle reflected the chaotic state of Kansas that summer. In early August, John Brown, with his son Frederick, joined a company of thirty Free-Staters led by General James H. Lane and Captain Samuel Walker that headed south from Nebraska City toward Lawrence, some 150 miles away.

The Browns soon broke off on their own with a group of followers that grew slowly over the course of the month. Focused on raising his own troop, Brown did not participate in the attacks on several proslavery settlements launched by other Free State forces between August 8 and 16. In mid-August he appeared in Lawrence, where he reportedly received a letter from John Jr., who expected to be released shortly by the grand jury and thus advised against a rescue attempt.

By the third week of the month Brown had organized the "Kansas Regulars," a small force he kept under tight discipline. He wrote bylaws for the group that reflected his military vision. He demanded sensible, moderate behavior on the part of his men, who were forbidden to fire guns indiscriminately, light fires after nightfall, or behave rudely. His Puritan prudishness came through in the following rule: "All uncivil, ungentlemanly, profane, vulgar talk or conversation shall be discountenanced." Captured foes were not to be harmed or executed unless they were first given a fair trial. At the same time, Brown opened the way for unrestricted pillaging, stating that antislavery soldiers could freely appropriate enemy property.

He put this rule into action a number of times, laying himself open to the charge that he was an outlaw. He urged his men to steal horses and cattle belonging to proslavery people. He himself rode a fine-blooded bay formerly owned by Dutch Henry Sherman.

Although such actions were hardly admirable, they were tame when compared with proslavery outrages committed that month. On August 17, a ruffian named Fugert, guzzling whiskey in a Leavenworth saloon, made a

$6 bet with his drinking partner that he could scalp an Abolitionist within two hours. He went to a public road, shot a Free State man who was driving a carriage, scalped him with a bowie knife while the man was still alive, and then pinned the scalp on a pole, waving it triumphantly through the streets of Leavenworth. In a copycat crime that day, another proslavery resident scalped a Free State teamster approaching the town. A resident who expressed horror at these deeds was told to run for his life and then was gunned down by his proslavery tormentors.

Even more appalling were new threats of a massive proslavery takeover of Kansas. President Pierce had appointed the Pennsylvania politician John W. Geary to succeed the outgoing Wilson Shannon as governor of the Kansas Territory. Geary would prove to be a judicious governor—too judicious, as it turned out, for Pierce and for his successor, James Buchanan, since he switched to the Free State side.

In the period between Geary's appointment in July and his arrival in Kansas on September 9, the proslavery element in the Territory did what it could to secure Kansas for slavery before he came. Missourians were furious that Pierce had not chosen John Calhoun as the new governor. Calhoun (unrelated to the famous South Carolina senator John Calhoun, who had died in 1850) was the rabidly proslavery surveyor-general of Kansas and Nebraska. According to a contemporary, he had "declared that he would kill an abolitionist with less compunction than he would kill a rat."

Pierce's failure to select Calhoun as governor prompted both Missourians and proslavery Kansans to call for an all-out war against Abolitionists. A group of Missourians led by Atchison and Stringfellow published an appeal to "all good citizens of Missouri and every other state" to join the militia and "expel from the territory" the antislavery "traitors, assassins and robbers" who were waging "a war professedly for our extermination." A similar proclamation was issued by Daniel Woodson, Kansas's acting governor, who called upon "all law-abiding citizens" to organize against Free State settlers.

There emerged a large proslavery force in Missouri, led by Atchison, and a renewed Kansas militia, commissioned by Woodson. On August 27, Owen Brown, recuperating in nearby Iowa, wrote to the North Elba family, "We hear lately that about three thousand Missourians have crossed at St. Joe and other places, and have gone armed into the Territory; that Governor Woodson has sent four hundred mounted men on to the frontier to intercept our volunteers."

These armies intercepted the mails and lived on livestock and provisions foraged from Free State farms. They hunted for antislavery leaders in the spirit of one of their spokespersons, the *Squatter Sovereign* editor Robert S. Kelley, who declared that he would not die happy until he had killed an Abolitionist. "If I can't kill a man," he said, "I'll kill a woman; and if I can't kill a woman, I'll kill a child!" The proslavery soldiers went on a murder spree, killing anyone suspected of Free State sympathies. According to one report, "the roads were literally strewn with dead bodies."

The revived proslavery aggression made John Brown more determined than ever to battle the ruffians. Hearing that Osawatomie would be attacked, he held council there on August 25 with James H. Holmes, a New Yorker who had moved west to join the vegetarian colony on the Neosho River but who instead became a Free State warrior in command of a company of Iowans. Also present at the Osawatomie meeting were the Free State captains Samuel T. Shore, Samuel Anderson, and James B. Cline with their companies.

At the meeting Brown again proved himself astute in matters of war. Whereas the others called the defense of Osawatomie unfeasible since nearly all its inhabitants had fled, Brown shrewdly argued that natural defenses such as the town's twin blockhouses and the nearby Marais des Cygnes River could be used effectively against a large invasion.

For the time being, however, his advice was ignored. The other captains went off in pursuit of a column of ruffians that was advancing along California Road. On August 26, Brown followed to give reinforcement and discovered that his Free State friends had routed the Missourians by surprising them in their camp. Told that other ruffians were plundering Free State homesteads in the area, he rounded up two dozen volunteers and went in search of them.

His eagerness for battle led to near disaster. Roaming through the woods, he lost his way and came upon what he thought was a secret camp of Missourians. He prepared an attack, then pulled up when he recognized the group as the company of his comrades Shore, Anderson, and Cline.

Unfazed by his blunder, he urged these captains to join him in a raid on proslavery settlements on Sugar Creek. Believing that enemy property must be appropriated for use in the war against slavery, he stole men's clothing as well as 150 cattle from the farm of the proslavery leader John E. Brown.

He took captive a number of proslavery soldiers. Instead of harming them, he released them almost immediately—not, however, until he had lectured them about the wrongness of their views. "You are fighting for slavery," he declared. "You want to make or keep other people slaves. Do you not know that your wicked efforts will end in making slaves of your-selves? You come here to make this a slave state. You are fighting against liberty, which our Revolutionary fathers fought to establish in this Repub-lic, where all men should be free and equal, with the inalienable rights of life, liberty, and the pursuit of happiness. Therefore, you are traitors to lib-erty and to your country, of the worst kind, and deserve to be hung to the nearest tree. . . . Go in peace. Go home and tell your neighbors and friends of your mistake. We deprive you only of your arms, and do that only lest some of you are not yet converted to the right." If he caught them again, he added, he would show no compassion.

On the afternoon of Friday, August 29, he reached a hill north of Osawatomie driving his herd of stolen cattle. When a friend asked where he got the livestock, he chuckled and replied that "they were good Free-State cattle now." As he set up camp on a ranch outside of town that evening, he could not know that the next twenty-four hours would bring events that would earn him national renown.

He had been right about the Missourians' plans. On August 23, Major General John W. Reid left Westport, Missouri, with a company of over three hundred, crossing into Kansas with the aim of destroying first Osawatomie and then Topeka and Lawrence. His troop expected, as one of his officers put it, "to clear the whole territory of Abolitionists before our return." Along the way Reid picked up other proslavery volunteers, includ-ing the Reverend Martin White.

When the Missourians reached the outskirts of Osawatomie early in the morning of August 30, they encountered on the road a tall, strong-looking man. It was Frederick Brown, who had spent the night with his Uncle Samuel Adair and who had risen at six to feed horses. According to Brown family tradition, Frederick gave Martin White a friendly greeting only to be cruelly shot down on the spot. A more likely scenario, based on eyewit-ness reports, was that Frederick, with his customary foolhardiness, walked steadily toward the Missourians, cried "I know you!" when he spotted White, and, ignoring commands to stop and reaching for his revolver, took White's bullet through the chest.

The shot roused the Adairs and their neighbors, the Garrisons and a Mr. Carr. Samuel Adair and David Garrison rushed out of their cabins and looked up the road and spotted something that Adair first thought was a blanket but which he soon recognized as his nephew's bleeding corpse. Adair immediately fled to the brush, where he hid until his children later reported that danger had passed. Garrison and Carr were not so wise. They headed toward their cabins, were spotted by the Missourians, and were pursued. Garrison was shot down and killed, and Carr received numerous bullet wounds.

John Brown was having breakfast at his hillside camp when the news came of Frederick's murder and the Missourians' approach to Osawatomie. Brown shouted, "Men, come on, we must meet them before they get to town." He and his follower Luke F. Parsons grabbed their Sharps rifles and rode toward town, leaving the rest of the company to finish breakfast. On the way he asked Parsons if he had ever been under fire. Parsons said he had not and asked for advice. Brown's philosophical reply would later become famous. "Take more care," he said, "to end life well than to live long."

By the time Brown reached Osawatomie, his remaining men and others led by James B. Cline and William W. Updegraff had joined him, giving him a force of around thirty-eight. Realizing that he would be vastly outnumbered, he distributed his men shrewdly, making use of natural defenses. He sent Parsons and ten others into one of the town's two blockhouses with instructions to pepper Reid from above. Before long, however, Parsons's group, deciding that the blockhouse was vulnerable, joined Brown in the thick forest that lay between the Marais des Cygnes River and the road on which the Missourians were coming.

Hidden in the brambles and trees, Brown's company wreaked havoc on Reid's mounted column as it advanced toward Osawatomie. Brown spread his men out in a line in the brush, telling them to shoot carefully and often. He paced back and forth, screaming commands. His efforts were effective, for Reid's large force was thrown into confusion, with horses rearing frantically and their riders falling wounded to the ground. The Missourians fired into the woods, generally with no result except stripping branches above the concealed Free-Staters. One bullet, however, grazed John Brown. He momentarily halted and asked Parsons to check him. When Parsons said he saw nothing, Brown grumbled, "Well, something hit me an awful rap on that shoulder. . . . I declare, I don't intend to be shot in the back if I can help it."

The Missourians counterattacked by dismounting and charging into the woods, led by the sword-wielding Reid. Overwhelmed, Brown's small group scattered, some fleeing along the riverbank toward town and others plunging into the river. Those that did the latter were easy prey for the ruffians. George W. Partridge was riddled with bullets, and four other soldiers—Charles Kaiser, Robert Reynolds, H. K. Thomas, and the fourteen-year-old Spencer K. Brown—were taken prisoner.

John Brown, Jason, and several others avoided injury by going along the river, then crossing it when they were out of the Missourians' range. John Brown hardly looked heroic in flight. Wading waist-deep across the Marais des Cygnes, he had a clownish appearance in his wide straw hat, with his coattails floating behind him and his hands stretched high above him to keep his revolvers dry.

When he and Jason reached the opposite bank, they turned and looked back at Osawatomie. Over General Reid's protest the ruffians had burned the town's houses, plundered the post office and stores, and taken possession of all the horses and cattle they could find. John Brown's face tightened as he saw the smoke rise from the smoldering remains of the houses and buildings he knew so well. He declared grimly, "God sees it."

He pondered his losses. The ruffians had razed Osawatomie. On his side, his son Frederick, David Garrison, George Partridge, and a man named Powers were killed. Three others were wounded and four were captured. Among the latter, three, including the young Spencer Kellogg Brown, were soon released. The fourth prisoner, Charles Kaiser, would not be so lucky. On September 1, two days after his capture, the Missourians shot him to death, evidently while giving him a mock chance to run for his life.

The battle, which Stephen Oates aptly calls "the Osawatomie disaster," left plenty for the proslavery side to crow about—and lie about. In a report filed the day after the battle, Reid claimed that only five of his men were wounded and that "we killed about thirty of them, among the number, certain, a son of old Brown, and almost certain Brown himself; [we] destroyed all their ammunition and provisions, and the boys would burn the town to the ground. I could not help it." Another proslavery version of the battle insisted that Brown had 200 soldiers, to Reid's 250, and that Reid managed to kill 31, including "the notorious John Brown," without losing a single man on his side.

John Brown also indulged in self-aggrandizing falsification, though he did not skew the numbers nearly as badly as did his opponents. In a letter home and in widely read newspaper article, he reported that with only twenty-six to thirty men he had faced a force of four hundred and had left "some thirty-one or two killed, and from forty to fifty wounded." This was only a slight exaggeration. Although the exact numbers are unknown, it is safe to say that with a group of some thirty-eight he had battled a force more than seven times larger, killing between twenty and thirty and wounding at least forty more.

He had lost the battle but had won a moral victory. The odds against him had been enormous, but he had accepted them bravely, knowing that he might die. He had inflicted significant damage by choosing his position wisely, and he had retreated only when defeat was certain.

John Brown had not won Kansas for freedom, but he had shown how freedom could be won. As Senator John J. Ingalls later declared, "The Battle of Osawatomie was the most brilliant and important episode in the Kansas war. It was the high divide of the contest. It was our Thermopylae and John Brown was our Leonidas with his Spartan Band."

It mattered little, from this standpoint, that Osawatomie was in fact a losing effort. For those excited about the novelty of an Abolitionist who ran against the stereotype of the cowardly Northerner, the battle was a success. John Brown had proven that the North could fight. This was the point of a letter John Jr. wrote to his father on September 8 from prison:

> The Battle of Osawatomie is considered here as the great fight so far, and considering the enemies' loss, it is certainly a great victory for us; certainly a very dear burning of the town for them. This has proved most unmistakably that "Yankees" WILL "fight." Everyone I hear speaking of you is loud in your praise. The Missourians in this region show signs of great fear.

The battle had only stiffened John Brown's resolve to answer proslavery aggression with violence. As he watched black smoke billow from the ruins of Osawatomie, he told Jason, "I have only a short time to live—only one death to die, and I will die fighting for this cause. There will be no more peace in this land until slavery is done for. I will give them something else to do than to extend slave territory. I will carry the war into Africa."

Carrying the war into Africa meant invading the South. Even after having experienced what was in truth a lopsided loss, he was determined to go forward with his long-term plan of battling slavery on its own territory.

He could now think again about that plan, because he had done his share to save Kansas. Although the Battle of Osawatomie did not swing the Territory away from slavery, it was an important link in the chain of events that did so. Within three weeks of the battle the newly arrived governor, John Geary, ordered the disbanding of the proslavery army in Kansas. The fact that his order was followed attests not only to his own leadership skills but also to the dreaded presence of the now-famous John Brown. The "great fear" of Brown that his son had noted among "Missourians in this region" helps to explain the ruffians' readiness to compromise with their enemies.

The man the Missourians feared was, as usual, more a symbolic than an actual threat. In the period just after Osawatomie, John Brown lurked in the background of the Kansas struggle, allowing others to take the lead while he collected followers and made plans to leave the Territory.

For about a week after the battle, Brown tried to fortify a Free State farm near Osawatomie but failed to do so because of disorganization and illness among his troops. From there he and Jason went to visit Ottawa Jones. Brown felt closer than ever to his Indian friend, whose farm had been destroyed by Missourians on the very day Brown had lost at Osawatomie. While the main part of Reid's army was fighting Brown, a fifty-man contingent surrounded Jones's house and drove Jones and his wife outside, burning down the house and slitting the throat of a houseguest, Nathaniel Parker, who avoided death only because the jugular vein was missed.

Brown camped for a few days near Lawrence along with Jason, the sick Luke Parsons, and others. Hearing that Free State leaders were about to meet in Lawrence, he entered the town on September 7, accompanied by Parsons, with Jason scheduled to join them the next day.

As Brown rode into Lawrence, excitement swept the town—as if the president had arrived, according to an eyewitness. Cheers erupted from many who recognized him as he proceeded on his gray horse, his rifle across the saddle. As usual, he took the tumult with indifference.

His mind was on a Free State meeting then taking place in Lawrence. He arrived midway through the meeting, at which James Lane and James A. Harvey proposed an assault on the proslavery town of Leavenworth. Although Brown was offered the command of the raid, he rejected it, concentrating for the moment on John Jr., who was released from jail on September 9. Colonel Harvey led the Free State attack, capturing two proslavery towns in Leavenworth County and seizing enemy provisions. Meanwhile, Brown's close ally Aaron Stevens raided the proslavery village of Osawkee, stealing arms and eighty horses.

While Brown was in Lawrence, an army of more than 2,700 Missourians initiated yet another massive invasion of Kansas. On September 14 a contingent of 200 approached Lawrence and opened fire on the town, rejoining the main force in nearby Franklin after a skirmish on the prairie against 300 Free-Staters. John Brown, as determined as ever to counteract proslavery aggression with valor, rallied Lawrence's residents. He visited the town's four earthwork defenses and stone fort and delivered an address on a dry goods box on the main street. He warned of an imminent assault by the Missourians and gave military advice. Keep silent, he advised; be patient, get a clear target, and aim low. He couldn't count the number of times, he explained, that he had escaped death because enemy bullets had flown high.

Fortunately, the advice proved unnecessary. The invasion of Lawrence, which probably would have resulted in a bloodbath among the outnumbered Free-Staters, was averted. John Geary, the new governor of Kansas, arrived in Lawrence on September 15 and issued several proclamations ordering the warring parties to disarm and disband. Visiting the proslavery army in Franklin, Geary warned that further violence would hurt the proslavery cause by tarnishing the image of Democrats running for election in November. Aiming to calm the stormy atmosphere of Kansas, he offered clemency to both sides.

John Brown, the most violent of the Free State fighters, profited from Geary's policy of mercy. He received a note from his ally Charles Robinson assuring him that he would not be arrested. "There will be no attempt to arrest any one for a few days," Robinson wrote, "and I think no attempt to arrest you is contemplated by [Geary]. He talks of letting the past be forgotten, so far as may be, and of commencing anew."

Charles Robinson is a representative figure in the John Brown story, for he embodied successively the overly positive and overly negative misreadings of Brown, which, when they came into conflict, influenced the course of American history. Robinson was the first major antislavery figure to endorse the mythic view of Brown as the godly savior of Kansas. In a fulsome letter of September 14 he wrote that Brown's record in the Territory "has been such as to merit the highest praise from every patriot, and I cheerfully accord to you my heartfelt thanks for your prompt, efficient, and timely action against the invaders of our rights and the murderers of our citizens." "History," he added, "will give your name a proud place on its pages, and posterity will pay homage to your heroism in the cause of God."

Robinson continued to idealize Brown until the late 1870s, when he publicly compared him to Jesus Christ. But when Brown's responsibility for the Pottawatomie killings became widely known shortly thereafter, he did a turnaround and became one of Brown's principal defamers. After his death his wife, Sara, financed a damning book on Brown by Hill Peebles Wilson that portrayed Brown as a depraved criminal who exploited the antislavery cause to unleash violent urges and to gain personal notoriety. This harsh view of Brown, repeated in numerous books over the years, has made it difficult to integrate Brown comfortably into histories of the Civil War era.

Robinson had the schizoid reaction that has created so much conflict over Brown. He viewed John Brown initially as a patriotic warrior and later as a wicked outcast—first as Osawatomie Brown, to be venerated as a national legend, and then as Pottawatomie Brown, to be considered a despicable pariah of history.

Neither image, as we have seen, accorded with the facts. Pottawatomie, gruesome and vile as it was, was John Brown's impulsive response to equally vile crimes committed by the proslavery side. Osawatomie was the scene of heroism but also of failure. In both cases Brown had an admirable goal—challenging the proslavery element in the Territory—but had only qualified success.

Yet if the truth about John Brown's Kansas record lay in the middle, not in extremes, it was the extremes that would fire the popular imagination and kindle civil war. When Brown left Kansas in late September, he was ripe for deification by the North and for vilification by the South.

9

The Promoter

Few people have experienced so dramatic a change of fortunes as John Brown did between September 1856 and June 1857. The hunted criminal was transformed into a venerated warrior, the frontier pariah into an urban celebrity courted by a small but influential cluster of Northern businesspeople and intellectuals. His astonishing rise in stature resulted from his savvy self-promotion before a select group of Northerners hungry for heroes. In a time of pervasive moral flabbiness, John Brown sold himself—and was regarded by a few—as a man of sterling principles.

Unique cultural conditions in the North, particularly in eastern Massachusetts, created his fame. Had these conditions not existed, he would have remained a minor player in American history. As it happened, he promoted himself precisely at the right moment and in the right cultural environment. The times called for an antislavery soldier who would stand up to the South.

In a larger sense there was a dire need for a self-reliant, sincere individual utterly dedicated to a cause. Both sides of the slavery struggle had produced craven compromisers—what Walt Whitman branded as "swarms of cringers, suckers, doughfaces, lice of politics." An alternative kind of person was needed. In 1855, Whitman had offered one in his poetic persona—the self-confident, democratic "I" of *Leaves of Grass*.

But Whitman's "I" was just a poet's creation. John Brown seemed to some to be the real thing: a living, breathing homespun American hero. His supporters were as unbothered by the fact that he espoused retaliatory violence as Whitman's were that his "I" identified with criminals, prostitutes, and fugitive slaves. In a time of compromise and evasion in high places, there was something refreshing about decisive action, even when it was illegal. Just as Whitman sang praise to someone who was "wicked, rather than virtuous out of conformity or fear," so John Brown, who would be hanged for treason, appeared to his admirers as a valiant rebel whose violence against the slave power was fully justifiable.

To realize his violent plans Brown needed arms and soldiers. He was keenly aware of the activities of the National Kansas Committee, which between July 1856 and January 1857 had raised some $85,000 in cash and over $100,000 in supplies for emigrants to Kansas.

Brown wanted to tap such resources for his own purposes. To exploit the widespread concern for Kansas he planned a fund-raising tour of the East. He needed material support for his future antislavery battles in Kansas, support that he felt he could redirect secretly to his long-cogitated invasion of the South.

It was an opportune time for him to head east. Kansas had quieted down under the sensible leadership of Governor John W. Geary. Armies on both sides had been disbanded, and emotions had cooled. At the same time, however, Kansas's fate was uncertain enough for Brown to solicit donations from easterners worried that slavery could still win in the Territory.

Although under indictment for the Pottawatomie killings, Brown thought he could slip out of Kansas without being noticed. He was wrong. He was still under the eye of federal authorities and would remain so for some time. He left Kansas in a teamster's wagon with his sons John, Jason, and Owen, crossing over into Nebraska before U.S. troops caught him. On October 7, Lieutenant Colonel Philip St. George Cooke wrote from a place near the Nebraska border, "I arrived here yesterday, at noon. I just missed the arrest of the notorious Osawatomie outlaw, Brown."

By October 10, Brown, shivering with ague and fever, reached Tabor, Iowa. This frontier town, which had been founded in 1848 by Abolitionists from Ohio, was a western station on the Underground Railroad. Welcomed as a guest in the home of the genial Quaker Jonas Jones, Brown was glad to be among like-minded folk again. The day after he arrived, he wrote to his family, "I am *through Infinite grace*, once more in a Free State; & on my way to make you a visit."

He wanted Tabor to be the training base for a volunteer army of anti-slavery warriors. But first he needed arms. His mind was on the emigrant aid societies in the East. He did not know that J. P. Root, an agent of the National Kansas Committee, had already sent from New York a wagon loaded with two hundred revolvers to be used for the Free State cause in Kansas. The guns would reach Tabor after Brown had gone east and would be stored for the winter along with other weapons and supplies in the house of the Reverend John Todd, a close ally. Eventually, the revolvers were turned over to Brown, ostensibly for use in Kansas. As it turned out, they became part of his arsenal for the Harpers Ferry raid.

After a week in Tabor, Brown felt strong enough to travel to Chicago. From there he went to Ohio, where Governor Joshua Giddings gave him a letter of introduction to potential funders. Continuing east, Brown stopped at Peterboro, New York, to consult with the antislavery philanthropist Gerrit Smith, and then went to nearby North Elba, where he saw Mary and his younger children for the first time in sixteen months. There is no record of this reunion, which must have been a deeply emotional one.

Early January 1857 found Brown in Boston, where he looked up Franklin B. Sanborn, the secretary of the Massachusetts State Kansas Committee. When Brown arrived at Sanborn's office on School Street, he unwittingly opened the door not only to Harpers Ferry but also to his future fame. Through Sanborn he gained access to arms and money for Kansas and, later, for Harpers Ferry.

Sanborn was instantly impressed by this "tall, slender, and commanding figure," who wore a brown broadcloth suit, a high leather collar, and gray overcoat with a cape. With his "military bearing" and intense Calvinism, he seemed to combine "the soldier and the deacon." Brown appeared to be "of the unmixed Puritan breed"—a modern Oliver Cromwell, thought Sanborn.

Excited, Sanborn wrote an Abolitionist friend, the Worcester minister Thomas Wentworth Higginson, urging him to come to Boston to meet Brown. Higginson had recently returned from Kansas and had organized a convention for antislavery disunionists to take place on January 15. Enticed by Sanborn's letter, he interrupted his schedule and visited Boston on January 9. He took so strongly to Brown that he soon became his most radical supporter.

Sanborn also introduced Brown to another antislavery minister, Theodore Parker. The learned Parker had gained notoriety as a clergyman so liberal that he was forced to preach in the Boston Music Hall instead of in a church. Even though his religious views were poles apart from those of the Calvinistic Brown, the two met on the common ground of antislavery violence. Parker had taken up arms in defense of fugitive slaves threatened with recapture, and he passionately supported slave revolts. He was thrilled to meet the militant Brown, whom he invited to a Sunday reception at his home.

At the reception Brown met William Lloyd Garrison. Garrison, a longtime pacifist, cited passages from the New Testament to argue for a nonresistant response to the slavery problem. Brown, quoting the Old Testament, made the plea for taking up arms to free the slaves. Uncomfortable with Garrison's nonviolent approach, Brown never made him privy to his planned invasion of the South. He was more in tune with three other Boston Abolitionists he met that month: Amos A. Lawrence, Dr. Samuel Gridley Howe, and George Luther Stearns.

The wealthy Lawrence, after whom Lawrence, Kansas, was named, was a chief donor to Eli Thayer's New England Emigrant Aid Society. He enjoyed hearing firsthand about the Territory's antislavery wars when Brown visited him on January 7. He found Brown "a calm, temperate and pious man, but when aroused he is a dreadful foe. . . . His severe simplicity of habits, his determined energy, his heroic courage in the time of trial, all based on a deep religious faith, make him a true representative of the Puritanic warrior." Although later he would have second thoughts about Brown, he was in the first flush of his enthusiasm, and he offered to give $1,000 a year to Brown's indigent family and the same amount annually to the antislavery cause in Kansas until freedom was ensured there.

Another Bostonian Brown called on, Dr. Samuel Gridley Howe, was a physician and social activist who in his twenties had gone abroad to fight for Greece in its revolution against Turkey and then for Poland in its rebellion against Russia. Upon his return to America he became a pioneer in the treatment of the mentally and physically challenged (most notably the blind deaf-mute Laura Bridgman) and together with his wife, Julia Ward Howe, was involved in many reforms, including antislavery. With Theodore Parker he formed vigilance groups to protect Boston's fugitive slaves. He had a leading role in the Massachusetts Kansas Committee, which on January 5 agreed to give Brown the two hundred Sharps rifles that were stored for the winter in John Todd's basement in Tabor, Iowa. The committee also gave Brown ammunition and a promise of $500 in expenses.

The committee's president, George Stearns, had made a small fortune as a factory owner and was caught up in the furor against the Fugitive Slave Act. For over a month he and his reform-minded wife, Mary, had housed a fugitive slave in the Evergreens, their mansion on twenty-six acres in Medford. He became a major contributor to the Free State cause in Kansas. When Frank Sanborn, secretary of the Kansas committee, brought John Brown to meet him in his Boston office, he and Brown instantly took to each other—"like the iron and the magnet," his son recalled, as each "recognized the other at first sight and knew him for what he was worth."

Eager to introduce the antislavery warrior to his family, Stearns invited Brown to Evergreens. Brown, despite his rough garb, struck Stearns's wife as having an "exactness and neatness" that "produced a singular air of refinement." Mary Stearns, a niece of the Abolitionist Lydia Maria Child, was every bit as devoted to the antislavery cause as her husband and even more enthusiastic about Brown than he. She found that Brown had "such an erect, military bearing, such fine courtesy of demeanor and grave earnestness, that he seemed to my instant thought some old Cromwellian hero suddenly dropped down before me." This impression was strengthened when he declared, "It is better that a whole generation of men, women, and children should be swept away than that this crime of slavery should exist one day longer"—said with such force that the Stearnses' son Carl, not yet three, remembered it as an adult.

Over dinner Brown told the family about his travails in Kansas and his victory at Black Jack. The twelve-year-old Henry Stearns was so moved that he handed Brown some pocket money and asked, "Captain Brown, will you buy something with this money for those poor people in Kansas, and some time will you write to me and tell me what sort of a little boy you were?" Brown promised to do so. The result was a long autobiographical letter he sent Henry six months later. Though ungrammatical and fragmentary, the letter had an appealing directness and power. When it was later published, Emerson judged it a "positive contribution to . . . the historical literature of the English language," and James Russell Lowell in the *Atlantic Monthly* called it "one of the finest pieces of autobiography extant."

Having made important contacts in Boston, Brown was ready to continue fund-raising elsewhere. But first he wanted to meet Charles Sumner, whose pummeling at the hands of Preston Brooks had happened the previous May. When he was taken to Sumner's apartment, he asked the senator, still in pain from the beating, to show him the coat he had been wearing when he was attacked. Sumner hobbled to the closet and pulled out a rumpled coat on which bloodstains were still visible. Brown said nothing. He tightened his lips and stared at the coat "as a devotee would contemplate the relic of a saint," as a witness reported.

In the third week of January, Brown took a train with Sanborn to New York to seek support from the National Kansas Committee. When the committee met in the Astor House on January 24, a debate over Brown's violent tactics flared up. Brown, with the backing of Sanborn, requested money and supplies for his company in Kansas. A resolution to give him $5,000 was proposed but met strong opposition from several who insisted that no arms should go to Brown since he might use them recklessly. When H. B. Hurd, the secretary of the committee, asked Brown if he was planning to attack Missouri or any other slave states, Brown equivocated. "I am no adventurer," he declared. "You all know me. You are acquainted with my

Brown's six principal backers, later known as the Secret Six.
Clockwise from upper left: George Luther Stearns, Gerrit Smith,
Thomas Wentworth Higginson, Samuel Gridley Howe,
Theodore Parker, and Franklin B. Sanborn.

BOYD STUTLER COLLECTION OF JOHN BROWN, WEST VIRGINIA ARCHIVES.

history. You know what I have done in Kansas. I do not expose my plans. No one knows them but myself, except perhaps one. I will not be interrogated; if you wish to give me anything, give it freely. I have no other purpose but to serve the cause of liberty."

In other words, trust me and ask no questions. The committee met him halfway, granting him $5,000 to be drawn upon for "any *defensive* measures that may become necessary" but deflecting the weapons issue by saying that the Massachusetts committee controlled most of the arms anyway. The money seemed like a real windfall, but in the end Brown received only $150, and that six months later, as the committee ran low on funds. By early April, Brown would write, "*I am prepared to expect nothing but bad faith from the National Kansas Committee.*" He did, however, get fourteen boxes of clothing, which were shipped to Tabor in March.

Brown took to the road again, going by way of Vermont and Rochester to Peterboro, New York, where he again visited Gerrit Smith. He had high hopes of getting a sizable donation from the wealthy landowner. Had he known Smith better, he would have been less confident. The mercurial millionaire had passed through many phases of antislavery activity, having successively advocated colonization, politics, nonresistance, and finally violence. The sack of Lawrence and the assault on Sumner had led to Smith's supposed rejection of pacifism. He announced that "hitherto I have opposed the bloody abolition of slavery," but now "I and ten thousand other peace men are not only ready to have it repulsed with violence, but pursued even unto death, with violence." Strong talk; but at the time he said these words he was vice president of the American Peace Society, and as late as May 1858 he gave a lecture to the society titled "Peace Better than War."

Given his vacillation, it is understandable that he was standoffish with Brown. Although he admired Brown's heroic qualities—so much so that he was later a member of the Secret Six—he must have regarded the Puritan warrior as a loose cannon, for he was stingy with him. Smith had already contributed $10,000 toward a regular Free State force in Kansas, and he was giving $1,000 annually to the National Kansas Committee. He had nothing to spare for vigilante action. But he wished Brown well and promised future support.

After a brief visit with his family in North Elba, Brown returned to Boston, where Sanborn had arranged for him to address the Massachusetts state legislature as part of an effort to get a $100,000 appropriation passed for Kansas. Brown appeared before the legislature on February 18 along with two other Kansas veterans, E. B. Smith and Martin Conway.

Introduced by Sanborn as a patriot with the blood of the Puritans and the Revolutionary generation in his veins, Brown made an impressive showing. In his speech Brown came down harshly on the border ruffians (saying nothing, of course, about Free State crimes, least of all Pottawatomie). With pathos verging on theatrics, he described the afflictions suffered by his sons. To show how John Jr. was tortured, he held up worn shackles and declared, "Here is the chain with which one of them was confined, after the cruelty, sufferings, and anxiety he underwent had rendered him a maniac—yes, a maniac." Recounting the murder of Frederick, he reported seeing "the mangled bodies of three men, two of which were dead and had lain on the open ground for about eighteen hours for the flies to work at, the other living with twenty buckshot and bullet-holes in him. One of those two dead was my own son."

He contrasted the threadbare state of antislavery Kansans with the wasteful expenditure of the federal government, which was spending half a million dollars annually to impose slavery on the Territory. To counteract the government's "tyrannical & Damnable" actions, he said, what was needed in Kansas was "good men, industrious men, men who respect themselves; who act only from the dictates of conscience; men who fear God too much to fear anything human."

He tugged the heartstrings of his audience, but to no avail. The legislature failed to pass a Kansas bill. Brown resumed his search for funds.

The search became frenetic. For a month he crisscrossed Massachusetts, visiting Concord, Springfield, and the Berkshire region, and Connecticut, making appearances at New Haven, Collinsville, Canton, Hartford, and elsewhere. To generate contributions, Brown published in the *New-York Tribune* and other papers an appeal titled "To the Friends of Freedom." He wrote, "I ask all honest lovers of *Liberty and Human Rights, both male and female*, to hold up my hands by contributions of pecuniary aid, either as counties, cities, towns, villages, societies, churches or individuals. . . . Will either gentlemen or ladies, or both, who love the cause, volunteer to take up the business? It is with *no little sacrifice of personal feeling* that I appear in this manner before the public."

The money came in small spurts: he raised $80 for three talks at Canton and Collinsville, $70 at Lawrence, Massachusetts, and $100 from a friend of George Stearns. Despite the scanty donations, he was gratified when a group at Canton sent to his North Elba home the old granite gravestone of his grandfather to be used as a memorial to the murdered Frederick; eventually it marked John Brown's own grave.

He was also encouraged by the prospect of receiving a new kind of weapon: a pike, consisting of a two-edged bowie knife attached to a six-foot pole, made for him by Charles Blair, a Collinsville blacksmith who had attended one of his lectures in early March. The day after the lecture Blair saw Brown in a drugstore exhibiting weapons he had seized from his opponents in Kansas. Brown held up a knife and commented that if fixed to a pole it would provide an excellent defensive weapon for Free State settlers in Kansas. He asked Blair how much it would take to produce such a weapon. Blair figured he could make five hundred pikes for $1.25 apiece and a thousand for $1.00 apiece.

A few days later Brown showed up at Blair's foundry and requested sample pikes. Blair made a dozen and sent them to Brown in Springfield. Approving the samples, Brown signed a contract with Blair on March 30, promising to pay $500 within ten days and $450 within thirty days thereafter for a thousand pikes. The delivery was delayed indefinitely, since Brown could pay only $350 of the first installment and a small second payment in late April. During the delay, the bowie-knife heads, two inches wide and eight inches long, were packed separately from the ash shafts. With no other payments made, the pikes remained undelivered until January 1859, when Brown took the necessary steps to procure them for use at Harpers Ferry.

Brown had once spoken of the need for a practical weapon that could be used by those unaccustomed to handling a rifle. Although he welcomed the guns donated to him, he believed that rifles and revolvers were ill suited to untrained fighters. The pike, a modernized spear, was his idea of a democratic weapon. He knew that the most fearsome slave insurrections, such as Nat Turner's, had occurred when slaves had attempted to slash their way to freedom. The pike was a perfect tool for slaves untutored in firearms.

Although the pikes never saw combat use, they proved to have immense symbolic value when placed in the hands of blacks liberated during the Harpers Ferry raid. For John Brown, they represented retributive justice for blacks. For the South, they were the ultimate symbol of Abolitionist-inspired slave rebellions.

The symbolism surrounding the pikes, however, paled in comparison to that surrounding John Brown himself. Not long after Brown ordered the pikes, Frank Sanborn took him to Concord, the home of Transcendentalism. No one shaped the John Brown image more strongly than did the Transcendentalists, the nation's leading intellectuals. Their admiration of him laid the basis for the later widespread deification of him in the North.

The relationship between this influential group and John Brown is an untold story in Civil War history. For a long time historians maintained that the Transcendentalists had little connection with antislavery reform and did not factor in the background of the war. Emerson, Thoreau, and their circle go unmentioned in the classic histories of the war by revisionists such as Allan Nevins and C. Vann Woodward. In the late 1950s, Stanley Elkins struck a common note when he announced that the Transcendental-ists "took next to no part in politics at all." "Not only did these men fail to analyze slavery as an institution," he argued, "but they failed equally to con-sider and exploit individual means for subverting it."

Many historians have echoed this sentiment. One characterizes Emer-son and his group as "monks sitting cross-legged on the floor" who espoused "the most conservative attitude of all" by choosing to "abstain entirely" from the antislavery movement. Another claims that the "philo-sophical bent" of Transcendentalism "ran against the grain of the most important development of the decade, antislavery politics."

Although this picture of the Transcendentalists as apolitical thinkers has been challenged, much remains to be done to restore the group's impor-tance to the war. Actually, had the Transcendentalists not sanctified the arch-Abolitionist John Brown, he may have very well remained an obscure, tangential figure—a forgettable oddball. And had that happened, the sud-denly intense polarization between the North and the South that followed Harpers Ferry might not have occurred.

Frank Sanborn ensured John Brown's fame by bringing him into the Transcendentalist circle that immediately welcomed him and eventually magnified him to Christ-like proportions.

The Brown backers Sanborn organized, later known as the Secret Six, had strong links to Transcendentalism. The three most radical members of the group—Sanborn himself, Thomas Wentworth Higginson, and Theodore Parker—were devout followers of the Concord philosophy. A fourth, George Stearns, was a good friend of Emerson and his crowd. A fifth, Samuel Gridley Howe, was on the fringes of the Concord circle. Of the six, only the Peterboro philanthropist Gerrit Smith was outside the Transcendentalist set.

Since the Harpers Ferry raid would not have come off without the sup-port of the Secret Six, four of whom were connected to Transcendentalism, and since Transcendentalists would later take the lead in establishing Brown's reputation, the Concord philosophy must be recognized as a force behind the events that led to the Civil War.

Notably, S. G. Howe and Gerrit Smith, the two members of the Secret Six who were furthest from Emerson, would prove the most cowardly in their behavior during Brown's imprisonment and trial for murder and trea-son. Fearing arrest for complicity, Howe published a disclaimer and left the country. Smith became so terrified that he was confined for a time in a lunatic asylum, and to his death he denied his involvement in the raid. By contrast, the four closest to Emerson stood their ground in defending Brown. Although two of them took brief trips to Canada, the group did what it could to aid the incarcerated Brown and carried on in his spirit after his death.

The Inner Four, as they might be called, were case histories in how Emersonian self-reliance, under the right conditions, could nurture tough Abolitionism, expressed in devoted support of the nation's most violent antislavery warrior.

Frank Sanborn was an integral part of the Transcendentalist group. Twenty-five when John Brown first called on him, he had been an intellectual prodigy in his youth, having read Plutarch's *Lives* and the complete works of Walter Scott and Lord Byron by age twelve. A religious liberal, he started out in Universalism and then embraced the Unitarianism-cum-Abolitionism of the radical ministers Thomas Wentworth Higginson and Theodore Parker.

Sanborn discovered Emerson's writings as a teenager and visited Concord for the first time in 1851, when he entered Harvard. He became so enamored of Transcendentalism that he claimed to have learned more from Emerson and Parker than from his Harvard professors. Upon graduating in 1855, he moved to Concord and became close to the leading literati. He ran a school there until 1863 and had among his students Emerson's three children, John Brown's daughters Anne and Sarah, and Bob and Wilky James, siblings of Henry, William, and Alice James. Thereafter, Sanborn became a newspaper editor and author. He developed into one the most important early historians of Transcendentalism, producing five books on Thoreau, three on Emerson, two on Bronson Alcott, and one on Theodore Parker. He also wrote the still-valuable *Life and Letters of John Brown*.

When Sanborn introduced John Brown to Thomas Wentworth Higginson in Boston, he was calling in an ally who, like himself, was grounded in Transcendentalism and Abolitionism. Like Sanborn, Higginson was a Harvard graduate who had discovered Emerson as a teenager and remained close to the Transcendentalists for much of his life. A Unitarian minister, he alienated his first congregation, in Newburyport, Massachusetts, because of his social radicalism and then found a willing audience at Worcester's Free Church, where he laced his sermons with vigorous Abolitionist rhetoric.

Higginson not only knew the Transcendentalists personally but also was close to them philosophically. He appreciated their many dimensions. For instance, he noted the difference between taking nature walks with

Thoreau, the naturalist, and taking them with Alcott, the idealist. Thoreau dwelt on the physical landscape whereas Alcott spoke in abstractions.

But Higginson saw that, despite their different temperaments, both men took self-reliant action when it came to protesting against slavery. For them as for others, Transcendentalism bred not complacency but courage. Higginson enjoyed describing Alcott's intrepidity during the Anthony Burns affair and again after the Harpers Ferry raid, when Alcott offered to help go rescue John Brown from the Charles Town jail. Thoreau, too, combined quietism and pluck. As Higginson noted, "In a similar way Thoreau, after all his seeming theories of self-absorption, ranged himself on the side of John Brown as placidly as if he were going for huckleberries."

Higginson himself was a prime example of how a Transcendentalist could combine philosophizing with reform activity. Like his friends Alcott and Thoreau, he loved taking contemplative walks in the wild. His poetic strain accounts for his sensitivity to the intensely private Emily Dickinson, for whom he sustained an ambiguous admiration during her lifetime that led to his pioneering editorship of her poems after her death.

At the same time, he was relentlessly energetic as a reformer. He was the most radical member of the Secret Six, urging John Brown to launch the Virginia plan early and publicly announcing his support of Brown after the raid failed. In Higginson, Emersonian self-trust fostered muscular activism. His risky efforts to rescue imperiled fugitives from slavery, notably Anthony Burns and Shadrach, were of a piece with his unflinching support of Brown and of his command of the first African American regiment during the Civil War.

The other clergyman in the Inner Four, Theodore Parker, was yet another example of how Transcendentalism bred social radicalism. The youngest of eleven children in a poor farming family, Parker, largely self-taught, passed the entrance exam to Harvard, though he could not afford to enroll. Still, he received college credit for his achievements as an autodidact, and in 1835 he was awarded a degree from the Harvard Divinity School.

Emerson had a momentous effect on him. In 1838, Parker heard Emerson deliver his famous "Address" at the Divinity School. Unlike many others present, who considered the speech sacrilegious, Parker was enraptured by Emerson, who, he said, "surpassed himself as much as he surpasses others in a general way." Parker's own sermons became so imbued with Transcendentalism that they too aroused controversy. "I preach abundant heresies," Parker boasted. "I preach the worst of all things, Transcendentalism, the grand heresy itself."

Once again, Transcendentalism went hand in hand with a militant reform stance. Like Higginson, Parker was deeply involved in several movements, including women's rights, temperance, and prison reform. His Abolitionism started mildly, as indicated by his rational "Letter to a Slaveholder" (1848), but flamed into rage with the passage of the Fugitive Slave Act of 1850. Even as he kept up his pursuits as a multilingual scholar and minister, he took part in attempted rescues of fugitive blacks and endorsed slave rebellions. Praising John Brown's effort to spark an insurrection by blacks at Harpers Ferry, he wrote, capitalizing his words for emphasis: "ONE HELD AGAINST HIS WILL AS A SLAVE HAS A NATURAL RIGHT TO KILL EVERY ONE WHO SEEKS TO PREVENT HIS ENJOYMENT OF LIBERTY."

George Stearns, the Secret Six member mainly responsible for contributing weapons and money to John Brown, was in some senses very different from Sanborn, Higginson, and Parker. They were Harvard-bred intellectuals; he was a rich businessman. They were fiery and poetic; he was stolid and practical. Still, he shared not only their animus against slavery but also their interest in Transcendentalism.

It is a testament to the stimulating effect of Transcendentalism that Stearns increasingly devoted himself to antislavery activism. Earlier in his career he had been an unabashed materialist, accumulating riches by producing linseed oil and, later on, lead pipes. His social conscience was aroused in 1854 when he heard Theodore Parker deliver his sermon "The New Crime Against Humanity," a blistering indictment of proslavery laws promulgated in the name of spiritual law.

Stearns's commitment to fighting social ills intensified when he met Parker's Transcendentalist colleagues in Concord. In the mid-1850s he was inspired by Emerson's address "The Conduct of Life," and he made a point of going often to the philosopher's lectures thereafter. His sons Henry and Carl befriended Emerson's son Eddy, often staying at his house in Concord or having him spend nights with them in Medford. Soon Emerson himself was a regular guest at the Evergreens.

It was Emerson who prepared the way for the Secret Six, for in 1856 he introduced Stearns to his Concord friend Frank Sanborn, who, along with Stearns, would form the nucleus of John Brown's six backers. Emerson also brought Stearns into contact with Thoreau and Alcott. Before long, George and Mary Stearns enjoyed their role as the patrons of the Transcendentalists. They received the Concordites, who in turn took them iceskating or berry-picking in their bucolic town. At a particularly memorable skating party in 1859, George Stearns hit the ice with Emerson and Thoreau.

Mary Stearns grew as close to the Concord literati as did her husband. She heard Thoreau deliver "A Plea for Captain John Brown," and she attended the service in Concord that the Transcendentalists organized on the day Brown was hanged. She later arranged to have Alcott write a small book entitled *Emerson,* bound in fine leather and presented as a birthday surprise to Emerson, who, though grateful, recoiled at seeing his name on the front jacket of so fancy a volume.

During the war the Emersons and the Stearnses united around the ideal John Brown had stood for: the liberation of enslaved blacks through violent war waged by an army consisting of both whites and African Americans. Stearns persuaded Emerson to go with Wendell Phillips to see Lincoln and argue for emancipation as a primary war goal. Stearns also spearheaded the movement to recruit black troops. Although he disagreed with Emerson on the issue of African American suffrage, which he supported in the face of Emerson's uncertainty, he never lost the respect of his Concord friend. When Stearns died in 1867, Emerson eulogized him as "a man for up-hill work, a soldier to bide the brunt; a man whom disasters, which dishearten other men, only stimulated to new courage and endeavor."

Courage in the face of disaster. Emerson admired it in Stearns after he had learned to admire it in John Brown. In his lecture on "Courage," delivered while John Brown was in prison, Emerson raised Brown to divine status.

The kind of courage Emerson had in mind was in some ways akin to his earlier notion of self-reliance, presented in his famous essay of 1841. But in other ways it was radically different. Like self-reliance, courage of the John Brown sort was grounded in unswerving self-trust. It had little to do, however, with whim or nonchalance. The Emerson of the late 1850s was interested less in brash caprice and self-contradiction than in sturdy defense of what he called "the eternal right" of the antislavery cause. In "Self-Reliance," Emerson had announced his individualism by mocking an Abolitionist as an "angry bigot" who paraded an "incredible tenderness for black folk a thousand miles off." In "Courage" he compared the age's angriest Abolitionist to Christ.

Why did Emerson and the other Transcendentalists idolize John Brown? Why did they single him out from the countless other traveling reformers who, in that age of the lyceum, swarmed over New England? Why wasn't he dismissed along with those "madmen, madwomen, men with beards, . . . Groaners, Agrarians, Seventh-day-Baptists, Quakers, Abo-litionists, Calvinists, Unitarians, and Philosophers" whom Emerson jibed, or with those "men of one idea, like a hen with one chicken" Thoreau com-plained about in *Walden*?

Ironically, the answer relates only partly to the two things that mattered most to Brown: slavery and race. On these issues the Transcendentalists were far behind him. He had lived and breathed antislavery commitment since early childhood. They were latecomers to it. They were ready to espouse it militantly only after the passage of the Fugitive Slave Act of 1850.

Even then, they did not share his main goal: the liberation of the slaves so that African Americans could live on equal terms with whites. Although most of them would come to espouse this aim in the period after Brown's execution, it was a slow process for them to put aside the racism prevalent in their era.

Each of them had shockingly racist moments. Emerson once wrote that God had built "insurmountable" racial barriers by assigning "different degrees of intellect to these different races," making it natural "that some should lead, and some should serve." Not only blacks but others as well were subjects of Emerson's bigotry. In the 1830s he wrote in his journal, "I think that it cannot be maintained by any candid person that the African race have ever occupied or do promise ever to occupy a very high place in the human family. Their present condition is the strongest proof that they cannot. The Irish cannot; the American Indian cannot; the Chinese cannot. Before the energy of the Caucasian race all the other races have quailed and done obeisance."

Nor were Alcott and Thoreau free of racism. Alcott introduced Emer-son to the pseudoscientific idea that blacks would disappear over time as a result of intermarriage with whites. Although in 1844 Emerson said that blacks were "susceptible of rapid civilization," he soon confessed being con-vinced by Alcott that "it will happen by & by, that the black man will only be destined for museums like the Dodo."

Thoreau put a wrinkle on the racial-extinction notion, suggesting that blacks might last but Native Americans would not. "The history of the white man," he wrote, "is the history of improvement, that of the red man a history of fixed habits of stagnation." As for blacks, they would survive, but only in an inferior role. He argued, "The African will survive, for he is docile, and is patiently learning his trade and dancing at his labor; but the Indian does not often dance, unless it be the war dance." Thoreau's poem "Our Country" asserted that the "red race with sullen step retreats," and "the Afric race [is] brought here to curse its fate" along with Irish and Germans, while the "manly Saxon" is "leading all the rest."

It would be redundant to record all such statements made by the members of the Secret Six, each of whom more or less accepted the white-supremacist attitudes of the day. Most surprising was Higginson. Progressive in his social views, he championed the causes of women and ethnic minorities and devoted himself to African American involvement in the Civil War. He was quick to notice his friends' racism, as when he wrote, "Emerson, while thoroughly true to the anti-slavery movement, always confessed to a feeling of slight instinctive aversion to Negroes; Theodore Parker uttered frankly his dislike of the Irish."

But Higginson himself never rose above prejudice. If he avoided Emerson's aversion to blacks, he shared Thoreau's condescension toward them, calling them "simple, docile, and affectionate almost to the point of absurdity." One night during the war, as he watched his black troops fall asleep, he jotted in his journal, "I feel as if they were a lot of babies in their cradles cooing themselves to sleep, the dear, blundering, dusky darlings." John Brown not only eschewed such racism but in fact was guided chiefly by blacks in the planning and execution of his antislavery activities.

If the Transcendentalists were so distanced from him in their racial attitudes, why did they endorse him with such fervor?

A look at their firsthand response to him reveals that they regarded him as a Cromwellian warrior against corrupt political institutions in the name of a higher law. If they magnified him to supernatural proportions, it was because they believed he might succeed where they had failed. They had tried for years to supplant their culture's materialism, conformity, and shady politics with spiritual-minded individualism. Like their favorite poet, Walt Whitman, they wanted to cleanse America by providing it with an alternative vision. They began to realize, however, that they were waging an uphill battle. They believed that John Brown was better equipped than they to win this battle. They recognized themselves to be philosophical observers, theorizing about principles. He was an actual soldier in the field, fighting for principle.

Their admiration for him was shaped by the historical moment. Had their alarm over worsening social conditions not reached an extreme level, they would not have viewed him as a potential savior of society. Had they not held special ideas about heroism, they would not have fixed on him as a hero.

It is often maintained that the Transcendentalists would not have supported John Brown had they suspected his role in the Pottawatomie murders. The evidence suggests, however, that they knew of it and yet embraced him anyway. A detailed report of the crime, and of Brown's involvement in it, had been on public record since 1856, when the Committee to Investigate the Troubles in Kansas described it on the floor of the United States House of Representatives in vivid testimony that was subsequently published.

Moreover, the Transcendentalists supported Brown even after his responsibility for the killings was widely talked about in the aftermath of Harpers Ferry. His vicious deed at Pottawatomie was mentioned at a huge anti-Brown rally in Boston, in a letter between two Southerners, and on the floor of the U.S. Senate, where on December 12, 1859, future vice president Andrew Johnson branded Brown as a murderer who "seems to have had a great passion for cutting off hands," exhibited by his gory methods at Pottawatomie.

Despite such open discussion of the bloody slayings, the Transcendentalists went on praising John Brown, and they adopted some of his radical views on slavery and race.

Whether or not they knew every detail of Pottawatomie is moot, since they were thoroughly familiar with—and supportive of—his overall violent strategy. When Sanborn took Brown to Concord in March 1857, Thoreau greeted Brown and spent an afternoon hearing about his martial exploits in Kansas. Thoreau was thrilled when, in answer to his request to see booty from the Battle of Black Jack, Brown pulled from a trouser leg a huge bowie knife he said he had taken from his proslavery opponent, Henry C. Pate. Emerson, returning from a western lecture trip, joined the conversation in midafternoon and was so taken with Brown that he invited him to stay at his home the following night. The conversation continued there, and arrangements were made to have Brown give a speech at the Concord Town Hall.

This speech prepared the way for the later canonization of John Brown. Brown gauged the Concord audience well, for his attack on nonresistance and his call for violence struck a chord among his listeners. Emerson wrote in his journal:

> Captain John Brown of Kansas gave a good account of himself in the Town Hall, last night to a meeting of citizens. One of his good points was the folly of the peace party in Kansas, who believed that their strength lay in the greatness of their wrongs, and so discountenanced resistance. He wished to know if their wrong was greater than the negro's, and what kind of strength that gave to the negro? He believes, on his own experience, that one good, believing, strong-

minded man is worth a hundred—nay, twenty thousand—men without character, for a settler in a new country; and that the right men will give a permanent direction to the fortunes of a State. For one of these bullying, drinking rowdies, he seemed to think, cholera, smallpox, and consumption were as valuable recruits. The first man who went into Kansas from Missouri to interfere in the elections, he thought, "had a perfect right to be shot."

From an hour-long speech Emerson here culls what he termed Brown's "good points," most of them related to violence. The "folly of the peace party" in opposing resistance; the right of blacks to avenge wrongs against them; the martial superiority of a principled person fighting against "bullying, drunken rowdies"; and, especially, the "perfect right" of border ruffians "to be shot"—these were the images Emerson highlighted with approval.

Elsewhere he reported that John Brown "believed in two articles—two instruments, shall I say?—the Golden Rule and the Declaration of Independence; and used this expression in a conversation here concerning them: 'Better that a whole generation of men, women, children should pass away by a violent death, than that one word of either should be violated in this country.' " In effect, Emerson was accepting Brown's vision of the abolition of slavery through apocalyptic bloodletting. Rather than recoil from Brown's violence, Emerson dwelt on it.

So did Thoreau, who was also at Brown's lecture. Did Thoreau know about Pottawatomie then? Perhaps so; his friends Alcott and Sanborn, who were there as well, assumed that Brown's statement about proslavery men having a right to be murdered was a reference to the Pottawatomie killings.

But, with Thoreau as with Emerson, exact knowledge of a specific violent act mattered less than approval of Brown's violent agenda. The murder image that Emerson and the others noted became in Thoreau's handling a moment of epiphany. "I noticed that he did not overstate any thing, but spoke within bounds," Thoreau wrote. "Referring to the deeds of certain Border Ruffians, he said, rapidly paring away his speech, like an experienced soldier, keeping a reserve of force and meaning, 'They had a perfect right to be hung.' "

In Thoreau's view Brown's violent assertions were all the more powerful because they were laconic. Thoreau recalled, "When I expressed surprise that he could live in Kansas at all, with a price set on his head, and so large a number, including the authorities, exasperated against him, he accounted for it by saying, 'It is perfectly well understood that I will not be taken.' "

Like Emerson, Thoreau was fully aware of Brown's violent tactics, publicly endorsing them. As Thoreau declared, "It was his peculiar doctrine that a man has a perfect right to interfere by force with the slaveholder, in order to rescue the slave. I agree with him. . . . I think that for once the Sharps' rifles and the revolvers were employed in a righteous cause. The tools were in the hands of one who could use them." In a seeming reference to Pottawatomie, Thoreau said that right-minded people must honor an antislavery hero like Brown "even though he were of late the vilest murderer, who has settled that matter with himself."

How did it happen that Thoreau, who had championed passive resistance in the 1840s, turned full circle to promote the nation's most violent Abolitionist? Why did Emerson, once dismissive of Abolitionism and other reform movements, do the same? Why did Alcott, an erstwhile champion of nonresistance, join them? It is crucial to probe their change, which explains why they and their fellow Transcendentalists pushed John Brown so vigorously.

The change can be attributed to three phenomena: the government's malfeasance of the 1850s, which prompted their disillusion and anger; the anarchistic individualism that they, along with other reformers of that decade, embraced; and a turnaround in cultural attitudes toward John Brown's historical prototype, Oliver Cromwell.

Between 1846, when President James Polk launched the Mexican War, and 1855, after various proslavery laws had been passed, the Transcendentalists' animus against the government, strong from the start, intensified into revolutionary anarchism. Before then, the Transcendentalists had espoused passive resistance, the typical antislavery protest gesture of the 1840s. The American Peace Society, founded in 1828, and the New England Non-Resistance Society, founded by William Lloyd Garrison a decade later, held that slavery must be opposed by pacifism. Many antislavery reformers embraced civil disobedience, allowing themselves to be taken to jail. Among the willingly incarcerated were the Abolitionist Stephen S. Foster, imprisoned for nonappearance in a military parade, and Nathaniel Allen, Erastus Brown, and Thomas P. Beach, all of whom did prison time for interrupting church meetings with antislavery statements.

These nonresistant protesters proudly assumed martyr roles. When Foster was jailed in May 1842 for civil disobedience, he announced, "My body is indeed incased in granite and iron, but I was never more free than at this moment; I have at length triumphed over every foe." Allen, likewise, wrote from his vermin-ridden jail cell, "I am better off than those for whom I plead. I am happy here, and I think I may be, in whatever situation my enemies may place me." Beach declared defiantly, "I want company here; I wish every jail in Massachusetts and New Hampshire filled with those who have boldness enough to go and charge upon these God-dishonoring corporations [i.e., churches] all the guilt" for slavery and other social ills.

In the early going, Transcendentalism was closely allied to nonresistance. Bronson Alcott attended conventions of Garrison's peace society. Stating in his diary, "I regard Non-Resistance as the germ of the New Church," Alcott instituted versions of nonresistance at the Temple School, where naughty students were asked to punish their teachers, and at Fruitlands, his short-lived utopian community where pacifism was preached. In 1843 he followed the lead of others when he was jailed after protesting against slavery by refusing to pay a poll tax.

Thoreau and Emerson espoused their own kinds of civil disobedience. During the 1840s, Thoreau famously withdrew from society by living for two years at Walden Pond and by refusing to pay his poll tax for six years, for which he spent a night in the Middlesex County jail in Concord. The antislavery reformer he then most admired was the New Hampshire pacifist Nathaniel P. Rogers, whom Lewis Perry describes as the "non-resistant of non-resistants" because he utterly rejected the vote, legislation, and physical force.

If, as Perry says, Rogers "out-Garrisoned Garrison" in his pacifism, Thoreau out-Rogered Rogers when in 1849 he produced his essay "Civil Disobedience." Virtuous people, Thoreau argued, would refuse loyalty to the American government as long as it is "the *slave's* government also." He not only bragged about his jail sentence, as had the previous reformers, but he rhapsodized about justified criminality. "Under a government which imprisons any unjustly," he wrote, "the true place is also a prison. The proper place to-day, the only place which Massachusetts has provided for her freer and less desponding spirits, is in her prisons."

Emerson had no jail term to boast of, but he shared the spirit of nonresistance. He supported the American Peace Society, addressing its convention in 1838, and six years later, in his address "Emancipation in the West Indies," he argued for calmness in dealing with slavery. "Let us withhold every reproachful and, if we can, every indignant remark," he advised antislavery reformers. "In this cause, we must renounce our temper, and the risings of pride." He pointed to the West Indies as a model of peaceful abolition. He described how England became progressively more enlightened about slavery until in 1833 it passed a law freeing the slaves on its islands. The emancipated blacks, too, were calm, accepting the news joyfully but quietly. Some whites had left the islands "anticipating insurrection and general murder," but, Emerson emphasized, there was "no riot, no feasting, . . . not the least disposition to gayety," as "tranquillity pervaded the towns and country." "I have never read anything in history more touching than the moderation of the negroes," he added, suggesting that a similarly tranquil abolition could be effected in America.

The Fugitive Slave Act of 1850 shattered the pacifism of the Transcendentalists. While a few other reformers, such as Adin Ballou and Garrison, would cling to nonresistance, the Concord set joined a growing movement toward antislavery violence. The movement was spearheaded by Henry C. Wright, later one of John Brown's most vocal defenders. A Massachusetts clergyman, Wright had been a Garrisonian pacifist but made a reversal in 1850, when he declared that every Northerner had the right "to arm himself with a pistol or a dirk, a bowie-knife, a rifle, or any deadly weapon, and inflict death with his own hand, on each and every man who shall attempt to execute the recent law of Congress, or any other law, made with a view to recapture and return to bondage fugitive slaves." Soon even some mainstream politicians—notably the Republicans Charles Sumner, William Seward, Joshua R. Giddings and Henry Wilson—were defending armed resistance to slaveholders.

To mention these figures, however, is to recognize how revolutionary the Transcendentalists became in the 1850s. The politicians talked about violence, but when it came to defending John Brown, they demurred.

The Transcendentalists were different. First they promoted the *idea* of righteous violence. Then they boldly promoted John Brown, the most violent anarchist of the era. Finally, they promoted his principles during the war.

The Transcendentalists' shift toward violence was begun by Theodore Parker, who formed a vigilance committee in Boston to fight those who tried to capture fugitive slaves. When Parker learned in 1850 that slave-hunters were pursuing two black members of his congregation, William and Ellen Craft, he armed himself, keeping a sword and a loaded pistol in his desk as he wrote his sermons. He organized antislavery mobs that intimidated the slave-hunters, who soon left town. He then remarried the Crafts, whose union in Georgia had been annulled. Handing each of them a sword during the ceremony, he had them vow, "With this sword I thee wed." He sent the pair by boat to England.

The case of the fugitive slave Anthony Burns in 1854 revealed graphically the Transcendentalists' turn toward violence. When Burns was confined in the Boston courthouse to await trial, Parker arranged for Burns's legal counsel while his fellow Transcendentalist Thomas Wentworth Higginson plotted a rescue. On May 26, Higginson, along with two blacks, led the battering-ram assault on the courthouse, setting off a scuffle with police in which a guard was killed. When the attack was repulsed, Higginson, wounded and bleeding, still wanted to fight, shouting to his fellows, "You cowards, will you desert us now?"

Another Transcendentalist there, Bronson Alcott, was even braver. Alcott had been walking by as the assault on the courthouse occurred. After talking with the injured Higginson, Alcott calmly walked unarmed up the courthouse steps and asked, "Why are we not within?" Getting no response from his cowed associates, he slowly descended the steps, firm despite the danger (Higginson later reported having heard a gunshot).

Although the two leading Transcendentalists, Emerson and Thoreau, did not participate in the Burns affair, their response to it proved, in the long run, to be even more significant than that of those who did. They were appalled when a Massachusetts judge approved the rendition of Burns, who was led in chains through the Boston streets by federal troops who took him to the ship that returned him to slavery. This implementation of the Fugitive Slave Act fanned Emerson's and Thoreau's rage against the government and pushed them toward a sympathy with anarchistic violence.

Neither of them acted upon this sympathy. They were *theorizers* of violence, not *committers* of it. But had they not first theorized, they never would have extolled the violent John Brown later on.

Thoreau's view was made clear in "Slavery in Massachusetts," a speech he gave at an Abolitionist rally in Framingham on July 4, a month after Burns had been returned to slavery. At the rally were most of the leading Abolitionists, including Garrison, who created a sensation when he publicly burned copies of the Fugitive Slave Act and the Constitution.

In his speech Thoreau did something even more shocking. Metaphorically, he burned all charters and laws, and he murdered the federal government. The Fugitive Slave Act? "Its natural habitat," he declared, "is in the dirt" along with "every venomous reptile." The Constitution? An outdated proslavery document; we must follow "a higher law than the Constitution." The press? A gurgling "sewer" clogged with "slime." Massachusetts? "Morally covered with volcanic scoriae and cinders, such as Milton describes in the infernal regions." America? Thoreau felt "a vast and indefinite loss." "I did not know at first," he added, "what ailed me. At last it occurred to me that what I had lost was a country." The solution? "My thoughts are murder to the State, and involuntarily go plotting against her."

Violent talk; but Thoreau was hardly ready to take violent action. His *thoughts* might murder the state, but he was not about to arm himself and enter the lists as an antislavery warrior. He had always retreated to nature for solace, and in his speech he did the same. He concluded with the consoling image of a white water lily growing from the mud. Just as the lily's "purity and sweetness" rises from "the slime and muck of the earth," so "purity and courage" could reappear in corrupt America, "notwithstanding slavery, and the cowardice and want of principle of Northern men."

Emerson also swung between violent imaginings and faith in nature. "America, the most prosperous country in the world," he said, "has the greatest calamity in the universe, negro slavery." Every bit as disgusted as Thoreau by the Fugitive Slave Act, he declared, "It is not easy to parallel the wickedness of this American law." For him, as for his friend, the law revealed the bankruptcy of all legislation: "These things show that no forms, neither constitutions nor laws nor covenants nor churches nor bibles, are of any use in themselves; the Devil nestles comfortably into them all."

Like Thoreau, Emerson called for aggressive individual action against a corrupt system. In a nation where rescuing fugitive slaves is considered treasonous, he wrote, "I submit that all government is bankrupt, all law turned upside down; that the government itself is treason." And "when the public fails in its duty, private men take its place." Emerson now prized armed resistance. He went so far as to maintain that California, where anarchy and vigilante justice ruled after the gold rush, "had the best government that ever existed," because "every man throughout the country was armed with knife & revolver & perfect peace reigned. Instant justice was administered to each offense."

He could talk about maintaining order with knives and revolvers, but he was no more likely than Thoreau to take up weapons himself. He, too, looked with hope to nature. "This law of nature is universal," he wrote; "gravity is only one of its languages; justice is another. . . . The sky has not lost its azure because our eyes are sick; the seas & waters are not wasted if the cholera has swept the men." Eventually, America would follow the universal cycle and rid itself of corruption, as nature did. "Nature is not so helpless but it can rid itself of every crime," he averred.

Emerson and Thoreau were in exactly the right frame of mind to embrace John Brown when he arrived in Concord in March 1857. He did what they only talked about. He did not just theorize about fighting the government; he had actually fought government troops in Kansas. He not only contemplated vigilante justice; he enforced it, using real weapons. If he was a lawbreaker, all the better, since law itself was a mockery—as evidenced yet again that same month by the Dred Scott decision, which stripped American blacks of social rights.

In their view he even had nature on his side. Emerson praised not only Brown's forceful tactics but also his closeness to nature. In the second part of his journal entry on Brown's speech, Emerson turned from violence to pastoralism. Painting a glowing picture of Brown's early career, he wrote:

> He had three thousand sheep in Ohio, and would instantly detect a strange sheep in his flock. A cow can tell its calf by secret signals, he thinks, by the eye, to run away, to lie down, and hide itself. He always makes friends with his horse or mule (or with the deer that visit his Ohio farm); and when he sleeps on his horse, as he does as readily as on his bed, his horse does not start or endanger him. . . . "God protects us in winter [in Kansas]," he said; "no Missourian can be seen in the country until the grass comes up again."

Brown's lapses as a farmer—for instance, his being "a rough herdsman," as his business associate Simon Perkins once commented—had no part in Emerson's picture. Emerson saw Brown as Brown saw himself: as the "Man on the farm," at one with nature, not as the mere farmer producing goods. In Emerson's rendering, Brown possessed an almost supernatural intimacy with nature. Brown could spot a strange sheep among three thousand. He understood cows' signals. He befriended horses and deer. Even the weather favored him. Small wonder that Emerson regarded Brown as wholly upright and protected by nature. "He stands for Truth," Emerson said, "& Truth & Nature help him unexpectedly & irresistibly at every step."

Thoreau, too, noted an uncanny closeness to nature in Brown, whom he called "a New England farmer" with "many original observations" of the natural world. "It is a pity," Thoreau said, "that he did not make a book of his observations."

The question remains, though: How could the Transcendentalists support John Brown despite his brutal crime at Pottawatomie? How could they worship him even after early November 1859, when the *New York Herald* reported that "he took five respectable men—heads of families—out of their beds at dead hour of night, and mutilated and murdered them in cold blood," and after Massachusetts Congressman Caleb Cushing in a speech in Faneuil Hall a month later described the anguish of Mahala Doyle and Louisa Wilkinson as they witnessed their loved ones killed by Brown, "his sword dripping with the gore of those slaughtered, inoffensive, peaceful, slumbering men and children"?

For an answer we must look beyond the Transcendentalists' violent impulses, which they never acted upon. We must consider their veneration of Brown's prototype Oliver Cromwell, the leader of the English civil wars and the ruler of England from 1653 to 1658.

Although John Brown's contemporaries compared him to many historical figures—Moses, Samson, Washington, Garibaldi, and Kossuth, to name a few—Cromwell was mentioned most often. To Frank Sanborn, Brown was "a Puritan soldier, such as were common enough in Cromwell's day, but have not often been seen since"; to George Stearns, he was "a Cromwellian Ironside introduced in the nineteenth century for a special purpose"; to Mary Stearns, "some old Cromwellian hero suddenly dropped down"; to Wendell Phillips, "a regular Cromwellian, dug up from two centuries"; to Richard Hinton, "a Puritan brought back from the days of Cromwell"; to James Hanway, "the Oliver Cromwell of America"; and so on.

Thoreau made the connection most eloquently: "He died lately in the time of Cromwell, but he reappeared here." His hard words about slaveholders were, Thoreau said, "like the speeches of Cromwell compared with those of an ordinary king," and his band of soldiers in Kansas missed being "a perfect Cromwellian troop" only because there was no clergyman worthy of joining it.

It is hardly exaggerating to say that Brown's supporters venerated him *because* they had previously venerated Cromwell. They were *prepared* to support him by their initiation into the Cromwell cult.

Cromwell was not easy to admire. For over a century after his death he was reviled as a murderer and a harsh dictator. By the 1850s, however, he was revered by some as a self-reliant hero.

Why the change in attitude toward Cromwell? The British author Thomas Carlyle had caused it almost singlehandedly. If John Brown could be favorably compared to Cromwell, it was because Carlyle had made Cromwell a figure worthy of emulation: not a heartless murderer or an intolerant fanatic but rather the embodiment of sturdy heroism and sincere religious devotion. The major blots on Cromwell's reputation—his massacre of innocent Irish during the civil wars or his abrupt dismissal of the Rump Parliament and his establishment of a military dictatorship—were shrugged off by the admiring Carlyle as excusable measures for stern times.

It was Carlyle's *On Heroes, Hero-Worship, and the Heroic in History* (1840) and his four-volume *Oliver Cromwell's Letters and Speeches with Elucidations* (1845) that caused the attitude shift. American reviewers noted Carlyle's radical departure from the long-standing view of Cromwell as "a sort of monster, of such horrid aspect and nature that to touch him at all is revolting." He had "been termed a regicide, a monster and a tyrant," the "quintessence of cant, falsity and the devil,— . . . a usurper, murderer, hypocrite and prince of liars."

What had made him especially problematic was the criminal excess of his assaults on Irish towns in 1849. In the name of God, Cromwell had "put to the sword," in his euphemistic phrase, thousands of Catholic priests, enemy soldiers, and unoffending villagers. After storming Tredah, Cromwell wrote: "I forbade [my soldiers] to spare any that were in arms in the Town, and I think, that night they put to the sword about 2,000 men. . . . I am persuaded that this is a righteous judgment of God upon these barbarous wretches [i.e., the Irish], who have imbrued their hands in so much innocent blood; and that it will tend to prevent the effusion of blood for the future."

Murder as "a righteous judgment of God." This was Cromwell's rationale in Ireland, as it would be John Brown's in Kansas. The rationale itself was not surprising. What made it unusual was that the age's leading thinkers accepted it.

For Carlyle the Irish bloodbath was a forgivable by-product of war carried out in the name of principle. Carlyle depicted Cromwell as the utterly sincere Puritan hero, "the soul of the Puritan revolt; without whom it had never been a revolt transcendently memorable, and an epoch in the world's history." The eighteenth century, Carlyle argued, had demonized Cromwell and other Puritans because it was a skeptical age that rejected religion. Carlyle revived the Puritans not because he accepted their Calvinistic doctrines but because he prized their sincerity and their resistance to tyranny. He wrote: "The Puritans to many, seem mere savage Iconoclasts, fierce destroyers of Forms; but it were more just to call them haters of *untrue* Forms."

Carlyle's version of Cromwell influenced the Transcendentalists and spread into American popular culture. If the Transcendentalists prized John Brown because he resembled Carlyle's Cromwell, it was because Brown had already shaped himself after Cromwell as he was described by the American writer Joel Tyler Headley, whose 1848 biography of Cromwell recycled Carlyle for the masses.

Brown was inspired by Headley's book, which he kept on his bookshelf next to the Bible. Headley portrayed Cromwell as a God-directed Calvinist whose murderous tactics were justifiable because they fostered the democratic spirit behind the American Revolution. For Brown, with his family roots in Puritan Calvinism and the American Revolution, the combination of religion, republicanism, and violence in Headley's book was liberating.

Not so for all readers. A contemporary reviewer complained that the book was half made up of "exaggerated descriptions of battle-scenes" in which "wholesale slaughter is bronzed over, until to many it ceases to be hateful. Human butchery is coolly described with such minuteness, that undisciplined minds will easily imbibe a gusto for blood."

Evidently, Brown had no such qualms, because he accepted the book's premise that bloody violence was admirable if waged in the name of religion and democratic revolution. He must have agreed with Headley's apologia: "Some may object to the battle-scenes of this work, . . . saying that I foster a spirit of war. To such, I have but one answer—the spirit of rebellion against oppression, and deadly hostility to it, I *design* to foster, and only hope to succeed. . . . Men have always been compelled to *hew* their way, with their swords, to freedom."

Brown admired such hewing the way to freedom in Cromwell (as reinterpreted by Carlyle and Headley), and he took such action in Kansas, where he used Cromwell's declaration: "Trust in God and keep your [gun]powder dry."

Having patterned himself after Cromwell, John Brown appealed to the New England intellectuals, who had been dreaming that someone like Cromwell would arise and make holy war against social corruption. When Emerson, for instance, said in his journal that to fight slavery people must become "citadels and warriors," he gave this example: "Cromwell said, 'We can only resist the superior training of the king's soldiers, by having godly men.' "

Hence the Transcendentalists' rapture over Brown's declarations that a principled few could defeat an unprincipled horde and that proslavery people had a perfect right to be killed. If the Concord group liked Carlyle's Cromwell, they loved his modern avatar, John Brown. For all his violence, Brown seemed, in Emerson's phrase, "the rarest of heroes, a pure idealist," or, in Thoreau's "a transcendentalist, above all a man of ideas and principles."

The theoretical warriors of Concord might rhapsodize over his heroism, but the actual warrior was thinking of the weapons, money, and supplies he needed. Brown was a man of "ideas and principles," to be sure, but he was an actor in history, not a spectator. He promoted himself so that he could reach a real end: the violent overthrow of slavery.

As zealously as Concord took to him, there is no evidence that he considered the town anything more than another stop on his fund-raising tour. The small amounts of money Emerson and other Concordites donated must have struck him as typical of the piddling contributions he had received in other New England towns. Little did he know that the Transcendentalists would turn into the most important contributors of all, lending their enthusiastic support in the first days after Harpers Ferry, when everyone else recoiled from him. Without them, as time would tell, history might have forgotten him altogether.

For now, he had his mind on practical concerns. One was his family, which, as usual, was stoically enduring near poverty in North Elba. When Amos Lawrence wired Brown that he was ready to contribute funds, Brown replied with a request for $1,000 to be used toward "an improved piece of land which with a little improvement I now have might enable my family consisting of a Wife & Five minor children (the youngest not yet Three years old) to procure a Subsistence should I never return to them; my Wife being a good economist, & a real old fashioned business woman." Lawrence, not expecting so large a request, backed off, explaining that he had just given $14,000 for a school in Kansas. But he said he would help Brown's kin should a crisis arise. "The family of Captain Brown of Osawatomie," he wrote, "will not be turned out to starve in this country, untill Liberty herself is driven out."

Over the next several months Lawrence gathered $1,000 from a dozen people, including Wendell Phillips, J. Carter Brown, and George Stearns. The money was slow in coming, but in late August, after a series of delays, a 160-acre land parcel was bought for the Brown family.

Meanwhile, Brown remained on the lecture circuit. He gave three talks in Worcester between March 21 and 26. In a speech in Connecticut, he said he was trying to raise some $20,000 to $25,000. He used black humor to provoke the citizens of his native state to donate to his cause. He declared: "I was told that the newspapers in a certain city were dressed in mourning on hearing that I was killed and scalped in Kansas, but I did not know of it until I reached the place. Much good it did me. In the same place I met a more cool reception than in any other place where I have stopped. If my friends will hold up my hands while I live, I will freely absolve them from any expense over me when I am dead."

His frustration deepened when Mary wrote from North Elba that his sons were abandoning the armed struggle against slavery. On March 31 he replied: "It was not at my solicitation that they engaged in it [fighting] at the first: & that while I may perhaps feel no more love of the business than they do; still I think there may be possibly in their day that which is more to be dreaded: if such things do not now exist." His words must have pricked his sons' consciences, for Owen, Watson, John, and Oliver, as well as William Thompson and his brother Dauphin Adolphus Thompson (the brothers of Brown's son-in-law Henry), would stand by him to the end.

Far less faithful was Hugh Forbes, a British soldier Brown hired as a drill instructor. Having fought under Garibaldi in the failed Italian revolution of 1848–49, Forbes sold silk in Vienna and then moved to New York around 1855, scraping by as a fencing instructor and part-time journalist. Like most European revolutionaries, Forbes hated slavery and sympathized with the Abolitionists.

When Brown met Forbes in New York in late March, he was predisposed to like him. He was impressed by Forbes's military experience and his commitment to arming American slaves. He admired Forbes's 1856 pamphlet *Duties of a Soldier,* a concise exposition of military principles reflective of Brown's own views. Just as Brown saw himself as an ethical warrior against depraved enemies, so Forbes painted a moral picture of war, calling it a conflict between Right and Wrong. Forbes wrote: "Right is that which is good true honorable just humane self-sacrificing—it is the precise opposite to Wrong. . . . Between Right & Wrong there can be no compromise." Just as Brown associated the U.S. Army with a corrupt federal government, so Forbes argued that it was the custom of "despotic governments to maintain large permanent armies of those living machines to stifle Right and to perpetuate Wrong." Forbes asked, "Will the soldiery of a republic consent to become living machines, & thus sustain Wrong against Right?"

Despite his clarion moral distinctions, Forbes turned out to be an opportunistic adventurer. His words about an "honorable," "self-sacrificing" principle of Right were belied by his actions. Brown, who was often too optimistic about those he believed in, offered Forbes $100 a month— excellent pay in an era of ten-to-twelve-hour workdays and $700 annual salaries—and invited him to draw off of $600 of Kansas contributions deposited in a Hartford bank. Forbes did so, siphoning off $120 for private purposes between April and August 1857. His immediate job for Brown was to translate a foreign pamphlet, *Manual of the Patriotic Volunteer,* for use at the Iowa training camp, but he dawdled on it, concentrating on trying to bring his destitute wife over from Paris to join their daughter in New York (he ended by sending the child to Paris instead). He did not show up in Iowa until August 9, four months after he had been put on Brown's payroll. Unstable and stubborn, he eventually became a Judas, turning against Brown and exposing his Harpers Ferry plan to people in high places.

Brown could not anticipate such betrayal when he hired Forbes in the spring of 1857, caught up as he was in the excitement of his eastern tour.

The tour was characterized by extreme ups and downs, and it was in a positive moment that Brown took Forbes on. By mid-April Brown reported to his family that $13,000 in supplies and cash had been contributed to his cause, and he expected to bring the amount to $30,000.

His excitement was checked when he learned that a United States deputy marshal passing through Cleveland was on his way to New England to arrest him for his Kansas activities. On April 15, Brown wrote a friend, "One of the U S hounds is on my track; & I have kept myself hid for a few days to let my track get cold. I have no idea of being taken; & intend (if 'God will';) to go back with irons in rather than uppon my hands."

He stayed for a week with Judge and Mrs. Thomas B. Russell, whose home on a Boston back street was a convenient hideout. Although sympathetic to Abolitionism, the Russells were not prominent in the movement and thus aroused little suspicion. They were fiercely protective of Brown. Mrs. Russell alone opened the front door and admitted only people she knew.

Brown stayed in an upstairs bedroom, barricading the entry with furniture. At night before retiring he checked the loads in his revolvers, once commenting, "Here are eighteen lives." He warned his hostess that if she heard noises at night to hide her young daughter and stay out of sight. He added wryly, "I should hate to spoil these carpets, too, but you know I cannot be taken alive." As usual, Brown was full of stories about Kansas, some of them laced so liberally with black humor that Mrs. Russell later recalled him as a funnyman.

He was aggravated, however, that his date with history was postponed. With the "U S hound" after him, his tour ceased and he boiled with frustration. While staying with the Russells, he wrote a bitter document titled "Old Browns *Farewell:* to the Plymouth Rocks; Bunker Hill, Monuments; Charter Oaks; and Uncle Thoms, Cabbins."

The title sarcastically brought attention to the fact that New England, with its ostensible dedication to liberty and equality, did little more than pay lip service to these ideals. Brown announced that he was returning to Kansas "*with a feeling of deepest sadness.*" He had tried mightily to arm and equip his "Minuet men," who had "suffered hunger, cold, nakedness, and some of them sickness, wounds, imprisonment in irons" while fighting for "a cause in which every man, woman, and child; of the *entire human family* has a *deep* and *awful* interest." Brown lamented that he could not "secure, amidst all the wealth, luxury, and extravagance of this 'Heaven exalted,' people; even the necessary supplies of the common soldier."

If Brown wrote this self-pitying statement to prompt further contributions to his cause, he succeeded. He read the "Farewell" aloud to Mary Stearns on one of her visits to the Russells, telling her he hoped that Theodore Parker would read it on Sunday to his congregation at the Music Hall. The document did not strike Mary as being appropriate for church, but she was deeply moved by it, especially when Brown told her that if he had only the money Boston spent on smoking and chewing tobacco in a single day, "I could strike a blow which would make slavery totter from its foundations."

Overcome with guilt, she suddenly thought that it was "mean and unworthy—not to say wicked—to be living in luxury while such a man was struggling for a few thousands to carry out his cherished plans." She related Brown's predicament to her husband, who immediately issued a promissory note for $7,000, to be used should a hundred "volunteer regulars" be needed for active duty in Kansas.

This generous contribution temporarily cheered Brown. On April 15 he wrote his son John that although "a good deal of discouragement" had left him "quite depressed," Stearns's money and Lawrence's subscription toward land for the North Elba family were promising developments. He said the same in a letter three days later to his cousin, the Reverend Heman Humphrey, and sketched out his current plans for securing Kansas for freedom. "First," he wrote, "we must *secure* the *good graces* of the U S Officers & Soldiers; at whatever cost: *not fight them.* Then we must *take Charge* of the first man we can *catch* attempting to enforce or put into operation those *abdominable Bogus enactments* [the proslavery Shawnee laws]. Then we must start a Free State Government under the Topeka Constitution."

Despite his conciliatory words, he was still committed to fighting federal forces as long as they were on the side of slavery. He was eager to return to the Territory to continue the battle. On April 30 he wrote an Albany friend that he found it "humiliating" to "go about in the attitude of a beggar," as he had been doing. He was returning to Kansas "without securing even an outfit." "I go with a *sad heart*," he added, "having failed to secure even a means of equiping; to say nothing of feeding men."

The complaint was not fully warranted. At about the time he made it, he was arranging to procure two hundred revolvers, to be added to the twenty-five already given him by the National Kansas Committee. He struck a deal with the Massachusetts Arms Company, which offered him the guns at $1,300, half the normal price, for the purpose "of aiding in your project of protecting the free state settlers of Kansas and securing their rights to the institutions of a *free America.*" Payment was arranged through the ever-generous George Stearns, who promised to pay for the guns in four months after he had raised the money through a subscription. The revolvers were later shipped to Brown in Iowa with the warning that they were to be used for no other purpose than to defend freedom in Kansas.

Brown was irritated by such stipulations. Time would tell that he was right to be so. Since January 1 he had raised some $23,000 for his Kansas effort, about $2,400 of it in cash and the remainder in supplies. Although this amount was impressive, Brown had to pay $550 for the pikes, $600 to Forbes, and much of the rest for traveling expenses. Some of the contributions came with red tape. For instance, Brown was never able to draw on Stearns's $7,000, as it was targeted for a troop of a hundred "volunteer regulars" should Brown need to call them to active duty in Kansas—an eventuality that never materialized.

But as he planned his return to his Iowa camp, Brown still dreamed of raising such a force. He wrote Augustus Wattles, a friend in the Territory, that he was glad that Kansans had so far refused "to *pollute themselves* by the *foul and loathsome* embrace of the *old rotten whore* [slavery]" and that he was ready to rejoin "the strife between Heaven and Hell" in the Territory. Wary of being traced by the authorities, Brown now signed his letters "Nelson Hawkins," the first of several pen names he would assume.

He was also cautious about visiting his family in North Elba, where federal "hounds" were apt to look for him. He spent nearly two weeks there in April, but by mid-month he was on his way west. He was in Peterboro on May 18 and made it to Cleveland four days later. He pushed on through Akron to Hudson, where a spell of fever and ague delayed him. His son Owen, then living in Hudson, joined him on his journey. In mid-June they went to Milwaukee and then Chicago, where they met up with Gerrit Smith, who donated $350 toward traveling expenses.

After attending the semicentennial celebration of the founding of Tallmadge, Ohio, on June 24, the pair proceeded to Iowa City. There they got word that Richard Realf, an English-born poet and antislavery soldier who had met Brown the previous summer in Kansas, was waiting in Tabor with nearly $100 donated by the National Kansas Committee. In Wassonville, Iowa, Brown and his son paid $786 for wagons and two teams of fresh horses that got them to Tabor by August 7. After all his expenses, Brown had only $25 to his name. Once again he lodged with the kindly Quaker Jonas Jones.

What had the eastern trip accomplished? Materially, it had been a mixed success. On the positive side, the weapons and other supplies Brown gained during the trip saw use not only in Kansas and Missouri but also at Harpers Ferry. On the negative side, hiring Forbes as drill instructor would prove to be a costly mistake, and the money he raised was negligible, given his heavy outlay.

But his symbolic gains were immeasurable. He had been promoting Kansas, and in the process he promoted himself. He had won the hearts of some of the most influential people in America—several of them wealthy, others in the intellectual elite, and all in search of a principled hero to counteract the nation's moral failings.

That the hero turned out to be a violent lawbreaker seemed all the better to those whose hatred of legal enactments had originated with the Fugitive Slave Act and had intensified with the Kansas-Nebraska Act and the Dred Scott decision. Such government-sponsored outrages against freedom and decency demanded violent vigilantism of the type John Brown had already provided and that he promised for the future.

None could foresee that the violence he introduced would soon engulf the entire nation.

10

Plotting Multiculturally

Although Brown had spent months raising funds for a war in Kansas, when he returned to the Territory in early August 1857 he found that the slavery issue was moving toward a peaceful resolution there. President Buchanan, perturbed by Governor Geary's Free State leanings, had replaced him in May with Robert J. Walker of Mississippi, who proved to be as judicious (and as disappointing to the proslavery administration) as Geary had been. Walker's six-month term as governor would exceed Geary's by only thirty days, but during his tenure Walker oversaw a state election that had positive results for the Free State side.

With Kansas being settled by ballots rather than bullets, John Brown pondered his next move. He stalled in Tabor, Iowa, for three months, recovering from malarial fever and a recent injury to his back. With the two hundred Sharps rifles that had been stored in Tabor, supplemented by the two hundred revolvers donated to him and the thousand pikes on order, he had plenty of weapons. But he lacked men and money—and a cause. Violence flared up occasionally in Kansas, but the calming influence of the Geary and Walker administrations had prevented large-scale invasions by border ruffians or U.S. troops of the sort that had once stirred Brown to action.

Brown's mood swings of the spring and early summer continued. On August 8 he wrote George Stearns that he was "quite unwell; & depressed with disappointments, & delays." The trip west had stripped him of money, his health was poor, and, worst of all, eastern donors were reneging. He had received only $260 of the $1,000 promised him in Hartford and a mere $25 of the same amount pledged in New Haven.

Two days later he wrote Stearns again, saying that he was delighted to hear that the North Elba tract had been purchased for his family with the money raised by Amos Lawrence. "This generous act has lifted a heavy load from my heart," he wrote. But he begged Stearns for cash: "I am in *immediate* want of from Five Hundred to One Thousand Dollars for *secret service & no questions asked. Will you* exert yourself to have that amount, or some part of it; placed in your hands subject to my order?"

As sympathetic as Stearns was, he was not about to give Brown so large an amount "no questions asked." He had always tied his contributions to activities in Kansas, and he had an edgy suspicion that Brown had other goals in mind.

He was right. Brown had long had in mind other goals—rather, one other goal—that he thought would lead to the downfall of American slavery. That was the invasion of northwestern Virginia and liberation of slaves in the region of Harpers Ferry. Shortly after Hugh Forbes, his dilatory drillmaster, arrived at Tabor on August 9, Brown began discussing the plan in earnest.

Brown and Forbes had strong differences about the Virginia plan, differences that revealed the divergent racial views of the two men. Brown's bold plan reflected his belief in the intelligence and the fighting spirit of enslaved African Americans. Forbes's conservative plan grew from his doubts about the capabilities of blacks. Brown's was progressive and multicultural; Forbes's was tinged with racism.

Brown maintained that a direct attack by twenty-five to fifty black and white men on a slave region would have instant, dramatic results. Slaves who had suffered years of cruelty and oppression would rise up at the first opportunity for emancipation. Within the first twenty-four hours of the attack, Brown figured, two hundred to five hundred blacks would join their liberators. Half of the freed blacks would help take over the federal armory at Harpers Ferry, seizing weapons and destroying arms factories. The other half would split into groups and raid other plantations, freeing additional slaves who would become new recruits. All would flee to the Allegheny Mountains, where natural defenses and guerilla warfare would thwart pursuers, even federal troops. Those blacks untrained in weaponry would be given pikes, scythes, shotguns, and other simple instruments; the trained ones would use Sharps rifles, as would the whites.

The invasion would spread south along the mountain chain, which ran deep into other slave states. Quick raids on plantations followed by retreat to the mountains would create an atmosphere of terror and insecurity that soon would destabilize slavery throughout the South. Brown's Northern friends would instigate a political movement to abolish slavery by law.

Southern congressmen and senators would join the movement because of the panic that had crippled their region.

Forbes found this plan quixotic. In his view, the initial raid should be undertaken not by a racially mixed force, which he thought would be weakened by blundering blacks, but by a band of carefully chosen, trained whites. Moreover, the attack must be launched with the expectation that enslaved African Americans would *not* respond favorably to their liberation. "No preparatory notice having been given to the slaves," Forbes said, "the invitation to rise might, unless they were already in a state of agitation, meet with no response, or a feeble one." Since a slave insurrection is "from the very nature of things deficient in men of education and experience," the raid that Brown proposed would be either a flash in the pan or would create anarchy. Liberated blacks could not be counted on to embrace their sudden liberation or act upon it responsibly.

Forbes's idea was to string a force of white raiders along the Northern slave frontier, especially on the borders of Virginia and Maryland, and make rapid forays on plantations. Instead of advancing south and establishing a colony in the mountains, the raiders would immediately send freed blacks north to Canada, so that pursuit would be impossible. The raids, made unpredictably once or twice a month and then every week, would create terror among slaveholders, who in time would want to rid themselves of slavery.

Brown's plan was far riskier than Forbes's not because Brown was foolhardy but because he was certain that blacks were capable of rising up, resisting capture, and forming a liberating army. When Forbes questioned him, Brown pointed to the history of African American culture, his main source of inspiration. Nothing, he said, terrified white Southerners more than slave insurrections. If Nat Turner with fifty men could hold a section of Virginia for several weeks, he declared, an ever-growing band of armed blacks and whites could topple slavery in the state and eventually throughout the South.

Although Brown pretended to go along with Forbes's so-called Well Matured Plan, inwardly he found it timid. He was beginning to regret having hired the suave adventurer. Not only had Forbes delayed in coming to Tabor, but he had been collecting a salary while doing nothing more than translating the *Manual of the Patriotic Volunteer.* Meanwhile, Brown had sent Forbes's pamphlet *Duties of a Soldier* to several of his eastern supporters but had not received the response he expected. Gerrit Smith politely wrote a friend that the pamphlet was "very well written" and that Forbes "will make himself very useful to our Kansas work," but such kudos were meaningless when Kansas had quieted down and Forbes had just two men, his employer and his son Owen, to train at Tabor.

The lack of personnel galled Brown. On his eastern trip he had met several men who had promised to join him, but they had proved as faithless as most of his financial donors. "Among all the good friends who promised to go with me," he wrote to Frank Sanborn, "not one could I get to stick by me and assist me on my way through."

Some of Brown's eastern supporters in turn became frustrated with him. Thomas Wentworth Higginson, always ready for rapid action, complained to Sanborn that Brown was dragging his feet. Even though Sanborn himself was beginning to have doubts, he appeased Higginson by writing him on September 11 that Brown was "as ready for revolution as any other man . . . but he needs money for his present expenses, and active support." Sanborn added: "I believe he is the best Disunion champion you can find, and with his hundred men, when he is put where he can raise them, and drill them (for he has an expert drill officer with him) will do more to split the Union than a list of 50,000 names for your convention, good as that is."

This statement was misleading. Brown was ninety-seven soldiers away from the hundred-man force Sanborn mentioned; his "expert drill officer" was in fact a money-grubbing opportunist; and Brown, far from being the nation's "best Disunion champion," dreamed of a united, racially integrated America.

Sanborn kept Higginson at bay with his equivocations and did his best to placate Brown, who hounded him for money. On October 1, Brown wrote, "I have all the Arms I am likely to need," but added that he had received only part of the $500 promised him by the Massachusetts Kansas Committee. To show that he knew how to spend wisely, he reminded Sanborn that he had paid $550 for "1000 superior Pikes as a cheap but effectual weapon to place in the [hands] of entirely unskilful, & unpracticed men."

He didn't have to convince Sanborn, who fully believed in him. But he did have to convince motivated men in the Territory to join him. He now eyed Kansas as a recruiting station.

Since early September, the Free State leader James H. Lane had been badgering Brown to come to Kansas to fend off possible border ruffian interference with the elections to be held there on October 5. Lane, still operating under the mentality of the 1856 Kansas wars, was itching for a fight. He envied the huge cache of arms Brown had in Iowa. He promised Brown teams, men, and money to help cart the weapons to Kansas. To sweeten the offer, he even appointed Brown brigadier general of the anti-slavery army he had raised.

Brown, his mind now on Harpers Ferry, begged off, citing poor health and inclement weather. He must have sensed that Lane wanted more than his weapons. The border ruffians did not interfere with the October election. Free State Kansans gained more than half of the fifty-two-member territorial legislature and defeated the proslavery delegate to Congress by over 4,000 votes.

The moment was favorable for Brown to raise an antislavery force. With large-scale military activity having ceased, there were many antislavery soldiers left over from 1856 who were hungry for more battles.

Brown went to Kansas to recruit such men. First he had to deal with Forbes, who was upset over not receiving his full salary and preoccupied with his family problems. On November 2, Brown took Forbes to Nebraska City and saw him off to the East. Forbes promised to set up a military camp in Ashtabula County, Ohio, to train Brown's recruits during the winter.

Brown, needing manpower, rolled into Kansas on a horse-drawn wagon with his son Owen on November 5. His money situation had stabilized somewhat. Lane had sent him $150 to attract him to Kansas, and E. B. Whitman, the territorial agent for the Massachusetts Kansas Committee, gave him $500 plus tents and bedding.

Whitman made the contributions with trepidation. He was unsure about Brown, who stayed with him in his home in Lawrence but left after two days without saying where he was going. Brown assured Whitman he would be in Kansas whenever a crisis arose, but he was evasive. Whitman later wrote a friend that he had seen Brown briefly in early November but "since then nothing has been heard of him and I know of no one, not even his most intimate friends, who know where he is. In the meantime he has been much wanted, and very great dissatisfaction has been expressed at his course and now I do not know as even his services would be demanded in any emergency."

Brown was scouring Kansas in search of recruits for Harpers Ferry. While staying with Whitman, he had sent for John E. Cook. A twenty-seven-year-old Connecticut native, Cook had been trained as a lawyer but had been attracted to Kansas by the slavery excitement. In the summer of 1856, just after the Battle of Black Jack, he had briefly teamed up with Brown. When summoned to Whitman's, he assumed that Old Osawatomie wanted him for more action in Kansas. Brown gave him no reason to think otherwise. He invited Cook to rejoin him in the fight against slavery, asking if there were others who might join as well.

Cook accepted the invitation and mentioned three friends—Richard J. Hinton, Richard Realf, and Luke F. Parsons—as possible recruits. It turned out that Parsons was the only one available. He and Cook met Brown outside of Lawrence and had a long discussion. A few days later Brown wrote Cook, telling him to come with Parsons to a spot near Topeka for another meeting. Cook and Parsons were told to bring along weapons and supplies, and to keep silent about the matter. This time Parsons did not come. Cook met Brown alone and camped with him for two days before going into Topeka. There they rounded up three more Kansas veterans: Aaron Dwight Stevens, Charles W. Moffett, and John H. Kagi.

Brown took his four recruits into the prairie northeast of Topeka, where he informed them they would be drilling that winter under Forbes in Ohio. For now they would stay in Tabor. Cook was sent back to Lawrence for additional men and money. He picked up $80 there and collected Parsons and Realf, with whom he traveled to Tabor, where he found Brown with the others as well as three more volunteers, Charles Plummer Tidd and William Henry Leeman, who had previously served under Brown, as well as Richard Richardson, an African American who had escaped from slavery in Missouri and had met up with Brown in Iowa.

There were now ten in the group: Stevens, Kagi, Moffett, Tidd, Richardson, Realf, Parsons, Leeman, Cook, and Owen Brown. They were adventurous men, all in their twenties except for Leeman, who was eighteen. They detested slavery and were committed to opposing it with violence. Still, they were stunned when Brown told them at Tabor that their ultimate destination was Virginia.

An argument broke out. Cook objected strongly to the Virginia idea. It was his understanding, he declared, that Brown had recruited him only for operations in Kansas and Missouri. Others made the same complaint. But Brown's magnetism and vision won the day. "After a good deal of wrangling," Cook recalled, "we consented to go on."

None of them, not even Brown, knew what he was getting into. It turned out that of this initial group, six would be among the twenty-one men who raided Harpers Ferry two years later. Two of them, John H. Kagi and William Henry Leeman, would be killed during the raid. Two others, John Brown and Aaron Stevens, would be severely wounded, then imprisoned, tried, and hanged. Three more—Owen Brown, Charles Tidd, and John Cook—would escape north; Cook would be recaptured and hanged.

These grim destinies were not foreseen in November 1857 as the recruits prepared to travel to Ohio, where they were to train that winter. At Tabor the men loaded the rifles, revolvers, ammunition, and supplies onto wagons to be shipped east. This matériel, after detours and long delays, would end up in Chambersburg, Virginia, at the Kennedy farm, the launching place for the attack on Harpers Ferry.

On December 4 the group embarked from Tabor on the long trip toward Ohio by foot, accompanying the heavily laden wagons. The winter weather was frigid, but the atmosphere among the travelers was warm. Each night around the campfire they sang songs like "From Greenland's Icy Mountains" and "The Slave Has Seen the Northern Star." Stevens, who had a wonderful baritone voice, led the singing, and Brown often joined in. Lively conversations sprang up. Racial prejudice; the effects of Abolitionism on the North and the South; the moral right to kill slaveholders; the cowardice of the Republican Party; definitions of sin; Shakespeare; Mormonism, Islam, and Greek orthodoxy—these and other subjects were debated as prairie wolves howled in the distance.

As the conversations showed, these men were intellectually curious. After Harpers Ferry, the Southern press would often describe Brown's followers as ignorant thugs or narrow fanatics. Such characterizations were off the mark. Kagi, for instance, had taught school and earned a law degree in Ohio before going to Kansas to fight slavery. Cook, in his pre-Kansas days, had attended Yale and clerked in the office of a famous New York lawyer. Most of the men were avid readers.

They were independent thinkers, too. Rarely did they agree on an issue, except slavery. And none of them accepted the religious views of their leader. John Brown could be called a fanatic, but not his followers. Although Cook was a regular churchgoer, he was the exception. The others rejected religion or sought replacements for it. John Kagi, according to a friend, was "an agnostic of the most pronounced type, so grounded in his convictions that he gave but little thought to what he considered useless problems." Surprisingly, Brown's son Owen was also a declared agnostic. Aaron Stevens, as noted, espoused spiritualism, in which he found evidence of an afterlife more convincing than in Christianity.

If the men had little sympathy for John Brown's Calvinistic doctrines, they found their real replacement for religion in John Brown himself. He believed that God had predestined him to free the slaves, using nature's God-built defenses, the Appalachians. His followers were caught up in his Puritan spirit, even as they dismissed his Puritan theology. They quarreled with him, and he shouted back ("Father starts an outrageous jawing about something which I said," Jason recorded in his diary on December 6). Several contested his Harpers Ferry plan. But in the end they willingly joined him in the cause he was ready to die for.

After an arduous 285-mile trip across Iowa, the caravan reached the town of Springdale, a quiet town amid gentle hills, about three days after Christmas. There, Brown tried to sell his horses to pay for the remainder of the trip to Ohio. He was unsuccessful, and he decided to set up the winter camp in Springdale. He stored his weapons with the Reverend John Todd and had his men board with Quaker residents who, though opposed to his martial tactics, endorsed his antislavery aims. The next month he arranged with William Maxson, an Abolitionist who had a farm in nearby Pedee, to house his men free for the rest of the winter in exchange for the teams and wagons Brown had brought from Tabor. Brown stayed in the home of Pedee resident John H. Painter, about half a mile away.

The group fell into a regular schedule that included military drills and educational activities. Brown had them study Forbes's *Duties of a Soldier.* In the absence of Forbes the experienced Stevens served as the instructor in weapons use and battle tactics, fashioning wooden swords for them to practice with. For entertainment and instruction, the men established a mock legislature, with elections, offices, and debates over issues such as, Why are the principles of 1776 forgotten in 1858, with all of America's social ills?

Monkey trials were held in which members of the group received black marks. Cook, a handsome man with blond hair and striking blue eyes, was strongly reproved "for hugging girls in Springdale Legislature." Less seriously, Owen Brown was charged with taking up with a local girl, Laura Wascott. Owen pleaded guilty to the charge and would have proposed marriage to Laura had he not sensed that his future as an antislavery warrior was uncertain. As it turned out, he remained loyal to her memory to the end of his long life.

Fights erupted. On February 9, Owen wrote in his journal, "Ugly words between Moffett, Cook and Leeman, much swearing and giving each other the lie." Nor were these three the only ones who quarreled. The sarcastic, overbearing Tidd loved needling the others, and his close friend Stevens, who had once nearly killed an army officer by bludgeoning him with a bugle, had a hot temper.

Most of the time, however, the men channeled their boisterousness into heated discussions. When they were in philosophical moods, they debated "evidence of truths, religious themes, mesmerism, ventriloquism, necromancy, spiritualism, psychology, electricity, spiritual existence after death, dread of death." At other times they took up scientific topics such as earthquakes and astronomy. In lighter moments they exchanged what Owen called "vulgar stories."

On one thing they agreed: the need for profound social changes that would bring justice to America's oppressed minorities. The most intriguing product of their discussions was a plan for an imaginary "State of Topeka," their utopian version of America. In this fictional state, true equality would reign, as opposed to the spurious equality of the American 1850s. The nation's discriminatory voting laws were challenged when the men passed a bill "conferring the right of suffrage upon all well disposed, qualified citizens, African and women," as Owen described it. This was a startlingly progressive idea. Calling Africans "citizens" defied the recent Dred Scott decision, and awarding blacks the vote anticipated the Fifteenth Amendment, which would come a dozen years later after a bloody war. Extending suffrage to women was equally daring; it anticipated the Eighteenth Amendment by more than five decades.

Most remarkable of all was the logo of the imaginary state. The group fashioned a state seal that showed a black man standing on a cannon and holding in his right hand a drawn sword, with the inscription JUSTICE TO ALL MANKIND. To make an angry, armed black man the state symbol was more than daring or progressive; it was revolutionary. It looked forward not to liberal legislation but to militant pronouncements by the likes of Robert F. Williams and Malcolm X.

John Brown, meanwhile, had his own militant pronouncement to make. He gave his men details of his planned raid on Virginia, without, however, mentioning his scheme to take over the federal arsenal at Harpers Ferry. Ordering the group to stay in Iowa for the winter, he traveled to Ashtabula County, Ohio, in mid-January. He found that Forbes had left for the East. It was not long before he learned that Forbes, disgruntled over the salary issue, had turned against him.

Forbes approached various antislavery figures in an effort to parlay his frustrations with Brown into cash for himself and his family. Unsure of who exactly was financing Brown, he spread his net wide, sending vituperative letters to Brown's supporters and leading Republican politicians in Washington. Time and again, he complained that Brown had paid only part of the salary he had promised. One of his first appeals, amazingly, was to Senator Charles Sumner, who knew almost nothing about Brown.

Forbes claimed that Brown was a scoundrel who had teamed with Eastern "humanitarians" in a dangerous scheme. In a surprise visit to another prominent senator, William H. Seward, he described Brown as a "very bad man" who "would not keep his word, . . . a reckless man, an unreliable man, a vicious man." To Samuel G. Howe he wrote, "The humanitarians and Brown are guilty of perfidy and barbarity, to which may be added stupidity. . . . I am the natural protector of my children, nothing but death shall prevent my defending them against the barbarity of the New England speculators." In May 1858 he approached Senator Henry Wilson on the floor of Congress, ranting about Brown's wickedness. Horace Greeley, the editor of the *New-York Tribune*, reported that Forbes "came to me (as to others) with complaints that he had been deceived, misled, swindled, beggared, his family turned into the streets to starve" by Brown.

Forbes's cries for help, made to people who knew him slightly or not at all, had little effect other than to discredit himself. Greeley, vaguely aware that Forbes had been paid to drill soldiers in the Territory, wrote, "I only know that he did nothing, and was practically worth nothing," and that his slurs on Brown were groundless. Seward felt that Forbes was "a man of an unsound mind or very much disturbed mind" and that his report about Brown was "very incoherent, very erratic." Brown himself treated Forbes circumspectly. After receiving a scathing letter from him, he communicated with him through a third party. Brown was still ready to go ahead with the Virginia plan soon, but the members of the Secret Six, with the exception of Higginson, demanded postponement until the Forbes storm had blown over.

Brown would have found it difficult to invade Virginia anyway until he had more money and men. He needed to rally his eastern supporters. But with Forbes on the rampage, he needed to do so quietly, without revealing his whereabouts.

Having spent very little time with his wife and family over the past three years, he was desperately homesick. On January 30 he wrote Mary, "The anxiety I feel to see my *Wife*; & Children once more; I am unable to describe." Going home, however, was risky, for it could lead to his capture and arrest as result of Forbes's revelations. "My reasons for keeping still," he wrote, "are sufficient to keep me from seeing my *Wife*; & Children: *much as I long to do so*." Wary of visiting North Elba, Brown hid out in Rochester at the home of his old friend Frederick Douglass, where he spent three weeks in February 1858.

Brown got his Virginia project in motion. He wrote his closest backers, asking them to meet him at the end of the month at the Peterboro home of Gerrit Smith. He explained to Higginson that he needed between $500 and $800 "for the *perfecting* of BY FAR the most *important* undertaking of my whole life." He said he had also written Sanborn, Stearns, and Parker, although he still wasn't sure about the intensity of their commitment. Were they real Abolitionists? "I suppose they are," he wrote tentatively. When Higginson asked for further details about the current project, Brown referred to the Underground Railroad: "Rail Road business on a *somewhat extended* scale is the *identical* object for which I am trying to get means. I have been connected with that business as *commonly conducted* from my boyhood and *never* let an opportunity slip. I have been opperating to some purpose *the past season;* but I now have a measure on *foot* that I feel *sure* would awaken in you something more than a *common interest* if you could understand it."

The railroad business "on a *somewhat extended* scale." The words understated dramatic differences between Brown's plot and the Underground Railroad. For decades, blacks who escaped from slavery on the Underground Railroad chose among four main routes that led north: the Atlantic coast, along sea passages and swamps that stretched from Florida to Virginia; the Appalachian Mountains, which went from the Deep South to upstate New York and northern New England; the Cumberland Mountains of Kentucky and other Southern states, leading up to Ohio and Michigan; and the Mississippi River Valley. In all cases, the goal was the North and freedom.

Brown's project was something altogether new: not a "railroad" passage to the white-dominated North but an armed invasion of the South, using the Appalachians as a shield for an ever-expanding colony of blacks. In early February he wrote his son John, asking him "to get good Maps & State statistics of the different Southern States." Found among Brown's papers in the aftermath of Harpers Ferry were slave statistics and the maps of seven Southern states, with the main slave counties marked as targets. Brown expected his revolution to spread like a wildfire from Virginia southward through Tennessee, Alabama, and Mississippi to Georgia and other states. Thousands of blacks would flee to him, establishing an independent mountain society that, if necessary, could last for years, like the durable maroon communities of Jamaica.

Such a multicultural society, Brown decided, needed its own constitution. When he was staying at Douglass's home, Brown wrote his "Provisional Constitution and Ordinances for the People of the United States."

This document has been roughly received over the years. Many regard it as proof of Brown's insanity. It was presented as such during Brown's trial by his lawyer, Samuel Chilton, who, to counter the view of it as treasonous, called it "ridiculous nonsense—a wild, chimerical production" that "could only be produced by men of unsound minds." Most commentators have agreed. Even those most sympathetic to Brown, such as Hermann Von Holst and Oswald Garrison Villard, have excoriated the constitution. Von Holst dismisses it as a "piece of insanity, in the literal sense of the word," a "confused medley of absurd, because absolutely inapplicable, forms." Villard considers it "a chief indictment of Brown's saneness of judgment and his reasoning powers."

Brown's effort to write a new constitution "for the people of the United States" seems, on the surface, an act of hubris at best. Considered against the background of the American 1850s, however, the document makes sense.

The American Constitution as it stood in that decade was a highly contested text. Abolitionists like Garrison and Phillips were calling it "a covenant with death and an agreement with hell" because it indirectly sanctioned slavery. Republican leaders like William H. Seward, in an effort to counteract the seemingly proslavery implications of the Constitution, had been insisting since 1850 that there was a "higher law" than the Constitution—the law of morality and justice. The South, in the meantime, based much of its argument in defense of slavery on the Constitution, pointing out that slavery had existed in twelve of the thirteen original American states, had been tolerated by the founding fathers, and had been supported by the Constitution's three-fifths clause and its passage about the return of fugitives.

This assumption that the Constitution was proslavery was strengthened immeasurably in 1857 by Chief Justice Roger Taney's ruling in the Dred Scott case that blacks were not American citizens.

By 1858, therefore, the nation's legal institutions—the Constitution, the Supreme Court, and the laws of the land such as the Fugitive Slave Act and the Kansas-Nebraska Act—were lined up in support of slavery. Given this pervasively proslavery legal landscape, it is understandable that John Brown, ardently and passionately opposed to slavery, would attempt to present to the United States a new constitution, one that awarded full rights and citizenship to America's oppressed minorities.

Those who lambast Brown's constitution are insensitive to its progressive treatment of race. Villard, for instance, sneers at the idea that a colony of blacks in the mountains would be able to build churches and schools. Villard writes, "The whole scheme forbids discussion as a practical plan of government for such an uprising as was to be carried out by a handful of whites and droves of utterly illiterate and ignorant blacks."

Brown's goal, however, was to build an American society in which blacks and other minority groups would *not* be "utterly illiterate and ignorant," one that considered them responsible, educable citizens on the same footing as whites.

This aim was made clear in the remarkable opening passages of Brown's constitution:

> Whereas, slavery throughout its entire existence in the United States, is none other than the most barbarous, unprovoked, and unjustifiable war of one portion of its citizens upon another portion, the only conditions of which are perpetual imprisonment and hopeless servitude or absolute extermination; in utter disregard and violation of those eternal and self-evident truths set forth in our Declaration of Independence: Therefore
>
> We, the citizens of the United States, and the oppressed people, who, by a recent decision of the Supreme Court are declared to have no rights which the White Man is bound to respect; together with all of the people degraded by the laws thereof, Do, for the time being ordain and establish ourselves the following Provisional Constitution and Ordinances, the better to protect our Persons, Property, Lives, and Liberties; and to govern our actions:

> ### ARTICLE I.
> #### *Qualifications for membership*
> All persons of mature age, whether Proscribed, oppressed, and enslaved Citizens, or of the Proscribed and oppressed races of the United States, who shall agree to sustain and enforce the Provisional Constitution and Ordinance of this organization, together with all minor children of such persons, shall be held to be fully entitled to protection under the same.

What made this passage extraordinary was that it imaginatively resolved the controversial issues of slavery and race that were left ambiguous in the American Constitution. The latter did not mention slavery by name. In Brown's constitution, in contrast, "slavery" was the second word (or first one, if "Whereas" was set aside). The American Constitution implicitly condoned slavery. Brown's document called it the "most barbarous, unprovoked, and unjustifiable war of one portion of its citizens upon another portion"—a statement notable not only for its definition of slavery as a state of war but also its declaration, in opposition to Chief Justice Taney, that blacks were citizens victimized by their white fellow citizens.

The attack on Taney became overt in the second paragraph, where Brown condemned "a recent decision of the Supreme Court" by which blacks were "declared to have no rights which the White Man is bound to respect." In the society imagined by Brown's constitution, full citizenship was granted not only to blacks but to *all* oppressed or marginalized groups. Brown made a point of including "all of the people degraded by the laws" of the United States, "whether Proscribed, oppressed, and enslaved Citizens, or of the Proscribed and oppressed races of the United States, . . . together with all minor children of such persons."

Brown's main focus, then, was America's most oppressed group, African Americans; but by implication he encompassed other maltreated groups as well, such as women, children, and Native Americans and other ethnic minorities. Brown's constitution was unprecedented with regard to its inclusiveness with regard to race, gender, and age. Given this, the remainder of the constitution, which outlined governmental officers and their duties, became equally noteworthy, since it was assumed that all ethnic groups or women could assume leading roles in the new provisional government.

Brown's government was a slightly revised version of the American government. It had three branches: the executive, consisting of a president and vice president; the legislative, with a House of Representatives; and the judicial, made up of a Supreme Court and lower circuit courts. There was a separate commander in chief of the armed forces, to be chosen by the executive branch. The cabinet consisted of secretaries of state, war, and the treasury.

The key difference between Brown's organization and the existing American government was that it was devoted to protecting the rights of all the "Proscribed and oppressed races of the United States." Brown's plan for ethnic minorities to have key roles in his government would be fulfilled during the convention of African Americans and antislavery whites he held in Chatham, Ontario, in May 1858. At the convention, which approved Brown's constitution, several blacks were elected as officers of the provisional government.

Though revolutionary, Brown's constitution was meant to reform, not supplant, the American system. Article 46 of the document, titled "THESE ARTICLES NOT FOR THE OVERTHROW OF GOV'M'T," said that the provisional constitution "shall not be construed so as in any way to encourage the overthrow of any State Government of the United States:

and look to no dissolution of the Union, but simply to Amendment and Repeal. And our flag shall be the same that our Fathers fought under in the Revolution." Like the Garrisonians, Brown wanted to jettison the American Constitution. Like Lincoln, he wanted to preserve the Union. Unlike both, he wrote a new constitution that affirmed an American Union based on racial equality.

His constitution was hardly unproblematic. Its behavioral rules give one pause. One of its articles said, "Profane swearing, filthy conversation, indecent behavior, or indecent exposure of the person, or intoxication, or quarrelling, shall not be allowed or tolerated; neither unlawful intercourse of the sexes." So much for free speech and civil liberties. Public officials who got drunk could be removed. Rape of female prisoners was punishable by death. Divorce was discouraged; incompatible couples must make every effort to stay together. "Schools and churches [were to be] established, as soon as may be, for the purpose of religious and other instructions; and the first day of the week regarded as a day of rest appropriated to moral and religious instruction and improvement." All persons "known to be of good character, and of sound mind and suitable age, . . . whether male or female" were "encouraged to carry arms openly."

In real life, enforcing such rules would have been impractical, if not impossible. But the society Brown envisaged was not a normal one. It reflected his preoccupations in a time of widespread social inequities and personal corruption. Brown's constitution reflected the full range of his Puritan values, from the radical to the prudish. Like rebellious Calvinists from Anne Hutchinson to Wendell Phillips, he defied established laws in the name of what he regarded as Christian justice. Like conservative Calvinists from Cotton Mather to Lyman Beecher, he insisted on moral rectitude. His imagined society featured racial and gender equality but also strictly enforced morality. In it people of all ethnic backgrounds would, he hoped, become educated, upright, and productive citizens.

It was apt that Brown wrote his new constitution at the home of Frederick Douglass. Not only was Douglass the most prominent black Abolitionist in America, but he was in a position, like no other American, to appreciate the unified, fully integrated America that Brown envisaged. Five years earlier Douglass had broken with Garrison over the issue of the Constitution. Because Garrison thought that the Union as defined in the Constitution countenanced slavery, he advocated disunion, or separation of the North and South. Douglass, in contrast, had come to see the Constitution as being antislavery in its spirit; he therefore endorsed perpetuation of the Union along with emancipation of the slaves and integration of blacks into white society—exactly what John Brown called for in his provisional constitution.

Douglass had come to identify with Brown in other ways as well. Despite the militancy of his autobiographical *Narrative* (1845), famous for the scene in which he had a fistfight with a cruel overseer, Douglass initially believed that slavery could be overcome peacefully. It was John Brown who changed his mind. Not long after Brown first revealed to him his plan for invading the South, Douglass abandoned his pacifism. He said of Brown: "My utterances became more and more tinged by the color of this man's strong impressions." By 1849, Douglass said he would welcome the news that blacks had arisen in the South and "were engaged in spreading death and destruction there."

Time would prove that Douglass was not as brave as his words. He refused Brown's invitation to join the raid on Harpers Ferry, much to Brown's dismay. After the raid Douglass criticized it and fled to Canada and then England. In later years he always distanced himself from Harpers Ferry.

But not from John Brown himself. He appreciated Brown's integrationist ideals as no one else of the time did. "Brave and glorious old man!" he called him. He explained that "with the statesmanship, civilization and Christianity of America, the negro is simply a piece of property, having no rights which white men are required to respect; but with John Brown and his noble associates, the NEGRO IS A MAN, entitled to all the rights claimed by the whitest man on the earth." Although Douglass wanted the world to know he had nothing to do with Harpers Ferry, he also wanted to say that the impulse behind it was noble. "History has no better illustration of pure, disinterested benevolence," Douglass said of Brown. "It was not Caucasian for Caucasian—white man for white man; not rich man for rich man, but Caucasian for Ethiopian—white man for black man—rich man for poor man—the man admitted and respected, for the man despised and rejected." Douglass, then, admired Brown's demand for what today would be called a multicultural America, one in which all ethnic groups lived in a society of equal rights and mutual respect.

Doubtless, Douglass admired the spirit of Brown's constitution. Two members of what would become the Secret Six were less sure. By February 18, 1858, Brown was in Peterboro at the elegant home of Gerrit Smith, where he had hoped to meet his eastern supporters to consolidate the funding of his Harpers Ferry raid. Of the six, only Smith himself and Frank Sanborn were present. In an upper story of Smith's house Brown read aloud his provisional constitution. Sanborn recalled, "It was an amazing proposition—desperate in character, wholly inadequate in its provision of means, and of most uncertain result. Such as it was, Brown had set his heart on it as the shortest way to restore our slave cursed Republic to the principles of the Declaration of Independence; and he was ready to die in its execution."

If the constitution was "wholly inadequate," Brown's plan for raiding Virginia was no better, in the eyes of Sanborn and Smith. The two listened dubiously until late one evening as Brown told them of his plan to set the South aflame with revolution by invading northern Virginia near the Alleghenies. Wisely, he kept from them the idea of taking the federal arsenal at Harpers Ferry; certainly they would have rejected outright a direct attack on the United States government.

As it was, they peppered him with objections, which he deflected with Puritan certitude. As Sanborn recalled, he and Smith spent hours "proposing objections and raising difficulties," but when they pointed out "the grand difficulty of all,—the manifest hopelessness of undertaking anything so vast with such slender means," Brown quoted the Bible: "If God be for us, who can be against us?" What he needed was between $500 and $800 to initiate the project in the spring. Toward dusk the next day his skeptical comrades trudged through the snow in the surrounding woods and fields, discussing Brown's plan.

Most likely it would fail, they agreed, but it was a heroic gesture. "We cannot give him up to die alone," Smith remarked; "we must support him." Smith promised to donate money to Brown and asked Sanborn to solicit funds from his Massachusetts friends. Sanborn said he would. But as he headed back to Boston on February 24, he remained skeptical. He later recalled, "It was done far more from our regard for the man than from hopes of immediate success."

Sensing Sanborn's doubt, Brown encouraged him in a letter, expressing joy that "you felt ½ inclined to make a common cause with me" and telling him "what an inconceivable amount of good you might so effect, by your *counsel, . . . your natural, & acquired* ability; for active service." Brown insisted that he would lose nothing even if he died during the invasion: "I expect to effect a mighty conquest even though it be like the last victory of Samson."

He now began to turn in earnest to the group from whom he expected the most enthusiastic support: Northern blacks. This was an innovative move. As mentioned earlier, most white Abolitionists of the day were racists who did not like working with blacks. Sometimes this prejudice was blatant, as in the case of the author Oliver Wendell Holmes, Sr., who declared that "the white man must be the master in fact, whatever he is in name," or the antislavery scientist Louis Agassiz, who said, "The brain of the Negro is that of the imperfect brain of a 7 month's infant in the womb of a white."

More surprising was the subtle racism that tainted the era's most important antislavery organization, Garrison's American Anti-Slavery Society. Only three blacks had sat on the group's sixty-three-person planning session in December 1831, and over the years little changed. Except for Frederick Douglass and a handful of other celebrities, few blacks were assigned prominent positions in the organization. Profound disillusion with the Garrisonians had led many black reformers to organize their own movement in the 1850s. Douglass himself had split with Garrison in 1853, and others followed. As the doctor and editor Martin R. Delany explained in 1854, blacks had expected that the Garrisonians would "take the colored man by the hand, making common cause with him in affliction. . . . But in all this we [blacks] were doomed to disappointment, sad, sad disappointment," since "we find ourselves occupying the very same relation to our Anti-Slavery friends, as we do in relation to the pro-slavery party of the community—a mere secondary, underling position."

John Brown, far from shunning African Americans, learned from them, worked with them, lived with them, and wanted to fight alongside them. His Virginia plan had derived principally from black culture—particularly slave uprisings and maroon life—and he received his main encouragement and moral support from blacks. He was so unusual for his time that a few African Americans were actually dubious of him, convinced that no white could possibly want to sacrifice himself for them.

The most common response to him among Northern blacks, however, was astonished enthusiasm. For instance, Dr. and Mrs. James N. Gloucester, the African American couple he stayed with in Brooklyn after leaving Gerrit Smith's in late February, were wholly behind the Virginia plan. Brown had withheld details of the plan from his white advisers. Not so with the Gloucesters, who learned and approved of the idea in all its militancy. Although Brown doubtless requested a donation from the well-to-do Gloucester, his main reason for seeing the doctor was to gain access to a network of other blacks who might join the fast-developing plot. While staying with the Gloucesters, Brown wrote Jermain W. Loguen, an African American preacher in Syracuse, requesting his advice and help. Loguen was a good person to consult, for he had recently rejected Garrison's nonresistance, proclaiming that he would "fight a slaveholder" should the opportunity arise.

As eager as Brown was to involve blacks in his plan, he didn't lose sight of his six white backers, his main source of funds. In early March he headed for Boston to confer with them. On the train ride there he fortuitously met another important white associate, Dr. Alexander Milton Ross. The thirty-six-year-old Ross was an Ontario-born physician and natural scientist who had turned against slavery at a young age and had devoted himself to its destruction in 1852 after reading Stowe's *Uncle Tom's Cabin*.

Ross had made several daring tours through the South, ostensibly to follow his avocation as an ornithologist but actually to arm slaves and direct them north on the Underground Railroad. He helped hundreds escape and once in Mississippi was arrested and nearly lynched by proslavery citizens. Largely forgotten today, Ross had a high reputation in his time, winning praise from Whittier, Stowe, and others. Wendell Phillips told him, "No higher exhibition of heroism or chivalry was ever displayed, than by you in your humane and daring raids into the slave states, to let the oppressed go free." A polymath, Ross also won the praise of Emerson, who said, "My brave Canadian knight is not only the deliverer of the slaves, but a lover of flowers, birds and old English poetry." During the war Ross was selected as Lincoln's confidential correspondent in Montreal, and he later received honorary knightships from several nations, including Russia, Italy, Greece, and Persia.

As a celebrity, Ross met many famous people, but toward the end of his life he singled out John Brown for special praise. He wrote, "I have been in the presence of many men whom the world calls great and distinguished, but never before or since have a I met a greater or more remarkable man than John Brown."

The admiration was mutual. The year before, while returning to Iowa after his eastern tour, Brown had stopped to see Ross, who was then in Cleveland. The two talked intensely for several hours, Ross relating his experiences liberating slaves and Brown presenting his idea of invading Virginia. Brown castigated "that class of abolitionists who, from their abodes of safety in the North, spoke so bravely in behalf of the oppressed coloured people of the Slave States, but who took good care to keep their precious bodies north of the Potomac." He argued that only by going into the South and sparking insurrections could one destroy slavery. He told Ross he had studied guerilla warfare and was confident that he could, "with a small body of picked men, inaugurate and maintain a Negro insurrection in the mountains of Virginia, which would produce so much annoyance to the United States Government, and create such a feeling of dread and insecurity in the minds of slaveholders, that slavery would ultimately be abolished."

When Brown again saw Ross on the train in March 1858, he gave more details of the Virginia plot. He said the raid would take place that fall. He was training a score of soldiers in Iowa, and he expected to get more recruits at the antislavery convention he was organizing in Chatham, Ontario. He had weapons for two hundred and had contracted for a thousand pikes. He told Ross that an invasion of the South had been his dream for two decades. Reiterating his plan for a mountain community in the South, he said he surely would attract a sizable population of blacks. "He felt confident," Ross recalled, "that the negroes would flock to him in large numbers, and that the slaveholders would soon be glad to let the oppressed go free; that the dread of a negro insurrection would produce fear and trembling in the Slave States; that the presence in the mountains of an armed body of Liberators would produce a general insurrection among the slaves, which would end in their freedom."

Heady talk; but first he had to tend to practical matters. On March 5 he arrived in Boston and met with five of his backers: Sanborn, Higginson, Parker, Howe, and Stearns. He told them he needed $1,000, soon. He also asked Sanborn to contribute a number of books, including a biography of Napoleon and Irving's life of Washington, to be read by his men back in Springdale. The books were easy to get, but not the money. Brown left Boston on March 8 with the assurance that every effort would be made to raise $1,000. But two weeks later he got word that Stearns had raised only $150, Parker $100, and Howe $50. By the end of April just $410 was on hand. Eventually, the Boston visit yielded him a total of $600, with much smaller sums from other cities—meager resources for an attempt to dismantle the South's peculiar institution.

Still, Brown remained calmly optimistic. Because of Forbes's revelations, Brown now wore a long beard and called himself Nelson Hawkins to cloak his identity. His appearance at fifty-eight was distinctive. Although he was now stooped, his gait was as purposeful as ever. His friend Richard Hinton said, "The whole form moved steadily onward, never swaying, but walking as if on a visible line, prearranged for the occasion. Everyone gave way; a crowd parted like the waters, as when a strongly driven boat presses through." His white beard softened his cragged face, giving him a grave dignity. His eyes had a keen alertness, "the look," Hinton noted, "of the uncowed man in constant danger and always on the watch, in some respects the 'hunted' look."

For all he knew, he *was* hunted, given Forbes's mischief. But this didn't stop his trip. He met up with John Jr. in Philadelphia; they moved on to New York, New Haven, and North Elba. He was with his family there the last week of March. By April 2 he was back in Peterboro at the home of

Gerrit Smith, who remained supportive. Three days later he was in Rochester, where his black friend Jermain W. Loguen joined him. With Loguen he went north to St. Catherines, Ontario, reaching there on the seventh.

At St. Catherines he made a point of seeing Loguen's friend Harriet Tubman. Born into slavery in Maryland around 1819, Tubman had escaped north in the 1840s and became a leader of the Underground Railroad. Fearlessly, she returned south many times, aiding the escape of some three hundred slaves, including members of her own family, whom she resettled in St. Catherines. Her character resembled John Brown's. She did not know fear, and she dedicated herself to those worse off than she. She was perhaps even more severe than he. She permitted no whining from those she guided north. To prevent her escape routes from being revealed, she threatened to shoot anyone who had second thoughts and tried to return to slavery.

Small wonder that Brown wanted to involve Tubman in the Virginia plan, either in the raid itself or in ushering to Canada some of the blacks he freed. He praised this African American woman highly. Race or gender did not matter: in his eyes, the high-principled Tubman was tougher than anyone he had ever met. Pointedly, he referred to her as "he" or "the General." On April 8 he wrote his son John, "I am succeeding *to all appearances* beyond my expectations. Hariet Tubman hooked on *his* whole team at once. He *Hariet* is the most of *man* naturally; that I *ever* met with. There is the most abundant material; *& of the right quality:* in this quarter; beyond all doubt."

The quality "material" in Canada included not only Tubman but also many others Brown would have liked to join him. Some 75,000 blacks lived in the British-governed Canada West, most of them ex-slaves who had fled there to enjoy their freedom. By all accounts, their resettlement was a success. A large majority of the blacks who settled there, especially in Toronto, Buxton, and Chatham, led productive lives. They established schools and churches. They entered the trades and also became doctors, lawyers, ministers, and businesspeople.

Brown spent three weeks in Canada trying to tap into this rich body of potential recruits. His most important contact was the distinguished black doctor and editor Martin R. Delany. Three times Brown sought him out until he found him. Delany promised to help attract Canadian blacks to the antislavery convention in Chatham that Brown was planning.

Getting Delany on board was a real coup. Delany was known to hate white antislavery reformers. The era's leading spokesperson for black pride, the Pittsburgh-based doctor branded both the Garrisonians and the colonizationists as racists with whom blacks should no longer work. He headed the black emigration movement, arguing that blacks must leave America in order to establish an independent nation free of prejudiced whites. He envisaged a mass emigration of blacks to the Caribbean, South America, or Africa. Eventually, his focus shifted, and during the war he became one of the North's first commissioned black officers.

John Brown had much to do with Delany's change from an angry black separatist to a warrior for an integrated Union. Delany found in Brown something he had never seen in a white: the desire to organize an antislavery movement cosupervised by blacks and whites and committed to the violent overthrow of slavery. If America could produce a man like Brown, Delany decided, it was a nation worth fighting for.

For Delany, Brown was a model of toughness. When Delany expressed surprise that Brown "was unable to effect [a militant antislavery convention] in the United States," Brown replied, "Why should you be surprised? Sir, the people of the Northern states are cowards; slavery has made cowards of them all. The whites are afraid of each other, and the blacks are afraid of the whites. You can effect nothing among such people. . . . It is men I want, and not money. . . . Men are afraid of identification with me, though they favor my measures. They are cowards, sir! Cowards."

Brown's words struck home with Delany, who thought Northern whites were spineless hypocrites and free blacks were toadies. He had once said sneeringly of his fellow blacks, "We cling to our oppressors like objects of our love." In Brown he encountered a white who was not only brave and unprejudiced but who also demanded self-respect and action from black people. Delany was ready to do what he could to help organize the Chatham convention, scheduled for the following month.

The choice of Chatham was apt. The principal town of the County of Kent, Chatham was a hub of culture and politics for Canadian blacks. It featured the Wilberforce Educational Institute, a well-known school for blacks, as well as a black-controlled newspaper and a number of churches for blacks. Many of its settlers were fugitives from the South and had known the horrors of slavery firsthand. Brown expected from Chatham's blacks a positive response to his call for antislavery volunteers.

First, though, he had to return to Springdale, Iowa, to retrieve his men, who had been training there over the winter. He made the trip west quickly, arriving in Springdale on April 25. The group had four new members. One, George B. Gill, was an Iowa native who had known Brown in Kansas. Well educated, with a literary bent, Gill would play a leading role in Brown's antislavery efforts but was prevented from being at Harpers Ferry due to illness. When he had joined the Springdale group earlier in the spring, he had brought with him another bookish young man, Stewart Taylor. This stocky, fresh-faced twenty-one-year-old was a Canadian who had emigrated to the United States at seventeen, moved west to fight slavery in the territories, and settled in West Liberty, Iowa. Convinced that he was predestined to battle slavery, he bravely participated in the raid at Harpers Ferry even though he felt he would be among the first to die—a tragically accurate prediction.

Brown's two other new volunteers, the brothers Barclay and Edwin Coppoc, were examples of that oxymoronic type, the fighting Quaker. The type was common enough in literature of the day—including, for example, novels such as Robert Montgomery Bird's *Nick of the Woods*, Melville's *Moby-Dick*, and Harriet Beecher Stowe's *Uncle Tom's Cabin*—but not in real life. Quakers had a long history of opposition to slavery and an even longer one of pacifism. Most of the Quaker residents of Springdale who hosted Brown's men admired their antislavery stance but opposed their use of arms.

The Coppoc brothers were exceptions among the Springdale Quakers. They had no qualms about taking up weapons against slavery. The brown-haired, short-bearded Edwin, twenty-two when he joined Brown's group in early 1858, was an athletic, daredevil type with great magnetism and a sense of humor. The tall, thin Barclay, two years his junior, was equally adventurous. Both would display great courage in the aftermath of Harpers Ferry, Edwin in the Charles Town prison and on the scaffold and Barclay during the grueling thirty-six-day escape through the mountains to Pennsylvania. The brothers, however, could not go with Brown and the others to Chatham; they stayed in Springdale with their aging mother, promising to join up with Brown later.

Shortly after noon on April 27, Brown and nine of his men headed east, traveling by train via West Liberty to Chicago, where they arrived at five the next morning. Their first experience in Chicago exemplified the kind of racism they were going to Chatham to combat. They went to the Massasoit House for breakfast only to be told that one of them, Richard Richardson, would have to eat by himself because he was black. Enraged, John Brown immediately led his men out of the hotel restaurant and took them to another one, the Adams House, where Richardson was accepted.

That afternoon the group boarded a train east that stopped at Detroit at 6 a.m. and reached Chatham a couple of hours later, on Thursday morning, April 29. Brown stayed in Chatham with the black poet James Madison Bell and then with the African American surveyor and engineer Isaac Holden.

Planning for the convention began immediately. Brown directed his men to write Wendell Phillips, Gerrit Smith, Frederick Douglass, and other prominent Abolitionists, inviting them to come to Chatham for the meeting and a public signing of his provisional constitution, to take place within the next ten days.

The invitation was wishful thinking. Brown should have heeded his own words to Martin Delany: "Men are afraid of identification with me, though they favor my measures." None of the familiar Abolitionist leaders came to Chatham.

Still, Brown was not disheartened by the outcome of the convention, which had two sessions, the first on Saturday, May 8, in a French schoolhouse and the second two days later in a Baptist church. To ensure secrecy the event was advertised as a rally to form a Masonic lodge for blacks.

Brown described it to his family as "*a good* Abolition *convention*," but the description was understated. It was unlike any other convention, Abolitionist or otherwise, that had ever taken place in North America. It was organized by a white man, attended largely by blacks, and designed to raise a black army to trigger an African American revolution that would wipe out slavery.

Thirty-four blacks and twelve whites attended the convention—a nearly three-to-one black-to-white ratio that suited Brown's plan well. The whites included, besides Brown and his son Owen, the Springdale contingent of Cook, Gill, Kagi, Leeman, Parsons, Moffett, Stevens, Taylor, Tidd, and Realf. The black man of the Springdale group, Richard Richardson, was there as well. Among the other blacks were Delany, Bell, and Holden, as well as the Detroit preacher William Charles Munroe, the Chatham printer Osborne Perry Anderson, and the reformer James H. Harris, later a congressman from North Carolina. These and the other attendees had never heard anything remotely like what John Brown said when he addressed the convention's opening session.

For two to three decades, he said, he had been forming a plan to dismantle the institution of slavery in the United States. The time had come for action. A force of blacks and whites would invade a slave section of Virginia. News of the invasion would spread rapidly among the area's slaves, who would flock to the liberators and hide in the mountains that ran deep into the South, forming a colony that would attract a growing number of fugitives. Slaveholders would be terrified into submission, and free blacks North and South would rush to join the revolution, while antislavery whites would apply political pressure to abolish slavery.

The plan could work, Brown declared. He had studied guerilla warfare and had learned that tiny groups could cripple huge armies through the effective use of terror tactics and natural defenses. He pointed especially to Haiti, where heavily outnumbered blacks had outwitted and humiliated the great imperial powers of Spain, Great Britain, and France successively, driving them from the island.

The colony of liberators and fugitives formed in the Southern mountains, Brown announced, would need a provisional constitution to live by until the American system was reformed. Brown had written such a document, to be discussed and voted on by those present at the convention.

An election of officers followed. The election brought another novelty: in Brown's provisional government, blacks and whites held office side by side. The black minister William Munroe, the presiding officer of the convention, served as the acting president of the provisional government. Another black, A. M. Chapman, was elected vice president, with John Brown as commander in chief, Richard Realf as secretary of state, George Gill as secretary of the treasury, and John Kagi as secretary of war. The corresponding secretary was Martin Delany, and there were numerous black congressmen, including Osborne P. Anderson and Alfred M. Ellsworth.

This provisional government has elicited little more than condescension or ridicule over the years—understandably so, if it is taken literally. Officers awarded their high-sounding titles had neither political experience nor a body of citizens to govern. Taken symbolically, however, the government had great significance. In the imaginary, capsule-sized America Brown had fashioned, African Americans occupied the presidency, the vice presidency, and many other offices. In the mountain colony he hoped to create, the racial barriers that imprisoned American blacks would fall. Political and economic avenues would be open to everyone, regardless of race or gender.

It was a revolutionary concept, utterly new in American history. But Brown did not intend the provisional government to be un-American. He saw it as a natural fulfillment of the ideal of equality announced in the Declaration of Independence. It was what the American government really *was*, underneath the racism and corruption that currently spoiled it.

Here he disagreed with several at the convention. All the articles of his constitution were quickly approved but one: Number 46, which stated that the provisional government was not intended "in any way to encourage the overthrow of any State Government, or of the General Government of the United States" or to bring about the "dissolution of the Union."

A number of blacks at the convention objected to this passage. George J. Reynolds, the leader of a radical all-black society known as the League of Liberty, called for the removal of the article, arguing that the American government should be overthrown. Delany, Munroe, and a few others seconded him.

A warm discussion followed. Against the criticism of the blacks, John Brown defended the article, which he called the cornerstone of his plan. He insisted that the American Union must be preserved, free of the various kinds of oppression, especially chattel slavery, that now threatened its existence.

He won the day. The provisional constitution was approved. All the signs pointed to positive results for the convention, which, Brown believed, would yield many black recruits for his invading army.

As usual, his optimism had got the better of him. The Chatham convention produced only one black who fought at Harpers Ferry: Osborne Perry Anderson. This bright, dignified mulatto had been born free in Pennsylvania, had entered the printing trade, and was working in Chatham when he answered the call to attend Brown's convention. He would survive the Virginia raid and write a gripping pamphlet about it. During the war he served in the Union army.

Why was he the only new recruit Brown gained, despite the enthusiasm at the convention? The main reason was that Brown had to delay the Virginia raid indefinitely because of the ongoing treachery of Hugh Forbes. The zeal created at the convention dissipated as even Brown himself grew unsure about timing and strategy.

The convention was barely over when shattering news arrived. Brown learned that Forbes had revealed the Virginia plot to several political leaders, including the Republican senators John P. Hale, William H. Seward, and Henry H. Wilson. Wilson wrote in alarm to Brown's backer Samuel G. Howe, advising that the arms donated to Brown for use in Kansas should be taken away and put "in the hands of some reliable men in that Territory." On May 14, George Stearns sent Brown a copy of Wilson's letter along with a warning that the arms contributed by the Massachusetts State Kansas Committee were to be used only for the defense of Kansas. Stearns said an agent of the committee would soon arrive in Chatham to make arrangements for reallocating the weapons.

Harpers Ferry was suddenly out of the picture, at least for the time being. The momentum Brown had gained at the convention was lost. He wrote Stearns a temporizing letter, assuring him that "none of our friends need have any fears in relation to *hasty* or *rash steps* being taken by us." He would avoid "*hasty* or *rash*" steps, but his backers wanted him to take *no* steps in the near future.

He could not have gone ahead with the project anyway, because he was out of money. On May 25 he wrote his family, "We are completely nailed down at present for want of funds, and we may be obliged to remain inactive for months yet, for the same reason. You must all learn to be patient." He had stayed on in Chatham, most of his men having left on May 11, the day after the convention ended. They had gone to Ohio, ready to accept even menial jobs to stay solvent. Jobs were difficult to find, since the country was still suffering from the economic panic that had begun the previous fall. Still, all but three of Brown's followers found employment.

Brown, meanwhile, was facing a return to his old venue of action, Kansas. Except for Higginson, his committee of backers believed that whatever plans he had for a Southern invasion must wait. The only way for Brown to quiet Forbes was to go back to Kansas, as if he were resuming the slavery wars there.

Still, the exhilaration of the convention had buoyed Brown's spirits. He speculated that Forbes must have had an inside informant at Chatham, but he did not grow depressed. He wrote his son Owen that he must "delay further action *for the present*" due to Forbes's disclosures but added confidently, "It is in times of difficulty that men show what *they are*. . . . Are our difficulties sufficient to make us give up one of the noblest enterprises in which men *ever* engaged?"

On May 20, Brown went to New York to meet with his core supporters. Five of them (all except Higginson) convened with him four days later at the Revere House and told him they had decided that in light of Forbes's activities he must return to the Territory. Sanborn expressed the feelings of the group when he wrote that "Wilson as well as Hale and Seward, and God knows how many more, have heard about the plot from F. To go on in the face of this is mere madness." The Virginia plan would be put on hold until the following winter or spring, by which time between $2,000 and $3,000 would be raised to supplement the $500 that was being donated to Brown right away.

The exception among the six was, as always, Thomas Wentworth Higginson. He insisted that despite Forbes the Virginia plot should be set in motion immediately. He wrote Brown: "I utterly protest against any postponement. If the thing is postponed, it is postponed for ever—for H.F. can do as much harm next year as this. His malice must be in some way put down or outwitted." Brown replied in agreement, charging Stearns, Smith, and the others with being timid. But when he met Higginson in Boston on May 31, he confessed that the Virginia campaign depended on the ongoing financial support of his inner circle.

There was no more talk of his weapons being confiscated. Even if the committee wanted them back, it would have a hard time finding them. Earlier in the spring John Jr. had arranged to have the weapons and supplies moved from Tabor, Iowa, to Ashtabula County, Ohio, where they were hidden until needed for Harpers Ferry. They were first secreted under piles of coffins in a cabinet shop in Cherry Valley and then were taken to nearby Wayne, where they were divided between a barn storeroom and a sugarhouse.

The Massachusetts Kansas Committee ceded the weapons to Brown, requesting him to keep details of his activities quiet so that no one on the committee could later be charged with complicity in a crime. As Smith wrote to Sanborn, "I do not wish to know Captain Brown's plans; I hope he will keep them to himself." Although the Secret Six supported the Virginia plot, opinions about its possible success ranged from Higginson's enthusiasm to the uncertainty of Sanborn and Stearns to Smith's outright skepticism. Later charges of an organized Northern conspiracy therefore had no substance even when leveled against Brown's closest supporters, who were divided in their views and had little knowledge of his activities after June 1858.

The postponement dispersed Brown's volunteers. At the beginning of June, Brown sent Cook to northern Virginia to settle in the Harpers Ferry area in order to reconnoiter for the eventual raid. Owen went to his brother Jason's home in Akron along with Tidd, Leeman, and Taylor; the latter two soon left and moved about in Ohio and Illinois. Stevens and Gill worked for a time near Cleveland, then headed west and stayed in Springdale before rejoining Brown later in Kansas. Although Gill would stick by Brown, he would not be at Harpers Ferry, claiming to have met delays while going there. Brown visited North Elba before traveling to Cleveland, where on June 21 he gathered his followers to distribute small funds and arrange for a temporary breakup.

Several abandoned the project. Realf was sent to New York to spy on Forbes; soon he went to England to raise funds but then disappeared, apparently having a change of heart. Parsons spent the summer in Wayne, Ohio, guarding the arms, but he lost interest in the Virginia plan when he learned that the point of attack was a federal arsenal. He returned to his home in Byron, Illinois, evidently heeding his mother's warning about his comrades: "They are bad men. If you have got away from them, now keep away from them." Moffett also quit; he must have soured on the plot, though his sister reported that unexpected obligations kept him from going to Harpers Ferry. Richardson, the only black in the original group, stayed in Chatham, choosing to settle there rather than continue as an antislavery soldier.

Brown himself set off for Kansas with Kagi and Tidd. By June 22 they were in Chicago and three days later they reached Lawrence. Brown's friend and future biographer James Redpath met Brown in a hotel there and barely recognized him. His white beard had filled out, giving him a patriarchal stateliness.

Part of his disguise was a new name. As Shubel Morgan he went to southern Kansas, apparently ready for immediate action but really biding time for the big moment.

11

Practice

On his return to Kansas in June 1858, Brown faced a new dilemma. The Virginia invasion, the only project on his mind, was delayed indefinitely. But to keep the plan alive he had to pretend to care seriously about Kansas and to suggest that he was there for the long term. If he did not, the loose-lipped Forbes might see through the feint and become ever more reckless in his revelations. Also, Brown risked losing his backers, who expected him to make a decent antislavery effort in Kansas in order to allay growing suspicions of him in Washington.

And so he got involved in Kansas, though his mind was on Virginia. He felt more strongly than ever the impulse to "take the war into Africa" by invading the South. But he had to repress that impulse. He had at least to *appear* to be the guardian of Kansas, as of old.

By reassuming the role, he had more to gain than preserving his financial support, important as that was. He also got the opportunity to practice for the main event. Before the year was out, he had staged a dramatic dress rehearsal for Harpers Ferry. He had stunned the nation by snatching out of bondage eleven Missouri slaves, whom he escorted over a thousand miles to freedom.

He needed no excuse for this brash move. In his mind the existence of slavery was justification enough for stealing slaves. But fortuitously (or, as he would have it, as God decreed) a specific justification was there. Two months before his return there occurred an atrocity—the slaughter of five Free State settlers by the Southerner Charles A. Hamilton—that provided him with ample reason for revenge.

Hamilton was a wealthy young Georgia native who had emigrated to Linn County, Kansas, in 1856 to support slavery there. He had watched bitterly the ascendancy of the Free State cause. He was appalled by the elections of January 1858, in which Free State Kansans elected forty-two of fifty-three members of the Kansas legislature, and by the appointment of James Wilson Denver as Kansas governor to replace Robert Walker; once again, the Buchanan administration appointed a proslavery Democrat who proved fair enough to consent to Free State victories when they occurred.

Hamilton thought the Free State surge could be slowed by an intimidating act of violence. On May 19, 1858, with some twenty-five followers, he seized eleven Free State men and corralled them into a gulch by the Marais des Cygnes River near the village of Trading Post. From a nearby slope, Hamilton readied his men to shoot the prisoners. The unflinching Free-Staters taunted their enemies, telling them they had better shoot to kill or beware of the consequences.

Hamilton gave the order to fire, and a volley of shots rang out. The Free State men tumbled to the ground. Five were killed immediately. Five others were wounded and lay so still that Hamilton left them for dead; one was unhurt.

As was usual in Kansas, most of the vigilante killers went unpunished. Of the twenty-odd men who fired on the defenseless Free-Staters, only one was prosecuted under the law. The rest went free, including the leader, Hamilton, who became a colonel for the Confederacy during the war.

The Marais des Cygnes massacre shocked slavery's foes nationwide. Whittier wrote for the *Atlantic Monthly* a moving poem, "Le Marais du Cygne," that described the killers as "foul human vultures" that "feasted and fled." In Kansas the Free State leader James Montgomery vowed revenge and gathered troops to retaliate. War was avoided only through the tact of Governor Denver, who declared a general amnesty for both sides and promised Montgomery to remove certain proslavery officials.

No one was better prepared to retaliate for the massacre than John Brown, who had proved at Pottawatomie he could answer blood with blood. He *did* retaliate for Hamilton's crime, but not immediately and not in Pottawatomie fashion. He saw that Kansas was moving inevitably toward freedom through normal political channels. There was no need now for arbitrary killing.

Brown wrote Sanborn in mid-July that he was "located on the same quarter section where the terrible murders of the 19th of May were committed; called the Hamilton; or Trading Post murders." Although diplomacy had calmed the region, the situation was volatile. "A constant fear of new troubles seems to prevail on both sides of the line," Brown wrote, "& on both sides are companies of armed men. Any little affair may open the quarrel afresh." But he was not about to provoke violence. He explained, "As I am not *here* to *seek* or to *secure revenge;* I do not mean to be the first to *reopen* the quarrel."

He opted instead for healing. Near the site of the massacre he and his men built a stone and wood building, which he called Fort Snyder, with a view across the border to Missouri that permitted surveillance of proslavery activities. Although he was suffering from the fever and chills of the ague (malaria), he played doctor to four of the five injured during the Hamilton massacre.

He saw that more killing was pointless. This was 1858, not 1856. Bleeding Kansas was in the past. He took the precaution of forming a military unit called Shubel Morgan's Company, but it was designed more for maintaining discipline than for pursuing war. The "Articles of Agreement" signed by fifteen men emphasized propriety and decorum. The first article announced, "A gentlemanly and respectful deportment shall at all times and places be maintained towards all persons; and all profane or indecent language shall be avoided in all cases." The second said, "No intoxicating drinks shall be used as a beverage by any member."

Brown restrained himself from shedding blood even when he had a chance to wreak revenge on his old enemy, the Reverend Martin White, who had killed his son Frederick two years earlier. One day when scouting near Pattonville, Missouri, with John Kagi and the blacksmith Eli Snyder, who had been wounded in the Marais des Cygnes incident, he came to a hill overlooking White's homestead. There in full view was the proslavery minister, reading in the shade. Snyder gave out an exclamation and said to Brown, "Suppose you and I go down and see the old man and have a talk with him." Brown looked hard at White, then shook his head. "No, no, I can't do that," he declared. When Snyder and Kagi pressed him, he said, "Go if you wish to but don't you hurt a hair of his head; but if he has any slaves take the last one of them." Kagi replied that he and Snyder wanted to visit White "without instructions"—that is, with freedom to kill.

Brown rejected the request. He had no interest in private revenge. As he once explained to James Hanway, "People mistake my objects. I would not hurt one hair of his [White's] head. I would not go one inch to take his life; I do not harbour the feelings of revenge. *I act from a principle.* My aim and object is to restore human rights."

Instead of using violence to intimidate proslavery Kansans, who now seemed partisans of a lost cause, he meditated the violent emancipation of slaves. He argued the point with his Free State friend Augustus Wattles. In Garrisonian fashion Wattles argued that violence was unnecessary for emancipation; time and persuasion would do the trick. Brown responded with a firm negative. He had heard all the arguments for nonviolence from Abolitionists in the East, he declared. None of them held up. No more than five slaves a year, he estimated, could be freed as a result of moral persuasion. "Peaceful emancipation is impossible," he insisted. "The thing has gone beyond that point."

He said these words at a time when the Republicans Abraham Lincoln and William Henry Seward were also predicting that the slavery crisis would have a dire outcome. On June 16, just before Brown reached Kansas, Lincoln had delivered his landmark "House Divided" speech at Springfield, Illinois. " 'A house divided against itself cannot stand,' " Lincoln declared. "I believe this government cannot endure, permanently half *slave* and half *free*." On October 25, when Brown had been in the Territory for four months, Seward said in a speech in Rochester, New York, that the clash over slavery was not an ephemeral one caused by "fanatical agitators." Instead, said Seward, "it is an irrepressible conflict between opposing and enduring forces, and it means that the United States must and will, sooner or later, become either entirely a slaveholding nation, or entirely a free-labor nation."

These became influential statements of the antislavery position. They provided rallying cries for Northern Abolitionists, and they prompted outrage among Southern fire-eaters. After Harpers Ferry, leading Southerners connected the incendiary images of the house divided and irrepressible conflict with the so-called Black Republican spirit that supposedly produced John Brown.

The connection, however, was spurious. Lincoln and Seward were *not* John Brown. They shared his deep hatred of slavery but little else. It was understandable that both of them would later distance themselves from Brown and vigorously denounce his violent methods.

For them opposition to slavery did not entail violence against the South. Lincoln stressed this point in a speech in Chicago delivered on July 10, 1858, just as Brown was settling into Kansas. Lincoln said that as much as he abhorred slavery, he thought the North must not meddle with it where it already existed. He explained, "I believe there is no right, and ought to be no inclination in the people of the free States to enter into the slave States, and interfere with the question of slavery at all." He repeated the idea in his well-publicized debates with Senator Stephen Douglas, held from August through November 1858, when Brown was hatching his slave-stealing plot. By what means could slavery be challenged? "Not war," Lincoln stated flatly, adding that Northerners would not dream of invading the South: "There is no danger of our going over there and making war upon them."

Lincoln would use this argument early in his presidency in a last-ditch effort to stave off war. To placate the South he went so far as to announce that he was willing to sign an amendment to the Constitution guaranteeing the perpetuation of slavery in the states where it already existed. His main concern, he maintained, was to prevent its further spread, though he believed it would disappear over time. "Let it alone and it will go down of itself," he told a Cleveland crowd in February 1861. The next month, in the First Inaugural Address, he said, "There needs to be no bloodshed or violence, . . . no invasion—no using of force against, or among the people anywhere." Even after the firing on Fort Sumter, he declared, "I have no purpose to *invade* Virginia or any other State," though soon enough he would be forced to call up 75,000 troops.

Seward, who would become Lincoln's secretary of state, was also a dove, despite his deep antislavery convictions. By "irrepressible conflict" he did not mean a war between the North and the South but rather what he saw as an inevitable collision between two incompatible labor systems, slave and free. His emphasis was economic. Slavery would disappear with "the salutary instructions of economy" and "the ripening influences of humanity," he insisted, not through violence. "I will adopt none but lawful, constitutional, and peaceful means, to secure even that end," he said. To reassure the South, he indicated that the North as a whole felt the way he did: "None claims that Congress shall usurp power to abolish slavery in the slave states. None claims that any violent, unconstitutional, or unlawful measure shall be embraced." He was as far from endorsing armed invasion as was Lincoln.

By nature conservative and conciliatory, Seward was the chief spokesperson for the notion that the federal government should protect slavery where it already was, ensuring that it did not expand further. Like Lincoln, he looked forward to slavery's ultimate extinction, gradually and at some distant time—perhaps in five decades, he once said (Lincoln guessed a century)—but not through force. Early in the war he saw himself as a peacemaker, offering concessions to the South, such as popular sovereignty in the territories, that made some Republicans view him as a traitorous Copperhead.

Far apart from Brown on the violence issue, Lincoln and Seward were distanced from him on the question of race. Though committed to improving the social condition of blacks, these Republican leaders did not escape the racial prejudice prevalent in the era. Seward, the son of a New York slaveholder, thought that blacks would never assimilate into mainstream society because of what he saw as their innate shortcomings; he once made a statement about an African American's "inferiority of race" that infuriated the black Abolitionist James McCune Smith, who thereafter refused to support Seward. "I gave up all hope in him when I read that sentence," Smith fumed.

Lincoln's views of blacks were also ambiguous. On the one hand, no nineteenth-century American advanced the cause of blacks more than he, since he shepherded the nation through the war that led to emancipation and African American suffrage. On the other hand, for much of his career he manifested racist attitudes characteristic of the time. In September 1858, in his fourth debate with Douglas, he announced, "There is a physical difference between the white and black races which I believe will for ever forbid the two races living together on terms of political and social equality." He insisted he had never met anyone who favored social and political equality between whites and blacks. (He had never met, nor would he ever meet, John Brown.) While he wanted to improve the status of blacks, he would not grant them full rights, at least immediately: "I am not in favor of negro citizenship," he stated. He remained an ardent colonizationist until the second year of the war, because, as he explained, "What I would most desire would be the separation of the black and white races."

John Brown's conviction that enslaved blacks must be freed through violence and then integrated fully into American society was therefore a far more radical stance than that taken by Lincoln and Seward. His activities of 1858 revealed new dimensions of his radicalism. On the way back to Kansas from the East, he had stopped in Wayne, Ohio, where his son John was then living, and founded the Black Strings, a new organization devoted to the liberation of slaves.

He designed the Black Strings to coordinate the activities of the Underground Railroad to improve its efficiency. Named for the black ribbons worn by its members so that they would recognize each other, the group had secret grips and signs. Although it did not reach its goal of becoming an influential national organization, it did spread to Boston, where members of the radical publishing firm Thayer & Eldridge joined it. In early 1860 in Ohio the group stymied a federal marshal's effort to seize John Brown, Jr., and make him testify before the Senate hearing on Harpers Ferry.

Despite its meager accomplishments, the Black Strings was, like the Chatham convention, a stride toward civil rights. The bylaws Brown wrote put a progressive spin on America's founding texts. Repeating the Constitution's guarantee of due process and the Declaration of Independence's assertion of human equality, Brown stipulated that anyone who wanted to join the Black Strings must agree "that the African and all other races of men are included in these provisions" and had to sign this statement: "I believe all mankind are created free and equal, without distinction of color, race, or sex, and are endowed by their Creator with certain inalienable rights. . . ." As in his provisional constitution for the Chatham meeting, Brown again demanded full citizenship rights not only for blacks but for all Americans, regardless of "color, race, or sex."

He promoted his progressive views whenever and however he could. In early July 1858, shortly after his return to Kansas, he delivered what he called "the most *powerful* abolition lecture of which I am capable" to a proslavery Missourian he caught spying on his camp. Informing the visitor that he had fallen into "a perfect *nest* of the most *ultra Abolitionists*," he told "the story of the Missouri invasions: threatnings, bullyings; boastings, driving off, beating robbing, burning out, & murdering of Kansas people," with the "most miserably Pro Slavery, rotten; & corrupt Administrations to back them up assist; & shield them while carrying forward their devilish work." He gave the man dinner, then told him to go home and report what he had been told. The Missourian never came spying again. Brown wrote drily to his son John, "I presume he will not soon forget the old Abolitionist 'mit de' White beard, on."

Pressed, as always, for money, Brown came up with the idea of turning his Kansas experiences into a popular book. One of the most popular genres of the period was the sensational "blood-and-thunder" narrative that featured fast-paced action laced with violence and gore. He had a model for such a book in Joel Tyler Headley's *The Life of Oliver Cromwell*, his favorite book about his favorite historical figure. Brown did not share the opinion of an essayist for the *Democratic Review* who excoriated Headley for detailing "wholesale slaughter" and "human butchery" in battle scenes whose "pernicious tendency . . . we deem almost equal to that of histories of criminals and pirates." For Brown, Cromwell was as justified in his Puritan-inspired violence as Headley was in describing it.

Brown felt equally justified in popularizing his Kansas battles. He had already tried to exploit their sensational appeal in lectures. In Chatham he had given a speech that was advertised as an exposé of "the Horrors Perpetrated . . . by the Missouri Border Ruffians & Pro-Slavers from the South," with the racy subtitle "PILLAGE—INCENDIARISM—BASE OUTRAGES &C &C."

He now wanted to weave such topics into a potboiler, to be cowritten with his friend Wattles, that would have mass appeal. He wrote John Jr. requesting "any & all the interesting facts about *yourself; & the family* that you can think of: or supply," with relevant letters and manuscripts. He hoped to produce "a narative *of most thrilling* interest, . . . in a book illustrated with engraving sketches of landscapes &c." The proceeds, he said, would go toward the family and his future antislavery efforts. He was confident of a large sale. He wrote, "I *am certain* from the manner in which I have been *pressed to narate;* & the greedy swallowing every where of what I have told; & complaints in the Newspapers voluntaryly made of my backwardness to gratify the public: that the book would find a most tremendous Sale." No matter that newspapers had complained of his sensation-mongering attempts to "gratify the public." The "tremendous Sale" of the volume would aid his long-suffering family while furthering the cause of freedom for black Americans.

The book did not come to pass. Brown's illness lingered through the rest of the summer and into the fall. On August 6 he wrote home: "Have been down with the ague since last date. . . . I have lain every night without shelter, suffering from cold rains and heavy dews, together with the oppressive heat of the days." To escape the elements he moved for four weeks into Samuel Adair's cabin, where John Kagi and William Partridge, an antislavery friend, nursed him until his fever left and his strength returned.

During his illness he had visitors. Richard Hinton called and was informed by Kagi of the plan to invade Virginia. When the surprised Hinton said all the invaders would be killed, Kagi declared that the cause was worth the sacrifice.

When Brown recovered, he went to see his Free State friend James Hanway, who lived near Pottawatomie Creek. The two fell into a discussion of Kansas in 1856. Inevitably, the Pottawatomie massacre came up. Hanway said that everyone who lived in the region now approved of it, viewing it as amply justified and effective in intimidating the enemy. His words fell on eager ears. Brown exclaimed, "Oh, I knew the time would come when people who understood the whole circumstances attending [the slaughter] would endorse it." Pacing back and forth with an intense look on his face, Brown declared, "I tell you, Mr. Hanway, that it is infinitely better that this generation should be swept away from the face of the earth, than that slavery shall continue to exist."

The blood he had shed at Pottawatomie was beginning to be fused in his mind with a vision of purgative violence in the nation as a whole. At a time when Lincoln's instinctive answer to slavery was "Not war," Brown's was the possible sacrifice of a generation of Americans. In time, events would force Lincoln to accept something like this viewpoint.

Brown did not like to wait for events to push him. He pushed, and events followed. He was anxious to put in motion the Harpers Ferry plan, which he referred to in his letters as a "mill" or "business." In September 1858 he wrote his backers, "It now looks as though but little business can be accomplished until we get our mill into operation. I am most anxious about that, and want you to name the earliest date possible, as near as you can learn, when you can have your matters gathered up. Do let me hear from you on this point (as soon as consistent), so that I may have some idea how to arrange my business. Dear friends, do be in earnest; the harvest we shall reap, if we are only up and doing."

But the time was not ripe. The Virginia "business" would not be accomplished until another year had passed. Brown spent much of the fall scraping together what funds he could. As usual, he met obstacles. He went to Lawrence and approached John T. Cox for arms and money. He wrongly believed that Cox was an agent for the National Kansas Committee, all of whose contributions Brown now assumed were owed to him. The issue became a sore point when Brown started collecting on promissory notes recently contributed to the Free State cause by Kansas farmers. When the national committee objected that Brown had no right to cash in the notes, the Massachusetts committee rushed to his defense, saying that he was entitled to at least some of the money. As a result, he did collect funds from a number of Kansas towns.

He was so preoccupied with fund-raising that he barely noticed what was happening politically in the Territory. He knew, as did most people, that slavery in Kansas was now being defeated in the voting booth. In April, Congress had passed the English bill, which offered rapid statehood and additional territory to Kansans if they approved the proslavery Lecompton constitution. This effort by the federal government to force slavery upon Kansas failed. When the English bill came up for a vote in Kansas on August 2, it was defeated by a staggering 10.5-to-1 margin. Brown was not surprised by the Free State victory. He wrote that he was sure John Jr. had heard of the "general result" of the election, which had "passed over quietly on this part of the Line."

The lull continued for most of the fall. Governor Denver resigned on September 7, but the truce he had made in June kept Kansas calm. The acting governor, Hugh Walsh, maintained the peace. In November, however, old tensions flared up. On the first of the month Brown wrote home, "Things at this moment look quite threatening along the line." Within two weeks his fellow Free State warrior James Montgomery had been indicted by a proslavery court for having destroyed a ballot box the previous January.

Suddenly, it was 1856 again. Montgomery, known to command as many as four to five hundred volunteers, rallied his troops and invaded Paris, Kansas, with the aim of destroying the indictment. John Brown and his group went to the outskirts of Paris with Montgomery, who returned having failed to locate the papers. Although Brown was not actively involved in the raid, the proslavery side hoped to use it as a pretext to arrest him. Acting Governor Walsh put a price of $500 on Brown's head and $300 on Montgomery's, sending a force led by the proslavery captain A. J. Weaver to arrest the two men. Brown was absent when the proslavery posse approached his home, but Montgomery and his friends caught wind of the attack and easily drove off the posse, bearing out Weaver's comment that "many of the people of the county are intimidated and afraid—some of old Brown and others of Montgomery."

Brown, writing home on December 2 that "the prospect of quiet was probably never so poor" in the region, drafted a peace treaty by which criminal charges against both Free State and proslavery Kansans would be dropped and hostilities would cease. On December 6 a slightly revised version of his treaty was passed at a convention at Sugar Mound. Tensions resurfaced, however, when it was learned that Benjamin H. Rice, a Free State settler who had been arrested the previous month and was still being held in Fort Scott, was not going to be released by his proslavery captors. On December 16, Montgomery, with some sixty-eight followers, attacked Fort Scott. Brown wanted to join the assault, but Montgomery found him overeager to burn the fort and refused his aid. Montgomery succeeded in freeing Rice, but shots were exchanged, and one proslavery man was killed.

The turmoil prompted immediate action by the new Kansas governor, Samuel Medary, who had assumed office on December 1. The alarmed governor requested from Washington four companies of federal cavalry as well as arms and ammunition for the Kansas state militia. John Brown went on the offensive. Expecting the proslavery troops to retaliate for Montgomery's raid, he went to Fort Snyder and readied his small force for battle.

He had two new recruits, both of whom had come over to him from Montgomery after learning of his plan to attack Virginia. Jeremiah Goldsmith ("Jerry") Anderson, an Iowan who had fought in Kansas for over a year, was a thin, dark-haired twenty-six-year-old whose quiet demeanor cloaked a fierce determination to combat slavery violently. He would become one of Brown's most loyal followers and would die bravely at Harpers Ferry. His comrade Albert Hazlett, three years his junior, was a fresh-faced, genial man with light curly hair who had moved from Pennsylvania to Kansas to join the Free State cause. Hazlett (who also went by the name of William Harrison) would escape Harpers Ferry but was recaptured, tried, and hanged.

Shortly after they joined Brown, Anderson and Hazlett got the kind of bold antislavery action they yearned for. They participated in an unprecedented event: John Brown's cross-country journey with eleven blacks whom he had liberated and whom he delivered to freedom in Canada.

Fired by the excitement over Montgomery, Brown reentered the fray. The opportunity came in mid-December when his Free State friend George B. Gill told him he had just been visited by a black man, Jim Daniels, who was held in slavery by a Missourian named Harvey G. Hicklan (or Hicklin). Daniels, disguised as a broom salesman, had snuck across the state line and reported to Gill that he, his pregnant wife, and their two children were on the verge of being sold to a Texas slave-owner. Brown assured Gill he would help Daniels.

He was true to his word. On the night of December 20–21, he rode with twenty men into Vernon County, Missouri. As he approached the Little Ossage River, he divided his party. Twelve went with him to the area north of the river and the rest with Aaron Stevens to the south side. The goal was to liberate slaves and, if necessary, take whites as hostages.

Brown took his division to Hicklan's farm and forcibly liberated Jim Daniels and his family. He also took property—horses, mules, oxen, bedding, and two old Conestoga wagons—some of which was to be used on the trek to Canada, the rest to be sold to pay expenses. He told his men to appropriate only property that had either been used chiefly by the enslaved blacks or produced by their labor. This property, he believed, belonged to the blacks themselves. His order, however, was neglected by some of his party, who stole watches and other personal possessions of Hicklan.

After loading the blacks onto the wagons, he went three-quarters of a mile to the residence of another slave-owner, John B. Larue. Finding everyone there in bed and asleep, Brown roused Larue and announced, "We've come after your negroes and their property; will you surrender or fight?" Larue, who had several well-armed Missourians staying with him, replied that he would fight. "All right," Brown declared, "we'll smoke you out, then." At that, Larue surrendered.

Brown took from this farm five more blacks and held Larue and a houseguest, Dr. Ervin, as prisoners. Brown's group stole horses, cattle, a wagon, clothing, bedding, and provisions. The freed blacks were joyful. One woman exclaimed with gleeful sarcasm, "Poor marsa! he's in a bad fix; hogs not killed, corn not shucked, and niggers all gone." When one of the males learned that it was over 1,000 miles to Canada and freedom, he whipped the oxen and said, "Oh, golly; we 'uns never get dar before spring!"

Stevens, meanwhile, had raided the home of David Cruise, a wealthy settler who owned a slave named Jane whom Jim Daniels had said he wanted to accompany his family north. When Stevens announced his intention to take the woman, Cruise let him in but, as Stevens later reported, locked the door and pulled a gun. Before he could fire, Stevens shot him. Cruise dropped to the ground and died soon thereafter. Stevens liberated Jane and stole livestock and provisions.

Brown and Stevens joined up at daybreak. Between them, they had eleven blacks representing four families: Jim Daniels with his wife and children; a widowed mother with two daughters and a son; a young man and a boy who were brothers; and a woman who had been forced to live separately from her husband. Toward the end of the two-and-a-half-month journey to freedom, the Danielses' joy was increased by the arrival of a son, whom they named John Brown Daniels.

The blacks were taken thirty-five miles to Augustus Wattles's cabin in Moneka, Kansas, near Osawatomie. Before joining them Brown lingered near the state line to watch for any Missourians who might try to retaliate for his act. Subsequently, the blacks were moved to the home of Dr. James G. Blount, near Garnett. There, Brown built strong earthwork defenses in case of attempted reprisal.

Missouri's governor, Robert M. Stewart, put a $3,000 price on Brown's head. To this, President James Buchanan added $250. Predictably, the offered rewards did not lead to the capture of Brown, who acted as though it were universally understood, in the words of his famous boast, that he would "not be taken."

It was this bravado—not so much the slave-stealing episode itself—that proslavery settlers found intimidating in Brown. On seven previous occasions Free State Kansans had invaded Missouri, but none of the raids came close to having the same impact as Brown's. His deed provoked panic among Missouri slave-owners, whose overreaction anticipated the paranoia that would sweep the South in the aftermath of Harpers Ferry. Many farmers immediately sold their slaves, fearing that Brown would steal them.

A contemporary writer, Orville J. Victor, described the slave-owners' frenzied reaction to Brown's deed, which caused "more of a sensation than any event of the year—firing the Southern heart to a degree of eruptive fury." "The panic which followed this sensation," Victor noted, "was quite ridiculous, considering its provocation. A stampede of slaves was apprehended; consequently the two counties of Vernon and Bates were soon cleared of their 'chattels,' which were sent to the interior or sent South for sale."

Brown's act prompted at least one copycat incident. In mid-January 1859 the Free State Kansan Dr. John Joy, along with his son Charles, abducted thirteen Missouri slaves. Unlike Brown, the Joys were caught and put into a Missouri prison, though Charles managed to escape from it.

One might have thought that Brown's daring deed would have elicited universal praise from Free State settlers, but it did not. Some of Brown's friends took him to task. Augustus Wattles and James Montgomery debated with him heatedly, arguing that he had needlessly inflamed passions in the region and had placed Kansans living near the border under the threat of violent retaliation.

For a while their fears appeared to be justified. The Missouri General Assembly threatened harsh reprisal and Governor Samuel Medary of Kansas denounced Brown before the Kansas legislature.

Brown felt compelled to defend himself against his critics. While staying in Moneka with Wattles, he wrote a document, "John Brown's Parallels," that became famous when it was printed in the *New-York Tribune* and the *Lawrence Republican*. In it, Brown defended his deed by comparing it with the Marais des Cygnes massacre.

Less than a year ago, Brown wrote, "eleven quiet citizens of this neighborhood" (he gave their names) "were gathered up from their work and their homes, by an armed force under one Hamilton, and, without trial or opportunity to speak in their own defense, were formed into a line, and all but one shot—five killed and five wounded. . . . *All were left for dead.* The only crime charged against them was that of being Free-State men." He noted that no action was taken against the killers by the state and federal authorities. Compare this, he wrote, to the rage that followed his benign act of liberating eleven slaves. "Eleven persons are forcibly restored to their 'natural and inalienable rights,' with but one man killed, and all 'Hell is stirred from beneath.' " The governors of two states and the president of the United States condemn the "dreadful outrage." He added, "All Pro-Slavery, conservative Free-State, and doughface men, and Administration tools, are filled with holy horror." He ended with emphatic understatement: "Consider the two cases, and the action of the Administration party."

He did not mention that, like Hamilton, he himself had gone unpunished for five murders. But in his mind his action in 1856 on the Pottawatomie was altogether different from Hamilton's in 1858 on the Marais des Cygnes. His was a direct response to recent proslavery violence and the long-term crime of the slave system itself. Hamilton's was an unprovoked slaughter committed at a time when fair elections were ushering the slavery crisis to a peaceful resolution.

Although the government's angry reaction described in "John Brown's Parallels" was real, the most tangible effect of the slave-stealing episode was a cessation of violence in the Territory. Kansans were weary of antislavery wars, and Missourians realized that slavery in Kansas was a lost cause. In January 1859, even as Brown hid out with his fugitives, the Kansas legislature passed an amnesty act for "criminal offences growing out of any political differences of opinion." As one commentator noted, Brown's liberation of the slaves "was the finishing blow to Missouri violence. . . . Frightened for the future security of their 'property,' the pro-slave borderers became suddenly peaceful, anxious to recover the good will of their too evidently invincible opponents, and bearing, with as good grace as possible, the unpalatable fortune of a Free State on their western border."

By the spring, the state Democratic convention at Tecumseh had adopted a platform asserting that "the Slavery question is practically settled in favor of a Free State, beyond the possibility of further controversy"— a pyrrhic victory for Abolitionists, however, since the platform also said, "We assert the original and essential inferiority of the negro race," and resolved "to prohibit Negro and mulatto suffrage, and exclude all free Negroes from the future State of Kansas." At any rate, Kansas was headed for admission into the Union as a Free State, although Southern lobbying in Congress delayed the action until 1861.

It was one thing to rid Kansas of slavery but quite another to rid America of it. Even as settlers in the Territory embraced peace, Brown pondered the forthcoming war that he feared was the only means of achieving universal emancipation.

He aired his ideas to the Free State Kansan William Phillips toward the end of January in Lawrence. Having left the eleven fugitives with a friend outside of Lawrence, Brown had gone into town to sell some of his stolen livestock and to buy supplies for the journey north. He stayed in the Whitney House and sent Kagi to Phillips's home with the request that Phillips come meet him. Phillips, angry at Brown for his latest antislavery venture, at first demurred but eventually went to Brown after receiving word that this was probably the last time the two would ever meet.

Immediately, they fell into a discussion of the history and probable future of slavery in America. Brown revealed an understanding of slavery as profound as Lincoln's. Four months earlier, Lincoln in his debates with Douglas had argued that by definition American democratic principles were opposed to slavery and that these principles had been increasingly betrayed in recent times, leading to a precarious hostility between the nation's sections. This was Brown's point to Phillips, though Brown foresaw a different outcome of the hostility than did Lincoln.

Brown reviewed the emergence of slavery from colonial times onward. He insisted that the founding fathers, even those who owned slaves themselves, envisioned the eventual abolition of slavery and registered their feelings in the Declaration of Independence and the Constitution, both of which were antislavery in spirit. An ardently proslavery feeling arose in the South only as its economy became dependent on its peculiar institution. When some Northerners began to object to slavery on moral grounds, there was talk of disunion, raising the specter of America being divided into two separate countries. Fearful of a possible conflict, politicians devised compromises that sacrificed the very principles America stood for.

"And now," Brown declared, "we have reached a point where nothing but war can settle the question." If a Republican was elected in next year's presidential election, he added, there was a strong possibility that the South would secede and try to gain recognition from foreign powers as an independent nation. The Union would be restored only through war. Even now, the Buchanan administration was planning for the contingency of war by shifting national arms to Southern locales.

Phillips was incredulous. Surely the stymieing of slavery in Kansas had helped. War could be averted; peace was possible. "No," Brown replied, "the war is not over. It is a treacherous lull before the storm. We are on the eve of one of the greatest wars in history. . . . For my part, I drew my sword in Kansas when they attacked us, and I will never sheath it until this war is over."

But wasn't Brown simply exacerbating the situation through his militant activities? Phillips demanded. Yes, Brown answered, but America's core principles were being abandoned. Action must be taken to restore these principles. He had decided upon attacking a Southern state to incite a servile rebellion that would spread and destabilize the institution of slavery.

Phillips raised the issue of race. "The negroes," he said, "were a peaceful, domestic, inoffensive race. In all their sufferings they seemed to be incapable of resentment or reprisal." Brown was too familiar with the history of slave revolts to accept this line. "You have not studied them right," he said, "and you have not studied them long enough. Human nature is the same everywhere."

Spartacus, he continued, could have toppled the Roman Empire had he conducted his servile insurrection correctly. Instead of remaining stationary in Italy so that his enemies could swoop down upon him, he should have either attacked Rome or retreated to the mountains, gathered his forces, and then defeated the Roman army. (Ironically, Brown would make Spartacus's mistake at Harpers Ferry, remaining in place too long and not fleeing at once to the mountains.)

When Phillips continued to be skeptical, Brown lashed out in frustration. Phillips asked Brown why he had invited him to talk if he knew they would disagree. Tears streamed down Brown's wrinkled, bronzed cheeks. "No," he said. "We must not part thus. I wanted to see you and tell you how it appeared to me. With the help of God, I will do what I believe to be best." He gave Phillips a strong handshake, and then they parted, never to see each other again.

Years later, after the war, Phillips wrote that everything Brown told him that day "has a strangely prophetic look to me now; then it simply appeared incredible, or the dream and vagary of a man who had allowed one idea to carry him away." The comment was accurate. At a time when leading Republicans like Lincoln and Seward dismissed war as a possible solution to the conflict over slavery, Brown's prediction may have seemed "incredible," a "vagary." But time proved Brown to be unusually perceptive in his understanding of the social and cultural forces that led toward what he said would be "one of the greatest wars in history."

After finishing his business in Lawrence, Brown rejoined his party of blacks. The news of his escapade had reached the East. Five of his six main backers greeted the deed with enthusiasm, seeing it as an appropriate warm-up for an invasion of the South. The exception was Samuel G. Howe, who, despite his own participation in foreign revolutions, thought Brown had gone too far in stealing the Missouri slaves. Although Howe remained a member of the Secret Six, his support for the projected Southern campaign waned.

On the opposite side was Gerrit Smith, for whom the Missouri raid banished doubts about Brown he had once had. Smith wrote his wife excitedly, "Do we hear the news from Kansas? Our dear John Brown is invading Kansas and pursuing the policy which he intended to pursue *elsewhere*." On January 22 he contributed $25 to Brown through Frank Sanborn, to whom he wrote, "I am happy to learn that the Underground Railroad is so prosperous in Kansas."

He should have said *Upper*ground Railroad. The unique aspect of Brown's march northward with the eleven fugitives was that it was done openly, for all the world to see. The mystique surrounding Old Osawatomie made him seem invulnerable.

He dared pursuers to try to catch him. A party that lay in ambush for him one night near Lecompton let him pass because, as one of his men reported, "it could not conceive of ours being the outfit that they were looking for," since Brown had taken no precautionary measures such as posting guards or deploying scouts. Such measures, in Brown's view, were unnecessary. He continued fearlessly on his journey north. A contemporary noted, "Though closely followed by men thirsting for his blood, as well as eager for the rewards, his slow march over the States was unimpeded—it was like a little triumphal procession."

The trip had comical moments. As Brown approached Topeka, he met a Free State friend, Jacob Willetts, who asked him if he needed anything. Brown said the blacks lacked shoes and food, which Willetts proceeded to gather in the neighborhood. He returned to Brown, whom he found shivering. Seeing that Brown was wearing thin summer pants, he said he had on just-purchased long underwear that he would gladly contribute to the cause of freedom. Brown accepted the offer. Willetts removed his underwear and gave it to Brown, who gladly put it on.

Sometimes the comical blended into the absurd. The so-called Battle of the Spurs showed that the Brown mystique could create ridiculous situations.

In the town of Holton in Jackson County, north of Topeka, Brown stopped over at the cabin of the antislavery settler Albert Fuller. Brown stayed there with Aaron Stevens and the eleven fugitives while Tidd and Kagi went to Topeka for supplies and volunteers. While Brown and Stevens were waiting in the cabin, they confronted federal troops led by a deputy marshal named Wood. Stevens had gone out to see if the recent heavy rains had affected the terrain when he ran into eight of Wood's men. The mounted federals asked Stevens if he had seen any blacks in the area. Stevens told the soldiers to follow him, and he would show them the fugitives. When he reached the cabin, he entered it alone and came out with a rifle, taking aim at the troop's leader and ordering him to surrender. He did, and the seven others wheeled and galloped off in fear.

This farce was the prelude to even greater silliness. Brown and Stevens stayed in Fuller's cabin for three days, when Tidd and Kagi returned with twenty recruits. The party pushed north, its prisoner in tow. Before long the group came to a creek on whose opposite bank were Wood and eighty men. Though outnumbered by nearly four to one, Brown decided to take on the federals. He arranged his men in double file and ordered them to ford the muddy stream. "Now go straight at 'em, boys!" he cried. "They'll be sure to run."

For anyone but Brown, the move probably would have spelled disaster—as it did more than once during the Civil War when soldiers blundered by trying to cross a river to engage the enemy, only to be picked off as they negotiated the difficult crossing. But as Brown's group labored across the rain-swelled stream, their would-be captors took flight. Seized by panic, they dug their spurs into their horses. Some soldiers, having lost their horses in the trees, leaped onto already-mounted horses, sitting on the animals' rumps behind their comrades. One terrified man grabbed the tail of a passing horse and was dragged off.

Those of Brown's men who had horses chased the enemy for six miles, returning with four prisoners and five horses. Meanwhile, Brown had gotten the fugitives' heavy wagon across the creek by having it pulled with long ropes.

The Battle of the Spurs bolstered the already powerful John Brown legend. As one newspaper said in its report of the battle, "Old Captain Brown is not to be taken by 'boys' and he cordially invites all proslavery men to try their hands at arresting him."

Brown's bravado, however, was not accompanied by vindictiveness toward his enemies. He treated his prisoners kindly, as he would during the standoff at Harpers Ferry. To lessen the possibility of his five prisoners escaping, he had them walk instead of ride, but to console them he walked with them, using the opportunity to lecture them on the wickedness of slavery. He reprimanded one of his men who taunted a prisoner, explaining the cowardice of harming a defenseless person.

Angry prisoners who spouted oaths prompted Brown's remark: "Gentlemen, you do very wrong to thus take the name of God in vain. Besides, it is very foolish; for if there is a God you can gain nothing by such profanity; and if there is no God, how foolish it is to ask God's curses on anything!" Thereafter, the prisoners joined Brown's group in morning and evening prayers. One of the five, described as "a wild, rattling, devil-may-care kind of fellow," confessed that he knew no prayers. Brown pressed him, saying that his mother must have taught *some* prayer. To the amusement of all, he recited, "Now I lay me down to sleep." After being released, the man reportedly declared that Brown "was the best man he had ever met, and knew more about religion than any other man." The prisoner, though, admitted that "it did go a little against his grain to eat with and be guarded by the 'damned niggers.' "

Brown shortly let the five go, leaving them to find their way home by walking. Brown crossed into Nebraska and headed for Iowa, where he could expect to meet antislavery friends who would arrange railway passage to Illinois and Michigan. The weather had turned wintry, and Brown's caravan struggled through windswept drifts. In Nebraska the group stayed overnight in a settlement of Otoe Indians. A marshal's posse was in constant pursuit, but Brown evaded capture. On the evening of February 5 he led his party into Tabor, Iowa.

His reception at Tabor was as frigid as the weather. Although he knew that the Quaker-dominated town disapproved of violence, he assumed that this haven of fugitive slaves would welcome him. To his surprise, two days after his arrival he was denounced at a public meeting, where slave-stealing was equated with robbery and murder.

Brown and Kagi attended the meeting. A resolution was proposed stating that "while we sympathize with the oppressed, and will do all that we conscientiously can do to help them in their efforts for freedom, nevertheless we have no sympathy with those who go to slave States to entice away slaves and take property or life when necessary to attain that end." Kagi, exasperated to the point of irony, offered a mock counterproposal: "Whereas, John Brown and his associates have been guilty of robbery and murder in the State of Missouri, Resolved, that we, the citizens of Tabor, repudiate his conduct and theirs, and will hereupon take them into custody, and hold them to await the action of the Missouri authorities."

The Taborites did not like the joke. They continued discussing what they should do. Brown and Kagi said no more and walked out of the meeting. They and their fellow travelers stayed in Tabor for four days, gathering supplies, and then pushed eastward.

During the next week they passed through Grove City and Des Moines. On February 20 they stopped in Grinnell, where they were enthusiastically received. For two days the town's residents housed and fed them free of cost, contributing supplies and $26.50 in cash. Each night, Brown and Kagi spoke before packed houses, receiving cheers for their rescue of the Missouri slaves.

Resuming their journey, they stopped briefly in Iowa City, where Brown had another chance to show off his courage. On the street he heard a proslavery mob orator giving a harangue in which he branded John Brown as "a reckless, bloody outlaw,—a man who never dared to fight fair, but skulked, and robbed, and murdered in the dark." He added, "If I could get sight of him I would shoot him on the spot; I would never give him a chance to steal any more slaves." Brown walked up to the speaker and said calmly, "My friend, you talk very brave; and as you will never have a better opportunity to shoot Old Brown than right here and now, you can have a chance." Brown handed two pistols to the speaker, inviting him to shoot as quickly as he pleased. The orator nervously looked around, then gave the pistols back to Brown and slunk away.

The next stop was Springdale, where the party arrived on February 25. A posse was still in pursuit, but Springdale, Brown's old haunt, was not about to allow him to be captured. Brown and his group remained there safely until March 9, when they were escorted under heavy guard to the railroad town of West Liberty, seven miles to the south. There they were put on a boxcar that was soon picked up on a train headed for Chicago. When they reached Chicago, the detective Allan Pinkerton hid them and arranged for another boxcar to haul them to Detroit.

The trip through Illinois and Michigan was relatively safe, since sentiment was strongly against the Fugitive Slave Act, and Brown was widely viewed as a hero. In Detroit, John Brown made an emotional parting with his group of blacks, now numbering twelve with the recent birth of John Brown Daniels. He put them on a ferry that took them across Lake Michigan to Windsor, Ontario.

He had brought them in eighty-two days over 1,100 miles, half of that distance on tortuous overland routes with crude wagons in wintry conditions. As he watched them carried to freedom, he said he could now die in peace, declaring, "The arm of Jehovah protected us."

12

Preparation

The dramatic slave-stealing episode had whetted the appetite of his backers for acceleration of the Virginia project. On March 4, Sanborn enthusiastically wrote Higginson about the slave rescue and reported, "He also says he is ready with some new men to set his mill in operation, and seems to be coming East for that purpose." Higginson and Parker expected the Virginia invasion to happen within a couple of months.

Brown wanted the same thing, but he knew that more preparations and fund-raising had to be accomplished before the "mill" could run smoothly. His wealthiest supporters were now more inclined than ever to send money his way, though they still preferred not to hear details of the Virginia plan. Between March and September 1859 he would receive some $1,200 from Stearns and $700 from Smith.

Having seen off the twelve liberated blacks in Detroit, Brown went with Kagi to Cleveland in search of personnel and funds. The city boiled with excitement over the fate of the so-called Oberlin rescuers, a large group of Ohio Abolitionists under indictment for violating the Fugitive Slave Act. The previous fall, a black man living in Oberlin had been seized by two slave-hunters who had identified him as a fugitive slave. An angry group of Oberlin professors, students, and black and white residents—thirty-seven in all—staged a rescue, snatching the fugitive from his captors and hiding him. The rescuers were widely cheered throughout Ohio's Western Reserve, a hotbed of Abolitionism, but denounced by proslavery Democrats like Clement L. Vallandigham, who called the incident an "insurrection."

When Brown and Kagi reached Cleveland on March 15, the rescuers were in jail awaiting their trial, which was scheduled for April 5. Protesters surrounded the prison, chanting Abolitionist slogans. Brown and Kagi visited the rescuers and were inspired by them, in particular by one of the blacks who spoke out forcefully against the Fugitive Slave Act.

On March 22, Brown gave a public speech about his Kansas experiences. Attendance was sparse, since the public was preoccupied with the Oberlin rescuers. Those who came, however, heard firsthand about Brown's penchant for vigilante violence. He declared that his stealing of the Missouri slaves was the kind of action he was ready to take at any moment. If anyone tried to stop him, he would violently resist arrest. As the *Cleveland Plain Dealer* reported, he had his own way of dealing with border ruffians: "He believed in settling the matter on the spot, and using the enemy as he would fence stakes—drive them into the ground where they would become permanent settlers." He did not mention Pottawatomie by name, but he came close to describing his action there. He insisted he had not killed anyone—technically true, perhaps, since James Doyle was probably dead when Brown shot him. But he admitted that "on some occasions, he had shown the young men with him how some things might be done as well as others; and they had done the business."

A few days after his speech he auctioned off the horses he had stolen in Kansas. To a purchaser who asked about title, he said the horses were to him as slaves were to a Vermont judge who insisted he would not view a slave as property until the owner produced "a bill of sale from the Almighty." Besides, he chuckled, these were good "abolitionist" horses now; he had "converted" them. The horses brought him $250, which he immediately sent to North Elba.

On March 25, Brown left for other parts of Ohio. John Kagi and Charles Tidd stayed on in Cleveland. They attended a tremendous rally against the Fugitive Slave Act that attracted over 10,000 people. They also recruited two black volunteers: John Anthony Copeland, a twenty-three-year-old Oberlin College student, and his uncle, Lewis Sheridan Leary. Both were from Raleigh, North Carolina, and had fled to Oberlin, where they resided and participated in antislavery activity, including the Oberlin rescue. The handsome, intelligent Copeland had been born free but became ferociously committed to aiding his fellows in bondage. He was destined to become one of John Brown's bravest volunteers, fighting strongly at Harpers Ferry and later facing his imprisonment and hanging with unblinking calmness. The well-educated Leary, a light-skinned mulatto, had escaped from slavery and lived in Oberlin with his wife and infant child. He, too, did not shrink from action at Harpers Ferry, where he was killed, his body riddled with bullets as it lay in the Shenandoah River.

After leaving Cleveland, Brown had gone to West Andover in Ashtabula

County, where he gave John Jr. instructions about bringing east several Kansans he had recruited for Virginia. Next he traveled to Jefferson, Ohio, where the antislavery congressman Joshua Giddings had arranged for him to speak at a Congregational church before a bipartisan political audience. Brown stifled his hatred of both the proslavery Democratic Party and the Republican Party, which he considered timid, and retold his Kansas experiences with enough power that most present contributed small amounts of money. He later had tea with Giddings and his wife, who added $3.

Every dollar helped, but he needed a stronger infusion of funds. Along with Jerry Anderson he went to upstate New York, stopping in Rochester before going to Gerrit Smith's in Peterboro, where he stayed from April 11 to 14. The once-dubious Smith was now totally on Brown's side as a result of the liberation of the Missouri slaves. The day before he left, Brown addressed a group of Smith's friends. Smith, too, gave an emotional speech. He confessed, "I was once doubtful in my own mind as to Captain Brown's course. I now approve of it heartily, having given my mind to it more of late." Several of his guests wept when he declared, "If I were asked to point out—I will say in his presence—to point out the man in all this world I think most truly a Christian, I would point to John Brown." He presented $400 to Brown, who received an additional $35 from the others present.

On the fourteenth he went to North Elba, seeing his family for only the second time in two years. He was there two weeks before traveling to Concord, Massachusetts, to renew his contacts among the famous cultural figures there. He and Jerry Anderson stayed with Frank Sanborn in the Charles Wetherbee house, directly across from Thoreau's home. Thoreau came to the Wetherbee house to see Brown, who in turn accompanied Sanborn in dining with Thoreau. As during his visit in 1857, Brown gave a public lecture in the Concord Town Hall. Emerson, Thoreau, and Alcott were among those in attendance. Brown talked about Kansas and dropped hints about Virginia. Without revealing his plans, he said he was prepared to strike a dramatic blow for freedom by running off slaves in an effort to render insecure the institution of slavery.

The Transcendentalists' enthusiasm for Brown was stronger than ever. They thought he looked like an apostle, with his flowing white beard, his intense grayish eyes, and his aquiline nose, slightly hooked above his firm lips.

Bronson Alcott's journal entry about the Town Hall speech, titled "Osawatomie Brown," typified the Transcendentalist view of Brown. For Alcott, as for Emerson and Thoreau, Brown embodied the higher law, principled violence, and self-reliance. Alcott spoke with Brown after the talk and found him "superior to legal traditions, and a disciple of the Right in ideality and the affairs of state." Brown told him that both he and Jerry Anderson carried weapons and would use them if necessary. Alcott calmly accepted the statement, just as he and his fellow Concordites had applauded Brown's announcement of warlike intentions against the South. Alcott believed Brown was "equal to anything he dares,—the man to do the deed, if it must be done, and with the martyr's temper and purpose." Alcott noted that Brown, despite his age, was "agile and alert, and ready for any audacity, in any crisis. I think him about the manliest man I have ever seen,—the type and synonym of the Just."

Alcott, who fancied himself an oracle of wisdom, was actually prepared to defer to Brown on the great questions of the day. Alcott felt that he could learn many things if he could have a long discussion with the Kansas warrior. "I am curious," Alcott wrote, "considering his matured opinions on the great questions,—as of personal independence, the citizen's relation to the State, the right of resistance, slavery, the higher law, temperance, the pleas and reasons for freedom, and ideas generally."

But Brown was pondering one idea, not "ideas generally." The Concord philosophers had gratified him with their moral support but had contributed a meager $10 to his effort. He could not know that within six months their moral support would be the chief reason he would be plucked from infamy and enshrined in history.

After celebrating his fifty-ninth birthday in Concord on May 9, he and Sanborn went to Boston to meet his backers there. Sanborn, perhaps embarrassed about the stinginess of his Transcendentalist comrades, gave him $25.

Brown's Boston experience proved opposite to his Concord one: it was spiritually discouraging but financially rewarding. Sanborn's unflagging enthusiasm was shared by the munificent Stearns, who made a generous donation. But the Secret Six, never unified anyway, were showing signs of strain. Higginson, still miffed about the delay of the Virginia invasion, did not come to Boston from Worcester, though he wrote Brown encouragingly, "I have perfect confidence in you. All you do will be well done." Parker remained keen but was out of the picture, stricken by the tuberculosis that would kill him within a year. Howe, having escorted Parker for a final stay in Italy, had returned to Boston via the South, where several plantation owners had hosted him. Still fuming over Brown's theft of the Missouri slaves, Howe recoiled at the thought of gracious Southerners being murdered by rebellious blacks unleashed by Brown. Seeing that Howe needed to be won over again, Brown wooed him and received his grudging approval. "Don't tell me what you are about to do or where you are going," cautioned Howe, who called Brown a man "of the Puritan militant order" with "a martyr's spirit." Brown visited his home, where he met his young, fiery wife, Julia Ward Howe. Julia, who would later capture the Calvinist-warrior spirit in "The Battle Hymn of the Republic," immediately typed Brown as "a Puritan of the Puritans."

A Puritan, yes—but Puritans, even the most revolutionary of them, were not usually gun-toting slave-snatchers and horse thieves who hinted publicly they had supervised killings. Boston had cooled on Brown. Although he received $25 from the celebrated lawyer John A. Andrew, he quarreled with a number of other former supporters. Senator Henry Wilson, whom he met in Boston's Bird Club, told him that the slave-liberation episode had hurt the antislavery movement. Brown went to nearby Milton to solicit money from the businessman John Murray Forbes, only to fall into an argument about the use of violence to free slaves. The wealthy Amos Lawrence, likewise, had grown dubious of "the Miles Standish of Kansas" because of his recent "stealing Negroes and running them off from Missouri," which suggested to him that Brown was a monomaniacal fanatic who would be hanged if captured in a slave state.

Brown accepted that grim possibility with jovial calmness. When he visited his friends the Russells, he gave maple candy to their baby daughter and balanced her on one of his palms. He laughed and said, "Now, when you are a young lady and I am hanged, you can say that you stood on the hand of Old Brown."

The risk of facing execution seemed preferable to him than further delay. He was disgusted by a convention of the New England Anti-Slavery Society he attended in Boston. "Talk! talk! talk!" he exclaimed. "That will never free the slaves. What is needed is action—action."

Action for him was imminent. He traveled on June 3 to Collinsville, Connecticut, to check with Charles Blair on the pikes, which he planned to put into the hands of the blacks he would liberate in Virginia. Blair had not completed the weapons, and he was reluctant to do so. He asked why they were needed, now that Kansas was at peace. Brown curtly replied that he could put them to use. Over the next few days he paid $450 to Blair, who had a workman complete the weapons. In early September 950 pikes were shipped to Brown's secret weapons depot in Chambersburg, Pennsylvania, and shortly thereafter to his farm hideout near Harpers Ferry.

Brown went home to North Elba for the last time on June 11. More than a year had passed since his sons Oliver and Salmon had told Mary that all the Brown sons had decided to fight no more. Since then, Brown had won back his oldest, the thirty-seven-year-old John, as well as Owen, three years younger. Now he was intent on recruiting other family members. He needed every hand he could get. Besides, strong family representation would make an important symbolic statement.

He knew that Jason, thirty-six, was not about to join him. The sensitive Jason had strongly opposed the Pottawatomie killings and considered the Virginia plan wrongheaded. Brown did not chide Jason, whom he described as "a most tender, loving, and steadfast friend" who, while "bashful and retiring," was "right" about most things and was both "morally and physically brave." Actually, Jason was timid by temperament. As he later confessed, "I have always considered myself the greatest coward, moral & physical, in our family."

Salmon was a different story. Brown had good reason to think he would go to Virginia. He was tough, stubborn, and ferociously antislavery. He had willingly participated at Pottawatomie, which he ardently defended to the end of his days. Why, then, did he refuse Virginia, despite his father's badgering? Evidently, he thought the raid had little chance of success. He once recalled having told his brothers, "You know father. You know he will *dally* till he is trapped" (an accurate prediction, if indeed he made it). Also, his wife, Abbie, opposed his going south. She was not alone; all the wives in the family, including John Brown's Mary, had considered antislavery violence mistaken ever since the death of Frederick and the insanity of John Jr. in 1856. But Abbie controlled Salmon to an unusual degree. According to one of his sisters, "She dominated him, and actually prevented his going to say goodbye to his brothers when they set out from North Elba . . . for fear that at the last moment he would join them."

Still, Brown took satisfaction in knowing that five from North Elba—his sons Owen, Oliver, and Watson along with William and Dauphin Thompson, brothers of his son-in-law Henry—were committed to joining the Virginia raid. The confident, authoritative Owen often spoke back to his father but remained deeply loyal to him, cheering him in trying moments. Owen's half-brothers Oliver and Watson, twenty and twenty-three respectively, were, like him, around six feet tall but were more muscular and athletic than he. Oliver had fought alongside his father at Black Jack. Watson was headed for Kansas in late 1856 when he stopped in Tabor, Iowa, and then returned east after learning his father had left the Territory. Both brothers were recently married: Oliver to Martha Evelyn Brewster, a hardworking woman from a thriftless, rabidly proslavery local family, and Watson to Isabella M. Thompson, of the antislavery North Elba clan that provided two soldiers for Harpers Ferry.

William and Dauphin Thompson were two of the youngest of the twenty children born to the farmer Roswell Thompson and his wife, Mary. Their brother Henry, who was married to John Brown's daughter Ruth and who had battled in Kansas, had decided against Virginia—a decision John Brown at first contested but then accepted when he saw that Henry and Ruth carried many of the family responsibilities in North Elba. The twenty-six-year-old William Thompson was a large-boned, fair-haired rustic with a gift for mimickry. Dauphin, five years his junior, was quiet and shy, with light blue eyes and blond curls. "He always seemed like a very good girl," joked Brown's daughter Anne.

When John Brown left North Elba around June 16, he was accompanied by Owen, Oliver, and Jerry Anderson (the rest would join up later). Within two days the group arrived in West Andover, Ohio. John Jr. had been guarding the weapons there. Under his father's instructions he shipped fifteen boxes, labeled MINING EQUIPMENT, containing 198 Sharps rifles and 200 Maynard revolvers to Chambersburg, Pennsylvania, where John Kagi, Brown's secretary of war, ran a cover operation, Isaac Smith & Sons, under the name of J. Henrie. From there the weapons would be shipped south for the Virginia raid.

John Jr. had never fully recovered the psychological blow he had received in Kansas in the summer of 1856. For a year he had suffered from insomnia and uncontrollable crying fits. With the day of decision for Virginia fast approaching, his anxiety returned. His father had expected him to join the attack but saw him beset by "the most depressing melancholy" and realized that he would be of no use in Virginia. Instead of going south, John Jr. was sent on a recruiting and fund-raising tour through the North. Predictably, given his mental state, the tour bore little fruit. Although he later claimed that the Virginia raid came earlier than he had expected, while he

Harpers Ferry.

was in Canada, and "otherwise I would probably have been captured or killed with the rest," his brothers "found it conspicuous that he always managed to keep out of danger," as his half-sister Sarah reported. The day of Harpers Ferry found him safely ensconced among family and friends on his Ohio farm.

His father followed the opposite instinct: to walk into the jaws of danger. After conferring with John Jr. in West Andover, he visited several other towns in Ohio, freely telling antislavery friends he was about to attack Virginia, though he withheld details. With Oliver, Owen, and Jerry, he then rode southeast through Pennsylvania, stopping briefly in Pittsburgh and Bedford before staying two days in Chambersburg to arrange with Kagi the reception of the weapons there.

By June 30, Brown and his three soldiers were in Hagerstown, Maryland, just south of the Pennsylvania border and twenty miles north of Harpers Ferry. They stayed the night in a tavern and then made their way carefully southward (part of the way on foot), arriving at Harpers Ferry on July 3.

Harpers Ferry was a town of some 2,500 situated at the confluence of the Shenandoah River, which ran deep into Virginia, and the Potomac River, which stretched southeast to and beyond Washington, some 60 miles away. Baltimore was 70 miles to the east by rail and Richmond nearly 170 miles south.

Ruggedly beautiful, Harpers Ferry occupied a small peninsula framed by towering cliffs. To the east stood the Maryland Heights, more than 1,200 feet tall, and to the west the equally precipitous Loudon Heights.

The business center of Harpers Ferry was a low area built around Shenandoah and Potomac streets. Homes were scattered up Bolivar Heights, which sloped northward above the town.

Despite its forbidding terrain, Harpers Ferry was centrally located and historically significant. A hub of the Baltimore & Ohio Railroad, it was connected to mainland on both sides by long bridges that permitted trains to carry cargo and passengers between the East Coast and Ohio, where rail links opened into the western territories.

In the era before the railroad, the town had been a ferry connection between Virginia and Maryland. Named after the Philadelphian Robert Harper, who had bought the local ferry service in 1747, it was George Washington's choice as the site of the United States Armory, which opened in 1796. By the time John Brown arrived there, it had established itself as the largest weapons-maker in the South. Hall's Rifle Works, on a small island in the Shenandoah, made over 10,000 stand of arms annually, and nearly twenty times that number was stored in the fenced and gated arsenal on Potomac Street.

Brown saw Harpers Ferry as an attractive target. By attacking the United States arsenal in Virginia, he believed he could bring attention to the irony of federal property being located in a slave state. He could steal weapons intended for the defense of a slave-supporting nation and put them in the hands of emancipated blacks, who would flee with him to the nearby mountains and use them against their former oppressors. As his daughter Anne explained, "It was father's original plan, as we used to call it, to take Harper's Ferry at the outset, to secure firearms to arm the slaves, and to strike terror into the hearts of the slaveholders; then to immediately start for the plantations, gather up the negroes, and retreat to the mountains; send out armed squads from there to gather more, and eventually to spread out his forces until the slaves would come to them, or the slaveholders would surrender to them to gain peace."

When he reached the Ferry, he consulted with John Cook, who had lived there for over a year, reconnoitering the arsenal and the surrounding region. The ebullient, light-haired Cook had befriended residents in the area and had won the heart of a local woman, Mary Virginia Kennedy. He had impregnated her, and they were married in the spring of 1859; soon a son was born. Cook had taken jobs as a schoolteacher, then as a canal worker on the Potomac River and a traveling bookseller. Excited about Brown's plan to attack the federal arsenal, Cook had gathered information about the armory and the town.

Brown needed a sizable but out-of-the-way place to house his soldiers and await more recruits. On July 4 he went across the Potomac to Maryland in search of summer quarters. On a mountain road he met John C. Unseld, a local slaveholder, and struck up a conversation with him. Introducing himself as Isaac Smith, his sons as Owen and Oliver Smith, and Jerry Anderson as Anderson, Brown told Unseld they were farmers from upstate New York who had come to Virginia to escape the uncongenial conditions of the North, where their crops had failed.

Unseld bought the story and helped Brown find housing. Brown was shocked to learn the high price of real estate in the area—$15 to $30 an acre (he had predicted a dollar or two)—and asked about rental possibilities. Unseld told him he knew of a farm for rent nearby. Five miles from Harpers Ferry, the farm, owned by the heirs of Dr. Booth Kennedy, was in a secluded area of Maryland on a little-traveled dirt road. There were two structures on the land, a dilapidated farmhouse and, across the road, a log cabin. Each was set back three hundred yards from the road and was partly concealed by shrubbery. After negotiating with Kennedy's widow, Brown agreed to pay $35, which gave him the houses and land until the following March—a mythical date, since Brown knew that by then he would be either dead or in the wilderness with his army of emancipated blacks.

Brown moved into the Kennedy farm with his two sons and Anderson. To help with housekeeping, Brown's daughter Anne and Oliver's wife, Martha, both sixteen, came from North Elba in late July. Recruits arrived slowly over the next month and a half. Early August saw the arrival of Watson Brown and William and Dauphin Thompson. Then others trickled in: Tidd, Stevens, Leeman, Hazlett, Taylor, and Barclay and Edwin Coppoc.

Later on, Osborne Perry Anderson, the African American printer Brown had recruited in Chatham, came, as did three other blacks: Dangerfield Newby, Lewis Sheridan Leary, and John A. Copeland. The thirty-four-year-old Newby was a tall, muscular mulatto from Virginia who dreamed of rescuing his wife, Harriet, and their seven children, held as slaves some thirty miles south of Harpers Ferry. Leary and Copeland, twenty-four and twenty-two, respectively, were natives of Raleigh, North Carolina, but had been raised in Oberlin, Ohio, where they were active Abolitionists and participated in the Oberlin rescue. Leary, a fugitive slave with a wife and child, was a bright, well-educated quadroon. Copeland, a cheerful, pious bachelor, viewed Brown's aim of freeing the slaves as an act of Revolutionary patriotism. Copeland wrote that Washington died "not for the white man alone, but for both black and white," and in the Revolution "the blood of black men flowed as freely as that of white men."

Living conditions at the Kennedy farm were primitive and crowded.

The farmhouse consisted of two rooms, one on the first floor and the other above it. The downstairs room served as kitchen, parlor, and living room. Upstairs was a dormitory, storage area, and military training space. Furniture was sparse. Boxes were used as seats, and the men slept on the floor. The dining table was made of rough boards.

Accustomed to wilderness camps, the men didn't mind the hard lifestyle. They divided their time between military preparation—which included studying Forbes's *Patriotic Volunteer,* readying rifles, and making belts and holsters—and desultory activity such as chatting, singing, and playing cards or checkers. They sang hymns like "Nearer My God to Thee" and sentimental ditties like "Faded Flowers" and "All the Old Folks Are Gone" (they changed it to "All the Dear Ones Are Gone").

They debated religion and other topics. Stevens had a copy of Thomas Paine's *Age of Reason* that he passed around for others to read. John Brown, tolerant as usual, encouraged the group to discuss Paine's skeptical ideas, even though they conflicted sharply with his unwavering Calvinism. The men kept up with the news by reading the *Baltimore Sun,* which Brown had subscribed to, and the newspapers and magazines that Kagi sent in bundles from Chambersburg.

Relations with neighbors were friendly. John Brown became known in the area for his kindness and skill, especially as a veterinarian of sick horses and cattle. Some Dunkers—a pacifist antislavery sect—lived nearby, and Brown regularly attended their church, serving as their preacher occasionally. Owen Brown spent hours talking with railroad workers and others in Harpers Ferry, befriending them and picking up information about slavery in the region.

Still, the group at the Kennedy farm was circumspect. Anne Brown sat for hours sewing or reading on the front porch, where she kept a lookout and heeded the mongrel pup, Cuff, who barked when strangers approached. At the first sign of a stranger, Anne signaled the men inside, and they grabbed their dishes or games and went quietly upstairs.

A constant source of concern was an indigent family, the Huffmasters, who lived down the road. The barefooted Mrs. Huffmaster, her four young children in tow, often appeared unexpectedly at the farm. "She was a worse plague than the fleas," Anne said. Usually, the men were able to escape to the attic before she entered, but more than once she saw blacks amid whites in the farmhouse. Her suspicion was aroused, and she wondered aloud if Isaac Smith, this farmer from New York, might not be running fugitive slaves to the North. But she didn't go to the local authorities.

The greatest source of tension among the recruits was Brown's revelation of why he had summoned them south: to attack Harpers Ferry. Although they had long been eager to raid Virginia to free slaves, few of the men knew of the plan to attack the federal arsenal. Tidd and several others pronounced the idea suicidal. Tidd was so upset that he left the farm for a week and stayed at Cook's place near Harpers Ferry to let off steam. Even Brown's sons Oliver, Owen, and Watson took the dissident side. Oliver had scouted Harpers Ferry and was convinced that it could not be taken and held, since it was positioned between rivers and cliffs that gave advantage to the enemy.

Arguments erupted. Kagi, the adjutant general, visited from Chambersburg and strongly supported the plan, insisting that an escape from the Ferry could be made before the enemy had mustered a counterattack. Cook agreed, as did Stevens, Anderson, and Leeman. Appalled by quarrel, John Brown temporarily quit as commander in chief, a rhetorical gesture that had its intended effect. Soon after relinquishing the post he was reinstated by the repentant company. His sons led the return to the ranks. As Oliver said, "We must not let our father alone." Owen told his father, "We have all agreed to sustain your decisions, until you have *proved incompetent*, & many of us will adhere to your decisions as long as you will."

The choice of Harpers Ferry as a target became the main sticking point for Frederick Douglass, who traveled south to discuss the matter with Brown for a couple of days in mid-August. Brown and Kagi met Douglass in a quarry near Chambersburg, Pennsylvania. Accompanying Douglass was Shields Green, a fugitive slave who was living at Douglass's home in Rochester and who had previously met Brown.

Brown invited Douglass to join the raid. He described the plan to seize the Ferry and then retreat to the mountains. Douglass rejected the idea. Harpers Ferry, he argued, must be avoided altogether, since it was "a trap of steel" from which escape would be impossible. Brown pleaded with his longtime friend. "Come with me, Douglass," he said; "I will defend you with my life. I want you for a special purpose. When I strike, the bees will begin to swarm, and I shall want you to help hive them."

Realizing that Brown was inflexible, Douglass refused the invitation. Shields Green, though, reacted differently. When Douglass asked him if he wished to return to Rochester or join Brown, Green declared, "I b'l'eve I'll go wid de old man."

With this simple statement, Shields Green unwittingly set a precedent in American history. By choosing probable death with a white man over safety and security with a black man, Green crossed a racial divide. He was rejecting the reasoned persuasion of the nation's most prominent African American and embracing the risky venture of a white man who was widely considered an outlaw. Frederick Douglass later admitted that while he was willing to live for blacks, John Brown was willing to die for them. It was this self-sacrificing heroism in Brown that Shields Green saw and responded to. If Brown was ready to die for blacks, Green was ready to die by his side.

Green got immediate exposure to this new kind of selflessness from whites when he was escorted back to the Kennedy farm by Owen Brown. A number of Virginians spotted Owen and Green in the woods and, suspecting that a fugitive slave was being led north, went for reinforcements. Owen put his black companion on his back and waded down a stream. When the Virginians returned to capture the fugitives, they didn't bother to search southward, assuming that a black man would not be headed in that direction.

The recruitment of Shields Green underscored a crucial aspect of Brown's plot: just as the plan was largely inspired by the history of blacks, especially slave revolts and maroon societies in mountains, so it depended on the direct involvement of blacks. Although Brown never said so, he must have been disappointed that only five blacks joined his raiding party. His ambitious convention of African Americans in Chatham had yielded only one recruit, Osborne Perry Anderson. Harriet Tubman had tried to rally Canadian blacks but to no avail. His friends Loguen and Garnet had not come through with certain blacks they had promised.

John Brown, however, did not surrender his conviction that African Americans, slave and free, were driven by a fierce desire for freedom and justice. This conviction led him that summer to write a new version of the Declaration of Independence, one that registered the rage that many blacks felt against their white oppressors. Dated "—— 4th, 1859," it was found after Harpers Ferry in Brown's carpetbag along with his provisional constitution, whose radicalism it more than matched.

As in the constitution, Brown at once identified racial injustice as the chief characteristic of the United States. Far from equivocating on the race issue, as had the founders when they excerpted Jefferson's attack on the slave trade from the original Declaration, Brown put the issue up front by titling his document "A DECLARATION OF LIBERTY BY THE REPRESENTATIVES OF THE SLAVE POPULATION OF THE UNITED STATES OF AMERICA." His opening paragraph boldly equated basic American ideals with the right of African Americans to rise up in revolt:

Dangerfield Newby

Lewis Leary

Shields Green

Osborne Anderson

John A. Copeland

John Brown's black soldiers at Harpers Ferry.

When in the course of human events, it becomes necessary for an oppressed People to Rise, and assert their Natural Rights, as Human Beings, as Native and Mutual Citizens of a free Republic, and break that odious yoke of oppression, which is so unjustly laid upon them by their fellow countrymen, and to assume among the powers of Earth the same equal privileges to which the Laws of Nature, and nature's God entitle, them; A moderate respect for the opinions of Mankind, requires that they should declare the causes which incite them to this Just & worthy the action.

Having put a patriotic imprimatur on slave rebellion, Brown devoted the rest of his Declaration to justifying this rebellion and outlining a society that truly reflected the American ideal of human equality. In his view the reasons for rebellion were everywhere. The history of American slavery, he wrote, is "a history of injustice and cruelties inflicted upon the Slave in every conceivable way. . . . It is the embodiment of all that is Evil, and ruinous to a Nation; and SUBVERSIVE of all Good."

American lawmakers, he insisted, have proven themselves to be "leeches," "Swarms of Blood Suckers, and Moths," "totally unworthy of the name of Half Civilized Men." All laws relating to slavery were foul blots on "any Nation, which claims to have the least shadow or spark of Civilization above the lowest, most inferior Canibal Races." Government itself had become "a cursed treasonable, usurpation," completely at odds with the American spirit. There was only one principle for Americans to pursue: "To secure equal rights, privileges, & Justice to all; Irrespective of Sex; or Nation," and to give enslaved blacks "our Liberty, and the Natural rights and immunities of faithful Citizens of the United States." Given the intransigence of the proslavery party, there seemed to Brown to be just one solution: violence. "We will obtain these rights or die in the struggle to obtain them," he wrote. "We make war upon oppression. . . . Nature is mourning for its murdered, and Afflicted children [i.e., oppressed blacks]. Hung be the Heavens in Scarlet."

Brown's declaration pointedly reversed the standard racial attitudes of the day. Most Americans thought that blacks were much closer to being animals or savages than were whites. Brown suggested that the opposite was true: in a nation whose laws endorsed slavery and discrimination, it was the whites who were barbarous and animalistic. Brown's identification with the African American point of view extended even to his use of pronouns—blacks in his Declaration were "we," whites were "they." While emphasizing injustice against blacks, Brown again included another oppressed group: women. Full rights must be extended to "all," he declared—not only without regard to race but also "Irrespective of Sex."

Another document found in Brown's carpetbag, titled "Vindication of the Invasion," tersely justified his immediate action, the assault on Harpers Ferry in an effort to free slaves. Brown used the past tense, as if the "Vindication" were his message to the world in case he died during the raid. Brown explained that the invasion, first, "was in accordance with my settled policy." Second, "it was intended as a discriminating blow at *Slavery*"; third, "it was calculated to lessen the value of slaves"; and, last, "it was (over and above all others) *Right*."

This explanation of motives, evidently intended to be read in the event of Brown's death, suggests that failure was a real possibility to him. He had good reason to entertain this possibility, other than the sheer difficulty of the enterprise. His men had loose lips. In particular, Tidd, Anderson, Leeman, and Taylor wrote letters to family and friends in which they explained their mission in Virginia. Leeman went so far as to specify to his mother that he was soon to invade Harpers Ferry in order to liberate slaves in the region. Brown's antislavery colleague Richard Hinton later collected, in his words, "a score of letters" in which Brown's recruits mentioned the plan. The talkative Cook, meanwhile, told Southern friends at the Ferry that soon there would be a "disturbance" or "active uneasiness" among the "darkies."

Brown was exasperated by the revelations. "Persons who do not talk much are seldom questioned much," he wrote home on August 2. A sound policy, but he had trouble enforcing it. It soon seemed that *John Brown and his followers are about to attack Harpers Ferry* was being trumpeted to the world. "If everyone must write some girl," he complained to Kagi on August 11, "or some other extra friend, telling or showing our location; and telling (as some have done) all about our matters; we might as well get the whole published at once, in the New York Herald. Any person is a stupid fool who expects his friends to keep for him; that which he cannot keep himself."

Actually, he had little to fear from the humble people who were receiving letters from his men. What he didn't know was that his plan was reported to one of the highest officials in the U.S. government, the secretary of war, John B. Floyd.

A letter of August 20, sent anonymously, informed Floyd that "*old John Brown*, late of Kansas," was secretly training a group of blacks and whites to attack Virginia in a few weeks in order to effect "the liberation of the slaves at the South by a general insurrection." The letter stated that Brown had a cache of arms and that one of his agents had been reconnoitering "in an armory in Maryland," with additional recruits slowly filtering into northern Virginia and settling near Harpers Ferry. The letter was written by three Quakers of Springdale, Iowa, led by David J. Gue, who had known Brown there and who claimed they wanted to "protect Brown from the consequences of his own rashness."

Whatever their motive, their letter had little effect. Floyd knew that there was no arsenal in Maryland. He didn't associate the "*old John Brown*" with the John Brown who had recently stolen slaves from Missouri. He doubted the letter's message. Blacks and whites teaming up to attack the South? Absurd. As a journalist later commented, "the statement was so indefinite and improbable as to cause no fears of such an outbreak." Floyd tossed the letter aside.

He could not have imagined that John Brown at that moment was near Harpers Ferry preparing an invasion. The firearms contributed by George Stearns and the Massachusetts Kansas Committee reached Brown in early September. Fifteen boxes containing 198 Sharps rifles, 200 Maynard revolvers, and percussion caps for the revolvers were carted in an old wagon from Chambersburg, Pennsylvania, to the Kennedy farm. (Brown was unaware that the revolvers were useless to him because they required special tape primings that had not been sent.) The boxes were stored in the log cabin across from the farmhouse. William Thompson, Watson Brown, and Jerry Anderson moved into the cabin to guard the weapons and, should a crisis arise, to have them readily available. By the end of the month the 950 pikes made by Charles Blair arrived and were stored upstairs in the farmhouse.

With the time for the attack approaching, Brown sent Martha and Anne back to North Elba. They left on September 29. They had been a great help—Martha as a cook and Anne as a lookout—and they had been caring companions of the men. Tidd liked to tease the pregnant, newlywed Martha and her husband, Oliver, by calling them "Mother and Father." Within a month of Martha's departure Oliver would be killed; shortly thereafter Martha's baby would die within days of being born, and then Martha herself would take sick and die as well. Tidd himself would survive Harpers Ferry only to die of enteritis in the Civil War.

Had Tidd known his fate, he would have considered himself lucky. He realized that the chances were good that he would be killed during the raid or face execution after it. Shortly before the attack he wrote his family: "This is perhaps the last letter you will ever receive from your son. The next time you hear from me, will probably be through the public prints. If we succeed the world will call us heroes; if we fail, we shall hang between the Heavens and the earth."

His acceptance of possible death was shared by the other recruits, even those who had initially objected to Harpers Ferry as a target. When Richard Hinton warned Kagi that the whole raiding party would "be killed," Kagi replied, "Yes, I know it, Hinton, but the result will be worth the sacrifice." The young Stewart Taylor assumed he would be the first to be slain; as Anne Brown recalled, the idea "did not seem to make him cowardly in the least, or act like flinching from what he considered his duty." On September 28, Jerry Anderson wrote home, "We will commence digging the precious metal some time next week without doubt." He explained: "Millions of fellow beings required it of us; their cries for help go out to the universe daily and hourly. . . . If my life is sacrificed, it can't be lost in a better cause." Five days later Leeman reported to his mother, "We are determined to strike for freedom, incite the slaves to rebellion, and establish a free government. . . . I am in a good cause and I am not afraid."

John Brown shared his men's combined cheer and resignation. On September 8 he wrote to his family, "I write to say that we are all well: & are getting along as well as we could reasonably expect." To his youngest child, who was turning six, he added, "*Ellen I want you to be very good.*" He knew he might soon be dead. After Anne left, he wrote her with an ominous request: "*Save this letter* to remember your father by."

Not that he had lost confidence in his project. To the contrary, he was overconfident. During his three months at the farm he did little to scout the region. True, he knew a lot about Harpers Ferry from Cook, who also had talked with some slaves in the area and had come to believe that blacks would swarm in revolt as soon as they caught wind of the raid. But Brown made no organized attempt to inform local slaves of his plot.

This may seem surprising, since the Harpers Ferry district was actually thin in its slave population, and Brown needed a firm response from every black he liberated. In the Ferry itself there were only 88 slaves and 1,251 free blacks in a total population of some 2,500. In the six-county area, including four in Virginia and two in Maryland, there were around 18,000 slaves (less than a third of them males) and 10,000 free blacks in a population of some 143,000.

An overwhelming response from liberated slaves, therefore, was by no means guaranteed. But Brown doubtless expected many free blacks to join their emancipated fellows. Also, the northwestern district of Virginia, which in 1862 would be admitted into the Union as the free state of West Virginia, contained many nonslaveholding whites who sympathized with Abolition. Brown must have counted on help from them.

Moreover, the fall was a good time to strike. It was the harvest season, when discontent among overworked slaves was at its height. Also, the region was caught up in a religious revival, and religious fervor was known to fuse with rebellious passions among slaves. The timing, then, was propitious.

Even had it not been, Brown would have predicted success. In his view, slaves needed no special circumstances to motivate them to rebellion. By definition, they longed to rebel as a result of their oppressed condition. He sensed a phenomenon described by the historian Eugene Genovese: Even apparently contented slaves would seize an opportunity to gain liberation through violence. Within every submissive Sambo lurked a recalcitrant Nat Turner. "Sambo existed wherever slavery existed," Genovese notes; "he nonetheless could turn into a rebel. . . . The personality pattern could become inverted and a seemingly docile slave could suddenly turn fierce." Brown maintained that all a slave needed to unleash rebelliousness was a weapon. "Give a slave a pike," he declared, "and you make him a man. Deprive him of the means of resistance, and you keep him down." He had 950 pikes on hand, ready to be distributed.

By early October, Brown was in the last phase of preparation. He went to Pennsylvania to confer with Kagi and John Jr. In Philadelphia he and Kagi were joined by a new recruit, Francis Jackson Merriam, from Boston. One-eyed and mentally challenged, the dark-haired, thin Merriam had sultry good looks and a ferocious hatred of slavery. Descended from a well-to-do Abolitionist family, he had long admired Brown. When Brown's African American associate Lewis Hayden approached him on a Boston street, describing the Virginia raid and requesting a donation of $500, Merriam declared, "If you tell me John Brown is there, you can have my money and me along with it." Merriam procured $600 from an uncle and went south, consulting with Brown in Philadelphia before going to Baltimore, where he spent two days buying 40,000 Sharps rifle primers, percussion caps, and other munitions. He then proceeded to the Kennedy farm, arriving there on the morning of October 16. He turned over to Brown the munitions and more than $250 in gold left over from his purchase, keeping something for himself, to facilitate his escape north to Canada after the raid.

Merriam brought to twenty-one the force of recruits. Brown had hoped for fifty, but further delay was counterproductive. On Saturday, October 15, 1859, he announced that the revolution would begin the next evening. Once again he had chosen the Sabbath for his violent antislavery work.

On the morning of the sixteenth Brown held a Bible service in the farm-house. He read passages about God's sympathy for the lowly and oppressed, and he asked divine aid in setting free enslaved blacks. A council of the men was convened at 10 a.m. Fittingly, Osborne Perry Anderson conducted the meeting—a significant decision on Brown's part, as it assigned prominence to his African American recruits, whom he considered crucial to the success of his project.

At the meeting Brown's provisional constitution was read aloud for the benefit of four present who were unfamiliar with it. Officers were appointed and tasks assigned. Owen Brown, Merriam, and Barclay Coppoc were to remain at the farmhouse as sentinels until the return of others who would help them cart the weapons to a schoolhouse near Harpers Ferry, where the arms would be distributed to those who flocked to the side of the liberators.

The remaining eighteen would conduct active operations. They would make the six-mile march to the Ferry silently in pairs spread apart. Cook and Tidd would fan out to cut telegraphs wires. Kagi and Stevens would take prisoner the watchman at the Ferry bridge, permitting their confeder-ates free access to the town. Watson Brown and Taylor would guard the Potomac bridge, using pikes and rifles to hold it until morning. Oliver Brown and William Thompson would do the same at the Shenandoah bridge. Jerry Anderson and Dauphin Thompson would take over the engine house on Potomac Street, taking prisoner the guard there. Hazlett and Edwin Coppoc would seize and hold the armory across from the engine house. Kagi (who would turn over his prisoner to the pair holding the engine house) would take over the rifle factory along with Copeland. Stevens and Anderson would go into the surrounding countryside to liber-ate slaves and take captive their masters, returning with their human booty to the Ferry to await further instructions from Captain John Brown.

In a typically dramatic gesture of racial symbolism, Brown ordered that when Colonel Lewis Washington was captured, he was to be forced to hand over to Osborne Anderson the famous sword that allegedly had been given to his great-grandfather, George Washington, by Frederick the Great. Once more Brown assigned a prime position to an African American. He wanted a patriotic weapon of white America, associated with the Revolu-tion, to be given to a black man by a descendant of George Washington.

With the jobs apportioned, Brown warned the men to resort to violence only when necessary. He reminded them how dear life was to them and their loved ones. "And in remembering that," he said, "consider that the lives of others are as dear to them as yours are to you. Do not therefore, take life of anyone if you can possibly avoid it; but if it is necessary to take life in order to save your own, then make sure work of it."

As dusk fell, the men primed their weapons. At 8 p.m. John Brown, white-bearded and fiery-eyed like an Old Testament prophet, faced them. In his firm metallic voice he commanded, "Men, get on your arms; we will proceed to the Ferry."

He led them outside and took the seat of the old wagon loaded with tools and supplies. With a flick of the reins, he urged his mule forward. The men formed pairs and walked behind. The night was chilly and drizzly, the road soft from the dampness.

In the grim silence of that black October night, the revolution began.

13

Problems

The raid on Harpers Ferry helped dislodge slavery, but not in the way Brown had foreseen. It did not ignite slave uprisings throughout the South. Instead, it had an immense impact because of the way Brown *behaved* during and after it, and the way it was *perceived* by key figures on both sides of the slavery divide. The raid did not cause the storm. John Brown and the reaction to him did.

Ironies abounded. One was that the first person killed by Brown's men was the African American railway porter Shephard Hayward—tragically incongruous in a war designed to liberate blacks. Another was the shooting of Fontaine Beckham, the mayor of Harpers Ferry known for his special kindness to blacks. The greatest irony was that John Brown, famous for demanding action while ridiculing "Talk! talk! talk!" failed in military action but created a huge effect because of how he *talked:* to his prisoners during the raid, to his interrogators after it, and to the world during his trial and from prison. He won the battle not with bullets but with words.

Coincidences abounded, too. The raid and its aftermath prefigured the Civil War in uncanny ways—it was almost the Civil War in microcosm. The town Brown had chosen to attack, Harpers Ferry, was a crucial location during the war. It changed hands thirteen times, and it was near the scene of some of the war's greatest battles, including Antietam and South Mountain. The officer who supervised the capture of Brown was Robert E. Lee, later the leading general of the Confederacy. Lee's retreat from the decisive Battle of Gettysburg would pass over the same road that Brown took to Harpers Ferry on the night of his attack. The lieutenant who demanded Brown's surrender was J. E. B. Stuart, later Lee's celebrated cavalry officer. Among the officers who supervised at Brown's hanging was Thomas Jackson, soon to become the renowned "Stonewall." Among the soldiers at Brown's execution was a dashing Southern actor, John Wilkes Booth, who hated Brown's views but envied the impact he gained through political violence. Someday he would emulate Brown, in reverse, by his own act of political violence.

As for the raid itself, it combined irony with coincidence. Ironically, Brown ended up engaging in exactly the kind of battle he had wanted to avoid: a direct, open confrontation with his slaveholding enemy. Had he followed his decades-old plan of retreating to the mountains to hide there and fight a guerilla campaign, his plan might have succeeded. Mysteriously, he delayed, and he opted for a macho fight to the death. Coincidentally, it was this mistaken choice of open, face-to-face battle that was a deciding factor in the Civil War. The South, in particular, failed to take full advantage of its mountains, where it could have launched effective guerilla raids, and chose instead open confrontations that made it especially vulnerable to the North's superior firepower.

Irony and coincidence, of course, are tidy patterns perceived in hindsight, through the lens of history. The way events unfolded during the thirty-six hours that Brown fought at Harpers Ferry was not tidy. It was increasingly random, and sometimes verged on chaos.

The operation started smoothly enough. While John Brown, driving the wagon loaded with tools and weapons, led eighteen soldiers down the winding roads that led to Harpers Ferry, nearly six miles away, Owen Brown stayed at the Kennedy farm with Barclay Coppoc and F. J. Merriam to control supplies and weapons. Cook and Tidd went ahead to cut telegraph wires east and west of the town.

When John Brown reached the bridge that stretched across the Potomac to the town, he had his most experienced soldiers, Kagi and Stevens, lead the way. Silently, the men advanced across the bridge, on which there were both railroad tracks and a wagon road. They encountered a watchman, William Williams. The aged, benign Williams recognized a few of them and chuckled, assuming they were at some kind of game. He was astounded when they took him prisoner and forced him across the bridge.

While Watson Brown and Stewart Taylor remained at the bridge to guard it, John Brown and the rest stole to the armory buildings that bordered the Potomac and seized the watchman there, Daniel Whelan, pinning him against a gate and ordering him to open it. When he refused to turn over the key, Stevens snapped the chain with a crowbar and forced open the lock. Whelan was told to keep quiet or be killed. Brown announced sternly, "I came here from Kansas, and this is a slave State; I want to free all the negroes in this State; I have possession of the United States armory, and if the citizens interfere with me I must only burn the town and have blood."

Hazlett and Edwin Coppoc hurried across the street and took the arsenal, which was unguarded. Oliver Brown and William Thompson went beyond the arsenal and occupied the Shenandoah bridge. Some of the other men took prisoner several people on the street and kept them in a building in the armory yard. Brown led a few half a mile up the Shenandoah to Hall's Rifle Works, easily overwhelming the elderly guard. Kagi and Stevens stayed there to hold the building, joined later by Leary.

It had not been two hours since the party had left the Kennedy farm, and already it had under its control the armory, the arsenal, and the rifle works. The road seemed clear to victory. All that was needed was for word to spread to local slaves, and soon the liberation force would be swelled by hundreds, perhaps thousands of emancipated blacks.

At least, that's what Brown thought. He sent a party into the countryside to liberate slaves and take captive their masters. Three whites (Stevens, Cook, and Tidd) and three blacks (Leary, Green, and Osborne Anderson) were assigned to the job. Brown wanted this important mission, which he believed would initiate the liberation of Virginia's slaves, to be undertaken by a racially mixed group.

The six liberators went five miles above the Ferry to the farm of Colonel Lewis Washington, the great-grandnephew of George Washington. At midnight they captured this scion of the Revolution and forced him to hand over to Anderson the Lafayette pistol and the sword of Frederick the Great.

They subjected Washington to further indignity when they declared they had come to free his slaves and take him to the Ferry as a hostage. Washington tried to appease Stevens by offering him whiskey. When the offer was refused, Washington broke down. He was taken to his own carriage, behind which was his four-horse farm wagon, now full of his slaves and their captors. Amid the sobs and cries of his family, the vehicles rumbled away.

The next stop was a nearby farm owned by John H. Allstadt. The raiders roused Allstadt and his eighteen-year-old son, broke into the house, and seized them, along with their six slaves, putting them in the wagon. They drove back to the armory, where they deposited their human booty shortly before daylight. By way of introduction, Stevens pointed to his leader and said, "This is John Brown." "Osawatomie Brown of Kansas," Brown added.

So far all had gone as planned. Brown was especially pleased to have Lewis Washington and the symbolic sword, which the next day he held during the battle against his would-be captors. He informed Washington of his antislavery mission and explained that he had taken him hostage because otherwise he might have proven "a troublesome customer." "And apart from that," Brown added, "I wanted you particularly for the moral effect it would give our cause having one of your name, as a prisoner."

The freed blacks were immediately assigned control over their former masters. Brown handed a pike to each of the blacks, giving instructions as to how to guard the whites to prevent escape. He ordered, "Keep these white men inside."

It was at this moment that difficulties began to arise. To this point Brown had moved swiftly and surely; after it he was slow and indecisive. Slowness doomed his project. To succeed he should have seized what weapons he could from the arsenal, gathered his men and hostages, and returned across the Shenandoah bridge to the schoolhouse, where the previously purchased weapons had presumably been brought by Owen and the others from the Kennedy farm. He would still have had time to raid other plantations and seize more slaves and hostages, as long as he kept up a rapid pace.

Within two hours he could have been in the Blue Ridge Mountains, with the night still dark and the people in the Harpers Ferry region confused over what had happened. The departure of many slaves and their masters would have created panic, which would grow into chronic insecurity if Brown eluded capture for some time and launched nocturnal slave-stealing raids, ever moving south. Brown would have succeeded in touching the South's most sensitive nerve: its horror of slave revolts.

But would his guerilla campaign cause the fall of slavery? There was the rub. Brown had always believed it would, because he was sure the revolution would be contagious. Enslaved blacks all over the South would catch the fever of revolt. They would violently cast off their shackles, and rush to the mountains to join his growing black colony, which might actually be able to create an independent society like the Jamaican maroons, organized under his constitution. The institution of slavery would shake from its foundations. The basic fear that many Southern whites had of their slaves would turn into paranoiac terror. To save their lives and their economy, Southerners would strike a compromise with the North on slavery. They would abandon it altogether or perhaps accept a program of compensated emancipation, by which slaveowners were paid for freeing their slaves within a certain time period.

This result, in Brown's mind, hinged on the response of the slaves. If they rose up determinedly, slavery would be destabilized; if they did not, the plan would fail.

Did John Brown stall fatally at Harpers Ferry because he had a sudden revelation in the early morning hours of October 17? The evidence suggests that the events that night challenged his long-standing belief that blacks would rise up with unanimous determination if given the chance.

The response of the freedmen was mixed at best. By several reports, most were confused, and several actually feared that they were being captured to be sold south. After the raid, the Southern press crowed about Brown's miscalculation of the blacks' reaction. "Indeed," a local paper reported, "Brown's expectation as to the slaves rushing to him, was entirely disappointed. None seem to have come to him willingly, and in most cases were forced to desert their masters." David Hunter Strother, the *Harper's Weekly* essayist who heard Brown answer questions after the raid, similarly wrote that Brown "confidently expected large reinforcements from Virginia, Kentucky, Maryland, North and South Carolina, and several other Slave States, besides the Free States—taking it for granted that it was only necessary to seize the public arms and places them in the hands of Negroes and nonslaveholders to recruit his forces indefinitely. In this calculation he reluctantly and indirectly admitted that he had been entirely disappointed."

Journalists repeated anecdotes that illustrated Brown's failure to win the freedmen to his side. Strother noted that when Brown put a pike in the hands of one slave and told him to strike for liberty, the latter allegedly exclaimed, "Good lord, Massa. I don't know nuffin 'bout handlin' dem tings." When Brown tried to force the pike upon him, he said he had a bad hand and exhibited a stump of a finger he had lost in a wheat machine. Later when Brown sent him out for water, he "broke the pitcher and fled for his life." According to Strother, when Brown asked the blacks if they hadn't heard of "John Brown of Kansas—old Osawatomie Brown? . . . this only frightened the Negroes more. They dropped the pikes, like the devil's gifts, and took to their heels, hiding everywhere under the straw ricks, barns, and stables."

One might be tempted to dismiss such stories as fabrications if they weren't confirmed by other evidence. During Brown's trial John Allstadt testified that the freedmen were given spears but "showed no disposition to use them." Later, in the engine house, Allstadt saw several blacks cutting portholes by Brown's order, but "the other negroes were doing nothing, and had dropped their spears; some of them were asleep nearly all the time." Lewis Washington, too, testified "that not a slave seemed to have a heart in the matter. The slaves themselves did nothing," except for one or two who cut portholes. Another hostage, the armory officer John E. P. Daingerfield, said he saw in the engine house a dozen blacks "armed with pieces which they carried most awkwardly and unwillingly. During the firing, they were lying about asleep, some of them having crawled under the engines."

To be sure, there were instances of blacks who joined the liberators enthusiastically. Osborne Anderson recalled that Lewis Washington's coachman, Jim, fought "like a tiger" and was killed in the battle against the proslavery troops. Anderson also said he met some slaves along a mountain road who joined Brown's force when they learned of its mission.

Still, it is difficult to avoid the conclusion that most of the blacks responded with indifference or fear. When Cook took some eleven freedmen with him to the schoolhouse to meet Owen and the others, it was not long before all of the blacks had fled back to their farms. In fact, the defense lawyers for Brown and his confederates cited the blacks' fear or apathy in an effort to refute the charge of inciting insurrection. One of John Brown's attorneys used this argument, and John Cook's lawyer, Daniel Voorhees, made it central to his case. Far from endangering slavery, Voorhees argued, the raid supported it. Witness the outcome, he said. A supposed Moses appears and promises freedom to the slave, but "the bondsman refuses to be free; drops the implements of war from his hands; is deaf to the call of freedom; turns against his liberators, and, by instinct, obeys the injunction of Paul by returning to his master!"

If we accept that the freedmen did not respond in the way Brown had anticipated, the question arises: Why did they not? Southerners, predictably, had a racist explanation. Strother insisted that Brown had put too much faith in "this good-humored, good-for-nothing, half-monkey race—the Negroes." The Virginian Edmund Ruffin wrote in his diary that "Brown made the general mistake of abolitionists & Yankees in ascribing the same feelings & impulses to negroes as if they were white men."

The history of slave revolts refutes the racist argument. Scores of times enslaved American blacks had risen up violently against their masters. But that was the key. *They* had risen up. They were not *led* by an outside party, least of all *whites*. The impulse for revolt came from within. It galvanized unpredictably, sporadically, at moments when a local group of slaves, usually under a charismatic black leader, were able to conspire and to act on the desire to fight their way to freedom.

Whites for them were oppressors, not liberators. A white man who led blacks and other whites against their white masters? This was an unknown being, bizarre and completely alien to slaves degraded by years of ignorance and forced submission. Even whites in the Harpers Ferry area dismissed an early report of the raid's antislavery intention. According to an eyewitness, the suggestion that this was "an Anti-Slavery movement" was "received everywhere with derision, . . . with doubt and incredulity," and "any and every other explanation was accepted in preference." Like the Virginians, an antislavery white man from the North who happened to be in Harpers Ferry the day of the raid was astounded when he first heard of it. He dismissed the story as "balderdash," explaining: "Any serious project of a great Northern movement on behalf of Southern slaves was then as far from credible and as strange to my ears as could possibly be."

Incredible and strange to him; far more so for the slaves. To be awakened late at night by whites, in consort with blacks, who offered weapons for liberation must have been a baffling experience for many of them.

There was also the specter of reprisal from their masters if the revolt failed. Especially since the Nat Turner insurrection of 1831, punishment of rebellious slaves had been swift and brutal. Eugene Genovese notes that by the 1850s Southern whites had closed ranks, making slave insurrection "virtually suicidal." Harrison Berry, a Georgia slave, argued in an 1861 pamphlet that blacks did not join Brown because they feared certain, horrible death if they were later recaptured. Berry wrote: "I can imagine that I can see gibbets all over the Slave-holding states, with Negroes stretched upon them like slaughtered hogs, and pens of light-wood on fire! Methinks I hear their screams—I can see them upon their knees, begging, for god's sake, to have mercy! I can see them chained together . . . and shot down like wild beasts. These are but shadows of what would have been done, had John Brown succeeded."

Whatever the reason, the freedmen did not exhibit the zest Brown had anticipated. Nor did the "bees swarm." Besides the few blacks who reportedly joined Osborne Anderson on the road, none are known to have volunteered to join Brown's group.

And so, Brown dallied. All that night and the next morning he would ignore Kagi and Stevens, who sent repeated messages from the rifle works saying that they all must leave immediately or else be trapped. The reality of the situation had hit him: his long-anticipated revolution of blacks was not happening. He resolved to stay in Harpers Ferry. If the bees began to swarm, he would try to use his hostages to negotiate an exit. If not, he would fight to the death.

Actually, matters in the Ferry had been deteriorating since midnight. Patrick Higgins, the night watchman, appeared at the Potomac bridge to relieve Bill Williams as usual. Higgins knew something was wrong when he found that the bridge lights were out and Williams was not around. Lantern in hand, he walked across the bridge. Two men commanded him to halt, but, as he later declared, "I didn't know what 'Halt' mint then any more than a hog knows about a holiday." One of the men (Oliver Brown, he later learned) took hold of him and said, "Come along."

Higgins went several steps with Oliver but spotted guns and pikes stacked against the bridge railing. The sight terrified him. He punched Oliver sharply in the right ear and shoved him against the rail. Breaking free, he ran toward the Galt House, a well-lit saloon not far away. Stewart Taylor, the other guard, raised his rifle and fired at him. Higgins's hat flew off as the bullet grazed his skull. He scrambled into the saloon and told the night clerk he had been wounded by invaders. The clerk assumed he was out of his mind with drink. Not long after, the saloon's barkeeper went out to investigate and was taken prisoner by Brown's men.

At 1:25 the eastbound Baltimore & Ohio train from Wheeling was heard chugging toward town, and the wounded Higgins ran to warn the conductor, Phelps, of the danger on the bridge. Phelps stopped the train. Two crew members ventured out to explore the situation but were driven back by gunfire. Phelps backed the train away from the bridge. Passengers peered nervously out of the windows into the darkness. Word spread of a strike by railway workers at the Ferry.

Shephard Hayward, a free black who worked as a baggage handler for the railroad, walked out onto the trestlework in search of Bill Williams. He found himself confronted by Oliver Brown and Taylor, who pointed rifles at him and ordered him to halt. Bewildered, Shephard turned and started walking back to the railway office. Brown and Taylor fired at him. A bullet ripped into his back just below the heart. Shephard crumpled onto the trestle, bleeding profusely. Higgins dragged him back to the office. A local doctor, John D. Starry, had been roused by the shot and made his way to the station. He tended to Shephard's wound but saw that it was mortal. After long agony Shephard would die at around noon the next day. A black man was the first casualty of the war for black liberation.

Toward morning Cook, Tidd, and Leeman drove Lewis Washington's wagon, loaded with freedmen, across the Potomac with orders to capture the slaveholder Terence Byrne and his brother, free their slaves, and then help those at the Kennedy farm transport weapons to the schoolhouse, to be available to the Harpers Ferry force when it fell back. The Byrne brothers were seized, and their emancipated blacks were pressed into service. Cook and Leeman held the Byrnes as prisoners while Tidd with the blacks went to the farm, picked up weapons, returned to pick up the Byrnes, and then proceeded to the schoolhouse. Cook stayed with one of the slaves at the schoolhouse to guard the arms while Tidd returned to the farm for the rest of the arms. Leeman and Thompson took the Byrnes to the armory, where the brothers joined the other hostages. Soon most of the weapons-filled boxes at the farm had been transported to the schoolhouse, where Cook and Tidd guarded them along with the blacks.

The weapons could be used only if John Brown retreated soon. But he did not. He stayed with his freedmen and hostages in the armory yard, apparently waiting for the insurrection to catch fire among blacks in the region. At 3 a.m. he sent word to Conductor Phelps that he was free to continue east. But Phelps did not dare take his train across a bridge still guarded by the armed men who had murdered Hayward. Phelps waited until dawn before continuing his journey.

By allowing the train to go on, Brown negated having cut the telegraph wires. At 7:05 Phelps halted the train at Monocacy and wired W. P. Smith, the master of transportation at Baltimore, saying that 150 Abolitionists had taken Harpers Ferry, killed the porter, and intended to liberate slaves. He warned Smith to stop all trains in the region and notify the secretary of war.

The message seemed absurd to Smith. At 9:00 he wired back: "Your dispatch is evidently exaggerated and written under excitement. Why should our trains be stopped by Abolitionists, and how do you know they are such and that they numbered one hundred or more? What is their object? Let me know at once before we proceed to extremities." From Ellicott's Mills, where the train arrived at 11:00, Phelps replied, "My dispatch was not exaggerated, neither was it written under excitement as you suppose. I have not made it half as bad as it is."

In the meantime, John W. Garrett, president of the Baltimore & Ohio Rail Road, had seen the conductor's earlier message and took it seriously. At 10:30 he telegraphed President James Buchanan, Governor Henry A. Wise of Virginia, and Major General George H. Stewart of the Maryland Volunteers, reporting that an insurrection was in progress at Harpers Ferry. Preparations were made for troop movement.

Frightful reports were spreading around the Harpers Ferry region. Dr. Starry, having tended to the dying Shephard Hayward as best he could, became the Paul Revere of the day. For hours he snuck around, spying on the raiders, whom he assumed to be robbers. At daylight he went to the home of the chief clerk of the armory, Archibald M. Kitzmiller, alerting him and galloping off to rouse other citizens. He flew up Bolivar Heights to wake up residents, then returned to the Ferry and got people to ring the bell in the Lutheran church as an alarm. Next he sent messengers to nearby towns to call out militia forces. He sped to Charles Town, eight miles away, where a militia company, the Jefferson Guards, was called up.

The subject of all the excitement was acting unexcitedly. In the early morning Brown exchanged one of his prisoners for breakfast for forty-five from the Wager House Hotel. Food was sent, though Brown, Lewis Washington, John Allstadt, and perhaps others did not touch it, believing that hotel employees might have poisoned it. Brown and most of his men would go through the whole day and night without eating, and with very little sleep.

Workers arriving at Harpers Ferry on that damp, gloomy morning were shocked to find the roads picketed by armed strangers and even more so to be seized and taken captive in the armory building. Among those taken were Armistead Ball, master machinist; Benjamin Mills, master armorer; and John E. P. Daingerfield, armory clerk. Altogether, Brown held around thirty-five prisoners. Freedmen, armed with pikes that many of them wielded uneasily, guarded the whites in the watchhouse of the armory.

The hostages were told that no violence was intended for them. Ball recalled John Brown declaring "that his object was not to make war against the people, and they would not be injured if they remained quiet; his object was to place the United States' arms in the hands of the black men, and he proposed then to free all the slaves in the vicinity."

Not long afterward, one of Brown's black soldiers, Dangerfield Newby, used his weapon with deadly effect. A well-to-do Irish grocer named Thomas Boerly had just left his home and was walking to work when Newby shot him. With blood gushing from his groin, Boerly fell to the street and died soon thereafter.

Over in the railroad office the wounded black porter Shephard Hayward writhed in pain. He begged for water, and Higgins, who was caring for him, ventured out to a water pump. On his return, he was hailed by William Thompson, who asked for a drink. Higgins gave him the bucket. Thompson pointed to two men on the bridge, one white and the other black, and said they were thirsty, too.

Higgins took the bucket to the bridge and recognized the white man as Oliver Brown, whom he had shoved against the rail the night before. Oliver said, "You're the buck that hit me last night, eh?" When Higgins replied affirmatively, Oliver announced, "Well, you did an unwise thing; it was only this leg that saved you." He exposed a deep cut on his left leg caused by the scuffle. Higgins asked, "What's all this fuss about, anyhow?" "Oh, it's a darkey affair," replied Thompson. To show his kinship with blacks, he pointed at Oliver's smiling black companion and added, "I am one, and here's another." Higgins shot back caustically, "I'm on a darkey affair, too, and that's to get water for a negro whom you have shot." "All right," said Oliver, "go along. He brought it on himself by refusing to obey orders."

If John Brown wanted to escape from Harpers Ferry, around noon was the latest he could do so. Up to then, he still had control of the town's two bridges, his only escape routes. But since early morning, citizens in the region had been scrambling to respond to the invasion. No one was sure of its cause or those behind it, but all knew that whites in league with blacks had taken over the town. The invading force was thought to be in the hundreds because of the key buildings that were seized and the lively gunfire coming from them.

Groups gathered to attack the invaders. Few had regular weapons. Thousands of arms were in the arsenal, but that building was in the hands of the raiders. People brought out their fowling pieces, muskets, rusty cutlasses, and squirrel guns. Since ammunition was scarce, many had to melt down pewter plates and spoons to fashion crude bullets.

At last, weapons were discovered in an unguarded armory workshop and distributed to some of the citizens, who improvised a multipronged attack. Half a dozen crossed the Potomac above the Ferry, walked down the path next to the Chesapeake and Ohio Canal, and attacked the raiders holding the railway bridge, who now numbered six. Another group took a position on the Shenandoah opposite the rifle works, while a third went to recapture the Shenandoah bridge. A fourth group was posted on the railroad tracks west of the Ferry to stop incoming trains.

Just as the citizen soldiers made their moves, they were reinforced by two militia companies from nearby Charles Town, the Jefferson Guards and the Botts Greys. Residents in Bolivar Heights were organized under Captain John Avis and Richard B. Washington. The militia and citizens stormed the bridges, overwhelming the sentinels and pushing into the town, where they took over the Wager House and Galt House.

Inside the armory Old Osawatomie kicked into action. "Men! Be cool!" he ordered. "Don't waste your powder and shot! Take aim, and make every shot count! The troops will look for us to retreat on their first appearance; be careful to shoot first." A force of Marylanders surged over the Potomac bridge and down the street toward the armory. Brown waited until they were within seventy yards and then barked, "Let go upon them!" His men fired in unison, quickly reloaded, then fired again. Several Marylanders fell. The others, thrown into confusion, retreated to the bridge, awaiting reinforcements.

In the action Dangerfield Newby was killed. He had joined Oliver and others to guard the Potomac bridge but had pulled back when the militia attacked. Before he could make it to the armory, he was shot in the lower part of the neck—either by a sniper who fired at him from High Street or, as Villard suggests, by the charging Richard Washington.

And so the first of Brown's men to die that day was the African American who had dreamed of freeing his enslaved wife, who was waiting for him with their children thirty miles south of Harpers Ferry. In a pocket he had a letter from her pleading, "Oh dear Dangerfield, com this fall without fail monny or no Monny I want to see you so much that is the one bright hope I have before me."

Newby's death was gruesome. According to a Maryland journalist, infuriated citizens desecrated Newby's corpse, cutting off the ears and the genitals and poking sticks into the bullet wound. The body was then shoved into a gutter, where it became food for roaming hogs. The journalist gloated over Newby's grim fate: "The King of Terrors himself could not exceed those hogs in zealous attention to the defunct Newby. They tugged away at him with might and main, and the writer saw one run its snout into the wound and drag out a stringy substance of some kind, which he is not anatomist enough to call by its right name. It appeared to be very long or elastic . . . one end being in the hog's mouth and the other in the man's body."

Newby's death was the prelude to another bloody scene. Militia companies stormed the rifle works, forcing Kagi and his comrades out the back door, where their only hope for escape was across the Shenandoah. Kagi and Leary waded into the river but were quickly felled by gunfire. Kagi died immediately, collapsing into the current. When Leary was shot in the back, Copeland dragged him out to a rock in midstream. Leary would linger until the next day, when he would die in a cooper's shop in Harpers Ferry.

Copeland was stranded on the rock in the middle of the river. A local man, James H. Holt, waded toward Copeland, pointed his rifle at him, and pulled the trigger; at the same time, Copeland tried to shoot back. Both rifles were wet and didn't fire. Holt made it to the rock. Onlookers expected a fistfight, but the shivering Copeland surrendered, and Holt led him ashore.

John Brown, still in the armory with more than thirty hostages, saw that military victory was impossible. His only options were surrender, negotiation, or a fight to the death. Surrender was not in his nature. Hoping to negotiate an escape, he dispatched Will Thompson and a prisoner under a white flag with the message that he would exchange his hostages for unimpeded passage with his men across the Potomac River.

His enemies were in no mood to parley. The flag of truce was ignored, and Thompson was seized and taken to the Wager House, where he was held prisoner. Brown, realizing his position was insecure, left Hazlett and Anderson to hold the armory, while he moved with his other men, the freedmen, and eleven of his most important hostages to the fire-engine house, a brick structure with three heavy oak doors. Later celebrated as John Brown's Fort, the engine house was where he made his last stand.

Brown again tried to negotiate, with dire results. He sent his son Watson, Aaron Stevens, and the armory clerk Kitzmiller out under a white flag. The two raiders were showered with bullets. Stevens, severely wounded, fell and would have died were it not for the surprising kindness of Joseph Brua, one of Brown's hostages. Brua rushed from the engine house, dragged Stevens to the railroad station for medical aid, and then, oddly, returned to Brown, resuming his status as a hostage.

Watson Brown, shot in the bowels, crawled back to the engine house and was pulled inside by his brother Oliver. Bleeding and in terrible pain, Watson lay helpless on the engine-house floor.

The tension was too much for the young Will Leeman, who wanted to wade across the Potomac to Maryland and escape. He told Brown that he would go to the schoolhouse to check on Cook and the others. Brown agreed, and Leeman dashed out of the engine house into the river. Militia men spotted him and fired. He fell wounded into the river and drifted downstream, managing to pull himself onto a rock. George A. Schoppert, a man from Richmond, waded out to him, holding his revolver high to keep it dry. He reached Leeman, who pleaded, "Don't shoot! I surrender!" Schoppert answered by leveling his gun and smiling. He blew away Leeman's face. For hours, Leeman's corpse, sprawled on the rock, was used for target practice by gleeful Southerners on both sides of the river. Eventually, the bullet-riddled body floated off.

John Brown was surrounded by twelve militia companies and hundreds of screaming civilians. In the engine house his black and white helpers had cut several portholes through which they fired. He released a heavy double door and lashed it open to have another crack from which to shoot.

His recruits across the Potomac knew the game was up. Early in the day Cook, armed with a shotgun and a revolver and accompanied by a freedman, had left Tidd at the schoolhouse to investigate the goings-on at the Ferry. He met a black woman who said there was shooting in the town. He reached a canal lock a mile above the Ferry kept by an acquaintance, George Hardy, who was now one of Brown's prisoners. Hardy's wife saw Cook and begged him to save her husband. Cook agreed to try and went on. He met two boys who reported that his comrades were encircled in the town. He sent his terrified black companion back to the schoolhouse to tell Tidd what was happening.

Hoping to help his comrades, Cook mounted a hill overlooking the Ferry and climbed a tree. He had a clear view of High Street, where he saw militiamen firing their rifles. To divert their attention, he shot into their midst. Several of them looked up and fired in his direction. Bullets whizzed by. One struck the branch on which he sat, snapping it. He tumbled fifteen feet to the ground.

Cut and badly bruised, he limped back to the canal lock, where William McGreg, a worker, informed him that his comrades faced a hopeless situation, since both bridges were out of their hands. Cook made it uphill and dined at the home of an Irish family who told him that all but seven of Brown's force at the Ferry, including Captain Brown himself, were dead. Cook accepted the story. He returned to the schoolhouse, which was full of weapons but was unguarded, locked, and shuttered. On the road to the Kennedy farm he met Tidd, Merriam, Barclay Coppoc, and Owen Brown, accompanied by a freedman. He went with them to the farm, where Tidd told him that he had left the other blacks guarding the schoolhouse but they had fled, returning to their homes.

Realizing that it would be "sheer madness" to try to rescue their comrades in the Ferry, the men prepared to escape. They grabbed some supplies and went into the woods behind the farm to get some sleep. When they awoke, they found that the black had fled. They climbed a mountain, waited until dark, then proceeded to the next mountain. They were resolved to escape by moving north through the wilderness, avoiding towns and people. The mountains that were to serve as the home of John Brown's colony of emancipated blacks became the escape route of his remaining soldiers.

The deaths of two prominent citizens that afternoon inflamed the locals. George W. Turner, a widely respected landowner who lived thirteen miles from the Ferry, was appalled by news of the outbreak, especially the abduction of his friend Lewis Washington. Grabbing a shotgun, he rode to the Ferry. As he was heading down High Street a bullet from a Sharps rifle struck him in the neck. Forty-five minutes later he was dead.

Not long afterward, Fontaine Beckham met the same fate. A railroad agent and the mayor of Harpers Ferry, Beckham was beloved by both whites and blacks. Although he held slaves, he had a clause in his will liberating them upon his death. He had spent the morning in the railway ticket office, helping the wounded Shephard Hayward and advising citizens to stay indoors until the danger had passed.

Beckham should have followed his own advice. Several times he went out unarmed to see the state of the battle. He peeped around a water tank when Edwin Coppoc in the engine house got a bead on him with his rifle. Coppoc fired twice at Beckham. The second bullet tore through his shoulder into his upper body, killing him almost instantly. Due to the danger, no one dared to retrieve his body until late that evening.

Beckham's death, which occurred around 3 p.m., sent the mob into an absolute frenzy. It was already a boisterous scene—many of the locals were well spiked with liquor—but now it became uncontrolled. The kind of moderation Beckham had preached was tossed to the winds.

The crowd took out its wrath on Will Thompson, who was still confined on the second story of the Wager House. Led by the saloonkeeper George Chambers and the militiaman Henry Hunter, who was Beckham's nephew, a group burst into the hotel and stormed upstairs to seize Thompson. The hotelkeeper's daughter, Christine L. Fouke, tried to save Thompson, pleading with the men to let justice take its course. Hunter glared at her. "Mr. Beckham's life," he growled, "is worth ten thousand of these vile abolitionists." She begged them at least to do their violent work outside.

They grabbed Thompson and lugged him out of the hotel. He shouted, "You may take my life, but 80,000 will arise up to avenge me, and carry out my purpose of giving liberty to the slaves." He was taken to the railroad trestle to serve as a rifle target. Bullets rained on him, and he collapsed on the trestle. His body was shoved into the river below, where it caught on the shallow bottom. It continued to be punctured by bullets for the rest of the afternoon. A local historian reported that Thompson "could be seen for a day or two after, lying at the bottom of the river, with his ghastly face still exhibiting his fearful death agony."

At the engine house, the device John Brown had used to gain space for shooting—lashing open double doors—proved fatal to his son Oliver. As Oliver peered out of the crack between the doors he saw someone leveling his rifle on the trestle wall and aiming at the engine house. Oliver raised his gun to shoot the man, who shot him before he could pull the trigger. Oliver doubled up in pain, wounded in the bowels. It would take him nearly twelve hours to die.

By late afternoon the engine house was completely surrounded. A militia company from Martinsburg, captained by E. G. Alburtis, nearly succeeded in capturing Brown. Alburtis led a vigorous charge on the armory that resulted in the liberation of the prisoners—perhaps as many as thirty—who had been left unguarded in the armory watch-house.

But Brown's party fired unceasingly and inflicted enough casualties to make Alburtis think better of attempting the final move. Alburtis pulled back to the bridge and awaited the federal troops that he knew were coming from Washington.

It was a testament to Brown's courage, and to the disorganization of the various militia companies, that with only a handful of men Brown could achieve a standoff against forces that now numbered in the hundreds. These forces grew even larger with the arrival toward dusk of two companies from Shepherdstown, Virginia, and three more from Frederick, Maryland. In the evening came a company from Winchester and five from Baltimore. With a united assault, the companies could have easily overwhelmed the engine house.

But they were not up to a deadly fight. The militia set up a loose picket on the engine house, then pulled back to await the troops from Washington. The citizens were full of rowdy rage. They cursed, whooped, and fired their guns in the air, as though bluster would finish the job. Their unruliness was fueled by drink; by all reports, many in the mob were intoxicated.

In their wildness, they were not as observant as they should have been. Around nightfall, Albert Hazlett and Osborne Anderson, who had been left at the arsenal when Brown moved to the engine house, managed to escape from the town. Evidently, the two had been careful not to draw attention to themselves since early afternoon, when everyone was focused on the engine house. As dusk fell, the two went out the back of the arsenal and crept along the riverbank to the hill outside of town. They then returned to town and crossed to Maryland in a skiff. They were soon at the Kennedy farm, where they tracked down the other fugitives.

As evening settled, negotiation again was attempted. A citizen, Samuel Strider, approached the engine house under a white flag and delivered to Brown a summons to surrender from Colonel Robert W. Baylor. Brown sent back a note repeating his earlier terms: if allowed passage with his men across the Potomac, he would release his hostages unharmed. Baylor found the terms unacceptable. Brown's surrender must be unconditional.

An officer of the Frederick militia, Captain Thomas Sinn, went to the engine house and talked with Brown. Once more Brown demanded passage to Maryland in exchange for prisoners, and again the proposal was rejected. Brown complained to Sinn that his men had been shot down like dogs. Sinn said they had gotten what they deserved, for they had violently taken over a town. Brown insisted he had shown forbearance by not massacring citizens, harming his prisoners, or shooting unarmed people during the battle. Sinn pointed out that Fontaine Beckham was unarmed when he was killed. Brown said he deeply regretted the killing.

Sinn left Brown and went to the Wager House. There he found Aaron

Four of John Brown's white soldiers at Harpers Ferry.
Clockwise from upper left: John H. Kagi, Aaron D. Stevens,
Oliver Brown, and Watson Brown.

BOYD STUTLER COLLECTION OF JOHN BROWN, WEST VIRGINIA ARCHIVES.

Stevens, who had been suffering for hours from his wounds and who was now being taunted by some citizens waving guns in his face and threatening to kill him. Stevens looked at them coolly without flinching. Sinn rushed over and pulled his tormentors away, sending them out of the room. He declared, "If this man could stand on his feet and there was a room full of such as you, he could clean you out in a second."

Stevens's courage was more than matched by that of his leader. In the engine house Brown now had just four uninjured men: Edwin Coppoc, Jeremiah Anderson, Dauphin Thompson, and Shields Green. Stewart Taylor, slain that afternoon, lay dead on the floor. Near him were Brown's wounded sons, Oliver and Watson. Oliver, groaning with pain, begged his father to shoot him to end the misery. Brown hushed him up, instructing, "If you must die, die like a man."

Brown himself was prepared to die. He knew that the cessation of fighting was just the lull before the final storm.

At 11 p.m. a company of ninety marines commanded by Brevet Colonel Robert E. Lee arrived at Harpers Ferry. Lee's first instinct was to make a midnight assault on the engine house, but he realized that this might needlessly endanger the hostages.

Soon he devised another plan. At dawn he would send his aide, First Lieutenant J. E. B. Stuart, to order the invaders' leader, then called "Smith," to surrender. If, as he predicted, Smith refused, Stuart would signal by waving his cap and soldiers would storm the engine house. Lee offered the honor of leading the attack to two militia colonels, but they didn't want to risk the lives of their unexperienced men. This was a job for the well-trained marines. One of the colonels told Lee, "You are paid for doing this kind of work." Lee asked his second lieutenant, Israel Green, if he wanted the privilege of "taking those men out." Green assented with delight.

Brown prepared to defend himself. He blockaded the doors and had his men prop loaded rifles by their portholes so that they wouldn't have to reload during a fight. He made sure that his prisoners were as comfortable as they could be under the circumstances, telling them again that he meant them no harm. He paced back and forth in the darkness. He still wore the sword of Frederick the Great. Forty hours without sleep was taking its toll, even on Brown, who normally could get by on three or four hours a night. But sleep was not an option when, as he believed, the enemy might attack at any moment. "Men, are you awake?" he asked repeatedly. "Are you ready?"

They were ready, but not willing. A remark made by one of the hostages, John E. P. Daingerfield, that Brown was committing treason, made Dauphin Thompson and Jerry Anderson wonder for the first time if they weren't involved in something terribly illegal. They asked Brown if their slave-liberation enterprise could be called treasonous. "Certainly," replied Brown. In that case, they announced, they would not fire another shot. It made no difference, Brown said, except that they would die like dogs instead of falling like men.

The night stretched on. At one point Brown called over to Oliver. No response. "I guess he is dead," Brown murmured.

As dawn broke, J. E. B. Stuart appeared at the engine house. When the door was opened about four inches, he was surprised to see a familiar face peering out at him. "Smith," he realized, was "old *Osawatomie Brown*, who had given us so much trouble in Kansas." Brown had a cocked carbine with which, he later said, he could have wiped out Stuart "like a mosquito"—but he forbore. Stuart delivered Lee's written demand for surrender. Brown ignored it and explained his terms at length with an eloquence that impressed Stuart. His message was the same as before: he wanted to be allowed to escape.

Stuart stepped aside and waved his hat. Lieutenant Green chose a dozen men for the attack. He rushed with them to the door of the engine house and battered it with sledge hammers, to no avail. Rifle fire came from within, but no one was hit.

Inside, John Brown was, in the words of Lewis Washington, "the coolest and firmest man I ever saw in defying danger and death. With one son dead by his side, and another shot through, he felt the pulse of his dying son with one hand and held his rifle with the other, and commanded his men with the utmost composure, encouraging them to be firm and to sell their lives as dearly as they could."

Seeing a heavy ladder in front of the building, Green and his men picked it up and used it as a battering ram. The right-hand door splintered in its lower section, creating a ragged hole through which Green charged, followed by his group. Green ran between two fire engines, circled back, and saw Lewis Washington, who pointed to a kneeling man loading a rifle. "This is Osawatomie," Washington said. Green lunged at Brown, making a thrust with his sword.

By pure accident, Brown did not die from the thrust. In the rush of leaving his quarters the previous day, Green had mistakenly brought a dress sword instead of his military saber. Also, he evidently struck a belt buckle or a bone, for the sword bent before piercing Brown deeply. Clutching the light sword with two hands, Green slashed Brown several times in the head, inflicting wounds.

The other marines had been squeezing through the hole. The one just behind Green, Private Luke Quinn, was killed by gunfire as he entered. The next marine fell with a bad facial wound. The casualties enraged the remaining soldiers, who stormed into the engine house. One felled Anderson with his bayonet, while another skewered Thompson to a wall. Anderson and Thompson, who hours earlier had told Brown they wanted to give

up fighting for a treasonous cause, both died. Reportedly, they shouted surrender as the marines swarmed in, but their cries went unheeded.

The time for bloodshed had ended. Lieutenant Green called off his men
and liberated the eleven hostages. They were, he said, "the sorriest lot of
people I ever saw. They had been without food for over sixty hours, in constant dread of being shot, and were huddled in a corner where lay the body
of Brown's son and one or two other of the insurgents who had been killed."
This was an exaggeration, since some of them had snacked the previous
morning when Brown had ordered the mass breakfast. But they were
indeed famished. As Lewis Washington emerged from the engine house, a
friend asked, "How do you feel?" "Feel!" exclaimed Washington. "Why, I
feel as hungry as a hound and as dry as a powder-horn; for, only think of it,
I've not had anything to eat for forty odd hours and nothing better to drink
than water out of a horse-bucket!"

Arrangements were made to have the freedmen returned to their masters. Edwin Coppoc and Shields Green were taken into custody. The dead
and wounded, except for the dying Watson Brown, were carried to a grassy
area near the armory.

Watson was laid on a bench in a room adjoining the engine house.
Folded overalls served as his pillow. Tending him was a Southern reporter,
C. W. Tayleure, who admired the young man's tranquil stoicism as much as
he disagreed with his social views. Years later Tayleure described the scene
in a letter to John Brown, Jr. "I remember how he looked," Tayleure wrote;
"singularly handsome, even through the grime of his all-day strug-
gles, . . . very calm, and of a tone and look very gentle. The look with which
he searched my very heart I can never forget."

The wounded warrior remained unruffled even when the reporter
grilled him. "What brought you here?" Tayleure asked. "Duty, sir," Watson answered. Tayleure retorted, "Is it then your idea of duty to shoot
men down upon their own hearth-stones for defending their rights?" Watson replied, "I am dying; I cannot discuss the question; I did my duty as I
saw it." Watson faded over the course of the day. He died early the next
morning.

The brave Watson had been too feeble to defend his views at length.
This was not true of his father. When John Brown was carried out of the
engine house, he bled so much that many spectators assumed he was
doomed. But the wounds turned out to be less serious than originally
thought (though serious enough to bother him later during his trial).

He was taken to the paymaster's office in the armory, where he lay on
crude bedding near his comrade Stevens, badly hurt. Both men were grimy

and heavily bandaged. Their hair was disheveled and matted, their clothes splotched with blood and gunpowder.

A gathering group of reporters and politicians questioned Brown. His remarks, natural and unpremeditated, had a disarming candor. He could not know that in the long run they would have as great an impact on the national scene as his raid had.

When questioned by the Virginia congressman Alexander R. Boteler, Brown accounted for the project's failure by pointing to the lackluster reaction among slaves and sympathetic whites. Boteler asked, "Did you expect to get assistance here from whites as well as from the blacks?" "I did," Brown answered. Boteler pushed the point: "Then, you have been disappointed in not getting it from either?" With grave emphasis Brown responded, "Yes. I—have—been—disappointed."

But he didn't dwell on the point. By early afternoon he found himself on a national stage. An artist for *Harper's Weekly* was on hand to sketch scenes of the interview. A correspondent from the Associated Press had come, as well as pressmen from many local papers. Soon the train brought dignitaries from Washington, Richmond, Baltimore, and elsewhere, among them the Virginia senator James Mason, the state's governor, Henry Wise, and the Ohio Democrat Clement Vallandigham. Also present were many who had been involved in the recent action, including Robert E. Lee, J. E. B. Stuart, and Lewis Washington.

It wasn't an easy audience. Even if Brown had been healthy and rested, he would have been justified in being nervous. All present were outraged by what he had done. Most were rabidly proslavery. A number would become leading figures of the Confederacy. Some had seen suspicious papers that had already been brought from the Kennedy farm, including his provisional constitution and a marked map of Southern states. In questioning Brown, several tried to lay verbal traps that would snare him into revealing more than he wanted to. Brown was variously cajoled, insulted, and damned. His sangfroid in the face of the hostility was remarkable, and it remained steady through the entire three-hour interview.

Right away Senator Mason tried to get him to identify his collaborators in the North. Who had financed the expedition? Mason asked. Brown purposefully lied—"I furnished most of it myself"—and covered himself by making a point he would repeat many times: "I cannot implicate others."

Then he diverted attention by making another favorite claim: He had delayed in leaving Harpers Ferry because he felt sorry for his hostages. He could have escaped, he insisted, but "I had thirty-odd prisoners, whose wives and daughters were in tears for their safety, and I felt for them." He had allowed the train to go on for the same reason. He did so "only to spare the feelings of those passengers and their families" and to show that his was not "a band of men who had no regard for life and property, nor any feelings of humanity." He had kept the hostages, thinking the townspeople would not fire at him, since they would not want to injure their friends.

But how about the killing of innocent people? asked Mason. "If there was anything of that kind done," Brown replied, "it was without my knowledge." He did not permit his men to fire on "those we regarded as innocent persons." Just ask the hostages, he said. They would vouchsafe that he often told his soldiers to hold fire, even when they were fired at.

A bystander exclaimed, "That is not so," and brought up the murder of the unarmed Fontaine Beckham. "See here, my friend," Brown responded disingenuously, "it is useless to dispute or contradict the report of your own neighbors who were my prisoners."

Mason again asked about Northern collaborators. Brown replied that he would "freely and faithfully" answer any question about himself, but not about others. Vallandigham, the proslavery congressman from Ohio, also attempted to wring a confession about Northern backers. "Mr. Brown," he asked, "who sent you here?" Brown declared, "No man sent me here; it was my own prompting and that of my Maker; or that of the devil, whichever you are pleased to ascribe it to. I acknowledge no master in human form"—an answer that seemed equivocal but actually was true, since even the most ardent members of the Secret Six had not sent him to attack a federal arsenal.

Having deflected the tough questions, Brown rode home on the easy ones. They were easy because they prompted answers that came from the deepest recesses of his soul. Mason: "What was your object in coming?" Brown: "We came to free the slaves, and only that." Mason: "How do you justify your acts?" Brown: "I think, my friend, you are guilty of a great wrong to God and against humanity—I say it without wishing to be offensive—and I believe it would be perfectly right to interfere with you, so far as to free those you wickedly and willfully hold in bondage." And: "I think I did right, and that others will do right who interfere with you at any time and at all times." The Golden Rule, he added, applies to all who would help others to gain their liberty.

"But you don't believe in the Bible," chimed in J. E. B. Stuart. Obviously he knew next to nothing about the Cromwell of America. Brown understated his response: "Certainly I do." Stuart pursued the religious theme. When Brown denied that he paid wages to his recruits, Stuart essayed a biblical pun: "The wages of sin is death." Brown swiftly turned on his foe: "I would not have said that if you had been a prisoner and wounded in my hands."

Stuart wasn't the only one present clueless about Brown's inner workings. A bystander: "Do you consider this a religious movement?" "The greatest service man can render to God," Brown declared. Bystander: "Do you consider yourself an instrument in the hands of Providence?" The Calvinist's simple answer: "I do."

How about his antislavery activities before Harpers Ferry? Bystander: Hadn't the Emigrant Aid Society sent him to Kansas? Brown's reply radiated self-assertion worthy of Emerson: "No, sir; I went under the auspices of John Brown and no one else."

Another gift from a bystander: "Upon what principle do you justify yourself?" Again, the Golden Rule; with this eloquent addendum: "I pity the poor in bondage that have none to help them." He was not here "to gratify any personal animosity, revenge or vindictive spirit. It is my sympathy with the oppressed and the wronged, that are as good as you and as precious in the sight of God."

Now his interrogators were uneasy. Was he trumping them on the religious issue? They shifted to questions about his activities in Ohio and elsewhere. By this time Brown was weary and bored. When a bystander asked if he had ever lived in Washington (he had not), he brushed off the question and got back to the racial issue: "I want you to understand that I respect the rights of the poorest and weakest of colored people, oppressed by the slave system, just as much as I do those of the most wealthy and powerful. This is the idea that has moved me, and that alone."

An officer tried to trap Brown with a racist comment: "Suppose you had every nigger in the United States, what would you do?" The easiest question of all. "Set them free." But that "would sacrifice the life of every man in this community." Brown had lived with blacks too long to accept this canard. "I do not think so," he stated.

A reporter for the *New York Herald* asked Brown if he had anything more to say. Brown said no, only that he felt perfectly justified in what he had done, since he was here "not to act the part of an incendiary or ruffian; but, on the contrary, to aid those suffering great wrong." With prophetic brilliance he declared: "I wish to say, furthermore, that you had better—all of you people of the South—prepare yourselves for a settlement of this question. You may dispose of me very easily. I am nearly disposed of now; but this question is still to be settled—this negro question, I mean. The end of that is not yet."

Nonplussed, Governor Wise reminded Brown that he was a criminal with blood on his hands and, as such, he should worry about the afterlife. Wise did not know that he was dealing with a lay theologian who had been weaned on the subtleties of Jonathan Edwards. Brown said he knew he did not have long to live. But whether his time left were fifteen years, fifteen days, or fifteen hours, "I am equally prepared to go." With an Edwardsean sense of the infinite, Brown added, "There is an eternity behind and an eternity before, and the little speck in the centre, however long, is but comparatively a minute. The difference between your tenure and mine is trifling and I want to therefore tell you to be prepared; I am prepared." In other words, it was the slaveholders, not those who opposed slavery, who should worry about hell.

If everyone present hadn't disagreed with Brown's views so strongly, they would have applauded. As it stood, he impressed his auditors greatly, even if he didn't convert any of them. The proslavery *Herald* noted, "He converses freely, fluently, and cheerfully, without the slightest manifestation of fear or uneasiness, evidently weighing well his words, and possessing a good command of language." Brown showed "no sign of weakness," reported the *Baltimore American*, even when surrounded by enemies; and "with the gallows staring him full in the face, he lay on the floor, and, in reply to every question, gave answers that betokened the spirit that animated him. The language of Gov. Wise well expresses his boldness when he said 'He is the gamest man I ever saw.' "

The comment was accurate: Governor Wise *was* impressed with John Brown. Not with what he had done or with what he stood for, but with how he behaved, how he spoke. When he returned to Richmond after Harpers Ferry, he said in a speech:

> They are themselves mistaken who take him to be a madman. He is a bundle of the best nerves I ever saw cut and thrust and bleeding and in bonds. He is a man of clear head, of courage, fortitude and simple ingenuousness. He is cool, collected, and indomitable, and it is but just to him to say, that he was humane to his prisoners, as attested to me by Colonel Washington and Mr. Mills, and he inspired me with great trust in his integrity, as a man of truth. He is a fanatic, vain, and garrulous, but firm, truthful, and intelligent. His men, too, who survive, except the free negroes with him, are like him.

Wise's proslavery friend from Ohio, Vallandigham, had a similar response:

> Cap. John Brown is as brave and resolute a man as ever headed an insurrection, and, in a good cause, and with a sufficient force, would have been a consummate partisan commander. He has coolness, dar-

ing persistency, stoic faith and patience, and a firmness of will and purpose unconquerable. He is the farthest possible remove from the ordinary ruffian, fanatic, or madman. Certainly it was one of the best planned and best executed conspiracies that ever failed.

Many other Southerners praised Brown after witnessing him. Southerners praising the North's most ardent Abolitionist? On the surface, the phenomenon was absurd. But the terms of their praise must be noticed. For them, Brown was not *right*. He had certain admirable *qualities:* toughness, honor, daring, and humaneness. He was, in short, what the South had long said a gentleman should be. He was the Southern gentleman in Abolitionist dress. As Vallandigham said, he "*would* have been" a consummate commander—"in a *good* cause."

As it was, his qualities were altogether misdirected. Governor Wise, who praised Brown's character as strongly as anyone, spoke for most Southerners when he branded Brown and his followers as "murderers, *traitors*, robbers, insurrectionists," and "wanton, malicious, unprovoked felons."

For Southerners who saw him at Harpers Ferry, then, Brown was a walking oxymoron: a humane murderer, a calm revolutionary, a traitor of impeccable integrity. He presented a new kind of puzzle. How would the South deal with an Abolitionist who had any good qualities at all, particularly qualities Southern men of honor were supposed to possess?

For that matter, how was the North going to deal with him? He was as unusual in the North as in the South, an Abolitionist who was unlike the others. The others were, by and large, pacifists; even when they talked about violence, they did not commit it. They were either disunionists who rejected the Constitution or politicos who prized the Union and the Constitution. They tended to be racists.

He was none of these. He wanted a racially integrated Union based on a revised constitution that provided equal rights for all, regardless of ethnicity or gender.

How, then, to deal with John Brown? The first impulse for both the North and the South was to dismiss him as an aberration. But he could not be dismissed. In the volatile political environment of 1859–60, Northerners and Southerners needed resonant symbols for their respective sections. John Brown became the most resonant symbol of all.

14

Pilloried, Prosecuted,
and Praised

He had lived. In the end, that's what mattered. Israel Green's chance mistake had saved him. By carrying a dress sword instead of his saber that day, Lieutenant Green had left John Brown with wounds in the side and head, some painful but none life-threatening.

Brown had lived to talk, to write, and to be hanged. It was for this reason more than any other that he influenced American history. To be sure, the Harpers Ferry invasion itself was a shocking event that would have made the headlines in any case. But had John Brown been killed, the affair would have gotten momentary attention but then have disappeared from view. It would have been recognized for what it was—a unique action by a solitary warrior who had little support in the North. It would have anticipated not the Civil War but isolated acts of violence such as Waco, Oklahoma City, and Ruby Ridge.

But John Brown *talked* in court. He *wrote* letters from prison. Then he *was hanged,* an event he looked forward to. Because his eloquent talk and forceful writing were observed by the entire nation through the press, his hanging made a difference. It became something much larger than the execution of a criminal. For many in the North it was the martyrdom of a saint. For many in the South it was a vindictive thrust at the whole North.

Brown made his greatest effect not with weapons but with words. As Thoreau said, words were his Sharps rifles, more powerful than any gun he carried at Harpers Ferry. Here is where Brown differed from other terrorists in history. Many advocates of political violence have called Brown their spiritual forefather. But Harpers Ferry was far more than a terrorist act. It was a cultural event. It became so because of the way Brown behaved and expressed himself and because of how his behavior and words were interpreted—in many cases *mis*interpreted—by leading figures in both the North and the South.

In the North both the Harpers Ferry raid and Brown himself were at first sharply denounced. The Concord Transcendentalists led in resuscitating his image by defending both the man and his deed. Slowly, a positive view of Brown the man, if not his deed, spread as Brown's writings and behavior in prison were made known through the press. By the time of his hanging, seven weeks after the raid, widespread sympathy resulted in reverent memorial services throughout the North.

The South quickly transformed Brown into something he was not: a representative of the antislavery North. Brown therefore created a paranoiac panic in the South, intensifying secessionist feelings and producing an ever-strengthening defense of the institution of slavery.

The earliest response to the takeover of Harpers Ferry was confusion. Misinformation was rife. At first, no one thought that Abolitionists had attacked the town to free slaves. How could such a story be believed? Nothing of the kind had ever happened before. Abolitionists were known to be pacifists. The South had long derided them as cowards.

And so, "any and every other explanation was accepted in preference" to the idea that this was "an Anti-Slavery movement," as an eyewitness reported. Many stories arose. Workers at the armory had gone on strike. Robbers had broken into the paymaster's office to take a strongbox holding $15,000. Laborers on the dam were expressing grievances. These and other rumors circulated early on Monday, October 17, the morning after the raid began.

False accounts were followed by distorted ones. The *Baltimore Patriot*, late on the seventeenth, reported "a negro insurrection of a very serious nature" at Harpers Ferry led by "250 whites, supposed to be Abolitionists," along with "some 100 negroes." The leader was "S. C. Anderson," who expected "a reinforcement of 1,500 men" soon.

The next morning, the eighteenth, the *Baltimore American* said that the town had been raided by "at least three hundred persons; that among them were several strapping negroes, who occasionally shouted out that they longed for liberty, as they had been in bondage long enough." The ringleader, Anderson, had arrived in the region "five or six days ago, and since that time has been driving around the place in an elegant barouche drawn by two horses."

A third paper was even vaguer. An "outlaw band" of 250 to 300 led by an "Andreas" had threatened to burn the town and kill everyone in it. The outbreak was either "a bold, concerted scheme to rob the government pay-house of funds" or "a demonstration of the Abolitionists connected with some negro affair."

The reports got wilder. According to a telegram from the baggage master of the train that had been stopped at Harpers Ferry, 250 whites and as many as 600 blacks, led by a William Smith, had attacked for an unknown reason. This story appeared in several Northern papers. Another widely reprinted story was that the supposedly black invaders were actually white robbers "painted as blacks" who had put "almost all the leading people of Harper's Ferry in jail," killed several of them, and "taken money from the vaults."

More accurate reports came, with headlines that screamed:

**HARPER'S FERRY. FEARFUL AND
EXCITING INTELLIGENCE!**

NEGRO INSURRECTION AT HARPER'S FERRY!!

**EXTENSIVE SLAVE CONSPIRACY IN
MARYLAND AND VIRGINIA!**

HUNDREDS OF INSURRECTIONISTS IN ARMS!

SEIZURE OF THE UNITED STATES ARSENAL AND WORKS!

**TELEGRAPH WIRES CUT—BRIDGE SEIZED
AND FORTIFIED!**

**DEFENDED BY CANNON—TRAIN SEIZED AND HELD—
FIRING ON BOTH SIDES—SEVERAL KILLED—
CONTRIBUTIONS LEVIED—TROOPS ON THE WAY!**

By Wednesday, October 19, the truth about the invasion was known. Reporters relayed nationwide the information the wounded Brown had given during his three-hour interview after being captured.

More information came from a militia company, the Independent Greys of Baltimore, which investigated the Maryland schoolhouse, where they found twenty-one boxes containing assorted weapons and supplies: Sharps rifles, revolvers, pikes, cutlasses, picks, shovels, tents, clothing, stationery, and medical kits. Also found were pockets maps of Kentucky and Maryland.

Each of the Greys appropriated a rifle and two revolvers; the rest of the material was loaded into wagons to be turned over to officials.

A detachment of marines under Lieutenant J. E. B. Stuart went to the Kennedy farm and seized incriminating papers: the provisional constitution, letters from Northern supporters, hundreds of copies of Forbes's *Patriotic Volunteer*, and seven maps of Southern states, marked to identify points of attack. Curious neighbors had already stolen many items before the arrival of the marines, who gave out pikes as extra souvenirs.

At the Ferry five men were in custody. John Brown had a gash in the kidney area and four in the head. Aaron Stevens suffered terribly from his wounds; several bullets were lodged in the upper half of his body. The other three—Edwin Coppoc, the twenty-four-year old Quaker, and the African Americans John A. Copeland and Shields Green—were not wounded.

After being held overnight in the armory guardhouse, the prisoners were, on the nineteenth, taken under heavy guard to the county jail in Charles Town, eight miles southwest of Harpers Ferry. Governor Wise quickly had them arraigned on three charges: treason against the state of Virginia, inciting slaves to rebellion, and murder.

The first charge made little sense. Brown had never been a Virginia citizen, had lived only briefly in the neighboring state of Maryland, and had attacked a federal property. How could he have committed treason against Virginia? The question would be brought up by his lawyers. Most legal historians agree that Brown should have been tried by the national government, not the state of Virginia.

Wise wanted to be expeditious and to make a statement. It so happened that the semiannual term of the district court under Judge Richard Parker had just begun. It was convenient to rush Brown and his men to trial in order to speed the all-but-certain guilty verdict.

The issue of states' rights was also involved. Ever since the nullification crisis of 1832, when South Carolina had refused to pay a federal tax, Southerners had defended state sovereignty. The states' rights ethos would feed into the South's secession from the Union and its formation of the Confederate States of America. By claiming John Brown for Virginia, Governor Wise was supporting his own state.

He also had a personal vendetta to satisfy. John Brown had embarrassed him. With only four men and some emancipated slaves, Brown had achieved a standoff against Southern forces that at their peak approached eight hundred. A thin, tobacco-chewing slaveholder with aspirations to the presidency, Wise supported dueling and the bowie knife, a weapon with which, he later boasted, the South could easily conquer the North. This

Henry A. Wise, governor of Virginia.

scrappy Virginian was not going to allow himself to be bested by an Aboli-tionist. He would make sure that John Brown hanged and that Virginia hanged him.

After Brown's capture Wise castigated the inefficient militia companies of Virginia and Maryland. As a local paper reported, "When the Governor was informed of the mere handful of men who had created all this bobbery he boiled over." He was so ashamed of the militia's performance, he said, that he would rather lose his right arm than have the South disgraced in such a way again. His son, O. Jennings Wise, later went to court against Colonel Robert W. Baylor, the main commander of the militia companies at Harpers Ferry on October 17. Wise charged Baylor with cowardice and dereliction of duty in not storming the engine house with his vastly supe-rior force.

Humiliated and bitter, Virginia flexed its muscles. On the evening of Brown's capture, Governor Wise read aloud from Brown's papers to lounging militia men and tipsy citizens in the Wager House at the Ferry. Crying out "Sons of Virginia!" Wise made a running commentary on the papers. Frustrated over Brown's refusal to reveal his sources in the North, Wise fabricated sources as he read. Many Northerners were behind the plot, he insisted. Brown was their agent. According to one observer, Wise said that "prominent persons and party-leaders in the North" instigated the attack. "The most innocent notes and letters," the eyewitness reported, "commonplace paragraphs and printed cuttings, were distorted and twisted by the reading and by the talking into clear instructions and positive plots."

The North did all it could to prove that such accusations of a widespread conspiracy were off the mark. In the hundreds of Northern newspaper articles written during the week immediately after the raid, not one wholeheartedly supported Brown. Few manifested any sympathy at all. The common theme was that Harpers Ferry was the work of a solitary madman.

A few examples reflect the overall Northern reaction. The *New York Evening Post* denounced Brown's "fanatical enterprise." Creating a story that would be widely repeated, the *Post* claimed that Brown's troubles in Kansas "drove him to madness"; as a result, "frenzied by the remembrance of his wrongs, his whole nature turned into gall by the bitter hatreds stirred up in Kansas, and reckless of consequences, he has plunged into the work of blood." The *Providence Journal* said of Harpers Ferry, "Such deeds are not countenanced here," explaining that the Kansas wars had "shattered the brains of a poor old man." The *New York Commercial Advertiser* called Brown a "madman" and declared, "The whole movement was inadequate to the end proposed," meriting only "ridicule and contempt." The *Chicago Press and Tribune*, calling the Virginia raid a "stark-mad enterprise" produced by "addled brains," insisted that Brown had no supporters in the North:

> A squad of fanatics whose zeal is wonderfully disproportioned to their sense, . . . commanded by a man who has, for years been as mad as a March hare, unite in making an insurrection at Harper's Ferry. . . . They are guilty of the most incomprehensible stupidity and folly as well as unpardonable criminality in all these acts. . . . There is not a public journal of any party, or public man of any shade of opinion found to approve their means or justify their end.

The latter point was accurate. Even those one might expect to have approved of Brown's effort—long-standing antislavery reformers—recoiled from Harpers Ferry. William Lloyd Garrison in the *Liberator* called

Brown's raid "a misguided, wild, and apparently insane, though disinterested and well intended effort." Horace Greeley's *New-York Tribune*, the most widely read antislavery paper, insisted that "this deplorable affair" was "the work of a madman" and predicted, "There will be enough to heap execration on these mistaken men." Saying that Brown had attacked slavery "in a manner which seems to us fatally wrong," Greeley explained that Kansas had driven Brown mad: "He was born of rapine, and cruelty, and murder."

Cruelty and murder in Kansas. Greeley was bringing attention to the incident that, more than any other, raised doubts about Brown's sanity and probity: the Pottawatomie killings.

In the weeks after the Virginia raid, debate over Pottawatomie raged in Kansas newspapers and leaked into eastern ones. The *Leavenworth Herald* called Brown a "miserable old wretch" who had committed an "atrocity . . . unparalleled in the history of crime. We allude to the massacre of the Wilkinsons and Doyles. . . . Brown, with five or six followers, dragged these persons, five in number, from their beds at night, split their heads open with sabers, in the presence of their wives, and then cut off their ears and fingers, and otherwise mutilated their bodies. The individuals had committed no offense—the only crime charged, was that they differed politically from Brown."

Similarly, G. W. Brown in the *Herald of Freedom* argued that the man who led the "mad" Harpers Ferry raid had, three years earlier in Kansas, "called from their beds at their several residences, at the hour of midnight, on the 24th of May, Allen Wilkinson, Wm. Sherman, Wm. P. Doyle, Wm. Doyle, and Drury Doyle. All were found the next morning, by the road side, or in the highway, some with a gash in their heads and sides, and their throats cut; others with their skulls split open in two places, with holes in their breasts with their fingers cut off. No man in Kansas has pretended to deny that Old John Brown led that murderous foray, which massacred those men." In response to this report, a council of antislavery Kansans issued a declaration that "according to the ordinary rules of war" the Pottawatomie episode was "not unjustifiable, but . . . was performed from the sad necessity which existed at that time to defend the lives and liberties of the settlers in that region."

Back east, most of those who had supported John Brown before the attack on Harpers Ferry now shrank from him in horror. Within two days of Brown's capture, several leading papers, including the *New York Times* and the *New York Herald*, printed the letters to Brown from Northern backers that J. E. B. Stuart had collected at the Kennedy farm. Among those published were ones from Gerrit Smith, S. G. Howe, George Stearns,

Frederick Douglass, Frank Sanborn, and Senator Henry Wilson. Soon thereafter, Hugh Forbes contributed to the *Herald* letters that further implicated several members of the Secret Six. The revelations created panic among Brown's supporters, especially when the *Herald* on October 27 called for the arrest of Smith and Douglass as "accessories before the fact."

In the Charles Town jail, John Brown calmly awaited martyrdom. His closest backers in the North did not share his passion for self-sacrifice.

Gerrit Smith had a mental collapse. The erratic philanthropist had drifted through many kinds of antislavery reform, some of them at odds with one another. A month before the Harpers Ferry raid he had published a militant prediction that slave insurrections would soon sweep the South. "For insurrections then we may look any year, *any month, any day,*" he wrote. "A terrible remedy for a terrible wrong! . . . For what portions are there of the South that will cling to slavery after two or three considerable insurrections shall have filled the whole South with horror?" These were bold words that came close to exposing his friend John Brown, whose plan to incite slave revolts he knew well.

But Smith was far from bold in the aftermath of Harpers Ferry. When he saw his private letters to Brown published in the New York papers, he set about destroying documents in his possession that linked him to Brown. His worst fears were realized when word came that he and Frederick Douglass might face criminal charges as "accessories before the fact." He could not sleep. His reason left him. A *Herald* reporter who visited him in Peterboro found him thin and flushed, with bloodshot eyes and an air of "hasty, nervous agitation, as though some great fear was constantly before the imagination." Smith refused to discuss the Virginia raid, exclaiming, "I'm going to be indicted, sir, indicted! If any man in the Union is taken, it will be me."

Overcome with irrational guilt, he declared that he was a heartless criminal personally responsible for all the bloodshed at Harpers Ferry. He had a delusional idea of going to Charles Town to join Brown in prison. On November 7, five days after Brown was condemned to death, Smith was committed to the New York State Asylum for the Insane in Utica, where he remained until December 29. Although he later recovered his sanity, his delicate condition gave him a medical excuse for not appearing before the Mason Committee, which on January 4 began a six-month investigation of Harpers Ferry.

For the rest of his life, even after the rehabilitation of Brown's reputation, Smith denied having had a close affiliation with Brown. When in May 1860 a Democratic group, the New York Vigilant Committee, publicly charged him with having conspired with Brown, Smith sued the group for $1.5 million in slander and published a letter in the *Herald* stating that he had had only a superficial familiarity with Brown. He charged his accusers with airing "the meanest, nakedest, and most atrocious lies"—a phrase that better described his own statements about Brown. The committee backed down, fearing it would lose the case. Smith kept up the denial game during and after the war. In the late 1860s his family filed other suits to suppress threatened revelations and in 1872 prevented Frank Sanborn from making a full disclosure by insisting that Smith would go insane again if the full truth were made known.

Smith was an extreme case of a common reaction to Harpers Ferry among Brown's former backers, who feared being punished as accomplices in crime. Four of them left the country to avoid possible capture.

Frederick Douglass, informed that two Virginia agents, authorized by President Buchanan, were coming to Rochester to interrogate him, fled to Canada on October 19 and from there sailed to England. He later sent a public letter to the Northern papers denying his involvement in Harpers Ferry. He called a charge that he had promised to join the raid "wholly, grievously, and most unaccountably wrong," declaring that he had "never made a promise so rash and wild as this" and that he would conspire against slavery only "when there is a reasonable hope of success." Referring to his famous flight from slavery—and evidently forgetting his intrepid battles against the cruel overseer Covey, powerfully recorded in his autobiography—he wrote, "I have always been more distinguished for running than fighting—and, tried by the Harper's Ferry insurrection test, I am most miserably deficient in courage."

The day after Douglass fled, Frank Sanborn left Concord for Quebec. On the twenty-first he wrote secretively to Higginson, "I am going to try a change of air for my old complaint; whether my absence will be long or short will depend on circumstance." "Burn this," he warned. His immediate aim was to cover up his key role in the Secret Six. Before going to Canada, he destroyed many manuscripts and letters that linked him to John Brown, and he continued the purge when he returned to Concord on October 26.

Two others who left the country were S. G. Howe and George Stearns. Howe, for whom the Virginia idea had always been an adventurous escapade rather than a deep commitment, shook with fear when his name began to be associated with Brown. He went to Stearns's Medford mansion and paced about nervously, confessing that he was on the verge of going insane. He pleaded with Stearns to accompany him to Canada. Stearns acquiesced, and by October 26 the two were in Canada, where they remained until after Brown's execution on December 2.

In November, Howe sent an astonishing statement to the *New-York Tribune* in which he denied prior knowledge of the Virginia raid. (Actually, he had known of the plan, except the choice of Harpers Ferry as the target, ever since Sanborn had described it to him on February 26, 1858.) In his statement he not only separated himself from the raid but questioned its wisdom and lied about Brown. "Rumor has mingled my name with the events at Harper's Ferry," he wrote. But, he continued, "That event was unforeseen and unexpected but by me; nor does all my previous knowledge of John Brown enable me to reconcile it with his characteristic prudence, and his reluctance to shed blood, or excite servile insurrection. It is still to me a mystery and a marvel."

These blatant falsehoods roiled Thomas Wentworth Higginson. "Is there no such thing as *honor* among confederates?" he wrote Sanborn, who tried to defend Howe. Of the Secret Six only Higginson and Theodore Parker firmly defended the Harpers Ferry raid. Higginson called it "the most formidable insurrection that has ever occurred." Although he was disappointed when the raid failed, he stood his ground, refusing to flee the country or destroy incriminating documents. At first, he reasoned that Brown would make more of an impact as a martyr than as anything else. Later he leagued with two others to plot a rescue of Brown from prison.

From Rome the dying Theodore Parker sent a public letter defending slave revolts. Parker wrote, "Of course I was not astonished to hear that an attempt had been made to free the slaves in a certain part of Virginia, nor should I be astonished if another 'Insurrection' or 'REBELLION' took place in the state of ——, or third in ——, or a fourth in ——. Such things are to be expected; for they do not depend merely on the private will of a man like Capt. Brown and his associates but on the general causes which move all human kind to hate wrong and love right. Such 'insurrections' will continue as long as slavery lasts."

Higginson and Parker were more closely associated with Transcendentalism than were their fellow Secret Six members. It is important to recognize that in the immediate aftermath of Harpers Ferry, *only* Transcendentalists strongly defended John Brown.

Had Transcendentalism not been in the picture, what would have happened? The tide of negative commentary on Brown that flooded the Northern press would have continued. With few opposing voices, negativity would most likely have won the day. Northerners, realizing that Brown acted alone, would have come to regard him as a mistaken eccentric. South-erners would have had no ground for charging the North with widespread sympathy for Brown, since the charge would be patently false. In the end, John Brown would have been dismissed as a curious anomaly of history—an early sketch of, say, the Unabomber. As it was, Brown became an intensely polarizing figure who influenced national events. In the early going, it was the Transcendentalists alone who rescued him from infamy and possible oblivion.

The powerful contribution of the Concord group to the recovery of Brown was recognized by many contemporaries. The first Brown biogra-phy, James Redpath's *The Public Life of Capt. John Brown*, featured in its ded-ication the names of Thoreau and Emerson, calling them, in loud capitals, "DEFENDERS OF THE FAITHFUL, WHO, WHEN THE MOB SHOUTED, 'MADMAN!' SAID, 'SAINT!' " Similarly, George Stearns's son, Frank, asserted, "Emerson and Thoreau were the first to come forward and say to the astonished world: 'He is not a madman, but a saint.' " Wen-dell Phillips recalled, "The crowning honor of Emerson is that after talking about heroism for so many years, when the hero, John Brown, came he knew him."

Among the Transcendentalists it was Thoreau who made the earliest and boldest moves on behalf of Brown. When the news of Harpers Ferry reached Concord on October 19, Thoreau was with Bronson Alcott and Emerson at the latter's house. Of the three, Thoreau was the least startled by the news.

The least startled, but the most moved. Thoreau went home and poured out his feelings in his journal. His response was instant and unequivocal: John Brown was a saintly hero, and anyone who criticized him was amoral or thick-headed. Having long believed that the principled individual was worthier than the strongest government, Thoreau seized upon Brown as the one person in America who had Right on his side.

His first words in his journal about Harpers Ferry revealed his convic-tion that this was no aberrant event to be dismissed lightly. It was a light-ning flash that revealed the corruption of the entire American system. In the first paragraph of his October 19 entry, he went directly to the social significance of the government's suppression of Brown. "When a govern-ment puts forth its strength on the side of injustice," he wrote, "as ours (especially to-day) to maintain slavery and kill the liberators of the slave, what a merely brute, or worse than brute, force it is seen to be! A demonia-cal force!"

In his entries over the next three days he pursued the theme. John

Henry David Thoreau.

Brown was the virtuous, sturdy individual willing to sacrifice his life for the ideal of liberty for millions of enslaved African Americans. Those who stood opposed to him—the government, the press, the parties, the churches, the people—were depraved and inhuman.

Were Brown and his men insane, as the newspapers said? Thoreau bristled with sarcasm. "The Republican editors, obliged to get their sentences ready for the morning edition,—and their dinner ready before afternoon,— speak of these men . . . [as] 'deluded fanatics, 'mistaken men,' 'insane,' or 'crazed.' Did it ever occur to you what a *sane* set of editors we are blessed with!—not 'mistaken men'; who know very well on which side their bread is buttered!" Also: "What has Massachusetts and the North sent a few *sane* senators to Congress for of late years? . . . All their speeches put together and boiled down . . . do not match for simple and manly directness, force, and effectiveness the few casual remarks of *insane* John Brown on the floor of the Harper's Ferry engine-house."

But Brown "won't gain anything," Thoreau had heard from his neighbors. "Well, no!" he responded. "I don't suppose he could get four-and-six-pence a day for being hung, take the year round. But then he stands a chance to save a considerable part of his soul—and such a soul!—when you do not. No doubt you can get more in your market for a quart of milk than for a quart of blood, but that is not the market that heroes carry their blood to."

From America's "most hypocritical and diabolical government," Thoreau heard questions: "What do you assault me for? . . . Why won't you cease agitation on this subject?" Thoreau answered with a tragic symbol of slavery: "The slave-ship is on her way, crowded with its dying hundreds; a small crew of slaveholders is smothering four millions under the hatches. . . . What is that I hear cast overboard? The bodies of the dead, who have found deliverance."

Thoreau noted the irony of Brown being denounced by antislavery Northerners but receiving high praise from his Southern captors, who loathed his cause but could not help but admire his character. "I have seen no hearty approbation for this man in any Abolition journal," Thoreau wrote, with accuracy. Meanwhile, he continued, witness the comments of Southerners who saw John Brown in action. "Governor Wise speaks far more justly and admiringly of him than any Northern editor that I have heard of."

Thoreau placed his hero among the greats of history. John Brown was Jesus: "Some eighteen hundred years ago Christ was crucified; this morning perchance John Brown was hung. These are two ends of a chain which I rejoice to know is not without its links." He was Cromwell: "He was one of that class of whom we hear a great deal, but, for the most part, see nothing at all—the Puritans. It is vain to kill him. He died lately in the time of Cromwell, but he reappeared here. Why should he not? Some of the Puritan stock are said to have settled in New England." He was an American patriot: "like the best of those who stood at our bridge once, on Lexington Common, and on Bunker Hill, only he was firmer and higher-principled than any that I have chanced to hear of as there." He was Emerson and Thoreau: "A Transcendentalist above all, a man of ideas and principles,— that was what distinguished him."

But not even the Transcendentalists—no one, for that matter—could match him: "He could not be tried by his peers, for his peers do not exist." Thoreau, not known for his humility, genuflected to Brown: "I rejoice that I live in this age, that I was his contemporary."

It was one thing to praise Brown in one's private journal. It was quite another to publicize one's sympathy at a moment when even some of Brown's most fervent supporters quailed with fear of arrest. Thoreau alone took the risk of publicly defending the "insane" Brown and his "deluded" followers.

He announced in Concord that on October 30 he was going to give a lecture in the town hall in support of John Brown. The county Republican Party and a Concord antislavery committee called the idea "impolitic and extreme." Thoreau replied sharply, "I did not send to you for advice, but to announce that I am to speak." When the day came and town officials refused to ring the bell summoning citizens to the lecture, Thoreau rang it himself. The talk he gave, "A Plea for Captain John Brown," integrated his journal entries with personal comments that made him seem closer to Brown than he actually was.

Just when those truly intimate with Brown, such as Gerrit Smith and Frank Sanborn, were trying to cover up their connection with him, Thoreau was going out of his way to suggest that Brown was his friend and confidant. More than this, he was eager to spread his views on Brown. He wrote friends in Worcester and Boston, asking them to arrange appearances for him. He delivered his talk in both places. In Boston he sought out publishers, trying to get the speech printed and distributed as a book. Although none dared publish it separately, it reached a large audience by being copied in newspapers. Just as important, it roused to Brown's defense the intellectual leaders surrounding Thoreau, notably Emerson, who had huge cultural clout.

And so Thoreau and his fellow Transcendentalists planted the seed that eventually grew into the North's veneration of John Brown. In *Walden*, Thoreau, describing the impact of an idea, wrote that "a tide rises and falls behind every man which can float the British Empire like a chip"—a notion that would be borne out by Mahatma Gandhi and Martin Luther King, Jr., both of whom would use a Thoreauvian concept, civil disobedience, to help float away social injustice. Thoreau and his fellow Concordites did their part to rid America of slavery by introducing a radically new idea: the leader of the raid on Harpers Ferry was not a lunatic but a hero.

Their idea was confirmed by John Brown's behavior during his trial and in prison. Not once during the six weeks between his capture and his hanging did Brown swerve from the cool courage and humanitarian earnestness he had exhibited in the postraid interview. Thoreau's praise was borne out by Brown's poise and eloquence.

Charles Town, where Brown spent his last days, was the government seat of Jefferson County, Virginia. A flourishing town of 1,600, it was the center of a fertile agricultural region known as the Garden of Virginia. Rich in history, the town was named after George Washington's brother Charles, who, like many other Washingtons, had settled in the area.

The Washingtons were slaveholders, as Virginians liked to point out. Virginia believed it was fulfilling its patriotic duty by bringing to trial the Northerners who had attacked its sacred institution, slavery.

On October 25, a week after his capture, John Brown was arraigned in the county courthouse in Charles Town. Eighty bayoneted militiamen escorted him and Edwin Coppoc, manacled to each other, from the prison to the courthouse, diagonally across the road. Still suffering from his wounds, Brown had to be supported but had an air of proud defiance. His eyes were swollen from the saber gashes in his head.

The presiding justice arraigned him on three counts: conspiracy to incite a slave insurrection, treason against the State of Virginia, and first-degree murder. When asked to plead to the charges, Brown rose and said defiantly: "I did not ask for any quarter at the time I was taken. I did not ask to have my life spared. The Governor of the State of Virginia tendered me his assurance that I should have a fair trial; and, under no circumstances whatever, will I be able to have a fair trial. If you seek my blood, you can have it any moment, without this mockery of a trial. I have had no counsel. I have not been able to advise with any one. . . . If we are forced with a mere form—a trial for execution—you might spare yourselves that trouble. I am ready for my fate. I do not ask for a trial. I beg no mockery of a trial—no insult—nothing but that which conscience gives, or cowardice would drive you to practise. I ask again to be excused from this mockery of a trial. I do not even know what the special design of this examination is. I do not know what is to be the benefit of it to the Commonwealth. I have now little further to ask, other than that I may not be foolishly insulted, only as cowardly barbarians insult those who fall into their power."

In effect, Brown was saying: "The justice system, with the proslavery laws it enforces, is corrupt and incapable of arriving at truth. Don't insult me. Go ahead and hang me right away." His remarks were ignored by the court but reached a nationwide audience through the Associated Press. They established the brazen tone he would maintain over the coming weeks.

The magistrates assigned two Virginia attorneys, Lawson Botts and Thomas C. Green, to serve as his counsel and asked Brown if he accepted them. His defiance continued. "I wish for counsel if I am to have a trial," he declared, "but if I am to have nothing but a mockery of a trial, as I've said, I do not care anything about counsel. It is unnecessary to trouble any gentleman with that duty." Botts and Green were assigned anyway, and the trial was set to begin the next day, Wednesday, October 26.

In the morning Brown and the other prisoners were brought for the Grand Jury's indictment. Armed guards and cannons encircled the courthouse. The badly wounded Aaron Stevens was placed on a mattress before the bench. John Brown lay on a cot near him, with Coppoc, Copeland, and Shields Green standing behind. Brown and Stevens were forced to stand when a true bill was read, repeating the charges of treason, murder, and inciting insurrection.

After it was decided that Brown would be tried first, the others were taken back to jail and Brown was left alone before the judge. Brown requested a short delay in the trial, in light of his enfeebled condition. He was improving, he said, but his kidney wound bothered him, and his head lacerations had affected his hearing. His request for a delay was rejected. He pleaded "not guilty" to all charges against him.

Brown was walking the next morning when he entered the court, looking healthier but still feeling frail. He lay down on a cot that had been provided for him. He witnessed the trial from there, standing up when addressing the court.

He was not the only curious sight. The whole trial, serious as it was, had an element of farce about it. One Northern reporter was amused by the "free and easy style of the Southern habits" in the courtroom, and another wrote, "The customs of this court are singular. They strike a Northerner with peculiar force. . . . There are very odd ways of conducting business."

Odd indeed. From start to close the courtroom was crowded with five hundred to six hundred spectators who ceaselessly opened peanuts and chestnuts, throwing the shells onto the courtroom floor. The accumulating shells crunched whenever anyone walked or moved their feet while seated. The spectators puffed cigars and spat tobacco juice on the floor. The air was thick with stale smoke. Periodically, a bailiff shouted that smoking was not permitted, but this resulted only in a momentary cessation, followed by mass resumption of cigar-puffing, interspersed with curses hissed at John Brown, such as, "Damned black-hearted villain! heart as black as a stove-pipe!"

The lawyers involved in the case had disparate personalities and habits. The state's prosecuting attorney, Charles B. Harding, was a bulky, bibulous man with a hooked nose and several days' growth of scraggly beard on his receding chin. Often he would present an argument against Brown, sit down and put his feet on his table, and then doze off while the rest of the trial went on. Once he snorted himself awake and cried out for tobacco; the bailiff rebuked him by saying, "Gentlemen must not talk in Court." Harding talked anyway. On the second day of the trial he accounted for bruises on his face by telling of a fistfight he had had the previous evening with a man he described as a "blind nigger." Impaired by alcohol, Harding lost track of his arguments and eventually was dismissed by the court. The tall, dignified Andrew Hunter took over the case and conducted a vigorous prosecution against Brown.

Presiding over the trial was Judge Andrew Parker, a short, affable man who was descended from a line of Virginia dignitaries. Though capable and distinguished, Parker contributed to the casualness of the scene. His table, on an elevated platform, was a chaos of law books, papers, and inkstands. Holding a tremendous book open on his lap, he tilted back in his chair with his legs on the table. Many others present assumed a similar position. As a reporter noted, Parker was flanked by eight county magistrates who sat with raised legs, "one or two using a fragment of his table for the support of their legs; the rest displaying an unmasked battery of boots all along the railing which edges the platform." The reporter continued: "Near the center of the room, lawyers sat around a table, many of them following the usual upward fashion, or passion, as it seems to be here, of legs."

A militiaman assigned to supervise security, Colonel J. Lewis Davis, was a pompous coxcomb who wore his long hair braided and tied in a swooping knot over his forehead. Haughty and shrill, he marched to and fro with a Sharps rifle he had pilfered from Brown's cache of weapons, barking at reporters and bothersome spectators. He and his fellow guards had the unusual duty of waking up two somnolent witnesses who often disturbed the court with their snoring.

It was in these bizarre conditions that one of the most important political trials in American history took place. Despite the relaxed atmosphere, most of the spectators—quite literally a peanut gallery—were fixated on the lawyers' arguments and especially on the recumbent Brown, whom they stared at with mixed loathing and awe.

Brown seemed the least interested person present. Most of the time he spent lying on his back, with his eyes closed, attentive to the procedures but apparently indifferent to their outcome. His sole desire was that the court recognize what he saw as the truth of the case: He had attacked Harpers Ferry for the noble purpose of liberating slaves, which he regarded as his divine, patriotic duty. He had treated his hostages well. The killings that occurred during the raid were regrettable but unforeseen by him.

When the chance came for him to plead insanity, he refused to do so on the grounds that he believed such a plea would be false. Before any witnesses were called, the defense attorney Lawson Botts read aloud a telegram from A. H. Lewis, one of Brown's Ohio acquaintances, reporting many cases of insanity in Brown's family. An aunt of John Brown on his mother's side had allegedly died of it, and a daughter of hers spent two years in a lunatic asylum. Two children of his mother's brother had spent time in an asylum, and a third child was hopelessly insane and under restraint. Also read before the court were affidavits from friends and relatives of Brown that claimed he was insane; most of them said he was a "monomaniac" on the subjects of slavery and religion.

The attempt to prove Brown insane came from Ohio Abolitionists who were trying to soften his sentence. Brown rejected the effort outright. He told the court that he regarded the insanity plea "as a miserable artifice and pretext of those who want to take a different course in regard to me, if they take any at all, and I view it with contempt more than otherwise. . . . If I am insane, of course, I should think I know more than all the rest of the world. But I do not think so. I'm perfectly unconscious of insanity, and I reject, so far as I am capable, any attempt to interfere in my behalf on that score." He admitted that there had been some insanity on his mother's side but none on his father's. He added that his first wife and his two oldest sons, John and Frederick, had shown symptoms of derangement. But Brown insisted that he was not insane himself.

Was he right? I believe so. What some of his acquaintances called "monomania" was a burning desire to topple slavery in the name of God and American democracy. Brown exhibited none of the symptoms—severe mood swings, disturbed sleep patterns, persistent sadness, loss of concentration, delusions, disengagement from life, and so on—that modern psychiatry associates with mental illness. During his weeks in the Charles Town prison, he slept soundly and maintained a cheerful demeanor. He wrote long, cogent letters to his family and others. His speeches to the court were eloquent and rational.

The insanity issue having been dismissed, witnesses were called to testify for and against Brown. Brown's principal lawyer, Thomas C. Green, was an angular, blustery man given to rapid-fire questions and rhetorical outbursts full of "whars" and "thars." From several of Brown's hostages he elicited the testimony that Brown had treated them well in the engine house, had acted bravely there, and had waged a defensive battle with the specific aim of freeing slaves. He argued that the charge of treason against Virginia made no sense. There had been no assault on the state's government and no attempt to establish a rival one. At any rate, he declared, Virginia had no jurisdiction over crime committed on federal property; this applied to the murder charge as well.

Green's formidable opponent, Andrew Hunter, was a relative of Fontaine Beckham, the beloved mayor of Harpers Ferry who had been killed in the raid, and the father of Henry Hunter, the young man who had led the capture and shooting of William Thompson. At once suave and grave, the six-foot-tall Andrew Hunter used rhetorical techniques to dominate a courtroom, shifting between subdued and impassioned vocal tones.

It did not matter, he argued, that Brown had been brave or civil to his hostages. Nor did his supposedly noble motives count. The fact was that Brown had kidnapped citizens of Virginia, had stolen their slave property, and had initiated a battle in which innocent lives were taken. As for the issue of Harpers Ferry being federal property, Hunter cited precedent. Historically, Virginia had assumed jurisdiction over crimes committed in the Ferry. Why should this case be different?

Around midnight on October 27 there arrived in Charles Town a young Boston lawyer, George Henry Hoyt, who had come ostensibly to join Brown's defense team but actually was a spy on behalf of a group of Northern Abolitionists led by John W. LeBarnes. Ardently antislavery, Hoyt accepted LeBarnes's plot to serve as a conduit between Brown and Northerners and to assess possibilities for a rescue attempt.

A twenty-one-year-old who looked nineteen, Hoyt had been chosen as a spy because LeBarnes had thought someone so young would be above suspicion. Actually, his youth betrayed him. Andrew Hunter wondered why Bostonians, with their rich legal resources, would send such a neophyte to defend Brown. Hunter wrote Governor Wise on October 28, "A beardless boy came in last night as Brown's counsel. I think he is a spy." Even the local newspapers saw through Hoyt. One mocked his lack of knowledge of Virginia's laws and cast suspicion on him: "An eye will be kept upon this *volunteer* gentleman, as it should be upon others, whether *volunteers* or not."

Hoyt quickly saw that a rescue effort would be fruitless, since the region teemed with armed patrols. "There is *no chance* of [Brown's] ultimate escape," he wrote LeBarnes. "There is nothing but the most unmitigated failure and the saddest consequence which is possible to conjure up to ensue upon an attempt at rescue."

Hoyt got more than he had bargained for when he showed up in Judge Parker's courtroom on October 28. He had trouble being accepted as a lawyer, for he had no papers validating his training. Parker at last let him join the defense team that sat beside Brown's cot, but it wasn't long before Hoyt faced a small crisis. During the testimony of Henry Hunter, John Brown lost his composure for the only time in the trial. Hunter proudly recounted his part in the killing of William Thompson, whom he had helped to drag from the Wager House and fling into the river. He explained, "I felt it my duty, and I have no regrets."

Outraged by Hunter's callousness, Brown rose to his feet and declared that the trial was unfair and that his lawyers were not handling his case well. Botts and Green had little choice but to announce their withdrawal from the case. Judge Parker accepted their decision, and the young Hoyt was left as Brown's sole counsel. But Hoyt had learned that two additional defense lawyers, Samuel Chilton of Washington and Hiram Griswold of Cleveland, would arrive the next morning, Saturday. He was granted an adjournment until then.

Chilton and Griswold arrived in time for the opening of the session and immediately requested a few hours' delay so that they could learn the facts of the case. Judge Parker denied the request, and the trial went forward. With the help of Brown, the lawyers continued the defense along previous lines. Several of Brown's hostages testified that they had been treated kindly and that Brown had told them his mission in Virginia was humanitarian, not murderous. Whenever his lawyers flagged, Brown questioned the witnesses. In the afternoon Chilton made a motion that Brown be permitted to defend himself against one charge at a time, since it was impossible to deal with treason, murder, and insurrection at once. This request, too, was rejected.

Closing arguments came on Monday. Griswold represented the defense. Brown, he argued, had had no previous connection with Virginia and thus could not have committed treason against her. The raid had failed signally and did not come close to sparking a slave revolt. The deaths that had occurred during the battle could not be called murders.

Andrew Hunter, driving home the prosecution's case in a crescendoing voice, vilified Brown. Ignoring, for now, the South's stance on states' rights, he insisted that treason against one state was treason against all the states. Brown had stolen slaves, had given them weapons, and had been all too clear about his violent plan, which, had it succeeded, would have turned Virginia into another blood-soaked Haiti. As for the murder charge, the death of Shephard Hayward might have been accidental, but the slaying of others, especially Fontaine Beckham, was deliberate.

The jury, which didn't need convincing anyway, took only forty-five minutes to reach a verdict. Guilty on all three counts. When the verdict was announced, the hundreds of spectators, who for days had assaulted Brown with imprecations, were silent, evidently in awe. Brown himself remained unruffled. Sentencing was put off for another day.

When the court reconvened on Wednesday, November 2, for sentencing, no one suspected that this would be a day of victory for John Brown. He achieved victory through his demeanor and—far more important— through his remarks to the court. These remarks were spread by the Associated Press throughout the nation. As Thoreau had said, words were Brown's strongest weapons.

Judge Parker asked Brown if he wanted to state reasons why he should not be sentenced. Brown rose and leaned forward with his hands on his lawyer's table. His eyes fixed on Parker, he said calmly,

> I have, may it please the court, a few words to say.
>
> In the first place, I deny everything but what I have all along admitted: of a design on my part to free the slaves. I intended certainly to have made a clean thing of that matter, as I did last winter, when I went into Missouri and there took slaves without the snapping of a gun on either side, moving through the country, and finally leaving them in Canada. I designed to have done the same thing on a larger scale. That was all I intended. I never did intend murder, or treason, or the destruction of property, or to excite or incite slaves to rebellion, or to make insurrection.
>
> I have another objection, and that it is unjust that I should suffer such a penalty. Had I interfered in the manner which I admit, and which I admit has been fairly proved—for I admire the truthfulness and candor of the greater portion of the witnesses who have testified in this case—had I so interfered in behalf of the rich, the powerful, the intelligent, the so-called great, or in behalf of any of their friends, whether father, mother, brother, sister, wife or children, or any of that class, and suffered and sacrificed what I have in this interference, it would have been all right. Every man in this Court would have deemed it an act worthy of reward rather than punishment.
>
> This Court acknowledges, too, as I suppose, the validity of the law of God. I see a book kissed, which I suppose to be the Bible, or at least the New Testament, which teaches me that all things whatsoever I would that men should do to me, I should do even so to them. It teaches me, further, to remember them that are in bonds as bound with them. I endeavored to act up to that instruction. I am yet too young to understand that God is any respecter of persons. I believe that to have interfered as I have done, as I have always freely admitted I have done, in behalf of His despised poor, I did no wrong, but right. Now, if it is deemed necessary that I should forfeit my life for the furtherance of the ends of justice, and mingle my blood further with the blood of millions in this slave country whose rights are disregarded by wicked, cruel, and unjust enactments, I say, let it be done.

He finished by saying that he now felt "entirely satisfied" with his trial but had no sense of guilt. "I never had any design against the liberty of any person, nor any disposition to commit treason or incite slaves to rebel or make any general insurrection. I never encouraged any man to do so, but always discouraged any idea of that kind."

This speech has won many admirers over the years. Emerson called it and the Gettysburg Address the two greatest American speeches. To be sure, Brown lied. The Missouri slave-stealing episode had *not* been accomplished "without the snapping of a gun"—Aaron Stevens had killed David Cruise. And Brown's denial of trying to incite a slave insurrection did not jibe with his long-standing plan for southward-sweeping guerilla raids by blacks based in the Appalachians.

But, then, the Gettysburg Address similarly glossed over disturbing details in the interest of making a higher point. Lincoln left out the bloody horrors of the Civil War, just as Brown minimized his bloody tactics. Lincoln wanted to consecrate the war by presenting it as a consummation of the American concepts of liberty and equality. Brown wanted to consecrate his violent acts by associating them with the Golden Rule and with the American ideal of freedom.

The power of what Alfred Kazin calls Brown's "great, lying speech" lies in its trenchant appeal to a higher law. Many antislavery activists of the 1850s echoed Senator William Seward's affirmation of a "higher law" to protest against proslavery legislation. But John Brown did it more powerfully than anyone else. He actually *had* violated the law, persistently and dramatically. He really *was* a lawbreaker.

In this regard his speech is even more moving than the Gettysburg Address, for it is deeply personal even while making a general statement. Lincoln, speaking for the nation, never mentions himself. Brown does so at every turn. In the excerpt above, "I," "me," or "my" are used thirty-seven times.

Rhetorically, Brown positions himself on the side of God. Far from seeming egotistical, he humbles himself. In a reversal of the popular image of him as "Old" John Brown, he declares that he is "yet too young to understand that God is any respecter of persons." He doesn't just say that God's law transcends unjust human laws. He personalizes the idea. "*I* see a book kissed, which *I* suppose to be the Bible, or at least the New Testament, which teaches *me* that all things whatsoever *I* would that men should do to *me*, *I* should do even so to them. It teaches *me*, further, to remember them that are in bonds as bound with them. *I* endeavored to act up to that instruction."

Coming after the withering remark that "*I* suppose" the Court acknowl-

John Brown, portrait by Nathan B. Outbank, based on
a photograph taken in Boston by J. W. Black in May 1859.

edges "the law of God," this statement is potent. Brown knew that Southerners prided themselves on their Christianity. They claimed that the Bible
ordained slavery. *Untrue*, he replied.

Untrue, he suggested, because Americans should know the real meaning of the Bible. Americans had revolted against tyranny. Americans sympathized with the downtrodden. They stood for liberty and justice for all. For
true Americans the most meaningful Bible passage is the one that asks us to
remember those in bonds. Americans knew that it was not "the rich, the
powerful, . . . the so-called great" who needed assistance but rather the
"despised poor," the weak and the oppressed.

And so John Brown brought both the Bible and America to his side. By
the time he declared that he was willing to forfeit his life—to "mingle my
blood further with the blood of millions in this slave country whose rights
are disregarded by wicked, cruel, and unjust enactments"—his Southern

auditors must have been struggling to define themselves. In what sense were *they* Christians or Americans? What law did *they* stand for?

No wonder there was silence in the courtroom when Judge Parker announced the sentence: death by hanging on December 2. Brown had hushed the swearing, tobacco-chewing spectators just as he would awe the nation when his remarks hit the newspapers.

Both the South and the North now saw that John Brown was far more than merely an irritating extremist who could be easily dismissed and quickly forgotten. He was a *Christian*, he was an *American*—or, at least, he was a credible impersonation of these.

Southerners now scrambled to denounce him. This new development resulted from his stunning deportment during the trial. Before then the South had thought it safe to follow the lead of Governor Wise, Lewis Washington, and Clement Vallandigham in praising Brown for his courage. What was the harm? There was nothing to fear from someone so obviously deluded as he.

But Brown's performance in the trial and in prison changed opinions in both sections of the country. The North began to see in Brown a hero—not an unblemished one, as Thoreau would have it, but a hero nonetheless. The South, in contrast, deemphasized what it had once seen as Brown's admirable qualities. He was too impressive to be praised. He now had to be handled as a villain pure and simple—a brave one, yes, but a villain through and through. And, the South wished to believe, his villainy embodied that of the "Black Republican" Party of the North.

In describing a devilish kinship between John Brown and the antislavery Republican Party, the South was following the lead of Northern Democrats who tried to get political mileage out of the Harpers Ferry affair. Local and state elections were held in November, and the Democrats smeared Republicans with the tar of Harpers Ferry.

Within a week of Brown's raid, a writer for the *New York Journal of Commerce* began the Democratic onslaught by insisting that the real source of Brown's aggression was the Republican Party, with its talk about "an irrepressible conflict," "Beecher's Bibles," and so on. The writer called the near-universal criticism of Brown in the antislavery newspapers just a cover-up for Republican involvement in the Virginia raid. "No wonder that some of the leading organs of Republicanism writhe under the disclosures at Harper's Ferry," the journalist wrote. "Well do they know that the sanguinary scenes of Harper's Ferry were but the carrying out of the principles inculcated by such journals." It was not enough for Republicans to say Brown was crazy: "To be sure he was crazy, and has long been so; but he is no more crazy than those by whom he has so long been encouraged in his bloody career." In Kansas, Brown had been a "paid hireling of the New England Republicans," who supported his murderous campaign there. And the support broadened: "After his boasts that pro-slavery men had met their death with his own hands, he visited New England, was received with open arms by leading Republican politicians, donations were collected for his support and future operations, and his action, brutal and murderous as it confessedly was, generally approved by the leaders in the Republican party," who then began "looking out for another field of labor," finding it in Harpers Ferry.

Another Democratic paper, the *Boston Courier*, joined the anti-Republican barrage. The *Courier* identified Brown as "one of the Kansas free soil ruffians, whose former exploits in that distracted territory were widely extolled, and became incorporated among the achievements and victories of the Republican party," which had now organized "this absurd yet traitorous insurrection." Reasonable citizens will "turn aside at once from leaders, whose political doctrines conduct to disorder, plunder, and murder."

The effort to link Brown with the Republicans became an organized movement. On November 18 the New York Vigilant Committee held a convention in Manhattan in which many speakers harped upon the supposed link. The speeches were reprinted in newspapers and also were published in a pamphlet called *Rise and Progress of the Bloody Outbreak at Harper's Ferry*. The argument was unequivocal: "The principle upon which John Brown and his allies acted, is the same which has been proclaimed by nearly all the leaders of the Republican party," especially William H. Seward with his notions of "a higher law" and an "irrepressible conflict." Brown and his men were simply the "misguided, guilty tools, of more subtle and dangerous men," i.e., the Republican leaders.

This view intensified when it caught on in the South. The *Richmond Enquirer* swiftly connected Brown's speech in court to Republicans, saying that Brown "may be insane . . . but there are other *criminals*, guilty wretches, who instigated the crimes perpetrated at Harper's Ferry. Bring these men, bring Seward, Greeley, Giddings, Hale, and Smith to the jurisdiction of Virginia, and Brown and his deluded victims in the Charlestown jail may hope for pardon."

The implication was that the Republicans, and by extension many Northerners, were lawbreakers who threatened national peace. One Southern paper said of the Harpers Ferry affair, "The time has come when the choice must be made by our Northern bretheren between peace and safety of the country, based upon the constitution and laws of the land, on the one hand, and Mr. Seward's dogmas of 'higher-lawism and irrepressible conflicts.' " Another agreed that "Harper's Ferry is just a manifestation of the horrific and wrong-headed doctrines of Black Republicanism," which should now be called "Brown Republicanism after John Brown."

In its growing panic, the South began to group together disparate anti-slavery factions, as though they were a unified enemy. A Virginia journalist wrote, "Abolitionism, whether it presents itself in the garb of religious bigotry, or political power; whether preached from the pulpit by Beecher and Phillips, or taught by Seward and Giddings, or sought to be carried out by the bloody hands of Brown and Anderson—no matter in what form, or by whom sustained—must be strangled and crushed if we are to live together in peace and harmony as members of the same political brotherhood."

Calls were made for Republican leaders to be punished along with Brown, their supposed agent. A Richmond paper carried an ad offering $50,000 for the head of "the traitor" Seward. Another paper reported that a group of a hundred Southerners was offering $2,500 apiece for the heads of Seward and Frederick Douglass and $25 apiece for the heads of some thirty other so-called Abolitionists, including Giddings, Beecher, Hale, Phillips, and Owen Lovejoy. In early December, on the floor of the U.S. Senate, Jefferson Davis, later the leader of the Confederacy, insisted that Seward should hang for his role in Harpers Ferry. "We have been invaded," Davis declared, "and that invasion, and the facts connected with it, show Mr. Seward to be a traitor, and deserving of the gallows." If Seward were not punished, Davis argued, "then John Brown, and a thousand John Browns, can invade us, and . . . the Black Republican Government will stand and permit our soil to be violated and our people assailed and raise no arm in our defense."

How accurate were the charges of the Republican Party's complicity in Harpers Ferry? If complicity means advance support or knowledge of the raid, the answer is clear: not accurate at all. If it means sympathy after the fact, the answer is equally clear: negligibly so.

Actually, there was a great distance between John Brown and the Republicans, as those who knew him well pointed out. James Redpath, the Northern journalist who had befriended Brown in Kansas, was stunned by the reports of an alleged Republican connection. "He *despised* the Republican party," Redpath wrote in the *Liberator.* "He had as little sympathy with Garrison as Seward." Indeed, Redpath had learned from Brown himself that the Virginia invasion was an *anti*-Republican move. Brown had told Redpath that if the Republicans gained office, the American people would grow complacent, assuming slavery would disappear peacefully. "The Republicans," Brown had said, "would become as conservative of slavery as the Democrats themselves. . . . Apathy to the welfare of the slave would follow; hence it was necessary to strike a blow at once."

Others close to Brown made similar points. Brown's Kansas associate Richard Hinton characterized the effort to link Brown with the Republicans as "ridiculous enough to breed Homeric laughter." Hinton had once addressed the issue at length with Brown's right-hand man, Kagi, who "stated that no politician, in the Republican or any other party, knew of their plans, and but few of the Abolitionists. It was no use talking, he said, of anti-slavery action to non-resistant agitators." Richard Realf, who had been an officer of Brown's provisional government, wrote a public letter to Greeley's *Tribune* calling the Republican conspiracy idea "wholly and altogether untrue." Realf pointed out that Brown had conceived of the plan many years *before* 1854, when the Republican Party was formed. Moreover, Realf added, Brown and his followers had no faith in the American political system, which they believed was corrupted by compromises with slavery. "Not one of Brown's original party voted," Realf recalled. "We opposed the action of the [Republican] party in every possible way, by speeches, and in every available manner."

Not only did Brown hate the Republicans; they mistrusted him, too. The Republicans presented themselves as peaceful antislavery activists who wanted to stop the spread of slavery but were willing to let it stand where it currently existed. They opposed the Garrisonian Abolitionists because they shied away from disunion. Nor could they tolerate Brown's violence, which they considered a threat to the Union. They prized the political process and criticized any anarchistic action that might tear the national fabric. Like most Americans of the day—and unlike Brown—they had conservative attitudes on race.

Small wonder that the Republican leaders backpedaled en masse from Brown when they learned that he had invaded Harpers Ferry. Shortly after the raid, one of Lincoln's advisers, Charles H. Ray, wrote the future president, "We are damnably exercised here about the effect of Old Brown's wretched fiasco in Virginia, upon the moral health of the Republican party! The old idiot—The quicker they hang him and get him out of the way, the better." From that time forward, Lincoln was careful to distance himself from Brown. He praised Brown's character but excoriated his methods. His famous Cooper Union address, the March 1860 speech that he claimed got him elected, contained an impassioned section disavowing any connection between the Republican Party and Harpers Ferry.

William Henry Seward viewed Brown with similar ambivalence. It was ironic that he, more often than anyone else, was named as Brown's political accomplice, for he disapproved of Brown-like violence perhaps more strongly than any other Republican. (He went on to become a chief dove in the Lincoln administration.) When he had talked in 1858 of an "irrepressible conflict" between free labor and slave labor, he never dreamed he would one day be charged with complicity in an armed invasion of the South. Both the conflict and its solution, he believed, were economic. By the same token, when he had vaguely spoken eight years earlier of a higher law than the Constitution, he could not have imagined that his name would one day be linked with that of a guerilla fighter who tried to put arms in the hands of rebellious blacks.

Seward was in Europe when Harpers Ferry occurred and was astonished upon his return home to find his name associated with Brown's. The idea that he had helped bring about Harpers Ferry, either actually or in principle, was as foreign to his thought—to use Emily Dickinson's words in another context—"as Firmament to Fin." He had once met Brown and found him honest but unbalanced. He was sufficiently moved by Brown's performance in court to express wonder at "the stoical firmness of the monomaniac" who "rises morally above his prosecutors so much that you almost forget his criminality." But he knew that he was widely considered the front-runner for the Republican presidential candidacy, to be decided in the spring. He was not about to allow his chances to be compromised with even the suggestion of sympathy with the controversial John Brown.

He did what he could to separate himself from Brown. He wrote an official disclaimer of any affiliation with Brown, to be produced whenever necessary. He described the Virginia raid as "an act of sedition and treason" performed by misguided men under the sway of "earnest though fatally erroneous convictions." When they were executed, he called their punishment "pitiable" but "necessary and just."

But Seward's efforts to repudiate Brown were not enough for Republican insiders, who realized that his position had been compromised by Harpers Ferry. Anyone who knew him personally was aware that the conspiracy charge was nonsense, but the Republicans had an election to win. They weren't going to risk everything on a perceived radical who, wrongly or not, was widely associated with Brown. On November 11, the Republican William Frazer wrote Lincoln, "Since the Humbug insurrection at Harpers Ferry, I presume Mr Seward will not be urged." Three days later another adviser, Mark Delahay, noted to Lincoln that Seward had not done well in the recent New York State election, explaining, "The Harpers ferry affair doubtless has to some Extent hurt us in New York." Delahay commented that this was good news for Lincoln who, "as an old line Clay Whig (born in Kentucky)," did not have to worry about being regarded as a radical or a Brown sympathizer.

Time proved Delahay right. Even though Seward was in fact every bit as moderate as Lincoln (more so, even), the supposed John Brown link had spoiled the New Yorker's chances with the electorate. Seward was Harpers Ferry's main political casualty, Lincoln its main beneficiary—though in time Lincoln, too, would be charged with being a John Brown man.

There were many other leading Republicans who had political careers to protect. They all took the same approach: keep Harpers Ferry at arm's length. One after another, they lined up to deny affiliation with Brown.

New Hampshire's John P. Hale, the first antislavery advocate elected to the U.S. Senate, publicly said of Harpers Ferry that he "deeply regretted this event; that it would embitter both sides; that Brown had really made war on the United States." He distributed a printed card in response to those who claimed he and other Republicans "knew all about Brown's projected outbreak at Harper's Ferry, encouraged it, are implicated in it; . . . and that we deserve a felon's fate on the gallows." His answer: "I can only reply by denying every word and syllable, and pronouncing the whole, from beginning to end, in general and in detail, false." No one in America, he added, was more appalled than he when he learned of the raid.

Joshua Giddings, the Ohio Republican who had met Brown on a number of occasions, wanted to publicize the fact that the Virginia plan never came up during these meetings. He wrote a disclaimer for the press: "To the public I will say, *that Brown never consulted me in regard to his Virginia expedition, or any other expedition or matter whatever.*"

Salmon P. Chase, the Republican governor of Ohio, assumed an attitude of condescending pity. Shortly after the raid he denounced Brown's "insane attempt." He conceded that he had once donated money toward Brown's Kansas effort, but that was his only tie to Brown. "Poor old man!" he wrote. "How sadly misled by his own imaginations! How rash—how mad—how criminal then to stir up insurrection which if successful would deluge the land with blood and make void the fairest hopes of mankind!"

Pity also characterized the response of Henry Ward Beecher, the period's leading antislavery preacher. In a sermon of November 3 he said of Brown, "I mourn for the hiding or obscuration of his reason. I disapprove of his mad and feeble schemes. I shrink from the folly of the bloody foray."

By December, around the time of Brown's execution, Republicans made a point of renouncing him on the floor of the Senate. The Illinois senator

Lyman Trumbull asked his colleagues whether any of them really believed "that the great Republican party is ready to put knives and pistols into the hands of slaves, to murder their masters?" He reminded his opponents that Republicans were "a conservative, Union-loving, Constitution-abiding people, loyal to the Constitution and to the Union, and are no ultraists in any sense of the word." Another Republican senator, Benjamin F. Wade, called it "exceedingly absurd to endeavor to implicate the Republican party in the acts of John Brown." Despite his undeniable virtues, Wade said, Brown "was misguided, he was demented, he was insane." Indeed, he added, "I have never yet heard of a man, woman, or child, that stood forth as a justifier of his raid upon Virginia."

Given this avalanche of attacks on John Brown—from Democrats, from Southerners, and from Republicans—where did the overwhelming approval that the North later showered on Brown come from? Who kept alive his reputation long enough for sympathy to take root?

Once more we must look to the Concord-Boston network of Brown supporters affiliated with Transcendentalism. Among the Transcendentalists, only Thoreau and Higginson had been unequivocally exultant when they first heard of Brown's raid. Emerson and Alcott were initially ambivalent. Five days after Brown was captured, Emerson wrote his son about "the sad Harpers Ferry business," commenting that Brown "is a true hero, but lost his head there." Three days later he wrote a friend, "For Captain Brown, he is a hero of romance, & seems to have made this fatal blunder only to bring out his virtues." Alcott wrote similarly ambiguous words about the raid in his journal, "This deed of [Brown's], so surprising, so mixed, so confounding to most persons, will give an impulse to freedom and humanity, whatever becomes of its victim and of the States that howl over it."

Brown's stellar performance in court and Thoreau's persuasive speech about Brown eradicated all such misgivings. By the first week of November, Emerson and Alcott were just as eager to defend Brown as were Thoreau and Higginson. Alcott contemplated a rescue effort. He discussed with Sanborn and Higginson possible ways of stealing south and freeing Brown from jail. Alcott offered to go to Charles Town on an exploratory mission; later he said he was ready to join a rescue party.

Emerson also wanted Brown to be rescued. "I must hope for his escape to the last moment," he wrote. But Emerson implemented an even more important form of rescue: a metaphorical rescue, one that plucked Brown from the obloquy that assaulted him from all sides.

Emerson was as well positioned as anyone in America to accomplish

Ralph Waldo Emerson.
LIBRARY OF CONGRESS.

such a rescue. Thoreau was eloquent about Brown, but he didn't come close to having Emerson's cultural clout. Known as a nature-loving recluse, Thoreau generated respect but also a few snickers when he launched his one-man campaign on Brown's behalf. The *Liberator* mixed praise and mild sarcasm in its report of Thoreau's speech on Brown: "This exciting theme seemed to have awakened 'the hermit of Concord' from his usual state of philosophic indifference, and he spoke with real enthusiasm for an hour and a half."

Although Emerson also was known to hold aloof from social questions, in his case aloofness actually helped. He didn't have the problem of Abolitionists like Garrison and Douglass or Republicans like Seward and Sumner, who had long been dragged over the coals by their proslavery opponents as a result of their outspoken views. The religious controversy that had surrounded Emerson's 1838 address at the Harvard Divinity School was a thing of the past. By the late 1850s, Emerson was widely regarded as America's leading intellectual, even by those who disliked his views. He was one of the nation's most popular lecturers, second only to Wendell Phillips in the fee he could demand as a speaker. As the *Atlantic Monthly* noted in 1860, "It is a singular fact, that Mr. Emerson is the most singularly attractive lecturer in America. . . . Mr. Emerson always draws." Even in 1871, after formidable speakers like Mark Twain had entered the field, the *Springfield Republican* could pronounce Emerson "the most widely known, the greatest, and the most attractive of all the present lecturers." An Emerson lecture was a cultural event.

When Emerson spoke, America listened. A pithy phrase from him could create shock waves. Countless people saw the American Revolution through his eyes, for his inspiring image of "the embattled farmers" on the "rude bridge" who fired "the shot heard round the world," in his poem about Concord, was universally known. His few antislavery speeches gained high visibility. After the assault on Sumner in 1856, he gave a talk that contained the exclamation: "As if every sane man were not an Abolitionist!" When this speech, with its curt interjection, was reprinted in newspapers throughout the nation, it aroused attention and swayed readers. The poet Ednah D. Cheney commented that the speech deserved "to be placed beside the famous orations of antiquity for its condensed power of thought and feeling, and for its influence in changing the minds of men." The same, Cheney noted, was true of several other Emerson speeches. Indeed, she wrote, "The influences of these [Emerson's] lectures, from 1835 to 1865, on the growing mind of Boston in those days, is simply inestimable. In the language of one of his hearers, 'His words not only fired the thoughts of his hearers, quickened their consciences, and pierced their hearts, but they modeled their lives.' "

He was unobtrusive, even withdrawn, but influential. Walt Whitman noted that Emerson was normally reserved in making pronouncements on social issues, but "when he did come out it was with the power, the overwhelmingness, of an avalanche." Similarly, Julia Ward Howe explained that although Emerson was wary of rushing headlong into an issue, "when he distinctly saw what to aim at, a single shaft from his bow flew far and hit the mark." After Emerson had given two widely reprinted speeches on John Brown in November 1859, Wendell Phillips begged him to keep up the Brown campaign, explaining, "You know what a vein and stratum of the public you can tap, far out of the range of our bore."

Phillips had good reason to be enthused over Emerson's contribution to Brown's cause. No person advanced this cause more than Emerson. Four years earlier Emerson had rescued the besieged Whitman from possible oblivion with the oft-reprinted statement "I greet you at the beginning of a great career," the impact of which Whitman himself compared to "one of the long range guns we read about," firing a bullet that "speeds on undistracted by anything either side of it through miles of landscape till it finally achieves the point aimed at." Now Emerson rescued the similarly besieged John Brown with an equally memorable remark.

The remark came in Emerson's lecture "Courage," which he gave before a large crowd at the Music Hall in Boston on November 8, five days after Brown's address to the Virginia court. Emerson began by pointing out a major lesson of Harpers Ferry: Southerners did not have a corner on courage. "The Southerners reckon the New Englanders to be less brave than they," he declared, but John Brown proved otherwise. And, unlike Southerners, Brown had Right on his side. Abolition, Emerson said, is unarguably right. Any ethical person is, by definition, an Abolitionist. Emerson asked rhetorically, "Why do we not say, with reference to the evil of the times, that we are Abolitionists of the most absolute abolition?—as every man must be; only the Hottentots, only the barbarians, or semi-barbarians, are not." Like Thoreau, he noted the instinctive admiration Brown elicited in his captors: "If Governor Wise be a superior man, and inasmuch as he is a superior man, he distinguished his captive John Brown." In their shared regard for courage, Emerson added, "Enemies become affectionate; become aware that they are nearer alike than any other two, and if circumstances did not keep them apart, they would fly into each other's arms."

Powerful statements. But they paled before Emerson's startling description of John Brown: "That new saint, than whom none purer or more brave was ever led by love of men into conflict and death,—the new saint awaiting his martyrdom, and who, if he shall suffer, will make the gallows glorious like the cross."

The phrase Emerson had coined for Lexington—the shot heard round the world—was also descriptive of the impact of his remark that Brown would "make the gallows glorious like the cross." The phrase was not original Emerson. As he was writing his speech on Brown, he had written in his journal, "Mattie Griffith says, if Brown is hung, the gallows will be sacred as the cross."

If Emerson plagiarized, it was fitting that he did so from Mattie Griffith, whom he once called "a brilliant young lady from Kentucky." In her views of race and slavery, Griffith was very much like Brown, even though she had approached them from the opposite end of the social spectrum. Born into a wealthy Kentucky family, she turned against slavery as a teenager when she witnessed a slave on her plantation being beaten by her grandmother. Just as the young Brown had first hated slavery when he saw a slave boy being beaten, so she moved from witnessing an act of cruelty to a commitment to Abolitionism. At nineteen she made a dramatic move by freeing all of the slaves she had inherited. They were so overjoyed at her kindness that they offered to continue to work for her and turn over their wages to her. She rejected the offer, willingly embraced poverty, and moved to Boston, where she struggled by as a writer. Among her writings was her *Autobiography of a Female Slave*, one of the most moving exposés of slavery written before the Civil War.

When aired publicly by Emerson, the "gallows glorious" phrase sped through newspapers North and South like a ricocheting bullet. It outraged Brown's opponents and inspired his supporters. It was the most polarizing statement made about John Brown. It added fuel to the already inflamed sectional tensions that led to civil war.

One of Brown's most vocal opponents, the *New York Herald*, did what it could to refute Emerson in its report of the speech. The *Herald*, proslavery and Democratic, was the nation's most widely read newspaper. After quoting the "gallows glorious" image, the *Herald*'s columnist joked that Brown, a "murderer," would doubtless have a conspicuous place in the next edition of Emerson's *Representative Men*. Then the writer brought up the two most controversial issues related to Brown. First, Pottawatomie. The columnist sneered at Emerson's proposal of "the apotheosis of John Brown, after he dies the death of a murderer on the gallows—a man of whom the leading journalists of his own party in Kansas had admitted, that he took five respectable men—heads of families—out of their beds at dead hour of night, and mutilated and murdered them in cold blood." Next, race. After Emerson's speech, John Brown's "gallows will be the emblem of nigger redemption, and bits of the rope with which he will be hanged, will be sold at enormous prices, and be venerated, like pieces of the cross. He will be regarded as a second Saviour, whose sacrificial blood has redeemed the black race."

For Brown's would-be supporters, in contrast, Emerson's endorsement of Brown was exactly what was needed: an imprimatur from the Sage of Concord. A typical response came from the Abolitionist Henry C. Wright, who asked in delight, "What means the almost universal applause bestowed on the remark of Ralph Waldo Emerson, the most prominent literary man, lecturer and moral philosopher in the nation, that the execution of the hero and saint of Harper's Ferry, 'Will make the gallows as glorious as the cross'?" To Wright and others who wanted to believe in Brown, the answer was that Brown *did* have redeeming qualities. Even Walt Whitman, who was ambivalent about Brown, extolled Emerson's "gallows glorious" image, which he called "sublime, ultimate, everlasting."

November 18, 1859, may be identified as the day when the roiling attitudes toward Brown separated into two main streams, one leading toward a primarily negative view of him and the other toward a primarily positive one. We have seen that the anti-Brown convention held that day in New York under the auspices of the New York Vigilant Committee gave tremendous impetus to the theory of a "Brown-Republican" conspiracy that would sweep the South. That evening Brown's Massachusetts supporters held a fund-raising rally for Brown's family in Tremont Temple that gave an equally strong push to the opposing idea that John Brown was a hero about to become a Christ-like martyr.

Once more it was Emerson who made the strongest statement on Brown's behalf. The halo of Brown's unforgettable court speech hung over the rally. Printed copies of the speech, along with a facsimile of Brown's signature, were sold for 10 cents at the door. Several speakers quoted from the speech. For the first time, a gathering of prominent figures had positive things to say about John Brown.

Not *wholly* positive. Some of the speakers assumed a praise-the-man-but-not-the-deed posture that soon characterized much Northern opinion. John A. Andrew, later the governor of Massachusetts, said he was not sure "whether the enterprise of John Brown and his associates in Virginia was wise or foolish, right or wrong; I only know that whether the enterprise itself was one or the other, John Brown himself is right." The next speaker, the Reverend J. Evan Mann of Old South Church, said that if Brown had asked him ahead of time whether he should go ahead with the Virginia raid, "I should have told him to refrain. I should have said to him, 'You will be performing an awful, a fool-hardy, a suicidal act.' " But now Mann was convinced that God "used this man, John Brown, as his sword to inflict a wound on the slave power," so that later generations "will say that from the time when John Brown hung between heaven and earth, we may date the beginning of the end of American slavery."

The speech of the Abolitionist Wendell Phillips fully endorsed Brown. A Calvinist himself, Phillips praised Brown as "a Calvinist of the old stamp. . . . It is the old Mayflower cropping out. . . . Wherever there is a fierce battle to be fought for an idea, you can trace its lineage back to old Plymouth Rock." As one whose progressive racial views almost matched Brown's, Phillips retold the story of Brown as a child, after meeting an intelligent black boy who was brutalized by whites, asking, "Why should a black skin make that difference between me and him?" His answer, Phillips insisted, was Harpers Ferry, through which "he said, for sixty years we have given the sword to the white man; the time has come to give it to the black." Phillips brought attention to the lesson Brown was giving the nation through his words, which were daily disseminated by the press. Phillips called Brown's postraid interview and court speech a new "anti-slavery catechism," with "the press printing that anti-slavery catechism to the number of 500,000 copies, forcing every American citizen to read it." Phillips continued: "Why, men say he should remember that lead is wasted in bullets, and is much better made into types. Well, he fired one gun, and he has made use of the New-York Herald and Tribune for a fortnight."

This was strong praise, but it paled in comparison to the glorification of Brown that came in Emerson's speech. "This commanding event which has brought us together," Emerson announced, "eclipses all others which have occurred for a long time in our history." John Brown, he continued, "is so transparent that all men see him through. He is a man to make friends wherever on earth courage and integrity are esteemed, the rarest of heroes, a pure idealist, with no by-ends of his own." Those who know him personally are "impressed alike by his simple, artless goodness, combined with his sublime courage." Rhapsodizing over Brown's words before the Virginia court, Emerson insisted that it was the *"reductio ad absurdum* of Slavery, when the Governor of Virginia is forced to hang a man whom he declares to be a man of the most integrity, truthfulness, and courage he has ever met. Is that the kind of man the gallows was built for?" Emerson noted that although the meeting had convened to consider relief for Brown's family, in fact "that family looks very large and very needy of relief," since it includes "almost every man who loves the Golden Rule and the Declaration of Independence, like him, and who sees what a tiger's thirst threatens him in the malignity of public sentiment in the slave states."

Emerson was soaring beyond politics to ideals and principles. But America was a nation in which ideals and principles were in harness to the politics and laws of the moment. When Emerson spoke these inspiring words, John Brown was in prison awaiting execution for treason and murder.

On November 18, Emerson helped to open the floodgates of Northern appreciation of Brown. Emerson offered a new equation. John Brown equals purity, holiness, and the highest idealism. No one except he and a few other Transcendentalists ever accepted all terms of the equation. But it wouldn't be long before some of the terms, in couples or triples with Brown in the mix, would win wide acceptance in the North—surprisingly so, given the initial hostility to Brown there.

Also on November 18 the New York Vigilant Committee had opened the way to Southern demonization of Brown. It had an equation of its own. John Brown equals the Republican Party equals Abolition equals pure evil.

John Brown was Christ. John Brown was Satan. In the not distant future, the two views would come into violent collision.

15

───────────

The Passion

Despite the social and political winds swirling around him—early signs of the national hurricane to come—John Brown did not crack or bend. In the Charles Town prison he slept soundly and remained alert and cheerful. He wrote letters to family and friends. "I do not think I ever enjoyed life better than since my confinement here," he wrote to Rebecca Spring, a Quaker sympathizer. He talked with visitors who came in a steady stream. He got along well with his jailer, Captain John Avis. He even befriended some slaveholders in the area who came to see him. The only people he sent away were Southern clergymen who offered their services. Slaveholding Christianity disgusted him.

Above all, he looked forward to his hanging. He had lived for enslaved blacks; now he wanted to die for them. He wrote his half-brother Jeremiah on November 12, "I am gaining in health slowly, and am quite cheerful in view of my approaching end,—being fully persuaded that I am worth inconceivably more to hang than for any other purpose." He added in a postscript: "I feel a thousand times more on account of my sorrowing friends than on my own account. So far as I am concerned, I 'count it all joy.' 'I have fought the good fight,' and have, as I trust, 'finished my course.' " He never showed fear.

The same cannot be said of the South. Its early self-assured attitude toward Brown dissolved, and it was seized by a panic that intensified as time passed. One source of anxiety was the fact that several of Brown's confederates had gotten away. Although two, Albert Hazlett and John Edwin Cook, were captured, five made it to the North: Osborne Anderson, Owen Brown, Barclay Coppoc, Charles P. Tidd, and Francis J. Merriam. There was fear that the band might regroup, gather more recruits, and attempt another desperate raid, perhaps elsewhere in the South. Posters were widely distributed with descriptions of the fugitives and promises of $1,000 reward for the capture of Cook and $2,000 for Brown, Barclay, Tidd, and Merriam.

Hazlett and Anderson, who were not known to the Virginia authorities, proved the most intelligent in the choice of escape routes. After they had stolen across the Potomac during a lull in the Harpers Ferry battle around dusk on October 17, they had found the Kennedy farm and the schoolhouse deserted. They climbed a nearby mountain and slept until they were awakened by gunfire early in the morning. From their height they saw a battle taking place near the engine house, though they could not know their captain was making his last stand before being captured. They waited some hours before they saw a militia company take over the schoolhouse, just below them.

Unable to locate the other escapees, they fled directly north, hugging main roads and railroad tracks. The route was risky but rapid. Within four days they reached southern Pennsylvania. Had they continued, Hazlett and Anderson could have both been soon out of danger, but Hazlett developed incapacitating blisters on his feet. He told Anderson to go on alone, realizing that his condition would retard their flight. They parted tearfully, agreeing to proceed separately and meet up later near Chambersburg, ten miles north. Anderson made it there quickly, while Hazlett limped north along the bed of the Cumberland Valley Railroad.

On October 22, four days after leaving the Ferry, Hazlett was captured near Newville, Pennsylvania, and was taken into custody in nearby Carlisle. He was held there until November 5, when he was extradited to Virginia, even though the evidence linking him to Harpers Ferry was circumstantial. He assumed the name William H. Harrison to hide his identity, and when he was put into the Charles Town jail his comrades pretended not to know him. The ruse did not work, for he would be convicted and executed. His black companion, Osborne Anderson, meanwhile, had sped north to freedom.

The other five fugitives, led by Owen Brown, chose a more arduous but safer course over mountains toward western Pennsylvania and Ohio, where people friendly to their cause lived. Pursued by bloodhounds, the men took precautions. They waded up streams to hide their tracks. They traveled only at night and did not light campfires for fear of being seen.

It was a difficult journey. Barclay Coppoc suffered from a lung ailment that slowed his pace, though he was mentally tough and did not complain during the thirty-six-day trek through the wilderness. Cook and Tidd argued hotly over strategies for escape. Francis Merriam, the frail scion of upper-class Boston, put on a brave face but found the tramp torturous.

Often Owen and Tidd had to carry him up streams or through bushes, bruising him severely.

Hunger besieged the men. Once when Owen Brown and Tidd were scouting ahead of the others, they smelled food being cooked in a farm-house in a nearby valley. Tidd, famished to the point of desperation, announced his intention to go to the house and request food. It was all Owen could do to prevent him from doing so. When the two returned to camp, the other three agreed with Tidd that someone should go to the house. Cook, glib and personable, was selected to make the attempt. He went to the house, where he was given dinner as well as bread, boiled beef, and a pie to take his comrades in the woods, who, he said, were hunters. His friends were overjoyed to have food, but before long he and Tidd were quarreling. Cook wanted to shoot game to keep up the hunting pretext. Tidd thought this would only attract unwanted attention.

Buoyed by his success in food-collecting, Cook grew foolhardy when the group approached Chambersburg, Pennsylvania. His boldness cost him his life. Telling his comrades he would again return with food, he de-scended the mountain and reached a field where he saw some men talking. One of them, Daniel Logan, recognized Cook from the description that had been circulated.

A shrewd mountaineer who was neutral on slavery, Logan was practiced in hunting down fugitive slaves and collecting bounty for them. He whis-pered to one of his companions, "That's Captain Cook; we must arrest him; the reward is $1,000." Cook approached the group, explaining that he was a hunter and wanted to replenish his food supply. Logan offered to take Cook to his "store" where there was food. Cook walked with them but immedi-ately found himself surrounded. After a brief struggle he was taken captive. He asked, "Why?" and Logan replied, "Because you are Captain Cook."

When Cook learned that Logan's only concern was the reward money, he told the bounty hunter that he had friends in Indiana and New York who would send more than $1,000 in exchange for Cook's release. Logan accepted the proposal and said the exchange could be handled by the Republican lawyer Alexander K. McClure. Logan went in search of McClure but, unable to find him, turned Cook over to a local sheriff and a Judge Reisher. Logan tracked McClure down but realized it was too late to make a deal, for the sheriff had received a requisition for Cook's arrest from Carlisle, thirty miles away.

By this time both the sheriff and Logan were sorry they had captured Cook, whose fearlessness they admired. Logan said that he hoped Cook would escape "reward or no reward." But the next day a county sheriff arrived along with a Virginia lawyer to take Cook into custody. Cook was put into irons and locked in a jail cell in Chambersburg.

McClure visited Cook and was struck by the bronzed young man, with blue eyes and long blond curls, who talked excitedly about emancipating the slaves. McClure later recalled that when he asked Cook if he would give up the antislavery fight should he escape, "his large, soft eyes flashed with the fire of defiance, as he answered, with an emphasis that unstrung every nerve in his body, 'No! the battle must be fought to the bitter end, and we must triumph, or God is not just.' "

The next morning, Friday, October 28, two days after his capture, John Cook was taken under heavy guard to a train that carried him to Charles Town. He arrived there in the afternoon, at the end of the second day of John Brown's trial. He was put into the Charles Town jail along with the other prisoners, who now numbered seven with the recent capture of Hazlett.

In the woods near Chambersburg, Owen Brown and the other three fugitives had been anxiously awaiting Cook's return. Tidd and Coppoc had not learned from Cook's mistake, for on the morning after Cook's capture they ventured into Chambersburg in search of food. They tapped on the window of Mrs. Mary A. Ritner's boardinghouse, where several of John Brown's men had stayed on their first trip to Harpers Ferry. Mrs. Ritner was alarmed when she looked outside and saw the two fugitives. "Leave, leave!" she cried. They said they needed food. She replied, "I can't help you, if you were starving, leave! the house is guarded by armed men!"

The two rejoined the others in the woods. The next day the men glumly heard the martial music that played as Cook was taken to the train, which they watched as it rolled off to Virginia. Deciding they had to speed their trip, the men discarded their rifles in a briar patch, keeping only their smaller weapons.

It was clear that Francis Merriam could not finish the trip by foot. He would have to risk taking a train. He still had some money left from the $600 he had drawn from his trustee and uncle, James Jackson, and he divided it among his comrades, refusing to keep more than $5 for himself. Owen Brown shaved off Merriam's beard and brushed his clothes in an attempt to disguise him. On a pitch-black night during a blinding snowstorm, Owen led Merriam to railroad tracks above Chambersburg and pointed him toward the next station, Scotland, five miles away. Merriam struggled through the blizzard and reached the station, where he caught a train headed northeast. He passed through Philadelphia and then proceeded to Chatham, Ontario, where he was in early December when John Brown was hanged.

The three remaining fugitives continued northwest through the hills of southern Pennsylvania. On November 4, twenty days after they had left the Kennedy farm, they came to a farmhouse near Bellefonte, Pennsylvania, where they were cordially admitted and fed. Owen posed as Edward Clark, Tidd as Charles Plummer, and Coppoc as George Barclay. When they asked about Harpers Ferry, the host was shocked at their ignorance, saying that the raid was the biggest news story in recent times. After a meal of flapjacks, the men settled near the fire and picked up a newspaper that described the raid and its aftermath. Tidd read aloud from the paper in a trembling voice. Owen Brown and Coppoc had to restrain their feelings as they heard the details of the dead and wounded at Harpers Ferry and the six who were on trial for their lives in Charles Town. Their host evidently had no clue of their identity—or pretended he didn't—for he told them that four escapees, with large bounties on their heads, were still missing.

The farther north the fugitives got, the safer they were. They were fed by friendly Quakers who asked no questions and pointed them on their way. But care still had to be taken. Once they were almost caught. Benjamin Wakefield, a Quaker farmer who had housed and fed them, saved them by sending them on to a relative forty miles away while giving their pursuers wrong directions. At last they reached Centre County, Pennsylvania, an area where several of Owen Brown's relatives lived. On November 24, the three parted ways, Owen going to his brother's place in Dorset, Ohio, Coppoc to Springdale, Iowa, and Tidd to Chatham.

Back in Charles Town, John Brown waited for his hanging while his six prison-mates began to face Judge Parker. The day previous to Brown's sentencing, Edwin Coppoc, who had fought by Brown's side in the engine house, was tried on the same charges as his captain. The next day, after Brown was sentenced, Coppoc was convicted on all three counts. Evidently because of Coppoc's Quaker beliefs, Governor Wise intervened on his behalf, requesting the Virginia legislature to commute his sentence to life imprisonment. The legislature refused, and Coppoc awaited sentencing.

On November 3, the two black prisoners, Shields Green and John A. Copeland, faced the court. Andrew Hunter prosecuted them with extra ferocity because of their color. In his view, they were especially culpable because they were blacks who had participated in the killing of whites.

Ironically, however, Green and Copeland fared better in trial than their white confederates due to the shrewdness of their defense lawyer, George Sennott, who had just arrived from Boston. Sennott was a more formidable opponent for Hunter than Hoyt had been, for, as a Democrat, he carried none of the Abolitionist baggage that had stymied the strongly antislavery Hoyt.

Sennott used a clever argument against the treason charge. By definition, he said, blacks could not commit treason—either against Virginia or the United States—because they were not citizens, according to the Dred Scott decision. The court conceded to him on this point and dropped the treason charge. Still, Green and Copeland were convicted on the other two counts.

That left Cook, Stevens, and Hazlett (who still called himself William H. Harrison). Governor Wise tried to have Cook and Hazlett tried in a U.S. court in nearby Staunton, believing that a federal court would uncover a conspiracy between the Harpers Ferry raiders and Northern Republicans such as Seward and Giddings. When Charles Harding, the alcoholic attorney on the prosecution team, heard that there might be a change of venue for Cook, he blustered furiously on the streets of Charles Town. "No, sir," he cried to anyone who would listen; "if the United States want him, they must wait till we get through with him. We caught him, and we mean to have the first chance at hanging him. The United States may take his dead body, if they choose."

The change of venue was not approved. Cook's trial went forward in the district court. Because the court's term ended on November 10, the trials of Stevens and Hazlett were delayed until the next one began, in February.

Cook's trial was controversial for a number of reasons. Of all the prisoners, Cook aroused the strongest hatred in the Virginians. To them he seemed treacherous and deliberately evil, because he had moved to Harpers Ferry over a year before, had befriended area residents, and had married a local woman who had recently borne his child—and all the while he was a spy intent on destruction and murder. A local newspaper, calling him the most depraved of "the hellish miscreants of Brown," recommended that he be lynched without trial: "He is a villain of the blackest hue, and should be placed outside the leniency and protection of the law. A court of justice should not be disgraced by the presence of such a black-hearted villain."

He didn't even appear to have the virtue of courage. Not only had he run away from the scene, but he allowed his lawyer to use a craven ploy to try to get him acquitted. Cook had rich relatives who disagreed with him on slavery but were still loyal toward him. They hired Daniel Voorhees, a defense lawyer known for his courtroom eloquence. A Democrat who later served as a senator from Indiana, Voorhees had a definite plan: to present his client as the guiltless tool of the scheming, murderous John Brown.

The baby-faced, blond-haired Cook looked like an innocent victim, and Voorhees played the idea to the hilt. Voorhees described John Brown as "the chief of criminals, the thief of property stolen, . . . a falsifier here in this court, . . . a murderer" in both Kansas and Virginia. Brown was guilty of "a thousand crimes," with a record of "grim-visaged war, civil commotion, pillage and death, disunion and universal desolation." This villain had mesmerized his young comrade: "John Brown is the despotic leader, and John E. Cook was an ill-fated follower of an enterprise whose horror he now realizes and deplores."

Moreover, Voorhees claimed, Cook was a pawn in a much larger conspiracy hatched by the Republican Party. A devoted Democrat, Voorhees appealed to the anti-Republican passions of his Southern listeners:

> Ministers, editors, and politicians—Beecher, Parker, Seward, Giddings, Sumner, Hale, and a host of lesser lights of each class—who in this court-room, who in this vast country, believes them not guilty, as charged in the indictments of all the courts, to a deeper and far more fearful extent than John E. Cook? . . . They put in motion the maelstrom which has engulphed him. They started the torrent which bore him over the precipice.

The jury doubtless nodded in agreement with these words. None of the arguments, however, contradicted the clear evidence of Cook's involvement in the raid. Cook was convicted on all counts.

When Cook, Coppoc, Green, and Copeland appeared before the judge on November 19 for sentencing, the blacks said nothing when offered the chance to say a final word in their defense. Cook and Coppoc, in contrast, still tried to save themselves. They insisted they had not known of Brown's intention to take over Harpers Ferry until shortly before the raid.

Perhaps Coppoc told the truth here, but Cook twisted facts. After all, he had willingly gone to Harpers Ferry in June 1858 and had been Brown's chief source of information. He was even more extreme than Brown in some ways. Impulsively, he had wanted to spread word about the forthcoming attack among local slaves—a risky notion that Brown rejected. He had also wanted to destroy arsenal buildings and burn the two main bridges during the raid, whereas Brown was not inclined to destroy property.

It is going too far, however, to charge Cook with hypocrisy or cowardice, as Frederick Douglass did when he commented, "It is a remarkable fact, that in this small company of men, but one showed any sign of weakness or regret for what he did or attempted to do. Poor Cook broke down and sought to save his life by representing that he had been deceived, and allured by false promises." Daniel Voorhees had done what any modern-day defense attorney would do—blame someone else in order to free his client. Once Voorhees had made the claim, Cook felt obliged to sustain it.

All four prisoners were sentenced to hang on December 16, Green and Copeland in the morning and Cook and Coppoc in the afternoon. When the sentence was announced, none of them quailed. Far from being cowardly, Cook faced death with a calmness that approached John Brown's. On December 9, a week before his execution, Cook reported in a letter home that his sleep and appetite were normal. He wrote, "There has not been one single instance in which I have felt or shown any signs of fear or nervousness since I have been here. Neither has my comrade, Coppoc, since he has occupied the cell with me, shown any such weakness or dread of death. We dislike the mode of death to which we have been doomed. But, notwithstanding, we are cheerfully and calmly awaiting our fate, and trust we shall meet it like men."

There was no nervousness on their part, but plenty of it on the South's. Was another Northern invasion brewing? Would attempts be made to rescue the prisoners? Would the prisoners manage to escape through their own efforts? Would slaves catch insurrectionary fever and launch a major revolt?

The trial and conviction of John Brown, instead of making the South feel more secure, actually amplified its fears. As the trial began, the *New York Herald* reported: "The excitement at Harper's Ferry, instead of subsiding, is daily increasing." The day after his conviction, a correspondent for the *Tribune* wrote from Charles Town:

> A feeling of irrepressible uneasiness still lingers here. The streets by day are filled with groups of people discussing, with profound seriousness, the chances of renewed attacks, escapes, and insurrections. Under the walls of the Court-House the debates often rise to a warmth at once betraying the alarm which will all attempt to conceal. At night, the thoroughfares are guarded by armed patrols, who arrest, without distinction, all persons who wander from their homes, unless immediate proof can be given of the innocence of their intentions. All strangers are regarded with particular suspicion.

The South began to arm itself. Its sudden resort to weapons was linked to the combined awe and loathing it felt for John Brown. Governor Wise gave a speech in which he repeated his former praise of Brown's courage but in the same breath ordered Virginians to take up arms. He distributed Brown's rifles recovered from the Kennedy farm among citizens whom he commanded to guard the Charles Town courthouse. He commissioned militia companies to patrol the streets of both Charles Town and Harpers Ferry. All Virginians, he declared, must be ready for military action: "I shall implore the people to organize to take arms in their hands and to practice the use of arms, and I will cause depots to be established for fixed ammunition along our borders and at every assailable point."

Many followed his request. Weapons were everywhere. The *Tribune* complained, "The prevalence of firearms is not always agreeable. The people are forever handling them." Strangers walking into barrooms often found themselves "confronted by half a dozen ugly muzzles from all directions. There seems to be a great fondness for the employment of Sharp's rifles."

Governor Wise was doing far more than protecting his community. He was gearing up for civil war. Evidently, he took seriously Brown's declaration that the South had better prepare itself for a settlement of the "negro question." Wise and his friend Andrew Hunter were convinced, as Hunter said, "that this Brown raid was the beginning of a great conflict between the North and the South, and had better be regarded accordingly." Wise's call for arms was "not alone for the protection of the jail" or the region, "but it was for the purpose of preparing for coming events."

Virginia spearheaded a military buildup throughout the South. In a study of the subject, the historian John Hope Franklin notes: "The greatest stimulus of military organizations in the South was provided by the fears aroused by John Brown. The effect of this fantastic attempt in 1859 to put an end to slavery was electrifying." In Georgia, the Carolinas, and elsewhere, volunteer militia groups sprang up, and regular militia outfits performed military drills with new fervor.

Although Governor Wise had an eye on the future, he also had real problems in the present. His immediate concern was that the prisoners might escape or be rescued.

Their jail was easy to escape from. Its flimsiness was well known. "The Charlestown jail is certainly a very infirm establishment," the *Tribune* commented. "Its walls bespeak decay, and its doors and windows tell of insecurity. . . . Unless the greatest watchfulness is exercised, the prisoners may find some means of escape."

The jail consisted of two small cell buildings with a narrow yard in back and an even narrower one in front. The jailer, John Avis, occupied a room to the left of the front entrance. Surrounding the jail was a fourteen-foot brick wall.

John Brown's cell, which he shared with Stevens, was the easiest to escape from, since it had a large chimney. A juror who visited the cell cried in dismay, "Two good Yankees could get these men out and away *so* easily!" Connected to Brown's cell was that of Green and Copeland, and next to that was Coppoc and Cook's. Hazlett first occupied a cell in the second building and was then moved in with Stevens after Brown was hanged.

Given the jail's vulnerability, it is not surprising that stories of impending rescue filled the air. On November 19 the *Baltimore American* noted, "Various rumors have been in circulation for the past few days in regard to an attempted rescue, by Northern fanatics, of Brown and his fellow-prisoners, but nothing reliable has been obtained, although it is believed by many intelligent and knowing gentlemen that the attempt will be made." Likewise, the *Richmond Enquirer* reported, "Rumors are rife that the rescue of the condemned prisoners is preparing, and that parties with such designs are in the neighborhood."

Governor Wise later claimed that he received 3,600 letters threatening rescue efforts during the sixty days Brown was in jail. Sixty letters a day—surely the number was inflated. That he did get many such letters, however, is indisputable. Hunter received similar ones, dividing them into two piles: "Contemptible Nonsense" and "Possible."

His ambiguous assessments were apt, in light of the wild rescue schemes that were aired. The boldest, and perhaps least practical, was concocted by the militant Abolitionist Lysander Spooner and some Boston confederates. Spooner wanted to kidnap Governor Wise and take him out onto the ocean in a boat to be held as ransom until John Brown was released. Spooner secured a tugboat, but the project failed for lack of funds. Another plan was a proposed land-based operation with Richard Hinton and John W. LeBarnes leading some sixty men in an assault on Charles Town. Under-funding killed that project too—which was just as well, for such an attack would surely have turned into a fruitless bloodbath for the invaders.

Some of the other plans were only slightly less outlandish. A "T.A.B" wrote from Ohio that he had seen an armed forced of 50 to 60 men headed toward the western border of Virginia, where 270 others would join them to swoop into Charles Town, break into the jail, and spirit the prisoners away. At different times, 500 would-be rescuers were said to be on their way from Kansas, 1,000 from Cleveland, 2,500 from New York, 7,000 from

Chicago, and 9,000 from Ohio. Even such numbers, if real, most likely would have produced failure, in light of the military preparations Wise had made.

Besides the rescue rumors, other occurrences in the Charles Town region created nervousness. A succession of fires broke out, giving rise to fears that a slave rebellion was brewing. The *Richmond Enquirer* reported: "Numerous acts of incendiarism have destroyed much property of the prominent and wealthy, as well as the poorer people. Night after night the heavens are illuminated by the lurid glare of burning property, which, with the exaggerated reports flying through the country, tends to increase the excitement."

The fires disturbed John Brown, who could see their glow from his cell. He wrote Mary on November 21, "There is now here a source of disquietude to me,—namely, the fires which are almost of daily and nightly occurrence in this immediate neighborhood." He was annoyed mainly because he knew they would be wrongly charged to blacks or antislavery whites in the area. "No one of them is the work of our friends," he wrote, "[but] we shall be charged with them."

The insecurity of the Charles Town jail would be confirmed a week after John Brown's execution, when Coppoc and Cook nearly succeeded in escaping from it. Charles Lenhart, an old Kansas friend, disguised himself as a Virginia militia volunteer and posted himself on the street in the back of the jail on the night of December 13, planning to lead his friends to the nearby Shenandoah Mountains. In the meantime, the two prisoners bored a hole through the wall behind their bed, using a bed screw and a knife that a jail guard had given them to cut a lemon.

All went as planned, except that Cook's relatives were visiting on the appointed day, and the escape was postponed until the next evening. Crawling through their hole on the night of the fourteenth, Coppoc and Cook found a pile of timber in the yard that had been used for John Brown's scaffold and was being saved for their execution. They mounted the pile and climbed the wall. Escape would have been easy, for they could have made the street below and gotten away quickly. A street sentinel, however, spotted them and fired at them. They clambered back into the jail yard and voluntarily gave themselves up to their jailer, John Avis.

Surrendering to Avis was easy for them; all the prisoners got along well with him. Although he had fought against them at Harpers Ferry and guarded them in jail, he treated them with respect and consideration. Short and heavyset, the middle-aged Avis had a pleasant face and a sincere manner. He was a principal reason why John Brown had no interest in escape or rescue.

Brown recognized Avis's integrity early on and pledged to him that he would not attempt to escape. Brown discouraged rescue efforts from the outside, for he knew that Avis would be hurt or killed if the jail were stormed. As Higginson wrote Brown's family in early November: "One thing we have ascertained: the prison is not hard to get out of. But Captain John Brown doesn't wish to come out, at present: and sends us the most earnest messages not to attempt it. . . . [He] thinks of himself as a prisoner 'on parole,' at present, because he has been treated so very indulgently by the jailor, never ironed, and allowed to see his friends without witnesses." Brown made the same point to a Boston journalist, who wrote, "He said that Captain Avis, his jailor, showed as much kindness in treating him, as he had shown courage in attacking him. 'It is what I should expect from a brave man.' "

His closeness to Avis was part of his overall satisfaction with his weeks in prison. Far from feeling gloomy or defeated, Brown was accepting and even joyous. He had done his life's work. It was time to die. He told a *Tribune* correspondent, "I do not know that I ought to encourage any attempt to save my life. I am not sure that it would not be better for me to die at this time."

To be sure, he had regrets. During his first few days in jail he admitted to Stevens that he had botched the raid. Had he ordered a quick retreat to the mountains, he would have succeeded. He explained that he had become preoccupied with his prisoners and with waiting for blacks and antislavery whites from the region to swarm to his side.

No matter. He could not change the past. He clung to his Calvinistic belief that God predetermined everything, including his hanging. As a reporter noted after interviewing him, "Captain Brown appears perfectly fearless in all respects,—says that he has no feeling about death on a scaffold, and believes that every act 'even all follies that led to this disaster, were decreed to happen ages before the world was made.' "

Some of his friends on the outside hoped that his hanging could somehow be avoided, but he disagreed with them. Wentworth Higginson wrote Brown's family that it was "a great thing, . . . a sign for the future" that the execution was delayed for a month. "The general impression now," Higginson wrote, "is that the sentence will be commuted to imprisonment. . . . They [the Southerners] cannot afford to give the North any martyrs to talk about, they say, the abolitionists will make too much capital out of it."

The opinion that Brown's sentence would be reduced became more widespread when Brown's supposed connection with the Republican Party gained wide acceptance. "There is a decided impression that John Brown will not be hanged," *Harper's Weekly* announced in mid-November. "Appeals for mercy to Governor Wise have been forwarded from highly respectable quarters. Most of these take the ground that Old Brown was a fanatic and a madman, and that it would reflect honor on the South to pardon his crime out of charity. It is urged that, after all, John Brown only carried into practical effect the teachings of the New York *Tribune*, and other Abolitionist organs, and that while the teachers escape unscathed, it is not worth while to execute the poor ignorant disciples. . . . Certain it is that the hanging of Brown would strengthen, and the pardon of Brown would discredit, the Northern Abolitionist party."

Similarly, the Democratic *Journal of Commerce* warned, "To hang a fanatic is to make a martyr of him and fledge another brood of the same sort. . . . Monsters are hydra-headed, and decapitation only quickens their vitality, and power of reproduction."

The same reasoning led others to hope that the execution of Brown would be carried out. Northerners who had criticized the raid thought that the gallows would make Brown the heroic martyr of the antislavery cause. Henry Ward Beecher declared in a widely reprinted sermon, "Let no man pray that John Brown be spared! Let Virginia make him a martyr! Now, he has only blundered. His soul was noble; his work was miserable. But a cord and a gibbet would redeem all that, and round up Brown's failure with a heroic success."

The last sentence expressed Brown's view. When he read Beecher's sermon in a newspaper delivered to the jail, Brown scribbled "Good" in the margin beside the sentence. Although Brown's other marginalia revealed his disapproval of Beecher's criticisms of the Harpers Ferry raid, he agreed completely with the notion of martyrdom.

Not that he boasted about it. To the contrary, his letters from jail are marked by humility. When he wrote that he was "worth inconceivably more to hang than for any other purpose," he had in mind the millions of suffering slaves for whom he was giving his life.

For this reason he thought he had succeeded in life, despite his many afflictions. Two weeks before his hanging he wrote his childhood teacher, the Reverend H. L. Vaill: "I have often passed under the rod of him whom I *call* my Father; & certainly no son ever needed it oftener; & yet I have enjoyed much of life, as I was enabled to discover the secret of this; somewhat early. It has been in making the prosperity, & the happiness of others my own: so that really I have had a great deal of prosperity. I am very prosperous still; . . . As I believe most firmly that God reigns; I cannot believe that anything I have *done* [*or*] *suffered or may yet suffer will be lost;* to the *cause of God or of humanity:* & before I began my work at Harpers Ferry; I felt assured that in the worst *event;* it would certainly PAY."

Small wonder that this letter—which, like most of Brown's prison letters, was printed in the newspapers—caught the eye of Henry David Thoreau. Like Thoreau, Brown championed a higher prosperity than a material one. Brown's errors in grammar and punctuation did not bother Thoreau, who affectionately recalled Brown having told him, "I know no more of grammar than one of your calves."

Thoreau viewed Brown's prison letters as models of literary excellence. "Where is our professor of *belles lettres* or of logic and rhetoric, who can write so well?" Thoreau asked. "He wrote in prison, not a history of the world, like Raleigh, but an American book which I think will live longer than that." The power of Brown's style lay in its sincerity. Thoreau wrote: "This unlettered man's speaking and writing are standard English. . . . It suggests that the one great rule of composition—and if I were a professor of rhetoric, I should insist on this—is to *speak the truth.* This first, this second, this third; pebbles in your mouth or not. This demands earnestness and manhood chiefly."

Brown's letters grew spontaneously from a prison experience that Thoreau thought was unmatched in American annals. "John Brown's career for the last six weeks of his life," Thoreau declared, "was meteor-like, flashing through the darkness in which we live. I know of nothing so miraculous in our history."

The meteor metaphor was apt. On November 15, while Brown was awaiting execution, an unusual astronomical event took place over the skies of the Northeast. A series of meteor showers appeared, highlighted by a tremendous meteor that raced in a bright streak across the morning sky and then exploded. The meteor was seen as far north as Albany, New York, and as far south as Fredericksburg, Virginia. When the meteor burst, it gave off what one journalist called "a series of terrific explosions, which were compared to the discharge of a thousand cannon."

Thoreau was not alone in comparing Brown to a meteor. Frederick Douglass said that Brown flashed across the cultural sky like "a splendid meteor." Herman Melville in "The Portent," his poem about Brown's execution, called Brown *"the meteor of war."* Walt Whitman featured Brown in his poem about 1859–60 titled "Year of Meteors."

Brown's meteoric light shone more brilliantly for Thoreau than for any of the other writers. For Thoreau, Brown was more of a star than a meteor; he was a fixture in American history, a cynosure for all to follow. And, Thoreau wrote, Brown showed his mettle while in prison and on the scaffold.

Neither Thoreau nor anyone else could have had *any* response to John Brown's words if they had not been printed in the press. Thoreau noted the irony that many proslavery papers unwittingly promoted Brown's antislavery message by reprinting virtually all of his spoken and written words. Of the immensely popular, proslavery *New York Herald*, Thoreau wrote, "It does not know of what undying words it is made the vehicle."

Unlike today, when political prisoners are typically cut off from any communication with the outside, the 1850s were an open time when prisons were porous. John Brown received many visitors in jail: friends, well-wishing strangers, curious enemies, and a steady stream of news reporters. The impressions of these visitors inevitably found their way into the press, as did his letters.

John Brown's statements reached the nation; over the telegraph, they reached the civilized world. With only slight exaggeration, the Abolitionist Henry C. Wright could say in early December 1859 that for the previous two months "John Brown, the friend of the slave, [had] edited every paper, presided over every domestic and social circle, over every prayer, conference and church meeting, over every pulpit and platform, and over every Legislature, Judicial and Executive department of government; and he will edit every paper, and govern Virginia and all the States, and preside over Congress, guide its deliberations, and control all political caucuses and elections, for one year to come."

Notably, Brown's prison letters did not pretend to be anything more than that: letters. That is because Brown was not pretending when he wrote them. He did not write for a national audience, even though he had one. He was beyond making "public" statements like the messages he had written to newspapers in 1857 during his fund-raising tour. Now he was expressing his private feelings. And his most private feeling was that God had assigned him to be the liberator of America's enslaved millions.

His first letter to his family, written on October 31, shows that his main concern was with America's blacks. He briefly reviewed the Harpers Ferry raid, mentioning only in passing the deaths of his two sons and others, and assured his loved ones that he was happy, reminding them to think of those less fortunate than they. "Under all these terible calamities," he wrote, "I feel quite cheerful in the assurance that God reigns; & will overrule all for his glory; & the best possible good. . . . Never forget the poor nor think anything you bestow on them to be lost, to you even though they may be as *black* as Ebedmelech, the Ethiopian eunuch who cared for Jeremiah in the pit of the dungeon; or as *black* as the one to whom Phillip preached Christ."

In other letters he continued to console them with regard to his coming death. Hanging was the best thing that could happen to him, he insisted, since it would "do vastly more toward advancing the cause I have earnestly endeavored to promote, than all have done in my life before." For Thoreau or Emerson the comparison between Brown and Christ was metaphorical, for they were not Christians. For him it was sincere and deeply felt. He wrote: "Remember, dear wife and children all, that Jesus of Nazareth suffered a most excruciating death on the cross as a felon, under the most aggravating circumstances. . . . May God Almighty comfort all your hearts, and soon wipe away all tears from your eyes! To him be endless praise! Think, too, of the crushed millions who 'have no comforter.' "

In comparing himself to Christ, he was not being vain. His prison letters are full of confessions of sinfulness. To his sisters Mary and Martha he wrote, "I feel astonished that one so exceedingly vile & unworthy as I am would even be suffered to have a place [among those] . . . who when they came to die (as all must:) were permitted to pay that debt of nature in defence of the right: & of Gods eternal & immutable truth." "My only anxiety," he wrote his wife, "is to be properly assured of my fitness for the company of those who are 'washed from all filthiness:' & for the presence of Him who is Infinitely pure."

When he called himself vile and unworthy, he was expressing Calvinistic humility, not guilt over his antislavery actions, even those that had involved bloody violence. Repeatedly, he said he had a clean conscience on that score.

Still, one wonders how he felt when he received an anguished letter from Mahala Doyle, who had lost her husband and two of her sons to Brown's followers at Pottawatomie. From Tennessee she wrote:

> I do feel gratified, to hear that you were stopped in your fiendish career at Harper's Ferry, with the loss of your two sons, you can now appreciate my distress in Kansas, when you . . . entered my house at midnight and arrested my Husband and two boys, and took them out of the yard and in cold blood shot them dead in my hearing, you cant say you done it to free slaves, we had none and never expected to own one, but has only made me a poor disconsolate widow with helpless children. . . . O how it pained my heart to hear the dying groans of my Husband & children.

In a postscript she added that her son John was now grown and would like nothing more than to be in Charles Town on December 2 to adjust the rope around Brown's neck.

Although Brown apparently did not answer Mrs. Doyle, he seemed to have settled the Pottawatomie matter in his mind, as is indicated by a discussion he had with one of his visitors, M. D. Lowry, a neighbor from his early Pennsylvania years. Lowry asked him how he responded to G. W. Brown's charge in the *Kansas Herald of Freedom* that Brown was "selfish, unjust, revengeful, mercenary, untruthful and corrupt." He could have added "murderous," because G. W. Brown had gained national attention with his revelations about Pottawatomie in his newspaper.

John Brown saw the gist of Lowry's question. Weighing his words, he replied, "Time, and the honest verdict of posterity will approve of every act of mine to prevent slavery from being established in Kansas. I never shed the blood of fellow man except in self-defence or in promotion of a righteous cause." This open-ended statement, which did not lie but did not tell the whole truth, suggests that Brown now considered his bloody career in Kansas justifiable in light of his overall mission.

His happiness over his imprisonment and impending death appears to be related to expiation for his violent deeds in Kansas. Sometimes this happiness could seem *too* intense, as when he wrote his sisters: "Oh my dear friends can you believe it possible that the Scaffold has no terrors for your own poor, old, unworthy brother? . . . I am weeping for joy: & gratitude that I can in no other way express."

His joy grew from his conviction that God had assigned him a new, milder role in the fight against slavery. A Quaker woman from Rhode Island wrote commending him for his "brave efforts in behalf of the poor oppressed" but added that "we, who are nonresistants, and religiously believe it's better to reform by moral, and not by carnal weapons, could not approve of bloodshed." In his reply, Brown emphasized that he had now left bloodshed behind him:

> You know that Christ once armed Peter. So also in my case I think he put a sword in my hand, and there continued it so long as he saw best, and kindly took it from me. I mean when I first went to Kansas. I wish you could know with what cheerfulness I am now wielding the "sword of the Spirit" on the right hand and on the left.

In his mind, when he was in Kansas he had been the sword-wielding Peter or the warrior Gideon; his work then was righteous violence. In the

Charles Town jail he was Christ about to sacrifice his life for a cause; his work now was martyrdom.

The Rhode Island woman's feelings about Brown—admiration for the man but not his deed—characterized many of the letters he received from the North. The Abolitionist and novelist Lydia Maria Child, for example, offered to come to Charles Town to care for him because she liked what he stood for, not what he had done. "Believing in peace principles," she wrote, "I cannot sympathize with the method you chose to advance the cause of freedom. But I honor your generous intentions,—I admire your courage, moral and physical." Offering her services, she explained: "I think of you night and day, bleeding in prison, surrounded by hostile faces, sustained only by trust in God and your own strong heart. I long to nurse you,—to speak to you sisterly words of sympathy and consolation."

Brown appreciated the offer but rejected it. He wrote her saying that he was tended by a "humane gentleman" and that she must not expose herself to needless danger. The expense of her trip could be better applied elsewhere. He asked her to donate 50 cents a year to his family.

Old friends visited him, but even they admired his spirit more than his recent actions. One day John Avis escorted into Brown's cell Judge and Mrs. Thomas Russell, with whom he had stayed in Boston. Mrs. Russell sewed buttons on his coat and sent his blood-stained clothing to be cleaned. Neither she nor her husband mentioned Harpers Ferry. As Mrs. Russell later recalled: "I did not talk about the raid with Capt. Brown. I had never sympathized with his ideas on such subjects, and had always avoided them in our conversation. But I loved *John Brown*."

His imperturbability struck her. Emotion came through understatement, not outcries. Of his sons who fell in the raid, he said, " 'I have seen my two boys killed, and,' he added, in his very measured, quiet fashion, 'not gently killed.' " Of Frederick Douglass, who, he said, had ruined a great opportunity, he declared, " '*That* we owe to the famous Mr. Frederick Douglass!' and he shut his mouth in a way he had when he thought no good."

But the main drift of his conversations with visitors was optimistic, not negative or nostalgic. Rebecca Spring, a pacifist Quaker from New Jersey, visited him in late November and found him contented. She had been disturbed when she arrived at the jail. At the entrance she saw a sign advertising 50 NEGROES FOR SALE, and upon entering Brown's cell she realized from a bloody towel that his head wound had not healed. Outside, a noisy mob threatened to invade the jail and lynch the prisoners.

In the mayhem John Brown was calm. He told his visitor, "I think I cannot now better serve the cause I love so much than to die for it; and in my death I may do more than in my life." He smiled when she exclaimed, "Then you will be our martyr!" He denied feeling vindictive toward anyone, including those who had killed his sons. She asked how he could stand the long days in prison. To surrender courage, he replied, would be to lose faith in his cause: "I do not believe I shall deny my Lord and Master, Jesus Christ; and I should if I denied my principles against slavery." He added, "I sleep peacefully as an infant; or, if I am wakeful, glorious thoughts come to me, entertaining my mind."

Many others came, some friendly, some hostile. Samuel C. Pomeroy, a freedom-fighter from the Kansas days, paid a visit, offering to organize a rescue. Brown gave the usual answer: "I am worth now infinitely more to die than to live." From Boston, George and Mary Stearns sent a sculptor, Edwin A. Brackett, to create a bust of John Brown. Sitting outside Brown's cell, Brackett made a sketch from which came the idealized white figure that became a fixture in the Stearnses' mansion.

Southerners, mainly militiamen, flocked to see the Abolitionist prisoner, as though he were one of P. T. Barnum's caged freaks. Brown took the opportunity to give antislavery lectures. As he reported to Rebecca Spring, "I have very many interesting visits from proslavery persons almost daily, and I endeavor to improve them faithfully, plainly, and kindly. I do not think that I ever enjoyed life better than since my confinement here."

One visitor he did not enjoy was Henry Clay Pate, the border ruffian he had defeated at Black Jack. Brown, resenting his opponent's gloating attitude, told Pate that he had met many braver people than he. Pate responded by calling Brown a villain.

Brown's main concern was his family. He begged visitors to go to the relief of his loved ones. His letters home mixed practical instruction with religious exhortation. Thoreau was particularly impressed by a letter of November 16 in which Brown instructed his wife on methods of educating their children. In *Walden*, Thoreau had called for practical rather than bookish education, advocating learning by doing.

Without having read *Walden*, Brown made a similar point. "I have always expressed a decided preference for a very *plain but perfectly practical* education for both *sons and daughters*," he wrote. What he wanted was "enough of the learning of the schools to enable them to transact the common business of life, comfortably and respectably," along with "thorough training to good business habits" and everyday skills. "You well know," he wrote, "that I always claimed that the *music* of the broom, washtub, needle, spindle, loom, axe, scythe, flail, etc., should first be learned, at all events, and that of the piano, etc., Afterwards." As always, he demanded that the girls be educated in the same way as the boys. He wanted his daughters to become "strong, intelligent, expert, industrious, . . . [and] matter-of-fact women."

Aware that several of his children had rejected the Calvinistic religion of their childhood, he devoted much space to preaching. He implored them to study the Bible and to realize their powerlessness before God. As a concession to their skepticism, he said they need not give up their reasonable questions about religion. But he insisted that his main consolation came from his religious faith. He wanted them to enjoy this consolation as well. Quoting John Rogers, a sixteenth-century Protestant martyr, he warned his children to "abhor that arrant whore of Rome." Using the third person, he announced, "John Brown writes to his children to abhor with *undiing hatred* also: that 'sum of all vilanies;' Slavery."

He never lost sight of the group he represented in prison: America's nearly 4 million chattel slaves. Assuring a Northern friend that he was in good cheer, he wrote, "*Men* cannot *imprison,* or *chain;* or hang the *soul.* I go joyfully in behalf of Millions that 'have no rights' that this 'great, & glorious'; '*this Christian* Republic,' is bound to respect."

Not only was he happy to die for the victims of the Dred Scott decision, but he declared that he would far prefer to be accompanied to the gallows by poor blacks than by Southern clergymen. As he wrote to George L. Stearns, "I have asked to be spared from having any *mock; or hypocritical prayers made over me,* when I am publicly *murdered:* & that my only *religious attendants* be poor *little, dirty, ragged, bare headed, & barefooted Slave Boys; & Girls;* led by some old *grey headed Slave* Mother."

Although he welcomed most visitors, he tried to stop the visit of the one he wanted most to see: his wife. The journey from North Elba, he knew, would eat into family expenses, and Virginia had become a dangerous place for strangers from the North. Besides, the emotion of seeing her might prove too much. As the young lawyer George Hoyt wrote to her, "Mr Brown fears your presence . . . might disturb the great serenity and firmness which he wills to have accompany him to the gallows."

But she did come, initially as part of a rescue plan. When Higginson discovered that Brown was adamant in his refusal to be rescued, he visited Mary Brown in North Elba, asking her to go to him and persuade him otherwise. She set out on the slow journey south. Higginson accompanied her to Boston and put her on a train to Philadelphia, where the Abolitionist J. Miller McKim and two others took over as her escorts. When Brown heard she was there, he encouraged her to come on to Charles Town, if she felt up to the trip. She wrote Governor Wise for permission to do so, and he granted it willingly.

When she arrived in Charles Town on December 1, the day before her husband's execution, her escorts were ordered to return north. A twenty-five-man cavalry guard, under the direction of Major General William B. Taliaferro, conducted her carriage to the jail. John Avis and his wife greeted her in the entrance room. Their manner was kind, but, under orders from Taliaferro, Mrs. Avis took her into a room and searched her for concealed weapons. Then she was led to John Brown's cell and let in. It was 3:30 p.m., less than twenty-four hours before he was to be hanged.

Emotion stifled talk. Husband and wife embraced tightly, holding each other for many minutes without speaking. John Avis, at the cell door, was the only witness, since Stevens had been temporarily moved to another cell.

Finally, she said, "My dear husband, it is a hard fate." He answered, "Well, well; cheer up. We must all bear it in the best manner we can. I believe it is all for the best." He asked her to tell their children that "their father died without a single regret for the course he has pursued—that he is satisfied he is right in the eyes of God and of all just men."

They talked at length, mainly about practical matters. Brown had asked General Taliaferro for two or three hours. Too long, the general said. But rules were forgotten. The reunion lasted four hours.

She noticed a chain around one of his ankles, causing him to wear two woolen socks on the foot to prevent chafing. She asked if she could have the chain to keep as a family relic at home along with John Jr.'s chain from Kansas. He said he had already made the request but had been refused.

They discussed plans for burial. He suggested that, to save money, she put his body, along with the bodies of Watson, Oliver, and the two Thompson boys, on a woodpile, burn them, and take their remains with her in a box for burial in North Elba. The idea repelled her. She wanted to take the bodies north for a proper funeral and burial. She had brought up the matter with Governor Wise, who had written her, "Sympathizing as I do with your affliction, you shall have the exertion of my authority and personal influence to assist you in gathering up the bones of your sons and your husband in Virginia, for a decent and tender interment among their kindred."

She mentioned that Gerrit Smith was still in the Utica asylum. Brown remarked, "He was a good friend, and I exceedingly regret his misfortune. How is he; have you heard from him lately?" She replied affirmatively, saying she had heard he was beginning to recover.

He had some ideas for a will, he said, and he wanted to go over them with her. He wanted to leave his surveyor's equipment to John Jr.; his silver watch to Jason; binoculars, a rifle, and $50 in cash to Owen, "in consideration of his terrible sufferings in Kansas and his crippled condition from childhood"; $50 to Salmon; his large Bible, containing the family record, to Ruth; Bibles to the rest of his children, his grandchildren, and his sons- and daughters-in-law; and $50 each to various people outside the family, mainly old business associates. The cash payments were to come mainly from his father's estate. Any monies left over were to be divided among members of the immediate family, as specified by Brown.

One important factor in their lives—the gathering whirlwind of opinions about Brown in the press—came up only once. Brown asked his wife to do what she could to expose as false the story that he had told Governor Wise that the raid on Virginia stemmed from revenge for personal losses.

The end of their time together approached. They had a quick dinner. John Brown finally exploded in anger. Why couldn't his wife spend the night with him? he demanded. What was the harm?

The plea was fruitless. His tantrum subsided, and his stoic calm returned. Mary prepared to leave. She asked to see the other prisoners. Avis was willing to take her to them despite strict orders not to. To avoid getting him into trouble, Mary dropped the request. She left a book, *Voices of the True-Hearted*, as a gift for Edwin Coppoc. Later Coppoc wrote her a letter thanking her for the book, expressing fond recollections of Anne and Martha at the Kennedy farm, and describing the last moments of Watson and Oliver.

As Mary left the jail, her husband said he hoped she would spend the rest of her days in North Elba. He again recommended practical education and strict religious instruction for their children. He handed to her his papers and the letters he had received in jail, and he instructed her to take his clothing back with her to North Elba.

Wanting to formalize his will in the morning, Brown asked Avis when the hanging would take place. "Eleven o'clock" was the reply.

After leaving the jail, Mary was taken back to the Wager House Hotel in Harpers Ferry. She did not want to witness the execution. She preferred to wait in the hotel until it was over and then accompany her husband's body by train to North Elba for a funeral service there.

The morning of December 2 broke clear and mild. "Did you ever see such beautiful weather in December?" wrote a local woman to her cousin. "Oh it is charming. How I would like to ride in the country to-day. Old Brown is to be hung to-day."

Old Brown acted as though he were too busy to think about his hanging.

After reading some of his favorite Bible passages, he sent a message to the state's prosecutor, Andrew Hunter, asking to see him. Although Hunter was busy preparing for the execution, he dropped his work and went to Brown. When he arrived at the jail, Brown told him he wanted to put his will in order. Hunter suggested that Brown write the will in his own hand, but Brown replied that he was busy answering letters and would rather dictate it to Hunter.

The will was done in an hour and a half. Hunter recalled, "As evidence of his coolness and firmness, while I was drawing the will he was answering letters with a cool and steady hand. I saw no signs of tremor or giving way in him at all." In addition to the terms he had discussed with Mary, Brown added a codicil for two new friends: "I wish my friends, James W. Campbell, sheriff, and John Avis, a jailer, as a return for their kindness, each to have a Sharp's rifle of those belonging to me, or, if no rifle can be had, then each a pistol."

At one point in the morning, Governor Wise's son, O. Jennings Wise, came to Brown's cell and asked if he wanted "the consolations of religion." Brown scoffed at the idea. Instead of being accompanied to the scaffold by a Southern clergyman, he declared, he would rather be joined "by barefooted, barelegged, ragged slave children and their old gray-headed slave mother." He added, "I should feel much prouder of such an escort, and I wish I could have it."

While Brown settled his affairs, Charles Town bustled with activity. At 7 a.m. carpenters fetched planks that had been stacked near the Baptist Church and transported them to a thirty-five-acre field on Rebecca Hunter's farm in the southeast end of Charles Town. There they built a scaffold. The platform—six feet high, twelve feet wide, and some sixteen feet long—was reached by a flight of twelve railed stairs. Near the front of the platform the workmen cut a hole with a trap door on hinges built to spring open when a rope was cut. Above the hole was a gallows, consisting of two stout posts, a crossbeam, and an iron hook from which dangled a noose of tarred hemp.

At eight, soldiers began organizing on the streets of the town. Governor Wise had taken extreme measures against possible last-minute rescue efforts. A week earlier he had summoned 1,000 state militia to Charles Town. From the Virginia Military Institute he procured the services of Thomas J. Jackson to help guard the hanging site with hundreds of cadets. From Washington came Major General Robert E. Lee with 264 soldiers, who were posted at bridges and along rivers in the region. In all, a force of nearly 3,000 were present on the day of the hanging. They were concentrated in Charles Town, with pickets encircling the town in a fifteen-mile radius.

No strangers, except for a handful of reporters, were allowed to enter the town. Unlike most executions, which were public events, this one would be virtually unwitnessed by citizens. Two lines of soldiers would surround the scaffold, and beyond that sentries fifty feet apart would stand guard. Cannon were trained on the prison, on the road to the execution field, and on the scaffold.

President Buchanan found these precautions "almost incredible," and the governor of Pennsylvania called them "utterly and entirely without foundation." But Governor Wise declared that he would "call out the whole available force of the state" if necessary, explaining that he believed "an attempt will be made to rescue the prisoners, and if that fails, then to seize the citizens of this State as hostages and victims in case of execution."

General Taliaferro went to the jail and told John Brown that his time was approaching. Brown dashed off a note to Mary suggesting an inscription for him, Watson, and Oliver on a gravestone in North Elba. He finished a letter to an Ohio friend. Captain Avis and James Campbell, sheriff of Jefferson County, appeared and escorted Brown out of the cell. Thanking them for their kindness and courage, Brown gave his silver watch to Avis and a Bible to Campbell. Then he went to see the other prisoners.

He told Green and Copeland to "Stand up like men, and do not betray your friends." Shaking their hands, he gave each of them 25 cents, saying he had no more use for money. He did the same with Coppoc and Cook, but the farewell was testy. Cook had said in court that Brown had forced him to go to Harpers Ferry a year before the raid. This was false, Brown insisted; Cook had gone voluntarily. After a brief argument they decided that they remembered differently. To Coppoc, Brown said, "You also made false statements, but I am glad to hear you have contradicted them." He reminded both men that they were dying for a good cause.

He then went to Stevens, who declared, "Good bye, Captain, I know you are going to a better land." "I know I am," Brown said; "bear up, as you have done, and never betray your friends."

Avis, Campbell, and some helpers led Brown outside. He was wearing a black hat, black coat and pants, white socks, and red slippers. As he stepped into the soft, springlike morning, his unruffled manner astonished all who saw him. "Brown appeared perfectly calm and collected," reported the *New York Times*. To his foes his calmness could seem sinister. One Southern

Thomas Hovenden painting, *The Last Moments of John Brown*
(1884), showing the apocryphal scene of Brown kissing a black
child as he leaves the Charles Town jail.

BOYD STUTLER COLLECTION OF JOHN BROWN, WEST VIRGINIA ARCHIVES.

journalist wrote, "Fierce as a gun-lock, cool as a sword, he makes no apolo-
gies, and yields no triumph to his enemies. . . . His face indicates unflinching resolution, evil passions, and narrow mind."

A press report about what happened next became accepted as fact. The
story was that as Brown descended the steps of the jail, he spotted in the
crowd a black woman holding her child. Brown bent over and kissed
the child. This final gesture of his love for blacks had an irresistible appeal
to those sympathetic to Brown. It appeared in many speeches, poems,
and essays on Brown. At least three artists portrayed it—most famously
Thomas Hovenden in his 1884 painting *The Last Moments of John Brown*,
reproduced as a popular Currier & Ives lithograph.

The story, however, was fabricated. Based on secondhand sources, it was reported as true by Edward F. Underhill of the *New-York Tribune*. Captain Avis, who was by Brown's side to the very end, denied its truth. Andrew Hunter, also present the whole time, averred: "That whole story about his kissing a negro child as he went out of the jail is utterly and absolutely false from beginning to end. . . . Nothing of the kind occurred—nothing of the sort could have occurred. He was surrounded by soldiers, and no negro could get access to him."

Actually, the story may be seen as an imaginative coupling of John Brown's stated desires with truth. Brown's willingness to give his life for blacks stood out in startling relief in the raid and its aftermath. He had said that he wished a slave mother and slave children could escort him to the gallows. In effect, his wish was granted, since countless people associated his final journey with his kissing the slave child.

If the story was fictional, one of Brown's actions as he left the jail proved disturbingly truthful. He gave a guard a note he had scribbled that morning. It read:

> Charlestown, Va. 2nd, December, 1859.
>
> I John Brown am now quite *certain* that the crimes of this *guilty, land: will* never be purged *away;* but with Blood. I had *as I now think: vainly* flattered myself that without *verry much* bloodshed; it might be done.

He had once believed optimistically that his action at Harpers Ferry would start an ever-spreading rebellion that would end slavery. His recent experiences had shattered his idealism. He now saw that only a bloody war would purge the nation of its greatest crime.

Sheriff Campbell pinioned Brown's arms at the elbows behind his back with a rope. Brown was led to the open furniture wagon that was to carry him to the scaffold. Mounted soldiers with bayonets stretched before and behind the wagon, which was pulled by two white horses. At the rear of the wagon the sheriff and his helpers lifted Brown onto a poplar box that contained his black walnut coffin. As the wagon rolled off, he sat on the box with Campbell, Avis, and the undertaker, Sadler, another of his friends from prison.

On the short journey Brown tapped his fingers on his legs and looked around him. When the wagon approached the gallows hill, the sun, filtered by high clouds, cast a luminous glow over the rolling Virginia landscape.

"This is a beautiful country," Brown said. "I have not cast my eyes over it before—that is, while passing through the field."

"Yes," Avis responded glumly.

Sadler remarked, "You're the gamest man I ever saw, Captain Brown."

"Yes," Brown replied, "I was so trained up; it was one of the lessons of my mother; but it is hard to part from friends."

The wagon reached the execution site. Brown was assisted off the wagon and led by guards to the scaffold. Next to it was the Virginia state flag. In the distance, at a corner of the field, the Stars and Stripes flapped in the breeze.

Brown was the first to mount the stairs and make the platform. Edmund Ruffin, who had arranged to be among the troops around the scaffold, commented, "His movements & manner gave no evidence of his being either terrified or concerned, & he went through what was required of him apparently with as little agitation as if he had been the willing assistant, instead of the victim."

Avis and Campbell joined Brown, who said to the jailer, "Sir, I have no words to thank you for your kindness." Avis responded with equal warmth.

As Brown turned and walked toward the middle of the platform, he surveyed the impressive scene before him. Two rows of soldiers, gaudily clad in different colors, surrounded him. The grassy field, with corn stubble still showing, dipped gently toward distant meadows and forested hills. Five miles away, the Shenandoah flowed below the majestic Blue Ridge Mountains, which had an Alp-like grandeur due to bright clouds perched on their peaks.

His hat was removed and a white linen hood was placed over his head. He was positioned on the trap door. Captain Avis pinioned his legs, adjusted the noose around his neck, and asked Brown if he wanted to give the signal that he was ready by dropping a handkerchief. Brown answered, "No; I am ready at any time; but do not keep me needlessly waiting."

But wait he did. Many of Brown's serious moments were tinged by absurdity, and this one was no different. The hanging was delayed as the troops that had escorted him from the jail sought their correct positions, designated by white flags on the field. In what must have seemed an eternity, Brown had to wait nearly ten minutes for the end to come. He stood straight and still.

At last Sheriff Campbell received word that the troops were ready. He hesitated, then raised a hatchet and cut the rope that held the trap door. When the drop opened, its hinges shrieked.

The rope was unusually short, and Brown fell only about two feet. His spinal column snapped in the fall.

After Brown fell, reported the *Tribune*, "There was but one spasmodic effort of the hands to clutch at the neck, but for nearly five minutes the

"The Execution of John Brown." Engraving in *Frank Leslie's Illustrated Newspaper*, December 10, 1859.
LIBRARY OF CONGRESS.

body jerked and quivered." The contortions were not extreme. A surgeon noted that Brown's legs did not shoot up convulsively, as was usual. Colonel John Preston of the Virginia Military Institute, who stood near the scaffold, gave this description: "His knees were scarcely bent, his arms were drawn up to a right angle at the elbow, with the hands clinched; but there was no writhing of the body, no violent heaving of the chest. At each feebler effort at respiration, the arms sank lower, and his legs hung more relaxed, until at last, straight and lank he dangled, swayed to and fro lightly by the wind."

Colonel Preston broke the silence by shouting, "So perish all such enemies of Virginia! all such enemies of the Union! all such foes of the human race!"

These were also the sentiments of a young volunteer in the Virginia Greys who stood nearby: John Wilkes Booth. Recalling Brown's execution, Booth later wrote, "I looked at the traitor and terrorizer with unlimited, undeniable contempt."

Booth, a thin, handsome actor, had canceled a Richmond performance and rushed to Charles Town to join the militia troops that would help guard Brown's scaffold. As much as he loathed Brown's views, he thought the

Abolitionist "terrorizer" had a kind of tragic grandeur. He later told his sister, to whom he presented a John Brown pike, that a part of him pitied Brown, who, he fancied, looked around from the scaffold in search of rescuers he expected to appear. "He was a brave old man," Booth said to her; "his heart must have broken when he felt himself deserted." Booth, a star of melodrama and a devotee of Southern romantic machismo, saw Brown's hanging as a twisted fantasy of hairbreadth escapes and cheap pathos.

Others destined to have important roles in history were present as well. On the outskirts of the scene was Robert E. Lee, directing the protection of access routes to Charles Town. In the execution field behind the double-lined soldiers cantered Captain Turner Ashby, later another prominent general for the Confederacy. The leader of the Virginia Institute cadets, Thomas J. Jackson, soon to become the legendary "Stonewall," said a prayer for John Brown. A devout Calvinist like Brown, Jackson realized with awe that Brown "might receive the sentence 'Depart, ye wicked, into everlasting fire.' " Jackson wrote his wife, "I hope that he was prepared to die, but I am doubtful. He refused to have a minister with him."

Brown's body was left hanging for more than thirty-five minutes. When it was hauled up and cut from the rope, it crumpled on the platform in a limp heap. Some fifteen physicians examined it to confirm death. The face was dark purple, and the noose had opened an inch-deep circular gash in the neck.

The body was carried down to the wagon and placed in the coffin. Before the wagon left the field, carpenters began to dismantle the scaffold so that its wood could be used for the executions of Cook and Coppoc two weeks later. A second scaffold would be built for the two black prisoners.

A somber cavalry procession escorted his body to Harpers Ferry, where Mrs. Brown awaited it. She had spent the morning sitting at a sunny window in the Wager House Hotel. At 11:15, a friend with her looked at his watch and said, "It is all over!" She wept convulsively but soon regained her composure. Her husband's body was put in the care of an army officer at the station of the Baltimore & Ohio Rail Road.

The next morning, Saturday, December 3, Mary Brown started out on her long journey north with the body of John Brown. When her party arrived in Philadelphia at around noon, it was greeted by a mob consisting mainly of Brown sympathizers, including many blacks, who struggled to catch a glimpse of his coffin. Fearing a racial incident, the mayor of the city sent a decoy coffin to a local morgue, while Brown's was secretly placed on a boat going to New York.

There, the corpse was restored, dressed, and iced by undertakers

McGraw & Taylor. On its arrival the body was in terrible shape. But after careful touching up, it had a dignified, lifelike appearance.

A public viewing of the body was held. One New York woman wrote, "Our entire block was filled with anxious men to see the body of John Brown." She gave her opinion on Brown's restored looks: "None of the pictures that I have seen do him justice. I never see a finer looking man of his age such a death too. His countenance was as serene as if asleep just red enough to look life like. When he come he was black in the face for they slung him in the coffin with all his clothes on with his head under his shoulder and the rope he was hung with in the coffin, and strange to say his body still warm, but the ice soon restored his looks and he went to his bereaved family all the better for his stop at M.Graw & Taylors."

Early Monday morning Mary Brown, who had taken a train to New York and spent a night with Brooklyn friends, resumed her trip north with her husband's body, which was in a new coffin (a Southern one was considered unacceptable). Accompanying her were the Abolitionists J. Miller McKim and Wendell Phillips.

The three stopped for a couple of hours in Troy, New York, at the American House, a temperance hotel that had been one of John Brown's favorite stopovers. Late in the afternoon they traveled to Rutland, Vermont, spent the night there, and pushed on at five the next morning. By the evening they had reached Vergennes, Vermont.

The following day they went by boat over Lake Champlain to Westport, New York. They started out by sleigh to Elizabethtown, twenty-five miles away, but a heavy rain turned the snow into dirty slush, and they had to finish the route by carriage. In Elizabethtown they left Brown's body in the local courthouse under the guard of six volunteers while they stayed in a hotel owned by the town's sheriff. Then came the grueling twenty-five-mile journey over steep mountain passes, which brought them to North Elba on the evening of Wednesday, December 7.

Mary Brown's arrival home prompted an emotional outburst among the family members. "Mother!" cried Anne Brown, crying uncontrollably. "O! Annie!" was the response, and mother and daughter rushed into each other's arms. Similar scenes occurred when the others appeared, first the thirteen-year-old Sarah, followed by the five-year-old Ellen, and then Oliver's widow, Martha, and Ruth, John Brown's oldest daughter. The only son at home was Salmon, twenty-three. After much sobbing, restraint returned. McKim and Phillips were introduced, and everyone sat for a meal, though little was eaten in the solemnity of the moment.

After dinner McKim reviewed the events of the past month, sparing painful details. He treated gingerly the issue of the failure to recover Watson's body, which had been given to the Winchester Medical College, and Oliver's body, which had been thrown in a box and buried by the Shenandoah River along with other victims of the raid. Although Watson's widow, Isabel, was sick and absent, Martha listened with aching interest to what was said about her husband's remains. McKim assured the grieving widow that every attempt would be made to retrieve both bodies and bring them to North Elba for proper burial. McKim turned to the topic of John Brown's bravery. Phillips amplified the theme. By the end of the evening the family had settled into a peaceful resignation.

The following day, December 8, a simple funeral took place. At 1 p.m. Brown's open coffin was placed on a table outside the front door. Family members and neighbors walked by to have a last look at Brown, whose face still appeared dignified. There followed a procession to the grave, near an eight-foot rock some fifty feet away from the house.

As the coffin was lowered into the grave, the family of Lyman Epps, the part African American, part Native American friend of Brown, sang Brown's favorite hymn, "Blow Ye the Trumpet, Blow!," with its stirring opening

> *Blow ye the trumpet, blow—*
> *The gladly solemn sound;*
> *Let all the nations know,*
> *To earth's remotest bound,*
> *The year of Jubilee has come.*

And so John Brown lay amid the jagged splendor of the Adirondacks, with the glistening Lake Placid nearby and the sheer Whiteface looming above the scene like a pale giant. It was a fitting place for John Brown to rest for eternity.

The Reverend Joshua Young of Burlington, Vermont, gave an impromptu sermon and said prayers for John Brown, his family, and the blacks he had died for. Next came McKim, who emphasized Brown's fortitude and the power of his words. Quoting Brown's statement about God's giving him the sword of the spirit to replace the sword of steel, McKim declared:

> And with the sword of the spirit what a work he has done. . . . And how admirably he has wielded it! None could resist him. His utterances were in the demonstration of the spirit, and with power. They have gone out to the world and are doing their work. . . . Thus, with

the sword of the flesh and the sword of the spirit John Brown has performed a double mission; and the handwriting that dooms the system
[of slavery] already flames out upon the wall.

Wendell Phillips likewise affirmed that Brown had killed slavery. "Mar-
vellous old man!" declared Phillips. "He has abolished Slavery in Virginia. . . . History will date Virginian Emancipation from Harper's Ferry."
In a seeming paraphrase of Thoreau, he added, "His words, they are
stronger even than his rifles. These crushed a State. Those have changed
the thoughts of millions, and will yet crush slavery."

Unable to shed his pacifism, Phillips added that Brown had shown slavery would disappear as a result of ideas, not force. "I do not believe slavery
will go down in blood," Phillips said. "Ours is the age of thought. . . . His
words,—they are stronger even than his rifles."

Brown would have appreciated most of these comments, but he would
have rejected Phillips's notion that slavery would disappear without violence. The nation's crimes, he had written just before his death, "*will* never
be purged *away;* but with Blood."

Actually, time would prove that both Phillips and Brown were right. It
would take the bloodiest war in America's history to abolish slavery. But
behind this war were powerful ideas that catalyzed soldiers North and
South, impelling them to action. The Civil War would be both a war of
steel and a war of the spirit. And the recent memory of John Brown was a
major factor in the war in both senses.

John Brown's body was mouldering in the grave. The time had come for
his soul to do its work.

16

Positions and Politics

At a service held in Concord, Massachusetts, on the day of John Brown's hanging, Henry David Thoreau declared that Brown embodied "transcendent moral greatness." Thoreau rhapsodized, "Almost any noble verse may be read, either as his elegy or his eulogy"; Brown was "one of those rare cases of heroes and martyrs for which the ritual of no church has provided."

Ten days later Senator Andrew Johnson of Tennessee expressed a very different sentiment in a speech before the U.S. Senate as it prepared to investigate the Harpers Ferry raid. Johnson announced, "I want these modern fanatics who have adopted John Brown as their Christ and their cross, to see what their Christ is. . . . This old man Brown was nothing more than a murderer, a robber, a thief, and a traitor."

The statements by Thoreau and Johnson illustrate how polarizing a figure Brown had become at the time of his execution. For Thoreau, speaking at a memorial service he had organized with Emerson and Alcott, Brown was on the level of Christ and other exalted beings. Brown's miraculous final weeks on earth, Thoreau believed, had carried him to spiritual heights that could not be described but only suggested. "The sense of grand poetry," Thoreau said, "read by the light of this event, is brought out distinctly like an invisible writing held to the fire." Thoreau read verses from Andrew Marvell and Aytoun's "Lays of the Scottish Cavaliers." Alcott read Plato and an ode he had written for the occasion. Emerson read Brown's speech to the Virginia court and selections from his prison letters. Others read statements made by Solomon and by Jesus Christ.

For Andrew Johnson, comparisons between John Brown and Jesus—or anyone else good, for that matter—were absurd and dangerous. Appearing on the national stage at a key moment, the future vice president of the United States launched a diatribe against Brown, whose true colors, he argued, were revealed at Pottawatomie in May 1856, when he supervised the murder of the three Doyles, Allen Wilkinson, and William Sherman. Johnson juxtaposed the bloody incident with rapturous eulogies coming from the North in the wake of Brown's execution. To prove Brown's connection with the slayings, Johnson quoted at length from several documents: Mahala Doyle's deposition in June 1856 and her recent letter to the imprisoned Brown; the Senate's report on Kansas in the summer of 1856; G. W. Brown's articles on Pottawatomie in the *Herald of Freedom*; and John Gihon's account of the incident in his history volume, *Geary and Kansas.*

It was at Pottawatomie, concluded Johnson, that "hell entered [Brown's] soul. . . . Then it was that he shrank from the dimensions of a human being into those of a reptile. Then it was, if not before, that he changed his character to a demon who had lost all the virtues of a man. And you talk of sympathy for John Brown!"

Thoreau and Johnson represented diverging streams of response to Brown. In time, the streams became overpowering rivers that swept Americans on opposite sides of the slavery divide toward war.

Brown's martyrdom became a common rallying point for Northern antislavery figures who had long been divided. We tend to generalize that the North was against slavery and the South for it and that the conflict between the two outlooks caused the Civil War. Actually, Northern antislavery opinion had long been fractured. Admiration for John Brown and the sorrow and anger provoked by his execution brought a semblance of unity to previously warring antislavery factions.

Since the late 1830s, there had existed six major antislavery groups in America: the Garrisonian Abolitionists; the antislavery political parties, ranging from the Liberty Party through the Free Soil Party to the Republican Party; the evangelical Abolitionists, centered around the New York reformers Arthur and Lewis Tappan; the colonizationists; the Christian perfectionists, especially the Oberlin group led by Asa Mahan and Charles Grandison Finney; and the black militants, such as Henry Highland Garnet and David Walker. A seventh group, the Transcendentalists, though not continuously active in the antislavery movement, contributed to it through their speeches and essays.

John Brown had supported the black militants but had had mixed feelings about the other groups. As for the groups themselves, they often fought, sometimes bitterly. "There Shall Be Division" was the headline of an 1839 article on Abolitionism in a Methodist paper, the *Zion's Herald,* just before the rift between the Garrisonians, the Tappanites, and the political Birneyites.

Contrasting views (no-government versus political action, come-outerism versus support of the church, anti-Constitution versus pro-Constitution, and so on) were enhanced by personal differences. Wendell Phillips respected William Lloyd Garrison but never felt close to him, partly due to differences in their backgrounds; Phillips was a wealthy Boston Brahmin and Garrison the son of an alcoholic drifter. Phillips befriended a fellow Bostonian, Edmund Quincy, but then the two had a falling out and avoided each other when they approached on the street. The fiery Charles Sumner was temperamentally at odds with the timid Hamilton Fish and the wily politician Thurlow Weed. As Parker Pillsbury wrote, "Being intensely human, abolitionists were intensely individual. . . . They felt as intensely as they thought. And so how could they but differ? . . . Many a discordant note . . . seemed to ring on down to the gate of the grave. . . . To the last, there were differences of opinion."

John Brown did not repair these differences. Rather, he became an inspirational center of attention. For the North to go to war, unified action was required. There had to be points of agreement between conflicting antislavery factions and individuals. John Brown was such a point.

He began to become so during his trial, when his fearlessness and eloquence won many Northern hearts. One important convert to his side was Garrison. As a committed pacifist who had once quarreled sharply with Brown, Garrison was not easy to win over, as evidenced by the articles on Harpers Ferry that he ran in the *Liberator.* In the first few weeks after the raid, most of the pieces he ran in his paper were harsh indictments reprinted from other papers, especially the *Journal of Commerce.* Garrison himself called the raid a "well-intended but sadly misguided effort," a "wild and futile" enterprise.

Despite his qualms over tactics, Garrison was a leading promoter of Brown's personal qualities. "Our views on war and bloodshed, even in the best of causes, are too well known to need repeating here," he said in a piece about Harpers Ferry. But in the same breath he extolled Brown as brave, honest, and self-sacrificing. Remarking on the self-possession Brown demonstrated in his postraid interview, Garrison asked, "Is there another man, of all the thirty millions of people inhabiting this country, who could have answered more wisely, more impressively, more courageously, or with greater moral dignity, under such a trying ordeal?"

When Brown was sentenced to hang, Garrison's American Anti-Slavery

William Lloyd Garrison.
LIBRARY OF CONGRESS.

Society issued a broadside declaring that on the day of execution Northerners should express sympathy, "whether by public meetings and addresses,
the adoption of resolutions, private conferences, or any other mode of
action,—for the furtherance of the Anti-Slavery cause." The broadside
continued, "In all the Cities and Towns of the North, let there be some
suitable and expressive form of manifestation. Among other things, let
there be a tolling of the bells for one hour."

Between then and December 2, two major pro-Brown meetings took
place: the November 18 meeting at Tremont Temple in which, as seen earlier, Emerson and others spoke; and, two days later, a rally in Natick,
Massachusetts, led by Henry C. Wright.

Wright had started as a Garrisonian pacifist but had become more militant during the 1850s. At the huge gathering in Natick on the evening of
November 20, Wright presented for approval a resolution in support of
John Brown. Passed the following day, the resolution held "that it is the
right and duty of the slaves to resist their masters, and the right and duty of
the people of the North to incite them to resistance, and to aid them in it."
In an open letter to the imprisoned Brown, Wright declared: "Virginia will
hang your body, but she will not hang John Brown. . . . By the gallows you
have triumphed. . . . Your execution is but the beginning of that death

struggle with slaveholders, which must end in striking the last fetter from the last slave."

Emboldened by Emerson's comparison of Brown to Christ earlier in the month, Wright pushed the image further. Noting that three decades of Christian preaching in America had failed to end slavery, Wright argued that Brown was more effective than Christ in this respect. "Christ," Wright said, "as represented by those who are called by his name, had proved a dead failure, as a power to free the slaves. John Brown is and will be a power far more efficient. The nation is to be saved, not by the blood of Christ, (as that is now administered,) but by the blood of John Brown, which, as administered by Abolitionists, will prove the 'power of God and the wisdom of God' to resist slaveholders and bring them to repentance. . . . Redemption is to come to the slave and his oppressors, not by the Cross of Christ, as it is preached among us, but by the gallows of Brown."

The November groundswell of support for Brown fed into the massive show of grief and sympathy throughout the North on December 2. In New York's Church of the Puritans a crowd that included Lewis Tappan and women's rights advocate Ernestine L. Rose attended a prayer meeting at 11 a.m., when Brown was executed, and a second meeting that evening in which the Reverend George B. Cheever praised Brown as a martyr like St. Stephen. In Lowell, Massachusetts, a large bell was carried up the streets on a cart and was rung by a black man. In nearby Worcester bells tolled from 10 a.m. to noon; later, some 3,000 people crowded into Mechanics Hall for a meeting in honor of Brown. An even larger gathering took place in Boston's Tremont Temple, where Garrison, Phillips, and others spoke. Garrison declared himself "a non-resistant" devoted to "the peaceful abolition of slavery" but added: "I am prepared to say: 'Success to every slave insurrection at the South, and in every slave country.' . . . Give me, as a non-resistant, Bunker Hill, and Lexington, and Concord, rather than the cowardice and servility of a Southern slave-plantation."

Cities and towns throughout the North recognized the significance of the day. Train passengers riding through Maine heard bells ringing in Portland and Gardiner. In Manchester, New Hampshire, there was a "brisk excitement" when Brown sympathizers rang the bell in the City Hall belfry and were ordered to desist by the mayor. At New Bedford, Massachusetts, John Wise was hanged from a tree in effigy, with a card stuck to one of his feet, on which was written, GOV. WISE—THE TRAITOR.

Emerson and Thoreau had opened the floodgates to comparisons between Brown and Christ. A Dover, New Hampshire, minister said of Brown, "The gallows from which he ascends into Heaven, *will be in our pol-*

itics, what the cross is in our religion. . . . To be hanged in Virginia, is like being crucified in Jerusalem—it is the last tribute which she pays to *Virtue!*" The *Milwaukee Free Democrat*, affirming "that John Brown is CRUCIFIED as the representative of an idea," cited Emerson: "The gallows of John Brown, said Emerson, will be glorified . . . like the cross, and so it will, because the gallows of John Brown, as the cross, is used to persecute ideas, or *great principles of enduring benefit* and necessity to humanity."

Some meetings endorsed Brown's character even as they expressed doubts about his violent actions. For instance, a memorial gathering in Providence, Rhode Island, passed a resolution that said, "While we most decidedly disapprove the methods he adopted to accomplish his objects, yet in his strong love for freedom, in his heroic spirit, in his fidelity to his convictions, . . . his dignified bearing, [we see a] noble spirit."

A characteristic service was held in Cleveland, where 1,400 people, a third of them women, met that evening in the Melodeon. The hall was draped with black crape. To the left of the stage was Brown's picture, captioned JOHN BROWN, THE HERO OF 1859. To the right were banners inscribed with the words THE END CROWNS THE WORK, REMEMBER THEM THAT ARE IN BONDS AS BOUND WITH THEM, and IF I HAD INTERFERED IN BEHALF OF THE GREAT, THE WEALTHY AND THE WISE, NO ONE WOULD HAVE BLAMED ME.

Typically, some of the evening's speakers criticized Brown's tactics. "I cannot say that his means were my means for the removal of slavery," said one. Another conceded that Brown "may have mistaken the *method*, the *time*, and the *place*" of the attack. But there was unanimity about Brown's virtues and his aims. Resolutions were passed branding slavery as "the sum of all villainies" and saying it could "only be subdued by giving it, in southern parlance, 'war to the knife, with the knife to the hilt.' "

Brown would have most appreciated the comments of an African American speaker, Charles H. Langston, who insisted that, above all, Brown stood for racial equality. Langston began by announcing that he never thought he would sing praise to a white person. "Why should I honor the memory or mourn over the death of any of the white people of this land?" he asked. "Remember the bitter, burning wrongs the colored people have received at their bloody hands." He pointed out that racism pervaded both the South and the North. Indeed, "so wide-spread and well nigh universal is the feeling of negro-hate in this country, that I had nearly made up my mind never to find one of the dominant race true to the principles of human brotherhood."

John Brown, he insisted, was unique. He was "a lover of mankind—not of any particular class or color, but of all men. He knew no complexional distinctions between God's rational creatures. . . . He fully, really and *actively* believed in the equality and brotherhood of man. . . . He is the only American citizen who has lived fully up to the Declaration of Independence. . . . He admired Nat. Turner as well as George Washington."

Many other blacks expressed similar feelings in the wake of Brown's death. A convention of African Americans held that day in Detroit issued a resolution saying "that we hold the name of Captain John Brown in the most sacred remembrance, as the first disinterested martyr who, upon the true Christian principles of his divine Lord and Master, has freely delivered up his life for the liberty of our race in this country. Therefore will we ever venerate his character, and regard him as our temporal redeemer whose name shall never die." Detroit's black churches were to be hung in mourning for a month. In Chatham, where Brown had publicly introduced his plan to invade the South, an assembly of blacks convened at 4 a.m., seven hours before the execution, and remained until late the next evening, expressing "very intense" sympathy for Brown.

It was fitting, given Brown's racial message, that among the most heartfelt services in his honor were those held in Haiti. The epoch-making slave revolts of Haiti had inspired John Brown; he in turn inspired Haitian blacks. A "grand solemn service" was held on January 20, 1860, at the Port-au-Prince Cathedral, which, like other buildings in the city, was draped in mourning. On its altar were the words, inscribed in gold, *À JOHN BROWN, MARTYR DE LA CAUSE DES NOIRS.* Many eulogies to John Brown were delivered, and there was a procession to a place called Martyr's Cross. For three days leading citizens of the city wore badges of mourning, and January 23 was set apart for "humiliation and prayer, in memory of the greatest cosmopolite that has been in existence the last century—John Brown."

Similar services were held in villages throughout the island. A subscription was taken up for Brown's family, and a paper proclaimed that any Haitian who did not contribute to "this great national work" deserved "shame and ignominy." Another paper extolled Brown as "the immortal benefactor of our race, the holy victim of our cause . . . greater than other philanthropists; . . . his sacred name will be pronounced with a holy respect." This was high praise, coming from a country that had a remarkable martyr of its own, Toussaint L'Ouverture. By 1863 there hung in the Haitian senate building a full-length portrait of Brown standing on a cloud, holding hands with two blacks, who placed a laurel wreath on his head.

The French novelist-reformer Victor Hugo was as deeply stirred by Brown's death as were the Haitians, whose history and culture he admired. Hugo sent an emotional letter about Brown, dated December 2, to the

London News. Soon newspapers throughout the world, including many in America, had reprinted the letter. American Abolitionists saw it as a document that would "be read by millions with thrilling emotions."

What made the letter significant was not only Hugo's celebrity but also his sincere love of America. Hugo did not hate the South and love the North. Instead, he hated slavery and loved America. His revulsion over Brown's execution was proportional to his respect for the American democratic experiment. "The more one loves, admires, reveres the Republic," he wrote, "the more heart-sick one feels at such a catastrophe." He was astounded that this horror occurred "not in Turkey, but in America!"

The execution of John Brown revealed America to be the greatest oxymoron in the world. In this unthinkable act, Hugo wrote, the world witnessed "the champion of Christ . . . slaughtered by the American Republic," "the assassination of Emancipation by Liberty," "something more terrible than Cain slaying Abel, . . . Washington slaying Spartacus!" "The murder of Brown," he wrote, "would be an irreparable fault. It would penetrate the Union with a secret fissure, which would, in the end, tear it asunder."

This was no momentary eruption on Hugo's part. He lingered on the topic for years. On December 11 he wrote that John Brown, a "rigid Puritan, sincerely religious," had won the grandest prize of all: becoming a martyr for a holy cause. A week later he confessed to a friend that he was "overwhelmed with grief" due to the "murders" of Brown and his associates.

Moved by the passionate response to John Brown in Haiti, Hugo wrote two open letters about Brown to the Haitian people. In the first, written on December 28, Hugo called Brown's hanging "among the calamities of history" and predicted, "The rupture of the Union will fatally follow the assassination of Brown. What an error! What a disaster!" "As to John Brown," he continued, "he was an apostle and a hero. The gibbet has only increased his glory, and made him a martyr." Like Brown, Hugo detested racism, and emphasized racial equality in his Haitian letter. "A white and a black republic are sisters," he wrote, "the same as a white and [a] black man are brothers"; and, "Black and white, all brothers, all equal."

As the quarrel over Brown intensified in America in the following months, Hugo realized that Brown's execution spelled the death of American slavery. On March 30, 1860, he wrote another letter to the Haitians predicting that

> slavery in all its forms will disappear. What the South slew last December was not John Brown, but Slavery. Henceforth, no matter what President Buchanan may say in his shameful message, the

American Union must be considered dissolved. Between the North and the South stand the gallows of Brown. Union is no longer possible: such a crime cannot be shared.

Hugo's interest in Brown did not flag, even after slavery was abolished. Five years after the Civil War, Hugo aired plans to write a novel about John Brown. The *New-York Tribune* objected to his idea "to write a romance of which the hero is to be John Brown," insisting that "the short, snappish, spasmodic sentences which Hugo puts into the mouths of all his heroes and heroines" would hardly suit someone as eloquent as Brown.

Although Hugo dropped the plan, he incorporated Brown into *Les Misérables*, his famous novel of 1862. At the climax of the novel, to illustrate the idea that the victor is "magnificent" and the martyr "sublime," he wrote: "For ourselves, who prefer martyrdom to success, John Brown is greater than Washington." One sees shades of Brown in Hugo's Christ-like protagonist Jean Valjean, who suffers for the oppressed, and in Enjolrus and his fellow revolutionaries, who fight against overwhelming odds on the barricades, just as Brown had fought in the engine house, and who die for a noble cause.

In 1874 Hugo, as the head of a committee of eleven French reformers, wrote a letter to Brown's widow along with a gold medal inscribed "To the memory of John Brown, judicially murdered at Charlestown, in Virginia, on the 2nd of December, 1859, and in commemoration also of his sons and comrades who, with him, became the victims of their devotion to the cause of Negro emancipation."

Another Frenchman, Pierre Vésinier, pushed beyond Hugo's reformism to an ultraradical interpretation of Brown. In his 1864 book *Le martyr de la liberté des nègres; ou, John Brown, le Christ des noirs*, Vésinier, later a leader of the Paris Commune, declared that American slavery, "that crime of crimes, . . . justifies everything, authorizes everything"—even mass killings of whites by blacks. Associating Harpers Ferry with slave revolts in Haiti and Jamaica, Vésinier insisted that every minute of Brown's thirty-odd minutes on the gallows must be repaid by 100,000 lives. "The negro race will exterminate the white race," Vésinier wrote; "it is necessary that one die so that the other may live." Since whites could not cultivate Southern soil, he argued, blacks should massacre the whites and take over the land: "The only desirable, just, useful, opportune, indispensable, solution is that the black race remain alone, in free possession of the soil, which it alone can cultivate."

Vésinier reached the fringe of sympathy for Brown. The mainstream

European reaction was much like that of antislavery Americans: however rash Brown's act may have been, his goals were admirable and his conduct above reproach. True, a few papers, such as the *Times* of London and the *Edinburgh Review*, denounced Brown, but in general, England and the Continent supported him. At an antislavery meeting in London on his execution day he was hailed as America's "first and greatest martyr—the martyr of negro freedom." The *Morning Star* of London called Brown "a stern, single-minded, God-fearing, Puritan-souled man, who has died for an idea, and that a disinterested and generous one." *Manchester*'s *Examiner and Times* remarked that "no man ever died in a nobler cause, or died more nobly" than Brown, adding that "his death cannot fail to deepen and embitter the hostility which divides the northern from the southern States, and to advance, by peaceful or by violent means, the cause of the Abolitionists."

What truly caught the attention of foreigners was new behavior on the part of the South, which had always been cocky and self-assured but was now approaching a state of panic. In an overview of the European response to Harpers Ferry, historian Seymour Drescher has found that "there was a very general conclusion that the South, by its overreaction, had helped transform a senseless adventure into an act of heroism and a political crisis." Typically, the *Liverpool Mercury* noted the "frenzied rage and terror" that had seized Virginia, revealing "the conscious weakness and rottenness" of slavery. "The so-called Abolitionist invasion of Virginia," commented the *Mercury*, "has had the effect of disclosing the frightful insecurity of a social condition based on Slavery; and it has brought out the character of a Slave-owning community in a light at once odious and ridiculous." England and France, where racism was less pronounced than in the United States, were shocked by the "colorphobia" the South exhibited, marked by senseless violence against blacks and antislavery whites. Brown, meanwhile, was lauded in Europe for his raw courage. "THERE WAS NO 'BUNKUM' IN BROWN" ran the headline of a *Morning Star* report of the "true grit" Brown exhibited on the scaffold.

Europe's recognition of the South's sudden sense of insecurity was shrewd. John Brown created what amounted to an identity crisis among Southerners. A main ingredient of the South's chivalric code was an assumed superiority in courage over the North. John Brown challenged this code. When Governor Wise declared that he would give his right arm to prevent a large Southern force from again being embarrassed by a small band of Northerners, and when his son took a local militia commander to court for cowardice, they manifested the shame and confusion Brown had caused, merely through his bravery.

Northern supporters of Brown rubbed his courage in the South's face. One of the first positive articles on Brown, a piece in early November 1859 by James Redpath in the *Boston Atlas*, did so with glee. Responding to the near-universal criticism of Brown that had been published to that date, Redpath noted that "there is one aspect in which the recent insurrection has not been hitherto viewed—in the light, I mean, of a *success*." As an effort to free the slaves, Redpath conceded, the raid was "if not an insane movement, . . . at least, an unsuccessful one." But as proof of the North's valor and the South's weakness, it was a revelation.

In Kansas, Redpath pointed out, John Brown had begun to expose the South's spinelessness. "Every one believed the South to be full of fighting pluck," Redpath said, but at Black Jack and elsewhere Brown "demonstrated . . . that she was only a cowardly braggart, after all; and now, to confirm our evidence, and convince the unwilling North of the undoubted, and the disgraceful truth, comes daily accounts of her shrinking and her quaking at Charlestown." In its embarrassment and shock, the South blew the raid out of proportion. Redpath wrote:

> Never before, among modern nations, did seventeen men, produce so terrible and universal a panic as Old Brown at Harper's Ferry. What a posse of policemen would have quelled in ten minutes; and reporters in the Northern States would have barely noticed,—has made fifteen States for nearly fifteen days to tremble in their breeches, and threatened to produce even more ridiculous results. They are not done quaking yet, I am very much afraid that *diapers* will be needed before the trial of Old Brown shall be finished.

Redpath concluded, "As a demonstration of the cowardice of the South, then, John Brown's exploit is a brilliant success."

When Brown remained brave up to his final moments, while Governor Wise timidly overguarded the execution, Northerners ratcheted up their jibes about the South's weakness. At a service for Brown in Manhattan, a minister was applauded when he declared that "Virginia's chivalry was nothing but a laughing-stock. Virginia could be whipped easily." A writer for the *Liberator* affirmed that Brown "has revealed the impotent timidity of the South," predicting that "like a nightmare, he will haunt her with troubled breath, till sleep shall be a stranger to her eyelids."

Such taunts roused the defenders of slavery to action. In the North, proslavery Democrats organized "Union meetings" in which John Brown was vilified. In the South, violence against blacks and against suspicious Northerners took on a new paranoid intensity.

The Union meetings in the North came in response to the pro-Brown rallies of November, rallies that took Democrats by surprise, since in the early going Brown had been criticized from all quarters (except Concord). In the wake of the Tremont Temple assembly, featuring Emerson and Phillips, and the Natick one, led by Wright, Boston conservatives launched a counteroffensive.

At a three-hour meeting on December 8, a large crowd in Faneuil Hall heard several speakers denounce John Brown and his followers as criminals and traitors. Edward Everett, the pompous orator who later would precede Lincoln on the podium at Gettysburg, compared John Brown's intended servile insurrection with the bloody horrors, rapes, and tortures of St. Domingo in 1791. Everett attacked Emerson, his former student at Harvard, for blasphemously comparing Brown, the murderer, to Christ, the savior of mankind.

Another speaker, Caleb Cushing, argued that Brown shared with Emerson, Phillips, and others a "monomania" on the subject of slavery. Cushing declared: "I know that the imputed insanity of John Brown is that his intelligence has become perverted, that his heart is gangrened, that his soul is steeled against everything human and conscientious by that same monomania, which pervades the speeches and writings of Wendell Phillips and Waldo Emerson. Are they insane?" He answered, "I know not," but pointed to Gerrit Smith, the lunatic supporter of Brown, as evidence of what effect the antislavery monomania had on the mind.

Inevitably, Cushing brought up Pottawatomie. He drew a melodramatic portrait of inoffensive Kansas families sleeping in their cabins when they were awakened at midnight "by the treacherous approach of armed assassins." Here was John Brown in action: "The husband—two husbands,—are torn from the arms of their wives, and ruthlessly slaughtered in cold blood. Nay, their youthful children are brained before their eyes." Cushing described Mahala Doyle and Louisa Wilkinson begging the invader to spare their loved ones, "But they spoke to a merciless heart, for they spoke to John Brown!" "That is the commencement of civil war in these United States," Cushing declared. And, he continued, it was in the same spirit that Brown raided Virginia, with the goal of subjecting "millions and millions of white men and white women to servile insurrection and civil war."

Similar anti-Brown assemblies were held in New York and Philadelphia. On the evening of December 19, a crowd of over 6,000 gathered in New

York's largest hall, the Academy of Music at Irving Place and 14th Street, to protest against "the treasonable raid of John Brown" and to give Virginia "more than a tacit assurance of the horror with which our people regarded the crimes of Brown, and of their sympathy with the victims of his raid." Outside the building 15,000 thronged the streets, as a band played and fireworks and bonfires lit the night. It was described as "the largest public meeting ever held in the city of New York" by the *Journal of Commerce* and as "the largest, the most enthusiastic, the most singular, and most instructive meeting ever held in New York" by the *Herald.*

The crowd that day heard that slavery was good and John Brown was evil. One speaker said, "I insist that negro slavery is not unjust. (Cries of 'Bravo!') It is not only not unjust, but it is just, wise, and beneficent. . . . I hold that the negro is decreed by nature to a state of pupilage under the dominion of the wiser white man in every clime where God and nature meant that the negro should live at all." Another pointed out that, actually, few Northeners completely supported Brown. "That there should be any," he said, "is a disgrace to a Christian age and country. But while those who approve the act are only a handful, revilers of all human laws and blasphemers against God, there are those—too many who, while they condemned *the act*, sympathize in some degree with *the man*," despite his "cold-blooded atrocity."

After the speakers, letters were read from notables who could not attend the meeting but supported its aim. Among those who had written were Franklin Pierce, Martin Van Buren, Millard Fillmore, and Winfield Scott. A typical letter stated that Brown's "pathway can be traced by bloody footprints along his whole career, from theft to murder," starting in Kansas, where "his course was marked by every species of wrong and violence," and culminating at Harpers Ferry, the scene of "stealth, fraud, robbery, murder, treason, and attempted insurrection." Even worse, this criminal "has been canonized by the blasphemous orgies of those who demand an anti-slavery Bible and an anti-slavery God," including one who declared "that the gallows would henceforward be more glorious than the cross and crucifixion."

The Union meeting in Philadelphia was in the same vein. On December 7 more than 6,000 people jammed into Jayne's Hall "to repudiate," in the words of one speaker, "the schemes of those who are striving to plunge the nation into the horrors of a civil war." Two 100-gun salutes were fired to herald the event, which was advertised by banners emblazoned DOWN WITH ALL TRAITORS, FACTIONISTS, AND DISUNIONISTS. An orator told the crowd, "We have no sympathy with that modern hero-worship which exalts crime and deifies a felon."

Various speakers endorsed the Union and the Constitution and denounced disunion and John Brown. Slavery was a fact of American life, they said. Brown only proved that slaves are contented with their condition, since he could not lure any to his side. Along with Brown, like-minded Abolitionists merited punishment, since he was carrying out "what for years has been promulgated in various parts of the North, in newspapers, from the pulpit, and the hustings." Mass executions were in order: "Let there be no sympathy with or for abolitionists of the John Brown stamp; but let them, wherever found, be legally condemned, and hung as high as Haman."

While Northern conservatives talked of hanging Abolitionists, Southerners actually hung them. Four of Brown's followers—Shields Green, John Copeland, Edwin Coppoc, and John Cook—were hanged on December 16. Once again, military companies guarded the jail and the gallows as the prisoners were carted on their coffins to the execution field. At 10:30 the two blacks, Green and Copeland, took the same trip their leader had two weeks earlier. Although they looked glum, they followed his example by walking firmly up the scaffold steps and saying kind words to their sheriff and jailer. Remaining strong through the preparations for hanging, Green prayed out loud and Copeland remained silent. When trap doors opened and the men dropped, Green's body moved little. Copeland's twisted and jerked on the rope for minutes before it went limp.

Two hours later came the executions of Coppoc and Cook. Before they left the jail, they visited the cell of Stevens and Hazlett, addressing the former by name and pretending not to know the latter. Stevens saw sad looks on their faces and said, "Good by, cheer up; give my love to my friends in the other world." Coppoc replied, "It is the parting from friends, not the dread of death, that moves us."

On the ride to the gallows, the men looked resigned and indifferent to their surroundings. Like their black comrades, they made a point of being brave at the end. A journalist reported that at thirteen minutes before one o'clock, Coppoc and Cook ascended the scaffold stairs "with a determined firmness that was scarcely surpassed by Capt. Brown." They said goodbye to their Southern friends. After the hoods were placed over their heads, Cook reached out and said, "Stop a minute—where is Edwin's hand?" When he found it, they shook hands vigorously. Coppoc exclaimed, "God bless you." The ropes were adjusted around their necks. Both of them asked the sheriff to be quick. He was. The two hung for thirty minutes, and then their bodies were put in black walnut coffins, to be shipped to relatives in the North.

The four hangings on December 16, horrible as they were from an antislavery perspective, at least resulted from a legal trial. The wave of violence against visiting Northerners that swept the South after the Harpers Ferry invasion was a different matter.

People suspected of Abolitionist leanings had long been targets of Southern attacks. After Harpers Ferry, however, anti-Northern violence took on a new virulence. The shock and fear John Brown had instigated fueled widespread panic among Southerners. Panic, in turn, fed into a paranoia vented in aggressive acts, ranging from imprisonment to torture to murder. Journalists throughout the nation were startled by the sudden surge of hostile behavior. In January 1860 the *National Era* noted:

> We should literally have no room for anything else, if we were to publish all the details of the whippings, tar-and-featherings, and hangings, for the utterance of Anti-Slavery opinions in the South, which the mails daily bring us. The reign of terror in that section is marked by atrocities equal to those which desolated France seventy years ago. It is not safe for a Northern man to travel through the South at the present time, for either business or pleasure.

Everywhere the South looked, it seemed to see another John Brown, prepared with pikes and guns to launch a midnight raid and steal slaves. The *New York Times* reported that "in consequence of the Harper's Ferry affair . . . panic pervades all classes of citizens; . . . suspicion and distrust are abroad. . . . The country is in fact but one degree removed from anarchy."

In Pulaski County, Virginia, a New Englander thought to be an Abolitionist was lynched by a mob that hung him from a tree until he was nearly dead, then revived him, and repeated the process four more times—"once each for Old Brown, Coppick, Cook, Stevens, and Hazlett," his tormentors said. He was ordered to leave the state and told that if he ever returned "he would have to take the sixth and final leap." In Columbus, Georgia, a William Scott was jailed and expelled from the state for "an open expression of sympathy for 'Old Brown,' and the possession of Beecher's incendiary sermons." In Easton, Pennsylvania, a man selling a biography of Brown received a dozen lashes and was forced to leave town. A mob in Milton, Florida, burned in effigy wax figures of John Brown and Jesus and the Apostles, with whom he was compared in the North. A Savannah shoe-dealer was tarred and feathered for having read with interest "the history of the trial of John Brown."

There was no Southern state in which John Brown's name did not come up in connection with such outrages. In Mississippi a man who praised John

Brown and denounced Governor Wise was shoved off a moving train. When a Pennsylvanian visiting a small Virginia town called Wise as big a fool as Brown, he was seized by two men and hanged from a tree. He was saved only when two others interfered, "his face . . . black from strangulation, and his neck bruised and discolored by the abrasion of the rope."

Even Northerners who had no sympathy for John Brown were targeted. One New Englander in South Carolina wrote the editor of the *New York Times*, "To avoid suspicion of being thought an insurrectionist or an emissary of John Brown, as Southerners think all the Northerners among them are, I had been especially careful not to say or do any thing that would at all alarm." This precaution did not save him from being tarred, feathered, and expelled from the state. William S. Bailey, a newspaper editor in Newport, Kentucky, had his press destroyed by a mob when the false story circulated of his "having correspondence with Brown at Harper's Ferry," even though he had known nothing of Brown until he read about the Virginia raid. Near Mobile, Alabama, two Italian organ-grinders, who knew little English, asked the way to the next town, and a wag wrote down "directions," which in fact was a "Fatal letter":

> To the Knowing Ones:
>   Pass my Italian friends. All right. Mum's the word.
>   John Brown, of Osawatomie.

At the next town they went into a tavern, presented their letter of recommendation, and were immediately stripped, tarred, and feathered.

Far from being covert or disguised, as many lynchings of the Ku Klux Klan era would be, such actions were openly reported and promoted by Southerners. The *Atlanta Confederacy* explained, "We regard every man in our midst an enemy to the institutions of the South, who does not boldly declare that he believes African slavery to be a social, moral, and political blessing"—if not, he "should be requested to leave the country." A Virginia postmaster announced unapologetically: "We are in the midst of a Reign of Terror here. . . . All men of Northern birth now here are under surveillance by the so-called Vigilance Committee; and any one suspected of thinking slavery is less than divine is placed under care."

Northern newspapers even mildly sympathetic to Brown were widely banned in the South. Many Southern post offices refused to distribute the *New-York Tribune*, the *Springfield Republican*, the *Albany Evening Journal*, the *New York Independent*, and other papers deemed subversive. Even some conservative periodicals, like *Harper's Weekly* and *Frank Leslie's Illustrated News-*

paper, were banned. The *Springfield Republican* lamented that "nearly all northern papers are now excluded from the South, except the *New-York Herald* and the *New-York Observer*, the one the organ of Pro-slavery diabolism and the other of Pro-Slavery piety."

"Black lists" of "Abolition houses," or businesses run by antislavery people, were circulated so that their products could be boycotted. These businesses were said to be "steeped and saturated in Sewardism, Brownism, Greeleyism, Helperism, and incendiarism." Westmoreland County, Virginia, passed a resolution to "adopt a strict non-intercourse in trade and commerce with the citizens and merchants of all the non-slaveholding States," and to "arrest and send out of the State . . . all itinerant venders of northern books, newspapers, periodicals, or any other articles of northern growth or manufacture." A main impetus behind the anti–John Brown Union meetings in the North was economic. Failure to sign up for such a meeting was "regarded as conclusive proof of infidelity to southern interests, while signing it was to be a way to southern favor."

Blacks were the greatest victims of the Southern reaction to Harpers Ferry. Stories of blacks maimed, tortured, and killed by Southern whites filled newspapers from mid-November 1859 through 1860. If many visiting Northerners seemed like John Browns, blacks were regarded as potential John Copelands or Shields Greens. Slaves who acted suspiciously or rebelliously were dispatched quickly, often by being hanged or burned alive. "These barbarities," commented the *National Era*, "proceed from fear. They indicate the sentiment of the Southern people in regard to the stability and strength of Slavery, and leave no doubt that, in spite of their professions to confidence in it, they in fact feel it to be a continual source of terror. Their fears make them suspicious, cruel, and intolerant."

Free blacks faced the double threat of violence and enslavement. In 1860 there were around 3.9 million slaves and 253,000 free blacks in the South. The panic induced by Harpers Ferry led several states to move against the latter. Maryland, where nearly half the black population was free, proposed to "terminate free-negroism" by giving free blacks the chance to either "enslave themselves" or leave the state—if they did neither, "they and their posterity [were to] be sold as Slaves for life." North Carolina passed a law requiring free blacks to choose between exile and slavery; similar bills almost passed in Florida and Georgia. Feeling arose in Alabama to enslave or expel all free blacks by January 1, 1862. Arkansas and Mississippi passed bills of this nature. The Mississippi law was particularly harsh: passed on December 7, 1859, it stipulated that free Negroes who had not left the state by July 1, 1860, would be sold into slavery. In Tennessee, railroad officials who permitted a free black to ride on a train unattended by a white citizen of the state were subjected to heavy fines.

As injustice to Northerners and blacks intensified, so did the South's demand for secession from the Union. Like anti-Northern violence, secessionist sentiment was not new in the South. In particular, the Compromise of 1850, despicable to antislavery Northerners for its fugitive slave provision, was equally vile to Southern extremists, who resented the ban against slavery in California and who called for disunion with the ardor of their Garrisonian opponents. There were temporary surges of secessionist feeling during the Frémont campaign of the 1856 and the slavery wars in Kansas.

It was not until the Harpers Ferry raid, however, that the secession movement became well organized. A core of Southern politicians—especially Edmund Ruffin of Virginia, William Lowndes Yancey of Alabama, and Robert Barnwell Rhett of South Carolina—led the way in making the case for secession. For these and other fire-eaters Harpers Ferry was a godsend. They had long called for secession, and they thought Brown's raid was exactly what was needed to push Unionist Southerners, still a vast majority, into their camp.

The secessionists manipulated the South's panic over Harpers Ferry to foster a general desire for disunion. They did so with such effectiveness that one contemporary journalist saw this John Brown–provoked secessionist impulse as the one constant of 1860:

> Early in the summer of 1860 it became evident to every dispassionate observer in the South that the country was swiftly approaching a great crisis. So dexterously had politicians managed the excitement which arose on the discovery of the plot of John Brown, that at the very beginning of the year a small and united party had been formed, having for its aim the immediate separation of the States. This party, following this well-defined object, was the only fixed thing in Southern society during the year. In the midst of all changes it was permanent.

A look at a typical fire-eater, the Virginia politician-farmer Edmund Ruffin, reveals how John Brown's raid was used to further the cause of secession. The wealthy Ruffin had connections and influence in the South. He was present at the hanging of John Brown, at many key Southern political conventions, and at the engagement at Fort Sumter, where he served in the Palmetto Guard. Ruffin wanted the South to secede and form a new nation based on slavery, an institution he considered so wonderful that he

Edmund Ruffin.

hoped whites would one day take over Africa and enslave its natives, who would then receive the blessings of Christian civilization. He wrote, "I deem enslavement to white & Christian masters, whether in or out of Africa, the only possible means for making them Christians."

When Ruffin heard on October 19, 1859, that an Abolitionist invasion had taken place at Harpers Ferry, he was delighted. For years he had been saying that Abolitionists were maliciously aggressive, but he had had little proof. Finally, proof arrived out of the blue. He wrote in his journal: "Incredible as it seemed at first naming, by rumor, it really seems now most probable that the outbreak was planned & instigated by northern abolitionists, & with the expectation of thus starting a general slave insurrection. I earnestly hope that such may be the truth of the case. Such a practical exercise of abolitionist principles is needed to stir the sluggish blood of the south."

Ruffin was overjoyed that John Brown had led the invasion of Virginia, for Brown could be presented as an Abolitionist villain of the darkest dye.

Ruffin knew of Brown's murderous career in Kansas—he discussed the Pottawatomie slayings in his journal—and he was exultant over Brown's plan to free slaves, arm them, and set them against their former masters. A large slave rebellion, Ruffin knew, was every Southerner's worst nightmare.

Henry Wise's praise of Brown's better qualities enraged Ruffin, as did the governor's criticism of Virginians for their cowardice. Ruffin knew that Wise was right: Brown was brave and the Virginians had acted weakly at Harpers Ferry. But Ruffin was concerned with image, and he wanted to publicize an image of Brown as the wicked representative of the North. It was not the South's business to praise him.

Ruffin's happiness grew as support for Brown strengthened in the North. He had previously been frustrated by the disunity of Abolitionists. Now, he wrote, "all these shades of opinion concur in one general import," as a "very general sympathy [is] intimated for the criminals, either directly or indirectly, through many of the northern states." Southerners at last had an identifiable, common foe—the "great majority of the northern people, [who] are so much the enemies of negro slavery, that they sympathise even with treason, murder, & every accompaniment of insurrection, & with the worst criminals acting therein, to overthrow slavery."

In turn, previously disunited Southerners were coming together. Ruffin noted, "Many persons, heretofore the most 'conservative,' or submissive to northern usurpations & aggressions, & clinging to the Union under all circumstances, are now saying something must be done by the south—& separation is admitted by others as the coming result." Ruffin used his social contacts to be present among the militia guarding Brown's scaffold. Although he admired Brown's courage, he was certain that the Abolitionist invader would soon be in hell.

When the execution prompted even stronger Northern sympathy for Brown, Ruffin realized that the opportunity for secession must be seized before it disappeared. Six days after the hanging, he wrote that "the conspiracy of the abolitionists, its outbreak in the invasion of Harper's Ferry, & the very general sympathy of the northern people with the murdered, afforded the best practical ground of dissolution that the South ever had— & that it ought not to be passed over. We ought to agitate & exasperate the already highly excited indignation of the south."

He did everything he could to transform Southern anger against Brown into an anti-Northern fever. He resorted to high drama. He procured a number of John Brown's notorious pikes, intended for freed slaves, and carried one of them wherever he went as a grisly advertisement of John Brown's dastardly intentions. He sent a pike to each of the governors of the slave states so that no one would forget the hostility and aggressiveness of the North toward the South.

The pike-distribution plan was carefully thought out. The day before Brown's hanging, Ruffin arranged with Colonel Alfred W. Barbour, the superintendent of the Harpers Ferry arsenal, to have fifteen pikes sent to the Washington office of Senator Clement C. Clay of Alabama for exhibition in the capital and distribution to the Southern governors. In mid-December Ruffin wrote an article for the *Richmond Enquirer* on Brown's pikes, announcing that "one shall be sent to every governor of the slave-holding states, to be placed in the legislative hall of each capitol." For each pike Ruffin composed a label that read, "Sample of the favors designed for us by our Northern Brethren." Accompanying each pike was a letter asking the governor to display the weapon prominently and permanently in the state capitol building, "there to remain, & be preserved, as abiding & impressive evidence of the fanatical hatred borne by the dominant northern party to the institutions & people of the Southern States, and of the un-scrupulous & atrocious means resorted to for the attainment of the objects sought by that party."

Ruffin's words were carefully chosen. They pushed toward generalization. John Brown's pikes represented the "fanatical hatred" harbored by the "dominant northern party" toward "the institutions & people of the Southern States." This statement, of course, was untrue. The pikes had *no* connection with *any* "northern party," dominant or otherwise. But Ruffin wanted to equate John Brown with the Republican Party and, by association, with the entire North. The pike, wreathed in secessionist rhetoric, was a vivid means of doing this.

Sending the pikes was especially important to Ruffin because of the 1860 presidential contest. Ruffin had looked forward to a Republican victory, which, he knew, would greatly increase the chances that his fellow Southerners would decide for secession. He was alarmed, however, when in the spring of 1860 Lincoln emerged as the Republican front-runner. In late May he lamented that the Chicago convention did not nominate a compelling candidate such as William Henry Seward, Benjamin Wade, or Salmon Chase "but Lincoln of Illinois, inferior in ability & reputation to all—& whom no one had mentioned before. I am sorry they did not nominate their ablest man, Seward, & so made their success more probable."

The chances for secession, Ruffin thought, were decidedly poor if a compromiser like Lincoln took office. Lincoln was not known as an Abolitionist, and he might be tolerated by the South, the place of his birth. In dismay Ruffin wrote, "I wish for the southern states to be forced to choose between secession & submission to abolition domination, though I greatly fear that, even if Lincoln shall be elected, not one state will thereupon secede."

With the prospect of secession dimmed by Lincoln's nomination, Ruffin kept reminding Southerners of John Brown. He rarely referred to Lincoln's party as the Republican Party. He called it either the "abolition party" or the "Brown-Helper party." Again, accuracy was of little importance. Ruffin merely wanted to yoke together incongruous people—the arch-Unionist Lincoln, the disunionist Abolitionists, the racist antislavery Southerner Hinton Rowan Helper, and the militant John Brown—in whatever way he could.

The John Brown pikes helped Ruffin stir up a secession frenzy. At a Southern convention held shortly after Lincoln's nomination, he put the pikes on display. He opened a box of "beautifully labeled" pikes that "were taken out, & seen by many of the southern delegates." As he showed the pikes, he reminded the delegates of the crucial need for Southern unity. He declared, "If the southern states & people can be brought together in one great & exciting contest, & separately from the northern, in this object, I trust that by next November, & the election of an abolitionist, some one or more of the Southern states will promptly secede."

By June 25, as he recorded in his journal, he had "disposed of 13 of the 15 pikes designed to be presented to the slave-holding states, placed in the charge of different gentlemen, members of Congress or delegates to the Convention, who will deliver them to the governors of the several states." He withheld the pike intended for Delaware, thinking it might not be appreciated there, and gave one pike to the city of Charleston, South Carolina, a center of secessionist feeling.

The efforts of Ruffin and other rabid disunionists to make political capital of Harpers Ferry fell on willing ears. Ruffin was justified in claiming that Brown's raid, once it began to receive wide support in the North, made even conservative Southerners think seriously about secession. Governor Wise declared that if the United States government refused to prevent such raids as Harpers Ferry, Virginia "must of necessity go out of the Union, and provide for her own defence." Three days after Brown's hanging, a Virginia newspaper noted that "the impression that a dissolution of the Union is inevitable is becoming more firmly fixed in the public mind every hour," and the South is "ripe and ready for secession."

The impetus John Brown and his eulogists gave to secession is registered in key documents leading up to the South's separation from the Union. The earliest one, the fall 1859 report of the Florida legislature's

Committee on Federal Relations, revealed the fury Brown and his endorsers had aroused. Sometimes called the first secession document, the Florida report made the same allegation Ruffin did: since John Brown was an evil emissary of the Republican Party and other Northerners, the South had little choice but to leave the Union.

The fact that the allegation was utterly baseless seems to have mattered as little to the Florida legislators as it did to Ruffin. The "theory and philosophy of the Black Republican party," the document read, had "its practical results in the bloody tragedy of Harper's Ferry." The Republicans' responsibility for the raid was revealed by the praise Brown got in the North:

> It was this [Republican] creed, and the mad prophets of its faith, that led to the invasion of Virginia by a band of robbers and murderers, and when, in expiation of their crimes, they were doomed to death by the just penalty of violated law, instead of receiving the merited execrations due the felon, they were hailed by their sympathizing friends in the North as heroes and martyrs in the holy cause of charity and philanthropy. . . .
>
> Nor does the sin and shame end here. The Christian Church has been desecrated, the House of God defiled, and the name and mission of the Saviour profaned by assimilating the blood of treason and murder to the redeeming blood of the Lamb of God.

Other Southern states followed Florida's lead in citing Northern support of John Brown as a main reason for disunion. To argue for secession Mississippi passed a resolution stating that among the crimes of Northerners was "that they have encouraged a hostile invasion of a Southern state to excite insurrection, murder, and rapine." A Georgia resolution, likewise, held that "the abolition sentiment of the Northern States . . . has prompted the armed invasion of Southern soil by stealth . . . for the diabolical purpose of inaugurating a ruthless war of the blacks against the whites . . . ; [and] has prompted large masses of Northern people openly to sympathize with the treacherous and traitorous invaders of our country." The governor of Tennessee wrote a public letter maintaining that the North has "under state patronage, . . . justified and exalted to the highest honors of admiration, the horrid murders, arsons, and rapine of the John Brown, and has canonized the felons as saints and martyrs."

It was not only proslavery secessionists who made the improbable link between the Republican Party and John Brown. Unionist Democrats did so as well. The most vocal of these, the Illinois senator Stephen Douglas, created a sensation when he made the claim on the floor of the Senate. The so-called Little Giant—the author of the Kansas-Nebraska Act, the adept debater who stood toe-to-toe with Abraham Lincoln, and the presidential aspirant—had high visibility. On January 23, 1860, he declared to his fellow senators: "I have no hesitation in expressing my firm and deliberate conviction that the Harper's Ferry crime was the natural, logical, inevitable result of the doctrines and teachings of the Republican party, as explained and enforced in their platform, their partisan presses, their pamphlets and books, and especially in the speeches of their leaders in and out of Congress." There was applause in the galleries.

As usual, Douglas pointed to the Republican leader, Seward, with his talk of an "irrepressible conflict." More important, in light of the future, he mentioned his fellow Illinoisan, Abraham Lincoln. Still smarting from Lincoln's devastating ripostes during their debates over slavery the previous year, Douglas now used a national platform to tar his opponent with complicity with the John Brown plot. Douglas quoted from Lincoln's "House Divided" speech and then offered an interpretation of it: "The declaration is that the North must combine as a sectional party, and carry on the agitation so fiercely, up to the very borders of the slaveholding States, that the master dare not sleep at night for fear that the robbers, the John Browns, will come and set his house on fire, and murder the women and children, before morning." Trying to scare his audience, Douglas asked: "Can any man say to us that although this outrage has been perpetrated at Harper's Ferry, there is no danger of its recurrence? Sir, is not the Republican party still embodied, organized, confident of success, and defiant in its pretensions? . . . The causes that produced the Harper's Ferry invasion are now in active operation."

The association between Lincoln and John Brown was repeated by others during and after the presidential race of 1860. Brown influenced the outcome of the election in an overall sense. The excitement over Harpers Ferry fractured the Democratic Party, which was now divided between the secessionist "National Democrats," who chose John C. Breckinridge of Kentucky as their candidate, and popular-sovereignty Democrats, who went with Stephen Douglas. The *Charleston Mercury* announced in April 1860: "The Democratic party, as a party, based upon principles, is dead. . . . It has not one single principle common to its members North and South." Old-time Whigs of the border states, promoting themselves as "anti-extremists," organized the Constitutional Union Party around John C. Bell of Tennessee. The Republicans created a four-way race by choosing the relatively obscure Lincoln, fearing that more controversial figures like William H. Seward or Salmon P. Chase would alienate the public.

It turned out that Lincoln won all eighteen Free States, while the slave states were divided among the other candidates. Lincoln won 40 percent of the popular vote and 180 electoral votes, as opposed to 72 electoral votes for Breckenridge, 39 for Bell, and 12 for Douglas. Lincoln tried to minimize the slavery issue, emphasizing a homestead bill and a protective tariff and using the benign slogans Vote Yourself a Farm and Free Speech, Free Home, Free Territory.

Still, his opponents did all they could to portray him as a rabid Abolitionist whose election would unleash more John Brown invasions of the South. After Lincoln was nominated, the pro-Breckinridge secessionist William L. Yancey said, "Suppose the Republican party gets into power, suppose another John Brown raid takes place"—in that case, Yancey declared, the South would soon be full of Northerners wielding pikes, revolvers, and Sharps rifles. *DeBow's Review*, calling for immediate secession in the case of a Republican victory, said of Lincoln:

> Just Heaven, upon what times have we fallen, when the seat of Washington is in danger of being occupied by this low and vulgar partisan of John Brown! Should that day arrive, is there not enough virtue in our people to shed the ignoble shackles, and proclaim themselves free?

The cries that Lincoln was a John Brown devotee swelled into a chorus. One proslavery spokesperson dubbed Lincoln "an Abolitionist; a fanatic of the John Brown type; the slave to one idea, who . . . would override laws, constitutions, and compromises of every kind." Another maintained that Lincoln got votes from "the fanatics who apotheosize John Brown." A third declared, "Our property has been stolen, our people murdered; felons and assassins have found sanctuary in the arms of the party which elected Mr. Lincoln." Even a moderate Southerner like Alexander Stephens could write to Lincoln that, though "personally, I am not your enemy," the South deeply distrusts the Republican administration as a result of "such exhibitions of madness as the John Brown raid into Virginia, which has received so much sympathy from many, and no open condemnation from any of the leading men of the present dominant party."

All such charges, of course, were false. The only people in the nation who gave "so much sympathy" to John Brown were the Transcendentalists, a small group unassociated with a political party. A good portion of the

North took an admire-the-man-but-not-the-deed position; few went beyond this tempered stance.

Lincoln, in fact, won the North by running an *anti*–John Brown campaign. In the early going, the people around him weren't sure how to deal with Brown. One adviser's worry about the effect of "Old Brown's wretched fiasco in Virginia" would have "upon the moral health of the Republican party" must have stuck with Lincoln, who never expressed enthusiasm for Brown. Shortly before Brown's execution, in a speech at Elwood, Kansas, Lincoln said he admired Brown's courage and unselfishness but stated that "no man, North or South, can approve of violence or crime." He added that the Harpers Ferry raid was both illegal and futile.

Even Brown's bravery on the scaffold did not melt Lincoln, who on the day after the hanging told a Leavenworth, Kansas, audience that "even though [Brown] agreed with us in thinking slavery wrong, that cannot excuse violence, bloodshed, and treason." Two days later Lincoln declared that he "believed the old man insane, and had yet to find the first Republican who endorsed the proposed insurrection."

Lincoln reserved his most emphatic denunciation of Brown for his most important campaign speech, his address at New York's Cooper Institute on February 27, 1860. That day Lincoln sat for portraits in the studio of Mathew Brady. When both the photographs and the speech were widely circulated, Lincoln said, "Brady and the Cooper Institute made me President."

He was hardly exaggerating. His audience of 1,500 that day included many movers and shakers, including Horace Greeley, William Cullen Bryant, and James Gordon Bennett. Lincoln made a wonderful impression—so much so that the *New York Times* called him "the greatest man since St. Paul." The speech was reprinted even in hostile papers like the *New York Herald*.

Hearers loved the speech's firmness, logic, and moderation. And on no subject was Lincoln as firm, logical, and moderate as on John Brown. Attacking those who linked the Republican Party with John Brown, he said:

> You charge that we stir up insurrections among your slaves. We deny it; and what is your proof? Harper's Ferry! John Brown!! John Brown was no Republican; and you have failed to implicate a single Republican in his Harper's Ferry enterprise. If any member of our party is guilty in that matter, you know it or you do not know it. If you do know it, you are inexcusable for not designating the man and proving the fact. If you do not know it, you are inexcusable for assert-

Abraham Lincoln before delivering his address at
the Cooper Institute. Photograph by Mathew Brady.
LIBRARY OF CONGRESS.

ing it, and especially for persisting in the assertion after you have
tried and failed to make the proof. You need not be told that persisting in a charge which one does not know to be true, is simply malicious slander.

Nor, Lincoln continued, was there any truth in those who insisted that
"our doctrines and declarations necessarily lead to such results" as Harpers
Ferry. *No* Republican doctrine supported Harpers Ferry. Republicans, he
pointed out, stood for noninterference with slavery where it currently
existed. A widespread slave insurrection could not occur in the South, he
argued. There were no means of communication that would make such a
coordinated revolt possible. Besides, there was truth in the oft-repeated
claim that some slaves had affection for their masters. As a result, no large

insurrection plot could get off the ground, since there would always be loyal slaves who would reveal the plot.

As for Harpers Ferry, Lincoln said: "John Brown's effort was peculiar. It was not a slave insurrection. It was an attempt by white men to get up a revolt among slaves, in which the slaves refused to participate. In fact, it was so absurd that the slaves, with all their ignorance, saw plainly enough it could not succeed."

In the speech that won the hearts of Northerners, then, Lincoln distanced himself from John Brown. He continued to do so throughout the campaign. In early March he told a Dover, New Hampshire, crowd, "The republicans were charged with being responsible for the John Brown raid, yet a Committee of Congress, with unlimited powers, has failed to implicate a single republican in his Harper's Ferry enterprise."

Lincoln was referring to the Senate committee, led by James M. Mason of Virginia, that had been organized in mid-December and ran an investigation of the Harpers Ferry affair from January 4 through June 14, 1860. Although Lincoln was accurate in saying that the Mason Committee did not implicate any Republicans, he failed to add that it did not implicate *anyone*, even Brown's closest supporters. The fact was, the Mason Committee merely went through the motions of an investigation, pretending to seek the truth but actually trying to put Harpers Ferry behind, so that tinderbox sectional passions would not flare into war.

After the Harpers Ferry raid Washington seemed on the verge of an explosion. For years an occasional weapon had been seen in the hands of a congressman, but now weapons were everywhere. As Senator James H. Hammond remarked, in both chambers of Congress "the only persons who do not have a revolver and a knife are those who have two revolvers." One Louisiana congressman threatened to bring a double-barreled shotgun into the House chamber. In the galleries, supporters of both sides were also heavily armed.

In this flammable atmosphere the Mason Committee knew it had to handle the Harpers Ferry matter with kid gloves. It questioned leading Republicans—William H. Seward, Joshua Giddings, John Andrew, Henry Wilson, and others—but quickly accepted their denials of complicity in the raid. It called several people Brown had known in Kansas, including Charles Robinson and Augustus Wattles, but skirted the volatile issue of Pottawatomie while concentrating on Brown's other activities there.

The committee treated the members of the Secret Six with telling laxity. Thomas Wentworth Higginson, Brown's most committed and knowledgeable supporter, was, incredibly, not called at all. Theodore Parker, dying of tuberculosis in Italy, was not asked to testify in writing. Gerrit Smith, although he had recovered his sanity, was excused from appearing by a doctor's note. To make sure he would not be implicated, Smith had his son-in-law, Charles D. Miller, publish a detailed denial of Smith's knowledge of the raid. Miller wrote, "No one feels deeper sorrow than does Mr. Smith, that his precious, nay idolized friend, was led into the mistake of shedding blood in his last attempt to get the slaves free."

The committee swallowed such lies-not only from Smith but also from the two Secret Six members who testified under oath, Howe and Stearns. Howe, who testified he had known nothing about the raid beforehand, later said of his interrogators, "In my case they were very unskilful and failed to get out of me some information which they might have been glad to have." Stearns testified that he had contributed weapons to Brown only for use in Kansas. Although he said he had some vague knowledge of Brown's designs elsewhere, he certainly had no suspicion that Harpers Ferry was a target.

Stearns even got off a joke at the expense of the committee's leader, James Mason. One day after a session Stearns encountered Mason while leaving the Senate. Mason asked if Stearns didn't feel guilty for sending weapons "to shoot our innocent people" in Kansas. When Stearns replied that he did so in retaliation for Southern aggressions, Mason remarked that Satan would question Stearns hard about this matter. Stearns shot back, "Before that time comes . . . he will have about two hundred years of Slavery to investigate, and before he gets through will say 'We have had enough of this business, better let the rest go.' " Mason laughed in spite of himself.

Another comedy, with serious overtones, surrounded the committee's effort to bring the final Secret Six member, Franklin B. Sanborn, to Washington to testify. When Sanborn refused the Senate's summons, an attempt was made to arrest him in Concord.

The effort failed, and, ironically, generated a symbolic victory for opponents of the committee. The Senate's sergeant-at-arms, Dunning R. McNair, delegated a deputy U.S. marshal, Silas Carleton, to arrest Sanborn and bring him to Washington. On the night of April 3, Carleton and three thugs spied on Sanborn from a barn near his house. Around 9 p.m., Carleton and his henchmen went to Sanborn's door, pretending to deliver a letter. When Sanborn appeared, the four men announced that he was under arrest. They handcuffed him and dragged him to a waiting carriage. The six-foot-four-inch Sanborn put up a lively struggle while his sister Sarah whipped the marshal's horses, which reared and jerked the carriage, preventing Sanborn's forced entry. A local blacksmith, hearing cries of murder, dispatched three schoolgirls who boarded with him to go through Concord ringing doorbells and spreading the alarm. Soon the whole town was aroused. Emerson arrived on the scene along with a judge who brought a writ of habeas corpus. The Concordites overwhelmed the four men, forcing them to unlock Sanborn's handcuffs and jeering at them as they ran off.

The next day Sanborn was brought before Chief Justice Lemuel Shaw in Boston. In a courthouse packed with antislavery spectators, including Walt Whitman and Wendell Phillips, Shaw dismissed the case by ruling that a sergeant-at-arms could not delegate authority to a deputy to make an arrest. Sanborn returned to Concord a hero. Thirteen guns were fired in his honor, and bells were rung. A rally was held in which Emerson, Higginson, and Thoreau praised Sanborn as a principled individual who stood in opposition to a corrupt federal government.

It was no accident that Transcendentalists took the lead in this episode, for they had remained active in the John Brown cause after the December 2 service Thoreau had organized. After Brown's execution, Mary Stearns pressed Emerson to write a life of John Brown. He felt he lacked the information to do so; the task fell to Brown's friend James Redpath, whose hagiographic book *The Public Life of Capt. John Brown* appeared in April 1860. Besides, Emerson was overwhelmed by the strong reactions, positive and negative, to his "gallows glorious" remark. He confided to Alcott, "We have had enough of this dreary business."

But Emerson continued supporting Brown. On January 6 he gave a speech on Brown at Salem that was even more rapturous than his previous ones. Emerson began by noting again Brown's uncanny power with words, saying that "his speeches and letters" reveal that he is a more powerful writer than "the best orators who have added their praise to his fame." Emerson wanted to suggest that what Brown stood for was as true as anything in the universe, like physical laws. When did Brown's plan to attack slavery originate? Emerson asserted, "I am inclined to accept his own account of the matter at Charlestown, . . . when he said, 'This was all settled millions of years before the world was made.' " For Emerson, this Calvinistic assertion of predestination was a metaphor for the eternal rightness of Brown's cause.

Brown's skills as a herdsman and farmer, Emerson suggested, revealed his closeness to nature. Was it true, as some politicians said, that few people in America felt sympathy for John Brown? "It would be far safer and nearer the truth to say that all people, in proportion to their sensibility and self-respect, sympathize with him. For it is impossible to see courage, and disinterestedness, and the love that casts out fear, without sympathy."

Sympathy for Brown, continued Emerson, was not only planted in right-minded people. It was a part of nature itself. Complaints about Abolitionism are pointless. "As well complain of gravity, or the ebb of the tide. Who makes the Abolitionist? The Slaveholder." The truth was crystal clear. Slavery was wrong. Abolitionism was right. There was no debate, no middle ground. "For the arch-Abolitionist, older than Brown, and older than the Shenandoah Mountains, is Love, whose other name is Justice, which was before Alfred, before Lycurgus, before Slavery, and will be after it."

Emerson and Thoreau did more than praise Brown. They contributed to his plot by aiding in the escape of Francis Merriam, who had been put on a train headed north in southern Pennsylvania by Owen Brown in November. Merriam had made it to Boston but, in a distracted state, missed a train to Canada and instead hopped a local one to Concord. There, Frank Sanborn, fearful of being caught as a Brown accomplice, turned Merriam over to Emerson and Thoreau. Emerson willingly lent his horse, Dolly, for the purpose of taking Merriam to the train in South Acton. Thoreau hitched Dolly to a carriage and drove Merriam to the station. Along the way, Merriam, in a crazed state, jumped out of the carriage in an attempt to run back to Concord to confer with Emerson. Thoreau forced Merriam back into the carriage and got him to the train, which took him to Canada.

Thoreau was not done with his efforts for Brown. He wrote another speech, "The Last Days of John Brown," which he delivered in Concord and then sent to be read by Richard Hinton at a July 4, 1860, service by Brown's grave in North Elba.

Evidently responding to the sectional squabbling over Brown in the presidential contest, Thoreau presented Brown as the ideal person who could bring together all America—indeed all humankind—if understood rightly. Thoreau recalled thinking before Brown's execution that "the man this country was about to hang appeared the greatest and best in it." Brown was the finest preacher: "How could they [ordinary clergymen] fail to recognize him, by far the greatest preacher of them all, with the Bible in his life and in his acts, the embodiment of principle, who actually carried out the golden rule?" Brown was the ultimate Transcendentalist. Witnessing the heroism of his final days, Thoreau said, "We . . . forgot human laws, and did homage to an idea. The North, I mean the living North, was suddenly all transcendental. It went behind the human law, it went behind the apparent failure, and recognized eternal justice and glory."

Perhaps "the living North" appreciated Brown, but Thoreau knew well enough that not all the North was living, in his sense of the word. There were Democrats: "The man who does not recognize in Brown's words a wisdom and nobleness, and therefore an authority, superior to our laws, is a modern Democrat. This is the test by which to discover him." Then there were those who regarded Brown as "an ordinary felon." "They have either much flesh, or much office," Thoreau intoned, "or much coarseness of some kind. They are not ethereal natures in any sense. The dark qualities predominate in them." A number, he quipped, "are decidedly pachyderma-tous." "How can a man behold the light who has no answering light?" he asked. "Show me a man who feels bitterly toward John Brown, and let me hear what noble verse he can repeat. He'll be as dumb as if his lips were stone."

It was just as well, Thoreau concluded, that Brown was not rescued, for then he would have taken up again a material sword, when he won his greatest victories with the sword of the spirit. Brown was still wielding this potent weapon: "Now he has not laid aside the sword of the spirit, for he is pure spirit himself, and his sword is pure spirit also." Brown did not die: "I meet him at every turn. He is more alive than ever he was. He has earned immortality. He is not confined to North Elba nor to Kansas. He is no longer working in secret. He works in public, and in the clearest light that shines on this land."

The clearest light in the land. This was wishful thinking. It was very well for Thoreau to offer his idealistic interpretation and to say that those who disliked Brown were "decidedly pachydermatous." But Thoreau was minimizing the political realities around him. John Brown *was* "more alive than ever," one *did* "meet him at every turn"—but he was alive both as a vil-lain and as a saint, driving a wedge into the nation and opening the fissure between the South and the North.

Thoreau's comments were like beautiful clouds floating above the gritty terrain of American life. While the Transcendentalists philosophized about John Brown, a profoundly divided America grappled over him at ground level. Brown lived, but he lived in everyday things: in angry letters, in con-tentious speeches, in headlines, and, as will be seen, in a wealth of popular writing and music.

He also lived in events. Between the Harpers Ferry raid in October 1859 and the firing on Fort Sumter in April 1861, Southern newspapers were filled with reports of slave revolts. Some of the stories were factual, some were based on rumor, and nearly all were amplified by the panic that had seized the Southern states. The peak periods of actual (as opposed to rumored) insurrections appear to have been from December 1859 to April 1860, from July through September 1860, and from mid-November 1860 to early 1861. Often the revolts were described as repeats of Harpers Ferry.

Just after the election of Lincoln in November, a Georgia politician made a typical declaration: "Take up your daily papers and see the reports of insurrections in every direction. Hear the telegram read which announces another John Brown raid."

The most serious insurrection occurred in Texas in July 1860. The exact nature and extent of the revolt may never be known, since news reports were, as usual, distorted by the post–Harpers Ferry hysteria. By a conservative estimate, the incident resulted in the deaths of ten whites and sixty-five blacks.

What is known is that in early July 1860 huge fires broke out in a number of neighboring Texas towns, including Dallas, Denton, and Pilot Point. It seems probable that at least some of the fires were set by rebellious blacks. Beyond this, nothing is certain except that a massive witch hunt followed. Blacks were rounded up and whipped for information. As in Salem in 1692, those who "confessed" were let go, while those who remained silent were killed, either by hanging or by being burned alive.

A number of blacks confessed after being tortured. The story they told was that a cadre of Northern whites had infiltrated Texas with the aim of inciting an enormous slave revolt that would lead to the liberation of all blacks in the state. The whites secretly distributed bowie knives and pistols among slaves. Black cooks were supplied with barrels of strychnine. The alleged plan was to terrorize the state by setting off fires and then on election day in early August to rise up in a coordinated rebellion. The armed slaves would butcher their masters and neighbors. Young white women would be kept as concubines for the liberated blacks. The cooks would use their strychnine to poison the food of the family they worked for. They would also pour poison into wells and public water systems. The end result would be either the toppling of slavery in Texas or the escape of freed blacks, along with their white leaders, to Mexico or elsewhere. In response to the story, many blacks and some suspicious whites were lynched.

True or not, the plot was played up in the Southern press, which was quick to label the insurrection an Abolitionist scheme inspired by John Brown. Many papers followed the lead of the *Savannah Republican*, which called it a "re-enactment of the John Brown affair." A reporter for a Waynesboro, Georgia, paper went so far as to claim, on no evidence, that Brown-like pikes were among the weapons given to the slaves. Southerners must not stand by, the journalist insisted, while their enemies "murdered by poison or abolition pikes and spears, their wives and children, and forced their fair daughters into the embrace of buck Negroes for wives."

The most elaborate connection between Harpers Ferry and the Texas troubles was made in a widely reported speech, "The Doom of Slavery in the Union," by John Townsend, a South Carolina state senator. Townsend claimed that John Brown had planned the Texas insurrection with the help of Northern Republicans and that the recently nominated Lincoln not only endorsed the plot but would use federal troops to make it succeed if he were elected.

Townsend reported that some months before Harpers Ferry, Brown and John Kagi wrote a "Plan for the Abolition of Slavery" to form associations of people who would help slaves rise up against their owners at any moment, and "the late insurrection in Texas was a development of this improved scheme of diabolical ingenuity, as well as an exemplification of the intense hatred which is cherished by the Abolitionists against the Southern slaveholder." Townsend continued: "By comparing the occurrences in Texas, until the plot was discovered and arrested, with these plans concocted by John Brown, we will be at no loss to understand the mode in which the Giddings and Garrisonian wing of the party intend, in future, to carry on this warfare." The plan was for the blacks to burn all the towns, rape the young women, destroy the farms, and "then on election day they were to be headed by John Browns, and march South for Houston and Galveston city, where they would all unite, and after pillaging and burning those two cities, the negroes were promised by these devils incarnate, that they would have in readiness a number of vessels, and would take them forthwith to Mexico, where they would be free."

The same "Abolition Aid Societies" that funded Brown and promoted Lincoln, said Townsend, were behind the Texas troubles. Many Southerners, he wrote, "believe that Lincoln is the head and representative of this Abolition Society, which sent John Brown to Virginia, and which is now giving us so much trouble here; and I believe I am not in the dark when I say that if Lincoln is elected, it will take five hundred thousand troops to inaugurate him President of the United States."

Townsend's equation of Brown, Giddings, Garrison, so-called Abolition Aid Societies, Lincoln, and the Texas plot was false in every respect. It was so wild that it wouldn't even work as historical fiction. But it showed how far the South's paranoia over John Brown could go.

Secessionists, predictably, reveled in reports of Abolition conspiracies in Texas, Alabama, and elsewhere. Edmund Ruffin wrote that he was happy to learn "from a northern correspondent in Texas, a statement of the late atrocities attempted & planned by northern abolitionists, in Texas." He was glad that "sundry other of the northern incendiary agents (or those so charged by the negroes, or by circumstances,) have been hung, in Texas &

in Alabama, which is the best result." He hoped that such an "Abolitionist" slave insurrection would happen in Georgia, which he found sluggish on secession and in need of provocation to take action with the other Southern states. He could barely find words to express his glee over the Texas plots, writing, "If but one-tenth of these plots & attempts be true, added to the attempt made through John Brown, it would be alone sufficient for a separation of the Union, to exclude northern emissaries & incendiaries from southern territory."

By early October 1860, with the election of Lincoln looming as a real possibility, much of the South was prepared to follow secessionists like Ruffin. Just a year earlier, this would not have been true. Unionism had still been strong then. The events of October 16–18, 1859, had caused a significant change in the Southern mood. On October 11, 1860, the *Charleston Mercury* spoke for much of the South when it connected John Brown, Texas, and the forthcoming Lincoln administration:

> If, in our present position of power and unitedness, we have the raid of John Brown—and twenty towns burned down in Texas in one year, by abolitionists—what will be the measures of insurrection and incendiarism, which must follow our notorious and abject prostration to Abolition rule at Washington, with all the patronage of the Federal Government, and Union organizations in the South to support it?

To many Southerners, there was only one alternative to the insurrections that must accompany Lincoln's ascendancy to power: separation from the Union. Few grasped what secession would entail. Secessionists like Ruffin assumed that separation could be achieved peacefully, as did their archrivals in the North, the Garrisonian disunionists. To be sure, there was increased activity among state militia companies, but this was regarded as a defense against further Abolitionist aggression, not as preparation for all-out war.

Unknown to most, something ominous was happening in the federal arsenals: weapons were being moved south. The head of the United States War Department, the Virginian John B. Floyd, who had received the letter of warning about Harpers Ferry two months before it occurred, recognized the relative military weakness of the South. Beginning in the late fall of 1859, he transferred weapons from arsenals in the North to ones in South Carolina, North Carolina, Alabama, Georgia, and Louisiana. In all, nearly 115,000 rifles and muskets were transported.

Evidently, Floyd intuited what Brown had stated: the slavery issue would be settled only by blood. If it was going to come to a fight, Floyd wanted the South to be prepared.

The South would be prepared, but so would the North. If John Brown had driven the South to a secessionist fury, he had at the same time carried the North toward unified action against slavery.

17

The Prophet

Would the Civil War have occurred had John Brown not been in the picture? Was war necessary, as Brown thought it was? Would the North have won the war if it did not have John Brown's example to follow? What would have happened to long-term relations between blacks and whites had Brown not existed?

In short, how would America have been different had this homegrown terrorist never been born?

These questions lead us to counterfactual history—how things *might have been* rather than how they were. Counterfactual history, or informed guesswork, is a useful exercise. It reminds us, among other things, how history resembles Frank Capra's film *It's a Wonderful Life*, in which an individual changes the world around him simply by existing. Emerson argues that institutions and eras are the lengthened shadows of a few individuals, such as Caesar, Christ, and so on. If these people had not lived, the events they set in motion would not have occurred, and the world would be a very different place. Can John Brown be called one of these influential individuals?

I suggest that he can—but largely because the contingency of his existence overlapped with specific social and cultural conditions that shaped reactions to him. Some of his influence came from him alone, some of it from responses to him, and some of it from chance.

What would have happened had he been killed during the raid? He would not have won the admiration of many Americans who witnessed his conduct during his final days. Even his survival of the raid did not guarantee he would have influence. Had the Transcendentalists not opened up the possibility of a positive response to him, he might have been lost in a tide of negative opinion.

Had Brown not become a visible figure, he would not have been seized upon by politicians of both sections, and there might not have been the fracturing of the Democratic Party that made possible the election of Lincoln. Had fire-eaters like Ruffin and Yancey not worked hard to keep Brown's controversial memory alive in the South, perhaps secession would not have occurred when it did. And had secession not happened, most likely the war would have been delayed.

Delayed, but, in my view, not avoided. I agree with John Brown on this point. War was needed to rid the nation of slavery.

Southern slavery was strengthening, not weakening, when Brown made his attack. The "needless war" doctrine of some historians, which holds that slavery would have soon disappeared anyway, is contradicted by several phenomena that occurred in the 1850s.

As difficult as it is for us to realize today, Southerners had come to regard slavery as a highly beneficial—indeed, essential—institution. In this sense they were different from previous generations of Southerners, who had considered slavery a useful but unfortunate system.

Jefferson had spoken for many earlier slaveholders when he advocated the eventual emancipation of slaves. In 1783 he had drafted a model constitution by which all children born to enslaved blacks after 1800 would be trained in crafts and then liberated when they reached adulthood, to be later deported. Although nothing came of the proposal, another one was made in 1796 by St. George Tucker, also a Southerner, who in *A Dissertation on Slavery* endorsed gradual abolition followed by the integration of freed blacks into white society, though without the rights to property or political participation. As late as 1831, plans for abolition were discussed in the Virginia legislature. Until then, most plans for abolition had come from slaveholders.

The shift in attitude came in the 1840s, when John Calhoun called slavery "instead of an evil, a good—a positive good," because it served whites while it civilized blacks. Calhoun made an argument that was often repeated: "Never before has the black race of central Africa, from the dawn of history to the present day, attained a condition so civilized and so improved, not only physically, but morally and intellectually."

Southerners now rationalized that blacks *needed* to be enslaved for their own good. One writer insisted that blacks were loyal and affectionate, and "they are also the most helpless [people]: and no calamity can befall them greater than the loss of that protection they enjoy under this patriarchal system." Jefferson Davis, the president of the Confederacy, explained in his opening address to the Confederate Congress that slavery had improved blacks immeasurably: "In moral and social condition they had been elevated

from brutal savages into docile, intelligent, and civilized agricultural labor-
ers, and supplied not only with bodily comforts but with careful religious
instruction. Under the supervision of a superior race their labor had been
so directed as not only to allow a gradual and marked amelioration of their
own condition, but to convert hundreds of thousands of square miles of
wilderness into cultivated lands covered with a prosperous people."

The supposed benefits of slavery were most fully described by Alexander H. Stephens, the Confederacy's vice president, in his famous "Corner-
stone Speech" of 1861. Slavery, Stephens affirmed, was one of the most
wonderful institutions ever conceived. The main difference between America's founders and today's Southerners, declared Stephens, is that the former, even when they were slave-owners, thought slavery was "wrong in
principle, socially, morally, and politically," and that "the institution would
be evanescent and pass away." Stephens challenged the founders unequivocally: "Those ideas were fundamentally wrong. They rested upon the
assumption of the equality of the races. This was an error. . . . Our new government [of the Confederacy] is founded upon exactly the opposite idea; its
foundations are laid, its corner-stone rests on the great truth, that the
Negro is not equal to the white man; that slavery—subordination to the
superior race—is his natural and normal condition." The Confederacy rep-
resents the acme of human history because it rests on this "divine" doctrine
of racial inequality. "This, our new government, is the first, in the history of
the world, based upon this great physical, philosophical, and moral truth."

A signal of the South's ever-strengthening devotion to slavery was its
call for a renewal of the international slave trade, which had been abolished
in 1808. In 1859, Alexander Stephens said, "It is useless to wage war about
more abstract rights, or to quarrel and accuse each other of unsoundness,
unless we get more Africans. . . . Negro slavery is but in its infancy."
DeBow's Review argued that "the law of Congress prohibiting the slave-
trade is palpably unconstitutional," and called for "the renewal of the
African slave trade, to fill up that vacuum in our population which will be
filled up by abolitionists if not by Negroes."

Southerners believed that they were doing Africans a favor by bringing
them to America to be enslaved. As a Georgia politician told a Democratic
convention, the slave-trader "goes to Africa and brings a heathen and
worthless man here and makes him a useful man, Christianizes him and
sends him and his posterity down the stream of time to join the blessings of
civilization." William Yowndes Yancey asserted, "I insist that *there should be
no more discrimination by law against the Slave-trade than against the Nutmeg-
trade of New England.*"

Actually, the slave trade *was* in full, illicit operation by the late 1850s. As historian Emerson David Fite has found, in 1859 between 35,000 and 40,000 Africans were shipped to Havana, the world largest slave market, for distribution in the Americas. Cargoes of blacks were landed in Florida, Georgia, South Carolina, and Texas. Despite the congressional prohibition of the slave trade and the threat of the death penalty for pursuing it, Fite notes that "the traffic was flourishing with impunity, and in the whole history of the country not one man had been executed for breaking the law."

The *Anglo-African Magazine* complained, "The re-opening of the African slave-trade is *un fait accompli;* it only remains for Congress to legalize it by rescinding all prohibitory laws, and abrogating the treaties entered into for its suppression."

Not only was the slave trade coming back, but slavery had become more profitable. Cotton production and cotton exports in the South nearly doubled during the 1850s. The value of field hands, which had averaged between $800 and $1,200 in 1850, reached $2,200 to $2,500 by 1860, a 100 percent leap.

The fact that slavery was becoming stronger suggests that it was far from disappearing on its own. In 1858, Abraham Lincoln suggested it would take a hundred years for slavery to vanish. Actually, forty or fifty years is a more likely estimate. Economics probably would have doomed slavery after the turn of the century. Slavery in America was far better adapted to an agrarian economy than to an industrial one. With industrialization and urbanization, slavery would have not made economic sense, even in the South, much beyond 1900.

But the proslavery ideology in the South not only would have survived but would have strengthened with the rise of "ethnographic science" in the 1860s and '70s. This specious discipline, which fed into eugenics, allegedly confirmed the inferiority of blacks and therefore would have bolstered the racism underlying slavery.

The South's ever-stronger faith in slavery would have inevitably come into conflict with the North's effort to stop its spread. Almost certainly, before the four or five decades had passed for slavery to disappear on its own, a war between the sections would have taken place. The later in the century the war came, the worse it would have been. Rising population would mean more troops—and thus more casualties—on both sides. Weapons technology would have improved sufficiently to wreak more havoc. At the same time, medicine would not have advanced enough to prevent most of the diseases that killed thousands in the Civil War.

In other words, as horrible a bloodletting as the Civil War was, a later war would have been even more devastating. Instead of some 620,000 deaths, there may have been a million or more. If the war had to come— and everything pointed to its inevitability—it was better that it came in 1861 than in, say, 1881.

One could argue that the Civil War was a "good" war in other ways, too. The 1850s had witnessed, in addition to growing tensions over slavery, rampant governmental corruption as well as widening class divisions and increasing violence on the streets of American cities. In this atmosphere, war served to purify the atmosphere like a violent thunderstorm. Walt Whitman recalled having been depressed about the state of the nation in the late 1850s, remarking that the war "saved" him and saved America by arousing idealism and social commitment. Although as a nurse in the war hospitals he witnessed gore and suffering as vividly as anyone, he would spend much of the rest of his life looking back at the war, which became an ever-fresh spring of inspiration for him.

Most important, the earlier America could rid itself of slavery, the better. The election of Lincoln alone did not ensure that war would break out. Lincoln was temperamentally averse to war. In 1857 he declared that to abolish slavery "not *bloody bullets*, but *peaceful ballots* only, are necessary," and the next year, in his debate with Douglas, he said, "There will be no war, no violence." Although he loathed slavery, he was not about to jeopardize the Union by provoking a war over it. The reason he supported the Fugitive Slave Act and proposed a constitutional amendment guaranteeing the preservation of slavery where it existed was that he wanted to strike a compromise with the South. He was, above all, a Unionist.

As such, he represented most Americans. Disunionist factions were small in both the North and the South. Not only did the arch-Unionist Lincoln win 40 percent of the national vote, but his rival Stephen Douglas, also an ardent Unionist, did well also. Although Douglas won only one state, Missouri, he was second among the four candidates in the popular vote, winning 30 percent. In other words, more than two-thirds of American voters wanted to preserve the Union. The only disunionist candidate, Breckinridge, received just over 18 percent. As one contemporary journalist noted, "The disunion movement has been set on foot by a comparatively small number of men in the Southern states," adding that Calhoun had pushed hard for secession but "his doctrines found no lodgment in the popular mind."

Disunionism, then, was relatively weak. It was only through a mighty push by fire-eaters that the South could be persuaded to secede in 1860. And their argument about the wicked aggressiveness of Northern Abolitionists would have carried little weight if John Brown had not attacked Harpers Ferry.

In our counterfactual picture, Brown emerges as a positive agent for change, because he forced a war that would have come anyway but could only have been worse than it was. Another lucky contingency was the presence of Lincoln on the national scene. Had his election, which partly resulted from the turmoil over John Brown, not happened, a lesser individual would have taken office. Lincoln had a rare combination of qualities: charity, discernment, humor, flexibility, and firmness. Had someone without these qualities, such as the wishy-washy Douglas or the timid Seward, been in control of the country when the South seceded, one could have predicted an abysmal result. Even with Lincoln in command, the South came close to winning the war. A President Douglas, advocating popular sovereignty, would have permitted the spread of slavery, which would have strengthened the South and perhaps set the stage for its victory in war.

Enough guesswork. As it happened, John Brown lived, and he influenced the course of American history because of the way he was received. We have seen that after an onslaught of negativism Brown was retrieved by a few admirers, revived to middling status by much of the North, and demonized by the South, which used him for its own political purposes. But that is only part of the story of his reception and influence.

As Brown gained celebrity during his trial and imprisonment, he became a figure of popular culture. During his six weeks in the Charles Town jail, "hundreds of persons," in his words, requested his autograph, but he refused them all, explaining that answering the huge demand would "deprive him of all the time that remained to him on earth." Harpers Ferry, meanwhile, became a tourist attraction. Rail passengers flocked there to gawk at the bullet-ridden engine house and to buy relics of the raid. Especially salable were pikes left over from the weapons cache at the Kennedy farm. Since the real pikes did not last long, a local entrepreneur produced fake ones that sold for as much as $2 to $3.

After Brown was executed, a syndicate reportedly bought planks of his scaffold for $900 and sold pieces of it to relic-hunters. Hucksters were soon selling worthless junk at a healthy profit. As one paper said, "One is led to suspect that there were as many John Brown gibbets for sale to a gullible public as specimens of Mayflower furniture."

Everything related to Brown was of interest. When his body lay in New York for two days on its route north, curiosity-seekers scrambled for items from the coffin, including pieces of the hanging rope, coffin screws, and a percussion cap. In the months after the hanging, pictures of Brown sold by the thousands, as did pamphlets of his prison letters. Lithographs of Brown were ubiquitous. A Philadelphia newspaper offered its subscribers a free color poster showing five key scenes of Brown's life. Even the association between Brown and Christ was commercialized; a traveler in the North noted in his diary, "In New England parlors a statuette of John Brown may be found as a pendant to the likeness of our Saviour."

Brown's appeal was lasting. James Redpath's *Public Life of Capt. John Brown* enjoyed a lively sale when it appeared in the spring of 1860, and his edited collection of eulogies of Brown, *Echoes of Harpers Ferry*, also sold well. During the war a John Brown pictorial envelope was issued, with Brown's portrait and a paraphrase of one of his statements: "I die for the inalienable right of mankind to freedom, whatever hue the skin may be."

After the war came the inevitable John Brown Cigar, in a box picturing a saintly looking John Brown framed by liberated blacks on one side and black slaves being whipped by an overseer on the other. In 1892 the Harpers Ferry engine house was dismantled, shipped to Chicago, and reconstructed for exhibition at the World's Columbian Exhibition, with 50 cents charged for admission and $1 for a memorial picture of Brown. The project was treated as a business venture: the John Brown Fort Museum Company was formed with a capital stock of $150,000 with the expectation, according to the *New York Times*, of "great possibilities in the way of earnings."

John Brown inspired an avalanche of literature and music. No one in American history—not even Washington or Lincoln—was recognized as much in drama, verse, and song as was Brown. Most of this expression was eulogistic. One piece, the war song "John Brown's Body," was unique in American cultural history because of the countless transformations and adaptations it went through. When Emerson said in 1865 that the name and fame of John Brown permeated the Civil War from start to finish, he doubtless had in mind the Brown-inspired music that was on the lips of tens of thousands of Union troops as they marched to battle.

In literature the antebellum period is known as the American Renaissance because of the extraordinary richness of the writings of Emerson, Thoreau, Hawthorne, Melville, Whitman, and Dickinson, among others. We have seen how John Brown affected two writers, Emerson and Thoreau. Although both had opposed slavery in the 1850s, it was not until they encountered Brown that their feelings about the slavery issue crystallized in sharp focus on an Abolitionist they believed could redeem America. Brown was the Cromwellian rebel against corrupt institutions they wanted to be. He did what they theorized about. They praised him, they promoted him, and when the war came, they continued to advance his principles.

Emerson, in particular, filled his journals with enthusiastic comments about the war, which, unlike most Northerners, he saw as a war for emancipation from the start. Long before Lincoln, Emerson wanted the war to free enslaved blacks, who, he hoped, would be awarded full rights as American citizens. Also before Lincoln, he called for the use of African American troops. Anticipating the stance of the postwar Radical Republicans, Emerson wanted to punish Southerners by confiscating their property.

For Emerson there was a refreshing lack of ambiguity about the war. The North was right; the South was wrong. Slavery must go, at any cost. The philosophical conundrums that had entangled Emerson in earlier works like "Circles" and "Experience" were replaced by certainty. The war, he wrote, "is a potent alternative, tonic, magnetiser, reinforces manly power a hundred & a thousand times." He continued, "War ennobles the Country; searches it; fires it; acquaints it with its resources; turns it away from alliances, vain hopes, & theatric attitudes . . . ; systematizes everything. We began the war in vast confusion; when we end it, all will be in system."

Although Melville was never as sure as Emerson was about either John Brown or the war, he regarded Harpers Ferry as a crucial historical event. In his story of 1855, "Benito Cereno," Melville had dealt with some of the issues that were important to Brown: slave revolts, racism, and black-white relations. The story dramatized an idea that fired John Brown: beneath the exterior of the apparently happy, loyal slave lurked the violent rebel. The main black character, Babo, appears through much of the story to be the affectionate slave who cares for his master. By the end he turns out to have been the ringleader of a slave revolt that toppled slavery on his ship. Melville probed the phenomenon of Nat Turner lurking within Sambo, to use Eugene Genovese's image. John Brown explored a similar possibility at Harpers Ferry, where he expected slaves to break out in violent revolt.

Small wonder that Melville was struck by John Brown. It is significant that Melville's career shifted notably in the late 1850s, just when he and the nation witnessed Brown's raid on Virginia. Eight years earlier, in *Moby-Dick*, Melville had portrayed Captain Ahab, who prefigured John Brown in that he was on a mad, heroic, impossible mission against an overwhelming enemy. Since then Melville had wandered through the ambiguities of *Pierre* and *The Confidence-Man*.

Never again, after that, would he write works as thematically murky as these novels. If John Brown and the war brought clarity to Thoreau and Emerson, they brought a kind of solidity and moral certainty to Melville, at least momentarily. In the six years after Brown's death, Melville wrote poems about the thing Brown cared about most: the struggle between the North and the South over slavery. When he collected his war poems as *Battle-Pieces*, he placed John Brown first in the volume just as he had been first in the war. Here is Melville's introductory poem, "The Portent":

> *Hanging from the beam,*
>   *Slowly swaying (such is the law),*
>   *Gaunt the shadow on your green,*
>   *Shenandoah!*
> *The cut is on the crown*
>   *(Lo, John Brown),*
> *And the stabs shall heal no more.*
>
> *Hidden in the cap*
>   *Is the anguish none can draw;*
> *So your future veils its face,*
>   *Shenandoah!*
> *But the streaming beard is shown*
>   *(Weird John Brown),*
> *The meteor of the war.*

Here was Melvillian mystery, but it was now concentrated on an actual person who had shaped the course of recent events. Melville's creative energies funneled through John Brown into the war, just as Emerson's had, albeit differently. John Brown was, in his own way, as evocative to Melville as Ahab had been. Unjustly executed for trying to do right, Brown was a symbol of the whole complex era: "*Slowly swaying (such is the law)*." Brown could be described only indirectly, through metonymies: he was a gaunt shadow, a wounded head, a streaming beard. And the metonymies pointed in several directions. The "*cut on the crown*" was, literally, Brown's head wound—perhaps Melville borrowed the image from an Edmund Clarence Stedman poem in which Brown receives "a cut on his brave old crown"— and, figuratively, a Christ image (the crown of thorns) as well as an omen of the bloody violence soon to overtake the nation. Similarly, the stabs that "*shall heal no more*" were Brown's saber gashes on his body, Christ's spear wound in the side, and the gory war to come. The "*anguish none can draw*" under the cap was not only John Brown's Christ-like suffering as he was hanged with the hood on his head but also the unknown miseries the nation was about to experience.

Brown was *"Weird John Brown"* in that he was larger than life, unknowable in his odd grandeur. This towering figure was *"the meteor of the war,"* because he flashed over the American landscape as an omen of the national conflict. Melville's special contribution in *Battle-Pieces* was to appreciate both sides of this conflict, to limn suffering and triumph among both Northerners and Southerners with sympathy. John Brown's values remained for him a measure of moral rectitude. Even when he praised Confederates, as in his poems on Stonewall Jackson, he tried to recognize their heroism by using John Brown as a touchstone of sincerity:

> *Stonewall!*
> *Earnest in error, as we feel;*
> *True to the thing he deemed was due,*
> *True as John Brown or steel.*

When Melville resumed writing fiction some thirty years later, in his unfinished novella *Billy Budd*, he still seemed to have Brown-related issues on his mind. The story of a well-intentioned man who lashes out at evil through impulsive violence is reminiscent of Brown, as are some particulars. When the wicked Claggart is killed by Billy's punch, Captain Vere exclaims, "Struck dead by the Angel of God; yet the Angel must hang!"— an image that recalls the irony of the pious, God-inspired Brown committing murder and hanging for it. Captain Vere's unusual nickname, "Starry Vere," recalls Dr. John Starry, the Virginian who first spread the news of Brown's raid. Billy is surrounded by Christ imagery, as Brown had been. Billy befriends his jailer and addresses him warmly at his execution, as did Brown. When after Billy is hanged spectators take pieces of his yardarm as though they were pieces of the cross, we think of those who took pieces of Brown's scaffold as though they were holy relics. Another similarity lies in the relative stillness of the two hanging bodies. Melville tells us that Billy barely has a spasm when he is hanged, just as Brown's body moved little.

Why was Melville still preoccupied with the hero of Harpers Ferry in the 1890s, long after Brown's death? Melville was caught up in cultural ironies that had deepened over time. Brown had died for the virtuous cause of emancipation, but with the collapse of Reconstruction in 1876, American blacks entered a long period of segregation and persecution. Brown, meanwhile, reached the nadir of his reputation in the 1880s, when a number of historians portrayed him as a bloody criminal. By the 1890s it could very well appear to a sensitive observer that Brown's virtue, in both his life and his death, had been ineffectual, for the many social evils he had challenged had reappeared, while his own reputation had suffered. Billy Budd, similarly, is a figure of ineffectual virtue. In life his goodness cannot prevent him from being hanged. In death it is obscured by the false reports of men—the only record of Budd is a naval chronicle emphasizing his depravity.

Whereas Melville pondered the meanings of John Brown, his friend Hawthorne did what he could to ignore Brown. This was difficult, for he lived in Concord, the center of Brown worship. Some members of his extended family, especially his Abolitionist sister-in-law Elizabeth Palmer Peabody, were avid fans of Brown.

In several ways Hawthorne was Brown's opposite. Brown devoted much of his life to the welfare of blacks; Hawthorne had little sympathy for blacks. Brown thought slavery could be combatted only through decisive action; Hawthorne was inactive on slavery, which he thought would disappear slowly over time. Brown hated doughfaces like Franklin Pierce; Hawthorne wrote a laudatory biography of Pierce, who was a chum of his from Bowdoin College days.

When in early 1860 Hawthorne returned to Concord after several years in Europe, he did not share his neighbors' excitement over the recently executed Brown. Later he visited Harpers Ferry as part of a Southern tour. He commented that Brown "won his martyrdom firmly, and took it firmly" but was a "blood-stained fanatic" who deserved his harsh sentence. "Nobody was ever more justly hanged," Hawthorne wrote. Anyone with common sense, he continued, "must have felt a certain intellectual satisfaction in seeing [Brown] hanged, if it were only in requital of his preposterous miscalculation of possibilities."

Walt Whitman, similarly, had a mixed opinion of Brown. Like most Americans, including Hawthorne, Whitman admired Brown's courage on the scaffold. In his poem "Year of the Meteors," describing the ominous atmosphere before the war, Whitman drew an imaginary portrait of himself at Brown's hanging:

> *I would sing how an old man, tall, with white hair, mounted the scaffold in*
>   *Virginia,*
> *I was at hand, silent I stood with teeth shut close, I watch'd,*
> *I stood very near you old man when cool and indifferent, but trembling with age*
>   *and your unheal'd wounds you mounted the scaffold.*

Late in life Whitman said of Brown, "Such devotion, such superb courage, men will not forget—cannot be forgotten." In the next breath, however, he confessed, "I never enthused greatly over Brown." He added, "I don't seem to like him any better now than I did then."

Why didn't Whitman, who in his poetry identified with fugitive slaves and even a murderous slave rebel, like John Brown? The answer lies in Whitman's devotion to the American Union. Though more progressive than Hawthorne on slavery, Whitman stood opposed to Abolitionism, which he considered a danger to the Union. Like Lincoln, Whitman regarded Brown as a zealot who threatened to rip America apart. Whitman in his poetry created an all-tolerating "I" who tried to identify with both sides of the slavery issue. Affirming "the union always surrounded by blatherers and always calm and impregnable," Whitman created a persona who announced himself "A southerner soon as a northerner, a planter nonchalant and hospitable, / A Yankeee bound my own way . . . / A Louisianan or Georgian, a poke-easy from sandhills and pines." If, as Whitman reported, his Abolitionist friends often got angry with him, it was because he refused to share their extreme stance on slavery, which, he knew, alienated Southerners.

Moreover, Whitman was not as far advanced on the race issue as was Brown. Accepting the then-popular idea that blacks would eventually die out because of their supposed physical inferiority to whites, Whitman said, "The nigger, like the Injun, will be eliminated: it is the law of the races, history. . . . A superior grade of rats come and then all the minor rats are cleared out." This idea is worlds apart from John Brown's notion of a racially integrated society.

The response of Whitman's reclusive contemporary, Emily Dickinson, to John Brown is hard to gauge. She rarely commented on slavery or the war, which from the perspective of her quiet life in Amherst, Massachusetts, seemed distant. Still, it is useful to speculate about her response. One piece of evidence I've unearthed indicates her father's reaction to Brown. Edward Dickinson, a lawyer who served as a U.S. congressman and Massachusetts state senator, sent a supportive letter to an anti-Brown Union meeting in Boston. He wrote: "I regard the tone of public sentiment, both at the North and the South, as intemperate and unpatriotic, and deserving of rebuke; and the conduct of many of the leading politicians in both sections as unworthy of respect or confidence of men who love the Constitution." He added that he would only support patriots who "will tend to strengthen the attachment of the people to the Union, . . . always keeping in view that our Government is based on reciprocal compromises, and that each portion of our country must respect these compromises."

In other words, Emily Dickinson's father was a fervent Unionist. A conservative one, too, for his letter retrospectively praises the old-time Whigs Henry Clay and Daniel Webster. When he wrote this letter in late 1859, his daughter Emily, apparently unbeknownst to him, was changing as a poet. Writing on sheets of paper that she would later sew together as booklets, she was making a dramatic move from the innocuous, jaunty style of her earliest poems to the dazzlingly experimental one of her mature phase.

Had the lightning stroke of Harpers Ferry, which split apart the nation, also expanded the fissure in the Dickinson household? We know that Emily rebelled against her stodgy father and mother in many ways, forging a poetry of freedom and rebellion, a lawbreaking poetry that took the restrictive hymn structure of her childhood and burst it with shocking metaphors and subversive ideas. Was she following the lead of the era's most famous lawbreaker, the ultimate rebel against corruption and compromise, an inspired criminal who, she knew, her father hated and who thus could shape her own private rebellion?

We may never know for sure. But it is perhaps meaningful that many of Dickinson's most adventurous poems were written within three years of the Harpers Ferry raid. And in her private rebellion against literary laws, Dickinson sought guidance from John Brown's most iconoclastic supporter: Thomas Wentworth Higginson.

Eighteen sixty-two, the year of Emily Dickinson's richest correspondence with Higginson, was also the year when she was most productive as a poet and when Higginson was perhaps the most radical man in America. He, more than anyone else, had carried forward John Brown's Abolitionist spirit. Brown had modeled himself after slave rebels and had led blacks into battles in order to free the slaves. Higginson, who had been Brown's most ardent supporter, had in the three years after his death advanced Brown's ideas by writing for his magazine, the *Atlantic Monthly*, a series of articles praising historic slave rebels like Denmark Vesey and the Surinam maroons, whom he compared to Brown. Also in 1862 he became the first colonel to lead blacks into battle. His journalistic accounts of his experiences as a leader of black troops would later be collected as *Army Life in a Black Regiment*. Besides militant Abolitionism, Higginson was devoted to other radical causes, such as women's rights and liberal religion.

Dickinson sent him poems and letters not only in reply to his "Letter to a Young Contributor," his *Atlantic* piece offering advice to writers, but also because she felt a deep kinship with him. If he was the most radical man in

America, she, in her own way, was the most radical woman. Their radicalism differed in emphasis and direction—his was aimed at changing society,
hers at revolutionizing poetry—but opened up mutual curiosity and
respect. True, he did not fully appreciate her quirky poetry, nor did she
embrace his radical social causes. But they shared a rebellious spirit.

"I read your Chapters in the Atlantic," she wrote him, "and experienced
honor for you—I was sure you would not reject a confiding question." Was
she referring to his articles on slave revolts, in which he praised John
Brown? We cannot say. Nor do we know whether her outpouring of 365
poems that year, including some of her most unconventional ones, was
given impetus by the John Brown-inspired radicalism that Higginson
embodied. Suffice it to say that, for the moment, she felt close to him. Her
1862 letters to him contained revealing confessions about her poetry and
her private life. She addressed him with unabashed admiration, calling him
"my Preceptor" and saying, "I have had few pleasures so deep as your opinion, and if I tried to thank you, my tears would block my tongue."

Besides being close to Brown's most zealous supporter, Dickinson may
have been inspired by Brown himself. Take these lines: "Much Madness is
divinest Sense— / To a discerning Eye— / Much Sense—the starkest Madness—." Did Dickinson have in mind the debate over Brown's sanity, in
which some labeled Brown a lunatic and others saw him as divinely sane?
Was she thinking of Brown in chains when she wrote, "Assent—and you are
sane— / Demur—you're straightway dangerous— / And handled with a
Chain—"? Or, to cite another poem: "Mine—by the Sign in the Scarlet
prison— / Bars cannot conceal!" Was this a veiled reference to imprisoned
Brown's ability to reach the world through his words, just as the reclusive
Dickinson hoped to do through her poetry?

And how about the one poem in which Dickinson deals directly with the
Civil War, "It feels a shame to be Alive—"? Was Brown on her mind when
she wrote it? It would seem so. Witness some sample verses:

> It feels a shame to be Alive—
> When Men so brave—are dead—
> One envies the Distinguished Dust—
> Permitted—such a Head—
>
> The Stone—that tells defending Whom
> This Spartan put away
> What little of Him we—possessed
> In Pawn for Liberty— . . .

It may be—a Renown to live—
I think the Men who die—
Those unsustained—Saviors—
Present Divinity—

In these lines Dickinson described Civil War soldiers the way the Transcendentalists portrayed John Brown. Emerson and Thoreau, known to have influenced Dickinson in other ways, seem to have had a strong impact here. Just as Thoreau said that Brown's death made other lives look trivial, so Dickinson expresses "shame to be Alive" in light of the heroic death "Permitted—to such a Head." Just as Thoreau said that Brown's peers do not exist, so Dickinson comments, "What little of him—we possessed— / In pawn for Liberty." Just as both Emerson and Thoreau found Christlike meaning in Brown's death, so Dickinson compares fallen soldiers to "Saviors" who "Present Divinity—" It was perhaps no accident that her preceptor, Higginson, was the strongest link between Brown and the Transcendentalists. Emily Dickinson, with her Transcendentalist take on American soldiers, was extending the meaning of John Brown to include the whole Civil War.

What Dickinson did obliquely, a myriad of popular writers did explicitly. It was largely due to the dissemination of Brown's image in popular culture that the war came to be widely associated with Brown. For the canonized poets and novelists, Brown was a ghostly figure whose influence was manifested in snippets and indirections. Not so for popular writers. For them, he was an ever-present spirit, aggressive, inspiring, and provocative.

At the start some authors tried to translate Brown's experiences into mass entertainment. In the weeks after the Harpers Ferry invasion, there appeared melodramas loosely based on Brown's life. The popular playwrights invented details they believed would add both spice and pathos to Brown's adventures. On November 15, 1859, the *Worcester Daily Spy* reported a performance the previous night of "an entirely new play" by J. H. Rogers called *Ossawatomie Brown; or, The Insurrection at Harper's Ferry.* "It is decidedly a 'sensation' drama and will please the masses," the *Spy* commented, adding that on opening night "the applause was vigorous and continued" for this "very lively performance." The play moves from Brown's home in Hudson, Ohio, to his camp in Kansas, which is burned down, killing Brown's wife and sons. In addition to this embellishment (Mary was never in Kansas, nor did any of the Browns die by fire), Rogers adds a "grand bowie-knife struggle" to the Harpers Ferry skirmish and an "Idiot Witness" to Brown's trial.

Another melodrama, also titled *Ossawatomie Brown; or, The Insurrection at Harper's Ferry*, by Mrs. J. C. Swayze, appeared the next month in New York and in Alexandria, Virginia. It is unclear if "J. H. Rogers" and "Mrs. J. C. Swayze" are the same writer. If so, s/he kept the original title but changed many details. The new play added several imaginary characters. As if the real John Brown did not have enough children, Mrs. Swayze gave him a new son, "Lewis," and two new daughters, "Julia" and "Alice," to go along with three actual ones depicted—Frederick, Oliver, and Watson. Instead of sticking closely to John Brown's life, which was fodder enough for a hundred plays, Swayze awkwardly interweaved fictionalized scenes from Brown's experiences in Kansas and Harpers Ferry with standard melodramatic vignettes of an Irish b'hoy and his sassy g'hal, an orphan who turns out to be a rich man's son, a fire that almost kills the main characters (who escape through a trap door), and the near rape of an innocent maiden by Black Jim, who is called a "Border Ruffian" but is a stock villain.

Throughout the play John Brown is treated with respect, but in tawdry contexts. In the opening scene, in North Elba, everyone calls him "Mr. Brown"—"for his larnin'," says the Irish girl Jeptha, who explains that "he talks like a 'lectioneer and raises the best cows in the hull United States." In Kansas the near rape of his daughter "Alice" and the murder of his sons "Lewis" and Frederick drive him to a violent frenzy. He vows revenge against all proslavery ruffians. Afraid of tarnishing her hero, Swayze fabricates a story about Pottawatomie, which Brown explains as follows:

> In the pursuit of vengeance, we drove those lawless ruffians to further deeds of violence and bloodshed. Whilst still evading our pursuit, they drew the inhabitants from their beds, brutally murdered them, and then left them to be counted as our victims. Thus we are in turn pursued . . . the people are infuriated—they swear 'twas we who committed last night's outrage.

In the rest of the play, Brown, driven by "a madness that has grown out of his misfortunes," moves with his followers to the Kennedy farm, invades Harpers Ferry, is captured and tried. He remains stoical in prison, saying, "the cause—the glorious cause—lives yet in the hearts of men who will follow in our footsteps."

Other Brown plays soon appeared. *John Brown; or, The Hero of Kansas and Harper's Ferry* seems to have been adapted from Swayze's play, with a similar plot, though some names are changed and Brown gets yet another daughter, "Amelia." *Pottawatomie Brown* was another play, starring an actress billed as "Lucille Western" in a Boston performance.

It may seem surprising, given Brown's adventurous life, that even more melodramas or sensational novels were not written about him. But Brown had stirred deep political passions that could not be comfortably expressed in such fast-paced, plot-driven genres. The overwhelming majority of imaginative writings about him were poems and songs. The divided opinions over Brown produced verse that was sharply contrasting in tone.

Proslavery poets and songwriters repeatedly lambasted him, using racist language. In the song "John Brown," P. H. Matthews crowed about the "great news" from Charles Town "about the hanging of old John Brown," which served as a lesson to "all you old men" and "abolitionists" who "wish to set the niggers free." Another Southern song, "The Fate of Old John Brown," asked: "If the Niggers had been free, John, / What would they get to do? / They know when they are well off, / And now they laugh at you." Similar mockery appeared in C. A. Boggs's song "John Brown," which joked: "Old Brown thought the niggas would sustain him; / But old Gov-'nor Wise, put spectacles on his eyes, / To show him the happy land of Canaan." Boggs noted that "Abolitionists are kicking up a dust" about Brown and that Governor Wise "would hang them freely . . . / If he catches them in the happy land of Canaan."

Some songs tried to squeeze proslavery comedy out of Brown's foray. A minstrel song, "Harpers Ferry" by Harry Fox, "the celebrated banjoist," announced: "At Harper's Ferry, dar's been a great sensation: / De white folks wanted to get de niggars off de Plantation." Brown, continued Fox, "thought the niggars all would run, and help him out in time. . . . / But instead of helping him, they all kept out ob sight." The scene was so funny, Fox said, that it was worth repeating: "If some fun you want to hab, give a nig a gun; / When the powder he does smell, oh Moses, wont he run!" Another wag satirized Brown's love for blacks in verses sung to the tune of the nursery rhyme "Ten Little Indians." The song began,

> *Old John Brown, he had a little nigger,*
> *Old John Brown, he had a little nigger,*
> *Old John Brown, he had a little nigger,*
>   *One little nigger boy.*

The song culminated in a supposedly humorous chant about "Ten thousand little nigger boys all armed with pitchforks eighteen feet long and commanded by *twenty thousand* abolitionists."

Racism laced with panic characterized another proslavery ditty, "Old John Brown, a Song for Every Southern Man," which depicted the failure of Brown's raid as an example for would-be "nigger-stealers." The song's repeated chorus was: "Old Ossawattomie Brown! / That will never pay, / Trying to come away down South, / And run the niggers away." The song gave details of Harpers Ferry and its aftermath, warning the South that Northerners "have their agents in the South, to run your slaves away." The song continued, "All you Southern darkies, a word to you I'll say," advising slaves to "always mind your masters, and never run away" and telling them to ignore "these Northern agents, they tell to you a lie, / They get you at the North, and starve you 'till you die." As for Brown and his men, they were in hell: "The devil standing down below, he calls for them to come, / It's no use now old John Brown, you can't get a chance to run."

This theme of Brown's allegedly satanic nature was a popular one in Southern songs, developed most fully in "John Brown's Entrance into Hell." Written in 1863 shortly after the Emancipation Proclamation was issued, the song revealed the South's bitterness over Brown, Lincoln, and the Republican Party. Brown was shown being greeted in hell by devils who sang joyful hymns, "For well they knew the lying thief, / Would make for them an honored chief." Satan himself embraced the new arrival: "Old Satan from his throne came down / And left his seat for Old John Brown." Satan welcomed Brown, declaring, "As often you've murdered, lied and stole / It did rejoice my burning soul." As cheers rang out "To hail the Abolition chief," Brown was introduced to Benedict Arnold and was assured that others would soon arrive, including Lincoln, Sumner, and Stevens. Lincoln would sit with Brown beside Satan, who prophesied: "John at my left, Abe at my right, / We'll give the heavenly hosts a fight; / A triune group we then shall be, / Yes, three in one and one in three." "In short," Satan says gleefully, "the negroizing clan, / Are traveling here to a man." Soon hell would be full of Brown's followers.

Richard S. Gladney made this equation of Brown with Northern politicians in his deadly serious poetic narrative *The Devil in America*, which held the Republican Party responsible for Brown's actions at both Pottawatomie and Harpers Ferry. His harsh words echoed the views of the Southerners who were using Brown to provoke secession.

To suggest that Brown was a tool of the Republicans, Gladney introduced his section on "Brown in Kansas" as follows: "Attempts the Black Republicans have made / To bring the issue on of endless strife." The Republicans, Gladney maintained, sent "paupers, criminals, and lawless men" to Kansas, among them John Brown, the head of "a savage, bloody clan." "Observe how great the feats which he perform'd," Gladney wrote, launching into a grisly account of the Pottawatomie massacre. Gladney pictured the Doyle family sleeping peacefully and awakened by Brown's men, who dragged the father and two sons outside and hacked them to death. The father was left "a cold and lifeless corpse, / And from his head and breast oozed out the blood." One of his sons lay nearby "with mangled breast, / And shatter'd head, and arms and fingers maim'd." Another was stretched out "with cleft and broken skull, / And from his side the purple torrent flow'd." Brown led his men to another cabin and similarly dispatched William Sherman, leaving him with a hand sliced off, his chest punctured, and "His skull twice widely cleft, his brains exposed, / There washing and floating in the stream." The "bloody fiends" then murdered Allen Wilkinson in a similarly gory way.

Pressing home the point that the Northern leaders sanctioned these atrocities, Gladney wrote:

> *The hordes of murderous men to Kansas sent*
> *Were but the pliant tools of other men,*
> *The troops sent forth by Black Republicans,*
> *By Sewer [sic], Phillips, Giddings, Garrison,*
> *And Parker, Emerson, and Gerrit Smith,*
> *And hosts of minor tools and satellites.*

Like other Southerners who manipulated Brown's image, Gladney conflated disparate Northern currents—antislavery politics, Garrisonianism, and Transcendentalism—and improbably put them under the umbrella of "Black Republicanism." The fact that *none* of the men he mentioned had supported Brown before Pottawatomie mattered to him as little as did the reality of the fragmented antislavery movement.

In the next part of the poem, "The Raid," Gladney insisted that "the demon Murder, thirsting still for blood, / Led Brown to search and plan a wider field." And so this "general of the Black Republicans, / From them receiving much 'material aid,'" planned and executed the assault on Harpers Ferry. The goal? Murder, pillage, and rape on a scale never before imagined. Brown wanted "to desolate a vast empire / By servile war and civil war combined," unleashing "savage hordes" of blacks who would rush

> *With brutal rage to murder men unarm'd,*
> *And foully violate their helpless wives,*

Then rip them open in their fiendish rage;
The fair and lovely maidens violate,
Then mangled leave them weltering in their blood;
Hoist writing infants on their bloody pikes,
Dash out their brains, or throw them in the flames.

This vision of the potentially catastrophic outcome of Brown's plans raised the nightmarish fear of interracial rape that lurked in the South's unconscious.

The John Brown who appeared in Northern poetry and song bore little resemblance to the South's version. Once Brown began to receive positive responses, the worst that Northern poets could say about him was that he had been driven mad by proslavery outrages in Kansas and that he engaged in an unwise but heroic effort to dislodge slavery in Virginia.

This was the theme of two of the earliest Northern poems, the anonymously published "Old Brown" and Edmund Clarence Stedman's "John Brown's Invasion, a Ballad of the Times," which both appeared shortly after Brown's sentencing. The former argued that after "that deed of murder done / In lawless Kansas" and the loss of his son there, "revenge became the mainspring of his life." Brown, "all disordered, moved by this alone," raided Harpers Ferry. The author felt "a saddening pity" for "the thought of him whom wrong had caused to err" but realized that Brown would be "martyr-crowned" in his death.

A similar ambivalence characterized Stedman's poem "John Brown's Invasion." In Stedman's view, Brown was a noble freedom-fighter in Kansas who went insane when proslavery ruffians killed two of his sons (Stedman wrongly said that John Jr. was killed along with Frederick). After the murders, Stedman relates, Brown shed no tears, but "his wild blue eye grew wilder," and "more sharply curved his hawk's nose," and now "Old Brown, Osawatomie Brown / Had gone crazy, as they reckoned by his fearful glare and frown." He "raised his right hand up to heaven, calling Heaven's vengeance down." And so, "Mad Old Brown" with "his eighteen other mad men" raided Harpers Ferry. He made a brave stand in the engine house, but his enemies "fired their souls with Bourbon whiskey, / Till they battered down Brown's castle with their ladders and machines." Brown "thrice was wounded by the bayonet and a cut on his brave old crown," and was forced to surrender.

Now, Stedman noted with sorrow, Brown was sentenced to hang. "But, Virginians, do not do it!" he warned:

And each drop of blood from Old Brown's life veins, like the red gore of the dragon,
May spring up like a vengeful Fury hissing through your slave-worn lands!
And Old Brown,
Osawatomie Brown,
May trouble you more than ever, when you've nailed his coffin down!

William Dean Howells, then a young antislavery journalist in Ohio, made a similar point in his poem "Old Brown." Brown's death, Howells affirmed, would only increase his power. Howells assured Brown: "Thy shouted name abroad shall ring, / Wherever right makes war sublime." "Oh, patience! felon of the hour!" Howells continued. Now Brown was on "the thorny path," wearing "the crown of thorns." But someday "men shall rise where slaves have trod," and "Over thy ghastly gallows tree, / Shall climb the vine of Liberty."

Biblical symbolism became a staple of the Northern poems about Brown. In "The Message to Pharror," anonymously published in the *Liberator* in mid-November 1859, Brown was associated with both Moses and Christ. He was the "serene and unshaken" Moses, standing "more kingly than Kings, before Pharoah's throne" and crying, "Send thy slaves forth in freedom! The Lord hears their moan!" He was also "this Jesus divine," the "Savior of men," who died for the others. His gallows was the cross, and his final days paralleled the passion of Jesus:

> *Thou man of deep sorrows, with grief well acquainted,*
> *Rejected, despised—we hail thee as "King"!*
> *Thy name branded "Traitor!"—with treason attainted,—*
> *We call thee "Deliverer, and Savior of men!*
> *Thy blood and thy loved ones" with purple shall clothe thee;*
> *Thy crown is a thorn-crown; thy scepter a chain!*

The Christ comparison had been first popularized by Emerson, whose image of the "gallows glorious as the cross" was often repeated. One poem declared: "John Brown, to help the helpless slave, / Counted all else but loss; / Henceforth that hateful gallows tree / Is glorious like the cross." Another predicted that history would remember Brown by "the scaffold— the modernized cross." "Rear on high the scaffold-altar!" proclaimed a third. "All the world will turn to see / How a man has dared to suffer that his brothers may be free!" For another, Brown and Christ were interchangeable:

> *For as that cross of shame*
> *Forever thence became*
> *Earth's holiest shrine;*
> *So must this gallows tree,*
> *Redeemed from infamy*
> *Become for bond and free*
> *A sacred sign.*

Such reverence increasingly typified the Northern poems about Brown. The early ambivalence over his alleged madness all but disappeared from the Northern verse.

The transitional moment was the day of his execution. It was then that the North fully realized that something extraordinary had been exposed: the South, despite its code of chivalric manhood, was not as strong as it pretended to be. Press reports of the execution, North and South, agreed that Brown was the calmest person in Charles Town that day.

His courage was later emulated by his comrades when they were executed. As seen, the four hanged on December 16—Copeland, Green, Coppoc, and Cook—were as firm as their leader had been on the scaffold. The same was true of the remaining two, Albert Hazlett and Aaron Dwight Stevens, who went to trial on February 2, 1860, and were executed on March 16.

Ever since he was captured in Pennsylvania and returned to Virginia, Hazlett had tried to cloak his identity. He went to trial as "William Harrison, alias Albert Hazlett." The cover-up did not work. Even though Hazlett had participated in the raid on Harpers Ferry—he had helped to hold the arsenal before escaping across the river—there was no evidence of his having done so. Still, he was convicted and sentenced to hang. He and Stevens were charged not with treason, as their confederates had been, but with advising slaves to revolt. Although their attorney, George Sennott of Boston, defended them ably, they did not escape their leader's fate.

A Northern plot was hatched to rescue the pair from the Charles Town prison. Higginson, Sanborn, Hinton, and others, having raised $1,800 for the purpose, went to Harrisburg, Pennsylvania, to launch a raid through the mountains. But Hazlett and Stevens, when told of the plan by a messenger disguised as a drunken Irishman, discouraged the idea. They liked their jailer, Avis, as much as Brown had, and feared he and others would be hurt were a rescue attempted.

Besides, both men were prepared to die. After his sentencing, Stevens wrote a relative, "I am cheerful and happy, ready to die at a moment's warning, although I would like to live as long as anybody." He added, "I am glad that I did not die of my wounds; for I believe that my execution upon the gallows will be a better testimony for truth and liberty." Hazlett, likewise, wrote the day before his hanging, "I am willing to die in the cause of liberty; if I had ten thousand lives, I would willingly lay them all down for the same cause. My death will do more good than if I had lived." Avis saw the two men pitching pennies in their cell. When Avis heard Stevens cry out happily, he asked, "What have you won?" Stevens said, "The privilege of selecting you to put the hangman's noose around my neck!" On the gallows, Stevens and Hazlett repeated the intrepid performance of the five who had gone before.

Poets eulogized them. "The last bloody act in the drama is o'er," wrote a black author. "The martyrs have gone to their rest, / . . . . They for others have lived, and for others have died, / The poor and despised of our race; / The tyrants of earth they have boldly defied— / In heaven they now have a place." Another writer lamented that Hazlett and Stevens were "Murder'd, Christ-like doing good" but affirmed, "They are here! / With us in the march of time, / Beating at our side!"

The coolness with which Brown and his followers faced death was an irresistible theme for Northern poets, who spread the news that the South, with all its surface bluster, was in fact cowardly. J. W. Pillsbury's poem "The Quaking South" pointed out that the South had long said that "worth and chivalry were fondly nurtured there," blazoning "the prowess of her gallant sons . . . far and wide." But now, Pillsbury wrote, "The lovely picture now reversed, and what do we behold? / Paleness is stamped upon each face— the blood is running cold: / A cry of insurrection is ringing wild and clear, / And boasted heroism now yields to inglorious fear."

The same idea governed a song titled "The Fright of Old Virginia. Being a Condensed Account of the Harper's Ferry Insurrection, October 16th, 1859." The song, consisting of nine verses of twelve lines each, interspersed with a four-line chorus, pounded on the theme of its title: once-boastful Virginia, so proud of its heroes, was made to quake by a small band of armed men who struck for freedom and died bravely. The chorus jibed the South's vaunted toughness:

> *Virginia is the state, you know,*
> *That never feared a mortal foe,*
> *But chivalry was rather low,*
> *When Brown came to Old Virginia.*

The song described Virginians "shivering" with fear from the start of the Harpers Ferry affair, when Brown's tiny band held at bay hundreds of indecisive militiamen, through his trial and imprisonment, when "that frightened clown" Governor Wise ordered a crackdown on suspicious Northerners in the region. It showed Brown calmly walking up the scaffold to meet his fate while surrounded by nervous soldiers who "trembled at each sound." Then "Brown died as every brave man dies, / A victim to that coward Wise / And shivering old Virginia."

The mockery came from all quarters. "Old John Brown," a poem in a Paterson, New Jersey, newspaper, said of Virginia: "Your lips with terror become white; / For every North wind's breath ye feel; . . . / And every midnight sound ye hear, / Your souls shall paralyze with fear!" From Nova Scotia came a mock-epic poem, "The Dragon and the Knight," in which the South shuddered before John Brown, who attacked slavery with his powerful sword:

> *All pale and paralyzed with terror,*
> *Back fell the multitude amazed,*
> *And never having known a hero*
> *With stare unrecognizing gazed.*

The *New-York Tribune* chimed in with "John Brown of Osawatomie," which declared to Southerners: "You're found . . . a brutal, cowardly crew!" ever since "At the wave of [Brown's] hand to a dozen men, two thousand slunk like hounds." A poet from Weymouth, Massachusetts, said to Virginians: "Shame to thy boasted chivalry!" for killing "The man who laid your folly bare, / And showed you where your weakness lay."

John Brown, therefore, gave the North a jolt of courage. For the first time, the North could say unequivocally that the South, for all its muscle-flexing, was more cowardly than it seemed. Also for the first time, it looked with admiration on an Abolitionist who assaulted slavery violently on Southern soil.

Brown was attractive, too, because he seemed to have a tender heart beneath his firm exterior. After all, he had stooped to kiss the slave child on the way to the scaffold—at least Northerners believed he had. Two poems in particular popularized this myth: John Greenleaf Whittier's "Brown of Osawatomie" and Lydia Maria Child's "The Hero's Heart."

As pacifists, Whittier and Child were uncomfortable with Brown's bloody tactics. But they respected his sympathy for the oppressed. They focused on the kiss story, which they believed illustrated Brown's gentle side. As Brown walked out of jail, wrote Whittier, "the bold, blue eye grew tender, / And the old harsh face grew mild, / As he stooped between the jeering ranks / And kissed the negro child!" This kindhearted act, Whittier indicated, made up for Brown's faulty methods: "That kiss from all its guilty means / Redeemed the good intent." Now, Whittier concluded, "Perish with him the folly / that seeks through evil good, / Long live the generous purpose / Unstained with human blood!"

Child was in the anomalous position of being closely associated with Brown while disapproving of his means for fighting slavery. A long-standing Abolitionist with ties to Transcendentalism, she had written to Brown when he was in jail offering to come and care for him. In a letter to him she expressed both admiration for his character and qualms about his methods. To get permission to visit Brown, she corresponded with Governor Wise and with the wife of Senator Mason. Although her visit never happened, the correspondence, which amounted to a debate over slavery, was published in Northern newspapers and later as a pamphlet, *Correspondence Between Lydia Maria Child and Governor Wise and Mrs. Mason of Virginia*, which sold 300,000 copies. Child's ambivalence toward Brown guided her editing of Harriet Jacobs's narrative *Incidents in the Life of a Slave Girl*. Jacobs had wanted to end her volume with a chapter on Brown, but Child prevented her from doing so, evidently to discourage any form of approval of Brown's violence.

In her poem on Brown, Child wrote that as Brown left the jail he saw not one friendly eye except that of a black girl who stared at his silver hair: "As that dark brow to his up-turned, / The tender heart within him yearned; / And, fondly stooping o'er her face, / He kissed her, for her injured race." Child reported that "Jesus smiled" at the scene, while angels waited to escort Brown to heaven.

The sentimentalized Brown that Child and Whittier presented, however, was not typical of the figure that appeared in most Northern poems. Although nearly all Northern poets saw Brown's sympathetic side, most emphasized his bracingly martial nature. Child could say that Brown had floated to heaven, but most Northern writers insisted that his spirit still stalked the earth, marching southward with his sword raised and his angry eyes burning.

Soon after the tide of Northern opinion shifted in Brown's direction, poets began insisting that hanging would not kill John Brown. One wrote, "Not any spot six feet by two / Will hold a man like thee; / John Brown will tramp the shaking earth, / From Blue Ridge to the sea." Another predicted that Brown would continue to haunt Virginia: "Will she not fear

the spirit from his tomb, / That when it strikes, will beat no empty air?"
A third wrote, "Escaped his earthly prison-house, / He's evermore set
free, . . . / His earnest spirit is not quelled or silenced for an hour; / His purposes shall ripen fast, / By large access of power." The liberation of Brown's
spirit after his execution spelled the death of slavery, maintained another:

> *By the Spirit abroad, by the still rising surge,—*
> *Dark land of the gallows, the chain and the scourge!*
> *Thy doom the most proud overwhelming shall be—*
> *Virginia! Virginia! Thy slaves shall be free!*

In effect, John Brown's soul was loosed upon the land, ready to grapple
with the South and kill slavery. The author of "The Dragon and the
Knight" depicted Brown hurling a "barbed, insinuating dart" into the
"dragon" of slavery, which now writhed in "fierce convulsions" as its death
approached. And, "When in the coming conflict, glorious / It totters to its
final fall, / *His* name will nerve the arm victorious, / And echo as the rallying call."

The prediction proved accurate. No name managed to "nerve the arm
victorious" as strongly as did John Brown's. At many key moments in the
war, his spirit was invoked for inspiration by the North.

John Brown seemed to stand at the very gates of the war, opening the
way for the Union armies. The first engagement summoned up a poetic
image of Brown as "the specter at Sumter," standing amid the falling Confederate shells:

> *There towered a spectral form!*
> *I knew by its proud erectness,*
> *By its calm determined mien,*
> *By the strong arms firmly folded,*
> *By the clear, deep eye serene,*
> *'Twas that old man, lion-hearted,*
> *Of the dark and terrible frown,*
> *The Genius of Retribution—*
> *Old Osawatomie Brown.*

This firm "Genius of Retribution" appeared often in the poetry of the
war. Shortly after Lincoln had called up 75,000 troops in response to the
South's attack on Fort Sumter, a poet for the *Tribune* advised the Union
soldiers:

Shrink not; the path, though toilsome,
Hath been trod by One before,
Who fought for Truth and Liberty
On old Virginia's shore;
He perished, but his memory
Is still our beacon-light;
This was his heart's true talisman—
"God speed the Right."

As the war progressed, the Calvinistic Christianity of John Brown came to define the rigors of war. An Edwardsean Calvinist, Brown had viewed God as an angry judge who had complete control of humans, who were totally depraved and merited eternal damnation. Walt Whitman, writing that "the real war will never get into the books," described "the seething hell and the black infernal background of countless minor scenes and interiors." As the carnage and devastation mounted on both sides, it seemed as though God were inflicting terrible punishment on the nation. A number of Northern poets suggested that the South was being punished for its "murder" of John Brown. From this perspective Harpers Ferry, which traded hands many times and was ruined in the process, epitomized the horrors of the war. The town John Brown had invaded provoked this Calvinistic outburst:

How has God's angry and visible frown
Blasted those regions where old John Brown
In glorious martyrdom laid down his life!
How swift is the punishment! God was defied:—
Say, shall the mockers in safety abide?
Look for your answer in War's fierce tide!

God, according to the poets, avenged Brown's execution not only by ruining Harpers Ferry but in more general ways as well. At a dark moment in the war, a poet for the *Liberator* wrote, "The earth looks sad and dreary, as if God with sin were weary; / . . . For [God's] ways are growing darker, and the times are more appalling." The reason? God's lingering anger over the death of John Brown. The poet retold the details of Brown's execution, then pictured him on the gallows: "He swings dead, dead, dead—the glorious soul has fled / Of Christ's well-beloved, martyred son!" The "thunders long, and loud, and deep" remind the poet that "God's voice was there, bidding the dark South prepare / For judgment on this crime—on this crime!"

For some, the war as a whole was John Brown writ large. "A Song for the Times, or John Brown" claimed that the South hanged Brown to quiet him, but his spirit was more alive than ever:

> *His mouth is hushed, his hand is still,*
> *But old John Brown they could not kill, Could not kill.*

> *For, now the soul of Old John Brown*
> *From North and West comes, marching down,*
> *With wild hurrahs, and roll of drums,*
> *And roar of cannon, lo! it comes! Lo! it comes!*

> *Oh! Great soul of Old John Brown!*
> *Through all the land, go thundering on,*
> *Till all our armies, all out towns*
> *Shall, all, be full of Brave John Browns, Brave John Browns!*

If the Union soldiers were "Brave John Browns," the poets believed, thousands monthly joined Brown in heaven after dying for the Northern cause. In a typical poem by Mary H. C. Booth, a Union soldier dying on the battlefield has a vision of being welcomed to heaven by Brown along with masses of other soldiers. The man finds himself in paradise among the blessed:

> *A hundred thousand soldiers*
> *Stood at the right hand of God;*
> *And Old John Brown, he stood before,*
> *Like Aaron, with his rod.*
> *A Slave was there beside him,*
> *And Jesus Christ was there;*
> *And over God, and Christ, and all,*
> *The Banner waved in air.*

"And now I'm dying, comrade," concludes the soldier, "And there is Old John Brown, / A standing at the Golden Gate, / And holding me a crown!

The abundant poetry and music about John Brown reflected the Northern mood and had a shaping influence on it. One song, "John Brown's

Body," with its stirring chorus of "Glory, glory hallelujah!," was the most popular song of the Union army and the parent of Julia Ward Howe's "The Battle Hymn of the Republic." It had an impact matched by few compositions in American history.

Written at the start of the war, in spring 1861, the John Brown song lasted in many variations until the end of the war and far beyond. As a Northern veteran later recalled, "It seized upon every blue-coated organization throughout the land with fascinating power, and it is certainly true that no song of the war became so popular." Lydia Maria Child, despite her mixed feelings about Brown, found the song irresistible when she first heard troops sing it in September 1861. She wrote her friend Whittier:

> Nothing on earth has such an effect on the popular heart as songs, which the soldiers would take up with enthusiasm, and which it would thereby become the fashion to whistle and sing at street corners. "Old John Brown, Hallelujah!" is performing a wonderful mission now. Where the words came from, nobody knows, and the tune is an exciting, spirit-stirring thing, hitherto unknown outside of Methodist conventicles. But it warms up soldiers and boys, and the air is full of it; just as France was of the Marseillaise, whose author was for years unknown.

Her puzzlement over the origin of the song is understandable. Once the song caught fire in the North, a number of people claimed authorship of it. Actually, the true story of its origin is stranger than any of the apocryphal ones.

The song, which eventually became a reverent eulogy of Brown's heroic Abolitionism, began as a joke. Ironically, its music came from a humorous ditty, "Say, Hummers, Will You Meet Us?," first sung to entertain a fire company in South Carolina, the cradle of secession. Methodists in the region heard it and changed its words to "Say, Brothers, Will You Meet Us?" which was widely sung at revivals.

The simple rhythmic melody got linked with John Brown when the Massachusetts 12th Regiment was stationed at Fort Warren near Boston early in the war. One of the soldiers, a short, humorless Scotchman named John Brown, was the butt of good-natured ridicule on the part of his comrades, who teasingly compared him to the deceased John Brown, saying "Well, now, ain't he lively for a corpse?" and "Hope I'll look as well for a dead man." One day a friend saw him and joked, "John Brown's dead." As the annoyed Scotchman walked away, someone else said, "Yet he still goes marching on." A singer who was present started up the "Say, Brothers" hymn and plugged in "John Brown's body lies a-mouldering in the grave," repeated three times. Another person laughed, and added, "But his soul goes marching on." By the evening all the soldiers in the fort were singing the song, making up new verses. The persecuted Scotchman, John Brown, sang as enthusiastically as anyone.

The song was written down and distributed. Eleven hundred soldiers sang it in a dress parade through Boston. The famous Gilmore's Band and the Germania Band received copies, and Oliver Ditson published sheet music. On July 28, 1861, the *New-York Tribune* printed the song. When the Massachusetts 12th marched through the streets of New York City later that summer, it thundered forth the John Brown song amid cheering throngs who lined the streets.

Before long, the Massachusetts 12th was the only Northern regiment that did *not* sing the song, which became too painful when John Brown, the much-teased but well-liked Scotchman, drowned after falling off a pontoon at Port Royal.

The rest of the Union army thought only of John Brown of Harpers Ferry when it sang the song, which was remarkably adaptable. The only constants in the song were "John Brown's body lies a-mouldering in the grave" and "His soul is marching on." The rest of the words changed according to the singers and the situation. Many of the early versions contained the following lines as well, each repeated three times: "He's gone to be a soldier in the army of the Lord"; "John Brown's knapsack is strapped upon his back"; and "His pet lambs will meet him on his way."

The song projected John Brown as a stern, fatherly spirit-soldier leading the way into battle with God supporting him all along. The image was one of unbending firmness but also of tenderness: on the way he met his "pet lambs," referring both to his farm animals and the Union soldiers, who were like his children or pets.

In variations the song became by turns caustic, hilarious, sadistic, or sober, according to the occasion—sometimes all at the same time. One popular version had all the above lines plus "They will hang Jeff Davis to a tree!" and "Now, three rousing cheers for the Union!" with the chorus slightly revised to "Glory Hally, Hallelujah!" and a "Hip, Hip, Hip, Hip Hurrah!" added at the end.

It was a song that lent itself to verbal riffs. In that respect it was much like the spirituals sung by slaves, who, as Frederick Douglass famously noted, made up words on the spur of the moment. Improvisation became a characteristic of African American music, as evidenced later by jazz and the blues, and it was a feature of the John Brown song as well.

Several variations were concocted by the black troops fighting for the North. Thomas Wentworth Higginson reported one evening of his black soldiers: "They got upon the John Brown song, always a favorite, adding a jubilant verse which I have never heard before, 'We'll beat Beauregard on de clare battlefield.' " With John Brown as the song's guiding spirit, it was apt that blacks used it to assert themselves. "Oh! we're de bully soldiers of de 'First of Arkansas,' " sang one regiment; "We are fightin' for de Union, we are fightin' for de law; / We can hit a rebel furder dan a white man ever saw, / As we go marching on."

The song transcended boundaries of race, class, and place. There even appeared a proslavery version, "I'm bound to be a soldier in the army of the South." By August 1862, an Illinois journalist could state, "The apotheosis of old John Brown is fast taking place" as a result of the song: "All over the country it may be heard at all times of the night or day in the streets of Chicago and all our other cities; it is the pet song among the soldiers in all our armies; more than a thousand verses have been composed and sung to the tune of old John Brown's soul is marching on."

Quintessentially egalitarian, the song was constantly refashioned by the masses. It fed on the passions of the moment. As a writer for *Harper's* noted:

> No poet could have written it. Such rudeness and wildness are beyond the conception even of Walt Whitman and the author of "Festus." One would say that it was written by the common soldiers who sang it as they advanced to battle; that it was an elemental tune, suited to the rugged natures that shouted its refrain as they resolutely faced death, with the confident assurance of immortality. The words are verbal equivalents of rifle-bullets and cannon-balls; the tune is a noise, like the shriek of the shell as it ascends to the exact point whence it can most surely descend to blast and kill.

As the war went on, more sophisticated versions of the song appeared. Some poets balked at the crudeness of the common versions. William W. Patton, appalled by the lighthearted line "We'll hang Jeff Davis to a sour apple tree," published a powerful version of the song in the *Chicago Tribune*. In his handling, John Brown was the valiant warrior who had died for "the sons of bondage" and who was now directing the Union armies from heaven. Widely reproduced, Patton's version became popular not only

among soldiers but also among celebrities like Wendell Phillips, who in his
speeches liked to quote from Patton's third verse:

> *He captured Harper's Ferry with his nineteen men so few,*
> *And he frightened "Old Virginny," till she trembled through and through;*
> *They hung him for a traitor, themselves a traitor crew,*
> *But his soul is marching on! Glory, Hallelujah!*

It seemed as though anyone on any occasion could come up with a new
spin on the song. William Lloyd Garrison penned a version for a July 4 celebration in 1862, saying that "the Lord our God" was leading the nation
through "the Red Sea of his justice," as "Our cause is marching on." As the
Emancipation Proclamation approached, J. M. Friend published "Proclamation Song," which announced that "John Brown, the dauntless hero,
with joy is looking on, / From his home among the angels he sees the coming dawn; / . . . When the slaves shall all go free!"

"The Battle Hymn of the Republic" was one more variation on the
theme. Julia Ward Howe, accompanied by the Reverend James Freeman
Clarke, was reviewing Union troops outside of Washington when a rebel
attack caused the troops to retreat. In the carriage ride back to the city, she
and Clarke cheered the soldiers by joining them in some of their favorite
songs, including "John Brown." Clarke suggested that she write new words
for the song. She said she had often tried to do so but had failed.

That night she slept soundly and awoke at 4 a.m. with the Brown tune
ringing in her head. She later recalled, "The melody of 'John Brown's Body'
kept running through my mind and I could not banish the catchy strains.
The song fairly tugged at me." In a rush of creativity, she scribbled down
some new verses and fell back to sleep. Within a few weeks, "The Battle
Hymn of the Republic" was published in the *Atlantic Monthly* and then in
newspapers nationwide. It was welcomed by the Union army and survived
the war as a national hymn.

Many previous versions of the John Brown song had come close to
deifying Brown; one, for instance, called him God's soldier who "shall stand
at Armageddon with his brave old sword." Julia Ward Howe took the further step of fusing the *meaning* of John Brown with the religious spirit
behind the Civil War. The wife of Secret Six member S. G. Howe, she had
known Brown well and considered him the archetypal Puritan. Her "Battle
Hymn" integrated his Calvinist vision with the North's mission.

The famous opening lines—"Mine eyes have seen the glory of the coming of the Lord: / He is trampling out the vintage where the grapes of wrath

are stored"—echo the spirit of John Brown's soul "marching on" without mentioning Brown himself. In Howe's hymn John Brown morphs into the God he had believed in: not the tender God of nineteenth-century Protestantism but the angry, just, warlike God of bygone Puritanism. This was a God who "hath loosed the fateful lightnings of His terrible swift sword," who was seen in the watch fires of soldiers' camps and who wrote "his righteous sentence" on "the dim and flaring lamps," who had "a fiery gospel writ in burnished rows of steel," who warned, "with you my grace shall deal," who was sounding the trumpet that never calls retreat, and who was "sifting out the hearts of men before His judgment seat."

If Brown had been "the last of the Puritans," a solitary Calvinist in a sea of liberals, the "Battle Hymn" announced that the wrathful, fateful Divine Judge of Puritanism was back in full force, symbolized by fire and steel, fighting on the side of the North. Christ is mentioned in the last verse as a supporter of Brown's goal of Abolitionism: "As he died to make men holy, let us die to make men free."

Brown powerfully influenced the war not only through the popular verse and music he inspired but because of the example he had set in his personal battle against slavery. Many have pointed out that the North fought initially to preserve the Union and eventually to free the slaves. The Northern war, that is, took on an increasingly Abolitionist tenor. John Brown's role in this shift is insufficiently appreciated. It could be argued that the war became more and more John Brown's war. It was largely because the North increasingly adopted Brown's aims and his tactics that it defeated the South.

Both before and after the war, Lincoln was identified by his opponents with John Brown. Shortly before Fort Sumter, a Southern newspaper, noting "a vein of coercion" beneath Lincoln's moderate exterior, announced sneeringly, "In the body of Lincoln the spirit of John Brown lives." Four years later, after Appomattox, a proslavery journalist lamented, "The Republican administration is simply a John Brown raid. The name of John Brown and Abraham Lincoln will indeed *go down to posterity together* . . . into the abyss of infamy and eternal shame." The writer grumbled, "The policy of the Republican party, since it came into power, has been a faithful carrying out of the work begun by old John Brown. The administration of Abraham Lincoln was a John Brown raid on the grandest scale; and it was no more. That is the place it will occupy in history."

The first comment made little sense; before the war Lincoln had little in common with Brown other than a hatred of slavery. The last two comments had a basis in truth; by the end of the war Lincoln had adopted much of what Brown had stood for.

At the start Lincoln did what he could to *avoid* tactics like those Brown had used in Kansas or at Harpers Ferry. Not only did he often denounce Brown during his campaign, but once he was elected, he specifically said he wanted to steer clear of an Abolitionist agenda because it recalled Brown, whom he considered extreme and divisive. Fearful of any controversial policy that might fracture of the Union, he said that supporting Abolition would be equivalent to launching a John Brown–like attack on the South. As the *Herald* reported in December 1861, "The President is resolutely determined to veto schemes whatever, involving the emancipation of negroes in a manner that they are turned loose upon the Southern States on an equality with white occupiers of the soil. He, on Saturday evening, uttered the following words:—'Emancipation would be equivalent to a John Brown raid, on a gigantic scale.' "

By the end of the war, Lincoln had not only emancipated the slaves but had conquered the South largely because he had directed what well might be called "a John Brown raid, on a gigantic scale."

To understand Lincoln's embrace of Brown-like methods, counterfactual history is again useful. A crucial moment in the war was the election of 1864. If Lincoln had lost that election, America might have turned out to be quite a different nation from what it became. The South had fought long and hard, and its morale showed little sign of flagging. At certain moments the South had come close to turning the tide of the war in its favor. A Northern victory, then, was by no means automatic.

Nor was Lincoln's in the 1864 race. Through the first four months of that year his chances looked poor. In early May 1864, he actually drafted a speech stating that "it seems exceedingly probable that this Administration will not be re-elected" and that he would cooperate with his successor, preserving the Union until the latter took office. As late as August, Horace Greeley could write in the *Tribune:* "Mr. Lincoln is already beaten. He cannot be elected. We must have another ticket to save us from utter overthrow."

If Lincoln's successor had been, say, a Peace Democrat like McClellan, a compromise might very well have been worked out whereby the South would have been granted the independent status it sought. The South, which had been the world's leading cotton producer before the war, would have flourished economically for some time.

As for Southern blacks, their fate would have been grim. Even if they were emancipated, they would remain virtually enslaved. The Thirteenth, Fourteenth, and Fifteenth amendments would not have been passed, and the horrors of Jim Crow and the Ku Klux Klan would have multiplied exponentially. Blacks would have been denied not only professional advancement but also geographical mobility, so that the great migration to northern cities would not have occurred.

There are two possibilities for what might have happened in the long term. The least likely, I believe, is that America would have remained disunified. However, had that happened, America would not have developed into the world superpower it became, because it would have lacked economic and political solidity. The second scenario—a civil war that would have come later in the century—would, as suggested above, have had horrific results. And, again, there was no guarantee that the North would have won. As it happened, Lincoln was elected, which set the stage for the North's victory, America's prosperity and strength, and the passage of the constitutional amendments that eventually led to civil rights.

The question becomes: What brought about Lincoln's election? Most historians agree that, without the victories of Sherman and other generals in the fall of 1864, Lincoln would probably not have been reelected. To the success of the fall campaign may be added two longer-term factors that contributed to the North's success: emancipation and the use of black troops.

In all three areas—emancipation, black enlistment, and Sherman-like fighting—John Brown had influence. A group of Brown's supporters were the earliest and strongest advocates of emancipation early in the war. At a time when Lincoln dismissed Abolition as "a John Brown raid, on a gigantic scale," Stearns, Sanborn, Phillips, and other followers of Brown formed the Emancipation League, demanding that freedom for the slaves must be a primary goal of the war.

Followers of Brown also led the way in raising black troops. In 1862, Brown's most generous funder, George Stearns, initiated a virtually one-man campaign to recruit blacks for possible enlistment. He worked ten to eighteen hours a day, visiting black communities throughout the North in an effort to generate interest in fighting for the Union. At first he was ridiculed, but in the end he managed, at great personal expense, to raise several black companies. He felt he honored Brown's memory by doing so. When Gerrit Smith contributed to the venture, Stearns thanked him for his help "to make this a true John Brown corps." Stearns was joyful at having created what he called two "John Brown regiments." Federal endorsement came his way when Lincoln's secretary of war, Edwin McMasters Stanton, noticed his work and appointed him an adjutant assistant general with the rank of major to recruit black soldiers nationwide. Stearns accepted the appointment, as historian Charles Heller notes, to "fulfill John Brown's dream of an army of African Americans liberating their brothers and sisters." In 1863, outraged at a reduction in the pay of African American soldiers, he persuaded Frederick Douglass to go to Stanton and Lincoln to lobby for equal pay.

When black enlistment became a federal program, it was fitting that the first to take regular command of a black regiment was Thomas Wentworth Higginson, Brown's most radical supporter. When Higginson was asked if he wanted to command the all-black First South Carolina Volunteers, he knew he was realizing a dream of his friend John Brown, who had championed blacks fighting for liberation. He declared that he "had been an abolitionist too long and had known and loved John Brown too well, not to feel a thrill of joy at last on finding myself in the position where he only wished to be."

The enlistment of black troops made a huge difference in the war, both strategically and symbolically. Douglass called black enlistment "the greatest event of our nation's history, if not the greatest event of the century." Ulysses S. Grant said, "I have given the subject of arming the Negro my hearty support. This, with the emancipation of the Negro, is the heavyest blow yet given the Confederacy. . . . By arming the Negro we have added a powerful ally. They will make good soldiers and taking them from the enemy weaken him in the same proportion they strengthen us." He added, "The South cares a great deal about it."

The South *did* care a great deal about it, for much the same reason that it had been terrified by Brown's plan to arm blacks. The South linked emancipation and arming blacks with social chaos and devastation. And it associated such calamities with John Brown. The fact that white and black soldiers marched south wreaking devastation while singing the John Brown song was a demonic realization of the South's deepest fears. A typical proslavery journalist called it "an abomination . . . when the New England soldiers marched through this city, they made it hideous as hell by singing and shouting '*John Brown's soul is marching on.*' " The song, continued the writer, embodied all the evils of the "Negro-worshipping" North. Was John Brown's soul marching on? he asked, and then hissed the South's answer:

> So it is, we have little doubt, *marching on* to the music of despotism, ignorance, revenge and lust, that swells up like a gorgon from the bottomless pit, out of the brazen throats of the Negro-worshipping mobs! *Marching on*, as a pestilence or a contagion, or a thing of horror

and death marches on! Behind its march are the wails of widows, the screams of children, the vain implorations of defenseless old men, and the humiliation of manhood. Before it, the insane gibberish and fantastic dance of Negroes, of both white and black complexion, making night and day hideous with infernal delight. Marching on!— alas, poor country! Alas, human nature! Why do we write these things now? Because we love, and we would save our country. Because we would bring our countrymen to their senses, by holding up the John Brown raid as a glass for them to see their faces in.

But holding the John Brown raid as "a glass for them to see their faces in" had come to mean something very different to Northerners than it once had. In the week just after the raid the Northerners had recoiled from the raid in horror. By the midpoint of the war, however, they began to look in the mirror and liked what they saw when they saw John Brown. For them, Brown's soul *was* marching on, at the very front of their ranks as they stormed south in a war of emancipation.

For that is what it had become. Historian James M. McPherson has found that by the third year of the war "most white soldiers" fought for "black liberty as well as Union." John Brown had said more than once that an entire generation of Americans might have to die for the slave to be free, and his last written words were that slavery would end only after "*verry much* bloodshed." He had foreseen an Abolitionist war, and an Abolitionist war is what eventually came.

For this reason Brown was increasingly associated with the North's goals in the war. As early as 1862 one writer noted, "Not a few of the Abolition papers are in the habit of referring to 'John Brown's soul' as the guiding star of this war, and they frequently express their satisfaction that 'his soul is marching on.'" The next year, a speaker at a British antislavery meeting made this observation about Brown's broadening impact: "That spirit that rises from his grave inspired at first only a few men; but, constantly widening in its influence, has at length leavened great masses, and now leads mighty armies in this tremendous war, which has at last avowedly become a war of emancipation. Well, indeed, may the negro sing:—'John Brown's body lies mouldering in the grave, / But his soul is marching on!'"

Another speaker at the meeting went even further. Brown's spirit did not merely "inspire" or "lead" the war. Rather, the war *was* John Brown. With every Northern attack on the South, Brown's life was being written: "Not yet is his life, or death, unfolded; but two millions of bayonet-pens are to-day busy writing his biography, and each month adds a new chapter to his life." "That old man's name is now the watchword in the greatest struggle in history," the speaker continued. One must be blind, he said, "who does not see in the United States army the million-grained ear of corn of which John Brown was the buried seed. . . . Every drum that beats in America is made of the skin of old John Brown. . . . It was John Brown that issued the first Emancipation Proclamation; it was by military necessity."

Emancipation achieved through violence: this had been Brown's goal, and now it was the North's. If Lincoln's election in 1864 resulted from the victories of his generals, it was because his generals had adopted some of Brown's tactics.

David Hunter was the first of Lincoln's generals who resembled Brown in his approach to war. Appointed the head of the Department of the South in 1862, Hunter said that Brown was "well known to me in Kansas." With Hunter, as with Brown, the aim of war was to liberate blacks, through extreme violence if necessary. He declared that the "great God of the Universe has determined that . . . the only way in which this war is to be ended" is "by advanc[ing] south, proclaiming the Negro free and arming him as I go." He enlisted the black regiment that Higginson commanded. A latter-day Puritan, Hunter shared Brown's admiration for Cromwell, once explaining that black soldiers had "religious sentiment . . . which [was what] made the soldiers of Oliver Cromwell invincible." Brown had murdered proslavery citizens under God's direction; in the same vein Hunter issued a decree, which he said was "ordered by an all-wise Providence," stating that he would "execute every rebel officer and every rebel slaveholder in my possession."

It was not until Hunter's strategy solidified in the "total war" doctrine of later Union generals that the North's victory was assured. According to this doctrine, elucidated by Sherman and carried out by him and several other generals, including Ulysses S. Grant and John Pope, virtually anything was fair game to gain victory in war. The Union had Right on its side. Aggressive action of any kind was justified to make sure that Right won. When the total-war strategy went into effect in the summer and fall of 1864, the North gained impressive victories, and Lincoln's reelection chances got a huge boost.

Critics of John Brown have often berated his policy of stealing the property of those he attacked. Such behavior, it is argued, brings into question his motives, making him appear to be a horse thief and vandal rather than a heroic liberator. It is true that Brown felt justified in seizing property of the "enemy" that might prove useful to his cause. But one cannot criticize him in this regard without criticizing the Union Army, which used a similar policy to win the Civil War. Total war meant attacking the whole South: not just its military forces but its economic centers, its transportation grids, and the property of its civilians. It also meant free appropriation of all Southern property and goods that Lincoln's generals believed would speed victory.

Sherman outlined the total-war strategy in 1863 when he wrote that in order to gain victory "we will remove and destroy every obstacle, if need be, take every life, every acre of land, every particle or property; . . . that we will not cease till our end is attained; that all who do not aid us are enemies, and that we will not account to them for our acts." He explained to his wife that his goal was "extermination, not of soldiers alone, that is the least of the trouble, but of the people also." She responded that she too desired "a war of extermination and that all [Southerners] would be driven like swine into the sea." To facilitate this brutal kind of war, Sherman, with Lincoln's approval, enlisted many roughs and criminals fresh from prison. Worlds apart from John Brown in his racial views, Sherman had as much contempt for blacks, Jews, Hispanics, and Native Americans as he did for the Southern rebels he hoped to destroy; within four months of Appomattox he would launch a campaign against the Plains Indians that amounted to attempted ethnic genocide.

In Sherman's famous march from Atlanta to the sea and then north through the Carolinas, he cut a swath of devastation across the South. John Brown had tried to be selective in the enemy property he stole. In contrast, Sherman admitted that only 20 percent of the robbery and ruin he caused was from military necessity. The remaining 80 percent, he boasted, was "simple waste and destruction" for the purpose of "making Georgia howl."

When the South charged the North with having committed atrocities, the response was that civilians' holdings, not civilians themselves, were targeted. In fact, however, many civilian deaths did result from Sherman's stated policy that "we are not only fighting hostile armies but a hostile people, and must make old and young, rich and poor, feel the hard hand of war as well as their organized armies." Although the exact number of civilian casualties that resulted from the "Hammer-and-Anvil" campaigns of Sherman and Grant is unknown, the fates of some 50,000 unaccounted-for Confederates can be surmised.

In some of the Border States, where guerilla warfare raged, both Union and Confederate troops committed atrocities against civilians that made Pottawatomie seem tame. Particularly in Missouri, soldiers on both sides not only slaughtered civilians but dismembered them, slicing off scalps, ears, noses, fingers, and toes and brandishing them as battle trophies. John Brown's most heinous action was emulated on a tremendous scale. Some

John Wilkes Booth.
LIBRARY OF CONGRESS.

might excuse the Civil War soldiers because they were using the tactics of violent intimidation during wartime and with the sanction of the government, whereas Brown was not. But in Bleeding Kansas in 1856, Brown felt that he was very much in a war, and there was no government (but God's) to which he could appeal.

Lincoln's reelection, which owed much to the Brown-like strategy of his generals, also provoked a Brown-like reaction in the man who would later assassinate him, John Wilkes Booth.

Booth was appalled when he realized in the fall of 1864 that Lincoln might return to office. For Booth, Lincoln was a vulgar, low warmonger, whereas John Brown was a grand, if politically misled, hero. Lincoln, Booth told his sister, was just a "Sectional Candidate" who if reelected would become the evil "king" of America:

> This man's appearance, his pedigree, his coarse low jokes and anec-
> dotes, his vulgar similes, and his policy are a disgrace to the seat he

holds. *Other brains rule the country. He* is made the tool of the North, to crush out, or try to crush out slavery, by robbery, rapine, slaughter and bought armies. He is walking in the footprints of old John Brown, but no more fit to stand with that great hero—Great God! No. John Brown was a man inspired, the grandest man of this century! *He* [Lincoln] is Bonaparte in one great move, that is, by overturning this blind Republic and making himself a king. This man's re-election which will follow his success, I tell you, will be a reign!

Although Booth's hatred of Lincoln typified the Southern attitude, his veneration of John Brown did not. How could Booth, who had said that at Brown's execution, "I looked at the traitor and terrorizer with unlimited, undeniable contempt," now call Brown a "great hero," "the grandest man of the century"?

We can begin to answer this question when we consider Booth's reaction to Lincoln's reelection in November 1864. In Booth's bitter view, the North had not only become *like* John Brown; it had gone far *beyond* John Brown in the breadth and intensity of its terror campaign against the South. As he wrote to his sister:

> When I aided in the capture and execution of John Brown (who was a murderer on our Western Border, and was fairly *tried* and *convicted*, before an impartial judge & jury—of treason—and who by the way has since been made a God[)]—I was proud of my little share in the transaction, for I deemed it my duty and that I was helping our common country to perform an act of justice. But what was a crime in poor John Brown is now considered (by themselves) as the greatest and only virtue, of the whole Republican party. Strange transmigration. *Vice* to be come a *virtue* simply because *more* indulge in it.
>
> I thought then, *as now*, that the abolitionists *were the only traitors* in the land, and that this entire party deserved the fate of poor old John Brown, not because they wish to abolish slavery, but on account of the means they have used to effect that abolition. If Brown were living, I doubt if he *himself* would set slavery against the Union. Most, or many, in the North do, and openly curse the Union if the South are to return and retain a *single right* guaranteed them by every tie which we once *revered as sacred*. The South can make no choice. It is either extermination or slavery for *themselves* (worse than death) to draw from. I would know my choice.

Booth was saying that as bad as Brown was—a murderer and a traitor now deified in the North—the Lincoln administration was much worse because it willfully embraced on a grand scale what had been deemed criminal in Brown. The isolated crime of "poor John Brown" had become "the greatest and only virtue, of the whole Republican party." Even Brown, Booth insisted, would not destroy the Union and devastate the South in order to wipe out slavery. Lincoln would.

What Booth did not realize was that Lincoln was every bit as committed to saving the Union as Brown was. The difference between the two was that Lincoln did not adopt Brown's violent, emancipationist tactics until more moderate methods had failed. By 1864, Lincoln *was* like Brown in his vision of a unified America that had rid itself of slavery through violence. In his Second Inaugural Address he used the same kind of Calvinist imagery yoked with apocalyptic antislavery passion that had characterized John Brown. Lincoln declared that a righteous God was in control who might very well demand that additional oceans of blood be spilled to rid the nation of slavery. But, he said, "if God wills that [the war] continue" until every drop of slave blood is repaid by another drawn with the sword, we must keep in mind that "the judgments of the Lord are true and righteous altogether." Like John Brown, he was now the Cromwellian warrior against slavery.

This was too much for John Wilkes Booth. Shortly before murdering Lincoln, Booth confessed that he had become "supremely unhappy with history itself" and that something "great & decisive" had to be done. Booth had become like John Brown, the angry terrorist—but in reverse. Brown had found the nation and its government aligned with slavery, which he wanted to topple with violence. Booth found the nation and its government aligned against slavery, and he wanted to strike out in violent protest.

This was why he had come to view Brown as a great hero. After all, Brown had changed history in a single stroke, like Brutus and many other Shakespearean villains Booth had played. Booth thought that perhaps he, too, could play a hero on the national stage. Who knew? Perhaps by shooting Lincoln he would become even grander than "the grandest man of the century," John Brown.

Booth was, of course, horribly mistaken. His last reported words, when trapped and killed in the barn of Richard Garrett's farm near Bowling Green, Virginia, were "Useless, useless," and they were true. By April 1865 the proslavery cause was useless, a thing of the past, gone with the wind.

John Wilkes Booth had lost. John Brown had won.

18

Posterity

As John Brown had predicted, America purged itself of its greatest evil, chattel slavery, through a massive bloodletting. Lincoln did what he had initially been reluctant to do: he launched what he called "a John Brown raid, on a gigantic scale" to emancipate the slaves.

After Lincoln's death, key questions faced the nation. How should the Southern states be reintegrated into the Union? To what extent should former rebels be punished? Above all, how should the 4 million freed blacks be handled? Should they be compensated for their sufferings? Should they be given full rights as American citizens?

Conservatives answered that the erstwhile rebels should be treated leniently and that the freedmen should be left to the mercy of the individual Southern states. Radicals insisted that the South must be harshly punished through Northern military occupation and the freedmen must receive full citizenship rights.

In the eyes of the South, many Northerners were flaming radicals whose anarchic, violent society had unleashed a cruel war on stable Southern institutions. A writer for *DeBow's Review* argued in 1866 that New Englanders were "fanatics, radicals, and destructives by inheritance, just the same people now as in the days of Cromwell's Independents, and of witch-burners and Quaker hangers two centuries ago; whilst we find the Southern people by inheritance, and continuous usage, . . . the most conservative people in the civilized world," having descended from "high-toned Monarchists, Legitimatists, Cavaliers, tories of the English stamp and descent, . . . and scions of the English gentry and nobility." The writer continued, "Opposed to innovation and change, the South was happy, peaceful, and contented, until assailed by Northern abolition." Tracing the faddish movements of the North to the revolutionary individualism of early Puritan New England, the writer declared that "there are now almost as many religions, isms, infidelities, and superstitions in New England as there are men. . . . These Radicals, with their tools, the German infidels [i.e., the Transcendentalists, who were strongly influenced by German philosophy], rule this nation, and if undisturbed in power, will soon ruin it. . . . The American Republic is near its end." Until Abolitionism became aggressive, the "Radicalism in the North [had been] checked, balanced, and sufficiently counterpoised hitherto by the excessive Conservatism of the South; but . . . now, the South being powerless, Northern Radicalism will have full swing and dominion, and, unless the South is speedily restored to the Union, will, by rash innovations and radical changes, destroy our present form of government."

In retrospect, John Brown appeared to be the most villainous Northerner of all. Conservatives took the side of Brown's old foe, Andrew Johnson, now president of the United States. A white supremacist who believed that the Southern states should be allowed to handle the freedmen issue by themselves, Johnson had been Brown's most visible critic. He had excoriated Brown in the Senate on December 12, 1859, describing the Pottawatomie killings in detail. After the war Johnson's supporters resurrected the speech in an effort to sully those who opposed his policies, especially the Radical Republicans in Congress. One editor, Charles Chauncey Burr, reprinted in his newspaper long sections of Johnson's speech on Brown. By way of introduction, Burr made this sour comment about the war's outcome and John Brown:

> The pulpits generally, and a majority of Republican papers, now boastingly rejoice that "*the North has vindicated the cause of John Brown, and wiped out slavery.*" Nor is this any foolish or unconsidered boast; it is strictly true. The policy of the Republican party, since it came into power, has been a faithful carrying out of the work begun by old John Brown. . . . The record of this party is in revolution and blood; in the revolution and blood inaugurated by John Brown. It has finished the raid which that prince of assassins and thieves, John Brown, began.

In the proslavery mind, the Republican Party, Lincoln's armies, and John Brown were amoral brutes. The North's claims to virtue were undermined by its worship of "that prince of assassins and thieves, John Brown." Having opposed Brown, President Johnson was in the right when he recommended leniency toward the defeated South.

Those infamous criminals, Brown and Lincoln, so the argument went, had followed in the footsteps of the Transcendentalists, the archpriests of the higher law. Proslavery Southerners had long viewed Transcendentalism as the epitome of the Puritan-based, lawbreaking individualism of the North. Just before the war, the Southern essayist William Falconer described what he regarded as anarchic New England Puritanism, which, he argued, fostered Northerners' devotion to "the *higher* or moral law, . . . which, in legislation, is called *higher-lawism*, and in their literature, constitutes that element recognized as *transcendentalism.*" Similarly, a writer for the *Democratic Review* indicted "this transcendental age," saying that "the Puritans of New-England" passed down "probably nineteenths of the strange, extravagant, absurd notions" of the North, including Abolitionism. Typical of the North's wildness was Seward, the "transcendental senator, whose conscience is above all laws, except of his own creating."

The Ohio Democrat Samuel S. Cox developed the point in a speech of 1863. Impugning "the Constitution-breaking, law-defying, negro-loving Phariseeism of New England," Cox generalized, "Abolition is the offspring of Puritanism. Until Abolition arose, the Union was never seriously menaced; the South was never endangered." The North's fanaticism was shown by the fact that its "Marseillaise is a hymn of apotheosis to John Brown—a horse-thief and a murderer." And the chief supporters of Brown, he continued, were those modern Puritans, the Transcendentalists, who absurdly put black people and white people on the same level. Cox got his proslavery audience laughing when he parodied the antislavery views of two leading Transcendentalists, Alcott and Emerson: "He [Alcott] being all in all, he holds himself personally responsible for the obliquity of the earth's axis. (Laughter.) Do you wonder, therefore, that he holds himself responsible for slavery in Carolina? Another [Transcendentalist], Emerson, holds that he is God; that God is every thing; therefore he is every thing. (Merriment.) Do you wonder, therefore, that since he makes the Negro a part of himself, he holds him to be his equal?"

As abhorrent as was Cox's tone, his summary of the Transcendentalists' radical social program was surprisingly accurate. Not only were the Transcendentalists Brown's strongest supporters, but their earlier racism had been replaced by Brown-like attitudes on slavery and race.

The views of the leading Transcendentalist, Emerson, are especially revealing. Emerson's statements that John Brown's name permeated the war and that Brown's court speech was as great as the Gettysburg Address show that he was still very much under Brown's sway during the war. This helps to explain why he peppered his journals with stinging remarks about the South and with demands for social rights for blacks. He was an early, ardent advocate of war for emancipation. The war made ethical matters simple, he maintained. The South was wrong about slavery and the North was right. Emancipation was justified by "the eternal right of it." Addressing the North, he wrote: "The difference between you & your enemies is eternal . . . yours to protect and establish the rights of men; and theirs to crush them." The North's duty, therefore, was to overwhelm the South: "Any & every arrangement short of forcible subjugation of the rebel country, will be flat disloyalty, on our part."

Most remarkable was how far Emerson had progressed on race. He sided with the most radical politician, Charles Sumner, on racial issues, and lamented what he saw as Lincoln's conservatism. He commented in 1862 that Lincoln "thinks emancipation almost morally wrong, & resorts to it only as a desperate measure, & means never to put radicals into power." In a stunning reversal of the message of the Dred Scott decision, Emerson wrote, "The [Southern] rebel has no rights which the Negro or white man is bound to respect." This assigning of a supreme position to blacks in league with antislavery whites recalled John Brown.

Also, Emerson was quick to take a stand on the vote for African Americans. "Let us agree," he wrote in 1862, "that every man shall have what he honestly earns, and, if he is a sane & innocent man, have an equal vote in the state, and a fair chance in society. . . . This time, no compromises, no concealments, no crimes . . . tucked in under another name, like, 'persons held to labor,' meaning persons stolen & 'held' meaning held by hand-cuffs, when they are not under whips." "The obvious remedy" for America's social problems, he argued, was "to give the Negro the vote."

After an 1864 meeting with Wendell Phillips, Emerson made this powerful assessment: "The two points seem to be absolute Emancipation—establishing the fact that the United States henceforward knows no color, no race, in its law, but legislates for all alike,—one law for all men:—*that* first; and, secondly, make the confiscation of rebel property final, as you did with the tories in the Revolution."

He went so far as to recommend that monetary reparations be paid to enslaved blacks after they were emancipated. He created a sensation when he read aloud his Abolitionist poem "Boston Hymn" on January 1, 1863, before the 3,000 in Boston's Music Hall and later at the John Brown party at the Stearnses' mansion. A paean to emancipation, the poem sent what was called "something like an electric shock" through the audience when Emerson read the following verse:

Pay ransom to the owner
And fill the bag to the brim.
Who is the owner? The slave is owner,
And ever was. Pay him.

Emerson was not just saying, "Pay freed blacks wages for their work." He was insisting that since the slave "ever was" the true owner of his own labor, "ransom" must be paid for past suffering—and the money bag should be filled "to the brim." Again, only John Brown would have made such a radical statement. Fittingly, Emerson contributed his poem to the Stearnses to be put in a commemorative album entitled *John Brown Album / Emancipation Evening / 1863*.

Emerson's radicalism on the issue of African Americans becomes clear when we compare his stance with that of others. Several who were otherwise forward-looking were surprisingly ambivalent about suffrage for blacks. William Lloyd Garrison, who tried to disband the American Anti-Slavery Society in 1863, believing its work completed, saw no advantage in giving blacks the vote. Like two other famous antislavery figures, William Henry Seward and Lyman Trumbull, Garrison thought that the South should be able to rejoin the Union easily, with freedmen left to the mercy of their former masters. Several Republicans who took a stronger position— including Thaddeus Stevens, Benjamin Wade, George S. Boutwell, and Jacob Howard—supported suffrage for blacks, but chiefly as a means of punishing the South. A few others, such as Charles Sumner, Horace Greeley, and Salmon Chase followed Lincoln's lead by endorsing black suffrage out of principle, but with qualifications and limitations.

Emerson, like John Brown before him, displayed no such reservations on the issue. None conceptually, but large ones in practice. His most radical statements were in his private journal. Ever averse to public lobbying, he refused offers to go on the warpath for African American suffrage. On the matter of race, he was a closet radical, not a public warrior. Here he differed sharply not only from Brown but also from his and Brown's mutual friend, George Stearns.

Just as Stearns had spearheaded the recruitment of black soldiers, so he led the way in the fight for African American suffrage. Although close to Emerson through much of the war, he was disappointed by the sage's reluctance to publicize his radical views. Deciding that "little more [was] to be expected from him," Stearns turned to another Transcendentalist, Bronson Alcott, who was eager to help out with the suffrage cause. Despite his worthy intentions, however, Alcott was temperamentally as reluctant to enter the political lists as was Emerson.

Stearns was left to carry on the battle virtually alone. He vowed to a friend that he would "advocate Negro suffrage with as much zeal and confidence too that we shall obtain it as we did emancipation last year." He did so in the spirit of the man for whom, as he liked to boast, he had bought John Brown's rifles to fight slavery. His biographer writes that in pursuing the vote for blacks Stearns aimed at achieving "the goal of the martyred John Brown."

Stearns perhaps did as much as Charles Sumner for black citizenship. As early as 1862, he took the first steps in establishing what became the Freedmen's Bureau, designed to aid emancipated blacks. After the war, when he saw that the conservative Andrew Johnson did not pursue the vote for blacks, he decided to advance the cause on his own. He founded a newspaper, the *Right Way*, which promoted full political rights for African Americans. Just as he had anticipated emancipation by forming his Emancipation League early in the war, so he formed the Impartial Suffrage Association, designed to influence Congress to readmit only those states that granted the vote to all their citizens "without regard to race and color." Although he would not see his dream come to fruition, since he died of pneumonia in April 1867, he contributed strongly to the movement for African American suffrage, which came with the passage of the Fifteenth Amendment in 1870. Emerson eulogized Stearns by saying that he "became, in the most natural manner, an indispensable power in the State." A measure of Stearns's goodness, said Emerson, was his closeness to "Captain John Brown, who was not only an extraordinary man, but one who had a rare magnetism for men of character, and attached some of the best and noblest to him, on very short acquaintance, by lasting ties."

Another of Brown's supporters, Samuel G. Howe, pursued the formation of the Freedman's Bureau when Stearns had gone on to other activities. Howe was one of three members of a commission that set the Bureau in operation after the war. As John Brown had gone to Chatham before Harpers Ferry, Howe visited blacks in Canada to get tips about how American blacks should regulate themselves and their society.

Given the importance of Brown's followers in the fight for the black vote, it is small wonder that Brown was sometimes seen as the controlling power behind Radical Reconstruction. The Northern journalist Sidney H. Morse in 1868 described the Civil War as a John Brown raid in a positive sense: a holy war for sectional and racial brotherhood. Brown's prison cell,

Morse wrote, was "the chapel of the Most High, and himself the high priest of his century." The John Brown song was the "song of cheer" that stirred Union soldiers "on every battlefield." Brown himself was "the irresistible, omnipotent man" who pointed the way to "universal rules of suffrage" that would guarantee equal rights to all Americans, irrespective of race or sex. "Looking at events to-day," Morse wrote anxiously, "the country seems yet groping in the path which Brown pointed out."

Morse had reason to be anxious. Although the future of African Americans looked bright, due to the Fifteenth Amendment and increasing political participation during the later 1860s and early '70s, Reconstruction collapsed in 1876. Eight decades of segregation and violence against blacks began.

It was no accident that the most negative portraits of Brown came during the years between 1880 and 1950, a time when Jim Crow and the Ku Klux Klan ruled in the South and were tolerated from afar in the North. During this period of rampant discrimination, Brown's struggle for racial equality held little appeal for leading white historians, many of whom were Southern in sympathy. As a result, Brown's alleged criminality and insanity stood out starkly, unrelieved by redeeming qualities.

The downturn of Brown's reputation began in 1883 with a debate over the role of the Transcendentalists, who were accused of using their cultural clout to rehabilitate the reputation of a common criminal. This was the argument of the Chicago minister David N. Utter, who in a widely read *North American Review* article charged the Transcendentalists with distorting John Brown by falsely idealizing him. It was the nation's misfortune, Utter argued, that Brown was promoted by writers "whose peers did not exist in America," who "have made our history and written it, and . . . have made our literature. They made the public sentiment that abolished slavery." Utter explained: "When these men said, John Brown is a hero and a saint, the bravest and the cleanest of all the heroes of ancient and modern times, there was nothing for it but to accept the verdict." These authors knew Brown was a lawbreaker but loved him for it: "The very fact that he had fought unlawfully added to his glory. No doctrine has ever been dearer to New England than the doctrine of the 'higher law.' This is an invisible and unwritten law which each man must find for himself, read and interpret for himself, and obey in his own way. If it leads him to disobey certain human enactments, so much the better." Blinded by their devotion to the higher law, Utter declared, the Transcendentalists brought ruin upon the nation by deifying a contemptible murderer.

Utter was answered by J. J. Ingalls, who defended the Transcendentalists and Brown's Kansas record. Pottawatomie, he insisted, was justified by proslavery outrages in Kansas. Ingalls berated Utter for "alleging that Ralph Waldo Emerson, Henry Thoreau, Theodore Parker, and other radical abolitionists, the makers of our history and literature, the trusted leaders of the North in the war for the Union, . . . conspired to impose a false verdict upon mankind" regarding John Brown.

When in 1885 a member of the Transcendentalist circle, Frank Sanborn, came out with *The Life and Letters of John Brown*, some took the opportunity to lash out again against the group, claiming that it helped bring about a terrible war by deifying Brown. Sanborn was vulnerable to such criticism, since he was both an unabashed fan of Brown and an admiring biographer of Emerson, Thoreau, Alcott, and others of the Concord group.

Especially harsh attacks came from the Roman Catholic Church, the largest church in America. Despite its size, the Catholic Church felt bitter toward the Transcendentalists, not only because of their indifference to Christianity but also because of their reputation as intellectual cynosures, a reputation Catholics coveted for themselves. The church's main organ, the *Catholic World*, lambasted the Concord thinkers in a review of Sanborn's volume on Brown. The opening sentences of the review set the tone of the attack:

> There is a small company of New England Radicals who have been posing for the last quarter of a century as the special depositaries of Divine confidence. It is on the question of Negro slavery that they assume to have shared the secrets of Providence. They advocated the most violent measures of emancipation while slavery was established by law. . . . When slavery at last was swept away, they began to believe that they had done it all themselves.

Because these radicals controlled "Boston literary circles," the reviewer lamented, "it happens that they have persuaded a considerable minority of the public to accept them at their own valuation." Noting that Sanborn had "long been a conspicuous member . . . of this complacent little company," the reviewer went into the details of Pottawatomie to show that the Transcendentalists exalted a mere assassin because of their dangerously subversive views on race, slavery, and individualism.

Although heartless in its lack of sympathy for Brown's social ideals, such criticism at least addressed the vital role of the Transcendentalists in salvaging Brown from obscurity. Over time both attackers and supporters of

Brown lost sight of this role. In the age of Freud, psychology replaced philosophy as the key to scholarly discussions. Allan Nevins, for instance, wrote that Brown was afflicted by "paranoia," and the only reason he was not permanently put in a prison for the criminally insane was that the nineteenth century "did not have the benefit of modern knowledge of mental derangement."

Historians indifferent to racial issues vilified Brown. Charles Robinson, one of Brown's Kansas admirers who turned negative when he learned the truth about Pottawatomie, launched an anti-Brown campaign that led to his wife's paying $5,000 to H. Peebles Wilson to write a negative book on Brown. The book, *John Brown, Soldier of Fortune: A Critique* (1913), argued that Brown's violence was motivated by a desire to steal and kill, not by antislavery feelings. This obtuse argument was reiterated by James Malin in *John Brown and the Legend of Fifty-six*, who presented Brown as a petty criminal devoid of deep antislavery commitment. Astonishingly, Malin wrote of Brown, "It is not necessary to assume that he entertained any long-cherished plan for the abolition of slavery."

The Brown-bashing continued through much of the twentieth century. Revisionist historians, who blamed the Civil War on misled fanatics, had little sympathy for Brown. In literary studies the New Critics depoliticized the Transcendentalists, losing sight of their social radicalism and emphasizing their style and philosophical ideas. The halo that Emerson and Thoreau had placed around Brown dimmed notably when Emerson and Thoreau were themselves presented as socially complacent writers distanced from the slavery issue. Robert Penn Warren, the Kentucky poet associated with the New Critics, wrote a 1929 book on Brown that depicted him as brave but lawless. Like many conservative writers of his day, Warren leaned toward Southern agrarianism and thus had little toleration for Brown.

The ambivalence with which Brown has been viewed by whites contrasts sharply with the enthusiasm of his reception by African Americans. No white person in American history has aroused such warm admiration from blacks as has John Brown. Public displays of this admiration began during Brown's imprisonment and have continued into modern times.

Two weeks before Brown's hanging, an organization of black women reached out to his wife, offering assistance. There was no group in America (except Native American women) who were in a weaker position to offer money than were black women. But such a group did make an offer in a November 23 letter to Mary Brown, whom they addressed as "our beloved sister." The group said that it had met recently in the house of Brown's old friend the Reverend Henry Highland Garnet and had agreed to take up a fund from black women around the nation to help support John Brown's surviving family. Assuring Mary that her husband was "the apple of [God's] eye," the writer of the letter told her, "Henceforth you shall be our own! we are a poor and despised people—almost forbidden, by the oppressive restrictions of the Free States, to rise to the higher walks of lucrative employment, toiling early and late for our daily bread; but we hope—and we intend, by God's help—to organize in every Free State, and in every colored church, a band of sisters, to collect our weekly pence, and pour it lovingly into your lap." What became of the offer is unclear. But for an organization of black women even to *offer* money to a white woman was unprecedented.

Around the time of this offer, Charles H. Langston, the black Abolitionist from Ohio whom Brown had tried to enlist for the Harpers Ferry raid, defended Brown passionately in a letter published in the *Cleveland Plain Dealer.* He wrote the letter ostensibly to quell rumors that he had conspired in the Virginia plot but actually to praise Brown. Unlike white politicians such as Hale or Giddings who denied sympathy with Brown, Langston made a caustic racial point coupled with a bold tribute:

> To speak of myself I have no political prospects and therefore no political fears! For my black face and curly hair doom me in this land of equality to political damnation and that beyond the possibility of redemption. But I have a neck as dear to me as Smith's, Hale's or Giddings', and therefore I must like them publish a card of denial. So here it is. But what shall I deny? I cannot deny that I feel the very deepest sympathy with the Immortal John Brown in his heroic and daring efforts to free the slaves.

Brown's "aims and ends," Langston argued, "were lofty, noble, generous, benevolent, humane and Godlike"—a realization of the Bible and the Declaration of Independence.

The memorial services held by blacks on the day of Brown's execution had none of the ambivalence of those organized by whites. Whereas the whites often expressed an attitude of praise-the-man-but-not-the-deed, the blacks extolled everything about Brown, including his raid. Huge gatherings of blacks assembled in all the Northern cities in a vast outpouring of praise.

The Detroit meeting was typical. Many of the city's blacks, a good portion of them fugitives from slavery, crowded into the Second Baptist

Church, where John Brown was honored by hymns, speeches, and a sermon. An "Ode to Old Capt. John Brown" was sung, and George Hannibal Parker, the president of the "Old Capt. John Brown Liberty League," gave the first of several addresses. A collection for Brown's family was taken, followed by the singing of the "Marseillaise" and a patriotic song, "On on to battle—we fear no foe." William Lambert read a resolution in praise of "our much beloved and highly esteemed friend, Old Captain John Brown," who "by his bold, effective, timely blow" had "freely delivered up his life to lay as a ransom for our enslaved race and thereby, 'solitary and alone,' he has put a liberty ball in motion which shall continue to roll and gather strength until the last vestige of human slavery within this nation shall have been crushed beneath the ponderous weight." The blacks present resolved to keep John Brown "in the most sacred remembrance" as "the first disinterested martyr for our liberty," and "to concentrate our efforts in keeping the old Brown liberty-ball in motion and thereby continue to kindle the fires of liberty upon the altar of every determined heart among men."

This prediction that Brown's raid would lead to a war to end slavery was made more consistently by blacks than by whites. The Baptist preacher J. Sella Martin, addressing a Boston meeting where, according to a reporter, "all the colored people of Boston and its vicinity were present," said that Brown's invasion spelled the death of slavery. "I have not the slightest doubt that this will be the result," Martin declared. "John Brown has died, but the life of Freedom, from his death, shall flow forth to this nation." Martin said he knew there was "some quibbling" over Brown's violent tactics by "men of peace principles." But not only was Brown's violence justifiable, Martin insisted; it was as admirable as the American Revolution—even more so, because of its implications for race relations. "I remember Concord, and Bunker Hill, and every historic battlefield in this country," Martin announced, "and the celebration of those events, all go to approve the means that John Brown has used; the only difference being, that in our battles, in America means have been used for *white* and that John Brown has used his means for *black* men."

During the war, John Brown occupied a special place in the hearts of African Americans. One black woman was quoted as saying, "We Negroes in the South never call him John Brown; we call him *our* Saviour. *He died for us.*" By a coincidence that Calvinists would have called a remarkable providence, one of the first black soldiers who died for the Union cause was named John Brown. When Thomas Wentworth Higginson's regiment attacked a rebel force on St. Simon's Island, Georgia, Brown led the charge and was the first to be killed. The soldier's father, as Higginson later wrote, "fully believes, to this day, that the 'John Brown Song,' which all the soldiers sing, relates to his son, and to him only."

The father was wrong literally but right in spirit. Although the song referred to no single soldier, it had special meaning for blacks. It was by far the favorite song among African American troops, who sang it everywhere. Most memorably, the 54th Massachusetts Regiment, under Colonel Robert Gould Shaw, thundered forth the song as it marched down Boston's State Street, headed south, on May 18, 1863, not long before its heroic attack on Fort Wagner, South Carolina. Shaw himself, though on the opposite end of the economic spectrum from Brown, resembled Brown in his willingness to die for freedom. He befriended his black troops, respected them, and died by their side at Fort Wagner, where he was buried with twelve of them. When Shaw's family requested his body, the Confederates replied snidely, "We buried him below his niggers," a phrase that became a badge of honor among Abolitionists sympathetic to blacks. Shaw's fate reminded the British writer Elizabeth Gaskell of the story about Brown kissing a black girl on his way to the gallows. "The dying blessing of the martyr," Gaskell wrote, "will descend from generation to generation, and a whole race will cherish the memory of that simple caress, so degrading as it seemed to the slaveholders around him."

The kiss *did* become a popular legend. More important, what the legend signified—John Brown's unmatched closeness to blacks—gathered new significance over time. A winding but unbroken thread of influences ran from Brown to the civil rights movement.

The thread began at Harpers Ferry. Just as the town epitomized the war, trading hands many times and being ravaged by both Northern and Southern troops, so in the postwar years it symbolized the spirit of Radical Reconstruction. Storer College, one the nation's first integrated institutions of higher learning, was founded there in 1867. Originally a project of the Freedmen's Bureau, the college received funding from the Maine businessman John Storer, who specified that the institution be run according to the principles of John Brown. No applicant would be refused on the basis of race or sex.

Storer College became the launching pad for vital efforts on behalf of African Americans. In 1881, Frederick Douglass gave a historic speech there in honor of John Brown, whom he described as having begun the war that ended slavery.

What made the speech important was that Douglass did not give blanket approval to Brown. Instead, he made a measured assessment of Brown in light of his historical contexts. Douglass distanced himself from the

Harpers Ferry raid, as he had decades earlier, insisting he was not directly involved in "this strange, wild, bloody and mournful drama." Douglass said that viewed alone, "as a transaction separate and distinct from its antecedents and bearings," the raid "takes rank with the most cold-blooded and atrocious wrongs ever perpetrated." But the same could be said, Douglass continued, of Sherman's march to the sea. Brown's violence, like that of Lincoln's generals, must be viewed historically. In resorting to violence, Brown was making up for centuries of outrages committed against American blacks. "The bloody harvest of Harpers Ferry," Douglass declared, "was written by the heat and moisture of merciless bondage of more than 200 years." Now, Douglass asserted, Brown may be called "our noblest American hero." Douglass stated: "He was a great miracle-worker, in his day, but time has worked for him a greater miracle than all his miracles, for now his name stands for all that is desirable in government, noble in life, orderly and beautiful in society. That which time has done for other great men of his class, that will time certainly do for John Brown."

Ironically, it was only two years after Douglass made this glowing prediction of Brown's future stature as an American hero that David Utter initiated the long series of negative commentaries that dragged Brown through the mud during the next several decades. But it was only whites who were negative. Black commentators continued to idealize Brown.

It is understandable that they did. The African American experience reached its nadir during the four decades after 1880. Blacks revered the memory of John Brown, viewing him as the only white American who fully identified with their cause.

During this period blacks faced segregation, disenfranchisement, and racist violence. In 1896 the Supreme Court gave its imprimatur to racial segregation in the case of *Plessy v. Ferguson*. Thirteen years later President Woodrow Wilson sanctioned segregation in the federal government. Throughout the South, restrictive voting laws virtually nullified the Fifteenth Amendment. Lynching of blacks was appallingly widespread. Between 1890 and 1910 more than 2,000 blacks were publicly murdered. The victims were often burned alive by mobs of cheering whites. The killers went unpunished. They justified their action on supposed threats of violence from blacks, invoking the stereotype of the savage black promoted in D. W. Griffith's 1915 film *Birth of a Nation*.

In this nightmarish atmosphere John Brown remained a major source of inspiration and encouragement to blacks. T. Thomas Fortune, the black editor of the *New York Age*, regarded Brown as a model of bloody revolution that blacks must follow. In May 1900, Fortune addressed a large African

American crowd that gathered in Brooklyn's Odd Fellows Hall to celebrate the hundredth anniversary of Brown's birth. Fortune extolled Brown as a martyr for freedom. Without Brown, Fortune insisted, the Civil War would not have occurred when it did. Very likely the North and the South would have compromised, and, Fortune said, "There would be slavery to-day." Brown established an example of the abolition of slavery through violence. "It cost tons of blood to put the Fifteenth Amendment into the constitution," Fortune pointed out, and "tons of blood" might also be necessary to avenge the discrimination and cruelty endured by modern blacks. In the twentieth century, American blacks must become like Brown, ready to sacrifice their lives for the cause of racial equality. Declaring that blacks were "on the verge of a greater crisis than any of former times," Fortune shook his fist and asked, "What are you going to do about it?" The crowd shouted its answer: "Fight! Fight!"

A similar militant message came from the black preacher Francis J. Grimke, who in December 1909 commemorated the fiftieth anniversary of Brown's death in a stirring address in the nation's capital. America, he declared, was "one of the most despicable countries in the world" because of its rampant racism. John Brown stood out as "one of these heaven-born heroes, one of earth's great martyrs to liberty, to human rights." Grimke continued: "It is impossible to overestimate the importance of the part which John Brown played in the great struggle for freedom in this country. He has placed the whole nation, and especially our race, under a lasting debt of gratitude to him." Insisting that Brown exhibited qualities "that as a race . . . we haven't got, I am sorry to say, in any large measure," Grimke told his black hearers: "We need to be dominated by a great purpose, as John Brown was. . . . We need the spirit of self-sacrifice which John Brown possessed. . . . We need the noble daring, the sublime courage which John Brown possessed."

Like Fortune, Grimke considered Brown the ur-source of justice for African Americans. Grimke said, "Out of the darkness, and the seeming triumph of the forces of oppression and injustice in 1859 when [Brown] was executed, there came the Emancipation Proclamation, and the great Amendments to the Constitution. . . . He it was who stirred the Anti-slavery leaders to action, and brought on the war, and inspired the men in Congress,—men like Sumner, and Stevens, and Wade,—and that moved upon the heart of Lincoln himself."

Though appreciative of Brown's role in sparking the war that ended slavery, neither Fortune not Grimke could have predicted his germinating influence on the civil rights movement. The thread that connected Brown and civil rights ran from Storer College through W. E. B. Du Bois and the Second Niagara Movement and beyond.

In 1896, the year of *Plessy v. Ferguson*, the Colored Women's League became the first of several African American organizations to make a pilgrimage to Harpers Ferry in order to visit Storer College and to honor Brown's memory. Other black groups followed. In 1906, W. E. B. Du Bois selected the site for the organizational meeting of the Second Niagara Movement, which became the National Association for the Advancement of Colored People (NAACP). Twelve years later the National Association of Teachers in Colored Schools convened there as well.

Of these pilgrimages to Harpers Ferry, the one made in January 1906 by the Second Niagara Movement had the most significance in the long run. Du Bois and the others called for an end to lynching and the abolition of unfair voting laws and other forms of racial discrimination. John Brown seemed spiritually present that day. The attendees made a ceremonial visit to John Brown's fort, which at the time had been rebuilt on a farm near Storer College. One of the speakers, Reverdy C. Ransom, averred, "Men like John Brown appear only once or twice in a thousand years. Like Mt. Blanc, the king of the mountains, he towers high above the loftiest figures of his time. . . . He had no predecessors, and can have no successors." Speaking of racism in his own era, Ransom said, "This nation needs to again to be aroused. The friends of truth and justice must be rallied."

It was Du Bois, the Harvard professor, who did the most among blacks to rally the nation. Du Bois often mentioned John Brown as his predecessor. He was not the first black intellectual who did so. The pioneering African American historian George Washington Williams had devoted a chapter of his 1883 book *History of the Negro Race in America from 1619 to 1880* to Brown. Saying that Brown ranked "among the world's greatest heroes," Williams wrote, "His immortal name will be pronounced with blessings in all lands and by all people till the end of time."

Du Bois translated reverence for Brown into activism on behalf of blacks. In the crucial years after the publication of *Souls of Black Folk* (1904) Du Bois meditated over Brown's legacy. He chose Harpers Ferry as the venue for the historic Second Niagara meeting, where he announced, "Here on the scene of John Brown's martyrdom, we reconsecrate ourselves, our honor, and our property to the final emancipation of the race which John Brown died to make free." In 1909, fifty years after the Harpers Ferry raid, Du Bois published what he considered his best book, *John Brown*. Passionate yet judicious, the volume pondered Brown's life in its relation to the

W. E. B. Du Bois.

condition of African Americans, past and present. In Du Bois's words, Brown was "the man who of all Americans has perhaps come nearest to touching the real souls of black folk."

For Du Bois, other white antislavery notables were admirable but still were tinged with racism. Lincoln, for instance, was a bundle of contradictions: "cruel, merciful; peace-loving, a fighter; despising Negroes and letting them fight and vote; protecting slavery and freeing slaves . . . —a big, inconsistent, brave man." Du Bois used no such qualifications about Brown, who had lived with blacks and had died for them. His true fellows, Du Bois insisted, were not white Abolitionists but rather black leaders such as Toussaint L'Ouverture, Gabriel Prosser, and Nat Turner. Du Bois gave an unequivocal verdict: "John Brown was right."

Also in 1909, Du Bois participated in the founding of the NAACP, the forerunner of the civil rights movement. In its long, vibrant history, the NAACP often looked back on John Brown. One of the group's founders, Dr. J. Max Barber, declared at the 1932 unveiling of a John Brown tablet at Storer College: "The ideals of John Brown are being carried forward by the National Association for the Advancement of Colored People." Barber added, "The N.A.A.C.P. is a direct descendant of the old League of Gileadites founded by John Brown. Its objects are the same, John Brown should be an inspiration to you in your fight for justice and self-respect."

Barber was right in mentioning John Brown as a forefather of the NAACP. Du Bois was not the only founding member of the group who was attracted to Brown. Another founder, Oswald Garrison Villard, was as well. The grandson of William Lloyd Garrison, Villard had antislavery passion in his genes. He, Du Bois, and four others led a racially mixed group that on February 12, 1909, organized the NAACP, then called the National Negro Committee. Villard also inherited his grandfather's commitment to non-resistance, which complicated his view of Brown.

Villard's book *John Brown, 1800–1859: A Biography Fifty Years After* (1910) was an impressive achievement, largely due to the tireless research of Villard's assistant Katherine Mayo. Still, Villard was neither a professional biographer nor a professional historian. He narrated the facts of Brown's life but did not link them to larger historical currents. A committed pacifist, Villard decried Brown's use of violence, especially at Pottawatomie. More surprisingly, given his closeness to Du Bois and the NAACP, he had little to say about Brown's progressive racial agenda. He was dismissive, for instance, of Brown's provisional constitution, which gave blacks complete citizenship rights.

Even a well-intentioned white liberal like Villard, then, could not pierce "the Veil" that Du Bois said shrouded African Americans. Du Bois wrote of the American black, "Within the Veil he was born . . . ; and there within shall he live,—a Negro and a Negro's son." John Brown had reached through the veil, but his white commentators found it difficult to follow his lead.

It was left to blacks to deeply appreciate Brown's racial message. In 1935, at a ceremony in North Elba, J. Max Barber, the editor who had founded the John Brown Memorial Association thirteen years earlier, unveiled a six-ton bronze statue of Brown, who was shown with his arm around a black boy. Emphasizing Brown's importance to American history, Barber predicted that "the coming centuries will hear of but three names of our civil war—Abraham Lincoln, the great emancipator; Ulysses S. Grant, the great general; and John Brown, the great forerunner of emancipation." Barber continued:

> Pushing up beside Lincoln must always appear the name of John Brown. . . . He it was who kindled the beacon fires of freedom on a thousand hills. He was the grim, grey herald of that awful conflict

which robed the nation in fire and blood. It was a conflict which had to come in order that we might have a new birth of freedom, a real birth of freedom. After John Brown there could be no peace with slavery in the land.

African American artists often chose Brown as a subject. The painters Horace Pippin, Jacob Lawrence, and Charles White produced portraits of him, and the sculptor Henry Bonnard a stone bust.

Among the many black poets who eulogized Brown were two leaders of the Harlem Renaissance, Langston Hughes and Countee Cullen. Hughes had a personal connection to Brown. His maternal grandmother had been married to two of Brown's black followers: Lewis S. Leary, who died at Harpers Ferry, and then Charles H. Langston, who had come close to joining the raid. Hughes considered Brown one of the true American heroes. "The Civil War that freed the slaves," declared Hughes, "really began with John Brown's Raid." Struck by the fact that Brown had fought alongside blacks, Hughes said, "John Brown's name is one of the great martyr names of all history and the men who fought with him rank high on the scrolls of freedom."

Countee Cullen extolled Brown in his 1942 poem "A Negro Mother's Lullaby (After a visit to the grave of John Brown)." Picturing Brown as an archangel sitting by Jesus on heaven's throne, Cullen described a black woman singing to her infant:

> *Though some may be bonded, you shall be free,*
> *Thanks to a man, Osawatomie Brown . . .*
>
> *Hushaby, hushaby, sweet darkness at rest,*
> *Two there have been who their lives laid down*
> *That you might be beautiful here in my breast:*
> *Our Jesus and . . . Osawatomie Brown.*

African Americans carried forth Brown's name not only in art and literature but also in society. In 1935, three years after Max Barber had linked the NAACP and Brown's League of Gileadites, the NAACP made a major stride toward one of Brown's goals—equal education for blacks—in a case in which the lawyers Thurgood Marshall and Charles Houston won entrance for a black student to the University of Maryland. Nearly two decades later the education issue turned the nation toward civil rights. In early 1954, seventeen states and the District of Columbia still mandated segregated schooling. The Supreme Court's decision on *Brown v. Board of Education*, announced on May 17 that year, banned school segregation and opened the way for the many reforms that followed.

The pacifist strategies of several civil rights groups, notably Martin Luther King, Jr.'s Southern Christian Leadership Conference, harked back not so much to Harpers Ferry as to the civil disobedience of Thoreau, Gandhi, and the Congress of Racial Equality. Still, the aim of the sit-ins and marches King inspired was the same as John Brown's: full justice for America's ethnic minorities. This similarity of aims led the poet Eli Siegel to write "They Look at Us," a poem picturing the antislavery martyrs together in heaven:

> *Martin Luther King*
> *Is with John Brown*
> *Look up: you'll see them both*
> *Looking down*
> *Deep and wide*
> *At us.*

Militant blacks, angered by the slow arrival of social justice, treasured the memory of Brown. Robert F. Williams, a leader of the Revolutionary Action Movement, carried around a copy of Thoreau's "Plea for Captain John Brown." Eldridge Cleaver, who rarely praised American whites, wrote in *Soul on Ice*, "From the beginning of the contacts between blacks and whites, there has been very little reason for a black man to respect the white, with such exceptions as John Brown and others lesser known." Of the same opinion was H. Rap Brown, who asserted that "John Brown was the only white man I could respect and he is dead." Floyd McKissick, the national chairman of the Congress of Racial Equality, insisted that men like John Brown were "exempt from the guilt of their people"; he explained that Brown "did as much in defense of black men as he would have done in his own defense."

For Malcolm X, Brown's violent response to injustice was a paradigm modern blacks must follow. "I don't go for any nonviolent white liberals," Malcolm said in January 1965. "If you are for me and my problems—when I say me I mean *us*, our people—then you have to be willing to do as old John Brown did."

The legal and social strides made by blacks in the late twentieth century were accompanied by a more positive view of Brown among whites. Anti–John Brown sentiment had crested during the era of Jim Crow and subsided with the rise of civil rights. Sympathetic, though still sometimes ambivalent, portraits of Brown emerged in Stephen Oates's 1970 biography *To Purge This Land with Blood* and Richard O. Boyer's 1973 *Legend of John Brown* (which followed Brown up to the Kansas years), and in three powerful novels: Bruce Olds's *Raising Holy Hell* (1995), Russell Banks's *Cloudsplitter* (1998), and Marilynne Robinson's *Gilead* (2004). Brown figured importantly in several seminal works on the Civil War, such as James McPherson's *Battle Cry of Freedom* and Ken Burns's *The Civil War*. Robert Kenner's informative PBS documentary, *John Brown's Holy War*, appeared in 2000. Useful primary sources were reprinted in two well-assembled collections of writings by and about Brown: Louis Ruchames's *A John Brown Reader* (1959; expanded and retitled *John Brown: The Making of a Revolutionary*, 1969), and Zoe Trodd's and John Stauffer's *Meteor of War: The John Brown Story* (2004).

However, historians—and Americans in general—are not completely comfortable with Brown, who remains an elusive, marginal figure. A 1996 collection of essays by modern historians titled *Why the Civil War Came* makes no mention of Brown, focusing instead on Lincoln and the Republicans. The discomfort many feel about John Brown has been expressed even by knowledgeable authorities such as the Kansas-based historian Jonathan Earle, who said in an interview of 2003: "If I were going to write a biography, one of the last people I'd want to write a biography about is John Brown. He's really interesting, but we've had 150 years of people in my business trying to 'get inside his head,' and I don't think we've done a very good job at all."

A key difficulty modern Americans have with Brown is that his goal— the abolition of slavery—was undeniably good, but his violent methods are hard to swallow. Indeed, John Brown's legacy is complicated by the fact that ever since his death he has been championed by fringe revolutionaries and agitators. The Fenians, a militant Irish group of the Civil War era, adopted Brown as their spiritual forefather, even though his Calvinism was distant from their Catholicism. To commemorate 1798, the year of their founding, the Fenians sang the John Brown song, changing its words as follows: "John Brown's knapsack was number 98."

American labor radicals honored Brown. On December 2, 1881, a New York convention of the Labor Standard American Auxiliary Association celebrated the anniversary of Brown's execution, distributing red cards inscribed with "His soul is marching on!" followed by the lines: "Yesterday,—'The abolition of chattel slavery.' / Tomorrow,—'The abolition of wages slavery.' " Four years later a similar meeting was held in New York by the International Working People's Association, which held up the Harpers Ferry raid as the model for socialist revolution. A Marxist speaker said of Brown, "The working classes must imitate him. The 'beasts of property and their hordes of adherents' must be annihilated."

Eugene V. Debs, the socialist who ran five times for the U.S. presidency between 1900 and 1920, revered Brown and his fellow Abolitionist Wendell Phillips. In a pamphlet titled *Negro Worker* he stated, "The greatest hero of them all was John Brown . . . [who], when the cross came, stood forth almost alone and struck the blow—the immortal blow that put an end to the most infamous of human institutions—slavery." The progressive lawyer Clarence Darrow also worshiped Brown. In a 1912 speech before the Radical Club in San Francisco, Darrow said, "No sordid motive ever moved [Brown's] life; his commander was the great Jehovah, and the outcome was determined since the morning the stars sang together and the world was new."

Mother Jones, the labor reformer variously known as "the most dangerous woman in America" and "John Brown in petticoats," was driven by her horror over poor working conditions for steelworkers to predict, "Some day, not in the far distant future there will come another John Brown and he will tear this nation from end to end if this thing does not stop."

The cultural revolution of the 1960s and '70s brought more radicals who claimed to follow in Brown's footsteps. Bernard Jerome Brous, who bombed AT&T radio towers in Nevada and Utah to protest against the military-industrial establishment, mailed a public letter to the *New York Evening Tribune* signed "John Brown of Harpers Ferry, commander-in-chief of the American Republican Army." Jean Libby, the editor of *John Brown Mysteries* and the leader of the leftist group Allies for Freedom, considered Brown a black nationalist who wanted to create an independent black nation. Further to the left, the Weather Underground in 1975 published a journal called *Osawatomie*. In the late 1970s, a Southern organization called the John Brown Brigade made several deadly attacks on the Ku Klux Klan.

Complicating Brown's legacy even further is the terrorism of recent times. The historian David W. Blight asks, "Can John Brown remain an authentic American hero in an age of Timothy McVeigh, Usama Bin Laden, and the bombers of abortion clinics?"

How can America, which regards terrorism as its greatest threat, admit to the fact that it was shaped by a terrorist of its own?

The question is a vital one, especially since a number of terrorists insist they acted in the tradition of John Brown. Violent right-to-lifers like Matthew J. Goldsby, John Burt, and Paul Hill venerated the memory of John Brown and claimed to act in his name. After bombing an abortion clinic in Pensacola Florida, Burt said: "Maybe like Harpers Ferry, where John Brown used violence to bring the evils of slavery into focus, these bombings may do the same thing on the abortion issue." As if echoing Brown's militancy, Burt added, "When the history of this period is written, it won't be the pickets or the letter-writers who will be the heroes. It's going to be the bombers." Hill, who received the death sentence for murdering an abortion doctor, wrote that Brown's "example has and continues to serve as a source of encouragement to me," and "the political impact of Brown's actions continues to serve as a powerful paradigm in my understanding of the potential effects of the use of defensive force may have for the unborn."

Timothy McVeigh, who killed 168 people by bombing a federal build-ing in Oklahoma City, was also a devotee of John Brown. As the journalist Dan Herbeck reported, "One of his big heroes was John Brown, who com-mitted some very violent acts during the 1800s in the effort to eliminate slavery in our country." Similarly, the author Gore Vidal noted, "McVeigh saw himself as John Brown of Kansas."

The connection between McVeigh and Brown has been hotly argued. For instance, a debate was posted online, titled "Was Timothy McVeigh Our John Brown?" between the historians Clayton Cramer and Paul Finkelman. Cramer took the affirmative side, arguing that both Brown and McVeigh responded with brutality against systems they regarded as bru-tal—one against the slave system, the other against the intrusive federal government whose tyranny, McVeigh felt, was exhibited at Waco and Ruby Ridge. Finkelman argued for the negative, saying that Brown attacked proslavery forces in a time when the political debate was stifled, whereas McVeigh slaughtered innocent people in an era when he could have made his point peacefully.

Other modern terrorists who have been compared to John Brown are Ted Kaczynski (the so-called Unabomber) and Osama bin Laden. The legal scholar Michael Mello compares the Unabomber's single-handed assault on technological industrialism with Brown's attack on slavery, suggesting that Kaczynski sparked a new environmentalism the way Brown spelled the end of slavery. Those who see Brown-like elements in bin Laden point to the latter's murderous campaign against a social system perceived as cor-rupt, launched by a charismatic fanatic in the name of God.

What are we to make of these comparisons between Brown and modern terrorism? To some degree they are valid. Terrorism, or murder to make a political point, is utilized by groups or individuals who feel that social change cannot be achieved through normal channels. Just as John Brown saw that decades of what he called "talk, talk, talk" had done nothing to halt slavery, so some modern terrorists stand opposed to social institutions or governmental systems that they feel have become overwhelming and impossible to challenge in any way other than through violence.

The idea that "one man's terrorist is another man's freedom fighter" is no less true now than it was in Brown's day. For some ardent foes of abortion, Paul Hill, who claimed to follow Brown, was a hero. Others thought that Timothy McVeigh carried out justice—Gore Vidal, for instance, disgusted by what he saw as an oppressive American government, compared McVeigh not only to Brown but also to Paul Revere, spreading the alarm that "The Feds are coming, the Feds are coming." Some militant Muslims, appalled by what they regarded as the decadence and corrupt imperialism of the United States, applauded bin Laden's destruction of the World Trade Center. In this sense, contemporary terrorists are no different from Brown, deified by some and demonized by others.

Still, it is misleading to identify Brown with modern terrorists. Actually, Brown would have disapproved of the use of violence by most of those who have proclaimed themselves as his heirs. It is important to recognize that many of the social ills that later bred radical violence plagued the nation in his time, but he went to war only over the issue of slavery.

Brown saw many things wrong with American society. In some respects social conditions were even worse then than in recent times. Americans were caught in the dizzying throes of a boom-and-bust economy, unregulated by federal programs, that left millions of poor people utterly without relief during times of economic decline, particularly between 1839 and 1842. Widening divisions between the pampered "upper ten" and the oppressed "lower millions" gave rise to labor groups and angry protest novels by George Lippard, J. H. Ingraham, and others. Native Americans, cruelly forced off their land by rapacious whites, journeyed west on the so-called Trail of Tears. Women were caught between the impulse to advance, signaled by the women's rights movement, and the reality of their political disenfranchisement and their entrapment in the home as a result of the "separate spheres" doctrine of capitalism. Incapacitated economically, city women were forced to turn in astounding numbers to the most lucrative job, prostitution. Because birth control was primitive, unwanted pregnancies abounded, and abortion was a vexed issue. In the absence of safe medical procedures, women seeking abortions risked their lives when helped on the sly by unprofessional people like New York's notorious Ann Lohman (aka "Madame Restell"), who was known as "the wickedest woman in New York" for operating a "house built on babies' skulls" on Fifth Avenue.

Political corruption was rife, as was noted by many observers, including Walt Whitman, who impugned the "swarms of cringers, suckers, dough-faces, lice of politics, planners of sly involutions for their own preferment to city offices or state legislatures or the judiciary or congress or the presidency." In America's cities the environment was a serious concern. Most city streets, still unpaved, turned to swampy muck in the winter and dust bowls in the summer. In an age before public sanitation, garbage was tossed into the city streets, where it rotted amid the feces of the animals. Not only horses but also pigs, cows, and sheep roamed through the cities. The lack of organized police and fire departments added to the precariousness of daily life.

In other words, there was plenty for John Brown to protest against. He *did* protest, as evidenced by remarks about corruption, women, Native Americans, and economic inequality in his writings. But slavery was the one thing that drove him to violence.

Why? Because slavery was a uniquely immoral institution that seemed cemented in place by law, custom, and prejudice. Bad economic times came and went. The status of women promised to change. Native Americans, although horribly maltreated, still had a measure of freedom. City conditions were improving as technology progressed. But slavery, the "sum of all evils," was there to stay, at least for the foreseeable future. And slavery was qualitatively different from all other social issues, since it deprived millions of their rights as Americans and their dignity as human beings. No other social phenomenon approached its wickedness. No other problem, Brown believed, called for the use of arms.

Brown had a breadth of vision that modern terrorists lack. He was an *American* terrorist in the amplest sense of the word. He was every bit as religious as Osama bin Laden—but was the Muslim bin Laden able to enlist Christians, atheists, or Jews among his followers? The Calvinistic Brown, reflecting the religious toleration of his nation, counted Jews, liberal Christians, spiritualists, and agnostics among his most devoted soldiers. Bin Laden's ultimate goal was the creation of a Muslim theocracy in which opposing views, especially Western ones, were banned. Brown's goal was a democratic society that assigned full rights to all, irrespective of religion, race, or gender.

Also, Brown possessed an eloquence unique among terrorists. When Thoreau said that Brown's words were more powerful than his rifles or when Emerson ranked his court speech with the Gettysburg Address, they were highlighting the power of his language. Perhaps Ted Kaczynski would have won more people to his side if he had published something more forceful than the meandering, garbled manifesto against leftism that he sent to newspapers. Similarly, Timothy McVeigh's final written statement, a handwritten copy of William Ernest Henley's poem "Invictus"—a work of self-serving machismo asserting one's power to survive in a harsh world (e.g., "My head is bloody but unbowed. / . . . I am the master of my fate; / I am the captain of my soul")—was on the opposite side of the rhetorical spectrum from the generous, other-oriented letters Brown wrote in prison. And Kaczynski and McVeigh are Shakespeares when compared with other modern terrorists, many of whom are anonymous suicide bombers, exploited devotees, or the like—faceless tools of a cause, not original inter-preters of one.

John Brown alone wielded both the sword and the sword-pen. His words sprang from deep wells of compassion for a race whose suffering he felt on his very nerve-endings.

The African American view of Brown as the selfless herald of emancipa-tion was memorably expressed in the 1964 book *The Negro Mood and Other Essays* by Lerone Bennett, Jr., a senior editor at *Ebony* magazine. Bennett wrote: "It is to John Brown that we must go, finally, if we want to under-stand the limitations and possibilities of our situation. He was of no color, John Brown, of no race or age. He was pure passion, pure transcendence. He was an elemental force like wind, rain and fire."

John Brown as "pure transcendence," as "an elemental force." This was Thoreau and Emerson again, but with a key difference. As an African American, Bennett prized Brown's racial program with an intensity the Concord philosophers lacked. Brown's violence, Bennett argued, retaliated for centuries of violence inflicted on American blacks:

> There was in John Brown a complete identification with the oppressed. It was his child that a slaveowner was selling; his sister who was being whipped in the field; his wife who was being raped in the gin house. It was not happening to Negroes; it was happening to him. Thus it was said that he could not bear to hear the word slave spoken. At the sound of the word, his body vibrated like the strings of a sensitive violin. John Brown *was* a Negro, and it was in this aspect that he suffered.

The statement "John Brown *was* a Negro," coming as it did from an African American, was one Brown himself would have singled out for praise. Brown's violent actions seem aberrant and insane if torn from their racial referents. Without the racial factor, Pottawatomie seems like heartless butchery and Harpers Ferry appears inane and quixotic. With the racial factor, both make sense. At Pottawatomie, Brown was responding to proslavery outrages: not only the sack of Lawrence and the caning of Sumner but the whole bloody history of America's cruelty toward blacks. At Harpers Ferry, he was tapping into Southern whites' deepest fear—slave insurrection—and protesting against the proslavery federal government in the process.

Brown's violence resulted from America's egregious failure to live up to one of its most cherished ideals—human equality. To expose this failure, Brown exercised the right of the individual to challenge the mass. In doing so he kept alive the revolutionary spirit that ran from Puritan antinomianism through the founding fathers' resistance to tyranny to the self-reliant nonconformity of the Transcendentalists.

It is this individualistic spirit that seems most threatened today. Lerone Bennett, in the same piece in which he announced that "John Brown *was* a Negro," posed the trenchant question: What happened to the America that produced Brown and other forceful rebels, such as Thomas Jefferson, Thomas Paine, and Wendell Phillips? Bennett wrote in alarm: "It may be that America can no longer produce such men. If so, all is lost. Cursed is the nation, cursed is the people, who can no longer breed indigenous radicals when it needs them." "What happened to that America?" Bennett asked. "Who killed it?"

These questions are even more urgent today than when Bennett asked them. America has become a vast network of institutions that tend to stifle vigorous challenges from individuals. Such challenges are needed if the nation is to remain healthy. There must be modern Americans who identify with the oppressed with such passion that they are willing to die for them, as Brown did. And America must be large enough to allow for meaningful protest, instead of remaining satisfied with patriotic bromides and a capitalist mass culture that fosters homogenized complacency. Unless America is ready at every moment to see its own failings, it is one step closer to becoming the tyrannical monster it pretends not to be.

Had John Brown and a few other forceful antislavery persons not been able to bring about the fall of slavery, one can only speculate about the terrible results. What would have happened if Brown had not violently disrupted the racist juggernaut that was America? As we have seen, even emancipation and manhood suffrage did not ensure the security of African Americans. It took nine decades of struggle for America to approach John Brown's goal of civil rights for all ethnic minorities. Even today the goal is not fully realized.

W. E. B. Du Bois's startling pronouncement thunders through American history. Indeed, "John Brown was right."

Notes

Abbreviations

AAS	American Antiquarian Society
ALLC	Abraham Lincoln Papers, Library of Congress
BPL	Boston Public Library
BSC	Boyd B. Stutler Collection of John Brown, West Virginia Archives
CEP	Henry David Thoreau, *Collected Essays and Poems*, ed. Elizabeth Hall Witherell (New York: Library of America, 2001).
EL	Ralph Waldo Emerson, *Essays and Lectures*, ed. Joel Porte (New York: Library of America, 1983).
KSHS	Kansas State Historical Society
JMN	*The Journals and Miscellaneous Notebooks of Ralph Waldo Emerson* (Cambridge, Mass.: Harvard University Press); vol. 12 (1976), ed. Linda Allardt; vol. 13 (1977), ed. Ralph H. Orth and Alfred R. Ferguson; vol. 14 (1978), ed. Susan Sutton Smith and Harrison Hayford; vol. 15 (1982), ed. Linda Allardt, David W. Hill, and Ruth H. Bennett.
LC	Library of Congress
OHS	Ohio Historical Society
Ru	Louis Ruchames, ed., *John Brown: The Making of a Revolutionary: The Story of John Brown in His Own Words and in the Words of Those Who Knew Him* (1969; New York: Grosset & Dunlap, 1971).
Ru2	Louis Ruchames, ed., *A John Brown Reader: The Story of John Brown in His Own Words, In the Words of Those Who Knew Him, and in the Poetry and Prose of the Literary Heritage* (London: Abelard-Schuman, 1959).
VC	Oswald Garrison Villard Collection of John Brown, Columbia University Library.

Preface

ix   "John Brown has loosened the roots": *The John Brown Invasion: An Authentic History of the Harper's Ferry Tragedy*, ed. Thomas Drew (Boston: James Campbell, 1860), p. 77.

ix   "If John Brown did not end the war": *Ru*, p. 298.

1. The Party

3   "the John Brown Party": For information on the John Brown Party, see Frank Preston Stearns, *The Life and Public Services of George Luther Stearns* (Philadelphia: J. B. Lippincott & Co. 1907), pp. 275–76; Charles E. Heller, *Portrait of an Abolitionist: A Biography of George Luther Stearns, 1809–1867* (Westport, Conn.: Greenwood, 1996), p. 143; and Elizabeth Powell Bond to Oliver Johnson, extract of letter in BSC.

3   "That hand-bill order": Letter from Robert H. Milroy to Abraham Lincoln, January 1, 1863; ALLC.

4   "make the gallows": *New-York Tribune*, November 8, 1859.

4   "the type and synonym of the Just": Journal entry of May 8, 1859, quoted in Franklin B. Sanborn, *The Life and Letters of John Brown* (Boston: Roberts Brothers, 1885), p. 505.

4   as Alfred Kazin suggests: "God's Own Terrorist" [review of Russell Banks's *Cloudsplitter*], *New York Review of Books*, April 9, 1998.

5   "I consider it the proudest act": F. P. Stearns, *The Life and Public Services of George Luther Stearns*, pp. 288–89.

5   "Abraham Lincoln, Slave-hound": *Liberator*, June 22, 1860.

5   "He has evidently not a drop": Wendell Phillips Garrison and Francis Jackson Garrison, *William Lloyd Garrison, 1805–1879* (New York: Century, 1889), 4:33.

6   "as a measure of justice": C. E. Heller, *Portrait of an Abolitionist*, p. 139.

6   The journalist James Redpath would later see: Merrill D. Peterson, *John Brown: The Legend Revisited* (Charlottesville and London: University Press of Virginia, 2002), p. 43.

8   The early biographers were mainly people: See especially James Redpath, *The Public Life of Capt. John Brown* (1860; Freeport, N.Y.: Books for Libraries Press, 1970); Richard J. Hinton, *John Brown and His Men* (1894; New York: Arno Press, 1968); and F. B. Sanborn, *Life and Letters of John Brown*.

8   In reaction, there arose a school of biographers: See Hill Peebles Wilson, *John Brown, Soldier of Fortune: A Critique* (Lawrence, Kans.: Cornhill, 1913); Robert Penn Warren, *John Brown: The Making of a Martyr* (New York: Payson & Clarke, 1929); and James C. Malin, *John Brown and the Legend of Fifty-six* (Philadelphia: American Philosophical Society, 1942). For similar negative criticism, see David N. Utter, "John Brown of Osawatomie," *North American Review* 137 (1883): 435–46; George Washington Brown, *The Truth at Last: History Corrected: Reminiscences of Old John Brown* (Rockford, Ill.: A. E. Smith, 1880); and Charles Robinson, *The Kansas Conflict* (New York: Harper & Brothers, 1892), pp. 329, 393–94, 487. For a useful review of the controversy over Brown, see M. D. Peterson, *John Brown*, especially chap. 3.

8   most notably Oswald Garrison Villard: O. G. Villard, *John Brown, 1800–1859: A Biography Fifty Years After* (Boston: Houghton Mifflin, 1910); and S. Oates, *To Purge This Land with Blood: A Biography of John Brown* (New York: Harper & Row, 1970). For a detailed look at Brown's early life, see Richard O. Boyer, *The Legend of John Brown: A Biography and History* (New York: Knopf, 1973).

8   "holds a position of impartiality": Albert Bushnell Hart, typed manuscript of book
     review (1910); BSC.

9   "the ideas of the time are in the air": *EL*, p. 627. The next quotation in this paragraph is
     from *EL*, p. 711.

9   "Great geniuses are parts of the times": Herman Melville, "Hawthorne and His Mosses"
     (1850), in "Reviews and Letters by Melville," afterword to H. Melville, *Moby-Dick*, ed.
     Harrison Hayford and Hershel Parker (New York: W. W. Norton, 1967), p. 543.

9   "John Brown and his raid": J. J. Chapman, "Doctor Howe," in *Learning and Other
     Essays* (New York: Moffat, Yard & Co., 1910), p. 131.

10 "John Brown! . . . Cause and Consequence!": A. Tourgée, *Hot Ploughshares* (New York:
     Fords, Howard & Hulbert, 1883), pp. 608–9.

11 Whitman, fearing the impending separation: See David S. Reynolds, *Walt Whitman's
     America: A Cultural Biography* (New York: Knopf, 1995).

11 "A man Caesar is born": "Self-Reliance," in *EL*, p. 267.

11 "He is more alive than he ever was": H. D. Thoreau, "The Last Days of John Brown,"
     in *CEP*, p. 428.

11 "It has been impossible to keep": *JMN* 15:468.

11 "a stupendous John Brown raid": C. C. Burr, "War Democrats—Their Crimes," *Old
     Guard* (New York) 1 (August 1863): 201.

12 "until every drop of blood": A. Lincoln, *Speeches and Writings, 1859–1865* (New York:
     Library of America, 1989), p. 687.

13 4 million members of his race: According to the census, in 1860 there were 3,953,696
     slaves in the United States. I have followed other scholars in rounding this figure off to
     4 million.

2. The Puritan

14 PURITANISM: "Worship of the North," unattributed political cartoon (1863); BSC.

16 Supposedly, it buttressed mainstream cultural values: This argument is most carefully
     developed by Sacvan Bercovitch in his books *The Puritan Origins of the American Self*
     (New Haven: Yale University Press, 1975), *The American Jeremiad* (Madison: Univer-
     sity of Wisconsin Press, 1978), and *The Rites of Assent: Transformations in the Symbolic
     Construction of America* (New York: Routledge, 1993).

16 "Abolition is the offspring of Puritanism": Samuel S. Cox, *Eight Years in Congress, from
     1857–1865: Memoir and Speeches* (New York: D. Appleton & Co., 1865), p. 282.

16 "this terrible Puritan war": "The Puritan War," *Old Guard* 1 (March 1863): 61. The fol-
     lowing quotation is on pp. 59–60.

16 "How peaceful and blest was America's soil": *Civil War Song Sheets*, ser. 2, vol. 1; LC.
     The next song quoted, "Disgrace & Shame," is in ser. 1, vol. 1.

17 "fertile forms of antinomianism": *EL*, p. 592. The next quotation in this paragraph is on
     the same page.

17 "Puritanism and nothing else can save this nation": *New Englander and Yale Review* 4
     (July 1846): 308.

17 "His Puritan Grandsire's sword": John Ross Dix, "My Northern Boy to the War Has
     Gone!" (New York: Charles Magnus, c. 1862), in *America Singing: Nineteenth-Century
     Song Sheets*; LC.

17 "the irreconcilable antithesis": Frank H. Alfriend, "A Southern Republic and a North-
     ern Democracy," *Southern Literary Messenger* 37 (May 1863): 283. See also Jan C. Daw-
     son, "The Puritan and the Cavalier: The South's Perception of Contrasting

Traditions," *Journal of Southern History* 44 (November 1978): 597–614; and William Robert Taylor, *Cavalier and Yankee: The Old South and American National Character* (New York: G. Braziller, 1963).

17 "at once a religious fanatic": J. Quitman Moore, "Southern Civilization; or, The Norman in America," *DeBow's Review* 32 (January–February 1862): 7, 8.

17 "the principles of [Northern] Calvinistic *insubordinatism*": "The Relative Political Status of the North and the South," *DeBow's Review* 22 (February 1857): 128.

18 "The institution of domestic slavery": George Fitzhugh, "Bonaparte, Cromwell, and Washington," *DeBow's Review* 28 (August 1860): 144.

18 "a benevolent system of tutelage": F. H. Alfriend, "A Southern Republic," pp. 286, 289.

18 "the history of Puritanism is a catalogue": S. S. Cox, *Eight Years in Congress*, p. 298.

18 "Everybody who ever saw a Puritan": G. Fitzhugh, "Bonaparte, Cromwell, and Washington," p. 142.

19 "He was, in truth, a calvinistic Puritan": Franklin B. Sanborn, *Recollections of Seventy Years* (Boston: Richard G. Badger, 1909), pp. 76–77.

19 "a Puritan of the Puritans": J. J. Ingalls, "John Brown's Place in History," article bound in book (1884), p. 148; BSC.

19 "In religion and character Brown": F. B. Sanborn, "John Brown, the Religious Martyr," speech of December 6, 1909, given at the Free Synagogue, New York, p. 10; BSC.

19 "a puritan brought back from the days of Cromwell": Quoted in Michael Fellman, *Inside War: The Guerilla Conflict in Missouri During the American Civil War* (New York: Oxford University Press, 1989), p. 17.

20 I find the *Mayflower* story plausible: Here I agree with R. O. Boyer, who in *The Legend of John Brown* (p. 168) cites the genealogical studies of Brown's family made by the Rev. Clarence S. Gee and by George F. Williams, who support the *Mayflower* story. However, O. G. Villard in *John Brown* (p. 10) disputes the story.

20 "a decendant on the side": *Ru*, p. 44.

20 "one of the best of mothers": "Owen Brown's Autobiography," ed. Clarence S. Gee (Lockport, N.Y.: ms. dated June 8, 1860), p. 2; BSC.

21 "the name of a good boy": "Owen Brown's Autobiography," p. 3. The next two quotations in this paragraph are also on p. 3. The quotations in the next three paragraphs are on pp. 3–4.

23 "Ever since, I have been an Abolitionist": "Owen Brown's Autobiography," in O. G. Villard, *John Brown*, p. 14.

24 "Whatsoever ye would that men": *Norton Anthology of American Literature*, A:389–90. The quotations from Woolman later in this paragraph are in A:620, 622.

24 "worse than if they were brutes": Theodore Dwight Weld, *American Slavery as It Is* (1839), edited by Richard O. Curry and Joanna Dunlap Cowden and published as *Slavery in America: Theodore Weld's American Slavery as It Is* (Itasca, Ill.: F. E. Peacock, 1972), p. 59.

24 "I believe in the Golden Rule, sir": In R. J. Hinton, *John Brown and His Men*, p. 424.

25 "Perhaps there has never been": "Owen Brown's Autobiography," p. 5.

25 "The disgrace of hanging": In Hinton, *John Brown and His Men*, p. 431.

26 "History will show": G. Fitzhugh, "Bonaparte, Cromwell, and Washington," p. 143.

27 "To hold any man in slavery": In Parker Pillsbury, *Acts of the Anti-Slavery Apostles* (1883; New York: Arno Press, 1969), p. 365.

27 "John Brown is almost the only radical abolitionist": Quoted in J. Redpath, *The Public Life of Capt. John Brown*, p. 69.

3. The Pioneer

29 "very harmonious and middling prosperous": "Owen Brown's Autobiography," in O. G. Villard, *John Brown*, p. 13.

30 "a wilderness filled with wild beasts": *Ru*, p. 44.

31 "When we came to Ohio": "Owen Brown's Autobiography," in O. G. Villard, *John Brown*, p. 13. The quotations in the next two paragraphs are also on p. 13.

31 "used to hang about them" and "was installed": *Ru*, p. 44.

32 "a thorough whipping": *Ru*, p. 44. The other quotations in this paragraph are on p. 45.

32 When Thoreau said that John Brown: H. D. Thoreau, "A Plea for Captain John Brown," in *CEP*, p. 398.

32 "was *excessively* fond of the *hardest*": *Ru*, p. 45. The quotations in the next paragraph are on p. 46.

33 "The effect of what he saw": *Ru*, p. 46. The quotations in the next paragraph are also on p. 46.

34 "quite full of self-conceit": *Ru*, p. 48.

35 "the very marked yet kind immovableness": *Ru*, p. 48.

35 "and how we had religious meetings": James Redpath, *Echoes of Harpers Ferry* (Boston: Thayer & Eldridge, 1860), p. 388.

36 "great, wise & good men": *Ru*, p. 47.

36 "Money became scarce": "Owen Brown's Autobiography," in O. G. Villard, *John Brown*, p. 7.

37 "eternal enmity to slavery": John Brown quoted in O. G. Villard, *John Brown*, p. 18.

37 "neat industrious & economical": *Ru*, p. 49.

38 But I cannot categorize John Brown: For arguments that Brown was insane, see especially Allan Nevins, *The Emergence of Lincoln* (New York: Scribner, 1950), II:5ff., 77–78, 92–93; and C. Vann Woodward, "John Brown's Private War," in *America in Crisis*, ed. Daniel Aaron (New York: Knopf, 1952), pp. 109–30. For a persuasive rebuttal, see L. Ruchames in his introduction to *Ru*, pp. 38–40.

38 "my guiding star": F. B. Sanborn, *The Life and Letters of John Brown*, p. 33. The next quotation in this paragraph is on pp. 33–34.

38 Although strict sabbatarianism was not rare: Actually, the Pottawatomie killings began just before midnight on Saturday May 24 and continued into early Sunday morning.

4. The Patriarch

41 "that his apprentices and journeymen": Letter from foreman to James Redpath, December 28 1859, in *Ru*, p. 171. The quotations in the next paragraph are on p. 172.

42 "Father had a rule": *Ru*, p. 182. The quotations in the following two paragraphs are on p. 183.

43 "often had . . . very affecting views": J. Edwards, *Personal Narrative*, in *Norton Anthology of American Literature*, A:475.

44 "the pursuit of the patriarchs": Quoted in R. J. Hinton, *John Brown and His Men*, p. 419.

44 He bought a two-hundred-acre parcel: There is some confusion about this date. Eighteen twenty-five is the year usually given for Brown's move to Randolph. Ruchames, however, provides convincing documentary evidence that 1826 was the year. See *Ru*, p. 172.

45   "for faithful service": Quoted in R. O. Boyer, *The Legend of John Brown*, p. 248.

45   "trifling thing": *Ru*, p. 184. The next quotation in this paragraph is also on p. 184, as is the one in the following paragraph.

46   "Thou shalt rise up before the hoary head": *Ru*, p. 185.

46   "good moral books and papers": *Ru*, p. 176. The following quotations in this paragraph are on p. 180.

47   "He was as enterprising": Quoted in R. O. Boyer, *The Legend of John Brown*, p. 230.

47   "He would never wear": *Ru*, p. 174.

47   "In his habits he was jocose": *Ru*, p. 175. The quotation in the next paragraph is on p. 174.

47   "no gentleman, let alone a clergyman": *Ru*, p. 173.

48   "a free use of pure wines": MS. Interview of Jason Brown by Katherine Mayo, December 13 and 14, 1908; VC.

48   "Our stupidity ingratitude": Letter from John Brown to Owen Brown, June 12, 1830; OHS.

49   "We are again smarting": *Ru*, p. 49.

49   "I have felt my loss verry little": Letter from John Brown to Seth Thompson, August 13, 1832; BSC. The quote in the next paragraph is also from this letter.

50   "It would be untrue": M. H. F., "A Brave Life," *Overland Monthly and Out West Magazine* 6 (October 1885): 863.

50   "Remember them that are in bonds": J. Redpath, *The Public Life of Capt. John Brown*, p. 45.

51   "I will be as harsh as truth": *Liberator*, January 1, 1831.

51   "misguided, wild, and apparently insane" and "utterly lacking in common sense": W. P. Garrison and F. J. Garrison, *William Lloyd Garrison*, 3:486, and *The Letters of William Lloyd Garrison* (Cambridge, Mass.: Harvard University Press, 1975), 4:661.

52   "No slave revolt": Eugene Genovese, *From Rebellion to Revolution: Afro-American Slave Revolts in the Making of the Modern World* (Baton Rouge: Louisiana State University Press, 1979), p. 11.

53   "a Nat Turner might be in every family": Statement made in the Virginia legislature in 1832 by James McDowell, quoted in Thomas Wentworth Higginson, "Nat Turner's Insurrection," *Atlantic Monthly* 8 (August 1861): 186.

53   "gigantic cannibal" and "A cry of horror, a cry of revenge": W. P. Garrison and F. J. Garrison, *William Lloyd Garrison*, 1:134–35. For a useful discussion of this topic, see Robert H. Abzug, "The Influence of Garrisonian Abolitionists' Fears of Slave Violence on the Antislavery Argument, 1829–40," *Journal of Negro History* 55 (January 1970): 15–26.

53   "We do not preach rebellion": *Liberator*, January 8, 1831.

53   "the first step of the earthquake": *Liberator*, September 3, 1831. The remaining quotations in this paragraph are also in this issue.

54   "The gleaming axe": *Liberator*, March 10, 1832.

54   "Another Dream": *Liberator*, April 30, 1831.

54   "Nat Turner and Cinques stood first": Quoted in J. Redpath, *The Public Life of Capt. John Brown*, p. 26.

55   As historian Henry Mayer has pointed out: Henry Mayer, *All on Fire: William Lloyd Garrison and the Abolition of Slavery* (New York: St. Martin's, 1998), pp. 308–9.

55   "How often have I heard him": Quoted in J. Redpath, *The Public Life of Capt. John Brown*, p. 26.

55   "Nothing so charms the American people": *Ru*, p. 84.

55   "terrible logic": *The Anglo-African Magazine, Volume I—1859* (New York: Arno Press, 1968), p. 386.

56   "Black John Brown": George Washington Williams, *History of the Negro Race in America* (1883; New York: Arno, 1968), 2:85. See Seymour L. Gross and Eileen Bender, "History, Politics and Literature: The Myth of Nat Turner," *American Quarterly* 23 (October 1971): 487–518.

56   "He considered it as much his duty": *Ru*, p. 175.

56   "He asked me how I would like": *Ru*, p. 186. The quotations in the next two paragraphs are on pp. 50–51.

57   "teaching slaves to read": P. Pillsbury, *Acts of the Anti-Slavery Apostles*, p. 436.

57   "Christian slaveholder" and "submit to considerable privation": *Ru*, p. 50. The quote in the paragraph after next is on p. 175.

61   "like a bomb-shell": *Ru*, p. 190. The next quotation is also on p. 190.

62   "Lynch him!": H. Mayer, *All on Fire*, p. 203.

62   "Accounts of outrages committed by mobs": "Address to the Young Men's Lyceum of Springfield, Illinois" (January 27, 1838), in A. Lincoln, *Speeches and Writings, 1832–1858* (New York: Library of America, 1989), p. 29. For an excellent account of this topic, see David Grimsted, *American Mobbing, 1828–1861: Toward Civil War* (New York: Oxford University Press, 1998).

62   "You may burn me at the stake": Edward Beecher, *Narrative of Riots at Alton*, ed. Robert Merideth (1838; New York: Dutton, 1965), pp. 86–90.

63   "mobocratic spirit": A. Lincoln, *Speeches and Writings, 1832–1858*, pp. 31–32.

63   "certainly a martyr": H. Mayer, *All on Fire*, p. 237.

64   "The brave Lovejoy": Bliss Perry, ed., *The Heart of Emerson's Journals* (Boston: Houghton Mifflin, 1926), p. 119.

64   "The crisis has now come": *Ru*, pp. 188–89. The quotations in the next paragraph are on p. 189.

65   "his determination to make war on slavery": O. G. Villard, *John Brown*, p. 46. Debunkers of John Brown have tried to disprove the story of the family pledge. Malin in *John Brown and the Legend of Fifty-six*, for example, argues that there is no record of the pledge in public documents—as if so private a matter would be reported in the newspapers! Others say that the pledge was retrospective wishful thinking on the part of Brown's children. Still, the fact that John Jr. and Jason separately recalled the event suggests its authenticity, as does the fact that several previous Brown biographers have accepted it after careful research. The date of the incident is uncertain, though everyone places it in the late 1830s. My guess is late 1837 or early 1838, just after the Lovejoy murder.

5. The Pauper

66   "It is now my settled purpose": Letter from H. Melville to Lemuel Shaw, October 6, 1849, in Jay Leyda, *The Melville Log: A Documentary Life of Herman Melville, 1819–1891* (New York: Harcourt, Brace, 1951), I:316.

66   "Poverty—be justifying": *Norton Anthology of American Literature*, B:2523.

66   "a mass of bombast, egotism": *Walt Whitman: The Critical Heritage*, ed. Milton Hindus (New York: Barnes & Noble, 1971), p. 61.

66   "If our young men miscarry": "Self-Reliance," in *EL*, p. 275.

67   "he that goes a-borrowing": B. Franklin, *The Way to Wealth*, in *Norton Anthology of American Literature*, A:520.

68   "functions are parcelled out": "The American Scholar," in *EL*, p. 54. The remaining quotations in this paragraph are also on p. 54.

69   "my extreme calamity": Letter from John Brown to Mary Brown, December 3, 1846; BSC.

69   "grew out of one root": Quoted in F. B. Sanborn, *The Life and Letters of John Brown*, p. 88.

71   "I have not yet succeded": Letter from John Brown to Dear Wife and Children, December 5, 1838; BSC.

71   "against this great curse": Quoted in O. G. Villard, *John Brown*, p. 47.

72   "I can only say that I still expect": Letter from John Brown to Seth Thompson, May 28, 1839; Henry P. Slaughter Collection, Atlanta University.

72   "I am now somewhat in fear": *Ru*, pp. 52–53.

73   "I have found it hard": *Ru*, p. 54. The next quotation is also on p. 54.

73   "I utterly deny": Letter from John Brown to George Kellogg, September 20, 1839; Chicago Historical Society.

73   "no less than a family": Quoted in S. Oates, *To Purge This Land with Blood*, pp. 45–46.

74   "and the interest thereon": F. B. Sanborn, *The Life and Letters of John Brown*, pp. 55–56. The next quotation is on p. 58.

74   "I started out in life": F. B. Sanborn, *The Life and Letters of John Brown*, p. 88.

75   "Bro. John Brown of Hudson": Quoted in S. Oates, *To Purge This Land with Blood*, p. 47.

76   "Both in and out of the game": Walt Whitman, *Complete Poetry and Collected Prose*, ed. Justin Kaplan (New York: Library of America, 1982), p. 30.

76   "Shoot him if he puts": Interview with Mr. and Mrs. Sherman Thompson, Hudson, by Katherine Mayo, December 20, 1908; VC.

77   "Divine Providence": *Ru*, p. 58.

77   "1 Pot Cracked 0.50": "Bankruptcy Inventory. John Brown, 1842 September 28," U.S. District Court of Ohio; BSC.

78   "a calamity from which father": *Ru*, p. 192.

78   "a steady, strong, desire": Quoted in O. G. Villard, *John Brown*, pp. 322–23.

78   "This has been to us all a bitter cup": *Ru*, p. 58. The remaining quotations in this paragraph are also on p. 58.

79   "Divine Providence seems to smile": *Ru*, pp. 60–61.

79   "because it was then the fashion": F. B. Sanborn, *The Life and Letters of John Brown*, p. 57.

81   "MY DEAR AFFLICTED WIFE": *Ru*, p. 45. The next quotation is on p. 46.

82   "Uncle John was no trader": F. B. Sanborn, *The Life and Letters of John Brown*, p. 65. The quotation in the next paragraph is on p. 57. The comment by Musgrave two paragraphs later is on p. 58.

82   "Father's favorite theme": Letter from John Brown, Jr., to F. B. Sanborn, November 11, 1887; BSC.

83   "the panic that now exists": *Ru*, p. 63.

84   "tried trade": Henry David Thoreau, *A Week on the Concord and Merrimac Rivers; Walden; The Maine Woods; Cape Cod*, ed. Robert F. Sayre (New York: Library of America, 1985), p. 377. The next quotation, from "Life Without Principle," is in *CEP*, p. 350.

84   "I am quite sensible of the truth": *Ru*, p. 68.

85   "We want to see every wool grower": Letter from John Brown to John L. Proudfit, January 13, 1847; BSC.

86   "no sofas, no cushions": *Ru*, p. 292.

87   "You have not enough devotional feeling": "Phrenological Description of John Brown as Given by O. S. Fowler," New York, February 27, 1847; KSHS.

88 "too blunt and free-spoken": Letter from John Brown to Mary Brown, March 7, 1847; BSC.

89 Le Roy Sunderland: For accounts of the Sunderland incident, see Henry Andrew Wright, "John Brown in Springfield," *New England Magazine*, May 1894, p. 279; and "An Old-Time Mesmerist," *San Francisco Bulletin*, July 1, 1885.

90 "a fine country, so far as I have seen": *Ru*, p. 77. The next quotation is on p. 78.

90 "many importunate letters": Letter from John Brown, Jr., to Simon Perkins, August 22, 1849; BSC.

90 "our Mr. Brown": Letter from John Brown, Jr., to Messrs. Bidwell and Perkins, August 22, 1849; BSC.

91 "Gentlemen," Brown declared: O. G. Villard, *John Brown*, p. 63.

91 "without a frown": *Ru*, p. 79. The next quotation is also on p. 79.

91 "thoroughly honest and honorable": O. G. Villard, *John Brown*, pp. 64–65.

92 "Junk Bottles": *Ru*, p. 83.

92 "To give you a full history": Letter from John Brown to Simon Perkins, October 20, 1851; BSC. The next quotation is from the same letter.

92 "One serious difficulty": Quoted in F. B. Sanborn, *The Life and Letters of John Brown*, p. 82.

93 "When I look forward": This and the other quotes in this paragraph are in *Ru*, pp. 87–88.

93 "appear to be a *little in advance*": Letter from John Brown to John Brown, Jr., August 26, 1853; BSC.

93 "through the infinite grace and mercy": *Ru*, p. 91.

93 "Yesterday I began my 54th year": Letter from John Brown to Henry Thompson and Ruth Brown Thompson, May 10, 1853; BSC.

6. The Plan

95 "the providence of God": A. Lincoln, *Speeches and Writings, 1859–1865*, p. 687.

95 "Indeed I tremble": "Notes on the State of Virginia," in *Thomas Jefferson, Writings* (New York: Library of America, 1984), p. 289.

95 "A dissolution": *The Diary of John Quincy Adams, 1794–1845*, ed. Allan Nevins (New York: Scribner, 1951), pp. 246–47.

95 "civil war": *Memoir and Letters of Charles Sumner*, ed. Edward L. Pierce (1877–1893; New York: Arno Press, 1969), 3:443.

96 "This nation is going steadily toward a war": *Boston Traveller*, July 8, 1856.

96 "liable to be drafted": *Documents of Upheaval: Selections from William Lloyd Garrison's* The Liberator, *1831–1865*, ed. Truman Nelson (New York: Hill & Wang, 1966), p. 43.

96 "to be 'led as a lamb' ": Quoted in Lewis Perry, *Radical Abolitionism: Anarchy and the Government of God in Antislavery Thought* (Ithaca: Cornell University Press, 1973), p. 234. The next quotation in this paragraph is on p. 53.

97 "If you are battling": *Proceedings of the American Anti-Slavery Society at Its Third Decade* (New York: Arno Press, 1969), p. 93.

97 "only by force": *The Works of John Adams, Second President of the United States*, ed. Charles Francis Adams (Boston: Little, Brown, 1850–56), X:315.

97 "a most iniquitous scheme": *Letters of Mrs. Adams, the Wife of John Adams*, ed. Charles Francis Adams (Boston: C. C. Little & J. Brown, 1840), I:24.

97 "be deemed a rebel": Quoted in Alice M. Baldwin, *The New England Clergy and the American Revolution* (Durham, N.C.: Duke University Press, 1928), p. 119.

98	"The relation between" and "If the slave states": Jabez D. Hammond, *Life and Opinions of Julius Melbourn* (Syracuse: Hall & Dickson, 1847), p. 105.

98	"10,000 men with an able commander": Letter from Jabez D. Hammond to Gerrit Smith, February 28, 1852, in Ralph V. Harlow, *Gerrit Smith, Philanthropist and Reformer* (New York: Henry Holt, 1939), p. 304.

98	"Think of the number": *Ru*, p. 84.

99	"I cannot afford to concede": Frank P. Woodbury, "The Former Years," *The American Missionary* 50 (November 1896): 341.

99	"always ready to invest": In C. E. Heller, *Portrait of an Abolitionist*, p. 97.

99	"Woe worth the hour": *The Poetical Works of James R. Lowell* (Cambridge, Mass.: H. O. Houghton, 1857), p. 264.

99	"Do you know": Frank Edward Kittredge, "The Man with the Branded Hand," *New England Magazine* 25 (November 1898): 366. The first quotation in the next paragraph is on p. 369.

100	"loathsome moral lepers": *The Poetical Works of John Greenleaf Whittier* (Boston: Houghton Mifflin, 1892), p. 112.

100	Alanson Work, James E. Burr: For an informative discussion of these and the other slave rescuers discussed in this paragraph, see Stanley Harrold, *The Abolitionists and the South, 1831–1861* (Lexington: University Press of Kentucky, 1995), chap. 4.

100	"form themselves into bands": L. Spooner, "Plan for the Abolition of Slavery"; Spooner Papers, BPL. The next two quotations in this paragraph are also from this document.

101	"a peace-maker": Letter from Lewis Tappan to Lysander Spooner, October 7, 1858; Spooner Papers, BPL.

101	"Immature-Impractical": Letter from H. R. Helper to L. Spooner, December 18, 1858; Helper Papers, Boston City Library.

101	"would be a good one": Letter from W. Phillips to L. Spooner, July 16, 1858, quoted in Herbert Aptheker, "Militant Abolitionism," *Journal of Negro History* 26 (October 1941): 470.

102	"The great obstacle": Letter from T. W. Higginson to L. Spooner, November 30, 1858; Spooner Papers, BPL.

102	"I had nothing to do": Letter from H. R. Helper to L. Spooner, October 8, 1859; Helper Papers, Boston City Library. For an account of Helper's racial views, see J. J. Cardoso, "Hinton Rowan Helper as a Racist in the Abolitionist Camp," *Journal of Negro History* 55 (October 1970): 323–30.

102	"the Brown-Helper party": *The Diary of Edmund Ruffin*, ed. William Kauffman Scarborough (Baton Rouge: Louisiana State University Press, 1972), I: 382.

103	"No doubt the African race": *Ru*, p. 259.

103	"Brethren, arise": *The Norton Anthology of African American Literature*, ed. Henry Louis Gates and Nellie Y. McKay (New York: W. W. Norton, 1997), p. 285.

103	"These mountains": *Ru*, p. 294. The quotations in the next three paragraphs are also on p. 294.

104	"though a white gentleman": Quoted in S. Oates, *To Purge This Land with Blood*, p. 63.

105	"Nat Turner, with fifty men": Quoted in J. Redpath, *Public Life of Capt. John Brown*, p. 206.

106	"A ravine is better": Quoted in Franklin B. Sanborn, "John Brown and His Friends," *Atlantic Monthly*, July 1872, p. 52.

106	"valuable hints": Quoted in O. G. Villard, *John Brown*, p. 53.

106	"acquainted as they were": J. H. Stocqueler, *The Life of Field Marshal the Duke of Wellington* (London: Ingram, Cooke & Co., 1852–53), p. 73. The next quotation in this paragraph is on p. 235.

106 "[Brown] would use natural": J. J. Nicolay and John Hay, "Abraham Lincoln: A History: Lincoln's Cooper Union Institute Speech," *Century* 34 (August 1887): 519.

107 "the first permanent inhabitants": In *Maroon Societies: Rebel Slave Communities in the Americas*, ed. Richard Price (Baltimore: Johns Hopkins University Press, 1979), p. 149. The quotations in the next paragraph are on pp. 152 and 162, respectively.

107 Richard Realf: *Report of the Select Committee of the Senate Appointed to Inquire into the Late Invasion and Seizure of the Public Property at Harper's Ferry* [hereafter cited as the Mason Report] (Washington, D.C.: n.p., 1860), p. 96.

107 "by heart": R. J. Hinton, *John Brown and His Men*, p. 66.

107 "to get together": *The Magnificent Activist: The Writings of Thomas Wentworth Higginson (1823–1911)*, ed. Howard N. Meyer (New York: Da Capo Press, 2000), p. 119.

109 "Surely no more convincing": "Hayti," *North American Review* 12 (January 1821): 115.

109 "In the case of Hayti": *Anglo-African Magazine* 1:187.

109 "The only race": *Wendell Phillips on Civil Rights and Freedom*, ed. Louis Filler (New York: Hill & Wang, 1965), p. 75.

110 "Some doubt the courage": *Wendell Phillips on Civil Rights and Freedom*, pp. 182–83. The next quotation in this paragraph is on p. 184.

110 "It was an attempt": *Report of Union Meeting in Faneuil Hall* (Boston: n.p., 1859), p. 15. The next quotation in this paragraph is on the same page.

110 Few slave rebels: See E. Genovese, *From Rebellion to Revolution*, p. 104.

111 "twenty years ago": *Ru*, p. 229.

111 His daughter Sarah recalled: O. G. Villard, *John Brown*, p. 55.

112 "fiends in human shape": *Ru*, p. 93.

112 "Anthony Burns must be released": J. Redpath, *The Public Life of Capt. John Brown*, p. 58.

112 "I think I may say" and "I know I can": Statement of Anne Brown Adams to Katherine Mayo, Petrolia, California, October 2, 1980; VC. The quotation in the next paragraph is also from this statement.

113 "he could easily maintain himself": Letter from Hugh Forbes to Samuel Gridley Howe, May 14, 1858, quoted in *New York Herald*, October 27, 1859; VC.

113 "the planters would pursue": Richard Warch and Jonathan F. Fanton, eds., *John Brown* (Englewood Cliffs, N.J.: Prentice-Hall, 1973), p. 54. The next quotation in this paragraph is also on p. 54.

114 "leap beyond his control": Letter from Hugh Forbes to Samuel Gridley Howe, May 14, 1858, quoted in *New York Herald*, October 27, 1859; VC. The quotations in the next paragraph are also from this letter.

115 "insane" and "fanatical" and "not so with the Negro": Henry Cleveland, *Alexander H. Stephens, in Public and Private: With Letters and Speeches, Before, During, and Since the War* (Philadelphia: National Publishing Co., 1866), pp. 722–23.

115 "To attempt to elevate": "Pen Pictures of Puritanism," *Old Guard* 4 (March 1866): 169. The next quotations in this paragraph are on pp. 170–71.

116 "prejudice at the North": C. Peter Ripley, ed., *The Black Abolitionist Papers*, Vol. IV, *The United States, 1847–1858* (Chapel Hill: University of North Carolina Press, 1991), p. 202. The next quotation in this paragraph is on p. 154.

116 "The prejudices of the north": *Park Street Address*, Boston, July 4, 1829; AAS.

116 "You see nothing": *The Black Abolitionist Papers*, p. 343.

116 "Nigger lips": *Negro Protest Pamphlets: A Compendium* (New York: Arno Press, 1969), p. 40.

117 "a man, woman or child": A. Lincoln, *Speeches and Writings, 1832–1858*, p. 637.

117 "Negro equality!": A. Lincoln, *Speeches and Writings, 1859–1865*, p. 29.

117 "I have studied": Quoted in David L. Smiley, *Lion of White Hall: The Life of Cassius M. Clay* (Madison: University of Wisconsin Press, 1962), p. 56.

117 "sufferers" and "it is possible": H. Mayer, *All on Fire*, p. 433. The next quotation in this paragraph is on p. 175.

117 *"they lack a practical exemplification"*: *The Black Abolitionist Papers*, p. 201.

118 "There may be counted": *The Black Abolitionist Papers*, p. 221.

118 "African high school": Letter from John Brown to Joshua Giddings, May 15, 1847; Huntington Library.

119 "devouring silly novels": *Ru*, p. 69. The quotations in the next two paragraphs are on pp. 71–72.

120 "I am the hounded" and "I am oppressed": W. Whitman, *Complete Poetry and Collected Prose*, pp. 65, 113.

120 "the odious stigma": *Negro Protest Pamphlets*, p. 20.

120 "The great fault": *The Black Abolitionist Papers*, p. 32.

120 "The elevation of the colored man": *The Condition, Elevation, Emigration and Destiny of the Colored People of the United States* (1852; New York: Arno Press, 1968), p. 87.

120 "individual manhood": *Anglo-African Magazine* 1:326.

121 "I do not often speak": "The Fugitive Slave Law," in the *The Essential Writings of Ralph Waldo Emerson*, ed. Brooks Atkinson (New York: Modern Library, 2000), pp. 779, 784.

121 "This law": "Slavery in Massachusetts," in *CEP*, p. 337.

121 "should feel justified": *Liberator*, April 11, 1851.

121 "I am frank to declare": *The Black Abolitionist Papers*, p. 64.

121 "so wicked, so atrocious": *The Black Abolitionist Papers*, p. 70.

121 "It now seems": *Ru*, p. 80.

122 "Now therefore come": Judges 7:3. The Gideon story is in Judges 6:1–8:35.

122 *"Do not delay"*: *Ru*, pp. 84–85. The quotation in the paragraph after the next one is on p. 86.

123 "John Brown was strong": Quoted in O. G. Villard, *John Brown*, p. 50.

123 "The mother, daughters": *Ru*, pp. 292–93.

124 "There were no drones": Salmon Brown, "My Father, John Brown," *Outlook*, January 25, 1913.

123 "the woman in him": *Ru*, p. 193.

123 "a branch of the United States League": *Ru*, p. 84.

124 "As citizens of the United States of America": *Ru*, p. 86.

124 "with the colored people here": *Ru*, p. 83.

124 "Colored people": *Ru*, p. 84.

125 "I was on some": *Ru*, p. 75.

126 In the North Elba census: *Census Notes* (North Elba, 1850); BSC.

126 "They never raise anything": *Ru*, pp. 228–29.

127 "a true friend" and "He'd walk up": Mary Lee, "John Brown Rests Amid the Mountains," *New York Times*, October 20, 1929.

127 Russell Banks's fine novel: *Cloudsplitter: A Novel* (New York: HarperFlamingo, 1998).

127 "There were a great many": Richard Henry Dana, Jr., "How We Met John Brown," *Atlantic Monthly* 28 (July 1871): 5. The quotations in the next five paragraphs are on pp. 7–8.

129 "This is the meal": W. Whitman, *Complete Poetry and Collected Prose*, p. 44. The next quotation is on p. 35.

129 "the man who of all Americans": W. E. B. Du Bois, *John Brown* (1909; Armonk, N.Y., and London: M. E. Sharpe, 1997), p. xxv.

130 "I never thought": *A Tribute of Respect, Commemorative of the Worth and Sacrifice of John Brown, of Ossawatomie* (Cleveland: n.p., 1859), p. 12.

131 "Keep these white men inside": MS. Interview of John Thomas Allstadt of Kearneysville, West Virginia, by Katherine Mayo, April 15, 1909; VC.

131 "Gerrit Smith's abortive attempts": *The Life, Trial, and Execution of Captain John Brown* (New York: Robert M. DeWitt, 1859), p. 9.

133 "their drinking, profanity": F. B. Sanborn, *The Life and Letters of John Brown*, p. 189.

133 "If you or any of my family": *Ru*, p. 94.

133 "After being hard pressed": *Ru*, p. 94.

135 "We are rejoiced": Letter from Ruth Brown to Mary Brown, November 15, 1854; BSC. The next quotation in this paragraph is also from this letter.

135 "There are slaves owned": F. B. Sanborn, *The Life and Letters of John Brown*, p. 198.

135 "The storm every day": Quoted in S. Oates, *To Purge This Land with Blood*, p. 92.

135 "The convention has been": F. B. Sanborn, *The Life and Letters of John Brown*, p. 194.

136 "d——d Abolitionists": Quoted in O. G. Villard, *John Brown*, p. 87. The remaining quotations in this paragraph are also on p. 87.

136 "I felt very much disappointed": *Ru*, p. 95.

137 "matters in general": Letter from John Brown to Mary Ann Brown, November 30, 1855; BSC. The next quotation in this paragraph is also from this letter.

7. Pottawatomie

138 "paranoia": Allan Nevins, *The Emergence of Lincoln* (New York: Scribner, 1950), II:92.

139 "I look upon the [Kansas-]Nebraska": Letter from A. Lincoln to Joshua F. Speed, August 24, 1855, in A. Lincoln, *Speeches and Writings, 1832–1858*, p. 361.

140 "Kansas is": Letter to the *Charleston Mercury*, quoted in F. B. Sanborn, *The Life and Letters of John Brown*, p. 165.

140 "If a set of fanatics": Daniel Webster Wilder, *The Annals of Kansas* (Topeka: G. W. Martin, 1875), p. 40.

141 "To those who have qualms": William Addison Phillips, *The Conquest of Kansas, by Missouri and Her Allies* (Boston: Phillips, Sampson & Co., 1856), p. 47.

141 "rough, coarse" and "groups of": Thomas H. Webb, *Scrap-Books of Kansas Happenings*, 14:35; KSHS. See also John H. Gihon, *Geary and Kansas: Governor Geary's Administration in Kansas: With a Complete History of the Territory Until July 1857* (Philadelphia: Charles C. Rhodes, 1857), esp. chaps. 4 and 8.

141 The *New-York Tribune* portrayed: See Michael Fellman, *Inside War* (New York: Oxford University Press, 1989), p. 14.

141 "We now have laws": D. W. Wilder, *The Annals of Kansas*, p. 57.

142 "We owe no allegiance": D. W. Wilder, *The Annals of Kansas*, p. 61.

142 "The border Missourians": [Hannah Anderson Ropes], *Six Months in Kansas* (Boston: John P. Jewett, 1856), see chap. 4.

142 "the lowest class of rowdies": This and the other phrases in this sentence are quoted in O. G. Villard, *John Brown*, p. 96.

142 "nigger-lovers" and "alone to the one idea": Quoted in M. Fellman, *Inside War*, p. 19.

142 "the best interests of Kansas": D. W. Wilder, *The Annals of Kansas*, p. 60.

143 "There is a prevailing sentiment": Quoted in J. C. Malin, *John Brown and the Legend of Fifty-six*, p. 516. The quotation in the next sentence is on p. 517.

144 "Arrived in Kansas": *Cleveland Leader*, November 29, 1883.

144 "We are Free State" and "They rode away": MS. Interview with Jason Brown by Katherine Mayo, December 13 and 14, 1908; VC.

144 "If any officer": Letter from John Brown, Jr., to Mary Brown, September 15 and 21, 1855; VC.

144 "Perhaps we shall all get shot": Letter from Wealthy Brown to Watson Brown, September 16, 1855; VC.

145 "The way they are served": J. H. Gihon, *Geary and Kansas*, chap. 8.

146 "TO ARMS!": D. W. Wilder, *The Annals of Kansas*, p. 56.

147 "matters in general": Letter from John Brown to Mary Ann Brown, November 30, 1855; BSC.

147 "We learn by their papers" and "Free state men": Quoted in O. G. Villard, *John Brown*, p. 119.

148 "Our present wants": *Ru*, p. 101.

148 "My sins are ever before me": Letter from Owen Brown to John Brown, January 26, 1856; BSC.

148 "We have just learned": R. J. Hinton, *John Brown and His Men*, p. 668.

149 "The Border Ruffians": *New-York Tribune*, March 1, 1856.

150 "We hear that Franklin Pierce": Letter from John Brown to Mary Brown, February 20, 1856; BSC.

150 "in readiness to act": Letter from John Brown to Joshua R. Giddings, February 20, 1856; VC.

150 "light up the fires": O. G. Villard, *John Brown*, p. 132.

150 "those miserable Missourians": Letter from Wealthy H. Brown to Louisa C. Barber, March 23, 1856; BSC.

151 "by all means come": Letter from John Brown, Jr., to Louisa C. Barber, March 29, 1856; BSC.

151 "For One I have no desire": Letter from John Brown to Mary Brown, April 7, 1856; KSHS.

152 "an Abolitionist of the old stock": Quoted in O. G. Villard, *John Brown*, p. 134.

153 "those damned Browns": *Ru*, p. 199. The remaining quotations in this paragraph are also on p. 199.

154 "I thought father was wild": *Ru*, p. 199.

154 "The Pottawatomie Rifle Company": James Hanway, "The Settlement of Lane and Vicinity," *Hanway Miscellanies*, vol. 4; KSHS.

155 "Sell husband, wife": F. B. Sanborn, *Recollections of Seventy Years*, p. 129. The remaining quotations in this paragraph are also on p. 129.

155 "He was a dangerous man": *Ru*, p. 215.

155 According to one report: *Ru*, p. 215.

156 "We are now in favor" and "In a fight, let our motto": *Squatter Sovereign*, April 29, 1856, and May 6, 1856, respectively.

156 "law-abiding citizens": J. H. Gihon, *Geary and Kansas*, p. 78.

156 Southern Rights: W. A. Phillips, *The Conquest of Kansas*, p. 297. The inscriptions in this paragraph are also on p. 297. The quotation in the next paragraph is on p. 296.

157 "This is the happiest moment" and "*Thus fell the abolition*": J. H. Gihon, *Geary and Kansas*, p. 85.

158 "wild and frenzied": James Blood, quoted in Appendix to *Reminiscences of Old John Brown*, in *John Brown Pamphlets*, 2:70; BSC.

158 "radical retaliatory measure": MS. Interview of Salmon Brown by Katherine Mayo, October 11, 1908; VC.

158 "We expect to be butchered": MS. Interview of Jason Brown by Katherine Mayo, December 13, 1908; VC.

158 "a big, savage, bloodthirsty Austrian": MS. Interview of Salmon Brown by Katherine Mayo, October 11, 1908; VC.

158 "Something *is going to be done*": MS. Interview of Jason Brown by Katherine Mayo, December 13, 1908; VC.

158 "Father, be careful": Quoted by George H. Grant, in Appendix to *Reminiscences of Old John Brown*, in *John Brown Pamphlets*, 2:71.

158 "chivalrous knight": *Memoir and Letters of Charles Sumner*, ed. E. L. Pierce, 3:446.

159 "At that blow": Quoted in O. G. Villard, *John Brown*, p. 154.

159 "Caution, caution, sir": Letter from James H. Hanway to Richard J. Hinton, December 5, 1859; KSHS.

159 "In the South": D. Grimsted, *American Mobbing*, p. 86. The quotations in the next paragraph are on pp. 91, 110, and 91, respectively. In the paragraph after that, the quotations are on pp. 91 and 92, respectively.

160 "Pistols, dirks": T. D. Weld, *American Slavery as It Is* (1839; Itasca, Ill.: Peacock, 1972), p. 108.

160 "The best way": Quoted in P. Pillsbury, *Acts of the Anti-Slavery Apostles*, p. 388.

161 "A feud is this way": Mark Twain [Samuel Langhorne Clemens], *Adventures of Huckleberry Finn* (1885; New York: W. W. Norton, 1977), p. 89.

161 "about thirty first-rate stripes" and "Every lick went": Quoted in D. Grimsted, *American Mobbing*, pp. 99–100.

161 HIT HIM AGAIN: John Hope Franklin, *The Militant South, 1800–1861* (Cambridge: Harvard University Press, 1956), p. 55.

161 "a pack of curs": Quoted in D. Grimsted, *American Mobbing*, p. 100.

162 "as long as one enemy": Quoted in Thomas H. Gladstone, *The Englishman in Kansas; or, Squatter Life and Border Warfare* (New York: Miller & Co., 1857), p. 278. The following quotations in this paragraph are on pp. 251 and 278, respectively.

162 "none was pushed harder": D. Grimsted, *American Mobbing*, p. 53.

162 "Abolitionists are like infidels": P. Pillsbury, *Acts of the Anti-Slavery Apostles*, p. 387.

162 "This was entirely unexpected": J. H. Gihon, *Geary and Kansas*, pp. 30–31.

162 "Boys, to-day I'm a Kickapoo Ranger": W. A. Phillips, *The Conquest of Kansas*, p. 295.

162 "It is only for some": T. Nelson, *Documents of Upheaval*, p. 120.

162 "the supremacy of the bowie knife": Quoted in H. Mayer, *All on Fire*, p. 449.

163 "Kansas would of course": *New Englander*, November 1859, p. 1069.

163 "We do not love to blush": Quoted in J. C. Malin, *John Brown and the Legend of Fifty-six*, p. 64.

163 "drunken ourang-outangs" and "duty to aid": Quoted in M. Fellman, *Inside War*, p. 15.

163 Of the fifty-two who died: The statistics in this paragraph are in D. Grimsted, *American Mobbing*, p. 248.

163 "brought Southern tactics": Albert D. Richardson, "Free Missouri. II," *Atlantic Monthly* 21 (April 1868): 498.

164 "tonight . . . will learn": Quoted in T. H. Gladstone, *The Englishman in Kansas*, p. 45.

164 "the wanton cowardice": Quoted in D. Grimsted, *American Mobbing*, p. 260.

164 "cowards, or worse": *Lawrence Daily Journal*, December 3, 1879.

164 "men of violence": *Wendell Phillips on Civil Rights and Freedom*, ed. L. Filler, p. 105.

165 "He was of the old Puritan stock": Quoted in Emerson David Fite, *The Presidential Campaign of 1860* (1911; New York: Kennikat Press, 1967), p. 10.

165 "good terrorism": Doris Lessing, *The Good Terrorist* (New York: Knopf, 1985); for a dis-

cussion of Lessing's idea, see Charles Townshend, *Terrorism: A Very Short Introduction* (Oxford: Oxford University Press, 2002), p. 20. See also Joanne Mariner, "Good and Bad Terrorism? (2002) at http://writ.news.findlaw.com/mariner/20020107.html.

166 Just as the populists: See, for example, J. J. Ingalls, "John Brown's Place in History," article bound in *John Brown Pamphlets*, 4:139; BSC.

166 "proposed to sweep the creek": *Ru*, p. 207.

167 "shoot & exterminate": Quoted in S. Oates, *To Purge This Land with Blood*, p. 122.

167 "a base conspiracy": Quoted in J. C. Malin, *John Brown and the Legend of Fifty-six*, p. 317. The next two quotations in this paragraph are on p. 312.

168 "Nearly all of the Indian agents": W. A. Phillips, *The Conquest of Kansas*, p. 16.

169 "I will have nothing to do with so mean an act": " 'Potawatomie': Statement by Jason, Second Son of John Brown," *Lawrence* (Kansas) *Journal*, February 8, 1880. The quotation in the next paragraph is also from this source.

169 "We want no houses": MS. Interview with Jason Brown by Katherine Mayo, December 28, 1908; VC.

169 "a great mistake": " 'Potawatomie': Statement by Jason, Second Son of John Brown," *Lawrence* (Kansas) *Journal*, February 8, 1880. The first two quotations in the next paragraph are also from this piece.

169 "did not want to mix up": *Ru*, p. 201.

171 "going back there": *Ru*, p. 201.

171 "fight fire with fire": Quoted in S. Oates, *To Purge This Land with Blood*, p. 133. The quotation in the next sentence is also on p. 133.

172 "Haven't I told you": *Report of the Special Committee to Investigate the Troubles in Kansas, 34th Congress, 1st Session, Report No. 200* (Washington, D.C.: Cornelius Wendell, 1856), *ex parte* testimony, p. 1193.

172 "You are our prisoner": *Report of the Special Committee . . . Troubles in Kansas*, p. 1197. The quotations in the next paragraph are on p. 1198.

173 "horribly cut and mangled": Quoted in S. Oates, *To Purge This Land with Blood*, p. 138. The next quotation in this paragraph is also on p. 138.

173 "There shall be no more": Quoted in O. G. Villard, *John Brown*, p. 165.

174 "an uncalled for, wicked act": *Ru*, p. 204.

174 "WAR! WAR!": *Westport Border Times*, May 30, 1856, reprinted in the *Kansas Weekly Herald* (Leavenworth) on May 31, 1856, and in the *Squatter Sovereign* (Atchison) on June 10, 1856.

174 "The blood-curdling story of the murder": *St. Louis Morning Herald*, June 5, 1856.

174 "robbers and assassins": Printed manifesto signed by some twenty proslavery Missourians and Kansans, August 28, 1856; VC.

174 "Brown, the notorious assassin": *Leavenworth City Journal*, August 7, 1856.

174 "Brown the notorious assassin and robber": *Squatter Sovereign*, August 26, 1856.

175 "John Brown, Sen., known as": *St. Louis Republican*, August 29, 1856.

175 "outrages were so common": W. A. Phillips, *The Conquest of Kansas*, p. 380.

175 "reign of terror": Statement by O. C. Brown, June 24 1856; KSHS.

175 "of brutal ferocity": J. H. Gihon, *Geary and Kansas*, p. 91. The other quotation in this sentence is on pp. 101–2.

175 "Some pro-slavery men": *Ru*, p. 33.

175 "the pro-slavery men were dreadfully terrified": "John Brown Once More," *Springfield Republican*, December 27, 1879.

176 "an organized band": *Kansas Weekly Herald*, June 14, 1856.

176 "Midnight murders, assassinations": *Squatter Sovereign*, June 10, 1856.

176 "With an eye like a snake": *Kansas Weekly Herald*, June 21, 1856.

176 "have secret military organizations": "The Voice of Kansas—Let the South Respond," *DeBow's Review,* August 1856, p. 189. The following quotations in this paragraph are on pp. 189 and 190.

177 "No; when I came to see": Quoted in O. G. Villard, *John Brown,* p. 165.

177 "accused of murdering": *Ru,* p. 102.

178 "There is no one": W. A. Phillips, *The Conquest of Kansas,* p. 332.

8. Pariah and Legend

180 "You endanger our lives": Quoted in O. G. Villard, *John Brown,* p. 167.

180 "We were heading down": W. A. Phillips, *The Conquest of Kansas,* p. 331.

180 "I have never knowingly injured": MS. Interview of Jason Brown by Katherine Mayo, December 13 and 14, 1908; VC.

181 "a maniac and in a terrible condition": MS. Interview of Jason Brown by Katherine Mayo, December 13 and 14, 1908; VC. The quotations in the next paragraph and the first quotation in the paragraph after that are also from this interview.

181 "no parallel in republican government": Quoted in O. G. Villard, *John Brown,* p. 196.

182 "decided, in a very cowardly manner": Letter from John Brown to his family, June 1856; BSC.

182 "If the cowardice and indifference": August Bondi, "With John Brown in Kansas," *Publications of the Kansas State Historical Society,* 8:281–82.

182 "Who goes there?": F. B. Sanborn, *The Life and Letters of John Brown,* p. 293. The quotations in the next paragraph are on p. 294.

184 "I would rather have the small-pox": J. Redpath, *The Public Life of Captain John Brown,* pp. 112–13.

185 "memories of what had once been boots": F. B. Sanborn, *The Life and Letters of John Brown,* p. 298.

185 "The Missourians!—They are coming!": W. A. Phillips, *The Conquest of Kansas,* p. 335. The quotation in the next paragraph is on p. 337.

186 "Hurrah! Come on, boys!": Quoted in O. G. Villard, *John Brown,* p. 208.

186 "Captain, I understand exactly": F. B. Sanborn, *The Life and Letters of John Brown,* p. 300. The next quotation in this paragraph and the quotation in the next paragraph are also on p. 300.

188 "acknowledge laws and institutions": A. Bondi, "With John Brown in Kansas," p. 282. The quotation in the paragraph after next is on p. 281.

189 "He was a great man": Letter from Samuel Walker to James Hanway, February 18, 1875; KSHS.

189 "He always impressed me as a sane man": Letter from Luke F. Parsons to J. H. Beach, April 21, 1913; BSC.

190 "in good keeping": *Ru2,* p. 96. The quotations in the next paragraph are on pp. 96 and 97, respectively.

191 "He was always an enigma": *Ru2,* p. 210.

191 "What a magnificent scene": *Ru2,* p. 211.

192 "a poetic and impulsive nature": *Ru2,* p. 212. The next quotation in this paragraph and the quotations in the next three paragraphs are also on p. 212.

193 "in the name of Franklin Pierce": *Ru2,* p. 98.

193 "Father was like a child": MS. Interview of Salmon Brown by Katherine Mayo, October 11–13, 1908; VC.

194 "There he is!": Diary of Samuel J. Reader, Topeka, Kansas, quoted in O. G. Villard, *John Brown*, p. 223.

194 "The Christian religion": R. H. Hinton, *John Brown and His Men*, p. 499.

195 "War! War!!": *Leavenworth Journal*, August 14, 1856.

195 "terror of all Missouri" and "old terrifier": *New York Times*, August 29 and September 7, 1856.

195 "Father . . . is an omnipresent dread": F. B. Sanborn, *The Life and Letters of John Brown*, p. 313.

195 "John Brown is coming!": MS. Interview of Mary Grant Brown of San Jose, California, by Katherine Mayo, September 24, 1908; VC.

195 "Brown was a presence in Kansas": MS. Interview of R. G. Elliott by Katherine Mayo, July 27, 1908; VC.

196 "All uncivil, ungentlemanly, profane": "John Brown's Covenant for the Enlistment of his Volunteer-Regular Company, August, 1856," app. B of O. G. Villard, *John Brown*, p. 664.

197 "all good citizens of Missouri": J. H. Gihon, *Geary and Kansas*, chap. 21. The next quotation in this paragraph is also in chap. 21.

197 "We hear lately that about three thousand Missourians": F. B. Sanborn, *The Life and Letters of John Brown*, p. 315.

198 "If I can't kill a man": J. H. Gihon, *Geary and Kansas*, chap. 21. The next quotation in this paragraph is in chap. 16.

198 "You are fighting for slavery": J. W. Winkley, *John Brown, the Hero* (Boston: James H. West, 1905), pp. 71–72.

199 "they were good Free-State cattle": F. B. Sanborn, *The Life and Letters of John Brown*, p. 327.

199 "to clear the whole territory": *Missouri Statesman*, September 5, 1856.

199 "I know you!": Testimony by Martin White before the Kansas House of Representatives, February 13, 1857, quoted in *Leavenworth Journal*, March 12, 1857.

200 "Men, come on": Quoted in O. G. Villard, *John Brown*, p. 243.

200 "Well, something hit me": Quoted in O. G. Villard, *John Brown*, p. 245.

201 "God sees it": Quoted in O. G. Villard, *John Brown*, p. 248.

201 "the Osawatomie disaster": S. Oates, *To Purge This Land with Blood*, p. 171.

201 "we killed about thirty of them": Missouri *Weekly Statesman*, September 5, 1856.

201 "the notorious John Brown": F. B. Sanborn, *The Life and Letters of John Brown*, p. 321. The quotation in the next paragraph is on p. 319.

202 "The Battle of Osawatomie": W. A. Phillips, *The Conquest of Kansas*, p. 298.

202 "The Battle of Osawatomie is considered": R. J. Hinton, *John Brown and His Men*, p. 670.

202 "I have only a short time": Quoted in O. G. Villard, *John Brown*, p. 248.

204 "There will be no attempt": F. B. Sanborn, *The Life and Letters of John Brown*, p. 329. The quotation in the next paragraph is on p. 330.

9. The Promoter

206 "swarms of cringers": W. Whitman, *Complete Poetry and Collected Prose*, p. 18. The quotation in the next paragraph is on p. 83.

207 "I arrived here yesterday": Quoted in O. G. Villard, *John Brown*, p. 261.

207 "I am *through Infinite grace*": *Ru*, p. 108.

208 "tall, slender, and commanding": F. B. Sanborn, *The Life and Letters of John Brown*, p. 341.

208 "of the unmixed Puritan breed": F. B. Sanborn, *Memoir of John Brown* (Concord, Mass.: J. Munsell, 1878), p. 45.

209 "a calm, temperate and pious man": William Lawrence, *Life of Amos A. Lawrence* (Boston: Houghton Mifflin, 1888), pp. 124–25.

209 "like the iron and the magnet": C. E. Heller, *Portrait of an Abolitionist*, p. 77.

209 "exactness and neatness": R. J. Hinton, *John Brown and His Men*, p. 721. The next two quotations in this paragraph are on pp. 721–22.

210 "Captain Brown, will you buy something": R. J. Hinton, *John Brown and His Men*, p. 721.

210 "positive contribution": Quoted in R. J. Hinton, *John Brown and His Men*, p. 28.

210 "one of the finest pieces": Quoted in appendix to H. Von Holst, *John Brown*, ed. Frank Preston Stearns (Boston: Cupples & Hurd, 1888), p. 221.

210 "as a devotee": James Freeman Clarke, *Anti-Slavery Days: A Sketch of the Struggle Which Ended in the Abolition of Slavery in the United States* (New York: Lovell, 1883), pp. 153–54.

210 "I am no adventurer": Letter from H. D. Hurd to George L. Stearns, March 19, 1857; KSHS.

212 "any *defensive* measures": Quoted in O. G. Villard, *John Brown*, p. 276. The next quotation in this paragraph is also on p. 276.

212 "hitherto I have opposed": Quoted in Ralph Volney Harlow, *Gerrit Smith: Philanthropist and Reformer* (New York: Henry Holt, 1939), p. 350.

213 "Here is the chain": R. J. Hinton, *John Brown and His Men*, p. 612. The next quotation in this paragraph is on p. 614.

213 "tyrannical & Damnable": Quoted in O. G. Villard, John Brown, p. 278.

213 "To the Friends of Freedom": *Ru*, p. 110.

215 "took next to no part": Stanley M. Elkins, *Slavery: A Problem in American Institutional and Intellectual Life* (Chicago: University of Chicago Press, 1959), p. 147.

215 "monks sitting cross-legged": Taylor Stoehr, *Nay-Saying in Concord: Emerson, Alcott, and Thoreau* (Hamden, Conn.: Archon Books, 1979), pp. 19–20.

215 "philosophical bent": Anne Rose, *Transcendentalism as a Social Movement, 1830–1850* (New Haven: Yale University Press, 1981), p. 219.

215 Although this picture of the Transcendentalists: See especially Albert J. von Frank, *The Trials of Anthony Burns: Freedom and Slavery in Emerson's Boston* (Cambridge: Harvard University Press, 1998); Len Gougeon, *Virtue's Hero: Emerson, Antislavery, and Reform* (Athens: University of Georgia Press, 1990); and Joel Myerson and Len Gougeon, eds., *Emerson's Antislavery Writings* (New Haven: Yale University Press, 1995).

217 "In a similar way": *The Magnificent Activist*, ed. H. N. Meyer, p. 572.

217 "surpassed himself": Quoted in Octavius Brooks Frothingham, *Theodore Parker, a Biography* (Boston: J. R. Osgood & Co., 1874), pp. 105–6.

217 "I preach abundant heresies": John Weiss, *Life and Correspondence of Theodore Parker* (Boston: Congregational Society, 1864), p. 101.

218 "ONE HELD AGAINST HIS WILL": *Ru*, p. 255.

219 "a man for up-hill work": *Remarks on the Character of George L. Stearns at Medford, April 14, 1867* (N.p.: printed broadside of 1867); VC.

219 "the eternal right": *JMN* 15:207.

219 "angry bigot": *EL*, p. 262.

219 "madmen, madwomen": *EL*, p. 1210.

220 "men of one idea": H. D. Thoreau, *Walden*, in *A Week* . . . , *Walden* . . . , *The Maine Woods, Cape Cod*, pp. 443–44.

220 "insurmountable" racial barriers: Quoted in Marjory M. Moody, "The Evolution of Emerson as an Abolitionist," *American Literature* 17 (March 1945): 29.

220 "I think that it cannot be maintained": *JMN* 12:152.

220 "it will happen by & by": *JMN* 13:286.

220 "The history of the white man": *The Journal of Henry D. Thoreau*, ed. Bradford Torrey and Francis H. Allen (1906; New York: Dover, 1962, 14 vols. in 2), 10:252. The next quotation in this paragraph is in 1:446. For a fine discussion of Thoreau and race, see Michael Meyer, "Thoreau and Black Emigration," *American Literature* 53 (November 1981): 380–96.

220 "red race with sullen step": *Collected Poems of Henry Thoreau* (Baltimore: Johns Hopkins University Press, 1964), pp. 134–35.

221 "Emerson, while thoroughly true": T. W. Higginson, *Contemporaries* (Boston: Houghton Mifflin, 1899), p. 271.

221 "simple, docile, and affectionate": *The Magnificent Activist*, ed. H. N. Meyer (New York: Da Capo Press, 2000), pp. 213–14.

221 "I feel as if they were": Tilden G. Edelstein, *Strange Enthusiasm: A Life of Thomas Wentworth Higginson* (New Haven and London: Yale University Press, 1968), p. 291.

222 A detailed report of the crime: See *Report of the Special Committee Appointed to Investigate the Troubles in Kansas; With the Views of the Minority of Said Committee* (Washington, D.C.: Cornelius Wendell, 1856), pp. 105–7.

222 "seems to have had a great passion": "History of Old John Brown," *Old Guard* 3 (July 1865): 330.

222 "Captain John Brown of Kansas": *JMN* 14:125–26.

223 "believed in two articles": J. Myerson and L. Gougeon, eds., *Emerson's Antislavery Writings*, p. 118.

223 "I noticed that he did not overstate": H. D. Thoreau, "A Plea for Captain John Brown," in *CEP*, p. 399. The quotation in the next paragraph is on p. 400.

224 "It was his peculiar doctrine": H. D. Thoreau, "A Plea for Captain John Brown," in *CEP*, p. 413. The next quotation in this paragraph is on p. 407.

224 "My body is indeed incased": P. Pillsbury, *Acts of the Anti-slavery Apostles*, p. 266. The next two quotations in this paragraph are on pp. 293 and 303, respectively.

225 "I regard Non-Resistance": Quoted in Lewis Perry, *Radical Abolitionism: Anarchy and the Government of God in Antislavery Thought* (Ithaca: Cornell University Press, 1973), p. 82.

225 "non-resistant of non-resistants": L. Perry, *Radical Abolitionism*, p. 118.

225 "the *slave's* government also": "Civil Disobedience," in *CEP*, p. 206. The next quotation in this paragraph is on p. 213.

225 "Let us withhold": *The Essential Writings of Ralph Waldo Emerson*, ed. B. Atkinson, pp. 753–54. The remaining quotations in this paragraph are on pp. 760–61.

226 "to arm himself": *Liberator*, October 4, 1850.

226 "With this sword I thee wed": Letter from Theodore Parker to Edward D. Cheney, June 28, 1859; Letterbook 4, Parker Papers, Massachusetts Historical Society.

227 "You cowards": Quoted in A. J. von Frank, *The Trials of Anthony Burns*, p. 68.

227 "Why are we not within?": *The Magnificent Activist*, ed. H. N. Meyer, p. 71.

227 "Its natural habitat": "Slavery in Massachusetts," in *CEP*, p. 337. The subsequent quotations in this paragraph are on pp. 343, 341, 345, and 346, respectively. The quotations in the next paragraph are on pp. 346–47.

228 "America, the most prosperous country": J. Myerson and L. Gougeon, eds., *Emerson's Antislavery Writings*, p. 57. The subsequent quotations in this paragraph are on pp. 57 and 83, respectively.

228 "I submit that all government": *JMN* 14:423.

228 "had the best government that ever existed": *JMN* 14:407.

228 "This law of nature is universal": *JMN* 14:394–95. The next quotation in this paragraph is on p. 410.

229 "He had three thousand sheep": *JMN* 14:126.

229 "a rough herdsman": F. B. Sanborn, *The Life and Letters of John Brown*, p. 57.

229 "He stands for Truth": *JMN* 15:68.

229 "a New England farmer": "A Plea for Captain John Brown," in *CEP*, p. 397.

229 "he took five respectable men": Quoted in S. D. Carpenter, *Logic of History: Five Hundred Political Texts: Being Concentrated Extracts of Abolitionism* (Madison, Wis.: S. D. Carpenter, 1864), pp. 71–72.

229 "his sword dripping": *Report of Union Meeting in Faneuil Hall* (Boston: n.p., 1859), p. 19.

230 "a Puritan soldier": F. B. Sanborn, *Memoir of John Brown*, p. 45.

230 "a Cromwellian Ironside": C. E. Heller, *Portrait of an Abolitionist*, p. 78.

230 "some old Cromwellian hero": Quoted in R. J. Hinton, *John Brown and His Men*, p. 721.

230 "a regular Cromwellian": Quoted in Robert B. Bonner, "Roundheaded Cavaliers? The Contexts and Limits of a Confederate Racial Project," *Civil War History* 48 (2002): 38.

230 "a Puritan brought back": Quoted in M. Fellman, *Inside War*, p. 17.

230 "the Oliver Cromwell of America": Quoted in R. J. Hinton, *John Brown and His Men*, p. 697.

230 "He died lately": H. D. Thoreau, "A Plea for Captain John Brown," in *CEP*, p. 398. The remaining quotations in this paragraph are on p. 399.

230 "a sort of monster": *American Whig Review* 3 (April 1846): 396.

230 "been termed a regicide": *New Englander and Yale Review* 4 (April 1846): 211.

231 "I forbade [my soldiers]": Thomas Carlyle, *Oliver Cromwell's Letters and Speeches with Elucidations* (1845; New York: AMS Press, 1969), II:60.

231 "the soul of the Puritan revolt": T. Carlyle, *Oliver Cromwell's Letters and Speeches*, I:12.

231 "The Puritans to many": T. Carlyle, *On Heroes, Hero-Worship and the Heroic in History* (first delivered as lectures from 1837 to 1840; New York: AMS, 1969), pp. 204–5.

232 "exaggerated descriptions": "Oliver Cromwell," *United States Democratic Review* 23 (October 1848): 334.

232 "Some may object": Joel Tyler Headley, *The Life of Oliver Cromwell* (New York: Baker & Scribner, 1848), pp. xii–xiii.

232 "citadels and warriors": J. Myerson and L. Gougeon, eds., *Emerson's Antislavery Writings*, p. 83.

232 "the rarest of heroes": *JMN* 14:334.

232 "a transcendentalist, above all": H. D. Thoreau, "A Plea for Captain John Brown," in *CEP*, p. 399.

233 "an improved piece of land": Letter from J. Brown to Amos A. Lawrence, March 12, 1857; BSC.

233 "The family of Captain Brown": Letter from Amos A. Lawrence to J. Brown, March 20, 1857; BSC.

233 "I was told that the newspapers": *Ru*, p. 109. The quotation in the next paragraph is on p. 111.

234 "Right is that which is good": R. J. Hinton, *John Brown and His Men*, p. 617. The remaining quotations in this paragraph are also on p. 617.

235 "One of the U S hounds": Letter from J. Brown to Eli Thayer, April 13, 1857; KSHS.

235 "Here are eighteen lives": F. B. Sanborn, *The Life and Letters of John Brown*, p. 512. The next quotation in this paragraph is also on p. 512.

235 "Old Browns *Farewell*": *Ru*, p. 114. The quotations in the following paragraph are on pp. 114–15.

236 "I could strike a blow": F. B. Sanborn, *The Life and Letters of John Brown*, p. 510. The first quotation in the next paragraph is also on p. 510.

236 "a good deal of discouragement": Letter from J. Brown to John Brown, Jr., April 15, 1857; BSC.

236 "First," he wrote, "we must": Letter from J. Brown to Heman Humphrey, April 18, 1857; BSC.

236 "humiliating" to "go about": Letter from J. Brown to William Barnes, April 3, 1857; BSC.

236 "of aiding in your project": Quoted in O. G. Villard, *John Brown*, p. 289.

237 "to *pollute themselves*": Letter from J. Brown to Augustus Wattles, April 8, 1857; BSC.

10. Plotting Multiculturally

239 "quite unwell": Letter from J. Brown to G. L. Stearns, August 8, 1857; VC.

240 "This generous act" and "I am in *immediate* want": Letter from J. Brown to G. L. Stearns, August 10, 1857; VC.

241 "No preparatory notice": R. Warch and J. F. Fanton, eds., *John Brown*, p. 50. The next quotation in this paragraph is also on p. 50.

241 "very well written": Letter from G. Smith to Thaddeus Hyatt, September 12, 1857; KSHS.

242 "Among all the good friends who promised": Letter from J. Brown to F. B. Sanborn, August 13, 1857; VC.

242 "as ready for revolution": Letter from F. B. Sanborn to T. W. Higginson, September 11, 1857; KSHS.

242 "I have all the Arms": Letter from J. Brown to F. B. Sanborn, October 1, 1857; BSC. The next quotation in this paragraph is also from this letter.

243 "since then nothing": Letter from E. B. Whitman to G. L. Stearns, February 20, 1858; KSHS.

244 "After a good deal of wrangling": *Confession of John E. Cook* (Baltimore: n.p., 1859), p. 6.

245 "an agnostic of the most pronounced type": R. J. Hinton, *John Brown and His Men*, p. 454.

245 "Father starts an outrageous jawing": "Journal of Another of Brown's Sons," *New York Times*, October 24, 1859.

246 "for hugging girls": "Diary of One of the Harper's Ferry Conspirators," *Richmond Daily Whig*, October 29, 1859.

246 "Ugly words between Moffett": "Diary of One of the Harper's Ferry Conspirators," p. 9.

246 "evidence of truths": "Diary of One of the Harper's Ferry Conspirators," p. 10. The remaining quotation in this paragraph and the quotations in the next paragraph are also on this page.

247 "very bad man": Testimony of William H. Seward, Mason Report, p. 253.

248 "The humanitarians and Brown": Letter from H. Forbes to S. G. Howe, April 19, 1858; reprinted in *New York Herald*, October 29, 1859.

248 "came to me (as to others)": F. B. Sanborn, *The Life and Letters of John Brown*, p. 427. The first quotation in the next paragraph is also on p. 427.

248 "a man of an unsound mind": Testimony of W. H. Seward, Mason Report, p. 253.

248 "The anxiety I feel": *Ru*, p. 118.

248 "My reasons for keeping still": Letter from J. Brown to F. B. Sanborn, February 17, 1858; Thomas Wentworth Higginson Collection, BPL.

248 "for the *perfecting* of BY FAR": Letter from J. Brown to T. W. Higginson, February 2, 1858; BPL. The next quotation in this paragraph is also from this letter.

249 "Rail Road business": *Ru*, pp. 118–19.

249 "to get good Maps": Letter from J. Brown to J. Brown, Jr., February 5, 1858; BSC.

249 "ridiculous nonsense": *The Life, Trial, and Execution of Captain John Brown*, p. 90.

250 "piece of insanity": H. von Holst, *John Brown*, ed. Frank Preston Stearns (Boston: Cupples & Hurd, 1888), pp. 109–10.

250 "a chief indictment": O. G. Villard, *John Brown*, p. 335.

250 "The whole scheme forbids": O. G. Villard, *John Brown*, p. 335.

251 "Whereas, slavery throughout": R. J. Hinton, *John Brown and His Men*, pp. 620–21.

252 "THESE ARTICLES NOT": R. J. Hinton, *John Brown and His Men*, p. 633. The quotations in the next paragraph are on pp. 631–32.

254 "My utterances became more and more tinged": Frederick Douglass, *Life and Times of Frederick Douglass* (Hartford: Park Publishing Co., 1882), p. 217.

254 "were engaged in spreading": Carter G. Woodson, *Negro Orators and Their Orations* (Washington, D.C.: Associated Publishers, 1925), p. 191.

254 "Brave and glorious old man!": *The Frederick Douglass Papers*, ed. John W. Blassingame and John R. McKivigan (New Haven: Yale University Press, 1979–92), 5:22.

254 "History has no better illustration": *Ru*, p. 289.

255 "It was an amazing proposition": Quoted in O. G. Villard, *John Brown*, p. 321.

255 "proposing objections": F. B. Sanborn, *The Life and Letters of John Brown*, p. 439.

255 "We cannot give him up": F. B. Sanborn, *The Life and Letters of John Brown*, p. 439.

255 "It was done far more": F. B. Sanborn, *Recollections of Seventy Years*, p. 147.

255 "you felt ½ inclined": F. B. Sanborn, *The Life and Letters of John Brown*, p. 444.

256 "the white man must be the master": Quoted in Louis Menand, *The Metaphysical Club* (New York: Farrar, Straus & Giroux, 2001), p. 16. The next quotation in this paragraph is on p. 109.

256 "take the colored man": M. R. Delany, *The Condition, Elevation, Emigration, and Destiny of the Colored People of the United States*, pp. 26–27.

256 "fight a slaveholder": Carter G. Woodson, *The Mind of the Negro as Reflected in Letters Written During the Crisis, 1800–1860* (1926; New York: Negro University Press, 1969), p. 267.

257 "No higher exhibition": Quoted in *Men and Women of the Time* (New York: Routledge, 1893), p. 2. The next quotation in this paragraph, by Emerson, is also on p. 2.

257 "I have been in the presence": Alexander Milton Ross, *Recollections and Experiences of an Abolitionist: From 1855 to 1865* (Toronto: Rowsell & Hutchinson, 1875), p. 24. The quotations in the next paragraph are on p. 22; the one in the paragraph after that is on p. 50.

258 "The whole form": R. J. Hinton, *John Brown and His Men*, p. 204. The next quotation in this paragraph is also on p. 204.

259 "I am succeeding": Letter from J. Brown to J. Brown, Jr., April 8, 1858; BSC.

260 "was unable to effect": R. Warch and J. F. Fanton, eds., *John Brown*, p. 42.

260 "We cling to our oppressors": *The Condition, Elevation, Emigration, and Destiny of the Colored People of the United States*, p. 205.

262 "Men are afraid of identification": R. Warch and J. F. Fanton, eds., *John Brown*, p. 42.

262 "a *good* Abolition *convention*": Letter from John Brown to Mary Ann Brown, May 12, 1858; BSC.

263 "in any way to encourage": R. J. Hinton, *John Brown and His Men*, pp. 631–32.

264 "in the hands of some reliable men": Letter from Henry H. Wilson to Samuel Gridley Howe, May 9, 1858; BSC.

264 "none of our friends need have any fears": Letter from John Brown to George L. Stearns, May 14, 1858; BSC.

265   "We are completely nailed down": F. B. Sanborn, *The Life and Letters of John Brown*, p. 456.

265   "delay further action": Letter from J. Brown to O. Brown, May 21, 1858; BSC.

265   "Wilson as well as Hale": Letter from F. B. Sanborn to T. W. Higginson, May 18, 1858; Thomas Wentworth Higginson Collection, BPL.

265   "I utterly protest": Letter from T. W. Higginson to J. Brown, May 7, 1858; Thomas Wentworth Higginson Collection, BPL.

266   "I do not wish to know": Letter from G. Smith to B. F. Sanborn, July 26, 1858, in F. B. Sanborn, *The Life and Letters of John Brown*, p. 466.

266   "They are bad men": Quoted in O. G. Villard, *John Brown*, p. 344.

11. Practice

269   "foul human vultures": J. G. Whittier, "Le Marais du Cygne," *The Poetical Works of John Greenleaf Whittier*, p. 185.

269   "located on the same quarter section": Letter from J. Brown to F. B. Sanborn, July 20, 1858; VC. The remaining quotations in this paragraph are also from this letter.

270   "A gentlemanly and respectful deportment": F. B. Sanborn, *The Life and Letters of John Brown*, p. 474.

270   "Suppose you and I": Letter from Eli Snyder to James H. Holmes, 1894; VC.

270   "People mistake my objects": Letter from J. Hanway to R. J. Hinton, December 5, 1859; KSHS.

271   "Peaceful emancipation is impossible": Mason Report, II:215.

271   " 'A house divided against itself' ": A. Lincoln, *Speeches and Writings, 1832–1858*, p. 426.

271   "fanatical agitators" and "it is an irrepressible conflict": "The Irrepressible Conflict: A Speech by William H. Seward, Delivered at Rochester, Monday, Oct. 25, 1858" (New York: New York Tribune, 1858), p. 2.

271   "I believe there is no right": A. Lincoln, *Speeches and Writings, 1832–1858*, p. 448. The next quotation in this paragraph is on p. 524.

272   "Let it alone": A. Lincoln, *Speeches and Writings, 1859–1865*, p. 206. The subsequent quotations in this paragraph are on pp. 218 and 236, respectively.

272   "the salutary instructions of economy": *The Life of William H. Seward with Selections from His Works*, ed. George E. Baker (New York: J. Redfield, 1855), p. 263.

273   "I gave up all hope": *The Black Abolitionist Papers*, IV:275.

273   "There is a physical difference": A. Lincoln, *Speeches and Writings, 1832–1858*, p. 637. The subsequent quotations in this paragraph are on pp. 675 and 478, respectively.

273   "that the African": Article in a newspaper [title unknown] in Ashtabula County, Ohio, October 20, 1899; Box 2, VC.

274   "the most *powerful* abolition lecture": Letter from J. Brown to J. Brown, Jr., July 9, 1858; BSC. The remaining quotations in this paragraph are also from this letter.

274   "wholesale slaughter": "Oliver Cromwell," *United States Democratic Review*, p. 334.

274   "the Horrors Perpetrated": Advertisement of a speech to be made by John Brown, *Oxford Herald* (Ingersoll, Canada), April 15, 1858; BSC.

274   "any & all the interesting facts": Letter from J. Brown to J. Brown, Jr., July 9, 1858; BSC. The remaining quotations in this paragraph are also from this letter.

275   "Have been down with the ague": Letter from J. Brown to Mary Brown, August 6, 1858; VC.

275   "Oh, I knew the time": J. Hanway, "Reminiscences" [1868], in J. C. Malin, *John Brown and the Legend of Fifty-six*, p. 333.

276 "It now looks as though": Letter from J. Brown to "Dear Friends, and Other Friends," September 10, 1858; BSC.

276 "general result": Letter from J. Brown to J. Brown, Jr., August 9, 1858, quoted in O. G. Villard, *John Brown*, p. 355.

276 "Things at this moment look": Letter from John Brown to Mary Brown, November 1, 1858; BSC.

277 "many of the people of the county": Letter from A. J. Weaver to Hugh S. Walsh, November 15 1858; KSHS.

277 "the prospect of quiet": Quoted in O. G. Villard, *John Brown*, p. 365.

278 "We've come after your negroes": R. J. Hinton, *John Brown and His Men*, p. 220. The next quotation in this paragraph and the quotations in the next paragraph are also on p. 220.

279 "not be taken": H. D. Thoreau, "A Plea for Captain John Brown," in *CEP*, p. 400.

279 "more of a sensation": O. J. Victor, *History of American Conspiracies: A Record of Treason, Insurrection, Rebellion, &c. in the United States of America, 1760–1860* (New York: James D. Torrey, 1863), p. 515. The next quotation in this paragraph is on p. 516.

280 "eleven quiet citizens": *Ru*, p. 122. The subsequent quotations in this paragraph are on p. 123.

281 "criminal offences": D. W. Wilder, *The Annals of Kansas*, p. 192.

281 "was the finishing blow": O. J. Victor, *History of American Conspiracies*, pp. 516–17.

281 "the Slavery question is practically settled": D. W. Wilder, *The Annals of Kansas*, p. 200. The next quotation in this paragraph is also on p. 200.

282 "And now": *Ru*, p. 224. The subsequent quotations in this paragraph and in the next five paragraphs are on pp. 225–26.

283 "Do we hear the news from Kansas?": Letter of January 10, 1859, quoted in Ralph Volney Harlow, *Gerrit Smith, Philanthropist and Reformer* (New York: Henry Holt, 1939), p. 403.

283 "I am happy to learn": Letter from J. Brown to F. B. Sanborn, January 22, 1859; BSC.

284 "it could not conceive of ours": R. J. Hinton, *John Brown and His Men*, p. 123.

284 "Though closely followed": O. J. Victor, *History of American Conspiracies*, p. 516.

284 "Now go straight at 'em, boys!": F. B. Sanborn, *The Life and Letters of John Brown*, p. 486.

285 "Old Captain Brown is not": *Leavenworth Times*, quoted in the *Lawrence Republican*, February 10, 1859.

285 "Gentlemen, you do very wrong": F. B. Sanborn, *The Life and Letters of John Brown*, p. 485. The remaining quotations in this paragraph are also on p. 485.

286 "while we sympathize with the oppressed": F. B. Sanborn, *The Life and Letters of John Brown*, p. 488. The remaining quotations in this paragraph are also on p. 488.

286 "a reckless, bloody outlaw": F. B. Sanborn, *The Life and Letters of John Brown*, p. 490. The remaining quotations in this paragraph are on pp. 490–91.

287 "The arm of Jehovah protected us": F. B. Sanborn, *The Life and Letters of John Brown*, p. 491.

12. Preparation

288 "He also says he is ready": F. B. Sanborn, *The Life and Letters of John Brown*, p. 493.

289 "He believed in settling the matter": *Cleveland Plain Dealer*, March 30, 1859.

289 "on some occasions": J. Redpath, *Public Life of Capt. John Brown*, p. 240.

289 "a bill of sale from the Almighty": F. B. Sanborn, *The Life and Letters of John Brown*, p. 494. The quotations in the next sentence are also on this page.

290 "I was once doubtful": F. B. Sanborn, *The Life and Letters of John Brown*, pp. 161–62.

291 "superior to legal traditions": F. B. Sanborn, *The Life and Letters of John Brown*, p. 504. The remaining quotations in this paragraph and the quotation in the next paragraph are also on p. 504.

291 "I have perfect confidence in you": Letter from T. W. Higginson to J. Brown, May 1, 1859; Thomas Wentworth Higginson Papers, BPL.

292 "Don't tell me what you are about": Quoted in S. Oates, *To Purge This Land with Blood*, p. 270. The quotation in the next sentence is on p. 271.

292 "the Miles Standish of Kansas": William Lawrence, *Life of Amos A. Lawrence, with Extracts from His Diary and Correspondence* (Boston: Houghton Mifflin, 1888), p. 130.

292 "Now, when you are a young lady": *New York Evening Post*, October 23, 1909.

292 "Talk! talk! talk!": F. B. Sanborn, *The Life and Letters of John Brown*, p. 131.

293 "a most tender, loving": F. B. Sanborn, *The Life and Letters of John Brown*, p. 600.

293 "I have always considered myself": MS. Interview of Jason Brown by Katherine Mayo, December 13, 1908; VC.

293 "You know father": MS. Interview of Salmon Brown by Katherine Mayo, October 11–13, 1908; VC.

293 "She dominated him": MS. Interview of Sarah Brown by Katherine Mayo, September 26, 1908; VC.

294 "He always seemed": R. J. Hinton, *John Brown and His Men*, p. 530.

294 "the most depressing melancholy": Quoted in S. Oates, *To Purge This Land with Blood*, p. 273.

295 "otherwise I would probably have been captured": *Sandusky Daily Register*, February 27, 1888.

295 "found it conspicuous": MS. Interview of Sarah Brown by Katherine Mayo, September 26, 1908; VC.

296 "It was father's original plan": R. J. Hinton, *John Brown and His Men*, p. 260.

297 "not for the white man alone": R. J. Hinton, *John Brown and His Men*, p. 510.

298 "She was a worse plague": Quoted in O. G. Villard, *John Brown*, p. 417.

299 "We must not let our father alone": R. J. Hinton, *John Brown and His Men*, p. 259.

299 "We have all agreed to sustain your decisions": Quoted in S. Oates, *To Purge this Land with Blood*, p. 280.

299 "a trap of steel": *Ru*, p. 296.

299 "Come with me, Douglass": See F. Douglass, *Life and Times of Frederick Douglass*, pp. 354–58.

299 "I b'l'eve I'll go wid de old man": *Ru*, p. 297.

300 "A DECLARATION OF LIBERTY": R. J. Hinton, *John Brown and His Men*, p. 638. The remaining quotations in this and the next two paragraphs are on pp. 638–39.

303 "Vindication of the Invasion": *New York Times*, October 22, 1859.

303 "a score of letters": R. J. Hinton, *John Brown and His Men*, p. 257. The quotations in the next sentence are also on this page.

303 "Persons who do not talk much": Letter from J. Brown to "Dear Wife & Children all," August 2, 1859; BSC.

303 "If everyone must write": R. J. Hinton, *John Brown and His Men*, pp. 257–58.

303 "*old John Brown*, late of Kansas": Mason Report, pp. 250–52.

304 "protect Brown from the consequences": MS. Interview of David J. Gue by Katherine Mayo, November 1907; VC.

304 "the statement was so indefinite": *Liberator*, October 21, 1859.

304 "This is perhaps the last letter": R. J. Hinton, *John Brown and His Men*, p. 561. The quotations in the next paragraph are on pp. 453, 532, 547, and 538, respectively.

305 "I write to say that we are all well": *Ru*, p. 124.

305 *"Save this letter":* Letter from John Brown to his wife and daughters, October 1, 1859; John Brown Papers, Huntington Library.

305 88 slaves and 1,251 free blacks: For the statistics in this paragraph, I am indebted to S. Oates, *To Purge This Land with Blood*, p. 274.

306 "Sambo existed wherever slavery existed": *Maroon Societies: Rebel Slave Communities in the Americas*, ed. R. Price, pp. 277–78.

306 "Give a slave a pike": J. Redpath, *The Public Life of Capt. John Brown*, p. 206.

306 "If you tell me John Brown is there": R. J. Hinton, *John Brown and His Men*, p. 570.

307 "And in remembering that": R. J. Hinton, *John Brown and His Men*, p. 282.

308 "Men, get on your arms": O. G. Villard, *John Brown*, p. 426.

13. Problems

309 "Talk! talk! talk!": F. B. Sanborn, *The Life and Letters of John Brown*, p. 131.

310 "I came here from Kansas": Mason Report, II:22.

311 "This is John Brown": MS. Interview of John Thomas Allstadt of Kearneysville, West Virginia, by Katherine Mayo, April 15, 1909; VC.

312 "a troublesome customer": Mason Report, II:40–42.

312 "Keep these white men inside": MS. Interview of John Thomas Allstadt of Kearneysville, West Virginia, by Katherine Mayo, April 15, 1909; VC.

313 "Indeed," a local paper reported: *Chambersburg* (Pennsylvania) *Valley Spirit*, October 26, 1859.

313 "confidently expected large reinforcements": *Harper's Weekly*, November 5, 1859. The quotations in the next paragraph are also from this source.

313 "showed no disposition to use them": *The Life, Trial, and Execution of Captain John Brown*, p. 73.

313 "that not a slave seemed to have a heart": *The Life, Trial, and Execution of Captain John Brown*, p. 88.

313 "armed with pieces which they carried": *The Life, Trial, and Execution of Captain John Brown*, p. 79.

314 "like a tiger": R. J. Hinton, *John Brown and His Men*, p. 511.

314 "the bondsman refuses to be free": *Address of Hon. Daniel Voorhees, of Indiana; Comprising His Argument Delivered at Charlestown, Va., Nov. 8, 1859, Upon the Trial of John E. Cook, for Treason and Murder* (Richmond: West & Johnson, 1861), p. 8.

314 "this good-humored, good-for-nothing": *Chambersburg* (Pennsylvania) *Valley Spirit*, October 26, 1859.

314 "Brown made the general mistake": Edmund Ruffin, "Conduct of the Negroes During the War, 1861–1865: Extracts from the Diary of Edmund Ruffin," *William and Mary College Quarterly Historical Magazine* 22 (April 1914): 262.

315 "an Anti-Slavery movement": "John Brown's Raid and Trial," *Harper's Weekly*, November 5, 1859, p. 713.

315 "balderdash": John G. Rosengarten, "John Brown's Raid: How I Got into It, and How I Got Out of It," *Atlantic Monthly* 15 (June 1865): 713.

315 "virtually suicidal": E. Genovese, *From Rebellion to Revolution*, p. 49.

315 "I can imagine": In Clarence L. Mohr, *On the Threshold of Freedom: Masters and Slaves in Civil War Georgia* (Athens: University of Georgia Press, 1986), p. 60.

316 "I didn't know what 'Halt' mint": Quoted in O. G. Villard, *John Brown*, p. 433.

317 "Your dispatch is evidently exaggerated" and "My dispatch was not": Document Y, *Correspondence Relating to the Insurrection of Harper's Ferry* (Annapolis: Published by the Maryland Legislature, 1860), pp. 1–2.

318 "that his object was not to make war": *National Intelligencer,* October 27, 1859.

318 "You're the buck that hit me": R. J. Hinton, *John Brown and His Men,* p. 289. The remaining quotations in this paragraph are also on p. 289.

319 "Men! Be cool!": R. J. Hinton, *John Brown and His Men,* p. 297.

320 as Villard suggests: See O. G. Villard, *John Brown,* p. 439.

320 "Oh dear Dangerfield": Quoted in S. Oates, *To Purge This Land with Blood,* p. 294.

320 "The King of Terrors": R. J. Hinton, *John Brown and His Men,* pp. 310–11.

321 "Don't shoot! I surrender!": Chester G. Hearn, *Six Years of Hell: Harpers Ferry During the Civil War* (Baton Rouge: Louisiana State University Press, 1996), p. 26.

322 "sheer madness": *Confession of John E. Cook* (Baltimore: n.p., 1859), p. 14.

323 "Mr. Beckham's life": *New-York Tribune,* October 29, 1859.

323 "You may take my life": In the *New-York Tribune* report of October 29, 1859, Thompson is quoted as having said "80,000,000," but that number seems improbable, especially since 80,000 appears in other contemporary records of his statement.

323 "could be seen for a day or two after": *The Annals of Harper's Ferry* (Hagerstown, Md.: Dechert & Co., 1869), p. 25.

325 "If this man could stand": Katherine Mayo, "A Lieutenant for John Brown," clipping from unidentified newspaper, 1909; BSC.

326 "If you must die": MS. Interview of John Thomas Allstadt of Kearneysville, West Virginia, by Katherine Mayo, April 15, 1909; VC.

326 "You are paid for doing this kind of work": Statement of Colonel and Mrs. John A. Tompkins to Katherine Mayo, Baltimore, February 24, 1908; VC.

326 "Men, are you awake?": John E. P. Daingerfield, "John Brown at Harper's Ferry," *Century* 30 (June 1885): 266.

326 "Certainly": J. E. P. Daingerfield, "John Brown at Harper's Ferry," p. 267; and J. G. Rosengarten, "John Brown's Raid: How I Got into It, and How I Got Out of It," p. 714.

327 "I guess he is dead": MS. Interview of John Thomas Allstadt of Kearneysville, West Virginia, by Katherine Mayo, April 15, 1909; VC. The exact time of Oliver Brown's death is unknown. Some sources suggest that he died within a half hour of being wounded. Allstadt's version seems to have the accuracy of an eyewitness account, since he was in the engine house that night.

327 "old *Osawatomie Brown*" and "like a mosquito": Henry B. McClellan, *The Life and Campaigns of Major-General J. E. B. Stuart* (Boston: Houghton Mifflin, 1885), pp. 28–30.

327 "the coolest and firmest man": Quoted by Governor Henry A. Wise in a speech in Richmond, October 21, 1859; VC.

327 "This is Osawatomie": Israel Green, "The Capture of John Brown," *North American Review* 141 (December 1885): 566.

328 "the sorriest lot of people I ever saw": I. Green, "The Capture of John Brown," p. 567.

328 "How do you feel?": Alexander R. Boteler, "Recollections of the John Brown Raid," *Century* 26 (July 1883): 410.

328 "I remember how he looked": Letter from C. W. Tayleure to John Brown, Jr., June 15, 1897; Maryland Historical Society.

329 "Did you expect to get assistance": A. R. Boteler, "Recollections of the John Brown Raid," p. 410.

329 "I furnished most of it myself": *Ru,* p. 126. The remaining quotations from this interview are on pp. 126–33.

332 "He converses freely, fluently": *Ru,* p. 125.

332 "no sign of weakness": *Baltimore American*, quoted in *New-York Tribune*, October 22, 1859.

332 "They are themselves mistaken": H. A. Wise, speech in Richmond, October 21, 1859.

332 "Cap. John Brown is as brave": *Boston Traveller*, 1859 (undated clipping); BSC.

333 "murderers, *traitors*, robbers": Message of Governor Henry A. Wise to the Virginia Legislature, December 5, 1859, Document 1, December 1859, *Journal of the House of Delegates*.

14. Pilloried, Prosecuted, and Praised

335 "any and every other explanation": *Harper's Weekly*, November 5, 1859.

335 "a negro insurrection of a very serious nature": *The John Brown Invasion*, ed. T. Drew, p. 5. The quotations in the next three paragraphs are on pp. 6, 7, and 9, respectively.

336 "HARPER'S FERRY. FEARFUL": R. J. Hinton, *John Brown and His Men*, p. 294.

338 "When the Governor was informed": *Harper's Weekly*, November 5, 1859.

339 "Sons of Virginia!": O. G. Villard, *John Brown*, p. 464. The subsequent quotations in this paragraph are also on this page.

339 "fanatical enterprise": *New York Evening Post*, October 18, 1859.

339 "Such deeds are not countenanced here": *Providence Journal*, quoted in the *Boston Traveller*, October 21, 1859.

339 "madman" and "The whole movement was inadequate": *New York Commercial Advertiser*, quoted in the *Boston Traveller*, October 21, 1859.

339 "stark-mad enterprise": *Chicago Press and Tribune*, October 21, 1859.

340 "a misguided, wild, and apparently insane": *Liberator*, October 21, 1859.

340 "this deplorable affair": *New-York Tribune*, October 28, 1859.

340 "miserable old wretch": *Leavenworth Herald*, October 29, 1859.

340 "called from their beds at their several residences": *Herald of Freedom*, October 29, 1859.

340 "according to the ordinary rules of war": *Lawrence Republican*, December 29, 1859.

341 "For insurrections then": Printed statement of August 27, 1859, in the Gerrit Smith Manuscripts, Syracuse University.

341 "hasty, nervous agitation": *New York Herald*, November 2, 1859. The next quotation in this paragraph is also from this issue.

342 "the meanest, nakedest": *New York Herald*, May 22, 1860.

342 "wholly, grievously": *Harper's Weekly*, November 12, 1859.

342 "I have always been more distinguished": "Letters to Antislavery Workers and Agencies," *Journal of Negro History* 10 (October 1925): 770.

342 "I am going to try a change": Letter from F. B. Sanborn to T. W. Higginson, October 21, 1859; Thomas Wentworth Higginson Collection, BPL.

343 "Rumor has mingled my name": *New-York Tribune*, November 16, 1859.

343 "Is there no such thing": Letter from T. W. Higginson to F. B. Sanborn, November 17, 1859; Thomas Wentworth Higginson Collection, BPL.

343 "the most formidable insurrection": T. W. Higginson, *Cheerful Yesterdays* (1895; New York: Arno Press, 1968), p. 223.

343 "Of course I was not astonished": *Ru*, p. 257.

344 "DEFENDERS OF THE FAITHFUL": James Redpath, *The Public Life of John Brown*, dedication page.

344 "Emerson and Thoreau were the first": F. P. Stearns, *The Life and Public Services of George Luther Stearns*, p. 181. The next quotation in this paragraph is on p. 379.

344 "When a government puts forth its strength": *The Writings of Henry David Thoreau*, ed. Bradford Torrey (1906; New York: AMS, 1968), 18:400.

345 "The Republican editors": *The Writings of Henry David Thoreau*, 18:406–7. The next quotation in this paragraph is on p. 414. The quotations in the next four paragraphs are on pp. 414–15, 409, 413, 405, 436, 406, 426, 420, 408, and 421, respectively.

346 "impolitic and extreme": Walter Harding, *The Days of Henry Thoreau* (New York: Knopf, 1985), p. 417.

347 "a tide rises and falls": *Norton Anthology of American Literature*, B:1981.

348 "I did not ask for any quarter": *The John Brown Invasion*, ed. T. Drew, pp. 25–26.

348 "I wish for counsel": *The John Brown Invasion*, ed. T. Drew, p. 26.

349 "free and easy style of the Southern habits": *New York Herald*, November 15, 1859.

349 "The customs of this court are singular": *New-York Weekly Tribune*, November 12, 1859. The quotations in the next four paragraphs are from the same issue.

351 "as a miserable artifice and pretext": *Harper's Weekly*, November 15, 1859.

352 "A beardless boy came in last night": Quoted in O. G. Villard, *John Brown*, p. 485.

352 "An eye will be kept upon this *volunteer*": *Charles Town Free Press*, quoted in *New-York Tribune*, November 12, 1859.

352 "There is *no chance*": Letter of George Henry Hoyt to J. W. LeBarnes, October 30, 1859, quoted in R. Hinton, *John Brown and His Men*, p. 367.

352 "I felt it my duty": *New-York Tribune*, October 29, 1859.

354 "I have, may it please the court": This speech was printed simultaneously in many newspapers. I have copied it from the *Boston Traveller*, November 5, 1859.

355 "great, lying speech": A. Kazin, "God's Own Terrorist," *New York Review of Books*, April 9, 1998.

357 "No wonder that some of the leading organs": *Journal of Commerce*, article reprinted in the *Liberator*, October 28, 1859. The remaining quotations in this paragraph are also in this issue.

358 "one of the Kansas free soil ruffians": *Boston Courier*, article reprinted in the *Liberator*, October 28, 1859.

358 "The principle upon which John Brown": *Rise and Progress of the Bloody Outbreak at Harper's Ferry* (New York: New York Democratic Vigilant Association, 1859,) p. 16. The quotation in the next sentence is on p. 15.

358 "may be insane": R. Warch and J. F. Fanton, eds., *John Brown*, p. 123.

358 "The time has come": Quoted in the *New York Times*, October 21, 1859.

359 "Harper's Ferry is just a manifestation": *Republican Vindicator* (Staunton, Va.), November 18, 1859.

359 "Abolitionism, whether it presents itself": *Valley Spirit* (Chambersburg, Pa.), November 9, 1859.

359 $50,000 for the head of "the traitor" Seward: Glyndon G. Van Deusen, *William Henry Seward* (New York: Oxford University Press, 1967), p. 216.

359 "We have been invaded": R. Warch and J. F. Fanton, eds., *John Brown*, p. 130. The quotation in the next sentence is on p. 129.

359 "He *despised* the Republican party": *Liberator*, October 28, 1859. The remaining quotations in this paragraph are also in this piece.

360 "ridiculous enough to breed Homeric laughter": R. J. Hinton, *John Brown and His Men*, p. 136. The remaining quotations in this paragraph are on pp. 675 and 137, respectively.

360 "We are damnably exercised": Letter from C. H. Ray to A. Lincoln, October 31, 1859; ALLC.

361 "the stoical firmness of the monomaniac": G. G. Van Deusen, *William Henry Seward*, p. 214. The quotations in the next paragraph are on p. 218.

361 "Since the Humbug insurrection": Letter from W. E. Frazer to A. Lincoln, November 12, 1859; ALLC.

361 "The Harpers ferry affair doubtless": Letter from M. W. Delahay to A. Lincoln, November 14, 1859; ALLC.

362 "deeply regretted this event": Quoted in J. M. B., "John Brown, Epitome of Career and Personal Recollections," *Christian Advocate*, October 28, 1909.

362 "knew all about Brown's projected outbreak": *Harper's Weekly*, November 12, 1859.

362 "To the public I will say": *Liberator*, October 28, 1859.

362 "insane attempt": Letter from S. P. Chase to Joseph H. Barrett, October 29, 1859; BSC.

362 "I mourn for the hiding or obscuration": R. Warch and J. F. Fanton, eds., *John Brown*, p. 106.

363 "that the great Republican party": *Remarks of Honorary Lyman Trumbull*, United States Senate, December 6, 7, and 8, 1859, pamphlet of December 1859, bound in *John Brown Pamphlets*, Vol. I; BSC.

363 "exceedingly absurd to endeavor": *Speech of Honorary Benjamin F. Wade*, United States Senate, December 14, 1859, pamphlet of December 1859, bound in *John Brown Pamphlets*, Vol. I; BSC. The remaining quotations in this paragraph are from this pamphlet.

363 "the sad Harpers Ferry business": *The Letters of Ralph Waldo Emerson*, ed. Ralph L. Rusk (New York: Columbia University Press, 1939), 5:178. The quotation in the next sentence is on pp. 179–80.

363 "This deed of [Brown's]": F. B. Sanborn, *The Life and Letters of John Brown*, p. 505.

363 "I must hope for his escape": *The Letters of Ralph Waldo Emerson*, 5:180.

364 "This exciting theme": *Liberator*, November 4, 1859.

364 "It is a singular fact": In Kenneth Walter Cameron, *Transcendental Log: Fresh Discoveries in Newspapers Concerning Emerson, Thoreau, Alcott, and Others of the American Literary Renaissance* (Hartford, Conn.: Transcendental Books, 1932), p. 148. The next quotation in this paragraph, from the *Springfield Republican*, is on p. 244.

365 "the embattled farmers": R. W. Emerson, "Hymn: Sung at the Completion of the Concord Monument," *Collected Poems and Translations*, ed. Harold Bloom and Paul Kane (New York: Library of America, 1994), p. 125.

365 "to be placed beside the famous": Quoted in *The Genius and Character of Emerson*, ed. Franklin B. Sanborn (1885; Port Washington, N.Y.: Kennikat Press, 1971), p. 28. The next quotation in this paragraph is on p. 20.

365 "when he did come out": Horace Traubel, *With Walt Whitman in Camden* (Philadelphia: University of Pennsylvania Press, 1953), 4:293.

365 "when he distinctly saw what to aim at": *The Genius and Character of Emerson*, p. 292.

365 "You know what a vein": James Brewer Stewart, *Wendell Phillips, Liberty's Hero* (Baton Rouge: Louisiana State University Press, 1986), p. 304.

365 "I greet you at the beginning": *Leaves of Grass, Comprehensive Reader's Edition*, ed. Harold Blodgett and Sculley Bradley (New York: New York University Press, 1965), pp. 729–30. The remaining quotations in this sentence are in H. Traubel, *With Walt Whitman in Camden*, 4:288.

366 "The Southerners reckon": R. W. Emerson "Courage," *New-York Tribune*, November 8, 1859. The remaining quotations in this paragraph and the quotation in the next one are also from this source.

366 "Mattie Griffith says, if Brown is hung": *JMN* 14:333.

366 "a brilliant young lady from Kentucky": *The Letters of Ralph Waldo Emerson*, 5:83.

367 "the apotheosis of John Brown": *Logic of History*, pp. 71–72.

367 "What means the almost universal applause": Henry Clarke Wright, *The Natick Resolu-*

tion; or, Resistance to Slaveholders the Right and Duty of Southern Slaves and Northern Freemen (Boston: n.p., 1859), p. 20.

368   "whether the enterprise of John Brown": *The John Brown Invasion*, ed. T. Drew, p. 99. The remaining quotations in this paragraph are on pp. 99–100. The quotations in the next paragraph are on p. 107.

369   "This commanding event": *Emerson's Antislavery Writings*, ed. L. Gougeon and J. Myerson, p. 117. The remaining quotations in this paragraph are on pp. 117–19.

15. The Passion

370   "I do not think I ever enjoyed life": Letter from J. Brown to Rebecca B. Spring, November 24, 1859; BSC.

370   "I am gaining in health": *Ru*, p. 142. The next quotation in this paragraph is also on p. 142.

372   "That's Captain Cook": R. J. Hinton, *John Brown and His Men*, p. 477. The next quotation in this paragraph is also on p. 477.

373   "reward or no reward": R. J. Hinton, *John Brown and His Men*, p. 478. The quotations in the next three paragraphs are on pp. 480 and 552, successively.

375   "No, sir," he cried: *The John Brown Invasion*, ed. T. Drew, p. 37.

375   "the hellish miscreants of Brown": *Charles Town Independent Democrat*, quoted in *New-York Weekly Tribune*, November 12, 1859.

376   "the chief of criminals": *Address of Hon. Daniel Voorhees, of Indiana*, p. 12. The following quotations in this paragraph and the one in the next paragraph are from pp. 13, 15, and 21, successively.

377   "It is a remarkable fact": *Ru*, p. 297.

377   "There has not been one single instance": R. J. Hinton, *John Brown and His Men*, p. 484.

377   "The excitement at Harper's Ferry": *New York Herald*, October 25, 1859.

377   "A feeling of irrepressible uneasiness": *New-York Tribune*, November 2, 1859.

378   "I shall implore the people": *The John Brown Invasion*, ed. T. Drew, p. 18.

378   "The prevalence of firearms": *New-York Weekly Tribune*, November 12, 1859.

378   "that this Brown raid was the beginning": R. J. Hinton, *John Brown and His Men*, pp. 377–78. The next quotation in this paragraph is on p. 378.

378   "The greatest stimulus of military organizations": J. H. Franklin, *The Militant South*, p. 189.

378   "The Charlestown jail is certainly": *New-York Tribune*, November 2, 1859.

379   "Two good Yankees": Quoted in O. G. Villard, *John Brown*, p. 512.

379   "Various rumors have been in circulation": Quoted in the *New-York Tribune*, November 22, 1859.

379   "Rumors are rife": Quoted in the *New-York Tribune*, November 22, 1859.

379   3,600 letters: See the *National Era*, February 9, 1860.

379   "Contemptible Nonsense": Quoted in O. G. Villard, *John Brown*, p. 518.

380   "Numerous acts of incendiarism": Quoted in the *New-York Tribune*, November 22, 1859.

380   "There is now here a source": *Ru*, p. 149. The next quotation in this paragraph is also on p. 149.

381   "One thing we have ascertained": Letter from T. W. Higginson to "Dear Friends" [the children of John Brown], November 4, 1859; BSC.

381   "He said that Captain Avis": *The John Brown Invasion*, ed. T. Drew, p. 42.

381   "I do not know": *New-York Tribune*, November 4, 1859.

381   "Captain Brown appears perfectly fearless": *The John Brown Invasion*, ed. T. Drew, p. 43.

381   "a great thing": Letter from T. W. Higginson to "Dear Friends" [the children of John Brown], November 4, 1859; BSC.

382   "There is a decided impression": *Harper's Weekly*, November 12, 1859.

382   "To hang a fanatic": Quoted in the *Liberator*, November 4, 1859.

382   "Let no man pray": *Echoes of Harper's Ferry*, ed. J. Redpath, p. 262.

382   "worth inconceivably more to hang": *Ru*, p. 142.

382   "I have often passed under the rod": *Ru*, p. 144.

383   "I know no more of grammar": H. D. Thoreau, "A Plea for Captain John Brown," in *CEP*, p. 397.

383   "Where is our professor": H. D. Thoreau, "The Last Days of John Brown," in *CEP*, p. 426. The next quotation in this paragraph is also on p. 426. The quotation in the next paragraph is on p. 422.

383   "a series of terrific explosions": *Harper's New Monthly Magazine* 37 (June 1868): 42.

383   "a splendid meteor": *The Frederick Douglass Papers*, ed. John W. Blassingame (New Haven: Yale University Press, 1985), p. 386.

383   *"the meteor of war"*: *Poems of Herman Melville*, ed. Douglas Robillard (Schenectady, N.Y.: New College and University Press, 1976), p. 34.

384   "It does not know of": H. D. Thoreau, "A Plea for Captain John Brown," in *CEP*, p. 409.

384   "John Brown, the friend of the slave": Letter from Henry C. Wright to Henry A. Wise, December 2, 1859; BSC.

384   "Under all these terrible calamities": *Ru*, p. 136. The quotations in the next two paragraphs are on pp. 140 and 161, respectively.

385   "I do feel gratified": Letter from Mahala Doyle to John Brown, November 22, 1859; BSC.

386   "selfish, unjust, revengeful": *The John Brown Invasion*, ed. T. Drew, p. 44. The quotation in the next paragraph is also on p. 44.

386   "Oh my dear friends": *Ru*, p. 161.

386   "brave efforts in behalf": *The John Brown Invasion*, ed. T. Drew, p. 47.

386   "You know that Christ": *Ru*, p. 137.

387   "Believing in peace principles": *The John Brown Invasion*, ed. T. Drew, p. 45.

387   "humane gentleman": *Ru*, p. 139.

387   "I did not talk about the raid": *Ru*, p. 247. The quotations in the next paragraph are also on p. 247.

387   "I think I cannot now": *The John Brown Invasion*, ed. T. Drew, p. 41. The remaining quotations in this paragraph are also on p. 41.

388   "I am worth now infinitely more": S. C. Pomeroy, letter to the *Christian Cynosure*, March 31, 1887.

388   "I have very many interesting visits": *Ru*, p. 155.

388   "I have always expressed": *Ru*, pp. 145–46.

389   "abhor that arrant whore": *Ru*, p. 166.

389   *"Men* cannot *imprison"*: *Ru*, p. 147.

389   "I have asked to be spared": *Ru*, p. 163.

389   "Mr Brown fears your presence": Letter from G. H. Hoyt to Mary Brown, November 11, 1859; BSC.

390   "My dear husband, it is a hard fate": *The John Brown Invasion*, ed. T. Drew, p. 63. The remaining quotations in this paragraph are also on p. 63; the quotations in the next five paragraphs are on pp. 63–64.

391 "Did you ever see such beautiful weather": Letter from "Alice" to "Dear cousin John," December 2, 1859; BSC.

392 "As evidence of his coolness and firmness": R. J. Hinton, *John Brown and His Men*, p. 390. The next quotation in this paragraph is on p. 394.

392 "the consolations of religion": F. B. Sanborn, *The Life and Letters of John Brown*, p. 622.

393 "almost incredible" and "utterly and entirely": Quoted in O. G. Villard, *John Brown*, p. 524. The quotation in the next sentence is on p. 523.

393 "Stand up like men": *The John Brown Invasion*, ed. T. Drew, p. 66. The remaining quotations in this paragraph are also on p. 66. The quotation in the next paragraph is on p. 67.

393 "Brown appeared perfectly calm": *New York Times*, December 3, 1859.

394 "Fierce as a gun-lock": F. B. Sanborn, *The Life and Letters of John Brown*, p. 729.

395 "That whole story about his kissing": R. J. Hinton, *John Brown and His Men*, p. 392.

395 "Charlestown, Va. 2nd, December": *Ru*, p. 167.

395 "This is a beautiful country": J. Redpath, *The Public Life of Capt. John Brown*, p. 400. There are several different versions of the following conversation. Although the versions occasionally differ in wording, they all express the same sentiments.

396 "His movements & manner": *The Diary of Edmund Ruffin*, I:369.

396 "Sir, I have no words": *The John Brown Invasion*, ed. T. Drew, p. 68.

396 "No; I am ready at any time": J. Redpath, *The Public Life of Capt. John Brown*, p. 402.

396 "There was but one spasmodic effort": *New-York Tribune* article on Brown's hanging, reprinted in the *Liberator*, December 9, 1859.

397 "His knees were scarcely bent": Letter from John Thomas Lewis Preston to Margaret Junkin Preston, December 2, 1859, in *The Life and Letters of Margaret Junkin Preston* (Boston: Houghton Mifflin, 1902), p. 114. The quotation in the next paragraph is also on p. 114.

397 "I looked at the traitor": Quoted in Ken Chowder, "The Father of American Terrorism," *American Heritage*, February–March 2000, p. 82.

398 "He was a brave old man": Asia Booth Clarke, *John Wilkes Booth: A Sister's Memoir*, ed. Terry Alford (1874; Jackson: University Press of Mississippi, 1996), p. 81.

398 "might receive the sentence": Mary Anna Jackson, *Memoirs of Stonewall Jackson* (Louisville: Prentice Press, 1895), p. 131.

398 "I hope that he was prepared": Quoted in Chester G. Hearn, *Six Years of Hell: Harpers Ferry During the Civil War* (Baton Rouge: Louisiana State University Press, 1996), p. 42.

398 "It is all over!": *The John Brown Invasion*, ed. T. Drew, p. 69.

399 "Our entire block was filled": Letter from Louisa Williamson to Jedidiah Williamson, December 8, 1859; BSC.

399 "Mother!": *The John Brown Invasion*, ed. T. Drew, p. 72.

400 "Blow Ye the Trumpet, Blow!": *The John Brown Invasion*, ed. T. Drew, p. 74. The quotation in the paragraph after next is on p. 76. The quotations in the two paragraphs after that are on pp. 77 and 78, respectively.

16. Positions and Politics

402 "transcendent moral greatness": H. D. Thoreau, "Services at Concord," in J. Redpath, *Echoes of Harper's Ferry*, p. 439. The quotations in the third paragraph are also on p. 439.

402 "I want these modern fanatics": *Speech of Andrew Johnson*, in *John Brown Pamphlets*, 8:15; BSC. The quotation in the sixth paragraph is on p. 13.

403 "There Shall Be Division": *Documents of Upheaval*, ed. T. Nelson, p. 153.

404 "Being intensely human": P. Pillsbury, *Acts of the Anti-Slavery Apostles,* pp. 495–96.

404 "well-intended but sadly misguided": *Liberator,* October 28, 1859. The quotations in the next paragraph are also in this issue.

405 "whether by public meetings": "Execution of Capt. John Brown," printed broadside of November 1859 (Boston), in *American Time Capsule: Three Centuries of Broadsides and Other Printed Ephemera;* LC.

405 "that it is the right and duty": H. C. Wright, *The Natick Resolution,* p. 3. The next quotation in this paragraph is on p. 4. The quotation in the next paragraph is on p. 9.

406 "a non-resistant": *Liberator,* December 9, 1859.

406 "brisk excitement": *Boston Herald,* December 3, 1859.

406 GOV. WISE—THE TRAITOR: *Boston Herald,* December 3, 1859.

406 "The gallows from which he ascends": The Rev. E. D. Wheelock, quoted in S. D. Carpenter, *Logic of History,* p. 65. The next quotation in this paragraph is on p. 69.

407 "While we most decidedly disapprove": *Speeches of Barstow, Day, Woodbury, and Davis* (Providence: n.p., 1860), p. 31; BSC.

407 JOHN BROWN, THE HERO OF 1859: *A Tribute of Respect, Commemorative of the Worth and Sacrifice of John Brown, of Ossawatomie,* p. 5. The remaining quotations in this paragraph are on pp. 5–6. The quotations in the next three paragraphs are on pp. 12, 2, 7, and 17–18, respectively.

408 "that we hold the name": *Liberator,* December 30, 1859.

408 "very intense": *Liberator,* January 6, 1860.

408 "grand solemn service": *The Anti-Slavery History of the John Brown Year* (n.p.: American Anti-Slavery Society, 1861), p. 164; BSC. The next quotation in this paragraph is also on p. 164. The quotations in the next paragraph are on p. 165.

409 "be read by millions": Quoted in Seymour Drescher, "Servile Insurrection and John Brown's Body in Europe," *Journal of American History* 80 (September 1993): 499.

409 "The more one loves, admires": *The Anti-Slavery History of the John Brown Year,* p. 160. The quotations in the next paragraph are on p. 161.

409 "rigid Puritan, sincerely religious": Proof sheet of V. Hugo's "Encore un mot sur le martyr John Brown," ed. Henri E. Marquand, December 11, 1859; BSC.

409 "overwhelmed with grief": Letter from V. Hugo to George David, December 20, 1859; BSC.

409 "among the calamities of history": V. Hugo, "Letter to the Republic of Haiti," December 28, 1859, reprinted in the *New-York Tribune,* March 3, 1860. The remaining quotations in this paragraph are from this letter.

409 "slavery in all its forms": F. B. Sanborn, *The Life and Letters of John Brown,* p. 631.

410 "to write a romance": Quoted in the *Boston Commonwealth,* June 25, 1870.

410 "For ourselves, who prefer martyrdom": V. Hugo, *Les Misérables* (1862; New York: Modern Library, n.d.), p. 1038.

410 "To the memory of John Brown": Quoted in J. C. Malin, *John Brown and the Legend of Fifty-six,* p. 352.

410 "that crime of crimes": Quoted in S. Drescher, "Servile Insurrection and John Brown's Body in Europe," p. 522. The remaining quotations in this paragraph are also on this page.

411 "first and greatest martyr": *The Martyrdom of John Brown* (London: Emancipation Society of London, 1863), p. 174.

411 "a stern, single-minded": *The Anti-Slavery History of the John Brown Year,* p. 157.

411 "no man ever died in a nobler cause": *The Anti-Slavery History of the John Brown Year,* p. 159.

411 "there was a very general conclusion": S. Drescher, "Servile Insurrection and John Brown's Body in Europe," p. 510.

411 "frenzied rage and terror": *The Anti-Slavery History of the John Brown Year*, p. 160.

411 "THERE WAS NO 'BUNKUM' ": Quoted in S. Drescher, "Servile Insurrection and John Brown's Body in Europe," p. 509.

412 "there is one aspect": J. Redpath, article from the *Boston Atlas* reprinted in the *Liberator*, November 4, 1859. The quotations in the next paragraph are also in this issue.

412 "Virginia's chivalry was nothing": *New York Times*, December 3, 1859.

412 "has revealed the impotent timidity": *Liberator*, December 30, 1859.

413 "I know that the imputed insanity": *Report of Union Meeting in Faneuil Hall* (Boston: n.p., 1859), p. 20; BSC. The quotations in the next paragraph are on p. 19.

414 "the treasonable raid of John Brown": *Official Report of the Great Union Meeting Held at the Academy of Music, New York, December 19, 1859* (New York: Davies & Kent, 1859), p. 3.

414 "the largest public meeting": *Journal of Commerce*, December 20, 1859, quoted in *Official Report of the Great Union Meeting*, p. 82. The next quotation in this sentence ("the largest, the most enthusiastic") is from the December 21, 1859, *New York Herald* and is quoted on p. 89 of this volume. The quotations in the next paragraph are on pp. 29, 32, and 53, respectively. The quotations in the paragraph after that are on pp. 79 and 80, successively.

414 "to repudiate": *Great Union Meeting, Philadelphia, December 7, 1859: Fanaticism Rebuked* (Philadelphia: Crissy & Markley, 1859), p. 4. The remaining quotations in this paragraph are on pp. 5 and 24, respectively. The quotations in the next paragraph are on pp. 49 and 55, respectively.

415 "Good by, cheer up": R. J. Hinton, *John Brown and His Men*, p. 405. The next quotation in this paragraph is also on p. 405.

415 "with a determined firmness": *The John Brown Invasion*, ed. T. Drew, p. 83.

415 "Stop a minute": R. J. Hinton, *John Brown and His Men*, p. 405. The next quotation in this paragraph is also on p. 405.

416 "We should literally have no room": *National Era*, January 12, 1860.

416 "in consequence of the Harper's Ferry affair": Quoted in William Lloyd Garrison, *The New "Reign of Terror" in the Slaveholding States, for 1859–60* (1969; New York: American Anti-Slavery Society, 1860), p. 99. The two quotations in the next paragraph are on pp. 140 and 122, successively.

417 "his face . . . black from strangulation": W. L. Garrison, *The New "Reign of Terror*," p. 93. The quotations in the next paragraph are on pp. 80, 66, and 96, successively.

417 "We regard every man in our midst": *The Anti-Slavery History of the John Brown Year*, p. 167.

417 "We are in the midst": W. L. Garrison, *The New "Reign of Terror*," p. 10.

418 "nearly all northern papers": *The Anti-Slavery History of the John Brown Year*, p. 194. The quotations in the next paragraph are on pp. 198 and 199, successively.

418 "These barbarities": *National Era*, January 12, 1860.

418 "terminate free-negroism": *The Anti-Slavery History of the John Brown Year*, p. 208.

419 "Early in the summer of 1860": *Continental Monthly* 3 (March 1863): 354.

420 "I deem enslavement": *The Diary of Edmund Ruffin*, I:451. The quotations in the next fourteen paragraphs are on pp. 349, 354, 357, 360, 377, 371, 378, 381, 382, 421, 473, 431, 432, and 438, successively.

423 "must of necessity go out of the Union": *Staunton* (Virginia) *Republican Vindicator*, December 9, 1859.

423   "the impression that a dissolution": *Chambersburg* (Pennsylvania) *Valley Spirit*, December 5, 1860.

424   "theory and philosophy": "Report" by Joint Select Committee on Federal Relations of the Florida Legislature, *Journal of Proceedings of the House of Representatives of the General Assembly of the State of Florida*, 1859. Available online at members.aol.com/jfepperson/florida.html.

424   "that they have encouraged": *The Annals of America* (Chicago: Encyclopedia Britannica, 1968–87), 9:204–5.

424   "the abolition sentiment of the Northern States": *The Confederate Records of the State of Georgia*, ed. Allen Daniel Candler (Atlanta: C. P. Byrd, 1909), 1:115.

424   "under state patronage": "First Message of Governor Isham Harris to the Tennessee Assembly," *Public Acts of the State of Tennessee, Passed at the Extra Session of the Thirty-third General Assembly, for the Year 1861* (Nashville: E. G. Eastman & Co., 1861).

425   "I have no hesitation in expressing": Henry Martyn Flint, *Life of Stephen A. Douglas: To Which Are Added His Speeches and Reports* (Philadelphia: John E. Potter, 1863), p. 160 of appendix. The quotations in the next paragraph are on pp. 168 and 164, respectively.

425   "The Democratic party": *Charleston Mercury*, April 16, 1860.

426   "Suppose the Republican party": E. D. Fite, *The Presidential Campaign of 1860*, p. 217.

426   "Just Heaven, upon what times": J. D. B. DeBow, "Presidential Candidates and Aspirants," *DeBow's Review* 29 (July 1860): 101.

426   "an Abolitionist; a fanatic": *St. Louis Democrat*, November 8, 1860, quoted in the *New-York Tribune*, November 12, 1860.

426   "the fanatics who apotheosize John Brown": Quoted in Arthur C. Cole, "Lincoln's Election an Immediate Menace to Slavery in the States?" *American Historical Review* 36 (July 1931): 747.

426   "Our property has been stolen": See Robert Toombs's Speech to the Georgia Legislature, November 13, 1860, in *Secession Debated: Georgia's Showdown in 1860*, ed. William W. Freehling and Craig M. Simpson (New York: Oxford University Press, 1992), pp. 31–50.

426   "personally, I am not your enemy": Letter from A. Stephens to A. Lincoln, December 30, 1860; LC.

427   "Old Brown's wretched fiasco": Letter from C. H. Ray to A. Lincoln, October 31, 1859; ALLC.

427   "no man, North or South": *The Collected Works of Abraham Lincoln*, ed. Roy P. Basler (New Brunswick, N.J.: Rutgers University Press, 1953), 3:496. The quotations in the next paragraph are on p. 497.

427   "Brady and the Cooper Institute": Quoted in Herbert Mitgang, "What Made Lincoln President," *New York Times*, February 7, 1960. The quotation in the next paragraph is also from this article.

427   "You charge that we stir up": A. Lincoln, *Speeches and Writings, 1859–1865*, pp. 122–23. The quotations in the next two paragraphs are on pp. 123 and 125, respectively.

429   "The republicans were charged with being responsible": *The Collected Works of Abraham Lincoln*, 3:553.

429   "the only persons who do not have": A. Nevins, *The Emergence of Lincoln*, II:121.

430   "No one feels deeper sorrow": Quoted in Ralph Volney Harlow, "Gerrit Smith and the John Brown Raid," *American Historical Review* 38 (October 1932): 56.

430   "In my case they were very unskilful": Letter from S. G. Howe to T. W. Higginson, February 16, 1860; Thomas Wentworth Higginson Papers, BPL.

430   "to shoot our innocent people": C. E. Heller, *Portrait of an Abolitionist*, p. 114.

430 "Before that time comes": Quoted in Franklin B. Sanborn, *The Personality of Emerson* (Boston: C. E. Goodspeed, 1903), pp. 87–88.

431 "his speeches and letters": *Emerson's Antislavery Writings*, ed. L. Gougeon and J. Myerson, p. 121. The remaining quotations in this paragraph and those in the next two paragraphs are on pp. 121–24.

432 "the man this country was about to hang": *Ru*, p. 272. The remaining quotations in this paragraph are on p. 273. The quotations in the next paragraph are on pp. 274–75, and the ones in the paragraph after that are on p. 277.

434 "Take up your daily papers": Quoted in Clarence L. Mohr, *On the Threshold of Freedom: Masters and Slaves in Civil War Georgia* (Athens: University of Georgia Press, 1986), p. 42.

434 "re-enactment of the John Brown affair": *Savannah Republican*, July 30, 1860.

434 "murdered by poison or abolition pikes": *Independent South* (Waynesboro, Ga.), September 26, 1860.

435 "Plan for the Abolition of Slavery": J. Townsend, *The Doom of Slavery in the Union: Its Safety Out of It* [speech of October 29, 1860, before the Edisto Island Vigilant Association] (Charleston, S.C.: Evans & Cogwell, 1860). The remaining quotations in this paragraph and the one in the next paragraph are from this speech.

435 "from a northern correspondent": *The Diary of Edmund Ruffin*, I:464. The remaining quotations in this paragraph are on pp. 464 and 470.

436 "If, in our present position of power": Dwight Lowell Dumond, *Southern Editorials on Secession* (Gloucester, Mass.: Peter Smith, 1964), p. 179.

436 nearly 115,000 rifles and muskets were transported: Robert Reid Howison, "History of the War," *Southern Literary Messenger* 34 (April 1862): 227.

17. The Prophet

439 "instead of an evil, a good": Quoted in Anson D. Morse, "The Cause of Secession," *Political Science Quarterly* 2 (September 1887): 488.

439 "they are also the most helpless": "Why We Resist, and What We Resist: The Two Opposing Views of the Great Issue Between the North and the South," *DeBow's Review* 30 (February 1861): 228–29.

439 "In moral and social condition": "Message of Jefferson Davis to the Provisional Congress of the Confederate States of America, April 29, 1861," in United States War Department, *The War of the Rebellion; A Compilation of the Official Records of the Union and Confederate Armies* (Washington, D.C.: Government Printing Office, 1893), ser. 4, 1:259.

440 "wrong in principle": Quotations in this paragraph are from H. Cleveland, *Alexander H. Stephens, in Public and Private*, pp. 717–29.

440 "It is useless to wage war": Quoted in John Elliott Cairnes, *The Slave Power: Its Character, Career, and Probable Designs* (New York: F. Foster & Co., 1863), p. 123.

440 "the law of Congress": *DeBow's Review* 3 (January 1860): 2.

440 "goes to Africa and brings a heathen": Quoted in E. D. Fite, *The Presidential Campaign of 1860*, p. 80.

440 "I insist that *there*": Letter from Henry Jarvis Raymond to William Yowndes Yancey, November 29, 1860, in *Disunion and Slavery, A Series of Letters to Hon. W. L. Yancey, of Alabama* (New York: n.p., 1861), p. 14.

441 "the traffic was flourishing": E. D. Fite, *The Presidential Campaign of 1860*, p. 78.

441 "The re-opening of the African slave-trade": *Anglo-African Magazine* 1 (September 1859): 301.

442 Walt Whitman recalled: Horace Traubel, *With Walt Whitman in Camden* (Carbondale: Southern Illinois University Press, 1982), 6:194–95.

442 "not *bloody bullets*" and "There will be no war": Quoted in Gabor S. Boritt, ed., *Why the Civil War Came* (New York: Oxford University Press, 1996), p. 13.

442 "The disunion movement": Letter from H. J. Raymond to W. Y. Yancey, November 29, 1860, in *Disunion and Slavery*, p. 9.

443 "hundreds of persons": *New-York Tribune*, November 30, 1859.

443 "One is led to suspect": *Topeka Capital*, March 29, 1884.

444 "In New England parlors a statuette": William Howard Russell, *My Diary North and South* (Boston: T. O. H. P. Burnham, 1863), p. 497.

444 "I die for the inalienable right": "John Brown" [pictorial envelope] (Stimson & Co., copyright holder); Graphic Arts File—Civil War Envelopes, New-York Historical Society.

444 "great possibilities in the way": "A Unique Speculation: Interesting to Stockholders of the John Brown Fort Company," *New York Times*, August 31, 1892.

445 "is a potent alterative, tonic": *JMN* 15:379. The next quotation in this paragraph is on p. 453.

445 to use Eugene Genovese's image: *Maroon Societies*, ed. R. Price, pp. 277–78.

446 "Hanging from the beam": *Poems of Herman Melville*, ed. D. Robillard, p. 34. The remaining quotations from this poem are also on p. 34.

446 "a cut on his brave old crown": E. C. Stedman, "John Brown's Invasion," *New-York Tribune*, reprinted in *The Liberator*, November 28, 1859.

447 "Stonewall!": *Poems of Herman Melville*, ed. D. Robillard, p. 71.

447 "Struck dead by the Angel of God": H. Melville, *Billy Budd: An Inside Narrative*, ed. Milton R. Stern (1924; Indianapolis: Bobbs-Merrill Educational Publishing, 1975), p. 95.

448 "won his martyrdom firmly": This quotation and the others in this paragraph are in James R. Mellow, *Nathaniel Hawthorne in His Times* (Boston: Houghton Mifflin, 1980), pp. 551–52.

448 "I would sing how an old man": W. Whitman, *Complete Poetry and Collected Prose*, p. 380.

449 "Such devotion, such superb courage, men will not forget": H. Traubel, *With Walt Whitman in Camden*, 4:206. The other quotations in this paragraph are on pp. 206 and 293, respectively.

449 "the union always surrounded": W. Whitman, *Complete Poetry and Collected Prose*, p. 8. The next quotation in this sentence is on p. 42.

449 "The nigger, like the Injun": H. Traubel, *With Walt Whitman in Camden* (1908; New York: Rowman and Littlefield, 1961), 2:283.

449 "I regard the tone of public sentiment": *Report of Union Meeting in Faneuil Hall*, p. 28.

451 "I read your Chapters": *Norton Anthology of American Literature*, B:2541. The other quotation in this paragraph is on the same page.

451 "Much Madness is divinest Sense—": Poem no. 435 in *The Complete Poems of Emily Dickinson*, ed. Thomas H. Johnson (Boston: Little, Brown, 1960), p. 209. The next quotation in this paragraph is also from this poem. The last quotation in the paragraph is from poem no. 528 (p. 258). The poem discussed in the next paragraph is no. 444 (p. 213).

452 "an entirely new play": *Worcester Daily Spy*, November 15, 1859. The quotations in the next sentence are in the issue of November 14.

453 "for his larnin' ": J. C. Swayze, *Ossawatomie Brown; or, The Insurrection at Harper's Ferry*, performed December 16, 1859, at the Bowery Theatre (New York: Samuel French,

1859), p. 3. The next quotation in this paragraph is on p. 10. The quotations in the next paragraph are on pp. 10 and 24.

454   "great news": P. H. Matthews, "John Brown," undated song sheet; BSC.

454   "If the Niggers had been free": "The Fate of Old John Brown. Air: John Anderson My Jo," undated song sheet; BSC.

454   "Old Brown thought the niggas": C. A. Boggs, "John Brown. Respectfully dedicated to the Young Monkey Crazy Association, and the public in general," undated song sheet; BSC.

454   "At Harper's Ferry, dar's been a great sensation": "Harpers Ferry" (New York: H. DeMarsan, n.d.).

454   "Old John Brown, he had a little nigger": *New York Post*, October 29, 1859.

455   "nigger-stealers" and "Old Ossawattomie Brown!": "Old John Brown, a Song for Every Southern Man," undated song sheet in *American Song Sheets*, ser. 1, vol. 7; LC.

455   "For well they knew the lying thief": "John Brown's Entrance into Hell" (Baltimore: C. T. A., 1863), song sheet; BSC.

455   "Attempts the Black Republicans have made": R. S. Gladney (pseud. Lacon), *The Devil in America: A Dramatic Satire* (Philadelphia: J. B. Lippincott, 1860), p. 142. The remaining quotations in this paragraph and the quotations in the next three paragraphs are on pp. 142–47.

457   "that deed of murder done": "Old Brown," *New-York Tribune*, reprinted in the *Liberator*, November 11, 1859.

457   "his wild blue eye grew wilder": E. C. Stedman, "John Brown's Invasion," *New-York Tribune*, reprinted in the *Liberator*, November 28, 1859.

458   "Thy shouted name abroad shall ring": W. D. Howells, "Old Brown" (November 1859), reprinted in *Echoes of Harper's Ferry*, p. 316.

458   "serene and unshaken": "The Message to Pharror," *Liberator*, November 18, 1859.

458   "John Brown, to help the helpless slave": R.W.T., "John Brown Is Gone!" *Liberator*, January 20, 1860.

458   "the scaffold—the modernized cross": Justita [pseud.], "The Virginia Martyrs," *Liberator*, March 30, 1860.

458   "Rear on high the scaffold-altar!": Dean [pseud.], "The Virginia Scaffold," *New York Independent*, December 1, 1859.

459   "For as that cross of shame": Benjamin H. Clarke, "John Brown Avenged," *Liberator*, June 27, 1862.

460   "I am cheerful and happy": R. J. Hinton, *John Brown and His Men*, p. 492. The remaining quotations in this paragraph are on pp. 496, 526, and 500, respectively.

460   "The last bloody act in the drama": Justita, "The Virginia Martyrs," *Liberator*, March 30, 1860.

460   "Murder'd, Christ-like": Richard Hinton, "They Are Gone," *Liberator*, March 23, 1860.

460   "worth and chivalry were fondly nurtured": J. W. Pillsbury, "The Quaking South," *Liberator*, December 9, 1859.

460   "Virginia is the state, you know": "The Fright of Old Virginia," undated song in *Civil War Song Sheets*; LC.

461   "Your lips with terror become white": "Old John Brown," *Guardian* (Paterson, N.J.), reprinted in the *Liberator*, December 9, 1859.

461   "All pale and paralyzed": "The Dragon and the Knight," *Halifax Sun*, reprinted in the *Liberator*, January 27, 1860.

461   "You're found . . . a brutal, cowardly crew!": "John Brown of Osawatomie," *New-York Tribune*, reprinted in the *Liberator*, November 25, 1859.

461 "Shame to thy boasted chivalry!": F. M. Adlington, "Thoughts, Suggested by the Sacrifice of John Brown," *Liberator,* March 29, 1861.

462 "the bold, blue eye grew tender": J. G. Whittier, "Brown of Osawatomie," *New York Independent,* December 22, 1859.

462 "As that dark brow": L. M. Child, "The Hero's Heart," song sung at an antislavery convention on January 26, 1860; reprinted in the *Liberator,* February 3, 1860.

462 "Not any spot six feet by two": Edmund H. Sears, "Old John Brown," *Monthly Religious Magazine,* reprinted in the *Liberator,* December 23, 1859.

462 "Will she not fear the spirit": A. P. C., "John Brown," *Anti-Slavery Standard,* reprinted in the *Liberator,* November 28, 1859.

463 "Escaped his earthly prison-house": *Liberator,* March 2, 1860.

463 "By the Spirit abroad": "Woe, Woe to Virginia!" *Liberator,* December 16, 1859.

463 "barbed, insinuating dart": "The Dragon and the Knight," *Halifax Sun,* reprinted in the *Liberator,* January 27, 1860.

463 "There towered a spectral form!": "The Specter at Sumter," *New-York Tribune,* March 19, 1861.

464 "Shrink not; the path": M. E. S., "God Speed the Right," *New-York Tribune,* May 8, 1861.

464 "the real war will never": W. Whitman, *Complete Poetry and Collected Prose,* p. 778.

464 "How has God's angry and visible frown": "John Brown's Avenger," *Liberator,* January 9, 1863.

464 "The earth looks sad and dreary": "The Martyr of Harper's Ferry," *Liberator,* January 3, 1862.

465 "His mouth is hushed": "A Song for the Times, or John Brown" (New York: H. DeMarsan, n.d.), *American Song Sheets;* LC.

465 "A hundred thousand soldiers": M. H. C. Booth, "I Think I'm Dying, Comrade," *New-York Tribune,* September 30, 1864.

466 "It seized upon every blue-coated organization": George Kimball, *Twelfth Massachusetts (Webster) Regiment Association* (Boston: n.p., 1903), pamphlet; VC.

466 "Nothing on earth has such an effect": *Letters of Lydia Maria Child with a Biographical Introduction by John Greenleaf Whittier* (Boston: Houghton Mifflin, 1883), p. 157.

466 "Well, now, ain't he lively": G. Kimball, *Twelfth Massachusetts (Webster) Regiment Association.* The remaining quotations in this paragraph are also in this pamphlet.

467 "They will hang Jeff Davis to a tree!": "Glory Hally, Hallelujah! Or the John Brown Song! Hip, Hip, Hip, Hurrah!" (Boston: Horace Partridge, n.d.), in *American Singing: Nineteenth-Century Song Sheets;* LC.

468 "They got upon the John Brown song": T. W. Higginson, *Army Life in a Black Regiment* (Boston: Fields, Osgood, 1870), p. 297.

468 "Oh! we're de bully soldiers": Lindley Miller, "Song of the First Arkansas," c. 1863, song sheet; SC.

468 "I'm bound to be a soldier": Arthur Fremantle, *Three Months in the Southern States, April–June '63* (Edinburgh: William Blackwood, 1863), p. 320.

468 "The apotheosis of old John Brown": *Mt. Carroll* (Illinois) *Weekly Mirror,* August 6, 1862.

468 "No poet could have written it": Edwin P. Whipple, "American Literature," *Harper's New Monthly Magazine* 52 (March 1876): 517.

468 "the sons of bondage": W. W. Patton (pseud. Plebs), "The New John Brown Song," *Chicago Tribune,* December 16, 1861. The next quotation in this paragraph is also from this source.

469 "He captured Harper's Ferry": W. W. Patton, "The New John Brown Song," *Chicago Tribune,* December 16, 1861.

469 "the Lord our God": H. Mayer, *All on Fire*, p. 537.

469 "John Brown, the dauntless hero": J. M. Friend, "Proclamation Song," *Liberator*, December 26, 1862.

469 "The melody of 'John Brown's Body' ": John J. McIntyre, "The Composer of 'The Battle Hymn of the Republic,' " typescript of a pamphlet published by William H. Conklin in 1916, p. 4; BSC.

469 "shall stand at Armageddon": H. H. Brownell, "John Brown Song."

469 "Mine eyes have seen the glory": J. W. Howe, "The Battle Hymn of the Republic," song sheet, c. 1865; BSC.

470 "a vein of coercion": *Charleston Mercury*, February 25, 1861.

470 "The Republican administration": "History of Old John Brown," *Old Guard*, p. 330. The quotation in the next sentence is on p. 324.

471 "The President is resolutely determined": *New York Herald*, December 10, 1861.

471 "it seems exceedingly probable": John G. Nicolay and John Hay, *Abraham Lincoln: A History* (New York: 1914), 9:251.

471 "Mr. Lincoln is already beaten": *New-York Tribune*, August 14, 1864.

472 "to make this a true John Brown corps": C. E. Heller, *Portrait of an Abolitionist*, p. 146. The remaining quotations in this paragraph are on pp. 150 and 151, respectively.

473 "had been an abolitionist too long": *The Magnificent Activist*, ed. H. N. Meyer, p. 20.

473 "the greatest event of our nation's history": "The Proclamation and a Negro Army: An Address Delivered in New York, New York, on 6 February 1863," in *The Frederick Douglass Papers*, ed. J. W. Blassingame and J. R. McKivigan, 3:549.

473 "I have given the subject": Letter from U. S. Grant to A. Lincoln, August 23, 1863; ALLC.

473 "an abomination . . . when the New England soldiers": "History of Old John Brown," *Old Guard*, p. 329.

474 "most white soldiers": J. M. McPherson, *For Cause and Comrades: Why Men Fought in the Civil War* (New York: Oxford University Press, 1997), p. 128.

474 "Not a few of the Abolition papers": "The Abolition Dead March," *Vanity Fair* 50 (1862): 164.

474 "That spirit that rises": *The Martyrdom of John Brown* (London: Emancipation Society of London, 1863), p. 2. The quotations in the next paragraph are on pp. 6 and 14, respectively.

475 "well known to me in Kansas": Edward A. Miller, Jr., *Lincoln's Abolitionist General: The Biography of David Hunter* (Columbia: University of South Carolina Press, 1997), p. 124.

476 "we will remove and destroy": U.S. War Department, *The War of the Rebellion: A Compilation of Official Records of the Union and Confederate Armies* (Washington, D.C.: Government Printing Office, 1890), ser. 1, vol. 30, part 3:698.

476 "extermination, not of soldiers" and "a war of extermination": *Home Letters of General Sherman*, ed. M. A. De Wolfe Howe (New York: Scribner, 1909), pp. 229–30.

476 "simple waste and destruction": U.S. War Department, *The War of the Rebellion* (Washington, D.C.: Government Printing Office, 1893), ser. 1, 44:13.

476 "we are not only fighting hostile armies": Basil Henry Liddell-Hart, *Sherman: Soldier, Realist, American* (New York: Praeger, 1958), p. 358.

477 "Sectional Candidate": A. B. Clarke, *John Wilkes Booth: A Sister's Memoir*, ed. T. Alford, p. 89.

478 "I looked at the traitor and terrorizer": Quoted in K. Chowder, "The Father of American Terrorism," p. 82.

478   "When I aided in the capture": A. B. Clarke, *John Wilkes Booth: A Sister's Memoir*, ed. T. Alford, p. 108.

479   "if God wills that [the war] continue": A. Lincoln, *Speeches and Writings, 1859–1865*, p. 687.

479   "supremely unhappy with history": *"Right or Wrong, God Judge Me": The Writings of John Wilkes Booth*, ed. John Rodehamel and Louise Taper (Urbana: University of Illinois Press, 1997), p. 146.

479   "Useless, useless": D. Grimsted, *American Mobbing*, p. 280.

18. Posterity

480   "a John Brown raid, on a gigantic scale": *New York Herald*, December 10, 1861.

480   "fanatics, radicals, and destructives": "The Impending Fate of the Country," *DeBow's Review* 6 (December 1866): 567. The remaining quotations in this paragraph are on pp. 567–68 and 562, respectively.

481   "The pulpits generally": *Old Guard* 3 (July 1865): 324.

482   "the *higher* or moral law": "The Difference of Race Between the Northern and Southern People," *Southern Literary Messenger* 30 (June 1860): 405.

482   "this transcendental age": "The Conspiracy of Fanaticism," *Democratic Review* 26 (May 1850): 400.

482   "the Constitution-breaking, law-defying": S. S. Cox, *Eight Years in Congress*, p. 283. The remaining quotations in this paragraph are on pp. 283, 296, and 298, respectively.

483   "the eternal right of it": *JMN* 15:207. The next quotation in this paragraph is on p. 219 of this volume. The quotations in the next three paragraphs are in the same volume and are on pp. 301, 296, 256, 302, 459, and 445, respectively.

483   "something like an electric shock": F. P. Stearns, *The Life and Public Services of George Luther Stearns*, p. 275.

484   "Pay ransom to the owner": *Centenary Edition, the Complete Works of Ralph Waldo Emerson* (1903–4; New York: AMS, 1979), 9:468. For a useful discussion of this poem, see Carl F. Strauch, "The Background for Emerson's 'Boston Hymn,'" *American Literature* 14 (March 1942): 36–47.

484   "little more [was] to be expected": C. E. Heller, *Portrait of an Abolitionist*, p. 194. The quotations in the next paragraph and the first quotation in the paragraph after that are on pp. 189, 192, and 208, respectively.

485   "became, in the most natural manner": *Remarks on the Character of George L. Stearns at Medford, April 14, 1867* (n.p.: n.p., 1867), pamphlet. The next quotation in this paragraph is also from this pamphlet.

486   "the chapel of the Most High": S. H. Morse, "The Second Day of December, 1859," *Radical*, December 1868, p. 458. The remaining quotations in this paragraph are on pp. 462 and 463.

486   "whose peers did not exist in America": D. N. Utter, "John Brown of Osawatomie," *North American Review* 137 (November 1883): 436. The subsequent quotations in this paragraph are on pp. 436 and 435, respectively.

487   "alleging that Ralph Waldo Emerson": J. J. Ingalls, "John Brown's Place in History," *North American Review* 138 (February 1884): 138.

487   "There is a small company": *Catholic World* 42 (January 1886): 515. The quotations in the next paragraph are on pp. 515–16.

488   afflicted by "paranoia": A. Nevins, *The Emergence of Lincoln*, II:93

488 "It is not necessary to assume": J. C. Malin, *John Brown and the Legend of Fifty-six,* p. 757.

488 "our beloved sister": Benjamin Quarles, ed., *Blacks on John Brown* (Chicago: University of Illinois Press, 1972), p. 80.

489 "To speak of myself": B. Quarles, ed., *Blacks on John Brown,* p. 14. The next quotation in this paragraph is on p. 12.

490 "Ode to Old Capt. John Brown": B. Quarles, ed., *Blacks on John Brown,* p. 23. The remaining quotations in this paragraph are on pp. 20–21 and 22, respectively.

490 "all the colored people of Boston": B. Quarles, ed., *Blacks on John Brown,* p. 26. The remaining quotations in this paragraph are on pp. 26 and 27, respectively.

490 "We Negroes in the South": *The Martyrdom of John Brown,* p. 14.

491 "fully believes, to this day": "Education of the Freedmen," *North American Review* 101 (October 1865): 547.

491 "We buried him below his niggers": Quoted in Elizabeth Gaskell, "Robert Gould Shaw," *Living Age* 80 (January 9, 1864): 70. The quotation in the next sentence is on p. 71.

492 "this strange, wild, bloody and mournful drama": *Ru,* p. 278. The remaining quotations in this paragraph are on pp. 281 and 283, respectively.

493 "There would be slavery to-day": "Crisis for the Negro Race," *New York Times,* June 4, 1900. The remaining quotations in this paragraph are also in this article.

493 "one of the most despicable countries": B. Quarles, ed., *Blacks on John Brown,* p. 93. The remaining quotations in this paragraph are on pp. 98–99. The quotation in the next paragraph is on pp. 102–3.

494 "Men like John Brown appear": B. Quarles, ed., *Blacks on John Brown,* p. 80. The next quotation in this paragraph is on p. 83.

494 "among the world's greatest heroes": B. Quarles, ed., *Blacks on John Brown,* p. 74.

494 "Here on the scene": Quoted in William E. Cain, "Violence, Revolution, and the Cost of Freedom: John Brown and W. E. B. Du Bois," *Boundary* 2 (Spring 1990): 319. Cain provides an insightful analysis of the relationship between Du Bois and Brown.

495 "the man who of all Americans": W. E. B. Du Bois, *John Brown,* p. xxv.

495 "cruel, merciful; peace-loving, a fighter": W. E. B. Du Bois, *Writings* (New York: Library of America, 1986), p. 1196.

495 "John Brown was right": W. E. B. Du Bois, *John Brown,* p. 338.

495 "The ideals of John Brown": *New York Times,* May 22, 1932.

496 "Within the Veil he was born": W. E. B. Du Bois, *Writings,* p. 507.

496 "the coming centuries": B. Quarles, ed., *Blacks on John Brown,* p. 111. The next quotation in this paragraph is also on p. 111.

497 "The Civil War that freed the slaves": B. Quarles, ed., *Blacks on John Brown,* p. 121. The next quotation in this paragraph is on p. 122. The poem by Countee Cullen quoted in the next paragraph is on pp. 119–20.

498 "They Look at Us": "Poems by Eli Siegel About Martin Luther King and America," *Southwest Digest,* January 9, 2003.

498 Eldridge Cleaver: The quotations in this paragraph from Cleaver, H. Rap Brown, and Floyd McKissick are in B. Quarles, ed., *Blacks on John Brown,* pp. 106–7. The Malcom X quotation in the next paragraph is on p. 107.

499 "If I were going to write a biography": J. Earle, discussion of Merrill Peterson's *John Brown: The Legend Revisited,* "The Kansas Territorial Experience" (Lawrence: University of Kansas, 2003).

499 "John Brown's knapsack was number 98": J. C. Malin, *John Brown and the Legend of Fifty-six,* p. 475. The first quotation in the next paragraph is on p. 476.

500 "The working classes must imitate": "Rich People to Be Annihilated," *New York Times*, December 5, 1885.

500 "The greatest hero of them all": In McAlister Coleman, *Eugene V. Debs* (New York: Greenberg, 1930), p. 43.

500 "No sordid motive": *San Francisco Bulletin*, December 10, 1912.

500 "Some day, not in the far distant future": Elliot J. Gorn, *Mother Jones: The Most Dangerous Woman in America* (New York: Hill & Wang, 2001), p. 238.

500 "John Brown of Harpers Ferry": "F.B.I. Questions 2 in Tower Blasts," *New York Evening Tribune*, June 20, 1961.

500 considered Brown a black nationalist: Quoted in K. Chowder, "The Father of American Terrorism," *American Heritage*, February–March 2000.

500 "Can John Brown remain": D. W. Blight, "John Brown: Triumphant Failure," *American Prospect* (2000), at www.prospect.org/print/V11/9/blight-d.html.

501 "Maybe like Harpers Ferry": Jon Nordheimer, "Bombing Case Offers a Stark Look at Abortion Conflicts," *New York Times*, January 18, 1985.

501 Brown's "example has and continues to serve": Lisa Belkin, "Kill for Life?" *New York Times*, October 30, 1994.

501 "One of his big heroes": Paul Finkelman vs. Clayton Cramer, "Analogies: Was Timothy McVeigh Our John Brown?" at hnn.us/articles/139.html.

501 "McVeigh saw himself": "Special Report: Timothy McVeigh," Edinburgh Festival (2001), at www.pastornet.net.au/jmm/articles/4647.htm.

501 "Was Timothy McVeigh": P. Finkelman vs. C. Cramer, "Analogies: Was Timothy McVeigh Our John Brown?" at hnn.us/articles/139.html.

501 Michael Mello: *The United States versus Theodore John Kaczynski: Ethics, Power, and the Invention of the Unabomber* (New York: Context, 1999).

502 "The Feds are coming": "Special Report: Timothy McVeigh," Edinburgh Festival (2001), at www.pastornet.net.au/jmm/articles/4647.htm.

503 "the wickedest woman in New York": Junius Henri Browne, *The American Metropolis: A Mirror of New York* (Hartford, Conn.: American Publishing Co., 1869), p. 582. The next quotation in this sentence is from Frank Moss, *The Great Metropolis, from Knickerbocker Days to the Present Time* (New York: P. F. Collier, 1897), p. 212.

503 "swarms of cringers, suckers": W. Whitman, *Complete Poetry and Collected Prose*, p. 18.

504 "My head is bloody": Quoted in Wayne Jackson, "Timothy McVeigh's 'Invictus,' " *Christian Courier*, June 18, 2001.

504 "It is to John Brown": B. Quarles, ed., *Blacks on John Brown*, p. 139. The remaining quotations in this and the following paragraphs are on pp. 139–40.

505 "It may be that America can no longer produce": B. Quarles, ed., *Blacks on John Brown*, p. 141.

Acknowledgments

I want to thank the kind and helpful staffs of various libraries: the Mina Reese Library at the Graduate Center of the City University of New York; the Baruch College Library; the Columbia University Library; the New York University Library; the New York Public Library; the New-York Historical Society; the Library of Congress; the Boston Public Library; the American Antiquarian Society; the Kansas State Historical Society; and the West Virginia State Archives. I greatly profited from the wonderful John Brown Web site of the Boyd B. Stutler Collection of John Brown at the West Virginia Archives, as well as other online resources, especially Making of America and American Memory.

I appreciate the intelligent input of my students at CUNY. I am particularly indebted to Mark McCullough, who tracked down and reproduced many Brown-related poems and songs for me.

My editor at Knopf, Jane Garrett, has facilitated this project with her usual professionalism and astuteness.

The idea for this book arose in a conversation I had years ago with my brother-in-law, Haig Nalbantian. He had a formative influence on the book and has encouraged me throughout the writing process.

My thanks to daughter Aline, who contributed good ideas about the jacket design.

Above all, I thank my wife, Suzanne Nalbantian. Her dedication to scholarship has inspired me, her intelligence has stimulated me, and her love has supported me.

Index

Page numbers in *italics* refer to illustrations.

Abolition Aid Societies, 435
Abolitionism
  black activism in, 5, 6, 9, 103–5, 111, 244
  divisive strains of, 403–4
  evangelical, 403
  JB's militant dedication to, 3, 4, 5, 7, 10,
    11, 13, 19, 24–8, 33–4, 36–9, 50–1,
    60–2, 64–5, 85, 95–6, 192, 220, 273–4,
    333
  journalism of, 51, 53, 59, 62, 64, 104,
    149, 157, 177, 183, 184, 188, 191,
    339–40, 359–60, 364, 404, 412, 458
  Lincoln and, 117, 139, 271–2, 281–2,
    422, 426
  opposition to, 11–12, 14–19, 26, 34,
    62–4, 412–17
  organizations in support of, 24, 36, 51,
    60
  pacifists and, ix, 4, 34, 51, 53, 56, 63–4,
    96–7, 162, 164, 177, 208–9, 224, 225,
    226, 404–5
  pioneers of, 3–6, 27–8, 34
  political forces of, 14, 64, 102, 118, 403,
    422–3, 424
  public events sparking involvement in,
    33–4
  "public teachings" of, 177, 178
  separation of North and South advo-
    cated in, 4, 51, 53
  support of militancy and violence in the
    cause of, 97–110, 403
"Abraham Lincoln, Slave-hound of Illinois" (Phillips), 5
Adair, Florilla Brown (JB's half-sister),
  144, 180, 181

Adair, Samuel Lyle, 144, 175, 177, 179–80,
  199
Adam, 21, 24
Adams, Abigail, 97
Adams, Anne Brown (JB's daughter),
  112–13, 123, *134*, 216, 294, 296, 297,
  298, 304, 305, 399
Adams, John Quincy, 50, 62, 95, 97, 98
"Address" (Emerson), 217
*Address to the Slaves of the United States of
  America* (Garnet), 103
Adirondack Mountains, 89, 125, 127
Adventures of Huckleberry Finn, The (Twain),
  117, 161
Aesop's Fables, 47
Afghanistan, 106
Africa, 23, 54, 71, 115, 420
African Americans
  admiration of JB by, ix, 12–13, 104,
    129–30, 131, 132, 488–99
  antislavery activism of, 5, 6, 9, 103–5,
    111, 244
  colonization advocated for, 5, 24, 36, 50,
    59–60, 62, 273, 403
  concept of financial reparation for, 101
  discrimination and violence against, 61,
    62, 102, 118, 417, 418, 492–3
  education and literacy of, 56–7, 118–19,
    251
  emigration movement of, 260
  free, 61, 89, 120, 418–19
  integration of, 36–7, 114, 260, 273
  JB's long-term impact on, ix, 4, 5, 12
  lynching of, 62, 170, 417, 492
  music of, 468

African Americans *(continued)*
  suffrage of, 5, 118, 134, 219, 247, 273,
    484–5
  Union Army service of, 5, 6, 102, 217,
    221, 264, 468, 472–4, 491
  virtual reenslavement of, 51, 102, 118
  see also civil rights movement; racism;
    slave revolts; slavery; slaves
Agassiz, Louis, 256
Age of Reason, The (Paine), 194, 298
Akron, Ohio, 76, 78–81, 88, 92–3
Albany Evening Journal, 417
Alburtis, E. G., 323–4
Alcott, Amos Bronson, 4, 216–20, 223–5,
    227, 290–1, 344, 363, 402, 431, 482,
    484–5
Alcott, Louisa May, 4
Allegheny Mountains, 25, 74, 105, 111,
    113, 240
Allen, Nathaniel, 224
Allies for Freedom, 500
Allstadt, John H., 311, 313, 318
Alton, Ill., 62–3
Alton Observer, 62
Amana community, 131
American Anti-Slavery Society, 36, 51, 60,
    64, 97, 117, 256, 404–5, 484
American Colonization Society, 36
American Party, 189
American Peace Society, 212, 224, 225
American Revolution, 19, 23, 297, 365
  Calvinism and, 26–7
  JB's ancestors in, 20, 25, 231
  slavery and, 23, 97
  social change after, 26–7
Amherst College, 20, 35
Amistad revolt, 54–5
Anderson, Jeremiah Goldsmith, 277–8
  death of, 277, 327–8
  at Harpers Ferry, 277, 290, 291, 294–5,
    297, 299, 303–5, 307, 326, 327–8
Anderson, Osborne Perry, 130, 262, 263,
    264
  escape of, 370–1
  at Harpers Ferry, 297, *301*, 307, 311,
    314–15, 321, 324
Anderson, Samuel, 198
Andrew, John A., 292, 429
Anglo-African Magazine, 55, 441
"Another Dream," 54
anti-Catholicism, 65, 189

Antietam, Battle of, 17, 309
antimiscegenation codes, 118
anti-Semitism, 189
antislavery movement, *see* Abolitionism
antislavery societies, 24, 36, 51, 60
Appalachian Mountains, 103–4, 245, 249,
    355
Appeal, 53, 103
Appomattox, Battle of, 476
Aptheker, Herbert, 107
Army Life in a Black Regiment (Higginson),
    450
Ashby, Turner, 398
Associated Press, 329, 348
Astromo, William, 70
Atchison, David Rice, 140–1, 158, 162,
    163–4, 197
atheism, 14, 15
Atlanta Confederacy, 417
Atlantic Monthly, 210, 269, 364, 450–1, 469
Autobiography of a Female Slave (Griffith),
    367
Avis, John, 319, 370, 379, 380–1, 390, 391,
    393, 395–6, 459–60

Badger, Joseph, 29
Ball, Armistead, 318
Ballou, Adin, 226
Baltimore American, 332, 335, 379
Baltimore & Ohio Railroad, 296, 316–17,
    398
Baltimore Patriot, 335
Baltimore Sun, 298
Banks, Russell, 127, 499
Barber, J. Max, 495–7
Barber, Thomas, 146–7
Barbour, Alfred W., 422
Barnum, P. T., 388
Battle Cry of Freedom (McPherson), 499
"Battle Hymn of the Republic, The"
    (Howe), 4, 5, 6, 292, 469–70
Battle-Pieces (Melville), 446–7
Baxter, Richard, 47
Baylor, Robert W., 324, 338
Beach, Thomas P., 224–5
Beckham, Fontaine, 309, 322–3, 324, 330,
    351, 353
Beecher, Henry Ward, 359, 362, 382, 416
Beecher, Lyman, 25, 253

Bell, James Madison, 261, 262

Bell, John C., 425–6

"Benito Cereno" (Melville), 445

Bennett, James Gordon, 427

Bennett, Lerone, Jr., 504–5

Berry, Harrison, 315

Bible, 48
   JB's devotion to, 19, 34, 40–1, 46, 50, 55, 59, 61, 93, 151–2, 208–9, 255, 307, 330, 355–6
   New Testament of, 40, 164, 208, 354, 355
   Old Testament of, 40–1, 42, 44, 93, 121–2, 151–2, 164, 190, 208–9, 308
   patriarchs of, 40–1, 44
   slavery as violation of, 27, 28
   study of, 21, 22, 25, 34, 40

Billy Budd (Melville), 447, 448

bin Laden, Osama, 106, 500, 501, 503

Bird, Robert Montgomery, 261

Birney, James Gillespie, 64

Birth of a Nation, 492

Black, J. W., *356*

Black Jack, Battle of, 181, 185–8, 189, 190, 191, 196, 210, 222, 243, 293, 388, 412

black nationalism, 500

Black Strings, 273–4

Blair, Charles, 214, 292

Blakeslee, Levi, 30, 32, 35, 37

Blight, David W., 500

Blithedale Romance, The (Hawthorne), 83

Blount, James G., 279

"Blow Ye the Trumpet, Blow!," 4, 56, 400

Boerly, Thomas, 318

Bondi, August, 182, 188–9, 194

Booth, John Wilkes, 310, 397–8, 477–9, *477*

Booth, Mary H. C., 465

Border Times, 174

Boston, Mass., 3–4, 6, 28, 51, 67, 70, 71–3, 188, 208–10, 258, 291–2
   anti-Brown rally in, 222, 413
   Bunker Hill in, 346, 406
   Faneuil Hall in, 229, 413
   Music Hall in, 3, 208, 366
   Old South Church in, 368
   Tremont Temple in, 3–4, 99, 368, 405, 406, 413

Boston Atlas, 412

Boston Courier, 358

"Boston Hymn" (Emerson), 3, 6, 483

Boston Traveller, 96

Boteler, Alexander R., 329

Botts, Lawson, 348, 350, 352

Boutwell, George S., 484

Bowdoin College, 448

Boyer, Richard O., 499

Brackett, Edwin A., 6, 7, 388

Bradford, William, 19, 31

Brady, Mathew, 427, *428*

"Branded Hand, The" (Whittier), 100

Branson, Jacob, 145–6, 156

Breckinridge, John C., 425–6

Bridgman, Edward, 177

Bridgman, Laura, 209

Brook Farm, 80, 83

Brooks, Preston, 155, 158–9, 161, 163, 210

Brous, Bernard Jerome, 500

Brown, Abbie (JB's daughter-in-law), 293

Brown, Amelia (JB's daughter), 81

Brown, Anna (JB's sister), 22

Brown, Anne (JB's daughter), *see* Adams, Anne Brown

Brown, Austin (JB's grandson), 133, 136

Brown, Austin (JB's son), 77, 78

Brown, Charles (JB's son), 59, 78

Brown, Dianthe Lusk (JB's wife), 37–8, 41, 46, 48–9, 351

Brown, Ellen, I (JB's daughter), 88

Brown, Ellen, II (JB's daughter), 94, 133, 305, 399

Brown, Ellen Sherbondy (JB's daughter-in-law), 86, 137

Brown, Erastus, 224

Brown, Frederick (JB's brother), 56, 58

Brown, Frederick, I (JB's son), 45, 46, 48

Brown, Frederick, II (JB's son), 128
   Kansas campaign of, 132, 137, 144, 148, 154, 171, 173, 177, 182–6, 187, 193, 195, 196, 199–200
   mental problems of, 38, 45, 46, 80, 88, 93, 148, 351
   murder of, 40, 45, 66, 144, 152, 179, 195, 199–200, 201, 213, 270, 293

Brown, G. W., 163, 340, 386, 403

Brown, H. Rap, 129, 498

Brown, Isabella M. Thompson (JB's daughter-in-law), 293

Brown, Jason (JB's son), 38, 65, 78, 80, 86,
    93, 133, 266, 293
  imprisonment of, 179–81, 187, 189
  JB and, 40, 42, 76, 81, 85, 174, 195, 202,
    203, 207, 245–6
  Kansas campaign of, 137, 146, 159, 166,
    169, 174, 177, 179–81, 187, 189, 195,
    200–3
Brown, J. Carter, 233
Brown, Jeremiah (JB's half-brother), 370
Brown, John, 87, 153, 190, 356
  aliases of, 258, 267
  animal affinity of, 45, 46, 79
  antimilitarism of, 33, 34
  antislavery passion of, 3–5, 7, 10, 11, 13,
    19, 24–8, 33–4, 36–9, 50–1, 60–2,
    64–5, 85, 95–6, 192, 220, 273–4, 333
  autobiographical letter of, 20, 210
  birth of, 23
  black activism promoted by, 5, 6, 9, 111,
    244
  burial of, 69, 126, 391, 393, 399–401,
    432
  business ventures of, 35–6, 41–5, 49,
    56–9, 66–7, 79–92, 94, 125, 126
  capture and imprisonment of, 6, 25, 67,
    160, 187, 216, 217, 219, 309, 328–9,
    334, 335, 337, 341, 358, 370, 380–4,
    403, 443
  character and personality of, 8–9, 10–11,
    19, 32–6, 41–3, 45–8, 66–8, 87–8, 91,
    94, 103–5, 111, 114–15, 118–21, 124,
    164–5, 181–2, 191–2, 209, 270, 332–3,
    407
  childhood and adolescence of, 28–37, 45,
    68, 168, 368
  children and family life of, 4, 37–8, 40–6,
    48–50, 56, 57, 59, 65, 73–4, 76–81,
    84–6, 88, 92–4, 123–4, 127–8, 208
  community building and leadership of,
    42, 44, 46–7, 48, 49, 59, 111, 124,
    125–32
  compassion and charity of, 42, 45–6, 49,
    50, 71, 270, 285
  cultural context of the achievements of,
    ix–x, 3–13, 14–15
  debating skills of, 47–8
  deeply religious Calvinist faith of, 5, 8, 9,
    12, 19, 21–8, 34–5, 38–9, 40–1, 43–4,
    47–8, 50, 55, 71, 75, 78, 81, 93–4, 102,

    148, 164–5, 188–91, 192, 194, 208,
    245, 253, 368
  early biographies of, 8, 183, 344, 431
  early resistance to Christianity by, 32, 34
  economic attitudes of, 67–9, 74–6, 82–5
  education and reading of, 32, 34–5,
    46–7, 106–7, 128, 164, 231–2, 274
  eleven Missouri slaves liberated by, 167,
    268, 278–80, 281, 283, 288, 289, 290,
    291, 304, 355
  European trip of, 90–1
  failed pursuits of, 66–7, 74–6, 82, 85, 88,
    90–1, 92, 125, 126
  financial and legal difficulties of, 28, 45,
    57–9, 67, 69–77, 82, 88, 90–2, 94, 112,
    124
  financial backing of, 4–5, 27, 99, 102,
    165, 208–18, 211, 221, 248–9, 254–5,
    257, 265, 266, 283, 291, 330, 340–2,
    343, 429–30
  fugitive slaves aided by, 37, 56, 59, 60–2,
    80, 86
  fund-raising and self-promotion of, 42,
    135, 174, 179, 193, 206–18, 222–3,
    232–3, 235–8, 239–40, 243, 248–9,
    254–5, 257–8, 274–5, 276, 288
  funeral of, 4, 391
  groundswell of popular support after
    death of, 404–13, 462–4
  hanging death of, 3, 4, 11, 55, 67, 95,
    130, 132, 187, 207, 309–10, 334, 338,
    343, 346, 362, 374, 379, 380, 383,
    392–8, 397, 402, 403, 404–5, 406–7,
    409, 410, 421, 423
  help and education of African Americans
    planned by, 56–7, 60–2, 118–19
  heroic and mythical status of, 4–5, 6, 7,
    8, 10, 11, 129, 132, 139, 178, 195–6,
    204–5, 206–7, 214, 222–3, 344–7,
    368–9, 402, 404–13
  humble lifestyle of, 28, 43–4, 47, 68–9,
    85–7, 126–7
  humor of, 47, 235
  illnesses of, 88, 239, 243, 275
  indictment of, 207, 337, 347–9, 351
  influences on, 5, 9, 18–19, 25–8, 51–2,
    54–6, 98–101, 106–11, 114, 164, 231–2
  land speculation of, 57–9, 69–70, 72,
    74–6
  lay ministry of, 42, 48, 49

"Man on the farm" image of, 68, 76, 79, 84, 229
marble bust of, 3, 6, 7, 388
memorial services for, 3–6, 12–13, 130, 402, 406, 407, 408, 412, 431, 432, 489–90, 493, 496–7
misreadings of the character of, 7–8, 178, 205, 335
music and literature based on, 444–70
Native American allies of, 31–2, 157–8, 168–9
New England family ancestry of, 19–23
as "Old Brown," 86, 355, 416, 457, 458
as "Osawatomie Brown," 195, 196, 205, 243, 290–1, 311, 313, 319, 327, 452
phrenological consultation of, 86–8
physical appearance of, 6, 35, 86, 193, 208, 256, 267, 399
physical exercise advocated by, 46
political alienation of, 50
powerful ego of, 34, 87–8
predestination belief of, 5, 25, 26, 41, 47–8, 55, 245
provisional constitution and government of, 8, 106, 249–55, 263–4, 274, 300, 333, 360
public antislavery commitment of, 65
Puritan heritage of, 18–22, 25, 27–8, 68, 93, 122, 153, 164–5, 188–9, 196, 208, 230, 231, 245, 253, 292, 346
racial and religious tolerance of, 33, 34, 103–5, 111, 114–15, 118–21, 128, 168–70, 189, 194, 256, 407–8
reformist sensibility of, 8, 9, 11, 12, 51, 80–1, 192
rewards offered for the capture of, 277, 279
sabbatarianism of, 38–9, 41, 42, 59, 173
sanity questions about, 6, 8, 9, 14, 38, 50, 138, 189–90, 190, 249–50, 339–40, 350–1, 357–8
souvenirs of, 443–4
tenderness vs. sternness of, 42–3, 45–6
vilification of, as murderer and terrorist, 6–8, 12, 14, 19, 52, 55, 174–5, 204–5, 222, 337–41, 357, 403, 412–17
violence and terrorism embraced by, 4, 6, 7, 8, 11, 12, 52, 54–6, 65, 67, 111, 122–3, 139, 149, 151–2, 159, 164, 165–6, 184

will of, 390–1, 392
wives of, *see* Brown, Dianthe Lus; Brown, Mary Day
wounding of, 200, 244, 327, 328–9, 336, 349, 387
writing style of, 32, 210, 334, 383–5
youthful revelations of, 33–4
Brown, John, trial of (1859), 130, 309, 347–57
arraignment and indictment in, 207, 337, 347–9, 351
closing arguments in, 353
conviction in, 66, 67, 353
defense attorneys in, 249–50, 348, 352–3
free and easy Southern customs at, 349, 350
hundreds of spectators at, 349, 353
insanity defense raised in, 38, 50, 249–50, 350–1
JB's demeanor and statements at, 347, 348, 349, 350, 351, 353–7, 358, 368, 402
JB's plea at, 348, 349
presiding judge at, 348, 350
press accounts of, 348, 352
prosecuting attorneys in, 349, 351–2, 353
security at, 350
sentencing at, 353–4, 357, 404–5
testimony in, 50, 313–14, 334, 350–1, 352–3
Brown, John, Jr. (JB's son), 93, 144, 273, 290, 293–5, 306, 328, 390, 391
childhood and adolescence of, 38, 42–3, 45, 57, 76, 78
education of, 61, 65, 78, 79, 81, 82, 86
imprisonment of, 179–81, 187, 189, 195, 196, 202, 203, 213
JB and, 40, 42–3, 57, 69, 76, 81–2, 85, 86, 90, 93, 133, 171, 202, 207, 234, 258–9, 266, 274–5
Kansas campaign of, 133, 135, 137, 142, 144, 148, 150–1, 154, 157, 158, 166, 169, 171, 173, 177, 179–81, 187, 189, 195, 203
marriage of, 86
political activism of, 142, 144, 148, 150, 154
temporary insanity of, 177, 179–81, 293, 294, 351

Brown, John (JB's ancestor), 20

Brown, John (JB's grandfather), 20

Brown, John (Scotchman), 466–7

Brown, John E., 198

Brown, Martha Evelyn Brewster (JB's daughter-in-law), 293, 297, 304, 399, 400

Brown, Mary (JB's ancestor), 20

Brown, Mary Day (JB's wife), 49–50, 127, 134–5, *134*, 292, 293, 488–9
   character and personality of, 49–50, 126
   childbearing and motherhood of, 49–50, 57, 59, 65, 81, 85, 133
   JB and, 49, 57, 72, 81, 88, 121, 124, 132, 137, 148, 177, 182, 208, 233, 248, 380, 389–91
   JB's body taken home by, 398–9

Brown, Nathan (JB's ancestor), 20

Brown, O. C., 175, 177

Brown, Oliver (JB's brother), 30

Brown, Oliver (JB's son), 40, 73–4, 88, 234
   death of, 40, 304, 323, 327, 328, 391, 400
   at Harpers Ferry, 292–5, 299, 304, 307, 311, 316, 318–19, 321, 323, *325*, 326–7
   Kansas campaign of, 136, 146, 177, 182, 193–4, 195

Brown, Owen (JB's father), 20–3, 22
   Abolitionism and racial tolerance of, 23, 27, 30–1, 34, 36–7, 60, 64–5
   Calvinist faith and principles of, 20–3, 25, 29–31, 65, 148
   civic activism of, 60, 74
   death of, 148
   early life of, 20
   farming, shoemaking, and tannery business of, 20, 21, 22, 29, 30, 32, 33, 34, 35
   JB and, 49, 51, 59, 64–5, 72, 84, 125, 136–7
   Ohio migration of, 29–31
   wives of, *see* Brown, Ruth Mills; Brown, Sallie Root

Brown, Owen (JB's son), 38, 126, 128, 266
   childhood of, 42, 43, 65, 88
   escape of, 370–4, 432
   at Harpers Ferry, 244, 293, 294–5, 298, 299, 300, 314, 322
   JB and, 40, 42, 76, 207, 237, 242, 244, 245–7, 262, 265, 266

Kansas campaign of, 132, 146, 148, 172, 173–4, 177, 180, 182, 193, 195, 207

Brown, Peter (JB's ancestor), 19–20, 29

Brown, Peter (JB's son), 74, 78

Brown, Reese P., 148

Brown, Ruth (JB's daughter), *see* Thompson, Ruth Brown

Brown, Ruth Mills (JB's mother), 21–2, 30, 32–3

Brown, Sallie Root (JB's stepmother), 32–3

Brown, Salmon (JB's brother), 22, 34–5

Brown, Salmon (JB's son), 59, 78, 391, 399
   at Harpers Ferry, 292, 293
   Kansas campaign of, 132, 135, 137, 153–4, 158, 171, 172, 182, 193–4, 195

Brown, Sarah (JB's daughter), 78, 111, *134*, 216

Brown, Spencer Kellogg, 200, 201

Brown, Tonny (JB's grandson), 136

Brown, Watson (JB's son), 57, 234, 400
   death of, 40, 328, 391
   at Harpers Ferry, 40, 293, 297, 304, 310, 321, *325*, 326, 328

Brown, Wealthy Hotchkiss (JB's daughter-in-law), 86, 135, 136, 144, 150–1

Brown, William Wells, 116

"Brown of Osawatomie" (Whittier), 461–2

Brown v. Board of Education, ix, 498

Brua, Joseph, 321

Bryant, William Cullen, 427

Buchanan, James, 197, 239, 269, 279, 282, 317, 342, 393, 409–10

Buford, Jefferson, 153, 156

Bunyan, John, 47

Burlington Mills Manufacturing Company, 92

Burns, Anthony, 34, 112, 217, 226–7

Burnside, Ambrose, 187

Burr, Charles Chauncey, 11–12, 16, 115, 481

Burr, James E., 100

Burt, John, 501

Bush Negroes, 108

Butler, Andrew P., 158

Butler, Pardee, 145, 156

Byrne, Terence, 316–17

Cabot Bank, 88, 92

Calhoun, John, 197

Calhoun, John C., 115, 197
Calvin, John, 18, 26
Calvinism, 5, 12, 29–30, 34
  doctrines of, 18, 21–2, 25, 43, 47–8
  impact of American Revolution on, 26–7
  JB's background and faith in, 5, 8, 9, 12,
    19, 21–8, 34–5, 38–9, 40–1, 43–4,
    47–8, 50, 55, 71, 75, 78, 81, 93–4, 102,
    148, 164–5, 188–91, 192, 194, 208,
    245, 253, 368
  orthodox vs. liberal, 18, 26–7
  self-flagellation of, 43, 93–4
Campbell, James, 393, 395–6
Canada, 170, 216, 241, 254, 258–65, 342,
  432
  flight of JB supporters to, 254, 342–3
  fugitive slaves in, 37, 80, 97, 118, 124,
    127, 259–60, 278–9
  JB's antislavery convention in, 167, 258,
    259, 260, 261–4, 265, 273
capitalism, 36, 41–5, 68–9, 76, 80, 83–4,
  126, 143
Capra, Frank, 438
Carasaw, William and Eliza, 127
Carleton, Silas, 430
Carlyle, Thomas, 230–2
Carpenter, O. A., 182–3, 187
Cary, Mary Ann Shadd, 120
Catholic World, 487
Cato, Sterling G., 153–4, 155, 166, 171
Cayahoga Indians, 31
Cayahoga River, 58, 70
Chamberlain, Amos, 75–6
Chambers, George, 323
Chaplin, William L., 100
Chapman, A. M., 263
Chapman, John Jay, 9–10
Charles I, king of England, 65
Charleston, S.C., 423
  aborted slave revolt in, 52, 97, 109
Charleston Mercury, 425, 436
Charles Town, Va., 130, 217, 317, 319,
  347–8, 363, 375, 378, 386–8, 392–3
Charles Town jail, 261, 373–92
  JB's imprisonment in, 6, 25, 67, 341, 351,
    358, 370, 380–4, 403, 443
  JB's letters from, 334, 351, 370, 380,
    382–9, 402
  JB's men in, 371, 373–7, 459–60
Chase, Salmon P., 362, 422, 426, 484
Cheever, George B., 406

Cheney, Ednah D., 365
Cherokee Indians, 168
Chesapeake and Ohio Canal, 319
Chicago, Ill., 208, 237, 261, 287, 422
Chicago Press and Tribune, 339
Chicago Tribune, 468
Child, Lydia Maria, 210, 387, 461–2, 466
Chilton, Samuel, 249–50, 353
Choctaw Indians, 168
Christianity, 24, 31, 164
  rejection of, 27, 188, 194, 245, 370
  revolutionary aspects of, 9, 26–8
  slavery and, 25–7
  see also specific Christian sects
Cilley, Jonathan, 160
Cinque, 54–5
"Circles" (Emerson), 445
civil disobedience, 188, 224–5
"Civil Disobedience" (Thoreau), 188, 225
civil rights movement, 36–7, 114, 118, 134
  impact of JB on, ix, 4, 5, 12, 129–30, 132,
    138, 273, 497–8
Civil War, U.S., 3, 58, 285
  battles of, 17, 187, 189, 309, 476
  black troops in, 5, 6, 102, 217, 221, 264
  casualties of, 187, 304, 441–2
  causes of, ix, 10, 14, 16, 56, 102, 138,
    165, 403
  deciding factors in, 310
  emancipation promoted as mission of, 6,
    102, 219
  JB as catalyst of, ix, 4, 10, 11–12, 39, 56,
    95–6, 139, 182, 187, 401, 404, 437,
    474, 493–4
  as large-scale "John Brown raid," 11–12,
    470–1, 478–9
  predictions of, 95–6, 151
  restoration of the Union paramount in,
    5, 12, 63, 102, 253, 271–2
  social and cultural issues of, 14–19
Clarke, James Freeman, 469
Clay, Clement C., 422
Clay, Henry, 36, 50, 160, 362, 450
Cleaver, Eldridge, 498
Cleveland, Ohio, 30, 35, 61, 130, 235, 266,
  272, 288–9, 407
Cleveland Plain Dealer, 289, 489
Cline, James B., 198, 200
Clingham, Thomas L., 160
Cloudsplitter (Banks), 499
Coleman, Franklin N., 145

Collins, Samuel, 145
colonization movement, 5, 24, 36, 50,
    59–60, 62, 273, 403
Columbus, Christopher, 31
communism, 82–3
Communist Manifesto (Marx), 80
Compromise of 1850, 34, 112, 149, 419
Concord, Mass., 4, 28, 214–16, 218–19,
    222–3, 232, 344–7, 402, 430–1
  Middlesex County Jail in, 225
  Town Hall in, 290–1
"Conduct of Life, The" (Emerson), 218
Confederate Army, 16, 112, 269, 468
  prominent generals of, 309, 398
Confederate States of America, 14, 329,
    359
Confidence-Man, The (Melville), 445
Congregational Church, 21, 30, 34, 37, 42
Congress, U.S., 67, 83, 112, 140, 150, 226,
    243, 248, 272, 276, 345, 429
  see also House of Representatives, U.S.;
    Senate, U.S.
Congress of Racial Equality, 498
Connecticut, 19–23, 25, 56, 73, 75
*Conquest of Kansas by Missouri and Her Allies,
    The* (Phillips), 191
Constitution, U.S., 4, 16, 18, 227, 361, 363
  due process clause of, 273–4
  fugitive slave clause of, 63, 250
  implicit acceptance of slavery in, 24, 63,
    96, 100, 115, 250, 251–2, 272
  rejection of, 64, 96, 100, 251–3, 333, 404
  three-fifths clause in, 24, 250
  see also specific amendments
Constitutional Union Party, 425
Continental Army, Connecticut 18th
    Regiment of, 20
Conway, Martin, 212
Cook, John E., 243–5, 246, 262
  escape and capture of, 324, 370–3
  at Harpers Ferry, 296, 303, 305, 307,
    310, 311, 314, 316–17, 321–2
  trial and execution of, 375–7, 380, 398,
    415–16, 459
Cook, Mary Virginia Kennedy, 296
Cooke, Philip St. George, 207
Copeland, John Anthony, 289, 418
  at Harpers Ferry, 297, *301*, 320
  trial and execution of, 348, 374–5,
    376–7, 415–16, 459

Coppoc, Barclay, 261
  escape of, 370, 371, 373, 374
  at Harpers Ferry, 297, 307, 310, 322
Coppoc, Edwin, 261, 337, 379
  at Harpers Ferry, 297, 307, 311, 323, 328
  trial and execution of, 348, 374–5,
    376–7, 398, 415–16, 459
*Correspondence Between Lydia Maria Child
    and Governor Wise and Mrs. Mason of
    Virginia* (Child), 462
Cortés, Hérnan, 31
"Courage" (Emerson), 188, 219, 366
Cox, John T., 276
Cox, Samuel S., 16, 18, 482
Craft, William and Ellen, 226
Cramer, Clayton, 501
Crandall, Prudence, 56
Creek Indians, 168
"Crime Against Kansas, The" (Sumner),
    95–6, 158
Cromwell, Oliver, 18–19, 164–6, 274, 475,
    480
  JB compared to, 19, 164–5, 208, 210,
    221, 224, 230–1, 330, 346
  JB's emulation of, 19, 164, 231–2
Cruise, David, 279, 355
Cuba, 54
Cullen, Countee, 497
cultural biography, 9–12
Cumberland Valley Railroad, 371
Cushing, Caleb, 229, 413

Daingerfield, John E. P., 313–14, 318, 326
Dana, Richard Henry, 127–9
Daniels, Jim, 278, 279
Daniels, John Brown, 279, 287
Darrow, Clarence, 500
Davis, Jefferson, 359, 439–40
Davis, J. Lewis, 350
Day, Charles, 49
DeBow's Review, 176–7, 178, 195, 426, 440,
    480
Debs, Eugene V., 500
Declaration of Independence, 12, 24–5,
    130, 223, 369, 408
  assertion of equality in, 24, 99, 263,
    273–4
  JB's version of, 300–3

Delahay, Mark, 361–2
Delamater, George B., 46, 47
Delany, Martin R., 120, 256, 259–60, 262, 263
Democratic Party, 8, 50, 120, 204, 357, 363, 425–6
  proslavery platform of, 29, 288
  Union meetings of, 412–13, 414–15
Democratic Review, 274, 482
Denver, James Wilson, 269, 276
Devil in America, The (Gladney), 455–7
Dickinson, Edward, 449–50
Dickinson, Emily, 49, 66, 217, 361, 449, 450–2
Dissertation on Slavery, A (Tucker), 439
Ditson, Oliver, 467
"Doom of Slavery in the Union, The" (Townsend), 435
Douglas, Stephen, 140, 425–6, 442, 443
  Lincoln debates with, 63, 139, 271, 273, 281–2, 425
Douglass, Frederick, 3–4, 25, 57, *105*, 120, 121, 132, 135, 256, 359, 364, 387, 473
  autobiography of, 342
  flight from slavery by, 342
  flight to Canada and England by, 254, 342
  on JB, ix, 86, 104, 123–4, 254, 262, 383, 491–2
  JB and, 103–5, 111, 112, 131, 134, 248, 249, 253–4, 299–300, 341
Dow, Charles, 145, 156
Doyle, Drury, 154, 172, 340, 403
Doyle, James P., 154–5, 166, 171–2, 289, 403
Doyle, John, 172, 386
Doyle, Mahala, 155, 171–2, 176, 229, 385–6, 403, 413
Doyle, William, 154, 166, 340, 403
draft riots, 160
"Dragon and the Knight, The," 461, 463
Drayton, Daniel, 100
Dred (Stowe), 107
Dred Scott decision, 23, 124, 228, 238, 247, 250, 389, 483
Du Bois, W. E. B., ix, 12, 129–30, 132, 494–6, *495*, 506
Duties of a Soldier (Forbes), 234, 241–2, 246

Ebony, 504
Echoes of Harpers Ferry (Redpath), 444
Edinburgh Review, 411
Edwards, Jonathan, 19, 21, 25, 41, 43, 47, 48, 151–2, 332
Edwards, Jonathan, Jr., 23, 25–6, 27
elections, U.S.
  of 1854, 149
  of 1858, 239, 242–3, 268–9
  of 1860, 422–3, 425–9, 434, 442
  of 1864, 471, 472, 477–8
Elkins, Stanley, 215
Elliott, R. G., 195
Ellsworth, Alfred M., 263
emancipation, 5, 34, 59, 60
  Lincoln and, 3, 4, 6, 12, 273, 469, 483
  of West Indian slaves, 34, 55, 225–6
"Emancipation in the West Indies" (Emerson), 225–6
Emancipation League, 6
Emancipation Proclamation, 3, 4, 6, 12, 273, 455, 469, 483
  celebrations of, 3–6, 12–13
Emerson, Eddy, 218
Emerson, Ralph Waldo, 9, 188–9, 215, 217–29, 257, 346, *364*, 402, 413, 452
  Abolitionist sentiment of, 3, 4, 6, 34, 55, 64, 121, 227–9
  JB defended by, 4, 32, 64, 66–7, 188, 210, 216, 219, 222–3, 228–9, 290, 344, 355, 363–9, 406–7, 431–2, 482–4
  philosophy of, 3, 4, 6, 10, 11, 17, 27, 64, 66–8, 84
  self-reliance concept of, 10, 11, 17, 64, 66–7, 188–9, 216, 217, 219
Emerson (Alcott), 219
"Emerson" (Higginson), 221
"End of the Wicked Contemplated by the Righteous, The" (Edwards), 48
England, 18, 23, 90–1, 116, 225, 226, 254, 266, 342
  civil wars in, 164–5, 230
Episcopalianism, 18, 26
Epps, Ann, 127
Epps, Lyman, 111, 127, 133, 400
Epps, Lyman, Jr., 127
"Eternity of Hell's Torments, The" (Edwards), 48
Evans, George Henry, 80, 192
Everett, Edward, 110, 413

"Execution of John Brown, The," 397
"Experience" (Emerson), 445

Falconer, William, 482
"Fate of Old John Brown, The," 454
Federalist Party, 32
Fenians, 499
Fifteenth Amendment, 5, 247, 472, 486, 492
Fillmore, Millard, 414
Finkelman, Paul, 501
Finney, Charles Grandison, 25, 60, 403
First Brigade of Kansas Volunteers, 147
Fish, Hamilton, 404
Fite, Emerson David, 441
Fitzhugh, George, 26
Florida, 99, 106, 107, 423–4
Floyd, John B., 303–4, 436–7
Forbes, Hugh, 113–14, 191, 234–5, 237–8, 240–2, 243, 244, 246, 266, 298, 337
    betrayal of JB by, 247–8, 258, 264, 265, 268
Forbes, John Murray, 292
Foreman, James, 41, 45, 47, 49
Fort Snyder, 270, 277
Fort Sumter, firing on, 63, 272, 419, 433, 463, 470
Fortune, T. Thomas, 492–3
Fort Wagner, 491
Foster, Abby Kelley, 97, 123
Foster, Stephen S., 97, 224
Fouke, Christine L., 323
Fourier, Charles, 83
Fourierism, 15, 83
Fourteenth Amendment, 472
Fowler, Orson S., 86–8
Fox, George, 11
Fox, Harry, 454
France, 90, 108, 411
Frank Leslie's Illustrated Newspaper, 417–18
Franklin, Benjamin, 47, 67
Franklin, John Hope, 378
Franklin, Ohio, 57–8
Franklin Congregational Church, 61–2
Franklin Land Company, 57–8
Franklin Mills, Ohio, 58–9, 70, 72, 73–4
Frazer, William, 361
Fredericksburg, Battle of, 187

Frederick the Great, 130, 307, 311, 326
Free Church, 60
Freedman's Bureau, 485
free love, 14, 15, 80
Free Soil Party, 64, 116, 145, 148, 150, 152, 155, 156, 403
Free State Hotel, 143, 146–7, 157
Free State Party, 148, 150, 176, 193, 239, 243
Frémont, John Charles, 419
Freud, Sigmund, 488
"Fright of Old Virginia, The. Being a Condensed Account of the Harper's Ferry Insurrection, October 16th, 1859," 460–1
"From Greenland's Icy Mountains," 245
Fruitlands, 225
Fugitive Slave Act of 1793, 60
Fugitive Slave Act of 1850, 5, 121, 122, 209, 226, 227, 228, 238, 250, 287, 288, 289
Fuller, Albert, 284
Fuller, Margaret, 86

Gabriel (slave), *see* Prosser, Gabriel
Gandhi, Mohandas K. "Mahatma," 347, 498
Garibaldi, Giuseppe, 113, 234
Garnet, Henry Highland, 103, 403, 489
Garrett, John W., 317
Garrett, Richard, 479
Garrison, David, 199–200, 201
Garrison, William Lloyd, 116, 118, 135, 250, *405*, 469
    Abolitionism of, 4, 24, 34, 50–5, 62, 63–4, 96–7, 138, 162, 227, 253, 360, 364, 403–5, 406
    antislavery journalism of, 51, 53, 59, 339–40, 359–60, 364, 404, 412, 458
    antislavery society of, 36, 51, 60, 64, 97, 117, 256, 404–5, 484
    1835 proslavery mobbing of, 34, 62, 63–4, 96, 111
    JB compared with, 50–2, 53–5, 138
    on Lincoln, 5, 12
    pacifism of, 51, 53, 55, 63–4, 65, 96–7, 162, 177, 208–9, 224, 225, 226, 404–5
Gaskell, Elizabeth, 491

Gaylord, Daniel C., 75, 76

Geary, John W., 197, 202, 204, 207, 239

Geary and Kansas (Gihon), 403

Geneva, Switzerland, 26

Genovese, Eugene, 52, 306, 315, 445

Gettysburg, Battle of, 187, 309

Gettysburg Address, 12, 355, 413, 482, 504

Giddings, Joshua R., 150, 208, 226, 290, 358, 359, 362, 375, 429, 435

Gihon, John, 403

Gilead (Robinson), 499

Gill, George B., 260–1, 262, 263, 266, 278

Gilmore's Band, 467

Gladney, Richard S., 455–7

Glanville, Jerome, 173

Gloucester, Dr. and Mrs. James, 256

God, 25, 26, 55, 61, 165
  grace of, 21, 72, 189
  judgment of, 5, 12, 21, 40–1, 93, 95, 174
  law breaking in the name of, 16–17, 121
  laws of, 40–1, 64, 121, 354, 355–6
  power of, 25, 406

Golden Rule, 24–5, 33, 223, 330, 331, 355, 369

gold rush, 228

Goldsby, Matthew J., 501

Grand River Institute, 78, 79, 81, 86

Grant, George, 155

Grant, John T., 177

Grant, Ulysses S., 12, 473, 475, 476, 496

Graves, William J., 160

Great Dismal Swamp, 107

Greece, 209, 257

Greeley, Horace, 149, 177, 248, 340, 360, 427, 471, 484

Green, Beriah, 59–60

Green, Israel, 326, 327–8, 334

Green, Shields, 299–300, *301*, 311, 326, 328, 337, 415, 418
  trial and execution of, 348, 374–5, 376, 415–16, 459

Green, Thomas C., 348, 351, 352

Griffith, D. W., 492

Griffith, Mattie, 366–7

Grimke, Francis J., 493

Grimsted, David, 159–60, 162

Griswold, Hiram, 353

Gue, David J., 304

guerilla warfare, 9, 106–10, 113, 187, 240, 257, 262–3, 310, 312, 361, 476–7

Haiti, 107–10, 263, 353, 409
  liberation of, 107, 108–10
  1791 slave revolt in, 97, 106, 108–9, 408, 410, 413
  Spanish and French in, 107, 108

Hale, John P., 264, 265, 358, 359, 362

Hall, Amos, 177

Hallock, Jeremiah, 21, 23, 27, 35

Hallock, Moses, 35

Hall's Rifle Works, 296, 311

Hamilton, Charles A., 268–70, 280–1

Hammond, Jabez D., 97, 98

Hammond, James H., 429

Hanway, James, 166–7, 177, 189, 230, 270, 275

Harding, Charles B., 349, 375

Hardy, George, 321

Harlem Renaissance, 497

Harper, Robert, 296

"Harpers Ferry" (Fox), 454

Harpers Ferry, Va., 295–6, *295*
  Bolivar Heights in, 296, 317, 319
  capture of JB at, 187, 328–9
  Civil War battle for, 112, 309
  federal arsenal at, 111–12, 113, 131, 240, 247, 255, 296, 299, 311, 312, 319, 320–1, 324, 330, 422
  JB's interrogation at, 309, 329–33
  JB's strategic choice of, 111–12, 113, 130–1, 296
  railroad hub in, 296, 316–17
  Wager House Hotel in, 318, 319, 321, 323, 324, 339, 391, 398

Harpers Ferry, Va., John Brown's raid on, ix, 3, 5, 7, 8, 9–13, 41, 129, 132, 167, 215, 222, 309–33, 420–1
  anti-Abolitionist frenzy stemming from, 102, 279, 335, 359, 412–19, 421–3
  contemporary accounts of, 331–2, 335–41
  death of JB's sons in, 66, 323, 327, 328, 384, 387
  denunciation of, 51, 63, 102, 337–41, 357–63
  distribution of pikes to blacks at, 14, 130–1, 214, 242, 292, 312, 313–14, 318
  escape of some JB forces from, 261, 278, 322, 324, 370–4
  failure of blacks to rally to, 312–15, 429

Harpers Ferry, Va., John Brown's raid on (*continued*)
historical antecedents and results of, 10–13, 109–10, 271
hostages taken at, 130–1, 307, 311–12, 318, 320, 322, 327–8, 329–30, 351–2, 353
ironies and coincidences of, 309–10
JB's arsenal for, 5, 208, 213–14, 237, 242, 245, 265–6, 294, 306, 336
JB's delays and mistakes at, 283, 310, 312–15, 319, 329–30, 381
JB's five black soldiers at, 109–10, 130–1, 244, 264, 289, 297, 299–300, *301*, 311, 314–15, 318–20, 324
Lincoln's reaction to, 63, 360–2
militia units at, 7, 314, 317, 319–22, 324, 336–7, 338–9
planning and recruiting for, 90, 101–7, 110–15, 131, 240–9, 254–68, 275–6, 288–308, 431
punishment of participants in, 3, 4, 11, 55, 67, 95, 130, 132, 187, 194, 207, 244, 278, 289, 309–10, 376–7, 398, 415–16
Senate hearings on, 273, 341, 402, 429–30
seventeen deaths at, 66, 96, 244, 261, 277, 289
skepticism about, 104–5, 113–14, 240–1, 245–6, 266
Sunday occurrence of, 38–9, 306
sympathy and support for, 101, 217–19, 233, 343, 363
twenty-two men engaged in, 3, 9, 244
ultimate failure of, 25, 66, 217, 353, 381
wounding of JB at, 200, 244, 327, 328–9, 334, 336, 349, 387
Harper's Weekly, 313, 329, 382, 417, 468
Harris, James, 173
Harris, James H., 262
Harvard, 13, 28, 103, 216, 218, 413
Divinity School of, 217, 364
Hasbrook, Josiah and Susan, 127
Hawthorne, Nathaniel, 43, 83, 448, 449
Hayden, Lewis, 100, 306
Haymaker, Frederick, 58–9, 61, 69–70, 77
Hayward, Shephard, 309, 316, 317, 318–19, 322, 353

Hazlett, Albert, 277–8, 311, 321, 324
escape and capture of, 324, 370–1, 373, 379
at Harpers Ferry, 278, 297, 311, 321, 324
trial and execution of, 278, 375, 415, 459–60
Headley, Joel Tyler, 164, 231–2, 274
Heller, Charles, 473
Helper, Hinton Rowan, 101, 102
Henley, William Ernest, 504
Herald of Freedom, 157, 340, 403
"Hero's Heart, The" (Child), 461–2
Hicklan, Harvey G., 278
Hickock, Laurens P., 64–5
Higgins, Patrick, 315–16, 318–19
Higginson, Thomas Wentworth, 27, 101, 107, 112, 208, *211*, 226–7, 248–9, 265, 266, 342, 343, 381, 450–1
black regiment commanded by, 102, 468, 473, 475, 490–1
JB supported by, 215–18, 221, 242, 258, 288, 291, 363, 389, 429, 431, 450
Hill, Elijah, 20
Hill, Paul, 501
Hinton, Richard J., 19, 107, 230, 244, 258, 303, 360, 379, 432
History of the Negro Race in America from 1619 to 1880 (Williams), 494
Holden, Isaac, 261, 262
Holly, J. Theodore, 109
Holmes, Oliver Wendell, Sr., 255–6
Holt, James H., 320
Homestead Act of 1862, 80
Hoskins, Alpheus, 70
House of Representatives, U.S., 222, 252
Houston, Charles, 497
Hovenden, Thomas, 394, *394*
Howe, Julia Ward, 4–5, 6, 209, 292, 469–70
Howe, Samuel Gridley, 4–5, 27, 209, *211*, 215–16, 248, 258, 264, 291–2, 340, 342–3, 469, 485
Howells, William Dean, 458
Hoyt, George Henry, 352–3, 375, 389
Hudson, David, 29, 30, 33
Hudson, Ohio, 29–34, 35–7, 42–4, 57–62, 64–5, 70, 73–4, 75, 237
Underground Railroad station in, 37, 60–2
Huffmaster family, 298

Hughes, Langston, 12, 497
Hugo, Victor, 10, 408–10
Hull, William, 33
human rights, 25–6
Humphrey, Heman (JB's ancestor), 20
Humphrey, Heman (JB's cousin), 236
Humphrey, Luther (JB's ancestor), 20
Hunter, Andrew, 349, 351–2, 353, 374–5,
    378, 392, 395
Hunter, David, 475
Hunter, Henry, 323, 351, 352
Hunter, Rebecca, 392
Hurd, H. B., 210–12
Hutchinson, Anne, 16–17, 253
"Hymn of Praise" (Mendelssohn), 3

"I" (Whitman), 206–7
Impartial Suffrage Association, 485
Impending Crisis of the South, The (Helper),
    101
Independent Greys militia, 336–7
Ingalls, John J., 202, 486–7
Ingraham, J. H., 502
Inner Four, 216–19
International Working People's Associa-
    tion, 500
"Invictus" (Henley), 504
Iowa, 195, 197, 207–9, 237, 257–8, 285–6
Ireland, 165, 230
Italy, 257, 291
    failed revolution of 1848–49 in, 113,
    234
"It feels a shame to be Alive—" (Dickin-
    son), 451–2
It's a Wonderful Life, 438

Jackson, Andrew, 50, 160
Jackson, James, 373
Jackson, Thomas "Stonewall," 309, 392,
    398
Jamaica, 107–8, 249, 312
    1831 slave revolt in, 108, 111, 410
James, Henry, Sr., 4
Jefferson, Thomas, 95, 98, 439
    racial policy of, 24, 26, 36, 439
    slaves owned by, 24, 32
Jefferson, Thomas and Jane, 127

Jesus Christ, 21, 65, 82
    JB compared to, 7, 67, 204, 219, 346,
        385, 402, 406–7, 413, 444, 458
    self-sacrifice of, 40, 63, 385, 387, 406
Jim Crow laws, 102, 118, 472, 486, 498
*John Brown, 1800–1859: A Biography Fifty
    Years After* (Villard), 496
*John Brown; or, The Hero of Kansas and
    Harper's Ferry*, 453–4
John Brown, Solder of Fortune: A Critique
    (Wilson), 488
"John Brown" (Boggs), 454
John Brown (Du Bois), 494–5
"John Brown" (Matthews), 454
*John Brown Album / Emancipation Evening /
    1863*, 484
John Brown and the Legend of Fifty-six
    (Malin), 488
John Brown Brigade, 500
John Brown Memorial Association, 496
John Brown Mysteries, 500
"John Brown of Osawatomie," 461
John Brown Reader, A (Ruchames), 499
"John Brown's Body," 3, 5, 7, 18, 444,
    465–70, 473–4, 491
"John Brown's Entrance into Hell," 455
John Brown's Holy War, 499
"John Brown's Invasion, a Ballad of the
    Times" (Stedman), 457–8
"John Brown's Parallels" (Brown), 280, 281
John Brown: The Making of a Revolutionary
    (Ruchames), 499
Johnson, Andrew, 222, 402–3, 481, 485
Johnson, Tom, 168
John the Baptist, 65
Jones, John Tecumseh "Ottawa," 157–8,
    170, 173–4, 180, 203
Jones, Jonas, 207, 237
Jones, Mother, 500
Jones, Samuel J., 145, 155–6, 157
Joy, Charles, 280
Joy, John, 280

Kaczynski, Ted, 501, 504
Kagi, John H., 244, 245, 262, 263, 267,
    270, 275, 281, 284, 286, 315, 320, 325,
    360, 435
    at Harpers Ferry, 288–9, 294–5, 298–9,
    303, 305–7

Kaiser, Charles, 200, 201
Kansas Free State, 157
Kansas Herald of Freedom, 386
Kansas-Nebraska Act of 1854, 97, 112,
    133, 139, 140, 143, 149, 168, 238, 250,
    425
Kansas Regulars, 196
Kansas Territory, 48
    as "Bleeding Kansas," 186–7, 270
    Brown's Station in, 132, 133, 136–7, 146,
        157, 184
    Hamilton Trading Post murders in,
        268–70, 280–1
    marauding proslavery border ruffians in,
        141–2, 144–9, 155–8, 159, 162–4,
        173, 178, 181–3, 191, 192, 195,
        196–7, 198, 200–1, 213, 223, 239,
        242–3, 274
    Native Americans in, 150, 154, 157–8,
        168–70, 194
    statehood of, 176, 193, 281
    struggle between Free State settlers and
        proslavery elements in, 45, 107, 112,
        113, 132, 136, 138–205, 207, 213, 236,
        239, 242–3, 268–70, 274, 276–7,
        281–2, 419
    see also Black Jack, Battle of; Osawatomie,
        Battle of; Pottawatomie Creek, Kans.
        Terr.; Wakarusa War; *specific cities*
Kansas Weekly Herald of Leavenworth, 176
Kazin, Alfred, 4, 355
Kelley, Robert S., 198
Kellogg, George, 73, 74, 76–7
Kennedy, Booth, 297
Kennedy farm, 245, 297–300, 304–7, 310,
    311, 312, 316, 322, 324, 329, 337, 371,
    374, 378, 391
Kenner, Robert, 499
Kent, Zenas B., 57–8, 71
Kentucky, 34, 80, 100
King, Martin Luther, Jr., 347, 498
King, William R., 140
Kitzmiller, Archibald M., 317, 321
Knox, John, 18
Ku Klux Klan, 417, 472, 486, 500

labor movement, 80, 499–500
Labor Standard American Auxiliary Associ-
    ation, 499

Lafayette, Marquis de, 130, 311
Lake Placid, 89, 125, 127, 128
land reform, 80, 192
Lane, James H., 143, 145, 147, 150, 156,
    157, 193, 194, 196, 203, 242–3
Langston, Charles H., 130, 407, 489, 497
"Last Days of John Brown, The"
    (Thoreau), 432
"Last Moments of John Brown, The"
    (Hovenden), 394, *394*
Laughlin, Patrick, 145
Law and Order Party, 155, 172
Lawrence, Amos, 143, 209, 236, 240, 292
Lawrence, Jacob, 497
Lawrence, Kans. Terr., 143, 145, 148–9,
    156, 169, 178, 182, 191, 196, 199,
    203–4, 209, 276
    Free State meetings in, 142, 203
    sack of, 155, 156–9, 162, 163–4, 167,
        173, 175, 180, 191, 193, 212, 505
Lawrence Republican, 280
League of Gileadites, 55, 98, 121–4, 497
League of Liberty, 263
Leary, Lewis Sheridan, 289, 297, *301*, 311,
    320, 497
Leavenworth, Kans. Terr., 143, 145, 147,
    148, 175, 196–7, 203, 427
Leavenworth Herald, 146, 340
Leaves of Grass (Whitman), 10–11, 64,
    206–7
LeBarnes, John W., 352, 379
Lecompte, S. D., 156
Lecompton, Kans. Terr., 154, 158, 191–2,
    284
Lecompton constitution, 149, 150, 152,
    153, 276
Lecompton Union, 157
Lee, Robert E., 187, 392, 398
    in capture of JB, 309, 326, 327, 329
Leeman, William Henry, 246, 262, 266
    death of, 244, 321
    at Harpers Ferry, 244, 297, 303, 316–17,
        321
Legend of John Brown (Boyer), 499
Lenhart, Charles, 156, 380
Lessing, Doris, 165
"Letter to a Slaveholder" (Parker), 218
"Letter to a Young Contributor" (Higgin-
    son), 450
Leyden, Holland, siege of, 20
Libby, Jean, 500

Liberator, 51, 53, 59, 339–40, 359–60, 364, 404, 412, 458, 464
Liberia, 36
Liberty Guards, 147
Liberty Party, 64, 403
Life and Letters of John Brown (Sanborn), 216, 487
Life and Opinions of Julius Melbourn (Hammond), 98
Life of Field Marshal the Duke of Wellington (Stocqueler), 106
Life of Oliver Cromwell, The (Headley), 164, 274
Lincoln, Abraham, 62, 116, 177, 219, 271–3, 360–2, *428,* 447
    antislavery of, 117, 139, 271–2, 281–2, 422, 426
    assassination of, 477, 479, 480
    colonization supported by, 36, 273
    Cooper Union Address of, 360, 427–9, *428*
    Douglas debates with, 63, 139, 271, 273, 281–2, 425
    1860 campaign and election of, 422–3, 425–9, 434, 436, 442
    1864 campaign and election of, 471, 472, 475, 477–8
    Emancipation Proclamation issued by, 3, 4, 6, 12, 273, 455, 469, 483
    First Inaugural Address of, 272
    Gettysburg Address of, 12, 355, 413, 482, 504
    in gradual progress towards Abolition, 5–6, 12, 34, 63, 95, 271–3, 275
    "House Divided" Address of, 271, 425
    JB linked to, 426–9, 470–1
    political opposition to, 5–6, 11–12, 14, 422–3, 425–7
    political rise of, 139, 436
    preservation of Union as paramount to, 5, 12, 63, 253, 271–2
    religious imagery of, 12, 95, 479
    Republican Party and, 422–3, 425–7
    Second Inaugural Address of, 12, 95, 479
    Union army troops called up by, 63, 272, 463
Lippard, George, 80–1, 502
Little Women (Alcott), 4
Liverpool Mercury, 411
Lives (Plutarch), 216

Logan, Daniel, 372–3
Loguen, Jermain W., 103, 256, 259
Lohman, Ann, 503
London News, 409
Lovejoy, Elijah P., 124
    murder of, 34, 62–3, 64–5, 98, 111
Lovejoy, Owen, 359
Lowell, James Russell, 32, 99, 210
Lowry, M. D., 386
Lundy, Benjamin, 51
Luther, Martin, 11

Madison, James, 32
Mahan, Asa, 60, 403
Mahoning Indian Trail, 30
Malcolm X, 12, 129, 247, 498
Malin, James, 488
Manchester's Examiner and Times, 411
Mann, J. Evan, 368
Manual of the Patriotic Volunteer, 234, 241, 298, 337
"Marais du Cygne, Le" (Whittier), 269
maroons, 106–8, 114, 131, 249, 312, 450
"Marseillaise," 490
Marshall, Thurgood, 497
Martin, J. Sella, 490
martyr de la liberté des nègres, Le; ou, John Brown, le Christ des noirs (Vésinier), 410
Marx, Karl, 80, 82
Marxism, 82, 500
Maryland, 114, 241
Maryland, University of, 497
Maryland Volunteers, 317
Mason, James M., 329–30
    Senate hearings of, 273, 341, 402, 429–30
Masons, 42
Massachusetts, 21, 25, 80
Massachusetts Arms Company, 236–7
Massachusetts State Kansas Committee, 208, 209, 212, 242, 243, 264, 266, 304
Mather, Cotton, 18, 253
May, Samuel J., 135
Mayer, Henry, 117
Mayflower, 19–20, 29, 368
McClellan, George B., 471
McClure, Alexander K., 372–3

McCrae, Cole, 145

McKim, Miller, 389, 399–401

McKissick, Floyd, 498

McNair, Dunning R., 430

McPherson, James M., 474, 499

McVeigh, Timothy, 500–1, 502, 504

Meadville, Pa., 44, 56, 168–9

Medary, Samuel, 277, 280

Mello, Michael, 501

Melville, Herman, 9, 10, 66, 99, 261, 383, 445–8

Mentzig, J. H., 171

Merriam, Francis Jackson, 306, 307, 310, 322

    escape of, 370, 371–4, 432

"Message to Pharror, The," 458–9

Meteor of War: The John Brown Story (Trodd and Stauffer), 499

Methodism, 11, 26, 47–8, 466

Mexican War, 34, 83, 194, 224

Mexico, 97

Miller, Charles D., 430

Millerites, 26

Mills, Benjamin, 318

Mills, Gideon (JB's ancestor), 20

Mills, Gideon, Jr. (JB's grandfather), 20

Mills, Lucius, 193–4

Mills, Peter (JB's ancestor), 20

Milroy, Robert H., 3

Milwaukee Free Democrat, 407

Misérables, Les (Hugo), 410

Mississippi River, 62, 63, 100, 132

Missouri, 112, 476

Missouri Compromise, 5, 10, 140

Missouri General Assembly, 280

Moby-Dick (Melville), 66, 261, 445

Modern Times community, 80

Moffett, Charles W., 244, 246, 262, 266

Montgomery, James, 276–80

Morgan, William, 42

Mormons, 26

Morning Star (London), 411

Morse, Sidney H., 485–6

Moses, 65, 230, 314, 458

Mott, Lucretia, 123

Munroe, Edward, 71

Munroe, George D., 71

Munroe, William Charles, 262, 263

Musgrave, Thomas B., 82, 91

"My Northern Boy to the War Has Gone," 17

Napoleon I, Emperor of France, 90, 106, 108–9

Narrative (Douglass), 57, 103, 254

National Association for the Advancement of Colored People (NAACP), 494, 495–6, 497

National Association of Teachers in Colored Schools, 494

National Era, 416

National Kansas Committee, 193, 207, 210, 212, 236, 237, 276

Native Americans, 29–32, 107, 442

    JB and, 31–2, 157–8, 168–9

    in Kansas, 150, 154, 157–8, 168–70, 194

    massacres by, 167, 170

    mistreatment of, 168, 210, 220–1, 500, 503

    U.S. campaigns against, 194, 500

"Nearer My God to Thee," 298

Nebraska City, Nebr. Terr., 193–4, 196, 243

Nebraska Territory, 193, 197, 207, 285

Negro Mood and Other Essays, The (Bennett), 504–5

"Negro Mother's Lullaby, A" (Cullen), 497

Negro Worker, 500

Nevins, Allan, 138, 215, 488

Newby, Dangerfield, 297, *301*, 318, 319–20

Newby, Harriet, 297

"New Crime Against Humanity, The" (Parker), 218

New Critics, 488

New England Anti-Slavery Society, 24, 292

New England Emigrant Aid Society, 132, 157, 209, 331

New England Non-Resistance Society, 96, 224

New England Wool Company, 73, 74

New Lucy, 132–3

Newman, William P., 121

New Richmond, Pa., 44–8

New York, 30, 54, 80, 103, 193

New York, N.Y., 20, 67, 70, 71, 265, 399, 414

    anti-Brown rally in, 413–14

    draft riots in, 160

    1712 slave uprising in, 52

New York Age, 492

New York Commercial Advertiser, 339

New York Evening Post, 339

New York Evening Tribune, 500

New York Herald, 229, 303, 331, 340–1, 342, 367, 369, 377, 414, 418, 427, 471

New York Independent, 417

New York Journal of Commerce, 357, 382, 404, 414

New-York Observer, 418

New York State Asylum for the Insane, 341, 390

New York Times, 181, 195, 340–1, 393, 416, 417, 427

New-York Tribune, 149, 177, 183, 184, 188, 191, 213, 248, 280, 340, 343, 360, 369, 377–8, 381, 382, 395, 396–7, 410, 417, 461, 467, 471

New York Vigilant Committee, 341–2, 358, 368, 369

Nick of the Woods (Bird), 261

North American Review, 486

North Carolina, 57, 107

North Elba, N.Y., 69, 89, 91, 132–6, 195, 197, 208, 212, 233–4, 249, 389
  JB's farm at, 89, 94, 125–6, *126*, 127–8, 239–40
  JB's final years and burial at, 69, *126*, 132, 213, 391, 393, 399–401, 432
  JB's settlement of blacks at, 111, 124, 125–30, 131–2

Northern states
  criminal mobs in, 159–60
  flight of fugitive slaves to, 37
  reform and creative ferment in, 15, 16–17, 115–16, 206, 480–1

Noyes, John Humphrey, 26

Oates, Stephen B., 8, 201, 499

Oberlin, Ohio, 288, 289, 297

Oberlin Collegiate Institute, 74–5, 111, 289
  antislavery advocacy of, 60, 289, 403
  founding of, 60

"Ode to Old Capt. John Brown," 490

Ohio, 20, 29–32, 94
  antislavery activities in, 37, 60–2, 80, 288, 289
  Ashtabula County in, 78, 243, 247
  black laws in, 60, 61
  Western Reserve of, 29, 30, 60–1, 288

Ohio River, 74, 100, 132

Ohio State Supreme Court, 75, 76

Oklahoma City bombing, 334, 501

"Old Brown," 457

"Old Brown" (Howells), 458

"Old Browns *Farewell*" (Brown), 235–6

"Old Capt. John Brown Liberty League," 490

Old Guard, 115

"Old John Brown," 461

"Old John Brown, a Song for Every Southern Man," 455

Oliver Cromwell's Letters and Speeches with Elucidations (Carlyle), 230–1

Oneida community, 131

On Heroes, Hero-Worship, and the Heroic in History (Carlyle), 230–1

Osawatomie, 500

Osawatomie, Battle of, 181, 187, 195, 196–203
  events leading to, 196–200
  failure vs. moral victory of, 196, 201–2

Osawatomie, Kans. Terr., 12, 132, 133, 143, 144, 152, 153, 176, 179–80, 182, 191
  Free State Convention in, 148

"Osawatomie Brown" (Alcott), 290–1

Ossawatomie Brown; or, The Insurrection at Harper's Ferry (Rogers), 452

Ossawatomie Brown; or, The Insurrection at Harper's Ferry (Swayze), 453

"Our Country" (Thoreau), 220–1

Outbank, Nathan B., *356*

Oviatt, Heman, 30, 58, 70, 72, 75, 76–7

Oviatt, Orson M., 35

pacifism, ix, 4, 51, 53, 55, 63–5, 96–7, 162, 177, 208–9, 224–6, 404–5

Paine, Thomas, 194, 298, 505

Painter, John H., 246

Palmetto Guard, 419

Paris Commune, 410

Parker, Andrew, 350, 352, 353–4, 357

Parker, George Hannibal, 490

Parker, Nathaniel, 203

Parker, Theodore, 27, 101, 102–3, 208–9, *211*, 215–18, 226, 248–9, 258, 288, 291, 343, 429–30

Parsons, Luke F., 189–90, 200, 203, 244, 262, 266

Partridge, George W., 200, 201, 275
Pate, Henry Clay, 176, 180, 182, 184–8, 222, 388
Patton, William W., 468–9
Peabody, Elizabeth Palmer, 448
Pennsylvania, 30, 44–8, 57
Perkins, Simon, 78–82, 83–4, 85, 88, 91, 92, 94, 229
Perkins & Brown, 103
Perry, Lewis, 225
Personal Narrative (Edwards), 43
Philadelphia, Pa., 413–15
Phillips, Wendell, ix, 27–8, 101, 102, 233, 250, 253, 257, 364, 365, 399–401, 413, 431, 483, 505
    Abolitionism of, 4, 5, 6, 118, 121, 219, 359, 404, 500
    on JB, ix, 109–10, 164–5, 230, 262, 368–9
Phillips, William, 145, 281–3
Phillips, William A., 175, 191–2
phrenology, 38, 86–8, 89, 117
Pickett, George, 187
Pierce, Franklin, 140, 149, 150, 152, 156, 193, 197, 414, 448
Pierre (Melville), 445
Pilgrims, 107
Pillsbury, J. W., 460
Pillsbury, Parker, 404
Pinkerton, Allan, 287
Pippin, Horace, 497
Pittsburgh, Pa., 30, 92, 150
Plains Indians, 476
"Plan for the Abolition of Slavery, A" (Brown and Kagi), 435
"Plea for Captain John Brown, A" (Thoreau), 188, 219, 347, 498
Plessy v. Ferguson, 492, 494
Plummer, William L., 162
Poe, Edgar Allan, 86
Polk, James K., 140, 224
Pomeroy, Samuel C., 388
Pope, John, 475
"Portent, The" (Melville), 383, 446
Potomac River, 111, 295, 296–7, 310, 316, 319, 320, 321, 324
Pottawatomie Brown, 454
Pottawatomie Creek, Kans. Terr., 41, 107
    JB's supervision of five murders at, 7, 8, 38, 96, 138–9, 149, 154, 155, 163, 164,

165–7, 171–8, 179, 183, 184, 195, 204, 207, 221–2, 223, 229, 269, 275, 280, 293, 340, 403, 413
Pottawatomie Rifle Company, 154, 157, 158, 169, 173, 180–1
Presbyterian Church, 21, 30
Preston, John, 397
proslavery
    forces dedicated to, 11–12, 14–19, 26, 34, 62–4, 412–17
    journalism of, 418
    violent mob action and, 34, 62–4, 96
    see also Southern states
Prosser, Gabriel, 52, 109, 495
Protestantism, 470
    conservative vs. progressive, 26–7
    revival meetings and, 21, 22, 24, 25, 61
    see also specific Protestant sects
Providence Journal, 339
"Provisional Constitution and Ordinances for the People of the United States" (Brown), 8, 106, 249–55, 263–4, 300, 333
    denunciation of, 249–50, 254–5
    provisional government created by, 263
    purposes and rules of, 252–4, 263–4, 274
Public Life of Capt. John Brown, The (Redpath), 344, 431, 444
Puritanism, 10, 16–22, 470
    Cromwell and, 230–2
    fusion of Protestantism and, 26
    JB's heritage of, 18–22, 25, 27–8, 68, 93, 122, 153, 164–5, 188–9, 196, 208, 230, 231, 245, 292, 346
    New England, 15, 16, 19–22, 27–8, 37, 116
    radical individualism fostered by, 16, 17, 19, 27–8, 115–16, 188
    reform ethic in, 16, 27–8
    subversive view of, 14, 15–19, 480–1, 482

Quaker City, The; or, The Monks of Monk Hall (Lippard), 80–1
Quakers, 11, 33, 51, 220, 246, 261, 286, 304, 337, 370, 374, 480
"Quaking South, The" (Pillsbury), 460

racism, 30–1, 51, 102
  Christianity and, 115, 116
  pervasiveness of, 115–21, 129, 333
  rhetoric of, 14, 15, 62, 115, 116–17, 142,
    273
  stereotypes of, 61, 103, 115, 155, 220–1,
    314
  Transcendentalism and, 220–1
  violence of, 62, 63, 170, 417, 418
  white supremacy belief in, 103, 143, 273
Radical Club, 500
Radical Political Abolitionists, 135
Raising Holy Hell (Olds), 499
Ram's Horn, 119
Randolph, John, 160
Ransom, Reverdy C., 494
Ray, Charles H., 360
Realf, Richard, 107, 237, 244, 262, 263,
    266, 360
Reconstruction, 102, 447
  Radical, 485–6, 491
Redpath, James, 6, 183–4, 267, 344,
    359–60, 412, 431, 444
Reeder, Andrew H., 149, 150
reform movements, 80, 218, 403
Reid, John W., 199, 200–1
religious revivals, 21, 22, 24, 25, 61
Representative Men (Emerson), 367
Republican Party, 8, 14, 32, 193, 195, 245,
    272, 346–7, 481
  antislavery platform of, 14, 64, 102, 139,
    150, 271, 357, 403, 422–3, 424
  formation of, 150, 360
  JB's exploits linked to, 357–63, 368, 376,
    382, 422, 424–5, 427–9
  Lincoln and, 422–3, 425–7
Revere, Paul, 502
Revolutionary Action Movement, 498
Reynolds, George L., 263–4
Rhett, Robert Barnwell, 419
Rhode Island, 23
Rice, Benjamin H., 277
Richardson, Richard, 244, 261, 262, 266–7
Richfield, Ohio, 77–8
Richmond, Va., 52, 397
Richmond Enquirer, 161, 358, 379, 380, 422
right-to-life movement, 500, 501, 502
Riler, Charles N., 156
*Rise and Progress of the Bloody Outbreak at
    Harper's Ferry*, 358

Ritner, Mary A., 373
Robinson, Charles, 147, 156, 157, 193,
    204–5, 429, 488
Robinson, Marilynne, 499
Robinson, Sara, 204
Rogers, J. H., 452
Rogers, John, 389
Rogers, Nathaniel P., 34, 225
Roman Catholic Church, 487
Roman Empire, 282–3
Root, J. P., 207
Rose, Ernestine L., 406
Ross, Alexander Milton, 118, 257–8
Ruby Ridge incident, 334, 501
Ruchames, Louis, 499
Ruffin, Edmund, 102, 314, 396, 419–24,
    420, 435–6, 439
Russell, Judge and Mrs. Thomas, 235–6,
    292, 387
Russia, 166, 209, 257

"Sambo's Mistakes" (Brown), 119–21
Sanborn, Franklin, 4, 5, 6, 19, 211, 255,
    269–70, 341, 342, 347, 363, 430–1
  support of JB by, 208–10, 212–16, 218,
    223, 230, 242, 248–9, 254–5, 258, 265,
    266, 283, 288, 290, 291, 487
Savannah Republic, 434
"Say, Brothers, Will You Meet Us?," 466
Sayres, Edward, 100
Scarlet Letter, The (Hawthorne), 43
Schoppert, George A., 321
Scott, Walter, 18, 216
Scott, William, 416
Scott, Winfield, 414
Second Niagara Movement, 494
Second Seminole War (1835–43), 107
Secret Six, 5, 27, 99, 102, 208–18, 211, 221,
    248–9, 254–5, 257, 265, 266, 283, 291,
    330, 340–2, 343, 429–30, 469
"Self-Reliance" (Emerson), 66–7
Selling of Joseph, The (Sewall), 24
Seminole Indians, 106, 107
Senate, U.S., 140, 159, 273, 362, 425
  investigation of Harpers Ferry raid in,
    273, 341, 402, 429–30
Sennott, George, 375, 459
Sewall, Samuel, 24

Seward, William Henry, 8, 14, 226, 247–8, 250, 264, 265, 271, 355, 358–62, 364, 375, 422, 425, 426, 429
  antislavery position of, 272–3, 358–9, 484
  as secretary of state, 272, 361
Shakers, 26, 73
Shakespeare, William, 479
Shannon, Wilson, 145–6, 147, 149, 197
Shannon's Sharp Shooters, 180
Shaw, Robert Gould, 6, 491
Shawnee Mission, Kans. Terr., 142, 144, 149, 168
Shenandoah Mountains, 380, 432
Shenandoah River, 111, 289, 295, 320, 396, 400
Sherman, Henry, 153, 154, 166–7, 170, 172, 173, 196
Sherman, Pete, 154
Sherman, William, 154, 158, 166, 173, 340, 403, 456
Sherman, William Tecumseh, 12, 472, 475, 476, 492
Shore, Samuel T., 183, 184–5, 187, 198
Sinn, Thomas, 324–5
"Sinners in the Hands of an Angry God" (Edwards), 25, 48, 151–2
Skillman, Isaac, 97
slave revolts, 9, 10, 14, 51–6, 105–10, 282, 314
  denunciation of, 53–4
  fear of, 53–4, 63, 110, 341, 433–4
  Indian allies in, 107
  prevention and suppression of, 52, 63
  punishment and retribution for, 52, 53, 55, 109, 110, 434
  support of, 53, 97–9, 343
  violence and terror of, 52, 53–5, 63, 108–10
  see also specific revolts
slavery, ix, 4, 9
  Christian views of, 25–7
  "civilizing" institution of, 15, 17, 18
  ending of, *see* Emancipation Proclamation
  Southern tradition of, 5, 24, 34, 54, 55, 114, 115
  violence inherent in, 64
  Western territories opened to, 112
"Slavery in Massachusetts" (Thoreau), 227

slaves, 110
  farm work of, 23
  fugitive, 23, 25, 34, 37, 56, 60–1, 80, 89, 103, 106–8, 226, 249, 372
  international trade in, 54, 71
  legislation limiting rights of, 5, 57, 60, 61, 112
  pursuit and capture of, 5, 60, 112, 121–3, 226–7, 300, 372
  rescue and help of, *see* Underground Railroad
  sale of, 52, 53
  torture and execution of, 52, 53, 54
Smith, E. B., 212
Smith, Gerrit, 74, 89, 97–8, 101, 211, 347, 413, 430, 472
  Abolitionism of, 97–8, 131, 135, 208
  JB and, 101, 125, 128, 208, 212, 215–16, 237, 241–2, 248, 254–5, 259, 262, 266, 283, 290, 340–2
  mental collapse of, 341, 390
Smith, James McCune, 118, 134
Smith, J. B., 13
Smith, W. P., 317
Snyder, Eli, 270
socialism, 82–3
"Song for the Times, or John Brown, A," 464
"Song of Myself" (Whitman), 76
Soul on Ice (Cleaver), 498
Souls of Black Folk (Du Bois), 494
South Carolina, 107, 156–7, 337
Southern Christian Leadership Conference, 498
"Southern Cross, The," 16
Southern states
  antislavery newspapers banned in, 417–18
  Norman "cavalier" tradition of, 17–18, 480
  secession of, 337, 419–24, 435–7
  slaveholding tradition of, 5, 24, 34, 54, 55, 114, 115
  violence and vigilante justice of, 159–61, 164, 170, 411, 413, 416–18
South Mountain, Battle of, 309
Spain, 54, 55
Spartacus, 282–3
spiritualism, 15, 194
Spooner, Lysander, 100–2, 379
Spring, Rebecca, 370, 387, 388

Springfield, Mass., 81–2, 84–6, *85*, 89, 91, 103, 124, 130

Springfield Republican, 417, 418

Spurs, Battle of the, 284–5

Squatter Sovereign, 156, 161–2, 175, 176, 198

Stanton, Edwin McMasters, 472–3

Starry, John D., 316, 317, 447

states rights, 14, 337, 353

Stauffer, John, 499

Stearns, Carl, 210, 218

Stearns, Charles B., 163

Stearns, George L., 27, *211*, 218–19, 230, 264, 340, 342–3, 430
  black regiments organized by, 6, 472, 484
  civil rights activism of, 5, 6, 13, 484–5
  JB and, 5, 24, 209–10, 213, 215, 218, 233, 236–7, 239–40, 248–9, 258, 266, 288, 304, 485
  JB celebration given by, 3, 4–6, 12–13, 483

Stearns, Henry, 20, 210, 218

Stearns, Mary, 6, 209–10, 218–19, 230, 236, 388, 431

Stedman, Edmund Clarence, 457–8

Stephens, Alexander H., 115, 426, 440

Stevens, Aaron Dwight, 203, 245, 246, 262, 266, 278–9, 284, 337, 381, 393
  at Harpers Ferry, 194, 244, 297, 298, 311, 315, 324–6, *325*, 355
  trial and execution of, 194, 244, 348–9, 375, 415–16, 459–60

Stevens, Thaddeus, 484

Stewart, George H., 317

Stewart, Robert M., 279

St. Louis Morning Herald, 174

Stocqueler, Joachim Hayward, 106

Storer College, 491, 494

Storrs, Charles Backus, 59–60

Stowe, Harriet Beecher, 36, 96, 107, 177, 257, 261

Stringfellow, B. F., 141–2, 161–2, 197

Strother, David Hunter, 313, 314

Stuart, J. E. B., 337
  JB's capture and, 187, 309, 326, 327, 330–1

Sumner, Charles, 14, 95–6, 226, 247, 364, 404, 483, 484, 485
  beating of, 155, 158–9, 161, 163, 175, 178, 210, 212, 365

Sumner, Edwin, 187–8, 190, 192–3

Supreme Court, U.S., 250, 252, 492, 498

Surinam, 107–8, 405

Swayze, J. C., 453

Tabor, Iowa, 207–9, 239, 244, 266, 286

Taney, Roger, 250, 252

Tappan, Arthur, 60, 101, 403

Tappan, Lewis, 60, 135, 403, 406

tariff laws, 83–4

Taylor, Stewart, 261, 262, 266
  at Harpers Ferry, 297, 303, 310, 326

Taylor, Zachary, 140

temperance movement, 48, 51, 218

Temple School, 225

Texas, 434–5

Thayer, Eli, 132, 143, 163, 209

Thayer & Eldridge, 273

Thirteenth Amendment, ix, 51, 472

Thomas, H. K., 200

Thomas, Thomas, 103

Thompson, Dauphin Adolphus, 234, 293, 294, 307, 326–8

Thompson, George, 34, 100

Thompson, Henry (JB's son-in-law), 91, 93–4, 135–6, 234, 293, 294
  Kansas campaign of, 136, 146, 154, 155, 172–3, 182, 187, 195

Thompson, Mary, 294

Thompson, Roswell, 294

Thompson, Ruth Brown (JB's daughter), 38, 79, 81, 86, 91, 93–4, 126, 128, 294, 399
  JB and, 45–6, 56, 135

Thompson, Seth B., 49
  JB's business deals with, 44–5, 58–9, 70, 72

Thompson, Stephen, 30

Thompson, William, 234, 293, 294, 304, 311, 317, 318, 320, 323, 351

Thoreau, Henry David, 67, 68, 192, 215–30, *345*, 366, 388, 403, 452
  Abolitionism of, 34, 64, 97, 121, 227–8
  JB defended by, 4, 11, 32, 64, 188, 219, 222–5, 228–30, 290, 334, 344–7, 353, 363–4, 383–4, 401, 402, 406, 431, 432–3
  philosophy of, 84, 94

Tidd, Charles Plummer, 244, 246, 262, 266, 267, 284

Tidd, Charles Plummer (*continued*)
  escape of, 370, 371–2, 373, 374
  at Harpers Ferry, 289, 297, 299, 300,
    304–5, 307, 310, 311, 316–17, 321–2
Times (London), 411
Todd, John, 207, 209, 246
Topeka, Kans. Terr., 143, 151, 191–3, 199,
  236, 244
To Purge This Land with Blood (Oates), 499
Torrey, Charles T., 98–9, 124
Torrington, Conn., 23, 71
"To the Friends of Freedom" (Brown), 213
Tourgée, Albion, 10
Toussaint, François Dominique "L'Ouver-
  ture," 107–10, 408
Townsend, J. Holland, 120
Townsend, John, 435
Townsley, James, 158, 171, 173–4, 175, 182
"To Wool Growers" (Brown), 83
Trail of Tears, 502
Transcendentalists, 4, 10, 11, 15, 188–9,
  214–30, 232–3
  defense and support of JB by, 4, 7, 32,
    64, 66–7, 188, 210, 214–16, 219–24,
    226–9, 232–3, 334–5, 343–7, 363,
    382–3, 426, 431–3
  pacifism of, 224–6
  racism of, 220–1
  social and political views of, 64, 68,
    215–30, 403, 481–5
  see also Alcott, Amos Bronson; Emerson,
    Ralph Waldo; Thoreau, Henry David
Trodd, Zoe, 499
Trumbull, Lyman, 363, 484
Tubman, Harriet, 259
Tucker, St. George, 439
Turner, George W., 322
Turner, Nat, 131, 306, 495
  background and character of, 52, 55
  1831 rebellion of, 52–6, 105, 111, 214,
    241, 315
  JB's emulation of, 54–6, 105, 114, 130,
    167–8, 241, 408
  trial and execution of, 53
Twain, Mark, 18, 86, 116–17, 161, 364–5
Two Years Before the Mast (Dana), 127

Unabomber, 344, 501, 504
Uncle Tom's Cabin (Stowe), 257, 261

Underground Railroad, 23, 37, 60–2, 98,
  99, 257, 259, 273–4, 283
  JB as agent of, 23, 37, 80, 87, 118, 121,
    122, 127, 249
Underhill, Edward F., 395
Union, 333, 415
  calls for separation of, 4, 51, 53, 96, 98,
    253, 337, 419–24, 435–7
  Kansas admitted to, 176
  Lincoln and preservation of, 5, 12, 63,
    253, 271–2
  secession of Southern states from, 337,
    419–24, 435–7
Union Army, 191
  blacks recruited for, 5, 6, 102, 217, 221,
    264, 468, 472–4, 490–1
  54th Massachusetts Regiment of, 6, 491
  First South Carolina Volunteers in, 473
  Lincoln's call-up of troops for, 63, 272, 463
  marching songs of, 7, 17, 18, 466–9, 491
  prominent generals of, 3, 12, 472, 473,
    475, 476, 492, 496
  strategic tactics of, 475–7
United States
  agrarianism in, 80
  capitalism in, 36, 41–2, 43, 45, 68–9, 76,
    80, 83–4, 126, 143
  class divisions in, 80
  concepts of patriotism vs. treason in, 66,
    99, 124
  concepts of success and failure in, 66–7
  democratic system of, 12, 17
  economic depressions in, 36, 69, 70, 73,
    88
  industrialization of, 68
  nativist sentiment in, 189
  police forces in, 63
  terrorism in, 334, 501–2
  unemployment in, 69
  see also Northern states; Southern states;
    Union
Unseld, John C., 297
Updegraff, William W., 200
utopian experiments, 80, 83, 131, 225
Utter, David N., 486, 492

Vaill, Herman L., 35, 382–3
Vallandigham, Clement L., 288, 329, 330,
  332–3, 357

Van Buren, Martin, 414
Vásquez de Ayllón, Lucas, 107
Vermont, 23
Vesey, Denmark, 450
   1820 slave revolt of, 52, 97, 109
Vésinier, Pierre, 410
Victor, Orville J., 279–80
Vidal, Gore, 501, 502
Villard, Oswald Garrison, 8, 250, 496
"Vindication of the Invasion" (Brown),
   303
Virginia, 52–6, 74–5, 80, 107
   plantations in, 52–3, 130, 240, 315
   slaveholding in, 74, 347
   Southampton County in, 52–3, 55
Virginia Military Institute, 392, 397, 398
Von Holst, Hermann, 250
Voorhees, Daniel, 314, 376, 377

Waco incident, 501
Wade, Benjamin F., 363, 422, 484
Wadsworth, Frederick, 58
Wadsworth, Tertius, 72–3, 76
Wadsworth & Wells, 70–1, 72–3
Wakarusa War, 146–8, 151, 152, 162
Wakefield, Benjamin, 374
Walden (Thoreau), 84, 188, 220, 347, 388
Walker, David, 53, 103, 403
Walker, Jonathan, 98, 99–100
Walker, Robert J., 239, 269
Walker, Samuel, 189, 194, 196
Walsh, Hugh, 276–7
War Department, U.S., 436
War of 1812, 31, 33, 113
Warren, Henry, 92
Warren, Robert Penn, 488
Wascott, Laura, 246
Washington, Charles, 130, 347
Washington, D.C., 100, 429
Washington, George, 110, 130, 131, 296,
   297, 307, 311, 408, 410
   slaves owned by, 24, 347
Washington, Lewis W., 314, 316, 328, 329
   on JB, 313, 327, 357
   JB's abduction of, 130–1, 307, 311–12,
   318, 322, 327
Washington, Richard B., 319, 320
Washington, Samuel, 130
Watkins, William J., 116, 117–18

Wattles, Augustus, 237, 270–1, 274, 279,
   280, 429
Watts, Isaac, 34
Weather Underground, 500
Weaver, A. J., 277
Webster, Daniel, 450
Webster, Delia A., 100
Weed, Thurlow, 404
Weeks, William R., 35
Weiner, Theodore, 158, 171, 172–3, 180,
   182
Weld, Theodore Dwight, 160
Wells, Joseph, 72–3, 76
Wesley, John, 11
Western Reserve Anti-Slavery Society, 60
Western Reserve Bank, 70
Western Reserve College, 23, 59–60, 64
West Indies, 107–10, 131
   emancipation of slaves in, 34, 55, 225
   slave revolts in, 107–10, 113
Westlands farm, 69–70, 72, 74–7
West Simsbury, Conn, 20–1
West Virginia, 111
Wetherbee, Charles, 290
Whedon, Benjamin, 30
Whelan, Daniel, 310–11
Whig Party, 50, 120, 139, 362, 425, 450
White, Charles, 497
White, Martin, 152
   murder of Frederick Brown by, 144, 152,
   199–200, 270
Whitefield, George, 24, 25
Whitman, E. B., 243
Whitman, Walt, 86, 116, 221, 365, 367,
   431, 503
   JB compared with, 10–11
   works of, 10–11, 66, 76, 120, 129, 206–7,
   383, 448–9, 464
Whittier, John Greenleaf, 10, 100, 257,
   269, 461–2, 466
Wightman, John S., 173
Wilberforce Educational Institute, 260
Wilkes, Warren, 139–40
Wilkinson, Allen, 155, 166, 167, 171,
   172–3, 177, 340, 403, 456
Wilkinson, Louisa, 229, 413
Willetts, Jacob, 284
Williams, George Washington, 494
Williams, Henry H., 170–1
Williams, Robert F., 247, 498
Williams, William, 310, 315, 316

Wilson, Henry H., 226, 248, 264, 265, 292, 341, 429
Wilson, Hill Peebles, 204, 488
Wilson, Woodrow, 492
Winchester Medical College, 400
Wise, Henry A., 160, 317, 329, 331–3, 337–9, *338*, 346, 352, 357, 366, 374–5, 378–80, 382, 390–3, 411–12, 417, 421, 423, 463
Wise, O. Jennings, 338, 392
women's rights, 15, 122, 218, 221, 247, 502–3
Wood, Captain, 180–1
Woodruff, Daniel, 113
Woodson, Daniel, 197
Woodward, C. Vann, 215
Woolman, John, 24

Worcester Daily Spy, 452
Work, Alanson, 100
World Trade Center attacks of September 11, 2001, 166
"Worship of the North" cartoon, 14–15, *15*, 17
Wouter van der Meulen, Peter (JB's ancestor), 20
Wright, Elizur, Jr., 59–60
Wright, Henry C., 97, 367, 405–6

Yale, 20, 98, 245
Yancey, William L., 160, 419, 426, 439, 440
"Year of Meteors" (Whitman), 383, 448–9
Young, Joshua, 400

A Note About the Author

DAVID S. REYNOLDS is Distinguished Professor of English and American Studies at the Graduate Center and Baruch College of the City University of New York. He is the author of *Walt Whitman's America: A Cultural Biography*, winner of the Bancroft Prize and the Ambassador Book Award and finalist for the National Book Critics Circle Award. His other books include *Beneath the American Renaissance: The Subversive Imagination in the Age of Emerson and Melville* (winner of the Christian Gauss Award and Honorable Mention for the John Hope Franklin Prize); *Walt Whitman; George Lippard;* and *Faith in Fiction: The Emergence of Religious Literature in America*. He is the editor of Whitman's *Leaves of Grass, 150th Anniversary Edition; A Historical Guide to Walt Whitman; George Lippard, Prophet of Protest: Writings of an American Radical, 1822–1854;* and Lippard's *The Quaker City; or, The Monks of Monk Hall*. He is the coeditor of *The Serpent in the Cup: Temperance in American Literature* and George Thompson's *"Venus in Boston" and Other Tales of Nineteenth-Century City Life*.

A Note on the Type

This book was set in Janson, a typeface long thought to have been made by the Dutchman Anton Janson, who was a practicing typefounder in Leipzig during the years 1668–1687. However, it has been conclusively demonstrated that these types are actually the work of Nicholas Kis (1650–1702), a Hungarian, who most probably learned his trade from the master Dutch typefounder Dirk Voskens. The type is an excellent example of the influential and sturdy Dutch types that prevailed in England up to the time William Caslon (1692–1766) developed his own incomparable designs from them.

Composed by North Market Street Graphics,
Lancaster, Pennsylvania
Printed and bound by Berryville Graphics,
Berryville, Virginia
Designed by Anthea Lingeman